MEN OF WAR

GREAT NAVAL LEADERS OF WORLD WAR II

MEN OF WAR

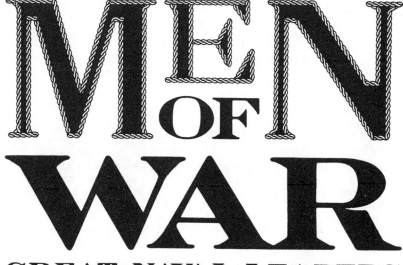

GREAT NAVAL LEADERS OF WORLD WAR II

Edited by

STEPHEN HOWARTH

With a foreword by
Admiral of the Fleet The Lord Lewin
KG, GCB, LVO, DSC

St. Martin's Press
New York

In memory of
Peter Kemp
Naval Officer and historian
11 February 1904–15 March 1992

Library of Congress Cataloging-in-Publication Data

Men of war / edited by Stephen Howarth.
p.   cm.
"A Thomas Dunne Book."
ISBN 0-312-08844-2
1. World War, 1939-1945—Naval operations.   2. Ship captains-
-Biography.   3. Submarine boat captains—Biography.   4. World War,
1939-1945—Biography.   I. Howarth, Stephen.
D770.M36   1993
940.54′5′0922—dc20   [B]   92-43299   CIP

First published in Great Britain by George Weidenfeld and Nicolson Limited.

First U.S. Edition: April 1993
10 9 8 7 6 5 4 3 2 1

Contents

Illustrations and Maps

Admiral Harold R. Stark – *Hulton-Deutsch Collection*
Admiral of the Fleet Sir James Somerville – *Hulton-Deutsch Collection*
Admiral of the Fleet Lord Fraser – *Hulton-Deutsch Collection*
Admiral of the Fleet Sir Philip Vian – *Hulton-Deutsch Collection*
Admiral Arleigh A. Burke – *Hulton-Deutsch Collection*

Part Six: Unsung Heroes
Admiral John Godfrey – *Weidenfeld & Nicolson Archive*
Captain Joseph John Rochefort – *US Naval Institute*
Vice Admiral Ben Moreell – *US Naval Institute*
Lieutenant-General Holland M. Smith – *US Defence Department (Marine Corps)*

Maps
The Sea War in the Pacific Hemisphere
The Sea War in the Atlantic Hemisphere

Contributors

JEFFREY G. BARLOW was a sergeant E-5 in the regular US Army from 1968 to 1970, serving in South Korea and the US Army Military History Research Collection at Carlisle Barracks, Pennsylvania. He graduated in History at Westminster College, Pennsylvania, and gained a PhD in International Studies at the University of South Carolina in 1981 for his work on *President John F. Kennedy and His Joint Chiefs of Staff.* Dr Barlow then joined the Heritage Foundation as a national security analyst, before becoming a military analyst for the National Institute for Public Policy/National Security Research Inc. Since 1987 Dr Barlow has been a member of the Contemporary History Branch, Naval Historical Center, Washington, DC, where he is writing an official history of the US Navy and national security affairs, 1945–63. Dr Barlow has contributed to several books on maritime strategy and American military power, and has recently completed a history of 'The Revolt of the Admirals', for publication in 1992.

EDWARD L. BEACH retired from active service in the US Navy in 1966 with the rank of captain and one distinguished career behind him. After graduating second in his Annapolis class, he made twelve submarine war patrols in the Pacific against Japan, sinking twenty-seven enemy ships and damaging a dozen more. He received seven personal decorations for valour in combat, including the Navy Cross (second only to the Congressional Medal of Honor). On shore-duty tours he was aide to General Omar N. Bradley, then Chairman of the Joint Chiefs of Staff, and naval aide to President Eisenhower. At sea he commanded five men-of-war, including the nuclear submarine USS *Triton*, in which he circumnavigated the world submerged in 1960. After retiring from the navy, Captain Beach spent eight years as Staff Director of the Senate Republican Policy Committee. Captain Beach is also well known as a historian and author, and has written ten books, including four national best-sellers and the prize-winning *The United States Navy: 200 Years.*

KEITH W. BIRD received his BA from Alma College and his PhD in Military History from Duke University. In 1969–70 he studied as a Fulbright Scholar and Duke University Exchange Student at the Free University in Berlin, and, as a fellow of the Militärgeschichtliches Forschungsamt, received a West German DAAD Fellowship in 1975. His articles and scholarly reviews have appeared in many journals including, among others, *American Historical Review, Armed Forces and Society* and the *Naval War*

College Review. Acknowledged as one of America's foremost specialists in German naval history, he is the author of *Weimar: The German Naval Officer Corps and the Rise of National Socialism* and *German Naval History: A Guide to the Literature*. Dr Bird has been assistant professor of History and Director of the Continuing Education Division, University of Bridgeport, and a member of the Editorial Advisory Board for the American Military Institute. He is currently the Provost and senior Vice-President of Academic Affairs at Hesser College, Manchester, New Hampshire.

DAVID BROWN was an aviator in the Royal Navy from 1957 to 1969. He then joined the Naval Historical Branch (Ministry of Defence), of which he became Head in 1977. His many publications include *The Royal Navy and the Falklands War* (1989) and *The Seafire* (1989). *The Seafire* in particular is acknowledged as the best book there has been on any naval aircraft.

PAOLO E. COLETTA earned his doctorate in British History from the University of Missouri, Columbia, in 1942. During World War II he served in destroyers in the Pacific; after the war he remained in the active USNR until his retirement in 1973 in the rank of captain. In his civilian life, meanwhile, he taught at the University of Missouri and at Stephens College, Columbia; at Brookings, South Dakota, State College; at the University of Louisville, Kentucky; and at the US Naval Academy, retiring from the last in 1983 after thirty-seven years of service. In addition to some eighty articles in historical and military journals, Captain Coletta is the author of several leading volumes in American political and naval history. In 1971 and again in 1990 he served as Senior Fulbright Lecturer in American History at the University of Genoa, Italy.

BENIS M. FRANK served as an enlisted Marine during World War II and took part in the invasions of Peleliu and Okinawa, as well as the occupation of North China. While still a member of the Corps, he graduated in History in 1949 with a BA from the University of Connecticut and subsequently worked in International Relations at Clark University. He was commissioned just before the Korean War and served in that country. On leaving the Corps he remained in the USMC Reserve until 1961, when he became a Corps historian. He pioneered the Corps' Oral History Program and headed it from 1966 to 1991, when he was appointed Chief Historian of the Marine Corps. Mr Frank is the author of several books and many articles and reviews on the Corps in the Pacific and later engagements – in particular *Okinawa; Touchstone to Victory, US Marines in Lebanon 1982–84* and (as co-author) *Victory and Occupation*, the fifth and final volume of the official *History of the US Marine Corps Operations in World War II*. He is currently overseeing the publication over four years (1992–5) of thirty-two monographs commemorating the Corps' operations in World War Two.

W. J. R. (JOCK) GARDNER is a serving officer in the Royal Navy, and a specialist in anti-submarine warfare. He joined the Royal Navy in 1964 and has served in a wide range of warships, from coastal minesweepers to aircraft carriers. His interest in naval history has resulted in papers on a number of topics such as the Battle of the Atlantic and the history of the Soviet ballistic missile submarine force. Work on the later subject led to the award of an MPhil degree in International Relations at the University of Cambridge in 1989. While there, he also edited the *Cambridge Review of International Affairs*. Currently working in the Ministry of Defence, his family home is in Hampshire.

Contributors

BODO HERZOG is one of Germany's leading experts in the history of the Kriegsmarine's U-boat arm. From 1943 to the end of the war he was a member of the Kriegsmarine, and from 1945 to 1947 worked under Royal Navy supervision in German Minesweeping Administration. From 1954 to 1986 he was Director of one of Germany's largest and oldest company archives. He is an extremely prolific author, with several hundred listed publications. The major ones include thirteen books published worldwide, of which the best known in English is *U-boats in Action, 1939–45*(1979). In 1981 Herr Herzog received the Rheinlandtaler in recognition of his contribution to regional industrial history. He has studied Otto Kretschmer's career for several decades and has interviewed Kretschmer many times.

DAVID HOBBS, a serving officer in the Royal Navy, entered Britannia Royal Naval College, Dartmouth, in 1964, qualified as a pilot in 1970, and has served worldwide in a variety of ships. These have included the LCT *Bastion*, in the Persian Gulf, and the aircraft carriers *Victorious, Hermes, Bulwark, Albion* and both the fourth and fifth *Ark Royal*. A recognized specialist in naval air matters, he has also written *Aircraft of the Royal Navy since 1945* and *Ark Royal: The Name Lives On*. At present he is serving in the Ministry of Defence (Navy) and working on an encyclopaedia of Commonwealth aircraft carriers.

STEPHEN HOWARTH, contributing editor of the present volume, is the author of several books on naval, maritime and general history. His works include *The Koh-i-Noor Diamond: The History and the Legend, The Knights Templar, Morning Glory: A History of the Imperial Japanese Navy 1895–1945, August '39: The Last Four Weeks of Peace in Europe, To Shining Sea: A History of the United States Navy 1775–1991*, and *Sea Shell: The Story of Shell's British Tanker Fleets, 1892–1992*. With his late father, the naval historian David Howarth, he co-wrote *The Story of P&O: The Peninsular and Oriental Steam Navigation Company 1837–1987* and *Nelson: The Immortal Memory*. He is currently working on an account of the Battle of Jutland. In addition, Mr Howarth writes articles, reviews and obituaries for a wide variety of periodicals, and is an active officer in the Royal Naval Reserve.

KIYOSHI IKEDA was educated at the Imperial Naval College, Etajima. Passing out in 1944, he became Gunnery Officer on board *Maya*, Submarine No. 47. From 1949 to 1952 he studied Law at Tokyo University and continued postgraduate studies there until 1957, when he became Professor of Modern European History in the Faculty of Law, Osaka City University, a post which he held until 1970, when he transferred to the same role at Tohoku University, Sendai. Since 1988 he has been Professor of International Relations at the School of International Politics, Economics and Business, Aoyamagakuin University, Tokyo. In addition to many translations from English into Japanese, Professor Ikeda is the author of many distinguished books on the history of the Imperial Navy, and is one of the world's leading experts in that field.

PETER KEMP was educated in the Royal Naval colleges of Osborne and Dartmouth. He served in the Royal Navy, mainly in submarines, until being invalided out in 1928. During World War Two he was recalled to service in the Naval Intelligence Division, where he worked in the Operational Intelligence Centre. In the five years before and five years after the war, he was a member of *The Times* editorial staff, and in 1950 became librarian and head of the Naval Historical Branch, a post he occupied until 1968. Between 1952 and 1962 he was also editor of the *Royal United Services Institute Journal*, and later published many books, including *Nine Vanguards*, *Victory at Sea*, *Brethren of the Coast* (with Christopher Lloyd), *The British Sailor*, *The History of Ships* and *The Campaign of the Spanish Armada* (1988). He also wrote several children's novels, and edited both the *Encyclopaedia of Ships and Seafaring* and the invaluable *Oxford Companion to Ships and the Sea*. He died on 15 March 1992.

ROBERT W. LOVE JR graduated in History at the University of Washington, gaining his doctorate in History from the University of California at Davis in 1975. Since that time Dr Love has been an associate professor of History at the US Naval Academy, Annapolis, specializing in Anglo-American naval diplomacy and recent naval strategy and policy. His publications include *The Chiefs of Naval Operations* (editor and co-author, 1980), *Changing Interpretations and New Sources in Naval History* (editor, 1980), and 'Fighting a Global War, 1941–1945' in *In Peace and War* (ed. K. J. Hagan, 1984). Dr Love's forthcoming books include *The History of the United States Navy* and *Journey to Pearl Harbor*, the latter being the first part of a two-volume work on the US Navy in the era of Admiral E. J. King.

JAMES M. MERRILL graduated from Pomona College in 1947, graining his MA from Claremont Graduate School two years later and his doctorate from the University of California in 1954. From 1952 to 1966 he was associate professor of History at Whittier College, and from 1966 to 1985 Professor of History and Marine Studies at the University of Delaware, where he has been Professor Emeritus since 1985. Professor Merrill has many important books to his credit, including histories of the US Navy, Army and Cavalry, studies of the Union Navy and river conflict in the Civil War, an account of the Halsey–Doolittle raid on Tokyo, and biographies of General William Tecumseh Sherman, Admiral Samuel Francis DuPont and Fleet Admiral William F. Halsey.

PETER PADFIELD trained for the sea on board HMS *Worcester*, serving subsequently as a navigating officer with P&O. In 1957 he served as a mariner in the transatlantic voyage of the replica barque *Mayflower II*. On his return to Britain after travelling in the Pacific, he took up writing and made his name as a naval historian with biographies of pioneer gunnery officers and a history of naval gunnery. He is the author of nineteen books, including *Himmler: Reichsführer SS*, the magisterial *Dönitz: The Last Führer*, and most recently *Hess: Flight for the Führer* (Weidenfeld & Nicolson, 1991).

ROGER PINEAU graduated from the University of Michigan in 1942 and enrolled for instruction at the Navy Japanese Language School, Boulder, Colorado. Commissioned as an ensign in the US Naval Reserve, from the summer of 1943 he worked in Naval Communication Intelligence in Washington DC. At the end of the war he was assigned as interpreter and analyst to the US Strategic Bombing Survey, Japan; thereafter he became assistant to Rear Admiral Samuel E. Morison in the preparation of the fifteen-volume official *History of United States Naval Operations in World War II*. In addition to many duties in both the regular and reserve forces of the US Navy, Captain Pineau has co-authored, translated or edited seven major works on the Pacific War and is acknowledged as one of his country's foremost specialists in that field.

Contributors

E. B. POTTER earned degrees from the University of Richmond and the University of Chicago and was awarded an honorary Doctorate of Letters by the former. During World War II he served at Pearl Harbor, attaining the rank of commander, USNR. Thereafter he joined the civilian faculty of the US Naval Academy and was for twenty years its chairman of Naval History. He has lectured at the army, naval and national war colleges and on television. On his retirement from active teaching in 1977, the Secretary of the Navy awarded him the title Professor Emeritus. Professor Potter co-authored and edited, with Fleet Admiral Nimitz, *Sea Power: A Naval History* and is the author of a history of the US Navy and of biographies of Admiral Arleigh Burke and Fleet Admirals Chester Nimitz and William F. Halsey.

CLARK G. REYNOLDS received his PhD in History from Duke University and has taught History at the US Naval Academy, the University of Maine and the US Merchant Marine Academy, heading the latter's Department of Humanities in the rank of captain, US Maritime Service. He is the author of *The Fast Carriers: The Forging of an Air Navy, Command of the Sea: The History and Strategy of Maritime Empires, Famous American Admirals, The Carrier War, The Fighting Lady: The New Yorktown in the Pacific War,* and *Admiral John H. Towers: The Struggle for Naval Air Supremacy.* For ten years Dr Reynolds served as curator of Patriots Point Naval and Maritime Museum, Charleston Harbor, South Carolina, before becoming Historical Consultant there. Since 1988 he has been a professor in and the chairman of the Department of History, University of Charleston (formerly College of Charleston), South Carolina.

DAVID ALAN ROSENBERG graduated from American University, subsequently receiving an MA and PhD with distinction at the University of Chicago. He has taught at the Universities of Houston and of Wisconsin-Milwaukee, served as a consultant to the Office of the CNO, and was author of a history of long-range naval planning for the Office of the Secretary of the Navy. From 1983 to 1985 he was a senior fellow at the Strategic Concepts Development Center at National Defense Univesity; from 1985 to 1990, a professor of strategy and operations at the US Naval War College; and in 1988 was awarded a five-year MacArthur Foundation Fellowship. Married with one daughter, Dr Rosenberg has published two dozen scholarly articles and chapters on the development of nuclear strategy, military affairs and naval history, and is currently completing two books: a biography of Admiral Arleigh Burke, and a history of American plans, policies and strategies for general war from 1945 to 1990. He is currently an associate professor of History at Temple University, Philadelphia, Pennsylvania, and is an Intelligence officer in the US Navy Ready Reserve.

B. MITCHELL SIMPSON III graduated in Law at the University of Pennsylvania in 1956, prior to twenty-one years' active duty in the US Navy, during which time he also gained his Doctorate in Law. Until 1970 he served extensively at sea in a variety of ships; from 1970 to 1977 he taught at graduate level in the US Naval War College and edited the scholarly professional journal *Naval War College Review*, before undertaking three years of advanced research in the College. Since 1980, when he retired from the navy, he has been in a civilian legal practice in Newport, Rhode Island. In addition to other books and learned articles, Dr Simpson's publications include a full war biography of Admiral Harold R. Stark.

THADDEUS V. TULEJA graduated from Rutgers University before enlisting, and later being commissioned as an ensign, in the US Navy. During the war he served in the Atlantic on convoy duty; in Casablanca as US Naval Liaison Officer with the French Naval Forces; in the Pacific as Navigating Officer of USS *Dawson*; and in the Atlantic as Executive Officer of USS *Merak*. As a naval reservist after the war he attained the rank of captain, before retiring in 1975. Meanwhile, in his civilian life, he joined the history faculty of St Peter's College, New Jersey. He taught there for many years and was recently named Professor Emeritus by the College. He is the author of three books of naval history (*Twilight of the Sea Gods, Climax at Midway* and *Statesmen and Admirals*), and has also been Visiting Professor of Naval History and Strategy at the US Naval War College, Rhode Island, and Visiting Professor of Military and Strategic Studies at Acadia University, Nova Scotia.

DAN VAN DER VAT was born in Holland and educated at the Cardinal Vaughan School, London, and Durham University. After graduating in Classics he went into journalism. He spent fourteen years (including ten abroad, of which five were in Germany) working for *The Times* of London. For six years thereafter he was chief foreign leader-writer for the *Guardian*. Now a full-time author specializing in naval history, he is the winner of two literary prizes. His books, commanding much critical acclaim, include *The Grand Scuttle, The Last Corsair, The Ship That Changed the World* and *The Atlantic Campaign, 1939–1945*.

GERALD E. WHEELER served in the US Navy during World War II as a 'blimp' pilot and later as an air navigator. Post-war, he continued to serve in the US Naval Reserve and rose to the rank of commander, while gaining his doctorate in American and Far Eastern History from the University of California at Berkeley. From 1952 to 1957 he taught at the US Naval Academy. From 1957 until his retirement in 1983 he was Professor of History at San Jose State University, California. For the academic year 1968–9 he was Ernest J. King Professor of Maritime History at the US Naval War College. Professor Wheeler's many publications include *Prelude to Pearl Harbor: The US Navy and the Far East, 1921–1931, Admiral William Veazie Pratt: A Sailor's Life* and *The Road to War: The United States and Japan, 1931–1941*.

MICHAEL WILSON joined the Royal Navy in 1948, and spent twelve of his thirty-one years' service as an active submariner, a period which included command of three submarines. After retiring with the rank of commander, he joined the Naval Historical Branch of the Ministry of Defence, where he worked as an historian. Now retired again, he lives in Norfolk. Commander Wilson has written several articles and two books about submarines: *Baltic Assignment* and *Destination Dardanelles*, both of which deal with the exploits of British submarines during World War One.

JOHN WINTON went to St Paul's School and joined the Royal Navy as a cadet at Dartmouth. He served in the Korean War, at Suez in 1956 and then in the Submarine Service for seven years, during which time his first novel, *We Joined the Navy*, was published. In 1963 he retired from the navy as a lieutenant-commander and became a full-time professional author. Since then he has written prolifically; he is literary editor of *Warship World* and, in addition to contributions to the *Naval Review*, the *Illustrated London News* and the *Daily Telegraph*, his list of published works to date includes thirteen novels and twenty-one books of naval history. Prominent among the latter are *The Forgotten Fleet*, a study of British naval operations in the Far East 1944–5, *The Victoria Cross at Sea*, biographies of Sir Walter Raleigh and Admiral Jellicoe, and most recently *The Naval Heritage of Portsmouth*. He is also an occasional publisher of naval history, including *Hands to Action Stations!: Naval Poetry and Verse of World War Two*, under his own imprint of Bluejacket Books.

JOHN F. WUKOVITS graduated in History at the University of Notre Dame in 1967, gaining an MA in History from the University of Michigan the following year. Since then he has taught History at secondary level, co-authored Middle School curricula in History and Geography, and in addition to reviews has published over ninety articles in newspapers, journals and magazines, including among many others *Military History*, *Naval History* and the US Naval Institute *Proceedings*. He has also written profiles of Fleet Admiral E. J. King (in *A Book of Days*, 1988) and Admiral of the Navy George Dewey (in *The Great Admirals*, 1990). In addition to teaching, Mr Wukovits is currently writing two books: a biography of Admiral Clifton Sprague, and, as part of the 50th anniversary series being published by the USMC Historical Center, an account of the Battle of Okinawa.

Foreword
by Admiral of the Fleet The Lord Lewin
KG, GCB, LVO, DSC

Looking back with the benefit of hindsight, the vital campaign in World War Two was the war at sea, a battle that lasted from 3 September 1939 to VJ Day. Shipping was the vital resource: to put it very simply, until the Allies could build ships faster than they were being sunk the land and air forces could not carry the war to the enemy in sufficient strength to ensure victory. North America was the arsenal from which manpower and material had to be convoyed to the operational theatres; command of the oceans had to be won before the campaigns that would win the war could be fought. The war had to be won on land; it could, however, be lost at sea.

Stephen Howarth and his contributors have assembled a portrait gallery of commanders with responsibilities ranging from Grand Strategy to close action, but their common concern, no matter on which side they fought, was defeat of the enemy in the battle for command of the sea. All are men who have earned their place in history because of their successes. I cannot fault their selection but reflect that chance must have played a part in ensuring some their place, or perhaps, to be fair, in excluding others. To have the flair for command, the ability to seize the initiative, is a great advantage, but to have the good fortune to be in the right place at the right time, blessed with adequate resources for the task in hand, is also important. So too, on the evidence presented, is a good relationship with both superiors and subordinates.

Reading the careers of those included in this book it is tempting to consider some 'might have beens'.

Admiral Sir Charles Forbes commanded the Royal Navy's Home Fleet in the early days of the war, handicapped in the disastrous Norwegian Campaign by bad strategic direction from Whitehall and short of air support. Admiral Sir Percy Noble fought the Battle of the Atlantic through the darkest days of 1941–2, short of escorts and long range aircraft, and before Ultra was providing its best intelligence. Forbes is accused by historians of errors of judgement; Noble is said to lack aggressive drive. Who is to say that with different timing, and more adequate resources, they might not have been just as successful as those who followed them – two of whom, Fraser and Horton, are included in this book?

xvi

Dönitz is rightly included, a truly aggressive and professional director of submarine operations. It chills the spine to think what his command might have achieved if the steel that went into the construction of *Tirpitz* and *Bismarck* – two ships that achieved nothing in the war against merchant shipping – had been devoted instead to building more U-boats, as he had advised.

Here, too, with equally strong justification, is Admiral Sir Bertram Ramsay. Recalled from retirement at the outbreak of war, he was an inspiring commander and a brilliant staff officer. He masterminded the almost miraculous evacuation from Dunkirk and was responsible for the detailed planning of three major invasions, North Africa, Sicily and Normandy. Yet because of a clash with his Commander in Chief, an officer of the old school who could not decentralize or make proper use of his staff, Ramsay retired before the war as a junior Rear Admiral. In happier circumstances who is to say he might not have become First Sea Lord – and perhaps better able to cope with the political infighting than either Pound or Cunningham.

Then there are the unsung heroes: Godfrey and Rochefort, victims of jealousy and political expediency; Moreell of the Seabees, whose men provided the unglamorous support on which successful operations depended; Holland M. Smith, the epitome of the US Marine Corps, who laid the foundations of victory in the Pacific Island Campaign but was ignored in its finale. I am glad that they have been included. There must have been many more candidates for this category.

This is a book to inspire ambitious young servicemen, but in studying the lives of these great men they should remember that it is the achievements of hundreds of thousands of sailors and marines at the sharp end – those who fed the guns, loaded the torpedoes, stumbled ashore on bullet swept beaches – on which the reputations of the 'Men of War' are founded.

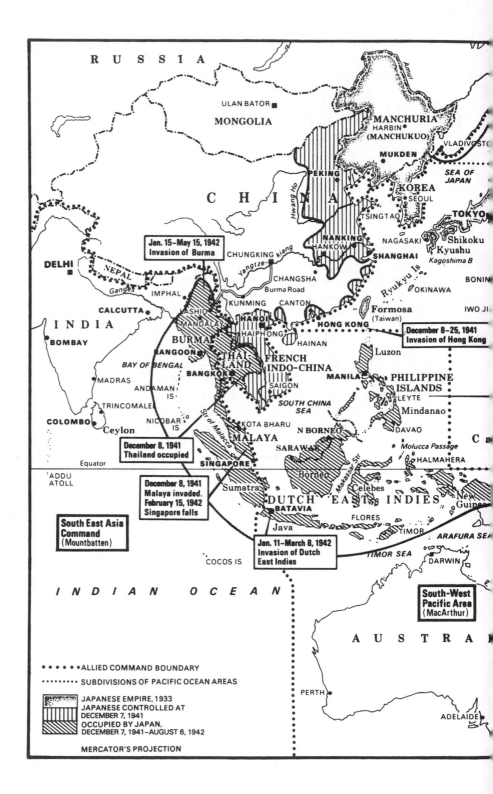

RUSSIA

ULAN BATOR ■
MONGOLIA

MANCHURIA
HARBIN ●
(MANCHUKUO)

VLADIVOSTO
MUKDEN ●

SEA OF
JAPAN

C H I N A

PEKING ■

KOREA
● SEOUL

TSINGTAO ●

TOKYO ■

Shikoku
NAGASAKI ● Kyushu
Kagoshima B

BONIN

DELHI ■

NEPAL

Jan. 15–May 15, 1942
Invasion of Burma

CHUNGKING kiang

NANKING ●
HANKOW ●

SHANGHAI ●

Hwang Ho

Yangtze kiang

CHANGSHA ●

Ganges

IMPHAL ●

Burma Road

CALCUTTA ■

ASHIO

KUNMING ●

CANTON ●

Ryukyu Is

OKINAWA

Formosa
(Taiwan)

IWO JI.

I N D I A

MANDALAY ●

HANOI ●

HONG KONG ●

December 8–25, 1941
Invasion of Hong Kong

BOMBAY ●

BURMA

HAIPHONG ●

HAINAN

Luzon

PHILIPPINE
ISLANDS

RANGOON ●

THAI
LAND

FRENCH
INDO-CHINA

MANILA ●

BAY OF BENGAL

BANGKOK ●

MADRAS ●

ANDAMAN
IS

SAIGON ●

LEYTE

Mindanao

TRINCOMALE

NICOBAR
IS

SOUTH CHINA
SEA

DAVAO ●

COLOMBO ■

Ceylon

Str of Malacca

KOTA BHARU ●

N BORNEO

MALAYA

SARAWAR

Molucca Passage

C a

HALMAHERA ●

December 8, 1941
Thailand occupied

Equator

SINGAPORE ●

Borneo

Makassar Str

Celebes

ADDU
ATOLL

December 8, 1941
Malaya invaded.
February 15, 1942
Singapore falls

Sumatra

DUTCH EAST INDIES

New
Guinea

BATAVIA ■

FLORES

South East Asia
Command
(Mountbatten)

Java

TIMOR

ARAFURA SEA

Jan. 11–March 8, 1942
Invasion of Dutch
East Indies

TIMOR SEA

COCOS IS

DARWIN ●

South-West
Pacific Area
(MacArthur)

I N D I A N   O C E A N

A U S T R A

PERTH ●

ADELAIDE ●

● ● ● ● ● ALLIED COMMAND BOUNDARY

● ● ● ● ● SUBDIVISIONS OF PACIFIC OCEAN AREAS

JAPANESE EMPIRE, 1933
JAPANESE CONTROLLED AT
DECEMBER 7, 1941
OCCUPIED BY JAPAN,
DECEMBER 7, 1941–AUGUST 6, 1942

MERCATOR'S PROJECTION

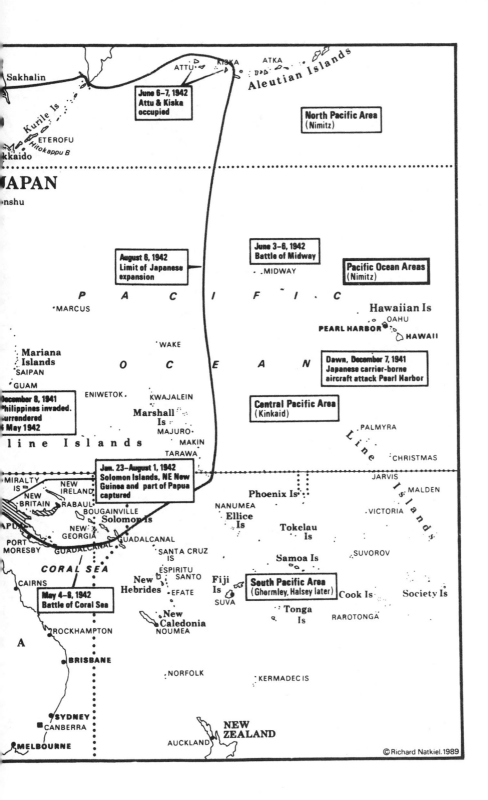

Sakhalin

ATTU ATKA
KISKA Aleutian Islands

**June 6-7, 1942
Attu & Kiska
occupied**

North Pacific Area
(Nimitz)

Kurile Is

ETEROFU
Hitokappu B
kkaido

JAPAN
nshu

**August 6, 1942
Limit of Japanese
expansion**

**June 3-6, 1942
Battle of Midway**

· MIDWAY

Pacific Ocean Areas
(Nimitz)

P   A   C   I   F   I   C
·MARCUS

·WAKE

Hawaiian Is
OAHU
PEARL HARBOR
HAWAII

**Mariana
Islands**
·SAIPAN

O   C   E   A   N

**Dawn, December 7, 1941
Japanese carrier-borne
aircraft attack Pearl Harbor**

·GUAM

**December 8, 1941
Philippines invaded.
surrendered
6 May 1942**

ENIWETOK·

KWAJALEIN

**Marshall
Is**
MAJURO·

Central Pacific Area
(Kinkaid)

·PALMYRA

l i n e   I s l a n d s
MAKIN
TARAWA·

·CHRISTMAS

**Jan. 23-August 1, 1942
Solomon Islands, NE New
Guinea and part of Papua
captured**

JARVIS

MIRALTY
IS
NEW
IRELAND
NEW
BRITAIN   RABAUL·
BOUGAINVILLE

Phoenix Is·
NANUMEA
Ellice
Is

·MALDEN

Line Islands

·VICTORIA

Solomon Is

APU
NEW
GEORGIA
GUADALCANAL

Tokelau
Is

·SUVOROV

PORT
MORESBY
GUADALCANAL

SANTA CRUZ
IS

Samoa Is

CORAL SEA

ESPIRITU
SANTO

New
Hebrides   ·EFATE

Fiji
Is
SUVA

South Pacific Area
(Ghormley, Halsey later)   Cook Is·

Society Is

CAIRNS

**May 4-8, 1942
Battle of Coral Sea**

Tonga
Is

RAROTONGA

·New
Caledonia
NOUMEA

A
·ROCKHAMPTON

·BRISBANE

·NORFOLK

·KERMADEC IS

·SYDNEY
·CANBERRA

·MELBOURNE

AUCKLAND

**NEW
ZEALAND**

©Richard Natkiel.1989

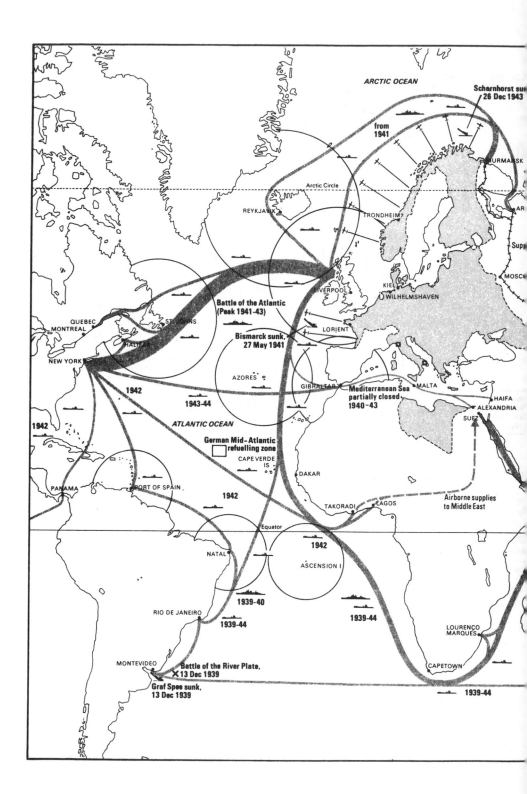

ARCTIC OCEAN

Scharnhorst sun[k]
26 Dec 1943

from
1941

MURMANSK

Arctic Circle

AR

REYKJAVIK

TRONDHEIM?

Sup[p]

MOSC[OW]

KIEL
WILHELMSHAVEN

LIVERPOOL

Battle of the Atlantic
(Peak 1941-43)

QUEBEC
MONTREAL

ST JOHNS

LORIENT

HALIFAX

Bismarck sunk,
27 May 1941

NEW YORK

1942

1943-44

AZORES

GIBRALTAR

Mediterranean Sea
partially closed
1940-43

MALTA

HAIFA

ALEXANDRIA

SUEZ

1942

ATLANTIC OCEAN

German Mid-Atlantic
refuelling zone

CAPE VERDE
IS

DAKAR

PANAMA

PORT OF SPAIN

1942

TAKORADI

LAGOS

Airborne supplies
to Middle East

Equator

1942

NATAL

ASCENSION I

1939-40

RIO DE JANEIRO

1939-44

1939-44

LOURENÇO
MARQUES

MONTEVIDEO

Battle of the River Plate,
X 13 Dec 1939

CAPETOWN

Graf Spee sunk,
13 Dec 1939

1939-44

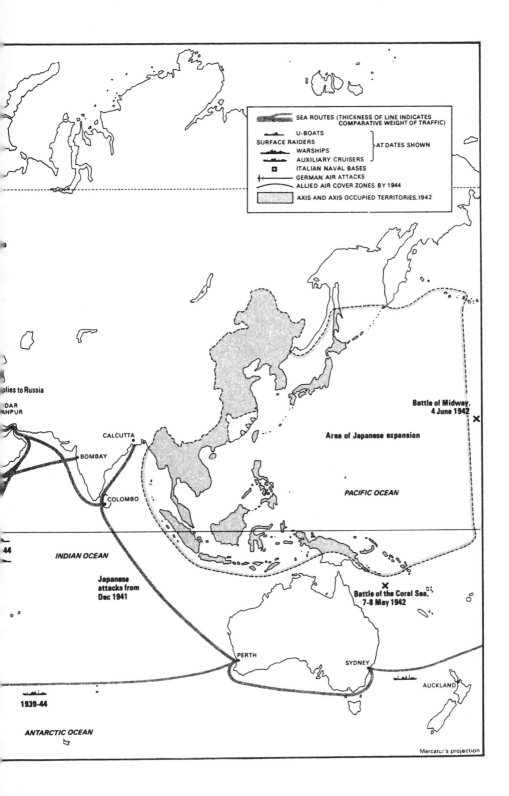

SEA ROUTES (THICKNESS OF LINE INDICATES COMPARATIVE WEIGHT OF TRAFFIC)

U-BOATS
SURFACE RAIDERS
WARSHIPS   AT DATES SHOWN
AUXILIARY CRUISERS
ITALIAN NAVAL BASES
GERMAN AIR ATTACKS
ALLIED AIR COVER ZONES BY 1944
AXIS AND AXIS OCCUPIED TERRITORIES,1942

plies to Russia
DAR
AHPUR

CALCUTTA

BOMBAY

COLOMBO

Battle of Midway,
4 June 1942

Area of Japanese expansion

PACIFIC OCEAN

44

INDIAN OCEAN

Japanese
attacks from
Dec 1941

Battle of the Coral Sea,
7-8 May 1942

PERTH

SYDNEY

AUCKLAND

1939-44

ANTARCTIC OCEAN

Mercator's projection

Introduction

by Stephen Howarth

Thinking of great naval leaders in most sea wars, those who spring most easily to mind are the fighting admirals and captains – the men who actually brought the war directly to the enemy. Many of the leaders written about in these pages were just such men; but not all.

One of the distinctive factors of World War Two at sea is that it was in many ways a war of electronics. The unprecedented speed and accuracy of available communications meant that, to a far greater degree than ever before, it was possible (though not always desirable) for the highest level of naval leadership to be exercised from shore positions, far removed from the actual scenes of battle, but often with rapid or even immediate effect upon them. Because of this – and irrespective of their success or failure – the most powerful naval leaders of the war were men whose front-line lives were for the most part over, but whose experience, skill and seniority qualified them to be commanders-in-chief. They did not necessarily face the shells, bombs, torpedoes and depthcharges of their enemies, but their individual and collective contribution to the sea war's wider direction were nevertheless vital.

An outline of the structure of this book will be useful. Its thirty-one chapters are divided into six groups; and in the first group – up front, as befits commanders-in-chief – we encounter the High Command: eight men (British, German, American and Japanese) who, whether as allies or enemies, between them masterminded the whole of the global war at sea.

Following them come four more groups which together include nineteen individual chapters. These studies reflect more, perhaps, of the traditional view of naval leadership: they show the sharp-end people, those who directed operations from the bridge of a warship at sea. But here again there is a difference, when compared to earlier naval wars. The bridges from which these men fought were by no means always in surface vessels armed with guns. The years 1939–45 showed vividly that naval conflict had moved permanently from two dimensions into three. No longer limited to the sea's surface alone, warfare had gone both underwater and into the air. Throughout World War Two, command of the seas included the depths and the heights, in a way never known before; not even the 1914–18 war – the Great War – could offer such widespread and critical use of submarine and aerial combat.

By 1939, submarines had already developed into weapons of utterly fearsome potential. During the next six years, they were put to terrible use in every naval theatre. At the same time, the traditional borderline between sea- and land-warfare became increasingly blurred. In the Pacific, close co-operation between soldiers, sailors and Marines became the norm, rather than something extraordinary; in the Mediterranean, the invasions of North Africa, Sicily and Italy marked the watershed of Axis power; and history's largest amphibious operation took place in Overlord, the Allies' cross-Channel invasion of Normandy in 1944. But perhaps the most spectacular confirmation of the new three-dimensional nature of modern sea war began in 1942. It was in that year – following decades of fruitless argument, and the cataclysmic attack on Pearl Harbor – that the US Navy shifted its emphasis from battle-ships to aircraft carriers.

Within months the carrier had swept the battleship from its ancient role as queen of the naval chessboard. The second group of chapters accordingly focuses on the Air Admirals: four men, experts all, who honed the use of the oceans' newly dominant weapon to perfection. It will be no surprise that these men are exclusively Japanese and American.

Following them in the third group come the Amphibious Admirals – four Americans and one Briton – and after them, a small but very select group: the Submariners. Here, for the first though not the last time, we go below the rank of admiral. Only three men are included, and just two nations are represented; but there can be little doubt that it was Germany and America which used this powerful, yet peculiarly cost-effective weapon to the greatest effect overall.

The fifth group of men is the largest and, it must be acknowledged, somewhat amorphous; but it is not always wise to try and force things or people into precise categories merely for the sake of tidiness. Thus, under the catholic umbrella of Anti-Submariners, Tactical and General, we have a further seven Britons and Americans who were leading exponents of their various skills: diplomacy; the hunting and killing of submarines; the direction of convoys; the handling of flotillas of small ships; and operational planning.

Observant mathematicians will have noted that, though there are thirty-one chapters in this book altogether, only twenty-seven have featured in these five groups so far. Taking station astern, the sixth and final group of chapters shows a quartet of men whose inclusion may at first seem to stretch the term 'great leaders' beyond its reasonable definition. It depends, of course, on what one means by a great leader; but here the term is taken to mean someone whose contribution to naval warfare between 1939 and 1945 was outstanding, whether or not the person concerned actually fought at the front. The final group therefore includes two outstanding intelligence officers; the creator of the US Navy's non-combatant Construction Battalions, the Seabees; and one US Marine Corps general. The group's title, Unsung Heroes, may be slightly unfair, but not very. More often than not, the men in it are overlooked by naval histories of this sort; and if their inclusion here is unusual it is all the more worthwhile, because the war could not easily have been won without them.

In these thirty-one chapters, the careers, contributions and styles of leadership of their subjects are described and assessed. Naturally they are almost all interrelated; and because the reader is not expected to start on the first page and go through to the last, there is a deliberate degree of overlap. Read in isolation, any single chapter will provide the reader with a sound understanding of its individual subject; read collectively, the thirty-one together provide a comprehensive coverage of the actions and characteristics of the men who led the global war at sea.

Looking now beyond the structure of the book to its content, Peter Kemp opens the High Command group with a thoroughbred study of Admiral of the Fleet Sir Dudley Pound, who, from the outbreak of the war in 1939 until shortly before his death in 1943, was Britain's First Sea Lord – the Royal Navy's most senior serving officer, equivalent to the US Navy's Chief of Naval Operations.

As will be seen in this and other chapters, Pound's career and character still provoke controversy: for example, by many people he is still best (or worst) remembered for the fate of Convoy PQ17, which, after being ordered by him to scatter, was two-thirds destroyed. Peter Kemp is particularly well suited to describe Pound: not only a highly skilled writer of naval history, Kemp was also a naval officer for many years, and, during the whole of Pound's tenure as wartime First Sea Lord, served in the Admiralty's Operational Intelligence Centre (OIC). Though he was considerably junior to Pound, the OIC brought them together. Such first-hand knowledge, hitherto unpublished, is increasingly rare, and correspondingly valuable. Encouraged to adopt a more personal tone than is usual in naval historiography, Kemp's chapter – thoughtful and modest, compassionate yet balanced – provides future writers with a resource which otherwise would have been unavailable, and demonstrates the true extent of Pound's success as overall guide of the Royal Navy during Britain's years of greatest danger.

Grand Admiral Erich Raeder was one year older than Dudley Pound, and, as Commander-in-Chief of Germany's *Kriegsmarine*, the Reich War Navy, was Pound's equivalent in rank, his counterpart in function and his almost exact contemporary in term of office.

A full generation before World War Two erupted, these two men had already faced each other in battle, at Jutland in 1916. Then, the forty-year-old Raeder had been Chief of Staff to Admiral Hipper (flag officer commanding the Scouting Forces of the *Hochseeflotte*, imperial Germany's High Seas Fleet), while Pound had been Captain of the battleship HMS *Colossus*. At that point, however, their similarities ended; and, as Keith Bird shows in his chapter on Raeder, many of their crucial and eventually fateful differences in

3

war management stemmed from the origin, prosecution and conclusion of World War One.

Because the High Seas Fleet scuttled itself in Scapa Flow in 1918, many German naval officers denied they had ever surrendered. But whatever gloss they put upon it, the inescapable fact was that Allied forces (including the Royal Navy) had won that war, and German forces (including the High Seas Fleet) had lost it. This left a long shadow in Raeder's mind and the minds of most of his colleagues, a shadow swirling with unfulfilled dreams, and an imprisoning tradition of building very large ships in order to seek a single decisive battle. At the outbreak of war in August 1939, the *Kriegsmarine* had on paper a timetable of construction which, when faced with the reality and actual consequences of Hitler's foreign policy, proved hopelessly unrealistic – incapable either of being achieved or of making a conclusive contribution to the Führer's goals. Like Napoleon, and with similar justice, Hitler has often been accused of failing to understand the uses of sea power. Alfred von Tirpitz, Raeder's spiritual and professional ancestor, spread the accusation, applying it to the whole German people. Keith Bird shows clearly that Raeder himself faces the same indictment; for under his leadership Germany's navy became neither a shield for merchant vessels – the primary function of any armed fleet – nor a coherent part of a national strategy, but something which existed and planned virtually for its own sake alone.

Fleet Admiral Ernest J. King of the US Navy had numerous flaws and weaknesses, but dreaming was not among them. The chapter by Robert W. Love Jr on the man who uniquely combined the role of Commander-in-Chief, US Atlantic Fleet, with that of Chief of Naval Operations is as energetic as King himself, and often as outspoken. One of the trickiest aspects within King's huge command was the problem of creating and maintaining a truly co-operative Allied war effort on a worldwide scale. That it succeeded as well as it did was no tribute to any forbearance of character on King's part; as Love has written elsewhere, 'King was accustomed to dominating those he worked with, either by his intellect, ability to work hard, or force of personality. He liked men he could not awe – *if* they worked *for* him.' In Britain, the generally received opinion of King is that he was a brilliant naval leader and a confirmed Anglophobe. Acknowledging that King did distrust British (especially English) leaders, Love has pointed out that he had his reasons: 'From his perspective in World War II the Royal Navy did *little* that was right . . . King was profoundly sympathetic with the Canadians, who felt on the whole that the RN and Pound treated them quite poorly.' These and similar questions are discussed at intervals throughout the book, without pretence that the contributors necessarily agree – which is as it should be. Among the motive forces of historical events, the personalities and prejudices of the participants rank highly. The same factors rank just as highly in subsequent writing on and interpretation of those events, and Robert Love's vigorous and vivid essay may be a salutary reminder to British readers that there are other points of view than their own.

Lasting only seventy-one weeks, the wartime career of Admiral of the Fleet Isoroku Yamamoto, Commander-in-Chief of the Combined Fleet of the Imperial Japanese Navy, was the shortest of these officers of the international High Command. Nevertheless, in some ways his brief career was the most important of them all; the part he played was world-historic in a manner unlike those of any of the other highest naval leaders here described – for he was the only one of them whose professional action precipitated war. If any single individual outside the realm of politics can be named as having transformed the war from one focused on Europe into a comprehensively global conflict, it is he, for it was he who conceived and planned the Imperial Navy's attack on Pearl Harbor.

Yet naming need not equate with blaming. For decades prior to the attack on Pearl, the form of Japan's political life – curious by most Western standards – had given to both the Army and the Navy ministers the right of direct access to the Emperor. That form also dictated that if either the army or the navy minister resigned and no replacement was forthcoming, the government must resign as well. Even so, all might have been well, had it not been customary for the ministers to be serving officers in their respective forces. Soldiers and sailors thus became politicians; and as a natural consequence the use of war as a political tool always ranked higher on the list of practical possiblities than it might otherwise have done.

After his long pre-war experience of Western countries, particularly America, Yamamoto argued long and hard against entering a prolonged struggle against them. To be sure, this was not from any pacifist motive, but because he was certain that Japan would lose any such conflict. Hence – when he and the Navy Minister, Admiral Yonai, eventually lost the argument with their militant colleagues and army counterparts – came the design against Pearl, which offered a better hope of brevity than any other plan. Yamamoto has been called the greatest admiral since Nelson; his attack on Pearl Harbor has been described as a strategic imbecility. As this chapter suggests, however, it may be more correct to view him as a completely professional naval officer trapped in an inescapable cultural dilemma.

If one had to use a single phrase to describe the wartime role of Admiral Chester W. Nimitz, it would be accurate to call him the Allies' principal naval administrator. This hardly sounds like the description of a fighting man, an impression which might appear to be confirmed by the observation in E. B. Potter's chapter that throughout Nimitz's long life there was only one single occasion (in April 1945) when he observed armed forces in combat.

But any image of Nimitz as merely a senior paper-shuffler would be wildly wrong, for, from his shore bases in Oahu and later in Guam, he was the man to whom fell the direct, grave responsibility of countering the work of Yamamoto and his successors. This responsibility began on New Year's Eve 1941, when, as replacement to the ill-fated Admiral Husband E. Kimmel, Nimitz hoisted his four-star admiral's flat in a submarine in the ravaged and utterly demoralized Pearl Harbor. For nearly four years thereafter – in what seemed at first to be a hopeless war – he commanded the sprawling Pacific Ocean Area and the increasingly huge US Pacific Fleet, until at last, on board the battleship USS *Missouri* on 2 September 1945, he accepted Japan's surrender in Tokyo Bay. In company with Admiral William D. Leahy (Roosevelt's wartime Chief of Staff, and a member of both the American Joint Chiefs of Staff and the Anglo-American Combined Chiefs of Staff) and Ernie King, Nimitz was promoted soon after the war to the rank of five-star fleet admiral. This was the first time such a high seniority had been conferred upon anyone in the US Navy, and emphasizes (if emphasis is necessary) the enormous value of Nimitz's job – and the skill with which he carried it out.

E. B. Potter, who served under Nimitz as a naval officer in Pearl Harbor for two of the war years, subsequently came to know him very well as a co-writer and friend. Based upon his prize-winning biography of the Fleet Admiral, his chapter (which might well have been called 'Nimitz's War') provides a superb summary of the major naval actions in the Pacific theatre, and a clear portrait of the Admiral and his particularly supportive style of leadership.

Though Admiral Raymond A. Spruance was not an aviator by training, it was he who led the American carriers against Nagumo at Midway (June 1942) and against Ozawa in the Philippine Sea (June 1944). He was a man of unusual intellectual power, and in both battles, as John F. Wukovits explains, his strategy and his tactics were brilliant. This was particularly so in the former battle; he was required to fight when he was not only severely outnumbered, but also without certain knowledge of where his enemy lay. Despite those great handicaps and others, he succeeded magnificently, winning one of the most remarkable victories in the history of sea war. There were four basic elements in his victory: courage, first and foremost; great determination; a timely input of luck; and – not least, but in notable contrast to his opponent Nagumo – decisiveness. Shortly thereafter he became Chief of Staff, and subsequently deputy, to Admiral Nimitz. Together they planned the counter-offensive against Japan, and from the spring of 1943 Spruance took command of those operations, attacking the Gilberts, the Marshalls and Truk, and on through other targets to the Philippine Sea, Iwo Jima and Okinawa. In the Philippine Sea, his pilots shot down 76 per cent of Ozawa's aircraft, yet Spruance was criticized for showing 'undue caution'. Today one can only say that some people are hard to please; he was certainly the most outstanding fleet commander of the war.

It was fortunate for Nimitz, and all the ships and men under his command, that the Imperial Japanese Navy failed to learn from the U-boat tactics employed by Germany. Karl Dönitz – successor to Raeder and ultimately successor to Hitler himself – began the war as a captain in charge of the U-boat arm. Little more than three years later he was a grand admiral in charge of the entire German Navy, with the U-boats specifically retained under his own personal control. Most submariners are aware of belonging to an elite, but probably none have ever been more so than those under Dönitz's command. He adored his boats and championed their crews, who responded with a level of commitment and devoted personal respect that has rarely been paralleled in naval history. How and why this came about is the theme of the chapter on Dönitz by Peter Padfield, a world-class expert on the Grand Admiral. Dönitz was 'an excellent officer', his fleet chief reported, 'of iron will-power, goal-oriented certainty and unwearying toughness' – a description which, though it sounds Teutonically overblown, was correct in every way. But so was a report written in 1930 by Admiral Wilhelm Canaris: Dönitz, he said, should 'take things more calmly and not set exaggerated demands, above all on himself'. This was the other side of the will-power, certainty and toughness. From 1935 Canaris was head of Wehrmacht intelligence, and in 1944 achieved fame as one of the principal plotters against Hitler's life. Despite his rank and role, Canaris could never have been called an enthusiastic Nazi, and when he suggested in that pre-war report that Dönitz was somewhat unbalanced, he actually revealed as much about himself as about his subject. Yet, between them, the two reports provide the key to Dönitz, a very nearly perfect product and example of his time and culture – a dedicated Nazi, inspirational leader and highly professional naval officer, who (fortunately for Britain and her allies) came to power too late to redress the strategic errors of his predecessors and superiors.

Finally in this section, we return to the Royal Navy, and to a man assessed by many of his contemporaries as Britain's greatest sailor since Nelson: Admiral of the Fleet Sir Andrew Browne Cunningham (later Viscount Cunningham of Hyndhope). Without sacrifice of historical accuracy, John Winton's chapter on A.B.C. – as Cunningham was known – is as bright and readable as anything Winton has written. Like Nelson (and, it must be admitted, like Dönitz as well), Cunningham had the gift of inspiring his subordinates with enormous personal loyalty. And, having already distinguished himself in World War One, when he won three DSOs, his name (again like Nelson's) first became internationally known because of his deeds in Mediterranean waters. Apart from some months in 1942 when he was head of the British Admiralty Delegation in Washington, he and his fleet – though always outnumbered – dominated that sea for four years, winning the victories of Taranto and Cape Matapan, sustaining Malta, and at last (in July 1943) accepting the surrender of the Italian fleet. Thereafter, Cunningham succeeded Dudley Pound as First Sea Lord; and thus the first group of chapters comes full circle, beginning and ending with the two men who, for six years, led Britain's war at sea.

In the second group of chapters, the Air Admirals, the most important aspect of the war's three-dimensional nature is studied in detail. James M. Merrill opens with an authoritative account of the war as fought by Admiral

William F. Halsey, one of the most charismatic and controversial of all the carrier commanders. He it was who, early in the Pacific War, launched the celebrated Doolittle raid against Tokyo, boosting American morale and earning national fame for himself; and he it was who, as the war drew to its end, left the beachhead at Leyte Gulf unprotected and exposed. His actions and nature have always attracted partisan support and criticism; Merrill's even-handed assessment is much to be commended.

Halsey was a very public man; his subordinate, Marc A. Mitscher, was not – which makes the chapter on him, by Clark G. Reynolds, all the more valuable. Slightly built, with a heavily wrinkled face and a gentle smile, Mitscher was nevertheless (in Halsey's words) 'a fighting fool' – a veteran pilot, one of the first in the US Navy to gain his wings; and a man who would go almost anywhere to attack the enemy, but would also do almost anything to bring his fliers safely back. TF 58 – the task force under his command – became legendary in its own time, known by the Japanese who had the misfortune to oppose it as 'the irresistible 58th'; and as Reynolds shows, the legend was fully justified.

Kiyoshi Ikeda (himself a former submariner in the Imperial Japanese Navy, and now one of Japan's most distinguished naval historians) writes on both Vice Admiral Chuichi Nagumo and Vice-Admiral Jisaburo Ozawa. As Yamamoto's leading carrier commander, Nagumo launched the attack against Pearl Harbor, and for six more months led the Fast Carrier Striking Force in an unparalleled series of conquests. However, he owed his position not to outstanding ability as a carrier commander, but to the Japanese naval system which gave the top job to the most senior man, regardless of background – and Nagumo was a torpedo specialist, not an aviator. Spruance, his opponent at Midway, was not a trained aviator either; but he probably had more brains, and certainly much more flexibility, than did Nagumo. Anyone like Nagumo who knows his job is beyond him, and yet cannot leave it, must be regarded as unfortunate; but in the long run it was the Japanese navy, and Japan itself, which was most hurt by the vagaries of the naval appointment system. By the time Nagumo was replaced by Ozawa in November 1942, the odds in carrier warfare had swung heavily against Japan; and that could be seen as Ozawa's own professional misfortune, for, though he was not an aviator either, he understood carriers in a way Nagumo never did, being the originator of the policy of using them in massed offensives. Undoubtedly the Imperial Navy's ablest strategic thinker, it fell to him to oppose TF 58 at the Battle of the Philippine Sea. There, his tactics were flawless; but the shortcomings of his predecessors, and America's vastly increased naval might, ensured his defeat, leaving him able only to lead his last – almost empty – carriers into the Battle for Leyte Gulf as a sacrificial decoy.

Amphibious warfare was by no means an exclusively American domain. However, it is at least arguable that US forces brought this form of combat to its most perfect form in World War Two, and so the third group, the

Amphibious Admirals, is dominated by Americans. First comes Admiral Richard L. Conolly, whose wartime career is ably described by Jeffrey G. Barlow. Origin-ally a destroyer man, Conolly learned amphibious work on the shores of Sicily and Italy. The experiments there were effective, the lessons well understood; and from October 1943 Conolly applied that experience throughout the Pacific, from Kwajalein to Lingayen Gulf, on every occasion welding his ships and men into teams of outstanding efficiency. As Thaddeus V. Tuleja relates, Admiral H. Kent Hewitt likewise earned amphibious eminence on the shores of Africa and the Mediterranean – Morocco, Algiers (where he worked in close co-operation with Cunningham), Sicily, Salerno and the south of France. Gerald E. Wheeler's subsequent chapter shows how, on the other side of the world, equal distinction was won by Admiral Thomas C. Kinkaid. As a wartime flag officer, Kinkaid's experience was very varied; after commanding cruiser screens for aircraft carriers he became a carrier task force commander, and as such performed so well that one could quite readily describe him as an air admiral. But he first came to public notice with the recovery of Attu in August 1943, and he won permanent fame with his command of the huge amphibious forces mustered for the invasion of Leyte – both amphibious operations; and thus in the end he must be seen as an amphibious commander, and a great one indeed.

So too was Admiral Sir Bertram Ramsay – the only non-American in this group. Having actually been retired from the service at the beginning of 1939, he returned to fill the billet of Flag Officer Dover. From the town's heights, it was often possible, on a clear day, to see German fortifications on the French coast, only twenty-two miles away across the Dover Strait. It was a sight guaranteed to galvanize anyone; but as Jock Gardner's chapter makes plain, Ramsay scarcely needed galvanizing. His first huge challenge was to manage the planning of Operation Dynamo, the evacuation of British troops from France. He and his colleagues met the challenge far more successfully than even they had hoped: though arms and equipment had to be abandoned, well over 300,000 men were brought safely back. Ramsay followed that with planning Operation Torch, the Allied invasion of North Africa and Husky, the invasion of Sicily, and was then appointed Naval Commander-in-Chief of the ultimate, Operation Overlord. 'The outcome', as Gardner says laconically, 'was successful; another triumph for the Ramsay method.' Ramsay's death, early in 1945, was a tragedy for the Allies; their luck was that he survived so long.

'The greatest of all amphibious commanders' is the judgement given by Paolo E. Coletta on the subject of his chapter, Admiral Richmond Kelly Turner. It is hard to disagree. In July 1942, when King sent him to the Pacific for the purpose, Turner had no experience and little knowledge of amphibious operations, and said so. 'You'll learn,' said King, and Turner did; over the next three years he led most of America's amphibious assaults across the Pacific, from Guadalcanal to Okinawa. He drank hard, swore hard, hit hard – and had a first-class brain. There were many tributes to his skill and bravery during his lifetime; but perhaps the most telling was the action of a Japanese general, Mitsuri Ushijima. When the invasion of Okinawa was about to take place, Ushijima decided – correctly – that his 80,000 troops would be unable to resist Turner's amphibians; and rather than face them on the beaches, he withdrew to the south of the island. As Coletta points out, the three most effective American naval forces in the Pacific were the carriers, the submarines and the amphibians; and, probably more than any other individual, Kelly Turner was responsible for the design, practice and refinement of amphibious assault doctrine. That is quite an epitaph.

With the fourth group of chapters we see just how effectively the Submariners, German and American, fought in the Atlantic and the Pacific. Bodo Herzog's chapter is another to benefit from personal knowledge of its subject: Commander Otto Kretschmer. Kretschmer's active wartime career was brief – his U-boat was sunk and he himself was captured in March 1941 – but his eighteen and a half months' activity at sea was such that he remained the most successful of all U-boat commanders in World War Two. In addition to his underwater exploits, Kretschmer exhibited considerable resourcefulness while a prisoner-of-war; and apart from his outstanding wartime record he is unusual in that Germany's defeat did not mark the end of his naval career – when it was allowed, he joined the Federal German Navy and eventually became an admiral. Commander Günther Prien, subject of the chapter by Dan van der Vat, was not so lucky: the attack on his boat (simultaneous with that on Kretschmer's) resulted in his death, in bizarre and somewhat macabre fashion. However, before that event, he too had been one of Germany's leading U-boat aces; and he figures here because, in addition to the remarkable tally of kills he built up, he allowed himself to be flaunted by the Nazi leadership as a shining example. He was; and, like it or not, that forms a further part of leadership.

Japanese submarines in World War Two had superb weapons – particularly the Long Lance torpedo, able to go further and faster than any Allied torpedoes, and far more difficult to detect. With them, as Admiral King remarked after the war, 'they might have raised hell with the West Coast–Hawaii convoys'. He then added, with feeling, 'Thank the Lord they did not understand or learn much about managing U-boats from the Nazis.' However, their American counterparts did. One of them, Edward L. Beach, followed a career of considerable distinction in submarines (including service in the Pacific War) with a literary career of comparable distinction. Here, his very individual chapter on Admiral Charles A. Lockwood Jr benefits not only from their shared naval background, but also from his personal knowledge of the Admiral. Beach makes vividly clear the frustrations of young submariners then, trying to wage war with inadequate weaponry; traces the huge efforts Lockwood made on their behalf; shows the staggering cost-efficiency they achieved; and leaves a powerful impression of the deep loyalty that Lockwood inspired. One set of statistics alone indicates the efficiency of the men under his command. His submarine crews represented only 1.6 per cent of the US Navy's total wartime personnel, yet they sank 55 per cent of the total merchant-ship tonnage and 29 per cent of the warship tonnage lost by Japan.

Naturally enough, the existence and threat of submariners bred anti-submariners; and the fifth (and largest) group of chapters opens with a study by David Hobbs of Captain Frederic Walker. He had once been passed over for that rank, but had he lived beyond 1944 he would almost certainly have become a flag officer. He was one of the Royal Navy's first professional anti-submariners, with eighteen years' experience by the time World War Two started. During the five years that remained to him, he introduced several novel tactics which became standard, and, using them, proved to be one of the best hunters, and killers, of submarines that the Royal Navy has had.

Michael Wilson follows with an illuminating chapter on Admiral Sir Max Horton. Horton was both a submariner and an anti-submariner – poacher turned gamekeeper, as his first biographer said. Setting a thief to catch a thief, though less flattering, would be an equally apt metaphor; and Horton succeeded equally well in both capacities. His many underwater victories in World War One and his inter-war experience qualified him perfectly for the role of Vice-Admiral Submarines at the outbreak of World War Two; and then, three years later, he began the work for which he is best remembered, the command of the Western Approaches – the area north-west of Ireland and Liverpool, towards which the life-sustaining convoys from America threaded their way across the Atlantic. To him is due much of the credit for the Allies' victory against the U-boats in the Battle of the Atlantic.

That victory – which paved the way for Overlord and the support of the entire Allied advance through Europe – was also, of course, due to (generally) good relationships between British and American forces; and there, as B. Mitchell Simpson III relates, Admiral Harold R. Stark did his life's best work. Having begun the war as Chief of Naval Operations, in March 1942 he became President Roosevelt's Commander, Naval Forces Europe. Despite its title, this was not a 'glamorous' fighting billet; but every child of the Allied nations should offer a prayer of thanks to his memory, for he proved to be a consummate and non-parochial diplomat. Envisioning America's likely fate if Britain fell, he smoothed their frequently fraught views of each other, and even contrived to keep the notoriously touchy General de Gaulle (and consequently all his followers) in good humour.

Like Ramsay, Admiral of the Fleet Sir James Somerville had been retired shortly before the outbreak of war. Like Ramsay again, he did not allow bureaucracy to get in the way; when the war began, he simply turned up at the Admiralty and started work. And like Ramsay yet again, he was soon down in Dover, where he helped his exhausted old friend. Thereafter, however, their paths diverged permanently, with Somerville going further and further afield. His command of the Mediterranean Force H included the unhappy duty of overseeing the bombardment of the French fleet at Oran. Subsequently he commanded the British Eastern Fleet in the Indian Ocean – a thankless task, for it did not begin to be an effective force until 1944; and finally he served as head of the British Admiralty Mission in Washington. David Brown's reasoned study of the man offers a refreshing and possibly contentious reassessment.

In 1939, aged fifty-one, the Third Sea Lord, Bruce Fraser, was a rear admiral. When the war ended six years later, he was a full admiral and a peer of the realm – Admiral Lord Fraser of North Cape. The title honoured his first really famous engagement, when, in the Battle of North Cape (26 December 1943), ships under his command sank the German battle-cruiser *Scharnhorst*. John Winton's second chapter – as lively as his account of Cunningham's life – demonstrates how Fraser's wartime career became one of the fullest and most varied that any naval officer could wish for. Starting with administration, it moved to classic action, and concluded with a uniquely close relationship with the US Navy in the Pacific. That brought with it the honour of representing Great Britain at the ceremony of Japan's surrender – an honour which many British sailors in the Pacific at the time felt Fraser had done little to deserve.

Admiral of the Fleet Sir Philip Vian was, for more than a year, subordinate to Fraser, both in the Indian Ocean and in the Pacific, during which time he commanded aircraft carriers. However (as with Admiral Nagumo), that was not really his forte at all. Vian was at his best when in tactical command of a flotilla of small ships – destroyers or cruisers. With such vessels he carried out the *Altmark* exploit; played a vital part in the pursuit of the battleship *Bismarck*; and helped sustain the beleaguered Mediterranean island of Malta. For him the less than completely welcome change of direction came after Overlord, in which he was Eastern Task Force commander – a role he filled so well that he was never given another chance to do the thing he liked best.

A comparable fate befell Admiral Arleigh A. Burke, subject of David A. Rosenberg's chapter – the final chapter in this group. Burke and his destroyer flotilla, the Little Beavers, became as famous in the United States as did Vian in Great Britain, and for a similar reason – like Vian, Burke was extremely good at handling a small-ship flotilla. It was during his brief time with the Little Beavers that he made his name and became a hero, by leading the Beavers into battle twenty-two times in four months, and sinking eleven Japanese vessels while shooting down nearly thirty Japanese aircraft. Now *that*, one might well say, shows leadership. It also shows the stuff of which legends are made; and legends can be baseless, or poised on feet of clay. Because of that, it should be said at once that Burke was not only a great *wartime* naval leader – after the war, he gave equally exemplary service both in Korea and for an unprecedented six years as Chief of Naval Operations. Considering that those stages of his career are often ignored in favour of the more 'glamorous' deeds with the Little Beavers, it is unfortunate that their detail cannot be given within the time-frame of this book; Burke's post-war naval service is worth considerable attention. But within the war years he demonstrated two great qualities which lead to his inclusion here. The first, as noted, was the instinctively brilliant way he handled his small ships; and the second was the patient, professional way he learned and carried out an entirely new job (one that, initially, he did not really want) as Chief of Staff to Marc Mitscher.

If that and later sections of Burke's life are often overlooked, his name is nevertheless widely remembered and honoured. The names of the four men whose wartime life stories make up the sixth and last group of chapters are, in the view of the present editor, all too frequently ignored, even by writers of naval history.

Who needs 'int' when it ain't? Perhaps one of the values of the intelligence branch, as viewed by other branches of the naval service, is that when something goes wrong intelligence can often be blamed – information, warnings, suggestions or advice were wrong, or were not supplied. In many navies, the work of the intelligence branch is accepted as merely normal when perfect, and derided as guesswork when mistaken. Its officers are not expected to stand up for themselves very much. As David Brown observes in his second chapter, the British Admiral John Godfrey spent the seven years between 1939 and 1946 in only two appointments, neither of which was sea-going; yet, as Director of Naval Intelligence (DNI) and subsequently Flag Officer Commanding, Royal Indian Navy, his influence was felt worldwide. However, as a brilliant DNI (for three years and nine months), his insistence on the department's independence brought displeasure from Churchill and opposition from his counterparts in the other services; and, shamefully, he was the only British admiral in World War Two not to be knighted. Likewise, it has been said of the American Commander (later Captain) Joe Rochefort that he 'made more difference, at a more important time, than any other naval officer in history'. This, of course, was because of his dazzling work in predicting the Battle of Midway. It was a virtuoso act, and he, unlike Godfrey, did achieve public honour, in the form of a Distinguished Service Medal; but the award was not made until ten years after his death. One of the themes of the chapter by Roger Pineau – himself a former member of US Naval Intelligence, a sometime subordinate and later friend of Rochefort – is the question of why it took so long for Rochefort's achievements to receive recognition.

If intelligence is a Cinderella within the armed services – an underfunded servant of the servants, ignored when working well, kicked whenever anything goes wrong and, above all, always assumed to be there and ready to work – then much the same applies to the US Navy's non-combatant Construction Battalions, the Seabees. Before the need for them arose, no one ever imagined them. Now they are there, no one can imagine them not being there. And no one can even begin to conceive how the Pacific War would have been won without them. But as Paolo E. Coletta describes, it was Vice-Admiral Ben Moreell who imagined the Seabees when they were not there; who set about inventing them; and who was ultimately responsible for all the airstrips, roads, harbours and hospitals that sprang up on the atolls and islands from Hawaii to

Okinawa. Because of that, though not one person in ten thousand has heard his name, he is one of the great naval leaders of World War Two.

He is also, as it happens, the last exclusively naval person in this book. It may at first seem odd to have a lieutenant-general listed in a book of naval leaders; but to include a representative of the US Marine Corps is right and proper, emphasizing the changed nature of naval war and saluting the invaluable contribution made by the Corps in the Pacific. That is not to say that Benis M. Frank's study of 'Howlin' Mad' Smith is a mere panegyric of one of the Corps' more colourful leaders; Frank is frank, if a small pun may be used, and does not gloss either the character of his subject or the often barbed and difficult relationship between Smith and his naval colleagues.

With Smith – last but certainly not least among these thirty-one leaders of naval war – the book concludes; and this Introduction may conclude with a few words of thanks: to David Roberts, of Weidenfeld and Nicolson, who conceived the idea; to all the contributors, who tolerated the editor's often lengthy correspondence and questioning; and to Marianne, the editor's beloved wife, who tolerated a haul which at times has seemed as long as World War Two itself. But the greatest thanks of all should go to the memories of all those whose courageous lives form the subjects of this book – the men who were the great naval leaders of World War Two.

PART ONE

High Command

1

Admiral of the Fleet

Sir Dudley Pound

GCB, GCVO
Royal Navy

1877–1943

by
Peter Kemp

*A*LFRED *Dudley Pickman Rogers Pound, born 29 August 1877. As a lieutenant RN, specialized in torpedoes during the development of this new and significant weapon. Until he reached the rank of rear admiral, his sea service was almost exclusively in battleships and battle-cruisers, stamping him as a 'big ship' officer. During World War I, commanded HMS Colossus in the Grand Fleet's 1st Battle Squadron. In her, present at the Battle of Jutland (31 May 1916). After the war, commanded HMS Repulse in the Atlantic Fleet, and later served as Chief of Staff to Admiral Sir Roger Keyes, Commander-in-Chief of the Mediterranean Fleet. Promoted to rear admiral in March 1926.*

After reaching flag rank, his naval career followed the almost classic path of advancement to the top naval commands, Admiralty staff appointments alternating with high commands at sea. He was promoted admiral in 1935, and in 1936 was appointed Commander-in-Chief in the Mediterranean, during the difficult years of the Spanish Civil War, following those of the Italian–Ethiopian War. In June 1939, because of the serious illness of Admiral Sir Roger Backhouse, the First Sea Lord, Pound was recalled to London to take his place as the professional head of the navy, being promoted admiral of the fleet a few weeks later.

Although only a small cog in a large machine, I was fortunate enough to spend the whole period of Pound's wartime service as First Sea Lord in the Admiralty's Operational Intelligence Centre (OIC), a new subdivision of the Naval Staff. Its brief was to receive and assess all intelligence of the enemy from all possible sources, and to keep our own fleets and squadrons at sea fully informed of all enemy ship and U-boat movements or possible intentions that might affect them. We also received advance information of plans for future operations, so that we could watch for any evidence of enemy concentrations which might endanger them. All this involved keeping an up-to-the-hour plot of the positions and movements of all ships and convoys at sea, the enemy's as well as our own. It gave us an overall and detailed picture of the progress of the war at sea as a whole, and the chance to observe Pound's strategical thinking in the direction of the sea war as it developed. He was a fairly frequent visitor to the oic, particularly during major operations and the big convoy battles in the Atlantic, as it was the only place in the Admiralty where all the intelligence information, all the ship positions and movements of both sides in every area of conflict, could be seen and assessed in one large room. I think we came to know Pound probably as well as any junior officers could ever know their admiral. Sadly, only two of the half-dozen or so who were in the oic from the start have survived the forty-five years since the war ended.

During the four years that Pound served as the wartime First Sea Lord, he was frequently criticized for his conduct of Britain's war at sea, and those criticisms have been frequently repeated since his death. Some were valid; others were not. The failure of the assault on Trondheim during the Norwegian operations of 1940; the escape through the English Channel of the *Scharnhorst*, *Gneisenau* and *Prinz Eugen* from Brest to Germany in early 1942; the disastrous scattering of Convoy PQ17 in July of the same year – these were three of the more important errors laid at his door. Any account of Pound's period as First Sea Lord must address these squarely and attempt to assess them fairly, as I shall try to do in this chapter. There were other more general reproaches, particularly his relations with Winston Churchill, and on these too I have some knowledge based on those four years of close contact with the sea war in all its aspects.

The oic was a new organization introduced in a limited form in 1938. It followed a suggestion put forward in 1937 by Admiral Sir William James, who had been in charge of Room 40 (where German naval signals were deciphered) for the last two years of World War One. He visualized a new and more sophisticated organization designed to avoid the mistakes and lost opportunities during that war in the use of such priceless information. It was based on a new section of the Naval Intelligence Division, with elements of the Operations, Trade and Signals Divisions incorporated in it. It was designed to deal only with immediate information of importance to the fleet, the longer-term aspects of such information remaining the responsibility of the individual staff divisions concerned.

Information came to the oic from many different sources – from agents of the Secret Intelligence Service serving abroad, from the naval attachés in the embassies of Allied and neutral nations, from the actual sightings of enemy ships (mainly by aircraft), from air reconnaissance photographs, from wireless bearings of enemy ship signals intercepted by the direction-finding stations ashore, and from breaks into the German Enigma cipher (which we knew as Ultra). These last came by direct teleprinter from the Government Code and

Ciphers School (GC & CS), which had moved out of London to Bletchley Park shortly before the outbreak of war. My own particular responsibility covered the positions of enemy ships from wireless bearings of their signals, though we were all privy to all other sources of information so that we could double up when required. The OIC also housed the Lower War Room, where an up-to-date combined plot of all ship positions and movements was maintained.

A complex communications system of direct telephone and teleprinter lines linked the OIC with all the naval home comands, the direction-finding stations, GC & CS, the headquarters of Fighter, Bomber and Coastal Commands, the Board of Trade, Lloyd's, the Baltic Exchange and similar authorities which might have something of value to contribute. And, most importantly, it had the authority to communicate direct with commanders-in-chief and the fleets at sea. The great importance of this was twofold: first, speed was essential in providing the fleets with new information; second, it gave us the ability to paraphrase our out-signals, thus safeguarding the sensitive sources of much of our information.

When Sir Ernle Chatfield retired as First Sea Lord in 1938 it was generally accepted in the navy that the choice of his successor lay between the Commanders-in-Chief of the Home (Sir Roger Backhouse) and Mediterranean (Sir Dudley Pound) Fleets. Pound, nearing the end of his time in the Mediterranean, was called to London to discuss strategy in that sea, and, during the visit, was told that the choice had fallen on Backhouse. So far as his own future was concerned, he was offered a choice between becoming Commander-in-Chief Portsmouth, a three-year appointment normally followed by retirement, or a fourth year of command in the Mediterranean, probably also to be followed by retirement. He had no hesitation in choosing the extra year in the Mediterranean, where he felt he had a more valuable part to play in continuing to train a major fleet for the war which all now recognized was coming – he was a notable fleet trainer. He was delighted to have been offered this choice, and indulged his life-long passion for shooting (second only to his passion for the Royal Navy) by buying himself a new gun in celebration. His family have stated that he had no great wish or ambition to become First Sea Lord, and none at all for a home port command.

When serious illness forced Backhouse to resign in June 1939 – he died a month later – the selection of Pound as his successor was a virtual certainty. There was no other senior admiral so highly qualified, and his recent experience in the Mediterranean (where his conduct of the fleet throughout the Spanish Civil War had been faultless in both the naval and political fields) was an added reason for bringing him home to fill the vacant post. There was little or no criticism among the senior officers of the fleet at his selection, but there was some surprise that a more charismatic admiral had not been chosen. Pound was generally regarded as a dour, unsmiling officer who kept himself to himself and who did not make friends easily. He had a daunting presence on the quarterdeck of his flagship, and his abrupt manner and proverbial silences could upset even senior officers who did not know his ways. He was addicted to do-it-yourself – and this made it difficult for him to delegate. He was known as a very hard driver, both of his staff and of the fleet he commanded, but it was equally recognized that he drove himself even harder.

Nevertheless, there was considerable criticism among the admirals of Pound's choice of Rear Admiral Tom Phillips – an officer who had not yet held a flag command at sea – as his Vice-Chief of Naval Staff. The position of VCNS was normally held by the senior vice admiral, and experience in command at sea was generally regarded as an essential prerequisite for so important a post in the Naval Staff. Phillips had a reputation as a brilliant staff officer, and Pound had much admired him when they served together in the Mediterranean on the staff of Sir Roger Keyes. He and Pound spent a good deal of time together in the OIC; we found Phillips somewhat abrasive, and at times impatient and rude. He also gave us the impression of refusing to listen to what others had to say before reaching a decision – so different from Pound, who was a patient listener. Pound had him promoted to acting vice admiral on his appointment, and this quick jump in rank also irritated the admirals.

Beyond his obvious naval qualifications, Pound brought to the Admiralty other qualities which fitted him uniquely for the work that lay ahead. Apart from a long-standing osteoarthritis of the left hip (which sometimes made sleep and rest difficult and painful and gave him a slight limp), he had quite phenomenal physical and mental stamina, and kept himself very fit. His capacity for work was tremendous, his patience inexhaustible and his loyalty to his superiors unquestioned. He brought to his new task a deep wisdom acquired through his years of service; if in 1939 the cards had fallen differently, he would have been an outstanding commander of a wartime fleet. He also brought a dedication to, and love of, the navy – a dedication and love so strong, they took precedence over everything, even over his own family.

From the start of his new appointment, Pound insisted that in Admiralty dealings with the other two services a compromise solution must be found in those cases where all three could not agree. There were some occasions when the Naval Staff felt aggrieved that their strong beliefs were sometimes sacrificed to the demands of the other two, but in Pound's view the overall strategy on sea, land and in the air could function efficiently only when the three services were working smoothly together. And if that called for compromise on some occasions, then compromise there must be. Looking back now at this policy it is impossible not to recognize that Pound was right and that, when the country was so hard-pressed during the early years of the war, any serious differences between the individual services could only have led to disaster. It was not, as some held, a policy of weakness but rather one of securing the fullest possible efficiency of the fighting capacity of the nation as a whole.

Part of Pound's brief as First Sea Lord laid down that he was 'responsible to the First Lord for the issue of orders to the Fleet affecting war operations and the movement of ships'. This particular duty is endemic in the organization of the naval service, and has a long historical background, stretching back to the sixteenth century. It rests on the fact that, unlike the other two services, the Admiralty is and always has been an operational headquarters. Generally a First Sea Lord leaves the conduct of naval battles to the man on the spot, the admiral commanding at sea, and limits his duty to ordering other squadrons or units, not under the admiral's direct command, to assist if necessary. He also keeps the admiral informed of any new intelligence or other event which may affect the course of the action. Today the speed and accuracy of communications makes this possible without causing any delay. It also enables the fleet to maintain wireless silence during operations, a necessary consideration as a wireless signal at sea can provide the enemy with bearings of the transmitter, and thus the position of the fleet.

Pound has often been criticized as a 'centralist', and, at times, of interfering unnecessarily in the course of operations at sea. Soon after he became First Sea Lord he wrote to Admiral Sir Charles Forbes, Commander-in-Chief Home Fleet, expressing his views. He asked 'that it be recognized that at times it will be necessary for the Admiralty to alter [fleet] dispositions but the Admiralty control will cease as soon as possible'. Forbes agreed that the necessity might occasionally arise, but argued that the Commander-in-Chief should retain the discretion whether or not to carry out the Admiralty's orders, as only the man on the spot would be able to appreciate the constantly changing conditions and circumstances which might be prevailing at sea, hundreds of miles from the Admiralty. 'If at all possible,' he wrote, 'information rather than an order should be passed.' When other flag officers expressed similar views, Pound stressed in reply that only in special circumstances would orders be issued from the Admiralty, and that, as soon as possible, control would be returned to the commander at sea. And there the matter rested.

All First Sea Lords must to some extent be centralizers in time of war, for it is only in the Admiralty that the whole picture of the developments of actual operations can be visualized and plotted as the various items of enemy movements, of new intelligence, of wireless direction-finding positions and so on are received. And only in the Admiralty is there space to accommodate together the various experts needed to study and analyse the new information and pass it quickly to the fleet. A flagship at sea in wartime can never have the physical space on board to carry sufficient specially trained staff to interpret all the complexities of modern intelligence, in addition to the wartime complement required to man and fight the ship.

A case which illustrates this aspect of operations was the chase and final destruction of the German battleship *Bismarck* at the end of May 1941. At the particular request of Admiral Sir John Tovey (then Commander-in-Chief Home Fleet) made to the First Sea Lord before the fleet sailed from Scapa Flow, the individual bearings of signals made by enemy ships were signalled to the flagship for plotting on board, instead of the position as obtained from the

Admiralty's plot. The reason was that he expected to have with him two destroyers with direction-finding receivers fitted on board, which would provide cross-bearings. In the event, though, neither was operational – but the original request was not cancelled.

A few hours after the *Bismarck*'s engagement with the *Hood* and *Prince of Wales*, the shadowing cruisers lost touch with her. Since she had been hit by the *Prince of Wales* during the engagement, it was thought that she might have abandoned her original objective of harrying the Atlantic convoys and have decided to return to Germany. For two days there was no sign of her, but fortunately, as British anxiety about her whereabouts was growing, she made a signal. As requested, we sent the original bearings to the Commander-in-Chief, and of course also plotted them in the OIC. The position obtained indicated to us that, instead of returning to Germany, she was making for a Biscay port. Unfortunately, the flagship had plotted the bearings on the wrong type of chart, giving a position some 120 miles or so to the north and indicating to the Commander-in-Chief that the enemy was taking a northabout route home to Germany – through the Faeroes gap, and down the North Sea to the Skagerrak and Kiel. Accordingly the fleet altered course, in fact away from the enemy, and widening the already considerable gap between the two forces.

Pound came down to the OIC to study the wireless position and to decide how to act on this new evidence of the enemy's intentions. By this time we had all got over our initial awe of the great man, and realized that his somewhat abrupt manner disguised not only an exceptionally keen naval brain but also a desire to listen to what we had to say. The plotting of wireless bearings in the OIC was at that time my responsibility, and I told him what I thought must have happened in the flagship to explain the fleet's change of course. He made no comment, but subsequent signals from the Admiralty confirmed that he had accepted the OIC's plot of the *Bismarck*'s signal. But by the time the fleet was back on course it was 130 miles astern of the enemy, with no hope of catching her.

That she was caught and sunk was entirely the result of Pound ordering other forces, not under the C-in-C's command, to concentrate on the Admiralty's estimated track of the *Bismarck*. There they found her, and disabled her to an extent that allowed the Home Fleet to reach her twelve hours later and sink her. In his official despatch on the operation, Tovey paid his tribute to Pound's vital contribution: 'The accuracy of the information supplied by the Admiralty', he wrote, 'and the speed with which it was passed were remarkable; and the balance struck between information and instructions passed to the forces out of visual touch with us was ideal.'

It was typical of Pound that he never took up with Tovey the mistake made in the flagship, realizing no doubt that they would work it out themselves. It was enough for him that the *Bismarck* had been caught and sunk.

But by no means all the operations at sea during the war ended as successfully as this. There were occasions when the Admiralty staff were at fault, particularly during the first two years of the war, when there had to be rapid expansion of

Naval Staff divisions to cope with the increase of activity, both of our own and of enemy forces. It took time to train the additional officers required to fill the gaps, many of them recalled from retirement, and as many more from the reserve organizations and civilian life. To some extent it was with a heavily diluted staff, lacking the speed and expertise that come only from training and experience, that Pound had to conduct the early war operations. Yet Pound relied on the Admiralty staff to a considerable extent to produce an accurate, current picture of the war at sea, on which to base his decisions for its conduct; and that there were (with the possible exception of the Norwegian campaign of early 1940) so few occasions of serious error either at sea or in the Admiralty – and even fewer of great consequence – says much for the soundness of his organization and training of the staff.

The Norwegian campaign was the first occasion on which Pound attracted specific criticism for his direct intervention in naval operations, particularly in his decision to withhold a naval covering force for the planned occupation of Trondheim in April 1940. Unlike several senior officers at this early stage of the war, Pound did not underrate the threat of air power against ships without fighter cover, and Trondheim lay well inland at the head of a fjord – within easy range of German airfields, and without any possibility of friendly fighter cover. Two earlier landings (at Namsos and Bandalsnes) had been achieved without opposition, and Pound persuaded his two fellow Chiefs of Staff that, in the light of those successes, the capture of Trondheim could be left to the land and air forces without risking the fleet to a heavy air attack. When the operation failed under strong German air attack, the blame was laid – at least in part – at the navy's door, in not providing a naval covering force. Pound accepted this criticism, though he never wavered from the view that the ships could not operate under threat of air attack, particularly in narrow waters, without strong fighter cover. He also held to the view that it was strategically unsound to risk ships unnecessarily in what was never going to become a major theatre of war.

The First Sea Lord naturally had many other duties and responsibilities. As Chief of Naval Staff (CNS), he was an active member of the Chiefs of Staff Committee, which met daily throughout the war under the chairmanship of the Minister of Defence. The overall brief of this committee (of which the Chief of Imperial General Staff and the Chief of Air Staff were the other two service members) was to advise 'His Majesty's Government on defence policy as a whole'. It was a brief which involved the formulation of the grand strategy under which the war was to be fought; the means by which that could be implemented; major and combined operations on land, sea and in the air; the advance planning of future operations; the allocation of resources; and every other aspect of the war as a whole.

A great weight of Admiralty business also rested on Pound's shoulders. The reading of signals from the fleet and other authorities; the daily work of the staff divisions inside the Admiralty; intelligence appreciations of enemy navies, and the speed and direction of their naval construction – all flowed across his desk, and he needed to know it all. Before the war, it had been decided that a Deputy First Sea Lord (DFSL) would be appointed on the outbreak of war to take much of the routine work of the Admiralty from the First Sea Lord, thus leaving him free to concentrate on the major issues. The choice of a DFSL had been made in anticipation of the outbreak of war, but ran into difficulties when the new Vice-Chief of the Naval Staff persuaded Pound not to go ahead with the appointment, on the ground that the DFSL (an admiral) would be senior to the VCNS (an acting vice admiral). This could cause problems. The VCNS suggested instead that a senior captain should be added to Pound's staff as a chief staff officer; but that would not work either, as an officer of that rank could have no authority to sign off letters for the First Sea Lord. It was not until July 1942 that Admiral Sir Charles Kennedy-Purvis was brought in as Pound's deputy, in a move to lighten the load.

Above all, in Pound's naval philosophy, was the need to build a sound relationship, based on mutual trust and respect, with the First Lord, his immediate political boss. On the declaration of war on 3 September 1939, Winston Churchill returned to the Admiralty to reoccupy the chair in which he had sat when World War One broke out in 1914. He was not an easy colleague, partly because his working day tended to be concentrated into the late hours of the night and small hours of the morning. The relationship between the two men began with a short period of mutual doubt, then developed into a real affection and admiration for each other, with a strong and unbroken mutual loyalty. In fact, neither could do without the other, Churchill providing the imaginative concepts and Pound restraining the First Lord's wilder ideas. Pound had his own method of dealing with the problem of voicing disagreement with doubtful propositions, a method which he explained to one of his staff when he commanded in the Mediterranean: 'Never say "No" unless it [the proposition] is really impossible. Say "Yes – and this is what it would mean in terms of resources and other commitments." Then they'll turn it down themselves.'

All Churchill's suggestions for new operations, however far-fetched, were sent by Pound to the Plans Division for examination and analysis. It meant extra work for the division, but it paid a big dividend in the relationship between the First Lord and his First Sea Lord. When Churchill left the Admiralty in May 1940 to become Prime Minister, he retained in his own hands the post of Minister of Defence, and the relationship between him and Pound continued in the Chiefs of Staff Committee.

All this meant a very long day's work for Pound. In 1939, when he came to the Admiralty as First Sea Lord, he was already sixty-two – a time of life when many men begin to slow down a little. His normal working day lasted from about 8.30 a.m. to around 2.30 a.m. the following morning, though whenever possible he took a short nap of about twenty minutes in an armchair after luncheon. He found that five hours' sleep at night was sufficient for him, though there were some occasions throughout the war when he had to be called at night, if events in the course of operations at sea or in the war on land raised a new naval problem.

Throughout his life, his chief recreations were shooting and fishing, two passions which had gone hand in hand with his love for the navy through all his years of service. On Saturday afternoons during the seasons for those sports, he would hope to get away from the Admiralty for exercise, fresh air and relaxation. It was not always possible, especially when large naval operations were under way, but, whenever it was, the short break from routine proved a valuable tonic. Allowing himself no more than seven days' leave a year, he invariably took the precious week during the shooting season, when he could enjoy the most physical and mental benefit.

Of all Pound's preoccupations during the years he served as First Sea Lord, the one which he considered basic to the outcome of the war in Europe was the Battle of the Atlantic: the long struggle against Germany's U-boats, defending the vital trade which flowed across the Atlantic. Almost from the start, he realized that before the war could be won it would be essential to ensure a risk-free transatlantic passage for the men, weapons and supplies that would be needed in Europe to win the final battle against Nazi Germany. It was a task for which the navy was singularly ill prepared. No studies had been made in the Admiralty of the similar campaign which had been waged in 1914–18, nor had any true analysis of the effect of convoy on trade been made. There was instead a confidence that with the development of Asdic (later known as sonar), which could detect a submerged submarine, the day of the submarine as a weapon of trade destruction was over. In 1936, this confidence was fortified by a declaration that Germany was renouncing submarine attacks on merchant shipping. In 1939, when she abrogated this promise, it was too late to build up an adequate force of convoy escorts before, later in that year, war was declared.

Although it had been announced that the Admiralty would introduce a system of convoy at the start of war, there were many naval officers who – in spite of Asdic – doubted the efficiency of convoy in conditions of modern submarine warfare. The sinking by the *U-30* of the Donaldson liner *Athenia* with the loss of 112 lives on the first day of war settled all doubts, but even then only a partial convoy system could be introduced: there were too few escorts, and none of sufficient endurance, to make possible a full system. It was not until July 1941 that end-to-end transatlantic convoy was finally achieved.

In 1940, Germany's invasion of Norway (followed quickly by the fall of France) brought a new dimension to the Battle of the Atlantic. U-boats operating from bases newly acquired or quickly constructed on the coast of Norway and in the Bay of Biscay were able to reach their Atlantic patrol areas much more quickly than from their earlier German bases. On each sortie, each boat could thus spend several more days in active operations against the convoys. There is a memory of Pound at that time, during a visit to the U-boat tracking room in the oic. Standing in front of a large wall chart of the Atlantic, he drew a wide sweep with his walking stick from the northern tip of Norway, round most of the Atlantic and back to the north-western tip of Spain. 'We have to hold them there,' he said of the U-boats, 'and then we'll drive them in.' It was said with such an air of decision and confidence that no one present could doubt the eventual fulfilment of his prophecy.

The German occupation of the northern half of France, coupled with a new French government suspected of pro-Nazi sympathies, raised a question-mark over the future of the French fleet. Although a few French ships had crossed the Channel to British ports as the German army advanced, the considerable majority, including all the modern capital ships, remained in French or colonial ports. While nothing could be done about those in French metropolitan ports, there were powerful squadrons including battleships and battle-cruisers at Dakar on the west coast of Africa and at Oran and Alexandria in the Mediterranean. The Cabinet in London decided that they must be confronted by a show of force and given a choice of continuing the fight against the Axis, of sailing with reduced crews to a French West Indian port or of demilitarization. The Chiefs of Staff were of course consulted, but, with the decision already taken by the Cabinet, their only task was to carry it out. And, as it had to be entirely a naval operation, the distasteful task of ordering such a confrontation backed up by force against a former ally fell to Pound. At Oran and Dakar, the operations degenerated into a shooting conflict. This caused a great deal of revulsion throughout Great Britain, and suspicions of misman-agement by the navy – suspicions which inevitably found their way back to Pound. In odd contrast, these unhappy incidents were applauded by most of the neutral nations around the world as evidence that Britain would continue the fight; but I do not think those reactions could have brought any consolation to Pound. He was never that sort of man.

With Italy declaring war in June 1940, the Mediterranean became a new theatre of war and added a new responsibility to Pound's already heavy load. It also brought the land war to North Africa, and a new naval burden of reinforcing the British army in Egypt with men and supplies. The short sea route through the Mediterranean and Suez Canal was effectively denied by the Italian navy and air force, and the supply convoys to Egypt had now to sail round the Cape of Good Hope, an addition of some thousands of miles to their perilous voyages. They also had to be very heavily escorted, as the start of their passage took them through the Bay of Biscay, where they were subject to attack not only by U-boats, but also by the German surface forces based in Brest.

Pound's strategy in the Mediterranean was based on the need to hold Malta at all costs. The narrow entrances to the Mediterranean at Gibraltar and Suez were already strongly held in British hands, and Malta, commanding the narrows of the central Mediterranean between the southern tip of Italy and the northern coast of Algeria, was the essential key to an ultimate victory. It divided the Mediterranean into two virtually separate halves, and at the same time denied to the Axis free use of the seaborne supply lines to their armies in North Africa. Their supply convoys had to be fought through against attack by British surface forces, submarines and aircraft based in Malta, and they suffered heavily. Although the cost in ships and lives in keeping Malta supplied and defended against Axis attacks was heavy and grievous, Pound never faltered in his determination to hold it and keep his Mediterranean strategy intact. When at the end of 1942 the time at last came to turn to the offensive, it was the fact that Malta was still held in British hands that ensured its ultimate success.

In the Atlantic, the bleakest years were 1941 and 1942. It seemed then that the growing production of anti-submarine frigates and corvettes was always relentlessly overtaken by the even greater production of U-boats, and there was a vast increase in the loss of merchant-ship tonnage. The evacuation of the British Expeditionary Force from Dunkirk in 1940 had cost dearly in the loss of destroyers and other small ships, and the subsequent threat of a German invasion across the Channel had resulted in a significant number of escorts being withdrawn from the Atlantic, while the threat lasted, to replace the lost ships. This in turn meant a temporary reduction of the already limited Atlantic convoy system, and sinkings of merchant ships increased. During the first five months of 1940, the average monthly loss to U-boats was 86,000 tons; for the rest of the year, that figure rose to an average of 251,000 tons a month; and in 1941 and 1942, the losses continued to rise to double that and more.

Yet in 1941 there was a gleam of light that gave promise of better things to come. A Commando raid on the Lofoten Islands in northern Norway, designed to destroy a large fish factory which produced glycerine used for explosives, was completely successful, and included the capture of the *Krebs*, an armed trawler. On board was an Enigma machine, the electro-mechanical machine used by all the German armed forces for ciphering their signals. It was a machine which embodied a wide variety of different settings, changed every twenty-four hours, so that in effect a different cipher was used for each day's signals. This added to the difficulties experienced by GC & CS in making significant breaks. They had been working on this machine since its first introduction, and though there had been some successes in breaking parts of the ciphers for short periods, the main problem had not yet been solved.

The machine taken from the *Krebs* had been considerably damaged, but its capture led to the thought that there might be other small German ships at sea which could also produce an Enigma machine. Specially fitted trawlers were employed as weather-reporting ships, and wireless bearings of their signals revealed two areas in which they operated – one north of Iceland, the other in the North Atlantic. Whether it was Pound who initiated the actions which resulted in their capture is not known, but certainly he was privy to it and made the necessary forces available. The first ship, the *München*, was taken in May 1941, followed a month later by the capture of the *Lauenberg*. Each of these produced an Enigma machine and other valuable material for GC & CS, but better than either was the capture of the *U-110* in the northern Atlantic on 9 May 1941. She provided not only her Enigma machine, but also a table of the daily alterations in settings to be used for the following month.

These various captures proved priceless; they provided a basis of new knowledge in solving the problem of the daily change of settings, and the expertise of GC & CS eventually provided the OIC with its most valuable and accurate source of information on German ships and U-boat positions, movements and intentions. Occasionally it took a day or two to reach decryption, but even that delay was acceptable, as the signals often pointed to future movements. Of course, it was not always possible to act offensively when the decrypted signals came in – the need always to protect the source of this information was paramount, and we were all well trained to use it with discretion, carefully disguised so that the enemy should not suspect that his cipher was vulnerable. It may be that some sort of suspicion arose in February 1942 within the U-boat arm as, alone among all the German fighting forces, they introduced a new mechanical element into their Enigma machines which made their signals unbreakable. Yet, within the year, GC & CS had redesigned and rebuilt their own machine, and by the end of the year had mastered the new cipher.

The last months of 1941 and the first of 1942 saw a further spreading of the war and new responsibilities for the First Sea Lord. The German invasion of Russia in 1941 brought a need to assist the new ally with supplies of weapons and aircraft, to try and stem the German advances towards Leningrad and Moscow. Since Russia could only be reached by sea, through the Arctic Ocean, this meant opening a new theatre of operations in those icy waters. The first of a series of convoys carrying supplies sailed at the end of September 1941. As the series built up into a regular supply route, the German reaction was to station heavy surface ships, U-boats and torpedo bombers in northern Norway. The passage of each convoy thus threatened to become a major naval operation.

At the end of 1941, yet another and more distant area of conflict was opened. From mid-1941, Japan's bellicose actions in South-East Asia (particularly the occupation of the naval base at Camranh Bay in Indo-China with the agreement of Vichy France) had virtually assured her the naval dominance of the South China Sea, with an obvious threat to Malaya and Singapore. The Chiefs of Staff Committee decided that these Japanese actions called for the reinforcement of the British Eastern Fleet, and Pound agreed to put forward proposals.

His plan was to send one of the modernized Mediterranean battleships and four older ones, reinforced later with two modern battleships and an aircraft carrier. These would be based in Ceylon, as a deterrent to any Japanese aggression against Allied shipping in the Indian Ocean. The planned force was all that could be spared at the moment, as we knew that the new German battleship *Tirpitz* was completing her trials in the Baltic and would soon be operational, and that in the Mediterranean the Italian battlefleet was still in being – even if a bit timid when there was any chance of battle.

But the Prime Minister thought differently. He preferred a more positive reaction to the Japanese threat, with a small powerful force of modern ships based at Singapore to deter Japan from any moves against Malaya. His belief was that the Japanese would not attack Malaya, but would use their navy against Allied trade in the area. He was backed up by the Foreign Office, which argued that politically a small force of modern ships on the spot would have a much greater deterrent effect on Japan than would a larger and more distant force of older ships in the Indian Ocean.

Pound protested strongly against this proposal, on two grounds. He disagreed with the Prime Minister's view that the Japanese would not attack Malaya; and such modern capital ships as were available were needed to meet the actual threats posed by the enemy in home waters and the Mediterranean, and could not be spared to act as a deterrent in the Far East where war had not yet begun. He was also convinced that to base the proposed squadron at Singapore instead of in the Indian Ocean was to take an unacceptable risk, unless we could be certain that the United States would declare war against Japan if she moved against Malaya. Washington could provide no such assurance.

However, another responsibility which Pound realized and accepted was this: that the Royal Navy was provided and maintained as an instrument of national policy, and that when the national need decreed a particular line of naval action, the navy must accept it, whatever its admirals might think. In this case, the political argument won the day, and it was decided to send the new battleship *Prince of Wales* and the aircraft carrier *Indomitable* from the Home Fleet to join the modernized battle-cruiser *Repulse* at Colombo. The three would then proceed together to Singapore.

Unfortunately, the *Indomitable* was unable to join the squadron, as she was damaged by running aground in the West Indies. The *Prince of Wales* and four destroyers reached Colombo on 28 November 1941 and, in company with the *Repulse*, reached Singapore on 3 December. In command was Sir Tom Phillips, Pound's former VCNS, now promoted to the rank of acting admiral. On arrival, he took over from Vice Admiral Sir Geoffrey Layton as Commander-in-Chief Eastern Fleet. Four days later, Japan's attack on Pearl Harbor took place; and three days later, both the *Prince of Wales* and *Repulse* were sunk by Japanese torpedo bombers. The Commander-in-Chief went down with his flagship.

'I was opening my boxes on the 10th when the telephone at my bedside rang,' Churchill wrote later in *The Grand Alliance*. 'It was the First Sea Lord. His voice sounded odd. He gave a sort of cough and gulp, and at first I could not hear quite clearly. "Prime Minister, I have to report to you that both the *Prince of Wales* and the *Repulse* have been sunk by the Japanese – we think by aircraft. Tom Phillips is drowned." "Are you sure it's true?" "There is no doubt at all." So I put the telephone down. I was thankful to be alone. In all the war I never received a more direct shock.'

Although there were a few murmurs in naval circles that the disaster showed Pound had not stood up to Churchill strongly enough, most accepted that the First Sea Lord had no choice on political grounds but to send the ships to Singapore. Yet there could be no disguising the wide criticism of Pound's selection of Phillips as Commander-in-Chief. For some reason, Churchill had lost confidence in Phillips as VCNS; his move from that post was therefore inevitable. Normally a VCNS can expect a top command at sea when he reaches the end of his staff appointment, but in some ways Phillips was not a normal VCNS in that he came to the post without any experience of an admiral's job at sea. Among the admirals, there was not only some resentment at his second jump in acting rank but, in addition, real concern that his lack of sea-going experience in a flag appointment in no way fitted him for so important a sea command. 'All the tricks still to learn, and no solid sea experience to fall back on,' as one senior admiral wrote to another.

Pound certainly liked Phillips personally, and had the highest regard for his abilities. It is also certain that Phillips was a brilliant staff officer and, like Pound, an exceptionally hard worker. At the Admiralty, they got on famously together. When Phillips left the Admiralty to take up his new command, Pound wrote in a farewell note: '. . . it will be a great comfort to know that there will be someone in the Far East who will make the most of the slender forces available, and in whom we have complete confidence'.

The decision to send such valuable ships to Sinagpore at this time of Japanese intransigence was one which Pound had always believed to be unsound. He felt this so deeply that it led him, in fact, into a small breach of protocol. He called a meeting of all the Sea Lords and other professional members of the Board of Admiralty to discuss the situation. The unanimous decision at the meeting – that it was strategically unsound to send out such an unbalanced force – resulted in a memorandum expressing the Board's view to A. V. Alexander, Churchill's successor as First Lord, with a request that it be forwarded to the Prime Minister. Whether Alexander sent it on is not known – probably he did not – but he pointed out that it was the duty of the First Sea Lord, and not the Board as a whole, to give professional advice to the government; that Pound had already done so; and that there the matter ended so far as the Sea Lords were concerned.

Opening hostilities in the Pacific and South-East Asia, Japan's attack on Pearl Harbor brought America into the war as a British ally. It also proved beyond any doubt that the British forces at Singapore, on which so much hope had been placed, had failed completely as a deterrent force; and in this new theatre of war the early months of 1942 were as bleak as the last month of 1941. Hong Kong had surrendered to the Japanese on Christmas Day of 1941; Singapore surrendered on 15 February 1942. The Japanese naval offensive swept on through the Netherlands East Indies and, though a small Allied naval force of American, Dutch, British and Australian cruisers and destroyers was formed, it was unable to stop the Japanese advance. Most of its ships were eventually lost in action.

Japan's attack on Pearl Harbor was swiftly followed by declarations of war against America by both Germany and Italy. The United States was thus drawn into the war in the West, and on 12 December 1941 Pound was in Washington, seeking from Admiral King [*q.v.*] (his opposite number in the US Navy) America's views on the two navies' future joint co-ordinated conduct of the maritime war as a whole. He found King to be a very sticky customer, generally unreceptive to British experience in the war so far, and a working relationship between the two men proved difficult to establish.

Before the end of Pound's visit, a small force of six U-boats arrived off the eastern seaboard of the United States to find a rich harvest of unescorted merchant ships, and particularly of tankers carrying oil from the Caribbean and Venezuelan fields, easily visible at night against the bright lights of the undarkened coast. Pound, with his experience of the Atlantic U-boat war, strongly advised King that the traffic be organized and protected in a convoy system, and offered to turn over ten corvettes trained in anti-submarine warfare as a nucleus around which an escort force could be built. The Americans, however, preferred their own system of surface and air patrols and hunting groups, which proved unsuccessful – indeed, they never even sighted a U-boat. Well over a million tons of shipping were sunk off the American seaboard, with almost as much again in the Caribbean and the Gulf of Mexico.

Pound was in despair over these vast and unnecessary losses, and asked Churchill to intervene directly with President Roosevelt. This had the desired result: a system of convey was introduced; almost at once, losses dwindled nearly to vanishing point; and within a month the U-boats, deprived of their easy targets, were withdrawn to operate in more profitable waters.

Nevertheless, in spite of all these extensions of the war into new areas of conflict, Pound's main preoccupation remained with the continuing battle against the U-boats in the Atlantic. He never interfered in the day-to-day conduct of the battle, confident I am sure that the OIC, working closely with its Trade Division element, had the situation well in hand. He was still a frequent visitor to the U-boat tracking room in the OIC, but only to keep himself fully up to date with events. Yet behind the scenes he was busy with new ideas and methods for training convoy escorts, and at the same time stimulating research and development into new anti-submarine weapons and new methods for their delivery.

During 1942, new hopes in the Battle of the Atlantic came when the large number of convoy escorts ordered in 1940 and 1941 reached completion, at last giving the opportunity of holding back numbers sufficient for full and systematic training before committing them to battle. Pound had appointed Admiral Sir Percy Noble as Commander-in-Chief Western Approaches (the operational authority conducting the Battle of the Atlantic) with instructions to introduce and perfect the new methods of training. The selection of Noble was a decisive factor in the coming victory. The new pattern convoy defence consisted of mixed groups of five or six frigates and corvettes which trained together to build up a group expertise in methods of hunting and attacking U-boats. The current completion rate of escorts provided sufficient numbers not only to form enough escort groups to keep the convoy cycle running with allowances for adequate rest and repairs, but also to form support groups. These could be sailed at short notice to augment the escort groups whenever a convoy was threatened with attack by a wolf-pack of U-boats.

New weapons were also just beyond the horizon. Of these, the ten-centimetre radar proved perhaps the most decisive, as it was undetectable by a U-boat's radar search receiver. A further development of sonar made it possible for the first time to determine the depth of a dived U-boat, while ahead-firing weapons (known as Squid and Hedgehog, firing salvoes of depth charges over the ship's bows) also for the first time allowed a U-boat to be attacked while still held in a sonar beam. A shallow-bursting depth charge was developed as well, which provided an ideal anti-submarine weapon for aircraft attacking a U-boat on the surface. By ordering small prefabricated aircraft carriers from American shipyards as an addition to the normal surface escort forces, it was hoped to achieve continuous transatlantic air escort. The first of these carriers arrived in October 1942, but, though they were used to give air cover for the Arctic convoys to north Russia, they were in fact rarely employed on escort duties in the Atlantic, because during the last months of 1942 Pound had won a notable decision.

The background to this was that in April 1941, though Coastal Command remained an integral part of the Royal Air Force, its operational control had been vested in the Admiralty. During 1942, the United States developed VLR (very-long-range) aircraft. Part of this production was allocated to Britain and promptly claimed by Bomber Command, to help maintain the bombing offensive against Germany. Recognizing their enormous potential value in Atlantic convoy defence, Pound argued strongly for a proportion of the VLR aircraft to be allotted to Coastal Command, but at first he could make no headway against Bomber Command's claim. But he was never one to give up when he knew that he was right. Finally, he convinced Churchill that convoy defence was at least as important in the long run as knocking down German cities. Churchill accordingly persuaded President Roosevelt to direct that a part of the British allocation must be earmarked for Coastal Command. Thus by the end of 1942 there were fifty-two VLR aircraft in Coastal Command, and more than double that figure by mid-1943. By basing them in Northern Ireland, Iceland and eastern Canada, it was possible to organize continuous air cover for every Atlantic convoy throughout its passage. This was not only a more sensible and economic solution than using aircraft carriers, but also a more effective deterrent against the U-boats as, being land-based, the VLR aircraft were not subject to the vagaries of carrier operation during periods of heavy weather in the Atlantic.

Earlier in 1942, however, there had been two setbacks for which Pound was widely criticized. The first, on 12 February, took place in home waters, causing something of a public outcry and a suspicion that the navy had been caught napping. The battle-cruisers *Scharnhorst* and *Gneisenau* and the heavy cruiser *Prinz Eugen* had been in Brest for many months, and the target of British bombing raids. The removal of these three powerful ships from the Atlantic seaboard, by some means or other, was much to be desired; their presence there had long caused anxiety in the Admiralty because of their threat of surprise surface attacks on the Atlantic. Believing that a British invasion of northern Norway was imminent, and that with these three ships at home Germany would be in a better position to counter it, Hitler had ordered his admirals to bring them home to Germany.

There was of course no such British plan; nor was it a secret in the OIC that the enemy was planning to bring the ships home. During the first ten days of February, we had observed the movement of German destroyers westward through the Channel, a big increase in German minesweeping activity along the French side of the Channel and a massive reinforcement of German fighter aircraft along the northern coasts of France and Belgium. It all indicated that a big naval operation was being planned, and the only one that fitted was to bring home the ships now at Brest. We considered it probable that the ships would make the passage up Channel at night and pass through the Dover narrows at first light in the morning. We anticipated that they would be steaming up Channel on the night of 11–12 February, as there would be a new moon (and therefore maximum darkness) and a strong east-going spring tide to help them in their passage and give them maximum depth of water over the British magnetic minefields.

Naturally Pound was kept fully informed. The possibility of a break-out from Brest was discussed in the Chiefs of Staff Committee, where he explained the Home Fleet's current commitments. All that was then available at Scapa Flow were two battleships, one battle-cruiser and one aircraft carrier. One of the battleships had in fact already sailed for the Clyde to escort a large troop and supply convoy en route through the Bay of Biscay for the Middle East. The other ships were needed to cover the new German battleship *Tirpitz*, now operational at Trondheim, which might at any time try to break out into the Atlantic or try to attack a convoy to Russia. Pound pointed out that, even if the Brest squadron were sighted at the start of its passage and the Home Fleet sailed at once, the nearest point of contact would be off the Dutch coast. There, the fleet would be sure to attract very heavy air attack from German bomber and fighter airfields in Holland. This was not a risk he was prepared to accept. All that the navy could provide in the Channel was a squadron of Fleet Air Arm torpedo bombers, six destroyers based at Harwich, and a few motor torpedo boats at Dover and Ramsgate.

The Chiefs of Staff agreed that the Home Fleet's present commitments must take precedence, and that the attempt to stop the German ships in the Channel must be mainly an air operation using high-level and torpedo bombers of the Royal Air Force, together with the small naval forces in the area. It was noted at the meeting that, as the bombing force available lacked training in attacking moving targets at sea, the chances of sinking or seriously damaging the German ships was slight.

The German departure from Brest was delayed by a British air-raid on the port, putting the ships behind their own schedule for the passage through the Channel, and similarly behind what we expected them to do. During the hours of darkness, three separate lines of search were flown by radar-fitted aircraft crossing the ships' estimated track. To give maximum cover, each line was flown by three or four aircraft consecutively. An unfortunate series of radar failures, combined with the cancellation of some of the follow-up aircraft, resulted in the German squadron remaining unobserved. Worse, the radar failures and cancellations were not reported to Dover, from where the whole operation was co-ordinated. As the night ended without any indication of enemy movements, this gave the impression that we had guessed the date wrong. It was not until about 10.30 a.m. on the 12th that the enemy ships were first sighted off the mouth of the River Somme. By then, it was too late to organize a co-ordinated air attack, as with no contacts reported through the night the preliminary aircraft concentrations had not been made. A series of piecemeal attacks by naval and RAF forces was made, but no enemy ship was hit. Later that day, before reaching the end of their passage, both the *Scharnhorst* and the *Gneisenau* hit mines. The *Gneisenau* was only slightly damaged and reached the Kiel Canal without difficulty; the *Scharnhorst* hit a second mine, and eventually limped into Wilhelmshaven on one engine.

There was widespread public and press dismay in Britain; it seemed that German warships could operate unscathed in what were widely considered British-controlled waters. On the face of it, the responsibility seemed to lie with the navy, and, if blame there were, it should naturally be directed at the man in control, the First Sea Lord. But, as always, Pound took it in his stride and remained silent. He knew that the decision not to hazard the Home Fleet in waters dominated by German air power was the only possible one in the circumstances, but, again as always, he took no steps publicly to justify his decision. He was content to leave it to history to make the final judgement.

The second setback of 1942 occurred in July. Pound then had to face a crescendo of criticism over the destruction of Convoy PQ17.

Strongly supported by the Commander-in-Chief Home Fleet, Pound had asked for the convoys to north Russia to be suspended during the summer months. At that time of year, there is perpetual daylight in Arctic waters, and losses of merchant ships and warships had been mounting – the latter including the two cruisers *Edinburgh* and *Trinidad*. The naval need to conserve the escort forces and merchant ships was clear; but, as in the discussions over the basing of the *Prince of Wales* and the *Repulse* at Singapore, the political argument – the need to maintain supplies to Russia – was held to override the naval need.

In the Admiralty it was thought probable that during the summer Germany would use her considerable surface forces already in Norway to make at least one big effort to annihilate a convoy. By the end of June it looked certain that PQ17 (which sailed from Iceland on the 27th) had been selected for this attempt. In the OIC we had been watching for signs, and had noted a significant movement of heavy surface ships northward. By 4 July, we knew that the battleship *Tirpitz*, the pocket battleship *Scheer*, the heavy cruiser *Hipper* and at least six destroyers had reached Altenfjord, the most northerly German base. Three merchant ships had already been sunk by air attack, leaving thirty still in the convoy, which was then about 350 miles north of Altenfjord, roughly twelve hours' steaming for the German squadron. It was at the extreme limit of its cruiser covering force, and far beyond the distant cover of the Home Fleet (which was also at sea), but it had a strong close escort of nineteen anti-submarine and anti-aircraft ships, of which six were Home Fleet destroyers.

Pound came down to the OIC during the evening of 4 July to ask whether the German squadron had sailed. He was told that the order to sail would come from Berlin by landline, and that there would be no wireless signals to put us on the alert. We would have to rely on Norwegian coast-watchers, whom we had found generally reliable. Although in these circumstances we could not be certain that the squadron had not yet left Altenfjord, we were about 90 per cent sure that, if it had sailed, we would know.

Pound left us without making any comment. We had no idea that the question he had in his mind at that time was whether to keep the convoy together with its escort, to give the maximum protection against U-boat and air attacks, or whether, in the face of the German surface threat, to order it to scatter.

It was an almost impossible decision to make, for if the German ships had sailed, the convoy and its escort force faced almost certain annihilation unless it was ordered to scatter at once; yet if it were scattered, it would break up into small groups of widely separated ships, very difficult to protect against U-boats and aircraft.

After leaving the OIC, Pound called a meeting of his senior staff. There, he explained the alternatives, doubtless reminding his staff that an order to scatter the convoy would be acting on negative intelligence – an assumption, not firm information – that the German squadron had left Altenfjord. The unanimous opinion of the meeting was that the surface threat was the greater, and that, as time was running short, the convoy should be scattered at once. This would achieve the highest degree of dispersion. Simultaneously, the cruiser covering force should be ordered to withdraw to the westward at high speed. Strong support for this action came from the VCNS, Vice Admiral Sir Henry Moore. Pound listened patiently; but the final decision still had to be his alone.

He accepted the advice of his staff meeting. A series of signals from the Admiralty ordered the withdrawal of the cruiser covering force and the scattering of the convoy. Unhappily, the wording and urgency of the signals gave the impression to those on the spot that the enemy was just over the horizon, and the six destroyers of the convoy's escort joined those of the withdrawing cruisers as a reinforcement for the surface battle they believed was coming. Even more unhappily, they remained with the cruisers when the battle did not materialize; they did not return to the scattered merchant ships.

I happened to be the duty commander OIC that night. I can remember vividly the feeling of dismay when the advance copies of the Admiralty's out-signals arrived on my desk, giving the OIC its first knowledge of Pound's decision. Possibly it was our own close association with the Atlantic campaign against the U-boats that had enhanced our confidence in the convoy system, and our belief that a well-organized and well-escorted convoy was in fact stronger than the sum of the individual strengths of its escort. Possibly, too, it was our belief that we would know if and when the German squadron sailed. In fact, it did not sail until the following morning, and was sighted and reported within an hour by two submarines on patrol, one Russian and one British. The German authorities, recognizing these signals as sighting reports, ordered the squadron to return. This made little difference to PQ17. By then, the U-boats and torpedo bombers were taking a heavy toll. Of the thirty ships still in the convoy when it scattered, eleven eventually reached safety in Russian ports; nineteen were sunk.

It is of course impossible to know what went through Pound's mind when he made the final decision. Perhaps he thought the escort commander would scatter the convoy into small groups of three or four ships, dividing the escorts among them to provide at least some protection from U-boat and aircraft attack. In the light of what actually occurred, it was obviously wrong to order decisive action on negative intelligence, particularly with all the various avenues of information channelled into the OIC and at Pound's disposal to give warning of the sailing of the German squadron. Again in hindsight, it would have been wiser to inform C-in-C Home Fleet and the Admiral commanding the cruiser covering force both of the facts as the Admiralty knew them and of Pound's appreciation of the dangers of surface attack. The final decision could, and perhaps should, have then been left to the man on the spot, in overall command of the operation. But Pound knew that the C-in-C would never order the convoy to scatter. In a telephone conversation with Admiral Tovey before the Home Fleet had sailed from Scapa Flow, he had mentioned the possibility that he might have to order the convoy to scatter if a surface attack appeared imminent. Tovey had protested strongly, on the ground that all the latest experience in these Arctic convoys pointed to the vital necessity for ships to keep well closed up, offering mutual support against the heavy air attack that was certain to take place. In Tovey's judgement, an order to scatter ships should not be given except as a last resort in the actual presence of attack by overwhelming surface forces. It could be this knowledge, added to the strong recommendation of his senior staff, that convinced Pound to intervene himself.

In the North Atlantic, although 1942 had been a desperately difficult year with U-boats sinking just on 5.5 million tons of merchant shipping, the year's end brought the first scent of victory in the long battle. American shipyards, adopting a design by the Sunderland Company of Newcastle-upon-Tyne, were producing prefabricated merchant ships with all-welded hulls at an astonishing rate, rapidly catching up with and eventually overtaking the losses in all theatres of war. Known as Liberty ships, they had a large carrying capacity and a remarkable ability to withstand war damage. The speed of their construction removed a fear that the present rate of sinkings by U-boats would ultimately result in too few ships to carry the supplies and reinforcements needed to continue the war.

With the new pattern of convoy defence through well-trained escort and support groups, the new anti-submarine weapons and continuous air cover, the U-boats themselves were beginning to take losses that, if continued, would cripple their campaign of mass attacks against convoys. There were also the first faint signs of a loss of morale among the U-boat officers and crews. In January 1943, at the Casablanca Conference of the Joint (i.e. British and American) Chiefs of Staff, these encouraging hints enabled Pound to declare that, now we had the measure of the U-boat menace, the worst of the war in Europe was over. This was soon to be confirmed by the enemy, for, looking ahead for a moment to May 1943, we can see in Admiral Dönitz's diary: 'Wolf-pack operations against convoys in the North Atlantic . . . were no longer possible . . . I accordingly withdrew the boats from the North Atlantic. We had lost the Battle of the Atlantic.' Pound did not keep a diary – it was probably against his principles as a serving officer in wartime – but, had he done so, two months earlier he could have written: 'We have won the Battle of the Atlantic.'

The hard years of 1941 and 1942 had imposed a tremendous strain on Pound, calling for extra long hours of work and correspondingly fewer of rest and recreation. The heavy losses, both of warships and of merchant ships, added to the strain. At one period in 1942 he told Admiral Cunningham [*q.v.*] (the senior Admiral at sea, and virtually certain to succeed him as First Sea Lord) that he was tempted to resign. Cunningham's reply was: 'Stick to your chair, Dudley.' Perhaps this expression of confidence in him during a period when so much seemed to be going wrong gave Pound back the urge to see his job through.

Although he aged visibly under the heavy workload, he still retained his steady outlook of sureness and authority, and never lost touch with what was happening at sea day by day. But, unknown to him or his doctors, a tumour – which was eventually to end his life – was growing in his brain. As is normal with the elderly, its growth was very slow, and was not yet enough to impair his physical or mental capacities in any way. During meetings of the Chiefs of Staff towards the end of 1942, he would sit there with his eyes closed. He was sometimes thought to have fallen asleep, but it was noticeable that at any mention of the navy his eyes opened at once and he was ready to take a full part in any discussion. The Army Chief of Staff, Sir Alan Brooke (later Lord

Alanbrooke), subsequently claimed that Pound actually did sleep during their meetings; others thought he stayed awake but closed his eyes merely to rest them during discussions in which naval affairs had no part.

That he was tired after three years of war was not surprising. He was the longest-serving Chief of Staff on the committee, and generally speaking Churchill gave his Chiefs of Staff a hard time, being not only Prime Minister but also Minister of Defence, and thus both their ultimate and immediate superior. The loyalty of the three Chiefs of Staff remained unswerving throughout, particularly after the appointments of Sir Alan Brooke and Sir Charles Portal as the army and air force Chiefs respectively. It is widely accepted that, with Pound, these three men formed the best Chiefs of Staff Committee that Britain has ever had to serve her. Before becoming Prime Minister, when he was in the Admiralty as First Lord, Churchill had, of course, worked with Pound, and thus had first-hand experience of his detailed knowledge and integrity. These characteristics continued in the Chiefs of Staff Committee, not only earning Churchill's respect and affection, but also enabling Pound to hold his own in any discussions with his formidable boss.

Pound was sixty-five by then, at the age when most men have retired from active life; and what was surprising was that, at least as far as we in the OIC could see, his undoubted tiredness did not affect his mental or physical stamina at all. He still retained the toughness of body and fortitude of mind that had carried him through so far, and he – and we as well – could now see quite clearly how his strategic direction of the war at sea was beginning to work out. We looked forward in confidence to the promise of rich dividends in the months ahead.

Beyond those criticisms of specific interventions in operations in the war at sea, which I have addressed, there have been others made by some writers since the end of the war. One is that Pound consistently failed to stand up to Churchill when the interests of the navy demanded that he should; another is that he hung on to office long after his failing health required a younger man to take over. Both are, I am sure, demonstrably false. Pound recognized that Churchill, as Prime Minister, was the irreplaceable national leader; but his great integrity ensured that he always gave his professional opinion fearlessly. In fact, when disagreements arose between the two, it was Pound's advice that more often prevailed. His great love for the navy was based on a lifetime of service, very strict self-discipline and an extreme professionalism which made it impossible for him not to speak his mind forcefully and with conviction when naval matters were discussed. As for his health, those in daily contact and who worked closest to him saw no real evidence of deterioration until the summer of 1943, when the brain tumour began to spread and take its toll. It was then that Pound told Churchill that he must resign. Certainly the long hours of his working day and the weight of responsibility he had to bear had made him very tired, but his habit of 'cat-napping' during the day when the opportunity occurred made up in some measure for his few hours of sleep at night, kept him going with remarkable resilience and did not lessen the clarity or value of his contributions to the Chiefs of Staff Committee.

Early in 1943, Pound was offered a peerage, but declined it on the ground that he was not sufficiently well-to-do to maintain it in civil life. The death of his wife in July of that year, after a long and happy marriage, was a heavy blow; from then on it was only will-power that enabled him to carry on. In August, when attending the Quebec Conference of the Joint Chiefs of Staff, his terminal disease manifested its first active symptom: a lack of feeling in the right leg. In Washington in early September, he told the Prime Minister he could no longer carry on as First Sea Lord. He returned to England, made his farewells to the Admiralty and the fleet, and died in hospital on Trafalgar Day, 21 October. The Prime Minister, after a perhaps shaky start in his relations with Pound when he was First Lord of the Admiralty, had the highest opinion of the First Sea Lord and insisted on walking behind the family in the funeral cortège from the Admiralty to Westminster Abbey. After the service there, Pound's ashes were scattered at sea.

Pound's four years as First Sea Lord are marked by the broad application of his strategic thought that led directly to the naval victories in the Atlantic and Mediterranean. Although there were occasional setbacks – in war there are always setbacks as the battle sways one way or the other – Pound's overall strategy held firm. It was directly responsible for the scuttling of the pocket battleship *Graf Spee* in the River Plate in December 1939; for the sinking of the *Bismarck* after an error at sea had lost her; and for the gradual hunting down of the armed raiders in both the North and South Atlantic. But the greatest of his achievements, and the one which must surely have brought him the most satisfaction, was the victory over the U-boats in the Battle of the Atlantic. That victory owed an immeasurable amount to a number of vital factors on which Pound insisted – proper training as soon as escorts were produced in sufficient numbers, in spite of the temptation to commit them to the battle at once; their reorganization into escort and support groups; the bringing under naval control, in 1941, of the RAF's Coastal Command; the supply of VLR aircraft to Coastal Command, ensuring continuous air coverage for the convoys; the encouragement of research and development of new, more efficient anti-submarine measures. Of equal importance in another theatre of war was his Mediterranean strategy of holding Malta, whatever the cost, against prodigious enemy assault, while using it as a base to harry the Axis supply lines to North Africa. It was this that produced the conditions which, in late 1942, made possible the British and American assault landings in Algeria and Morocco, which in turn – linked with the British Eighth Army's offensive from Egypt – led to the total defeat of the Axis in that continent. In the Far East, though sadly shattered by the decision to use

Singapore as a base instead of Colombo as he had advised, his strategy was being reactivated at the time of his death with the formation of a new East Indies fleet in the Indian Ocean.

Pound did not live to see the full reward of his four years in chief command. But, before he died, at least he saw the total withdrawal of the U-boats from the North Atlantic trade routes, no longer able to bear the losses they were enduring at the hands of the surface and air escorts. He saw too the start of the great build-up of armies and supplies that crossed the Atlantic in safety for the final assault on Europe in 1944, which brought the war there to an end. In the Mediterranean he saw the driving back of the Italian fleet, the reopening of the short sea route to the east through the Suez Canal, the capture of Sicily, the advance up the mainland of Italy, and – just – the surrender of the Italian fleet. And he would surely have savoured Admiral Cunningham's signal to the Secretary of the Admiralty on that occasion: 'Be pleased to inform Their Lordships that the Italian battlefleet now lies at anchor under the guns of the fortress of Malta.'

From the start of the war in 1939, we in the OIC had seen a good deal of Pound. No doubt we all had our own personal opinions of him on various issues, but, after some hesitation during the first year when we did not quite know what to make of this grave and silent man, I think we would have been unanimous in recognizing the growing confidence he inspired in us all, even during the bad years of 1941 and 1942. Much of his work was hidden from us; although the results usually filtered through to us fairly quickly, we did not see into his own office, into the Chiefs of Staff Committee, into his work behind the scenes of hard training and the encouragement of new methods and weapons of naval warfare. Although we were all deeply involved with our own particular responsibilities within the OIC, I think that we were all able to appreciate from fairly early on that his strategic thoughts and decisions must inevitably lead to the final victory.

And behind all the brusqueness there must have been a kindly man. One morning I found on my desk a large package containing a copy of Richard Walton's history of Anson's voyages around the world in 1740–4 – a copy which had been published in 1748. Accompanying it was a note written in the green ink which all First Sea Lords use in the Admiralty. 'I saw this in a bookseller's shop in the Charing Cross Road yesterday,' it said, 'and, knowing that you are interested in naval history, thought you might like it. D.P.' I found it deeply touching that an admiral of the fleet, and a man who bore so great a burden of responsibility, should have had the time and the thought to remember one of the more junior members of the Naval Staff in the Admiralty.

But, when the last fatal illness struck, I think from what we had seen and learned of Pound that – much as all the recent successes in the Atlantic and the Mediterranean would have pleased him – his greatest satisfaction would surely have been the knowledge that he was turning over to his successor not only a navy that had been tempered in battle and was now confident of victory, but also a streamlined Admiralty staff which, through his professional training and inspired by his example, would continue to operate as though on oiled wheels for the new First Sea Lord. It was no mean legacy.

2

Grand Admiral

Erich Raeder

German Navy

1876–1960

by
Keith W. Bird

*E*RICH *Raeder was born on 24 April 1876 in Wandsbek near Hamburg. Entered the Naval Academy in Kiel, in 1894; served in the Far East (1897–8) on* SMS *Deutschland. Appointed to German Naval War College for staff training, 1903–5; posted to Tirpitz's News Bureau (Nachrichtenbüro) in the Navy Office, 1906–8.' Assigned as navigation officer aboard the Kaiser's yacht* Hohenzollern. *First Admiralty staff officer on the staff of the Scouting Forces of the High Seas Fleet, 1912–17; Chief of Staff for the Scouting Forces to Admiral von Hipper, 1917. Fought at Heligoland Bight and Jutland. Commanded light cruiser* Cöln, *January–October 1918. Chief of the Naval Office's (later Admiralty) Central Bureau, November 1918–June 1920. Involved in the German armistice discussions at Spa (September 1918) and the reorganization of the navy after the war. Promoted to captain, 1919. Implicated in the naval command's support of the right-wing Kapp Putsch March 1920; spent two years (1920–2) in the Naval Archives and wrote two of the three volumes on cruiser operations for the official naval history. Honorary doctorate from Kiel University, 1926. Rear admiral, August 1922. Headed the navy's Education and Training Department (Inspekteur des Bildungswesens), 1922–4. Final sea duty: commander of the Light Naval Forces (North Sea), September 1924–January 1925. Named Chief of the Baltic Naval Station in Kiel, February 1925; promoted to vice admiral, April 1925. Chosen to head the navy (Chef der Marineleitung) with the rank of admiral, October 1928. Concluded that the problems of the Imperial Navy and the Reichsmarine stemmed from the lack of centralized authority and command – a situation which he ruthlessly addressed in quickly establishing his authority and independence in the administration of naval affairs.* [1]

[1] Kurt Assmann and Walter Gladisch, *Aspects of the German Naval War*, Naval Intelligence Division – British Admiralty, NID 24/T237/46 (copy US Navy). In this report, written shortly after the war by two

In June 1935, following the renaming of the navy from the Reichsmarine to the Kriegsmarine, *Raeder's title became Commander-in-Chief (Oberbefehlshaber der Kriegsmarine). In 1937, he was awarded the gold Party Emblem by the Führer at the launching of* Bismarck. *Promoted grand admiral, 1 April 1939.*[2]

'Today the war against England and France broke out which, according to the Führer's previous assertions, we had no need to expect before 1944.' On 3 September 1939, Admiral Erich Raeder, Commander-in-Chief of Adolf Hitler's *Kriegsmarine* – the War Navy – felt bitterly betrayed by his Führer: 'the surface forces . . .', he continued, 'are so inferior in number and strength . . . that they can do no more than show that they know how to die gallantly and thus are willing to create the foundations for later reconstruction'.[3]

Though it was by no means clear that the conflict which had just begun would develop into a world war, it was obviously going to be a major one, and Raeder felt his fleet was badly under-prepared. Nevertheless, in his gloomy assessment of its chances against the vastly superior naval forces of France and Britain, he reflected more than merely defeatist resignation. While he clearly anticipated defeat, he was determined that Germany's mistakes of the Great War would not be repeated. There would be no surrender, nor even another grand scuttle – his unready forces might be destroyed, but they would go down with their flags flying, and until then they would be fully committed to the

---

of Raeder's colleagues, the authors describe how he made the navy 'a self-sufficient organism with all reins of administration firmly in his hands' and the results of this policy for his failure to allow anyone other than himself to deal with Hitler.

[2] There is currently no critical biography of Raeder. In addition to his memoirs, *Mein Leben*, 2 vols (Tübingen, 1956 and 1957), the best treatments of Raeder are contained in larger studies of the German navy, notably: Keith W. Bird, *Weimar, the German Naval Officers Corps and the Rise of National Socialism* (Amsterdam, 1977); Jost Dülffer, *Weimar, Hitler und die Marine. Reichspolitik und Flottenbau 1920 bis 1939* (Düsseldorf, 1973); Holger Herwig, *Politics of Frustration: The United States in German Naval Planning, 1889–1941* (Boston and Toronto, 1976); Michael Salewski, *Die deutsche Seekriegsleitung, 1935–1945*, 3 vols (Frankfurt/Main and Munich, 1970–5); and Gerhard Schreiber, *Revisionismus und Weltmachtstreben. Marineführung und deutsch-italienische Beziehungen, 1919–1944* (Stuttgart, 1978). Schreiber continued his research with two articles which sparked a considerable controversy over the continuity of the navy's *Weltanschauung*, over two world wars and the similarity of aims between the navy and Hitler: 'Zur Kontinuität des Gross- und Weltmachtstrebens der deutschen Marineführung', *Militärgeschichtliche Mitteilungen*, xxvi (2, 1979), pp. 101–71, and 'Thesen zur ideologischen Kontinuität in den machtpolitischen Zeilsetzungen der deutschen Militärgeschichte', ed. Manfred Messerschmidt et al. (Stuttgart, 1982). For bibliographical analysis of the themes and interpretations of Raeder and German naval history see Bird's *German Naval History: A Guide to the Literature* (New York, 1985), and 'The German Navy in World War II' in James J. Sadkovich (ed.), *World War II Naval History: A New Assessment of the Major Combatants* (Westport, Connecticut, 1989). The most complete general survey of the war at sea and Raeder's policies is represented in the projected ten-volume *Das Deutsche Reich und der Zweite Weltkrieg* (Stuttgart, 1979–).

[3] 'Reflections of the Commander-in-Chief, Navy on the Outbreak of War, September 1939', *Führer Conferences in Matters Dealing with the German Navy*, vol. 4 (Washington, 1947).

struggle. During the previous few years, he had progressively lost control of Germany's naval rearmament programme to Hitler; now, confronted with the consequences of the Führer's foreign policy, his most urgent wish was that, whatever its immediate fate, the Kriegsmarine should show itself worthy of participation in what he believed would be the inevitable next stage of Germany's expansionist politics.[4]

His statement echoed German naval feelings of 1918 and 1919. Then, in the face of its defeat by Britain, the Imperial Navy proposed a 'death ride' against the Royal Navy, and, by scuttling itself in Scapa Flow, satisfied its own sense of honour. He had always believed that this provided – in his own words – the 'important basis for the rebuilding of the navy'.[5]

Raeder's many contacts with Hitler before the war had led him to believe that the Führer was thoroughly aware of the importance of sea power for the future of Nazi Germany's expansionist programme, and the conflict against the maritime powers that would inevitably ensue. For both men, the symbol of the navy's value as a political instrument was the battleship, and Raeder had eagerly sought to woo the Führer with plans for 100,000-ton super-battleships.[6] But, influenced by the failure of the High Seas Fleet in the Great War, neither the Admiral nor his naval colleagues had been willing to confront the operational and strategic issues that would arise if war with England occurred before 1944; and so, when war began unexpectedly early, the navy's first concern was the question of national strategic objectives.

Once England and France declared war on Germany, Raeder's hard-won victories in securing special priority for his ships dissolved in favour of Hitler's *Blitzkrieg* and the necessity of shifting resources to the Luftwaffe. Throughout his remaining tenure as naval chief, Raeder sought every opportunity to influence the course of the war to suit the needs of the navy vis-à-vis the other services – even to the point of what one historian has called 'criminal folly' in trying to divert Hitler's attention to the economic war against British and American sea power.[7]

Raeder's claims (and those of his post-war supporters) that Hitler never understood sea power were in large measure justified. Even so, the naval command was also at fault; it never developed a comprehensive concept of naval strategy and offered no real solutions to the problems of how to break the

[4]In the spring of 1940, Raeder reaffirmed the necessity of the navy's aggressive strategy. 'A navy which undertakes daring actions against the enemy and suffers losses through this will be reborn on an even larger scale.' If this did not occur, stated Raeder, the navy's existence after the war would be at stake. Salewski, *Seekriegsleitung*, vol. I, p. 523.

[5]Raeder, *Mein Leben*, vol. I, p. 168.

[6]See Bird, *Weimar*, pp. 278–85, for Raeder's contacts with Hitler and the Nazi Party, and Düllfer's *Weimar, Hitler und die Marine* for plans for the navy's battleships and their relationship to Hitler's plans for *Weltmacht*.

[7]See Herwig's criticism of Raeder's efforts to pursue his Mediterranean strategy in spite of Hitler's plans to invade the Soviet Union. *Politics of Frustration*, p. 216.

British blockade and how to overcome Germany's lack of strategic bases.[8] Indeed, the inclusion of Erich Raeder among the 'great naval leaders' of World War Two lies less in the accomplishments of the navy he commanded for fifteen years than in his role as the symbol of the failure of German naval leadership in the era of the world wars. Before studying Raeder's conduct of the German naval war from September 1939 to his resignation in 1943, it is therefore appropriate to return to a much earlier time.

Raeder's tragedy was that he never escaped from the heritage of Tirpitz's grandiose fleet-building plans and the unfulfilled promises of the High Seas Fleet in 1914–18. Indeed, from the first attempt to create a German navy in 1848, its leaders were caught between the realities of having to plan on the one hand for short-term solutions to naval strategy and operations, and, on the other, for the long-term goal of establishing a *Weltflotte* that could compete successfully against the other battlefleets of the world – in particular those of Britain and, after the Great War, the United States. The threat to other powers represented by Germany's aggressive statecraft and geography never allowed the time required to construct the navy both Tirpitz and Raeder envisioned. Moreover, this 'atrophy of strategic thought', noted by Herbert Rosinski, a German naval planner from 1932 to 1936, persisted through two world wars with both Tirpitz and Raeder building fleets without formulating a grand naval strategy which would incorporate Germany's needs or capabilities.[9]

The concept of German sea power (*Seegeltung*), which provided the ideological basis for the naval officers and the supporters of navalism, not only reinforced the conviction that 'a great nation is determined by the scale of its navy' but also confirmed the 'political exclusiveness and homogeneity' of the Imperial Naval Officer Corps.[10] The continuity of the navy's global ambitions and fleet-building programmes has been well documented through the archives and personal papers of its naval and political leaders.[11]

In evaluating Raeder's leadership of the navy during the Third Reich, and the first forty months of World War Two, it is necessary to understand how his policies were shaped by Germany's naval and political tradition as well as by his own ambition and personality. The story of the navy and its fate becomes a

[8]Raeder drew attention to Hitler's ignorance of naval matters beginning as early as March 1933 in a reference to Hitler's being a native of Austria (Dülffer, *Weimar, Hitler und die Marine.* p. 204), a point he and Dönitz made repeatedly at the Nuremberg Military Tribunal and in their memoirs. Karl Jesko von Puttkamer depicts Hitler as a 'coward at sea' and criticized the Führer's lack of understanding for issues of naval strategy. *Die unheimliche See. Hitler und die Kriegsmarine* (Vienna and Munich, 1952).

[9]Herbert Rosinski, 'German Theories of Sea Warfare', *Brassey's Naval Annual 1940* (London, 1940), p. 90.

[10]Cf. Schreiber's essays on the navy's *Seemacht* ideology, 'Zur Kontinuität des Gross- und Weltmachtstrebens', pp. 101–71, and 'Thesen zur ideologischen Kontinuität', and Herwig's seminal study of the Imperial Naval Officer Corps. *The German Naval Officer Corps, A Social and Political History, 1890–1918* (Oxford, 1973), p. 265.

[11]Cf. Bird, *German Naval History*, esp. pp. 3–56, 571–94.

study of Raeder and his direct personal and autocratic administration of naval affairs. Indeed, as one historian has agreed, after 1928 the navy became Raeder and Raeder the navy.[12] The attempts of Raeder and his supporters in their post-war accounts to blame Hitler and the military High Command for Germany's 'continental strategy' echoes Tirpitz's lament in 1919 that 'the German people have never understood the sea'.[13] However, the inability of Raeder and the naval command to influence Hitler's strategy concealed the fact that the navy itself was held captive by the Tirpitz tradition of the battlefleet, with its focus on the battleship and the 'decisive battle' to decide the fate of German sea power. Thus the German Navy never kept pace with the technological progress in naval warfare made by its enemies – especially in naval aviation and radar. Raeder's emphasis on getting his ships built at any cost ultimately led to the navy's failure to develop a 'clear naval strategy'. This failure had direct consequences on operations planning as well as ship construction and armaments priorities. Indeed, the navy never produced any maritime strategy to explain how German sea power could assist in Germany's bid for continental power – a necessary prerequisite to Germany's becoming a global sea power. Raeder's Mediterranean strategy, proposed as a 'war-winning' alternative to the invasion of the Soviet Union, actually represented not only the bankruptcy of his policies since 1928, but also his inability to see how the navy could make any meaningful contribution to the war effort other than the 'heroic' sacrifice of all of its forces. Moreover, his acceptance and accommodation of Hitler and National Socialism always represented a means towards a greater end. As with his mentor, Tirpitz, in World War One, who resigned when his influence had waned, Raeder increasingly found himself embroiled in events which he had helped to start but could no longer control.

Fleet Building in the Third Reich

During the period of the Weimar Republic, the navy's war games and rebuilding plans reflected its refusal to surrender its dreams of becoming a major sea power with a fleet large enough to challenge the Royal Navy and project its power on a global basis. But Raeder was a skilled tactician in naval political affairs, and used his government's and army's support for a defensive role – the protection of the Baltic and the sea link between the Reich and East Prussia – to secure support for the navy's rebuilding programme. With the approval of the first *Panzerschiff* programme, the navy quickly shifted its focus to a two-front war against Poland and its ally France. The *Panzerschiff* (Germany's 'pocket battleship', built under the 1935 Anglo-German Naval Treaty limitations of 10,000 tons to replace its ageing pre-dreadnought capital ships) was not only a 'prestige factor' but would 'enable the German navy to

[12]Salewski, *Seekriegsleitung*, vol. 1, pp. 108–9.
[13]See Alfred von Tirpitz, *Erinnerungen* (Leipzig, 1919), p. 387.

carry on every form of sea warfare and prevent it from degenerating into a coastal force'.[14] The problem of fitting the pocket battleship into German naval strategy and tactics was not really solved until the ship joined the fleet in 1930. The navy's demands for parity with France were not so much the results of a careful strategic analysis of its role in natural defences; rather, they were a means of furthering its long-term objectives – goals that reflected its own enthusiasm for a long-term fleet-building programme, more than the government' and army's plans for Germany's future naval power. Raeder was content at that stage to prepare the foundation for the expansion that would inevitably come once Germany 'recovered' from democracy, which he viewed as its political malaise.[15]

Envisioning a two-front war against Poland and France, the navy's aggressive blue-water war games and ambitious overseas plans during this period demonstrated Raeder's rejection of the limited role assigned to it by the pre-Nazi government and the army. This role required the navy only to maintain the sea link between East Prussia and the Reich. The concentration on France served several major functions for Raeder. The demands for parity with France ensured that the navy would not be relegated to a coastal navy, but instead would enable it to build the nucleus of a much larger fleet. Raeder's manipulation of foreign policy to serve his naval interests culminated in the 1932 *Umbau* (conversion) plan which was to maximize the naval limits permitted under the treaty. The plan also assumed a revision of the treaty and called for an aircraft carrier, U-boats and a fleet air arm. The concomitant increase in officers and personnel would ensure the foundation for future expansion. In spite of criticism within the navy that the opportunity for major growth had not been fully exploited, such relatively modest plans continued to disguise Raeder's ultimate objectives. Going far beyond the requirements of national defence, these perpetuated the weakness the navy had had in the Tirpitz era: naval expansion was detached from any grand national strategic planning. The gap between material reality and future possibilities began to widen. Under Hitler, it would become critical: his short-term diplomatic and military initiatives threatened (and eventually crushed) Raeder's long-term dreams.[16]

Nevertheless, with Hitler's rise to power, the dream of a 'world fleet' appeared to be within the navy's grasp. Its yearning for a strong national leader, who came from a unified broad-based movement of all the people, was itself a legacy of the Tirpitz era. Hitler's 'national revolution' appeared to fulfil the condition for the German people to achieve its '*Weltpolitische* destiny'. The

[14]Assman and Gladisch, *Aspects of the German Naval War.*

[15]For Raeder's and the naval officer corps' views of democracy and the promise of the Nazi state see Bird, *Weimar*, pp. 282–97.

[16]See Werner Rahn, *Reichsmarine und Landesverteidigung, 1919–1928* (Munich, 1976) and Gerhard Schreiber's 'Die Rolle Frankreichs im strategischen und operativen Denken der deutschen Marine', in Klaus Hildebrand and Karl Werner (eds), *Deutschland und Frankreich, 1936–1939* (Munich and Zurich, 1981).

correspondence between Raeder and the former officers of the Imperial Navy document the 'affinity for fascism' which existed in the fleet.[17] During Hitler's rise to power, Raeder was aware of the appeal of the Nazi emphasis on national defence and unity and saw the potential of the Nazi movement for the navy. The integration of the navy into the Third Reich was therefore no problem for Raeder; controlling the enthusiasm of the younger officers was more difficult since it interfered with his timing and style in dealing with Hitler.[18]

When Raeder first met Hitler in April 1933, he had already formed an impression of the Führer's attitudes towards the navy which reinforced the Admiral's conviction that here was another politician to be 'educated' to Germany's needs for sea power. For a long time, Raeder mistakenly believed that Hitler could be 'directed' to a proper understanding and that the 'independence' of the navy was due to Raeder's emphasis on obedience and loyalty.[19] In October 1932 Raeder had written to retired Rear Admiral Magnus von Levetzow, who had close contact with Hitler and Göring, to complain about Hitler's criticism of the Tirpitz fleet, and his anti-battleship and naval rearmament remarks in August of that year. Raeder called these attitudes 'criminal' and 'foolish', warning Levetzow that Hitler had endangered 'all the threads that we have spun'. Hitler, Raeder charged, would relegate the fleet to a coastal navy, restricted to the North Sea; he did not understand that a navy could not be fashioned overnight.[20] Levetzow sought successfully to reassure Raeder that Hitler would be receptive to rebuilding the navy, and encouraged Raeder to continue to provide information which Levetzow would pass on to his Nazi friends.[21]

Raeder was fully aware that Hitler did not support a forced naval build-up, and that he wished ostensibly to avoid conflict with England. Göring's close relationship with Hitler and his role as the Reichskommissar for Aviation meant that Raeder also had to contend with a new and powerful rival. Raeder's goals in 1933, therefore, were to convince Hitler that the navy's rebuilding programmes were modest and could be useful as a political instrument in the Führer's continental policy. The tradition of the navy's role as an 'alliance factor' (*Bündnisfähigkeit*) – which Tirpitz used so skilfully to disarm his domestic opponents – was emphasized by Raeder in his first face-to-face meeting with the new Chancellor. The expansion of the navy, he quickly emphasized to Hitler, was not directed against England.[22] From Raeder's

[17]Schreiber's 'Thesen zur ideologieschen Kontinuität'.
[18]Bird, *Weimar*, pp. 287–94.   [19]Ibid.
[20]Raeder to Levetzow, 26 October 1932, Levetzow Nachlass, Box 7, Bd. 35, Bundesarchiv-Militärarchiv.
[21]Cf. Levetzow's reply to Raeder, 26 October 1932, Levetzow Nachlass, Box 7, Bd. 35, Bundesarchiv-Militärarchiv. Levetzow referred to Raeder as his 'high-placed informant' and told Hitler of his 'closeness' to the chief of the naval command. See Bird, *Weimar*, p. 279.
[22]See 'Konzept Admiral Raeders für einen Vortrag beim Reichskanzler undatiert (Ende März 1933)', Sammlung Raeder, 12, BAMA reprinted in Salewski's 'Marineleitung und politische Führung, 1931–1935', *Militärgeschichtliche Mitteilungen*, x)2, 1971), pp. 153–5.

standpoint, however, his goal was clear – to secure his fleet through a series of tactical moves with Hitler, utilizing personal contact (which the army command never attempted to establish with Hitler); to assure the period of peace necessary for fleet construction; and to avoid the military, political and diplomatic problems that had accompanied the Tirpitz programme. It is not clear to what degree Raeder 'persuaded' Hitler – but the Admiral happily reported to his officers that Hitler 'is firmly convinced of the navy's great importance, not least as an influential factor in international affairs'.[23]

Actually, Raeder's subtlety was lost on a Führer who himself had long-term goals that already included a *Weltflotte* on a scale similar to that envisioned by the Admiral. For the short term, Hitler's initial reception of Raeder and the navy assured the loyalty of the navy while the Führer moved to consolidate his power. Less than a year later, Raeder felt sufficiently confident of Hitler's support and the thrust of the Nazi *Wehrhoheit* (sovereignty of arms) in foreign policy to propose a fleet of eight battleships, three aircraft carriers, eighteen cruisers, forty-eight destroyers and seventy-two U-boats to be completed by 1949. The principal theme was, again, parity with France – a formula that would give Germany a period of time to build the foundation from which it could challenge the Royal Navy once again. In order to avoid a naval race similar to that of the 1897–1914 Tirpitz era, Raeder sought a fixed ratio of the German fleet to the British of 35 per cent (which in practical terms meant parity with France, as fixed by the 1922 Washington Naval Agreement).[24]

Although there was some impatience within the navy over a 35 per cent ratio, Raeder failed in an attempt to increase it to 50 per cent, as the final terms of the 1935 Anglo-German Naval Treaty demonstrated. It was true that the Germans were now allowed to build 100 per cent of British submarine strength, but among some circles in the navy – officers who were perhaps more willing than Raeder to recognize the consequences of the growing threat to England represented by Hitler's expansion of the army and the creation of the Luftwaffe[25] – not even this clause could completely quiet unrest. Raeder's *Ressorteifer*, his desire to defend and expand his department and sphere of influence, coupled with the belief that he was on the verge of achieving the fleet that Tirpitz had wanted, repeatedly caused him to ignore internal criticism of the navy's construction plans, and to remain silent when Hitler's aggressive diplomatic moves threatened his timetable. His tenacity with Hitler did succeed in securing approval for secret increases in the size and armament of ships and in

[23]For the history of the Anglo-German agreement see Dülffer, *Weimar, Hitler, und die Marine*, p. 249.

[24]Ibid., pp. 279–354.

[25]The 100 per cent clause for submarines reflected the size of the Royal Navy's submarine force and the fact that Germany was already engaged in U-boat construction by means of subassemblies and would quickly exceed the 35 per cent ratio in any case. For internal criticism of the treaty, see ibid., pp. 331, 346–8, and Dönitz's memoirs, *Zehn Jahre und Zwanzig Tage*, 7th rev. edn (Munich, 1980), p. 15.

June 1934 he felt confident enough to mention openly to Hitler the ultimate aim of the navy – development of the fleet 'later poss[ibly] against E[ngland]'.[26]

The naval treaty of June 1935 with England was understood by Raeder not to constitute a rejection of the navy's ambitions; instead he regarded it as 'provisional', corresponding both to his needs and to those of Hitler. The Admiral attempted to assure his officers that the Anglo-German treaty would accelerate naval construction by five years from the 144,000 tons originally allowed by the Versailles Treaty to 520,000 tons.[27] Unfortunately, he had not fully considered the impact of naval construction on the capacity of German shipyards and the Reich's overall economic situation as Hitler forced the pace of rearmament. Shortages of labour and raw materials, especially steel, acted as a significant brake on the naval programme and forced Raeder to lobby intensively with the Führer to increase the priority for the navy.[28] As Hitler's diplomatic initiatives increasingly brought the question of conflict with England into the foreground, Raeder pressed even harder for the navy's interests, believing that the Führer valued its role in the first phase of his continental strategy. It was not until the Czechoslovakian crisis of May 1938, however, that Raeder openly allowed discussion and planning for war with England – and this was not only a full six months after Hitler had acknowledged (at the November 1937 Hossbach Conference) that a war with England was possible, but no less than four years after Raeder himself had recorded the anti-British bias in his fleet-building programme.[29] The taboo against planning for a naval war against England was finally lifted; the previously unthinkable became a reality for the naval command. While Raeder's subordinates urged him to oppose Hitler's risky diplomatic moves, the Admiral remained silent rather than jeopardize what he had won for the navy. Caught between their dreams of the distant future and the reality of having to plan how best to use the few ships available to them, Raeder and the naval command responded with plans for a 'cruiser war' with raiders and U-boats deployed to disrupt British shipping. Such a plan militated against the battlefleet that Raeder was intent on creating, yet no change was made in the naval programme, nor was any decision made regarding the role and type of U-boats or naval aircraft to be built. To resolve Germany's poor geographical position and secure 'access to the open sea', Raeder's staff also called for the

[26]See Salewski, *Marineleitung*, pp. 140–56, and Dülffer, *Weimar, Hitler und die Marine*, pp. 288–99. The standard interpretation assumes that it was Hitler, not Raeder, who mentioned that the navy might be used against Britain. See Wilhelm Deist, *The Wehrmacht and German Rearmament* (Toronto and Buffalo, 1981), p. 123.

[27]Dülffer, *Weimar, Hitler und die Marine*, pp. 315, 348.

[28]Ibid., pp. 457–8. Raeder noted in spring 1938 that the most tonnage that the Imperial Navy had under construction at any one time was 200,000 tons compared to the Kriegsmarine's 520,000.

[29]Deist, *Wehrmacht and German Rearmament*, p. 79. For the 'Turn against England', see Salewski, 'England, Hitler und die Marine', *Vom Sinn der Geschichte* (Stuttgart, 1976), Schreiber, 'Zur Kontinuität', pp. 123–31, and Dülffer, *Weimar, Hitler und die Marine*, pp. 434–534.

acquisition of overseas bases or the extension of Germany's coastal base to include the French, Dutch and Danish coasts – proposals that ignored the navy's short-term (six years) prospects in terms of the size of the fleet.[30]

The final resolution of the navy's deliberations in its construction plans culminated in the so-called Z-Plan, presented to Hitler in January 1939. This envisioned that, by 1948 at the latest, the fleet should include ten battleships, four aircraft carriers, fifteen *Panzerschiffe*, five heavy cruisers, sixty-eight destroyers and 249 U-boats. With this force, the naval planners believed Germany could defeat the Royal Navy, and perhaps the US Navy too.[31] The Z-Plan continued the navy's unrealistic assessment of a war against Great Britain and the difficulty of rationalizing the role of the battleship in such a war. Moreover, the appeal of the Z-Plan was such that little thought was given to what would happen if war began before 1944–5, when the fleet was scheduled to be completed. In spite of a major crisis in the shipbuilding industry (with an average of over twelve months' delay as of December 1937), Raeder altered neither his plans nor his demand for an increase in the navy's share of resources. Hitler continued to insist on the building of battleships and forced the pace of construction which in late 1938 had already led to Raeder threatening resignation.[32] By sacrificing the navy's plan for the development of an independent air arm Raeder gained Göring's support and won naval priority 'over all other Reich and export orders';[33] but barely seven months later, the Kriegsmarine found itself at war with England.

Raeder had achieved (at least on paper) the goal of his mentor Tirpitz – the approval for the creation of a first-class battlefleet. But it was a hollow achievement, not least because – at a time when Germany faced many deficiencies, including a shortage of diesel oil – it ignored the strategic and economic demands of such a navy. Raeder's bitterness at the start of the war reflects how deeply conscious he was of the failure of his political and strategic aims. It presaged, too, how little influence he was to have on the conduct of the war.

As indicated earlier, it was the fault not only of Hitler, but also of the naval command, that Germany never developed a comprehensive concept of naval strategy. Faced with the reality of war, the naval command offered no real

[30]Salewski, *Seekriegsleitung*, vol. 1, pp. 45–50, and Herwig, *Politics of Frustration*, pp. 191–3.

[31]Dülffer, *Hitler und die Marine*, p. 569, and Herwig, *Politics of Frustration*, pp. 193–4, argue that the 'Z-fleet' was designed to support Germany's bid for world hegemony.

[32]For a description of the Z-Plan, see Dülffer, *Weimar, Hitler und die Marine*, pp. 497–505, and Salewski, *Seekriegsleitung*, vol. 1, pp. 57–60. Herwig argues that the Z-Plan was designed with the United States in mind as well as England and was not meant 'to define the ultimate strength of the German navy' as later construction programmes were to reveal. *Politics of Frustration*, p. 193. By December 1937, the navy was anticipating delays of three to twenty-two months in the completion of its ships with the average delay of just over one year. Dülffer, *Weimar, Hitler and die Marine*, pp. 428–34, 568–9. With these problems it would be difficult, if not impossible, to reach the strength of the British by the target date of 1942.

[33]Dülffer, *Weimar, Hitler und die Marine*, pp. 497–502.

solution to the questions either of how to break the British blockade or of how to overcome Germany's lack of strategic bases.34 Along with Hitler's refusal in 1938–9 to allow more U-boats to be built (which Raeder and his junior officers proposed as an immediate deterrent to buy more time for fleet building), in favour of completing the battleships, the naval command rejected unrestricted submarine warfare as an alternative strategy because of the belief that a future U-boat war would have to be fought according to international Prize Rules (that is, warning ships before attacking) and the belief that anti-submarine warfare had made significant advances since World War One.35 The strategy envisioned by the 1939 Z-Plan was the strategy that Raeder tried to implement, in spite of the few ships available to him at the start of the war. It was this. As a result of the 1938–9 winter manoeuvres, the so-called 'double-pole' strategy was evolved, calling for attacks on the British sea lanes and operations against the Royal Navy in the Baltic Sea. If successful, this would enable even limited German task forces to win a 'decisive battle' over an enemy weakened by having to divide its own forces to protect its worldwide commerce and empire. Thus the navy expected to have strategic success in the economic war, but only tactical success against the blockade.36

Raeder's conception of seeking operational possibilities within the total theatre of operations – the 'multiplicity' (*Vielseitigkeit*) factor – fitted well with the navy's intention to seize the initiative and attack the British on a global scale.37 His determination to seize the initiative in a conflict with England was

34In spite of his praise of the naval command's efforts to formulate an effective naval strategy, Salewski still questions the aim of these efforts if the lifelines to England were never seriously threatened. Cf. Wolfgang Wilhelm's 'Zufuhrkrieg mit Panzerschiffen', *Marine Forum*, LV (5, 1980), pp. 140–5. Critics of Salewski who feel that he identifies too closely with the naval command in labelling the Atlantic strategy as a 'daring, first-rate plan' and its failure as tragic include Edward Wegener, 'Die deutsche Seekriegsleitung, 1935–1945', *MOV-Nachrichten*, XLV (1970), pp. 211–15. Wegener believes the naval command to have been as 'continental minded' as Hitler and objects to Salewski's description of using capital ships in commerce war as an 'offensive' naval strategy instead of 'defensive'. Wolfgang Wegener (Edward Wegener's son) called the Z-Plan 'Nothing more than cruiser warfare escalated to gigantic proportions'. See Herwig's introduction to *Naval Strategy of the World War* (Annapolis, 1989), p. xlvii. Wegener's *Naval Strategy* was originally published in 1929.

35For the German 'lessons of the war' see Philip K. Lundeberg's 'The German Naval Critique of the U-boat Campaign, 1915–1918', *Military Affairs*, 27 (Fall, 1963), pp. 105–18. Cf. Carl-Axel Gemzell, *Raeder, Hitler und Skandinavien: Der Kampf für einen maritimen Operationsplan* (Lund, 1965), p. 290. In 1937, Raeder argued that submarines had never been 'decisive' and were only important in a secondary role. The guiding principle for Raeder's naval politics was the building of large battleships. See 'Denkerschrift über den Flottenbau, 1926–1933', III M 151/1, *Bundesarchiv-Militärarchiv*.

36See Salewski, *Seekriegsleitung*, vol. I, pp. 45–50, and Herwig's discussion of the 'England Memorandum' of 25 October 1938 by Vice-Admiral Guse which concluded that commerce warfare was of primary importance but the naval command would not 'expect very substantial successes from an offensive naval war with U-boats only'. *Politics of Frustration*, p. 192.

37See Salewski, *Seekriegsleitung*, vol. I, p. 23, for reference to Raeder's 3 February 1937 lecture on 'Fundamentals of Naval Warfare'. This lecture should be considered more carefully in any future analysis of the origins and development of Raeder's naval strategy.

reflected in the operations orders positioning the *Deutschland*, *Graf Spee* and eighteen U-boats in the North Sea and the Atlantic in August 1939. Raeder hoped to use these ships and the remainder of the fleet (two battleships, one *Panzerschiff* (pocket battleship), thirty-nine U-boats and a handful of cruisers and destroyers) to buy time until additional U-boats could be built. Meanwhile, enemy naval forces, even if inferior in strength, were to be attacked only if fighting them contributed to the primary objective – that is, winning the commerce war. German mining operations in the North Sea were designed to disrupt merchant traffic, and Raeder ordered frequent changes of the operational areas to disperse British warships further. His belief that only quick and decisive action by the navy and the Luftwaffe could force England to sue for peace was frustrated by serious technical difficulties with torpedoes, as well as mechanical problems which affected the cruising range and readiness of a number of the new warships. The latter proved to have a decisive impact on operations throughout the war, while the torpedo problem and Hitler's initial restrictions on U-boat operations were to rob the navy of a number of potential successes.[38]

The successes that *were* achieved could not be exploited in any major way, because of the limited numbers of the new magnetic mines then available, and chronic rivalries and disagreements with the Luftwaffe. As the navy feared, the Luftwaffe's inaccurate dropping of mines – often on to mud flats, which prevented their self-destruct mechanisms from activating – aided the British considerably. By recovering such mines, they soon learned how to counter them.[39]

Raeder's struggles with Göring over the tactical use of air power in support of naval operations seriously crippled the U-boat war, mine warfare and the deployment of the *Lufttorpedo*. The navy had neither the numbers nor the types of aircraft necessary to conduct an offensive naval war such as Raeder envisioned against the Royal Navy and British commerce, and his constant attempts to establish an independent naval air arm were continually thwarted by Göring. The crews of the Luftwaffe were not sufficiently prepared in training or equipment to support the naval war against the British blockade fully, and communications were so poor that once, early in the war, the Luftwaffe managed to sink two *German* destroyers.

This struggle with Göring continued throughout Raeder's tenure. In January 1941, during one of Göring's hunting vacations, Raeder seemed to have won a major victory when he managed to have the Luftwaffe's long-range reconnaissance squadron 1/KG 40 provided with twelve Fw 200c aircraft to support the U-boat war. But on his return from holiday, Göring prevailed

---

[38]The torpedo crisis and the criticism of the pre-war shipbuilding programme were answered by Raeder in a memorandum of 11 June 1940 in an attempt to quell growing criticism within the officer corps. The translated text appears in Cajus Bekker, *Hitler's Naval War*, ed. and trans. Frank Ziegler (Garden City, NY, 1974), pp. 375–6.

[39]Salewski, *Seekriegsleitung*, vol. 1, pp. 141–7.

upon Hitler to establish, in March 1941, a new command (Fliegerführer Atlantik) that would control all aspects of naval air support in the Atlantic commerce war. This sounded grand, yet by the autumn of 1943, British air superiority and the lack of German aircraft made it impossible for this group to fulfil any of its objectives in the war against enemy shipping.[40] The limited German air reconnaissance further enhanced the effectiveness of British Special Intelligence (code breaking) in steering Allied convoys away from U-boats. As it was, in mid-1941, Raeder's war diary noted that because of strengthened convoy defences it took three times as many U-boats to achieve the same success as earlier.[41]

For Raeder and Göring, the issue was more one of principle than fighting a war. For example, although the months-long struggle in 1940–1 over who would control air torpedoes involved the German navy's entire torpedo stock, that in fact consisted of only five torpedoes.[42] Nevertheless, for Raeder this issue was directly tied into his plans for the future building of his naval air arm and the deployment of torpedo planes in the Atlantic. After the stunning successes of Japanese carrier forces at Pearl Harbor and in the first phase of the Pacific War, the navy's bitterness against the Luftwaffe became even more pronounced – but it had been Raeder who had continually pushed for battleships over aircraft carriers and delayed construction of the navy's only aircraft carrier, the *Graf Zeppelin*, until Germany's declining resources and the military situation precluded any further work.[43] Although Raeder did not initially see aircraft carriers as a main factor in his short-term strategy, the lack of development in naval aircraft was as much due to the technological failure of the navy in all areas of naval warfare. Even a prototype carrier for experimental purposes might have spurred the Luftwaffe and Hitler to develop carrier aircraft earlier than 1942. In 1940, however, when the Führer showed a brief enthusiasm for aircraft carriers (including 'jeep' carriers) following Japan's success, Raeder's long-term building plans still focused on the battleship – twenty-five battleships to eight aircraft carriers in the first stage – and, as a result, the navy could not take advantage of the situation at all.[44]

The First Phase: September 1939–March 1940

World War Two began with a surprise naval bombardment by the pre-dreadnought battleship *Schleswig-Holstein* against Polish defensive positions

[40]Gerhard Hümmelchen's *Die deutschen Seeflieger, 1935–1945* (Munich, 1976), pp. 62–6, 85–6.

[41]Dönitz, *Zehn Jahre*, pp. 127–37. For the role of Special Intelligence see Patrick Beesly's *Very Special Intelligence: The Story of the Admiralty's Operational Intelligence Centre 1939–1945* (London, 1977). The British Admiralty used 'Special Intelligence' to describe information derived from decrypting enemy signals and not 'Ultra'.

[42]Hümmelchen, *Seeflieger*, p. 86.   [43]Herwig, *Politics of Frustration*, p. 242.

[44]In addition to Salewski's evaluation of the navy and Hitler's plans for aircraft carriers in *Seekriegsleitung*, see Wilhelm Hadeler's 'Die Flugzeugträger in der deutschen Marine, 1934–45', *Marine Rundschau*, LIII (5, 1956), pp. 62–169.

on the Westerplatte, which blocked the navy's access to Danzig's harbour. This battle lasted seven days. Far harder than the Germans expected, the army and the Luftwaffe were eventually required to relieve the badly mauled naval landing forces. In retrospect, this action (little known except in Poland, where it represents a national symbol of resistance) foreshadowed all the German navy's major failures in World War Two. Not only did it lack any detailed plans for the attack on Poland, but the army forced it into a position of providing artillery support for German troops in Danzig – a task it did not want and was unprepared to carry out. Neither service saw the strategic importance of the Westerplatte until it was too late. The resulting poor communication between the two services, and the failure of either the naval command or the army to provide up-to-date intelligence about the Polish defences, led to high losses for the *Schleswig-Holstein*'s landing forces. The Polish resistance soon became a prestige issue for both sides. In an attempt to please an impatient Hitler, Göring ordered (on his own initiative and without co-ordination with the army or navy) a devastating Stuka attack that would have forced a capitulation – *if* it had been promptly followed up by another ground assault.[45] The failure of the German High Command to understand the importance of combined operations in World War Two, and the independence that both Raeder and Göring sought to maintain, would have serious consequences on the course of the war in all theatres.

Faced almost at once with the problems of the British–French declaration of war, Raeder immediately and radically revised the navy's building programme. Only the nearly finished *Bismarck*, *Tirpitz* and *Prinz Eugen* would be completed; instead of further capital ships, the emphasis would be placed on U-boats. Since the most urgent task was organizing logistics and securing resources for short-term stop-gap measures (such as mine warfare and disguised merchant ships), all weapons development virtually ceased. This factor badly impeded German development of radar and new U-boat types – weapons which might otherwise have had a significant effect on the war.[46]

Once the navy found itself in conflict with England, Raeder pressed Hitler vigorously to lift the restrictions placed on the operations of both the surface fleet and U-boats. With the limited number of forces available to him, Raeder did not want to give the Allies time to organize their defences; nor did he wish to lose the opportunity for quick and decisive attacks against enemy commerce. For Raeder, the conflict had become an economic war and he recognized that the war of attrition was a double-edged sword. He knew that sooner or later his surface forces would be sunk, or damaged for long periods of time, and he therefore pressed continually for unrestricted submarine warfare against *all*

---

[45]See Bertil Stjernfelt and Klaus-Richard Böhme's *Westerplatte* (Freiburg, 1979).

[46]See Salewski, *Seekriegsleitung*, vol. II, p. 306, for the navy's reliance on 'inspired improvisations' and the emphasis on 'will' and 'heroic struggles'. Herwig points out how both German arrogance and a lack of training contributed to an underestimation of the enemy – particularly the US. *Politics of Frustration*, p. 199.

commerce bound for England – a policy that he knew must ultimately bring the United States into the conflict. Hitler, however, continued to believe that he could reach a 'political understanding' with England and France, and only gradually lifted the restrictions to allow more offensive action against enemy shipping and warships.47

It was not until 23 September 1939 that Hitler allowed *Deutschland* and *Graf Spee* to commence operations. Results were modest, and in November *Scharnhorst* and *Gneisnau* were sent into the North Atlantic to relieve pressure on *Graf Spee* and force the British to disperse their forces. In December, however, *Graf Spee* was sunk by scuttling – the exact fate Raeder intended none of his ships to meet. Worried about the effect on national morale if *Deutschland* was also sunk, Hitler renamed the pocket battleship *Lützow* upon her return.

Raeder and the naval command were not pleased with the results of the six-day sortie of *Scharnhorst* and *Gneisenau*, and criticized the fleet chief, Admiral Wilhelm Marshall, for being too cautious and not aggressive enough. The loss of *Graf Spee* less than a month later caused further problems with both Raeder and Hitler. Aware of criticism within the navy and outside over the decision of *Graf Spee*'s commander, Langsdorff, to scuttle his ship without a fight, Raeder issued a directive saying that 'the German warship fights with full deployment of its crew until it is victorious or until it goes under with flag flying'.48

For Hitler, the defeat of *Graf Spee* reinforced his fear of losses at sea. His belief in the prestige factor of capital ships, and the propaganda value the British derived from each victory over the German navy, strengthened his determination to control all deployment of naval forces – especially the surface vessels. Raeder and his advisers were acutely aware that the surface navy had to justify its existence, especially if it wished to receive future support. The victories of the U-boats in sinking the aircraft carrier *Courageous* and battleship *Royal Oak* only underlined the need for the surface fleet to make a serious contribution to the war effort.49

The Norwegian Campaign (Weserübung) April–June 1940

With the army and Luftwaffe making ready for the war in the west – a task in which the navy could play only a minor and indirect role – a series of events involving Scandinavia presented Raeder with a major opportunity (and risk) which could determine both the immediate and long-term future of his fleet.

Originating in the writings of Wolfgang Wegener's post-World War One assessment of Germany's naval strategy, the navy's interest in obtaining bases in Norway increased as British plans to invade that country became more

47Salewski, *Seekriegsleitung*, vol. 1, pp. 227–34. For an example of Hitler's caution against provoking 'incidents' see Gerhard Wagner (ed.), *Lagevorträge des Oberbefehlshabers der Kriegsmarine vor Hitler 1939–1945* (Munich, 1972), pp. 286, 301. Dönitz supported Hitler's position against Raeder's urging of a more aggressive stance towards the us Navy.

48Salewski, *Seekriegsleitung*, vol. 1, pp. 160–4.   49Ibid.

evident during the period November 1939–April 1940.⁵⁰ At the opening of the war, the Nazi–Soviet Non-Aggression Pact of August 1939 made Raeder hope for co-operation in establishing a German naval base on the Russian Arctic coast.⁵¹ Because of that, and because of the navy's limited forces and its emphasis on U-boat warfare, Raeder at first ignored Norway's potential as a base for improving the navy's strategic position outside British blockade lines. A series of conferences with Hitler, beginning in October 1939, alternated between – at one extreme – Raeder's aggressive proposals to occupy Norway, and, at the other, his statement (in February 1940) that the maintenance of Norwegian neutrality might be the best option. His concerns over Norway can be related to his primary goal of ensuring that the navy's share of resources, both short-term and long-term, would not diminish. Having failed in late 1939 to win priority for the naval war against England, or to divert the Führer's attention from the impending land and air offensive in the west, Raeder – though he knew the risks involved – now loyally supported Hitler and the Norwegian planning of the OKW (*Oberkommando der Wehrmacht* – Army High Command). In late November, Hitler acknowledged this loyalty and offensive spirit, praising the navy collectively and Raeder individually, and noting how much the navy had contributed to the war effort despite its small size.⁵² Raeder was thus fully committed, despite his doubts and those of the SKL (*Seekriegsleitung* – Naval High Command) over an operation which (though he had helped to initiate it) he now said 'breaks all the rules of naval war theory'.⁵³ For Raeder, the Weser Exercise (Weserübung) no longer represented merely military issues but called for the navy to follow the 'political realities and necessities with the utmost speed' – a pattern of resistance and acquiescence that Raeder would follow throughout his tenure with Hitler.⁵⁴

The element of surprise resulted in a stunning tactical success: the occupation of Norway in the early summer of 1940. But this was at the cost of very heavy losses for the small German fleet (one heavy cruiser, two light cruisers, ten destroyers and six U-boats). Moreover, the strategic gain proved to be slight after the army's quick defeat of France provided the navy with more suitable bases to support Atlantic operations. But the victory in Norway did ensure the flow of Swedish iron ore; it protected the U-boat training grounds

⁵⁰Wegener was a member of Raeder's Naval Academy 'Crew' (1894) whose theories on 'seapower as a product of fleet and position' condemned the navy's strategy in World War One and called for bases in Scandinavia and the Channel and French Atlantic coasts as the means to challenge Britain for control of maritime communications in the Atlantic. Wegener was a consistent critic of both Tirpitz and Raeder – the latter who sought to deny his ideas and his writings despite their influence on the officer corps (Raeder himself borrowed Wegener's theories freely without giving him any credit). For the Raeder–Wegener feud see Herwig's introduction to Wegener's *The Naval Strategy of the World War*, pp. xv–lv.

⁵¹Salswski, *Seekriegsleitung*, vol. 1, p. 52.

⁵²*Lagevorträge*, p. 93. Cf. Carl-Axel Gemzell, *Organization, Conflict and Innovation: A Study of German Naval Strategic Planning, 1888–1940* (Lund, 1973), pp. 395–414.

⁵³Gemzell, *Organization, Conflict and Innovation*, p. 413.

⁵⁴Ibid., p. 413. Cf. Raeder's briefings with Hitler for 9 and 26 March 1940, *Lagevorträge*, pp. 85–9.

in the Baltic; and, not least from Raeder's point of view, it provided the navy with its first major feat of arms in the war. Against that, it brought the new problem of defending conquered Norway. Henceforward, both the Führer's belief that Norway would be the 'zone of destiny' of the war and the navy's stubborn adherence to its Norwegian position, without regard to any 'sober strategic analysis', diverted valuable resources for the rest of the war.[55]

In the success and sacrifices of the navy during the Norwegian campaign, a number of issues and problems emerged that were to have serious consequences for the conduct of the war and Raeder's command of the navy. Raeder's disagreements with Hitler over the handling of the Norwegian occupation (Raeder wanted to conclude a peace treaty with Norway) became, in the Grand Admiral's words, 'one of my main reasons for resigning'.[56] The still unsolved torpedo problems saved a number of British ships; the lack of co-operation with the Luftwaffe continued to plague naval operations. The torpedo problem would not be fully solved until late 1942. It was, however, the deficiencies in Raeder's organizational structure and its methods of drafting and conveying operational orders which ultimately led to the end of the surface fleet and to Raeder's resignation in January 1943.

The command problems between the naval command in Berlin, the shore command and the commanders at sea were primarily responsible for the disappointing results of Operation Juno (June 1940) in which *Gneisenau* and *Scharnhorst* found themselves unexpectedly in the middle of the British evacuation from Norway. This operation was designed to ease pressure on German forces in Narvik and attack enemy forces and supply ships while protecting German supply convoys. With Hitler following the operation closely, forces under Admiral Marshall quickly sank the British aircraft carrier *Glorious*, but a British torpedo damaged *Scharnhorst* and Marshall decided to retire his forces to Trondheim, thus allowing the British evacuation forces to escape. Raeder had expected Marshall's task force to remain at sea as long as possible to maintain strategic pressure against the British sea lines of communication. Marshall's decision to ignore his orders, based on his own judgement of the situation, was sharply criticized by Raeder and the SKL, and did not bring the results which would support the navy's claims for its capital ships. The sinking of *Glorious*, at first hailed as a victory for the 'capital ships', was now regarded as a stroke of luck in an operation in which Marshall had recklessly exposed his forces to enemy submarines. The contradiction between the offensive spirit and freedom of action promised by Raeder to the

[55]Salewski's analysis of the motivation behind Weserübung includes the military and political (justification of the navy's future existence) deliberations of the naval command and the impact of the German 'victory' on subsequent naval operations. *Seekriegsleitung*, vol. I, pp. 173–212. Walter Hubatsch's Weserübung (Göttingen, 1960) ponders the most detailed description of the Norway invasion.

[56]Raeder, *Mein Leben*, vol. II, p. 220. Cf. Hermann Boehm's *Norwegen zwischen England und Deutschland* (Lippoldsberg, 1956).

fleet commander, and the demand for strict adherence to operational orders, resulted in conflicting interpretations over how to conduct the mission as well as what the objectives were. After a sortie by *Gneisenau* and *Hipper* on 10 June – a sortie that lasted only two days – Marshall was dismissed. His replacement, Vice Admiral Günther Lütjens, was admonished to conduct an 'active, offensive advance' – but another British torpedo attack badly damaged *Gneisenau*, and Raeder finally had to accept that he would have to suspend further surface operations until the repairs to the battleships could be completed. The stakes were high: Hitler's close following of these operations and his fear of losses, coupled with Raeder's concerns that only successes could justify the surface fleet, ensured that. Yet it would not be until the autumn of 1940 that the navy could return to the Atlantic and implement Raeder's strategy for the second phase of the surface war.[57]

The High Point of Surface Operations: October 1940–May 1941

With the fleet no longer tied to German ports or forced to use the exposed Shetland–Bergen narrows to reach the Atlantic, Raeder ordered its full deployment, hoping to produce the 'maximum disorganization of the enemy's supply and convoy systems'.[58] Beginning by sending out the two pocket battleships *Admiral Scheer* and *Admiral Hipper* in October and November 1940, Raeder hoped to provide more substantial proof of the value of the surface fleet and the navy's 'tip and run' strategy. The second sortie of German battleships (Operation Berlin, in early 1941) appeared to demonstrate the validity of this strategy. The battleships *Gneisenau* and *Scharnhorst* stayed at sea for over two months (28 December 1940–22 March 1941) and sank twenty-two merchant ships, including fifteen from one convoy which had been dispersed. As predicted, the British were forced to cover convoys with battleships. Combined with the successes of U-boats and six auxiliary cruisers, the naval command, flushed with victory, believed that it had seized the initiative in the naval war on a global basis.[59] But the mechanical problems of the surface fleet did not improve, and the

[57]Salewski, *Seekriegsleitung*, vol. 1, pp. 160–4. See Bekker, *Hitler's Naval War*, pp. 96–166. See Salewski's analysis of Operation Juno from the perspective of the naval command, *Seekriegsleitung*, vol. 1, pp. 201–11, and the rebuttal of the Fleet Commander, Wilhelm Marshall, 'Zur deutschen Seekriegführung, 1939–40', *Marine Rundschau*, LXIX (1972), pp. 55–79. Cf. Heinrich Schuur's 'Auftragserteilung und Auftragsdurchführung beim Unternehem "Juno" vom 4.bis 10.Juni 1940', *Führungsprobleme der Marine im Zweiten Weltkrieg* (Freiburg, 1973).

[58]See *Lagevorträge*, p. 147.

[59]The navy's claim to its 'global' war was also supported by the voyages of the nine German raiders, the auxiliary cruisers (*Hilfskreuzer*), which sank 7 per cent of the total tonnage sunk by the U-boats and created a diversion far out of proportion to their numbers. See August Karl Muggenthaler's *German Raiders of World War II* (Englewood Cliffs, NJ, 1977).

navy's new base at Brest, which had seemed to promise so much for Atlantic operations, was being heavily bombed by the RAF. As a result, the *Panzerschiffe* were pulled back to Kiel in April 1941. This move marked the first stage of what would become Raeder's 'strategic withdrawal' from the Atlantic bases. No serious command problems developed during the autumn and spring campaigns as commanders were given orders (to which they rigidly adhered) not to take any risks when encountering any heavy forces of the Royal Navy.[60]

With the battleships *Bismarck* and *Tirpitz* and heavy cruiser *Prinz Eugen* nearing completion, Raeder looked forward eagerly to deploying his 'battle-group strategy'. This was supposed to enable the Germans to attack convoys protected by battleships. Raeder's impatience, however, culminated in Rheinübung, the first and last voyage of *Bismarck* in May 1941.[61] *Bismarck*'s availability in spring 1941 was expected to provide the basis for the first test of the battle-group strategy against enemy commerce, but repairs to *Scharnhorst* and *Gneisenau* meant delays that Raeder found unacceptable. In spite of criticism within the navy over the piecemeal approach to surface operations, he believed that a raid by *Bismarck*, the showpiece of German capital-ship technology, could maintain the momentum in the surface war and support the other commerce-raiding forces and U-boats.

Another major factor was Raeder's desire to produce successes for the new battleships as quickly as possible, in order to regain the Führer's favour for the navy's capital ships. Instead, of course, after a long chase, *Bismarck* was sunk. Raeder knew that the Royal Navy was fully aware of the surface threat posed by the new German battleships and was moving vigorously to counter the German strategy. British naval and land-based air forces and radar were also becoming increasingly effective. The dependence of surface operations on tankers (Operation Berlin had required seven tankers to supply the two battleships) and the limited availability of fuel were weaknesses that Raeder knew would also eventually affect the Atlantic War – possibly to the extent of ending any opportunities to demonstrate the worth of the surface navy.[62]

The *Bismarck* operation also revealed that the 'inner contradictions' of German naval orders remained unresolved. Remembering the fate of Admiral

---

[60]Salewski, *Seekriegsleitung*, vol. I, pp. 383–95. Raeder found the technical problems 'shocking' with frequent mechanical breakdowns and cruising ranges well under expectations (for example, *Admiral Hipper*'s effective range was only 4,430 sea miles, not 7,900). See Herwig, *Politics of Frustration*, pp. 216–17. M. J. Whitley's 1985 *German Cruisers of World War II* (Annapolis) covers the design of light and heavy cruisers and their wartime operations (the light cruisers were too lightly built to operate as commerce raiders and the 8-inch-gunned type did not have the endurance necessary for extended independent operations).

[61]The most recent assessment of Exercise Rhine is Baron Burkhard von Müllenheim-Rechberg's *Schlachtschiff Bismarck* (Frankfurt/Main and Vienna, 1980). A revised and expanded version was published in 1987. The author was the senior surviving officer of the *Bismarck*.

[62]See Salewski, *Seekriegsleitung*, vol. I, pp. 387–95 and 'Zweite Phase der Seekriegführung bis zum Frijahr 1941' by Bernd Stegemann in *Das Deutsche Reich und Zweite Weltkrieg*, vol. II, pp. 351–9.

Marshall, the Fleet Commander, Admiral Lütjens, rigidly followed his orders to avoid any unnecessary risks in confrontations with British naval units. As a result, he failed to exploit his victory over the *Hood* and finish off the *Prince of Wales*. His half-hearted leadership and his pessimism over each setback hindered his ability to analyse objectively his options or opportunities. Having been detected and shadowed by the Royal Navy at the start of the operation, the element of surprise was lost. But Lütjens was overly influenced by what he regarded as superior British radar, and, failing to realize that he had actually eluded his pursuers, he revealed his position by radioing for instructions from Berlin. Forced to continue, Lütjens resigned himself to carrying out Raeder's final orders to fight to the last shell.[63]

The End of Raeder's Atlantic Strategy and Retreat to the North: June 1941–December 1942

Exercise Rhine was the culmination of Raeder's command of the naval war. Although it appears that he was prepared to take the risk, Raeder and the SKL did not consider that the loss of *Bismarck* would be either 'unexpected' or a 'fatal blow'. Indeed, if that occurred, it would be thoroughly consistent with his desire to engage the enemy offensively and boldly until all the capital ships were sunk or no longer operational.[64] When *Bismarck* actually was sunk, however, Hitler saw it not as an heroic end but as the severe practical loss it really was. No longer prepared to support any further losses of prestige, morale and capital equipment, the Führer placed restrictions on all surface operations. This not only signalled the end of Raeder's Atlantic strategy but led directly to the Grand Admiral's resignation in January 1943. Raeder hoped that major naval victories would have assisted him in his attempts to divert Hitler from his decision to invade the Soviet Union in the spring of 1941. Instead, Hitler's control over deployment of the capital ships from May 1941 to February 1942 reflected Raeder's (and the navy's) waning influence. Raeder's efforts to continue the surface war in the Atlantic after *Bismarck* were also doomed by two other factors. First was the systematic elimination of the German supply system, a process made possible by a major breakthrough which enabled the British to read Germany's coded naval signals as rapidly as the Germans themselves. Second was the RAF's hammering of German ports, which put the fleet out of action until February 1942.[65] All in all, the forty-seven Allied ships sunk by the German surface fleet represented a small contribution to the commerce war when compared to the achievements of the

[63]See Salewski, *Seekriegsleitung*, vol. 1, pp. 387–95.
[64]Ibid., and Müllenheim-Rechberg, *Schlachtschiff Bismarck*, pp. 149–63.
[65]For the role of Special Intelligence in the sinking of the *Bismarck* and the destruction of the navy's supply system, see F. H. Hinsley, *British Intelligence in the Second World War: Its Influence, Strategy and Operations* (New York, 1979).

auxiliary cruisers, U-boats and Luftwaffe. Raeder was painfully aware, but could not openly admit, that his fleet's victories were a dismally low return on the expense and attention paid to the capital ships.[66] Moreover, the construction and repairs of the capital ships (as well as their fuel) diverted valuable resources and labour from the U-boat war – a situation that renewed the conflict between Raeder and the commander of the U-boats, Karl Dönitz [*q.v.*], over which arm of the navy should receive priority.[67]

As Raeder and the SKL struggled with these problems, Hitler resolved the naval command's indecision by ordering the fleet either to sail from Brest to Norway via a risky and bold 'Channel dash' or to disarm the surface ships and send the guns and crews overland to Norway, to be used as protection against the long-feared British attack. For Raeder, a choice like that was no choice. Quickly, he and the SKL began to envision new 'strategic and operational' opportunities for the surface fleet in northern waters.[68] Cerberus, the 'operation cover' for the Channel dash of February 1942, was a tremendous tactical success but a strategic failure.[69] The British could now concentrate on Germany's naval forces in the north, thus increasing the risks to German surface units attacking the Allied convoys to Murmansk. The difficulties of surface combat in the northern waters soon became apparent, and, along with the growing fuel and oil crisis, the question of the role to be played by the capital ships became critical. By 1942, the planning of all naval operations was dictated by the availability of fuel.[70] Surface operations against the Murmansk convoys PQ17 and OP15 (Operation Rösselsprung) were ineffectual, compared to the successes of the U-boats and the Luftwaffe against these convoys. The success of the Japanese at Pearl Harbor and the sinking by Japanese air power of the *Renown* and *Prince of Wales* in December 1941 had convinced Hitler that battleships were obsolete and useful only as batteries to defend Norway against invasion. In August 1942, Raeder's last attempt to deploy any warships in the Atlantic was denied by the Führer, who continued to be obsessed with the strategic importance of Norway. With the army facing a major disaster at Stalingrad and the Allies landing in North Africa in November 1942 instead of Norway, Raeder sought once again for permission from Hitler to attack. This set the stage for his final confrontation with the Führer.[71]

[66]Stegemann, 'Zweite Phase der Seekriegführung Frühjahr 1941', vol. II, pp. 351–9.

[67]*Lagevorträge*, pp. 322–5.

[68]See Salewski, *Seekriegsleitung*, vol. II, pp. –52, for his summary of the navy's plans to accommodate Hitler and develop a 'new' strategy for the surface fleet.

[69]Gerhard Bidlingmaier, 'Vor 20 Jahren: Unternehmen "Cerberus"', *Marine Rundschau*, LIX (1962), pp. 19–40, and J. D. Potter, *Fiasco: The Break-Out of the German Battleships* (London, 1970).

[70]See Hans-Jürgen Zetzsche, 'Logistik und Operationen. Die Olversorgung der Kriegsmarine und die Rolle des Dr. Freidrich Fetzer 1935 bis 1943', *Marine Forum* (1987), pp. 430–4.

[71]Salewski, 'Das Ende der deutschen Schlachtschiffe im Zweiten Weltkrieg', *Miltärgeschichtliche Mitteilungen*, VI (1972), p. 53.

Raeder's Search for Alternatives: May 1940–December 1942

In the spring of 1940, Raeder and his staff began the process of digesting the gains brought about by the successful occupation of Norway and the fall of France. The navy now had the French Atlantic and Channel ports and the possibility of a settlement with France which might involve concessions of colonies in Africa and the Middle East – even, perhaps, use of the French fleet.

In the euphoria of victory, Raeder and his close advisers did not concern themselves with Hitler's avowed statements about seeking an understanding with England. Instead, they had already focused on the United States as the navy's ultimate rival for maritime supremacy. Raeder's naval planners even contemplated a future German–Japanese conflict in the Far East for the final battle to decide which of those two Axis partners would be 'an oceanic naval power of the first magnitude'.[72] Envisaging the European continent in German hands, a German colonial empire in Central Africa and German control of the North Sea, Mediterranean, Black Sea and Baltic Sea, Raeder's staff called for a fleet of 60–80 battleships, 15–20 aircraft carriers, 100 cruisers and 500 U-boats supported by a commerce raiding fleet of 115 cruisers.[73] These plans have been too quickly dismissed by some scholars and former naval officers as 'fantasies'; they actually reflected the ultimate aim of German naval policy since Tirpitz, which Raeder continued. The building programme revealed the continuing influence of the American Admiral Alfred T. Mahan (whose theories had informed much of naval thought at the end of the nineteenth century), and undervalued the role that aircraft carriers, submarines and naval air power would play in World War Two and in future navies.[74]

During the interlude between the defeat of France and the June 1941 invasion of the Soviet Union, Hitler proved willing to discuss the navy's proposals, especially the seizure of the Atlantic islands, including Iceland, the Azores, the Cape Verde Islands and the Canaries. Growing American support for Britain and the fall-off in the U-boat tonnage war led Raeder to the conclusion in the autumn of 1940 that an alternative strategy to the Atlantic War was needed. The result was his so-called 'Mediterranean strategy', which

---

[72]Herwig, *Politics of Frustration*, p. 208.   [73]See Schreiber, 'Zur Kontinuität', pp. 101, 171.

[74]See Salewski's analysis of these plans in his chapter 'The Alternative to Reality: Dreams and Utopias', *Seekriegsleitung*, vol. I, pp. 234 ff. Schreiber treats the navy's plans to create a 'world fleet' more seriously. The 'first stage' would include twenty-five battleships, eight aircraft carriers and 400 U-boats. By August 1941, with the anticipation of future conflict with the United States and Japan, the navy envisioned a fleet of 60–80 battleships, 15–20 aircraft carriers, 225 cruisers and 500 U-boats and approximately 1,250 other support ships. See 'Zur Kontinuität', pp. 127–8, 147–8. Cf. *Seekriegsleitung* for the other wartime exercises in naval planning and construction, particularly the 'crowning document' of the continuity thesis in German naval history, Admiral Saalwächter's 1944 report on the navy's needs for bases to continue its global war. See Salewski's *Seekriegsleitung*. Herwig, *Politics of Frustration*, p. 208, argues that such plans 'revealed the fateful addiction of Hitler's admirals to the concepts of Mahan and Tirpitz'.

he continually advocated from then until the spring of 1941. This he saw as the best means of attacking England indirectly (and blunting the effects of the American aid), and as an alternative to Hitler's invasion of the Soviet Union.[75]

It is against the background of Raeder's struggle to find alternatives in the face of America's 'undeclared naval warfare' against Germany that German invasion plans of England (Operation Seelöwe – Sea Lion) must be judged. Although Raeder never fully endorsed Sea Lion, he had been the first to raise the idea in May 1940 with Hitler, having directed his staff to begin a study of its feasibility as early as November 1939. Hitler at first showed little interest, his horizons being already focused on the east and a possible rapprochement with England. It was not until he finally issued a definitive directive on 16 July 1940 for preparations for a landing to be completed by the middle of August that Raeder began to point out the difficulties inherent in the cross-Channel invasion – particularly the transport problems. While the army began to show some enthusiasm in July 1940, the two services differed over whether the invasion should be on a broad front – the army's preference – or a narrow one, as the navy wished. Both services awaited the outcome of the Battle of Britain, and the air superiority that both considered a precondition for any invasion. By September, Hitler made the decision to postpone the operation indefinitely. A thankful Raeder agreed with his Führer, but urged that the invasion preparations and the air attacks against England should be continued as a means of keeping pressure on the British. In the final analysis, Sea Lion was a bluff, a propaganda ploy and a diversion for other military operations. Raeder's first preference, as always, was to concentrate the navy's resources on the surface and U-boat war against England. Nevertheless, he had loyally (though without conviction) diverted resources to the preparations for Sea Lion in the event that his Führer had ordered the invasion. During this same period he had also rebuffed Hitler's proposal to invade southern Ireland and Iceland as viable alternatives in the attempt to force England to the bargaining table.[76]

On 6 September 1940, with Sea Lion behind him, Raeder presented his Mediterranean strategy to Hitler and Germany's military leaders. The origins

[75]Herwig, *Politics of Frustration*, pp. 211–14.

[76]The most recent analysis and summary of Operation Sea Lion is Hans Umbreit's 'Direkte Strategie gegen England', *Das Deutsche Reich und der Zweite Weltkrieg*, II, pp. 368–74, which concludes that in spite of momentary interest in actually carrying out the invasion the major purpose of Sea Lion was a means of 'psychological warfare'. Salewski, *Seekriegsleitung*, vol. I, pp. 270–5, points out the navy's 'scepticism' in spite of the extensive preparations. Raeder's use of Sea Lion with Hitler is closely related to the navy's assessment of its position vis-à-vis the army and Luftwaffe and the overall German command structure and allocation of resources. Raeder's 'manoeuvring' in this matter should be more closely studied in regard to his advocacy of a Mediterranean strategy. For more details on Sea Lion itself see Karl Klee, *Das Unternehmen Seelöwe* (Göttingen, 1959) and Walter Ansel's *Hitler Confronts England* (Durham, 1960). Andreas Hillgruber's *Hitlers Strategie* (Frankfurt/Main, 1965) places invasion planning within the context of the Führer's military and political *Programm* and argues that an invasion was seriously considered in the period July–September 1940. Hitler awaited not only the results of the air war against England (German air superiority was the major prerequisite for an invasion) but to see whether England could be made to sue for peace without Sea Lion.

of this plan lay in Raeder's assessment that the 'short war' against England had been lost and that with American support the naval conflict would be a long struggle. Against that, in Raeder's grand strategy, the possibilities presented by co-operation with Vichy France, Spain and Italy could result in Germany's control of Gibraltar, the Suez Canal, the Atlantic islands and the French holdings in north-west Africa, thereby turning the Mediterranean into an 'Axis sea'. Raeder argued that such a strategy was essential before America formally entered the war – a development that he regarded as inevitable. Its success would at the least prevent any British intervention in the Balkans and ensure Germany's access to raw materials and supplies. With control of the French colonies and the Atlantic islands of Portugal and Spain, the navy would also be able to expand its opportunities in the Atlantic War from safer bases than those in the French ports, which were constantly being attacked by the RAF. Furthermore, America might be discouraged in the short term and England forced to sue for peace.

These were heady possibilities. However, between July and December 1940, Raeder's ultimate goal in all his dealings with the Führer was to restart the Z-Plan and begin the preparations to construct the surface fleet necessary to fight a global war. Raeder deliberately kept alive Hitler's interest in the Atlantic islands by assuring his Führer that the navy could successfully support German plans to occupy the Canaries, Azores and possibly the Cape Verde Islands. He also encouraged Hitler's idea of utilizing the Azores as a base for long-range bombing of America – the operation, he acknowledged, was risky, but 'can succeed with luck'.[77] As the surface fleet began to return to the Atlantic campaign in the autumn of 1940 and with *Bismarck* ready in the spring of 1941, Raeder hoped for successes against the British that would support his ambitions. Best of all for his present and future goals, his Mediterranean strategy would not involve any significant commitment of the navy's limited resources and would not affect the Atlantic campaign. The primary forces necessary would be from the army, Luftwaffe and the Italian armed forces. Raeder's ideas, however, were predicated on successful diplomatic negotiations in October and November 1940 with Spain, France, Russia and Italy – none of which produced satisfactory results. These failures only hardened Hitler's resolve to solve the 'Russian question'.[78]

Raeder's efforts to realize his strategy as an alternative to the invasion of the Soviet Union also reflected his personal views that co-operation with the Soviet Union was more desirable than conflict. The Nazi pact with Communist Russia (23 August 1939) had brought both strategic and logistic advantages to Raeder which he was quick to utilize. The German use of the northern sea route in 1940 and 1941 and the loss of the French fleet in June 1940 meant that the Royal Navy had to patrol sea lanes in both the Atlantic and the Pacific, as well as to protect its own home shores against a possible German

77Herwig, *Politics of Frustration*, p. 214.   78Ibid.

invasion. Without Russia's substantial fuel and material support, Germany could not have carried on the naval campaign against England in 1939–41.[79] War between Germany and the Soviet Union therefore would bring no advantage to the navy's priorities; it would serve only to increase the threat in the Baltic to the U-boat training grounds. As with the German attack in the west in May 1940, the navy could foresee no real role for itself in a German victory over the Soviets. Hitler mollified Raeder by assuring him that the war in the east was 'preventive', to preclude a Soviet threat to German-occupied Norway. The Führer also argued that a quick victory in the east would be a blow against Britain, and would free Japan to occupy the attention of the United States in the Far East. More importantly, Hitler assured Raeder that the 'primary front' would continue to be against Britain, and that once Russia was beaten the 'blockading' of Britain would resume in full force. It followed that the navy would receive increased priority for its Z-Plan.[80]

In the event, what actually happened was that – encouraged by the army's initial victories in the Soviet Union in July 1941 – the Führer shifted Germany's armaments production to the navy's U-boats and the Luftwaffe.[81] In spite of his claims to the contrary, Raeder did not fundamentally disagree with Hitler over the need to expand in the east as a stepping stone to the *Weltmacht* both he and Hitler envisioned, but he would have preferred to delay such a move until the 'democratic' powers had been defeated.[82]

Raeder's preoccupation with pushing his Mediterranean strategy and the surface war did not sit well with Dönitz, the U-boats' commander. Dönitz had opposed Raeder's Mediterranean concept on the grounds that it diverted resources from the main theatre of operations – the Atlantic commerce bound for Britain. Dönitz had also continued to press for more resources devoted to U-boat construction and opposed the diversion of U-boats for other duties, such as weather reporting, the support of surface operations and defensive protection against possible invasions – the latter in part making up for the lack of naval air support.[83] He had repeatedly asked for twenty-nine new

---

[79]See Tobias Philbin's 'Soviet–German Naval Relations 1939–1941: Totalitarian Powers in Control and Conflict', unpublished Master's thesis, Defense Intelligence College, 1985.

[80]Cf. *Lagevorträge*, p. 154. Salewski, according to Schreiber (*Das Deutsche Reich und der Zweite Weltkrieg*, vol. III, p. 211), overstates Raeder's opposition to Barbarossa. In November 1940, Raeder only recommended a 'postponement' until the 'victory over England'. Philbin, 'Soviet–German Naval Relations', suggests that Soviet–German naval co-operation and actual deliveries of Soviet oil to the navy may also have contributed to Raeder's 'opposition' to an attack on the Soviet Union at this time.

[81]Walter Hubatsch, (ed.), *Hitlers Weisungen für die Kriegsführung, 1939–1945* (Frankfurt, 1962), pp. 136 ff.

[82]Schreiber's 'Der Mittelmeeraum in Hitlers Strategie 1940', *Militärgeschichtliche Mitteilungen*, XXVIII (2, 1980), pp. 69–99, demolishes the myth of Raeder's Mediterranean strategy and argues that the Mediterranean was simply a 'sideshow'. Schreiber's contributions to *Der Mittelmeeraum und Sudosteuropa*, vol. III of *Das Deutsche Reich und der Zweite Weltkrieg* (Stuttgart, 1984), represent the best summary to date.

[83]*Lagevorträge*, pp. 145–6.

submarines per month, but in 1941 had received only an average of fifteen per month.[84] Even with the limited numbers of U-boats at sea, Raeder and Dönitz had never resolved the issue of whether the U-boat war was a 'tonnage war' (Dönitz's strategy of sinking as many ships as possible wherever they could be found with little risk) or a commerce war, in which the U-boats were directed to those targets that had the greatest potential for a 'decisive impact' (that is, interrupting supplies to the Mediterranean or to the Soviet Union). Raeder never definitely dealt with this issue because, after the *Bismarck* episode, the U-boat was the sole offensive weapon the navy possessed and which Hitler allowed it to use more or less freely. (This was especially the case after America entered the war.) Dönitz himself did not share the 'old navy's' concern for its future post-war building plans; nor did he support Raeder's machinations with Hitler, except for what they did to increase U-boat production. These conflicting views of the navy's nature and function created a situation which neither admiral ever forgot or forgave.[85]

Raeder's other major battle with Hitler (fought concurrently with his attempts to promote the Mediterranean concept) was over the navy's insistence on declaring war against the United States. With the creation of the US Navy's Support Force, Atlantic, for convoy duty in March 1941 and the American declaration of war zones in the Atlantic, Raeder argued with Hitler that it was necessary to exploit American weaknesses before Germany's naval forces were depleted and America expanded its fleet into a two-ocean navy.[86] Hitler, however, continually ordered his navy to 'avoid *every* incident' with America until the situation in the east was clarified.[87] The Allied occupation of Iceland in July 1941 drove Raeder to demand from Hitler the right to attack American ships and he ordered his staff to prepare plans for war with the United States. For Raeder, a declaration of war seemed essential if the Battle for the Atlantic was not to be lost. Not only did he fundamentally disagree with his Führer over this issue, but he also actively encouraged an accommodation with Vichy France that would bring French naval support to bear on the Atlantic War before America could mobilize its vast resources – an action that was directly against Hitler's hopes of an Anglo-German alliance against the US at the expense of the French.[88] Recalling the arguments used in World War One, the navy urged meeting force with force and, in spite of Hitler's attempts to have Japan join in the war against the Soviets, even resorted to urging their Japanese counterparts to provoke war with the United States at sea.[89]

[84]For details of the navy's U-boat construction programmes, see Eberhard Rössler's *The U-boat* (London and Melbourne, 1981), pp. 124–5.

[85]For naval command and U-boat command issues, see Salewski, *Seekriegsleitung*, vol. I, pp. 265, 405, 436–9; vol. II, p. 295; vol. III, p. 373, and Peter Padfield, *Dönitz: The Last Führer* (London and New York, 1984), p. 241.

[86]Salewski, *Seekriegsleitung*, vol. I, p. 489, and Herwig, *Politics of Frustration*, pp. 221–2.

[87]Herwig, *Politics of Frustration*, p. 224. Cf. *Lagevorträge* p. 296.

[88]See Herwig, *Politics of Frustration*, pp. 228–30.   [89]Ibid., p. 233.

From May 1940, when France fell, to December 1941, Raeder's actions reflect his willingess to involve himself and the navy in policies and initiatives which were against the Führer's expressed wishes and orders. The discrepancy between (on the one hand) his efforts to involve Germany in a war with America and (on the other) the resources he actually commanded reflects Raeder's goal to keep the naval war – and therefore the role of the navy – in the forefront, regardless of the fact that Germany's future was being decided in the east. While Dönitz requested twelve large U-boats to attack shipping off the American coast in December 1941, Raeder would commit only six to the German 'drum beat' against America (Operation *Paukenschlag*).[90] Raeder's *Ressorteifer* (the defence and expansion of his sphere of influence), like Tirpitz's, led him to place personal interest (which he saw as synonymous with the navy's interest) and the long-term goal of German sea power ahead of Hitler's short-term diplomatic and military requirements. The lack of co-operation and planning with the army in their campaigns – first against Poland, then the western offensive and finally Barbarossa, the invasion of Russia – was carried over into the Luftwaffe–navy rivalry and co-operation with Italian naval allies. Moreover, Raeder proved that he and his staff were thoroughly imbued with negative and crude racial attitudes concerning both American and Italian national character.[91] The navy's distrust of the Japanese, no doubt inherited from the 'yellow peril' era of Kaiser Wilhelm II, also affected those two allies' discussions of dividing the world at a line running north to south at 70° longitude; Raeder's staff opposed such a division as an 'unacceptable expansion of the yellow sphere of influence'. German admirals had always thought big – as General Halder remarked wryly, 'These people dream in continents.'[92]

Raeder's Final Battle

Late in 1942, while the Führer was preoccupied with the siege of Stalingrad, Raeder and the SKL knew they must make more use of the surface fleet. Otherwise, continuing inactivity would damage morale, and lack of success would imperil future construction programmes of capital ships. They saw an opportunity in the shape of resumed surface attacks on the Murmansk convoys. Hitler agreed to these attacks being restarted, and on New Year's Eve 1942 he closely followed what appeared to be the making of a major German

---

[90]Ibid., p. 240. Cf. Dönitz's version, *Zehn Jahre*, pp. 193–203.

[91]See Salewski, *Seekriegsleitung*, vol. I, pp. 486–7. See Schreiber's *Revisionismus und Weltmachtstreben* for the navy's relationship with its Italian ally.

[92]Herwig, *Politics of Frustration*, p. 239. Raeder and the naval command continued their attempts in 1942 to argue the case for a global war in concert with Germany's allies, Japan and Italy. The navy's strategic planning (which Salewski refers to as the *Grosse Plan*) failed just as Raeder's attempts to influence an 'alternative strategy' in 1940–1 had, and would not have been, according to Salewski, 'war-decisive' but 'in the best case' would only have dragged out the war and ended in defeat. See *Seekreigsleitung*, vol. II, pp. 72–107.

victory (Operation Regenbogen – Rainbow).93 It seemed strange that the navy could not, or would not, provide him with progress reports, and it was only from a British broadcast that he learned that the German surface ships had failed to achieve any success. Not surprisingly, he was furious, and summoned Raeder to his headquarters. Naturally enough, Hitler felt that information was being deliberately withheld from him and that the entire action demonstrated the uselessness of the fleet; that the capital ships were nothing but a breeding ground for revolution, idly lying about and lacking any desire to get into action. It was, he said, his 'irrevocable decision' to pay off the fleet and put the personnel, weapons and armour-plating to better use. Admiral Theodor Krancke (Raeder's representative at the Führer's headquarters) and Hitler's naval adjutant, Captain Karl Jesko von Puttkamer, managed to delay Raeder's meeting with the Führer until 4 January 1943, hoping that Hitler by then would have cooled down, and allow the navy time to reconstruct what had happened.94

Raeder came to the meeting armed with carefully prepared reports, but he never had a chance to discuss them. Instead, Hitler delivered an hour and a half's tirade, giving his own interpretation of German naval history. In his view, the 'real reason' for lack of any notable contribution by the High Seas Fleet during World War One was that the navy 'lacked men of action who were determined to fight with or without the support of the Kaiser'. Unlike the army, Hitler charged that the navy 'has always been careful to consider the number of their own ships and men as compared with the enemy before entering an engagement. The army does not follow this principle. As a soldier,' Raeder's official report on this meeting added, 'the Führer demands that, once forces have been committed to action, the battle be fought to a decision.'95 Having insulted the fighting spirit of the battlefleets in both world wars and citing what he regarded as the ignominious end of the High Seas Fleet in revolution and scuttling at Scapa Flow, Hitler then outlined for Raeder the questions he wanted answered regarding the demobilization of the capital ships.96

Once Hitler had finished, Raeder requested a further immediate meeting in private (*unter vier Augen*) with him. This was granted, and Raeder at once tendered his resignation. He had come to this point several times before with Hitler, but this time Raeder's sense of honour, of duty to the fleet and of sheer weariness prevailed. Stepping down was the only alternative left to protect the

93Dudley Pope's *73 North* (London, 1958), provides an excellent overview of the background, battle and aftermath of Regenbogen for both the British and the Germans. Cf. Salewski's description of the operation, *Seekreigsleitung*, vol. ii, pp. 199–201.

94Pope, *73 North*, p. 272.

95'Besprechung des Ob. d. M. beim Führer am 6. 1. 1943 abends in Wolfsschanze', *Lagevorträge*, p. 453.

96Ibid., p. 454. See Raeder's description of these events in his memoirs, *Mein Leben*, vol. ii, pp. 286–90. Cf. Salewski, *Seekriegsleitung*, vol. ii, pp. 202–24.

navy; yet both Grand Admiral and Führer realized that for Raeder to resign in the middle of a war without a publicly acceptable reason could not be countenanced. Raeder skilfully provided a grateful Hitler with a face-saving explanation for his departure – he would become inspector-general, an honorific post that would keep him associated with the navy. Further, he would use 30 January, the anniversary of his tenth year of service under the Führer, as the date of transition to his successor. This would serve to demonstrate the navy's and Raeder's association with the National Socialist 'movement'. Hitler agreed with Raeder's proposal and asked, accepting his resignation, for two recommendations for his replacement.[97]

Raeder's account of this meeting carefully observed that 'it should not be considered a degradation [of the navy] if the Führer decides to scrap the large ships'.[98] This was such a radical shift that it must have been a pre-emptive move, attempting to defuse what could have been disastrous loss of morale in the surface fleet. For as Raeder now had to accept, Hitler saw the U-boats as the most important branch of the navy both in the previous war and in the present one. Along with the U-boat, he believed, the role of aircraft and lighter surface ships had made capital ships obsolete – similar to the role of the cavalry in the army.[99]

Using as a vehicle the memorandum which Hitler had requested at their 6 January meeting, Raeder's last act as Commander-in-Chief of the Kriegsmarine was to prepare the defence for the surface fleet. This document, drafted by Raeder's senior officers and carefully edited by him, was written as much for posterity as it was for the Führer; it amounted to a justification of Raeder's leadership and the history of the German navy in general. Its final version, with a brief covering letter written by Raeder to Hitler, contained the Admiral's last testament to his concept of German naval strategy as he had envisioned it before 1939, and as it had evolved during the war. Raeder argued correctly that the navy had succeeded in threatening British sea communications and thereby had forced the enemy to deploy resources for the protection of the North Atlantic sea route. He also (and equally correctly) argued that the entrance of Italy and Japan into the war had stretched enemy naval resources to the limit. It followed that the dismantling of the German battlefleet would constitute a 'bloodless victory' for the enemy, who would be able to concentrate forces either on the Mediterranean or against the Japanese navy. Germany's own coastline would be undefended; the U-boat war would be endangered. The report tactfully pointed out the Luftwaffe's manifold deficiencies in supporting naval operations, as well as the improbability that it could protect coastal shipping. In response to Hitler's questions as to the 'advantages' of scrapping the big ships, the report quantified what Raeder

---

[97]'Besprechung des Ob. d. M. beim Führer am 6. 1. 1943 abends in Wolfsschanze', *Lagevorträge*, p. 454–5.
[98]*Lagevorträge*, p. 453.   [99]Ibid.

considered to be a 'small gain in personnel and material which ... cannot outweigh the grave political and naval consequences that would result'.[100]

Cogent though the memorandum was, Raeder learned later that Hitler was totally unmoved by it. Worse, the navy's aircraft-carrier programme was cancelled as well. Although Raeder and the SKL had been briefed by Krancke as to the Führer's initial comments, Hitler gave his official decision not to Raeder but to Admiral Dönitz at their first command conference on 25 January 1943. All ships larger than destroyers were to be paid off. All construction projects were to cease; so were all repairs, except for those ships to be retained for training purposes; and all resources thus made available were to be diverted to the U-boat war.[101]

It was a staggering command: Germany's surface fleet – still proud of its traditions and believing in its own future – was being ordered to dismantle itself virtually entirely. Coming from the Führer himself, there could be no worse indictment, and 'in view of the political and psychological effect' the naval command tried to restrict the dissemination of these orders to the smallest possible number of officers.[102]

On 30 January 1943, Raeder gave his final address to the officers of the naval command. The Grand Admiral summed up his career as Commander-in-Chief thus:

> the entire time in Berlin has been a period of very difficult, continuous battles; only the battle front changed over the course of time. In the beginning there was a struggle against the ministries such as Groener and von Schleicher, struggles in the beginning against the army ... then against the Luftwaffe.[103]

Raeder also castigated Reichsminister of Armaments Fritz Todt and his successor, Albert Speer, who (although they had promised to help the navy) 'never failed' to create more difficulty. The most glaring omission from Raeder's list of foes was Adolf Hitler, but every officer in the room was aware of the Führer's sharp criticism of the navy's 'big ships'. Raeder's actions and words, however, left no doubt that he regarded 'absolute loyalty to the authority in the state' as the surest means of guaranteeing both the navy's independence and its interests.[104]

In the final analysis, the consequences of Operation Rainbow were not simply the 'fall' of Raeder and the end of the surface fleet. Raeder recognized that he was not prepared in health nor inclination to participate in the

---

[100]Raeder to Hitler, Berlin, 14 January 1943, and 'Die Bedeutung der deutschen Überwasserstreit-kräfte für die Kriegführung der Dreiermächte', *Lagevorträge*, pp. 456–64.

[101]*Lagevorträge*, pp. 465–70. Cf. Pope, *73 North*, pp. 300–1.   [102]Pope, *73 North*, p. 303.

[103]'Ansprache des Grossadmiral Raeder zur Niederlegung des Oberkommandos am Januar 1943', III, M 1005/7, Bundesarchiv-Militärarchiv.

[104]Ibid.

integration of the navy into the 'total war' of the Third Reich. He sensed that his loyal departure would help, not hinder, the fleet's relationship with Hitler, and clear the way for the next generation to carry the torch for German sea power. The Führer's focus on the 'big ships' had closely reflected the 'battleship psychosis' under which the older officers suffered and, in spite of the Führer's disappointment over the wartime deployment of the fleet, Raeder could assume that it might last only for the duration of the war. After that Hitler would again want his symbols of prestige, the battleships, to carry the flag to his *Weltreich*.[105]

January 1943 also represented a major turning point unrecognized by either Raeder or his successor. Their twin preoccupations – Raeder's with his ships and Dönitz's with his U-boats – resulted in the navy's failure to keep pace with the changing and technologically complex world of naval warfare. This was one of Hitler's criticisms in the aftermath of Operation Regenbogen. Particularly in the areas of code breaking and radar development, especially after 1943, the Germans were hopelessly mismatched in the naval environment, regardless of exhortations for more aggressive 'charge and attack' tactics (*Ran an der Feind*) and references to 'spirit' and 'will' in continuing the struggle.[106] Historians and apologists have, like Raeder, generally directed attention to what the navy's strategy *could* have been, if it were not for Hitler – his 'premature war', his restrictions on naval operations, his rejection of Raeder's strategic alternatives for the conduct of the war (for example, the Mediterranean versus the Soviet Union). The blame for Germany's naval failure in World War Two – like the responsibility for World War Two as a whole – can thus be conveniently placed on Hitler alone. But that is too simple; it would be much closer to the truth to say that under Raeder's leadership in peace and war, when he was the navy and the navy was him, his emphasis on the long-term goal of fleet building led to technological backwardness. It was this, more than Hitler, that led on to the naval failures.

Although Raeder gave two possible choices to Hitler as his successor, Admirals Carls and Dönitz, there could be no surprise about Hitler's decision. Carls, senior to Dönitz and commander of Group North, represented Raeder and the 'old navy', while Dönitz represented the 'new navy' that Hitler envisoned with its emphasis on the U-boat war. Hitler did not expect that Dönitz would disagree with him as to the fate of the capital ships. Moreover, Dönitz's successes with the U-boats and the enemy's reaction to this threat

---

[105]For the impact of the 'battleship psychosis' see Salewski's 'Das Ende der deutschen Schlachtschiffe in Zweiten Weltkrieg', pp. 53–73. Cf. Admiral Gerhard Wagener's rebuttal of Salewski in 'Überlegungen der deutschen Marineführung zum Einsatz und Verlust der Schlachtschiffe während des Zweiten Weltkrieges', *Militärgeschichtliche Mitteilungen*, xv (1, 1974), pp. 99–108.

[106]See F. Ruge's description of Dönitz, *In vier Marinen* (Munich, 1979), p. 260. Ruge concludes that Dönitz was 'clearly under [Hitler's] influence' (p. 268). Cf. Schreiber, *Revisionismus und Weltmachtstreben*, p. 377, and Salewski, *Seekriegsleitung*, vol. II, pp. 309, 487, 531, 551–4.

were in sharp contrast to the record of the surface navy. Dönitz's personality was also an advantage; his enthusiasm and optimism were better suited for a Führer who was increasingly confronted by defeat after defeat. Dönitz also had friends 'at court', such as Albert Speer, who had constantly clashed with Raeder over attempts to rationalize the armaments industries. Although Raeder personally found Dönitz's 'conceit and pushiness insufferable', nevertheless he counted on Dönitz to maintain the navy's cohesiveness and its independence against the army and Luftwaffe.[107]

In spite of Raeder's post-war criticism of his former U-boat commander, Dönitz did not, in fact, disappoint him at the time. Under Dönitz, the navy survived the war intact and loyal, and the fighting tradition of the U-boats, torpedo boats and destroyers created the foundation for a future German navy. Although he appeared to repudiate Raeder in his first directive as Commander-in-Chief ('considerations of how the navy should appear after the war have no value'), Dönitz's fanatical devotion to the U-boat war won respect and resources for him and the navy from the Führer.[108] Dönitz's plan in 1943 for building 2,400 U-boats in five years remained in the best (or worst) traditions of the Tirpitz Plan and Raeder's 'utopian' building programmes of 1939 and 1940; the sole essential difference was that U-boats would replace the battleship as the core of the fleet. Like Raeder, Dönitz continued to compete with other defence priorities for the scarce labour and materials available to the crumbling Third Reich, even at the expense of the total war effort.[109]

Dönitz's credibility with Hitler was such that he managed to persuade the Führer to permit further use of the surface ships. If nothing else, this partial reversal of Hitler's earlier complete opposition ensured that the fleet would die gloriously, as did *Scharnhorst* in December 1943, in the last foray by a German capital ship against the enemy. In this sense, Dönitz carried out the wishes of Raeder and the officers who had served in the old Imperial Navy.

The sinking of *Tirpitz* in November 1944 by British bombers marked the effective end of both the German fleet and the remnants of Raeder's strategy. Only three German capital ships survived the war – *Prinz Eugen*, *Lützow* and *Nürnberg*. Even without the British successes in code breaking which shortened the war against Dönitz's U-boats, the sheer weight of Allied technical and material superiority would have overwhelmed the German U-boat fleet. From May 1943, the navy was loyally fighting a holding action, believing that its sacrifices were tying down enemy forces and, in accordance with Raeder's wishes, 'dying gallantly' to prepare the foundation for yet another rebirth. This was no more than he had predicted in September 1939; and yet, given his own absolute belief in the Tirpitz tradition, his consequent

---

[107]See Padfield's description of Raeder–Dönitz relations in *Dönitz*, pp. 261–4. Raeder, *Mein Leben*, vol. II, p. 291. One officer wrote enthusiastically after Dönitz 'saved the battleships' in his 26 February 1943 meeting with Hitler that 'Perhaps 31 December 1942 was not the last chapter in the history of German navalism [*Flottengedanken*] after all.' Salewski, *Seekriegsleitung*, vol. II, p. 237.

[108]See Salewski, *Seekriegsleitung*, vol. II, pp. 226–40.   [109]See Padfield, *Dönitz*, pp. 302–3.

shaping of the navy in peace and his use of it in war, it is hard to imagine what other fate could realistically have been in store, whether the war had come early or late.

Inspector-General of the Kriegsmarine, *1943–5. Received regular briefings from representatives of all three services. Visited his Führer immediately after the attempt on Hitler's life in July 1944 to quiet any rumours about his involvement in either the opposition to Hitler or the planning of the coup. Arrested by the Soviets and flown to Moscow, July 1945. Charged by the International Military Tribunal at Nuremberg on three counts: 'Conspiracy to Wage Aggressive War', 'Waging Aggressive War' and 'War Crimes', November 1945. Found guilty on all three counts, 30 September 1946. Sentenced (19 October) to life imprisonment. Taken to Spandau Prison in Berlin, 18 July 1947. With Raeder's health deteriorating, his supporters were able to secure his release, 26 September 1956. Wrote two volumes of memoirs (*Mein Leben*), 1956 and 1957. Died in Lippstadt, 6 November 1960, aged eighty-four. Buried in Kiel, 11 November 1960 – the forty-second anniversary of Germany's armistice at the end of World War One.*[110]

[110]Salewski's analysis of the defence of the navy at Nuremberg (the final 'battle of the German navy, 1939–1945') is the best summary to date. *Seekriegsleitung*, vol. II, pp. 529–602. Cf. Raeder's version of the International Military Tribunal and the final years of his life as a 'vindication' of his career. *Mein Leben*, vol. II, pp. 306–35.

3

Fleet Admiral

Ernest J. King
United States Navy

1878–1956

by
Robert W. Love Jr

*E*RNEST *Joseph King, born 23 November 1878, in Lorain, Ohio, of a Scottish
father and English mother. Entered US Naval Academy, Annapolis, 1897.
Served in cruiser* San Francisco *during Spanish–American War, 1898, and saw
some action. Near top of class academically; shone in military performance. Rapidly
established a reputation for extreme arrogance, highly volatile temper, intemperate
risk-taking and absolute inability to tolerate those less competent than himself. Would
also stand up to superior officers, even at danger to his own career. All these
simultaneously sprang from and produced a nearly total dedication to the US Navy.
Served early on as navigator in converted gunboat* Eagle, *battleships* Illinois *and*
Alabama, *and protected cruiser* Cincinnati, *from which last he observed the 1904–5
Russo-Japanese War. Won gold medal of US Naval Institute for article on reform of
shipboard organization, 1909; most of his recommendations were adopted and remain
in force. Taught ordnance at Naval Academy; hitched his star to Rear Admiral Hugo
Osterhaus and prospered as his aide and flag secretary. Several years' battleship and
cruiser service; promoted lieutenant-commander, 1913. Commanded destroyer*
Terry, *1915. Promoted commander, 1917; temporary captain, September 1918;
rank confirmed, 1921.*

*World War One service produced deep-seated suspicion of British political motives
and low opinion of Royal Navy. Between the wars, he thoroughly regenerated the US
Navy's Postgraduate School. Buying a house in Annapolis for himself, his wife and six
children, he remained highly ambitious. Commanded a submarine flotilla, 1922, and
New London Submarine Base, 1923; introduced practice (still maintained) of reading
semi-annual fitness reports to officers with instructions on how to improve. He himself
drank heavily, bullied his juniors in every way to force them up to his professional
standards, and, though devoted to his children, was constantly and publicly unfaithful*

75

to his wife. Highly respected but widely feared and disliked. Under Rear Admiral William A. Moffett, gained his pilot's wings, May 1927 (at age forty-eight); served as Moffett's assistant Chief of Aeronautics; argued vigorously with Moffett and asked to be relieved. Became head of Hampton Roads Naval Air Station, and (in 1930) commander of new aircraft carrier Lexington. *Highly successful. Following Moffett's accidental death (1933), lobbied hard and successfully to be his replacement as bureau chief. Also promoted rear admiral, 1933. Returned to sea 1936, commanding land-based patrol planes of Base Force; took charge of Battle Force aircraft carriers, 1938. Devised new multi-carrier tactics successfully used in World War Two. Having hoped to become* CNO, *instead was appointed (August 1939) to the General Board. Commanded US Navy's Atlantic Neutrality Patrol, December 1940; billet upgraded to Commander-in-Chief Atlantic Fleet, February 1941, with the rank of admiral.*

'We are preparing for – and we are now close to – those active operations (commonly called war) which require the exercise and utilization of the full powers and capabilities of every officer in command status,' sixty-two-year-old Admiral King announced to the Atlantic Fleet on 31 January 1941. Summing up his years of experience, he warned that it would be 'essential to extend the knowledge and the practice of "initiative of the subordinate" in principle and in application until these are universal in the exercise of command'. For nearly a year, under some of the most difficult circumstances imaginable, he tried to instil this approach into the Atlantic Fleet. The United States was officially neutral in the European War. Politically, the situation was extremely delicate. From mid-summer 1941, Britain and Russia were allied in the Treaty of Mutual Assistance, and most Americans supported Britain's cause, but saw little difference between Hitler's Germany and Stalin's Russia. Public opinion and Congress supported measures intended to defend Britain, although President Franklin D. Roosevelt's decision to extend Lend-Lease to the Soviets was controversial, and the opponents of American entry into the war still held sway on Capitol Hill. However, F.D.R. and the Chief of Naval Operations, Admiral Stark [*q.v.*], intended to use the Atlantic Fleet to create incidents at sea which they hoped would lead to a German declaration of war against the United States.

Accordingly, King's missions in 1941 were to prepare the Atlantic Fleet to escort British merchant convoys from Canada and the United States to Britain, to conduct escort and evasive routeing operations when the navy began to participate in the convoy campaign, and to ready the Atlantic Fleet to mount an amphibious offensive against Hitler's Europe. Fully in agreement with the CNO's 'Europe first' strategy, King's distrust for the British nonetheless soon began to show. He criticized Churchill not for resolving to fight, but for fighting everywhere and for adopting a grand strategy of dispersion. Reasoning that Britain's problem with the U-boat was largely of her own making, King firmly resisted the Admiralty's attempts to draw the US Navy into secondary theatres such as the Mediterranean and the Indian Ocean. He was as eager as

Errest J. King

F.D.R. to establish mooring-points in the Atlantic to support Atlantic Fleet anti-raiding and escort operations, but he played a large role in dissuading the President from occupying the Portuguese Azores in June. Instead, King favoured the occupation of Iceland, despite Stark's opposition, and helped to convince Roosevelt to approve Operation Indigo in July 1941. King organized the occupation forces and established a destroyer pool to operate from Reykjavik. The Admiralty's mishandling of its aircraft during the poorly managed hunt for the *Bismarck* and other break-outs also led King to establish a powerful battleship–carrier task force, which he held poised to rescue the Royal Navy from the Germans if Hitler decided to send the *Tirpitz* into the Denmark Strait.

Following the Argentia Conference summit which King organized and attended, F.D.R. ordered the Atlantic Fleet to begin escorting Icelandic–American–British convoys on 1 September. Three days later, the *U-652* attacked the destroyer *Greer* while on anti-submarine patrol, and she responded with depth charges. Six weeks later, after King had formed several ocean escort groups for the run between Halifax and Iceland, the new destroyer *Kearney* was damaged by German torpedoes, and on 31 October the *U-552* sank the old four-stacker *Reuben James* during an escort operation. 'There are grim facts to be faced,' King told a friend, referring to the navy's outdated escort and anti-submarine doctrines, the overall weakness of the Atlantic Fleet's ocean escort groups, and the urgent need for more escorts, patrol bombers and carrier-based air power to combat the U-boat offensive. Heeding Stark's warning that eventually the navy would have to support an Anglo-American invasion of occupied Europe, King established a new Atlantic Amphibious Force under an extremely able figure, Rear Admiral H. Kent Hewitt [q.v.], who began to devise new specialized equipment and landing craft while training Marine and army divisions in the fast-developing art of shore-to-shore amphibious operations. King arranged the forces and launched the search for new Atlantic Fleet doctrines in escort, anti-submarine and shore-to-shore amphibious operations, but most of this was promise in December when King shifted his flag to Main Navy, the navy's Washington headquarters, to take on even greater responsibilities.

A few days after Congress declared war, Navy Secretary Frank Knox flew to Pearl Harbor, conducted his own investigation of the débâcle there, and returned to Washington with a proposal which F.D.R. approved for an immediate reorganization of the navy's High Command. Knox picked the chief of the Bureau of Navigation, Admiral Chester Nimitz [q.v.], to relieve Admiral Kimmel in command of the Pacific Fleet, and named King to the new billet of Cominch – Commander-in-Chief of the US fleet. Reaction in the fleet was jubilant. 'King is a man of action,' wrote Captain Charles Cooke upon learning the news. 'He could do things!' Knox told a friend. 'Lord, how I need him.' King would 'transform the mental attitude . . . of the navy from a defensive to an offensive posture'. King had no hand in Nimitz's selection, but he did get to name his own relief, Admiral Royal Ingersoll, an inspiring figure who in December took command of the Atlantic Fleet. In January 1942, Roosevelt reorganized the old Army–Navy Joint Board, creating the Joint Chiefs of Staff, which included General George C. Marshall, the army Chief of Staff, his principal air deputy, General Henry 'Hap' Arnold, Admiral Stark and Admiral King as Cominch. There was inherent trouble in these hasty arrangements. F.D.R. wanted the CNO to craft grand strategy and superintend shipbuilding while Cominch directed fleet operations, but neither Stark nor King found a satisfactory way to divide these closely knit functions. A solution was finally cobbled together by someone, perhaps Knox, who admired and valued both men. King would relieve Stark as CNO while keeping his hat as Cominch, while Stark would revive Admiral Sims' World War One billet as commander of US Naval Forces in Europe. By the end of March 1942, these arrangements were in place.

As Cominch–CNO, King was the most powerful professional military executive in American history, and he performed a role unique among World War Two commanders. As Cominch, he exercised immediate operational command of the Pacific, Atlantic and Asiatic Fleets. As CNO, he directed the most massive warship-building programme in the history of warfare. He was responsible not only for training and preparing a navy of over three million officers and men, but also for a Marine Corps which expanded into 'a second army' of 500,000 amphibious troops. Without doubt, the Marines were 'King's personal army', as one Englishman charged. Both the navy and Marine Corps created large land- and sea-based air forces, logistics commands and immense shore-based training commands, all of which fell under King's supervision. To direct the navy's shipbuilding and shore establishment, he selected Admiral Frederick Horne, an outstanding administrator. This surprised many people who knew that King and Horne simply did not like one another. But, recognizing that Horne possessed an extraordinary talent for organization and for getting things done, King put aside his personal feelings, gave Horne the enormous responsibility and did his best to get along. King found in his friend, General Thomas Holcomb, an extremely able comman-dant so dedicated to Marine Corps ways that when his four-year tour expired in 1943, in the middle of the war, he rejected King's and Roosevelt's personal entreaties and insisted on retiring so as to make way for a younger Marine. King heartily approved of Holcomb's selection of General Archibald Vandegrift, another fighter, the great hero of Guadalcanal, as his successor. King's well-known support for the Marines was repaid when, upon being asked by F.D.R. to join the JCS, Holcomb refused on the grounds that King would fairly advance the Marine Corps' views.

King sensed from the start that the navy would be best served if he spent most of his time on JCS and Cominch business, that is, devising strategy and conducting inter-service and Allied military diplomacy. To run the fleet from Cominch, he needed and chose subordinates who would stand up to him, men who did not fear his fiery rages. He acted to ensure that he was open to the best new ideas and officers from the fleet by arranging for the entire Cominch staff, with two exceptions, to rotate from the fleet to Washington and back again. The only two permanent members of his staff were Admiral Richard Edwards, a submariner who handled administration, and a newly minted rear admiral, Charles M. Cooke, who served as Cominch's Chief of Staff and the navy's main strategic planner throughout the war. Among all World War Two high commanders, King alone grasped the key relationships among industrial mobilization, new technologies and modern, multi-dimensional combined arms strategy. What often damaged him was that he invariably approached problems with an icy, impersonal detachment and brusque directness which many found off-putting – and which often defeated his own purposes. General Marshall, King's great army counterpart, did not pretend to understand the science behind an internal combustion engine or the atomic bomb, but, unlike King, Marshall was a superb military diplomat, a fine public speaker and a respected negotiator.

Soon after Pearl Harbor, the JCS first wrestled with the great problems of wartime grand strategy when they confronted Churchill and his chiefs at the Arcadia Conference (December 1941 to January 1942). F.D.R. reaffirmed his agreement with Stark's 'Europe first' strategy; King, Stark and Admiral Sir Dudley Pound [*q.v.*] of the Admiralty hammered out a new agreement on Lend-Lease transfers to the Royal Navy; and the Combined Chiefs of Staff agreed to study Operation Gymnast, a plan to invade French North-west Africa. They also established an American–British–Dutch command in the South Pacific to stem the tide of the Japanese offensive along the Singapore–Philippines line. King thoroughly distrusted Marshall's Christmas Day proposal for a unified command with 'one man in command of the entire theater – air, ground, and ships' in the ABDA (American–British–Dutch–Australian) area, but Stark did not object so King agreed in a 'lukewarm' fashion to support the scheme.

The ABDA accord soon led the CCS to divide the world into several operational theatres. India and the Middle East were bastions of exclusive British interest, whereas Churchill readily agreed that the Pacific, South-West Pacific and South Atlantic should become American commands. However, when Churchill proposed a combined Atlantic command, on the basis that in the North Atlantic, Europe and the Mediterranean the Allies shared interests, King stoutly rejected it. Unity of command was 'not a panacea for all military difficulties', he warned, although some 'amateur strategists' including the aged Secretary of War, Henry Stimson, were advancing the concept. The navy had 'no intention whatever of acceding to any unity of command proposals that are not premised on a particular situation in a particular area at a particular time for a more or less particular period', King declared, but ABDA's creation established a precedent that he never successfully reversed. He had no use for mixed multinational or even multi-service commands – other than the historic navy–Marine Corps team.

King approached the problem of crafting strategy in a more doctrinaire manner than did any of his peers – except for the narrow-minded Allied generals commanding the bomber forces. Like Marshall, King realized that waging war on behalf of a large democracy meant that the navy and Marines had to minimize casualties, but he saw no contradiction between that requirement and the need to conduct a material-intensive war by applying the principle of economy of force. 'We should determine on a very few lines of military endeavor and concentrate our efforts on these lines,' he told F.D.R. on 5 March 1942. This concept ran counter to Churchill's grand strategy of dispersion, and King knew it. King was also aware that the success of a grand strategy based on economy of force would require tremendous flexibility. 'The very few lines of US military effort may . . . be shifted in accordance with developments but the total number should be kept at very few.' How to get Roosevelt to accept this approach and overrule Churchill's habit of dispersing the Allied military effort around the world would be the greatest negotiating problem the JCS faced in World War Two.

King viewed Germany and Japan as posing radically different problems for the Allies. Admiral Stark, in his 1940 'Plan Dog', had argued that Germany could win the war by defeating Russia, holding Europe and menacing Britain. King agreed. On these grounds, he supported sending Lend-Lease material to Russia – although he would clearly have preferred a more calculated approach to the Soviets than F.D.R.'s dewy-eyed diplomacy would permit. Early in the war King agreed to detach a task force built around the new fast battleship *Washington* and her screen to reinforce the Admiralty's cover for the north Russia convoys, and he lent support to General Marshall's plan to establish a large Persian Gulf command to create a Lend-Lease pipeline through Iran to the Red Army in southern Russia. On the other hand, Admiral King reasoned that Russia could not defeat Germany alone, and so he was an early backer of Stark's case for an Allied invasion of France. Gymnast never appealed to King, and when in March 1942 General Marshall proposed instead to mount Operation Sledgehammer, a British-based cross-Channel invasion of Normandy in the autumn of that year, the Admiral quickly agreed to throw the growing Atlantic Fleet behind this strategy. Marshall flew to London and, for the moment, the British signed on as well.

No American military leader, least of all Admiral King, ever questioned the capacity of the United States to bring Japan to book, but how this was to be done caused all manner of controversy. Soon after he became Cominch, King outlined his concept for the campaign to Admiral Nimitz and Admiral Thomas Hart, the able Commander-in-Chief of the small Asiatic Fleet. 'Our primary concern . . . is to hold Hawaii and its approaches (via Midway) from the westward and to maintain its communications with the West Coast. Our next care in the Pacific is to preserve Australasia [Australia and New Zealand] which requires that its communications be maintained – via eastward of Samoa, Fiji, and southward of New Caledonia.' From these 'strong points . . .

we can drive north-west from the New Hebrides into the Solomons and the Bismarck Archipelago after the same fashion of step-by-step advances that the Japanese used in the South China Sea'. It was within the context of developing these lines of approach that King devised a way to disrupt the furious Japanese offensive.

'The Japanese have demonstrated a capacity for powerful mobility beyond anything we are prepared to offer,' Cooke warned in January 1942. 'They have moved from one thing to another with a continuous . . . tempo contemplated in some of our plans but declared impossible by practically all the planners and by external criticisers.' The stinging raid on Pearl Harbor resulted in almost no military benefit to the Japanese since the old American battleships which were sunk or damaged were simply too slow to operate with the carriers or the new fast *North Carolina*-class battleships in the Western Pacific. And, as navy planners predicted, Japan's invasion of the Philippines forced Admiral Thomas Hart to withdraw his Asiatic Fleet to the Dutch East Indies where he prepared to make a last stand. King and Stark expected to give up these forward outposts, but they also wanted to prevent the Japanese from overcoming the Allied island bases in the South Pacific and to hold Midway, which King believed to be threatened by Japan's movement into the Gilberts. These concerns led the Pacific Fleet to mount the abortive mid-December relief expedition to Wake Island which ended in yet another fiasco. Roosevelt sarcastically condemned the entire affair. Confidence in Washington in the eagerness of the Pacific Fleet to engage the enemy quickly hit a new low and Stark's position was therefore again undermined.

King believed the ABDA fiasco to be the result of two factors. First, the Allies had only weak forces to obstruct Japan's furious offensive. Second, they chose an unusually inept figure, General Archibald Wavell, for the ABDA command. He allowed the enemy to land on the Kra Peninsula, lost Singapore and wasted his few ships uselessly shuffling troops from one defeat to the next. Admiral Thomas Hart, a true fighter who was given the ABDA naval command, was outraged when a tug-of-war erupted between the British and the Dutch over how to use the small Asiatic Fleet to defend the remnants of their empires. The Japanese advanced to the south-west in three movements: the western thrust slammed into South-east Asia, the central advance struck along an axis from the Philippines to Borneo, and the eastern wing pierced the Molucca Sea. Hart's ships won the small battle off Balikpapan on 24 January, but in the meantime Wavell, a disreputable conniver, intrigued behind his back and at length Churchill persuaded F.D.R. to order Hart to return home. The Dutch Admiral who replaced Hart soon after blundered into the Java Sea, mishandled his ships and was soundly thrashed by the enemy. The Dutch East Indies and the Philippines surrendered a few weeks later. King never forgave the British for sabotaging Hart, and his attitude thereafter towards the Dutch was openly scornful.

Marshall and King now divided the Pacific basin into two American commands: the South-West Pacific fell under General MacArthur, who had retired to Australia, and the Pacific Ocean Area came under Admiral Nimitz. King had known MacArthur for many years – and thoroughly distrusted him, to the extent that Marshall accused the Admiral of adopting a 'policy of hate' towards the egocentric General. King liked and respected Nimitz, but agreed with Cooke's assessment that 'Chester was not too smart.' Nimitz's many years in the Bureau of Naval Personnel suggested to King that he was a 'fixer', overly willing to compromise and accept substandard performance. King carved out a special South Pacific naval area and, when Stark went to London, instructed Vice-Admiral Robert Ghormley, who had been in Britain for two years, to set up an area headquarters in New Caledonia.

Weeks before the collapse of the ABDA command, and months before the fall of the Philippines, Admiral King crafted an overall strategy for containing the Japanese advance in the Pacific. To dislocate the enemy's offensive balance, he intended to launch a series of raids against weakly defended points along Japan's Pacific Front. At the same time, he wanted to garrison a line of island bases in the South Pacific in order to secure the sea line of communications from Hawaii to New Zealand and Australia. 'The Navy wants to take all the islands in the Pacific,' complained Brigadier-General Dwight D. Eisenhower, the new head of the army War Plans Division, and 'have them held by Army troops, to become bases for Army pursuit planes and bombers. Then the Navy will have a safe place to sail its vessels.' This pejorative description of King's concept illustrated the continual opposition the Admiral faced from the War Department in obtaining garrison troops for the South Pacific bases and army air force aircraft to support the movements of the fleet.

If the Japanese Fleet ventured beyond the protection of its land-based aircraft, then King intended to challenge them with his few carrier task forces in battles of attrition. Admiral Nimitz, who took command of the Pacific Fleet at the end of 1941, was uneasy about this ambitious plan and acutely aware of the constant threat to Hawaii from another Japanese attack. However, in January 1942 Nimitz found himself under unremitting pressure from King for 'some aggressive action for effect on general morale'. Early that month, navy intelligence placed the Japanese carriers in the South-West Pacific, so King decided to relieve some of the burden on the ABDA command by mounting diversionary raids into the Central Pacific. On 20 January, he instructed Nimitz to send a task force to raid Wake Island. Nimitz assigned this mission to Rear Admiral Wilson Brown in the *Lexington*, but the loss of a fleet oiler meant the mission had to be postponed. Meanwhile, King had persuaded Marshall to reinforce the army garrison on Samoa, and it sailed from the west coast in late January 1942 escorted by *Yorktown*'s task force, under Rear Admiral Frank Jack Fletcher. When the escorts reached Samoa, Nimitz decided to send Fletcher north to rendezvous with Admiral Halsey [q.v.] in the *Enterprise*. Together they were to raid Japanese positions in the Gilberts and Marshalls. The cancellation of Brown's raid on Wake made it imperative that Halsey's raid on the Marshalls be 'driven home'. Halsey's daring raid on the Marshalls in early February was followed by Fletcher's attacks on the Gilberts and Brown's strikes on Japan's airbase at Rabaul and Lae and Salamaua, her New Guinea strongpoints. It would take one more action, however, for the raiding strategy to pay off.

King's raiding strategy climaxed in April 1942 in the spectacular Tokyo Raid. The notion of retaliating against Japan's home islands had been raised in some of the earliest Allied discussions of Pacific strategy after Pearl Harbor, and in January 1942 Captain Francis S. Low of the Cominch staff prepared a plan for a two-carrier attack against Tokyo. King believed this to be impractical, since the range of all American carrier bombers was less than that of the patrol planes which defended the Japanese homeland. However, when Low suggested launching a group of army air force medium-bombers from a carrier deck for a one-way mission from the North Pacific over Tokyo and on to airfields in China, King convinced Arnold to back the mission and the ball started to roll. The carrier *Hornet* stood out of San Francisco Bay in late March with the B-25 bombers on her flight deck, rendezvoused with Halsey in the *Enterprise*, and the task force brought Tokyo under attack on 18 April. The raid was an enormous boost to American morale, and a devastating blow to the prestige of Japan's military leadership. King did not expect any of the carrier raids to inflict significant damage. His purpose was rather to unsettle and disconcert Japan's High Command and dislocate their overall strategy. They reacted by hastening the entry of the Japanese Fleet into the Coral Sea and agreeing to Admiral Yamamoto's [*q.v.*] plan for the Midway operation.

The first chance King saw for the Pacific Fleet to engage the main Japanese fleet on favourable terms emerged on 15 April, when he learned that an enemy carrier division was to arrive at the fleet base at Truk later that month. Within three days he warned Nimitz that the Japanese intended to advance during the first week in May against Port Moresby, an Australian stronghold on the southern coast of New Guinea's Papuan Peninsula. Intelligence led to the clear conclusion that 'an offensive in the Southwest Pacific is shaping up'. Fletcher's *Yorktown* task force had been in the South Pacific since February, but King now directed Nimitz to hold him there during April, and arranged for Rear Admiral Aubrey Fitch in the carrier *Lexington* to join Fletcher at the end of the month. But now the price of the Tokyo Raid began to haunt King. His earlier decision to send Halsey with both the *Enterprise* and the *Hornet* into the North Pacific on the Tokyo Raid had inadvertently resulted in a division of the Pacific Fleet's decks when Nimitz most needed them to be concentrated. Directed by King to defend Port Moresby and the Coral Sea, Nimitz reluctantly decided on 22 April that, a day or two after Halsey returned to Pearl Harbor, he was to put to sea again, steam into the South Pacific and join Fletcher to help him deal with the Japanese offensive, although it seemed clear to King and Nimitz that these reinforcements would not arrive in the Coral Sea on time.

When Fletcher met the Combined Fleet in the Coral Sea, his squadrons devastated both enemy air groups and sank a small carrier, but the Japanese located Captain Frederick Sherman's *Lexington* and sent her under in return. The Japanese gained a tactical victory, sinking more tonnage than the Americans, but Fletcher won a strategic victory by thwarting the invasion of Port Moresby. However, King was angered by Fletcher's poor dispositions, his failure to use the weather to mask his carriers and the 'apparent lack of aggressive tactics of his force'. Nimitz stoutly defended Fletcher claiming the faults could 'be charged partly to the lack of sufficiently reliable combat intelligence' and partly to 'the necessity for replenishment of fuel and provisions'. Expecting another Japanese stroke to fall on the Americans in the immediate future, King was unwilling to shake up the Pacific Fleet or overrule Nimitz for the moment. On the other hand, in Captain Sherman, King had found another fighter in the Coral Sea, and soon promoted him to flag rank, in spite of the loss of the *Lexington*. 'We seem to have stopped the advance on Port Moresby for the time being,' King told Admiral Pound, but the 'battle of the Coral Sea was merely the first round of an engagement which will continue'.

On the day after Fletcher entered the Coral Sea, Admiral Yamamoto's plan to attack Midway was approved in Tokyo. He believed this would induce King to send his remaining carriers into the Central Pacific where the Combined Fleet would destroy them. American radio intelligence provided King with contradictory clues in early May regarding Japan's strategy, and little news about Yamamoto's tactical deployments. Captain Redman and his Pacific Fleet counterpart, Commander Joseph Rochefort [*q.v.*], directed their efforts against the top-secret JN25 naval code, but they were diverted by a bitter personal struggle pitting one code-breaking group against the other for status, prestige and the dominant voice in Pacific intelligence matters. Redman presented King with an estimate of Japanese strategy for the coming months which predicted a renewal of the offensive in the South Pacific during the late summer, and on 12 May King warned Marshall that a powerful Japanese 'force is training for another campaign or large operation to be initiated the last of May or the first part of June'. Although King had no 'information as to the nature or direction' of this thrust, he was 'inclined to believe that the enemy will first proceed with the Moresby operation' but admitted that 'between June 1st and 5th it could arrive near Alaska, the West Coast, Hawaii, or any of the island positions on the line to Australia, New Guinea, or Australia itself'.

Within a few days, however, Rochefort became convinced that Yamamoto intended to seize Midway Island. This assessment, which differed from Redman's prediction, was endorsed by Nimitz. King now had to select the most probable Japanese option. His views were coloured by Nimitz's continued opposition to the deployment of the American carriers in the South Pacific and by his own determination to resist Japan's offensive against the Hawaii–Australia line of communications. Before the *Yorktown* limped back to

Pearl Harbor after the Battle of the Coral Sea, King had instructed Nimitz to send Halsey and the *Enterprise* on a new raid against the Marshalls on 16 May. Citing Rochefort's intelligence, Nimitz tried to cancel this raid, but King insisted that it proceed. To circumvent King's orders, therefore, Nimitz broadcast a secret message to Halsey on 16 May, instructing him to send out patrol planes which would be spotted by the Japanese. Since Nimitz was enjoined by King not to risk his carriers against land-based bombers, Nimitz had an excuse to give to King when Halsey retired to Hawaii. Unclear about Nimitz's purposes, Halsey obeyed, his planes were sighted and he duly informed Nimitz and King that the *Enterprise* was withdrawing to Oahu.

When King received this message he had to make one of the hardest decisions in the war. He did not wholly trust Nimitz's judgement and strongly disagreed with him about South Pacific strategy. On the other hand, Nimitz was either responsible for the Pacific Fleet or he was not. Also, King had immense faith in the old Pacific Fleet carriers, whose F4F Wildcat fighters had already won a three-to-one exchange ratio with the vaunted enemy Zero. Nevertheless, if he allowed Nimitz to deploy the carriers *Hornet*, *Enterprise* and *Yorktown* to defend Midway and Yamamoto learned what was afoot, the Japanese might divert their fleet into the Coral Sea and overrun Port Moresby. This is what Redman's code breakers in Washington were predicting. 'The majority of our effective forces had been operating in the South Pacific,' King wrote, 'and the primary question was whether some should be left there . . . or whether all our carriers should be concentrated at Pearl Harbor.'

To verify Rochefort's prediction, King checked with Pound in London, but the British replied that the enemy did not intend to conduct major operations in the near future. Either the British were lying or their code breaking was very poor, King reasoned. Since 'Nimitz was certain that they [the Japanese] were going after Midway and Hawaii', on 17 May he moved decisively by agreeing to Nimitz's plan to concentrate the American carriers and ambush the Japanese when they closed on Midway atoll. The battle off Midway on 4–8 June 1942 cost the Japanese four carriers, over 200 aircraft and some of their most experienced naval aviators. Whereas the Japanese did not possess the shipbuilding capacity to replace these four carriers for six years, soon after the battle King told Nimitz that the first of sixteen new 27,000-ton *Essex*-class carriers would put to sea before the end of the year. Japan's military planners never truly came to grips with America's industrial superiority with the result that, after Midway, Japan no longer stood among the Great Powers.

On 10 June, two days after the rival fleets withdrew from the Central Pacific, King went up to the White House and persuaded F.D.R. to agree to mount a quick counter-offensive against Japan in the South Pacific. Although King later stressed that this step was simply 'an immediate result of the Battle of Midway', the greater strategic issue was in reality far more complex. The British were now backsliding on the promise to invade France in the autumn of 1942, and King and Marshall confronted the likelihood that there would be no major Atlantic operation that year. This caused King to allocate some of the new large LSTS (landing ship, troops) and smaller landing craft to the Pacific Fleet to allow Nimitz to mount a minor stroke that would increase the pressure not only on Japan, but also on the British ally. This became the Guadalcanal operation. King had to argue long and hard to get Marshall to agree to it, and Captain Low observed that in return for the army's co-operation in the South Pacific, King 'was forced to make commitments to Marshall for subsequent transfers of naval units to the Atlantic' to support the invasion of North Africa. F.D.R. had already warned the JCS that it would be 'unwise to attempt a major offensive in the Pacific area' during 1942, so King disingenuously portrayed the Guadalcanal counter-stroke as a mere shift from the 'defensive' to the 'defensive–offensive' phase of the war against Japan.

The objective of the invasion of Guadalcanal, codenamed Watchtower, was to begin a campaign against Rabaul in New Britain, the hub of Japanese air power in the South Pacific. King vested overall direction of the campaign in Vice Admiral Ghormley, who had only recently set up his headquarters in Nouméa, French New Caledonia. Nimitz's stout defence of Fletcher's handling of the carriers in the Coral Sea moved King to suspend judgement about relieving Fletcher, and Fletcher's performance off Midway seemed to justify this vote of confidence. After that engagement, Nimitz nominated Fletcher for promotion to vice admiral and proposed that he continue to command the carriers during the Guadalcanal operation. King winced and dallied. On 14 July, the carriers, with Fletcher in command, sailed for their rendezvous with the Watchtower invasion transports at Fiji. The next day, King relented, promoted Fletcher and agreed to allow him to hold on to the carrier command. Ghormley, who only now came to grips with the enormity of the Watchtower offensive, failed to force any coherent battle plan on his subordinates to fend off an expected enemy counter-attack; instead he began to beg King (in vain) to postpone the invasion. Nimitz, ever cautious, joined the chorus. King stood firm; there would be no postponement.

Fletcher's task force, composed of the three carriers *Enterprise*, *Saratoga* and *Wasp*, steamed into position to cover the landing of General Vandegrift's Marines on Guadalcanal and nearby Tulagi on 7 August 1942. Tulagi was quickly overrun. On Guadalcanal, Japanese support troops and workers – numbering about 2,000 – fled into the jungle, and an airstrip (later named Henderson Field) quickly fell to the invaders. In spite of minimal loss of his aircraft, Fletcher withdrew the carriers and the new fast battleship *North Carolina* – the most powerful ship in the South Pacific at the time – from Guadalcanal the following day. In the early hours of 9 August, a Japanese cruiser–destroyer slipped past radar picket destroyers, entered the sound between Guadalcanal and Tulagi, advanced on Rear Admiral Richmond Kelly Turner's [*q.v.*] anchorage, and off Savo Island sank one Australian and three American cruisers. The sound was soon given the macabre name of Ironbottom. The loss of life stunned King, but neither Nimitz nor Ghormley provided him with a clear picture of the action. King had hand-picked Turner, an aggressive leader, for the command of the Pacific Amphibious Force. Doubting that Turner was wholly responsible for the débâcle, and not wishing to discourage his admirals from risking their ships, for the moment King held his wrath in check.

Vandegrift's Marines sharply repulsed a series of enemy counter-attacks against Henderson Field, but in Ironbottom Sound the struggle for Guadalcanal in late August and September grew grim indeed. In a remarkably sloppy action, Fletcher bloodied a Japanese carrier raid in the Battle of the Eastern Solomons, but the *Enterprise* was damaged. The *Saratoga* too was attacked by an enemy submarine at the end of the month and had to retire to the west coast for repairs. Fletcher was slightly wounded in this action, and King took the opportunity to order him to return to Washington. From there he was eventually reassigned to the less demanding North Pacific Area. The catalogue of loss continued: in mid-September, Captain Forrest Sherman had to abandon the carrier *Wasp* after she was mortally wounded by another enemy submarine. Only the *Hornet* was left to provide offshore air support to the Marines on Guadalcanal. When these losses – still kept from the public – became known in Washington, the struggle for Guadalcanal assumed an importance that neither King nor F.D.R. had anticipated. F.D.R. was 'frankly . . . pessimistic at the moment about the whole situation', and warned that the loss of Guadalcanal could devastate American public morale.

Nimitz now demanded more ships and aircraft, and on 7 September – during one of their bi-monthly conferences in San Francisco – he complained to King that the South Pacific badly needed reinforcements. While planning the offensive against Guadalcanal in July, King had estimated that the Americans could overrun Rabaul by the end of the year, and he later confessed that he was thoroughly 'surprised by the violence and persistence of the Japanese reaction to our movement into the Solomons'. Pointing out to General Marshall that the navy had 'gone much beyond our commitments' towards meeting the needs of Operation Torch, the forthcoming invasion of North Africa, King insisted that more army air force pursuit planes and bombers be sent to the South Pacific. However, both Marshall and Arnold had opposed the Guadalcanal operation from the start, and now Marshall told King that 'the reinforcements which you propose can only be effected by diversions from Torch', a step the army Chief of Staff would not take. Despite King's badgering, Roosevelt refused to intervene and resolve this impasse for over a month, by which time it was evident that losses in the South Pacific would adversely affect the Democrats in the upcoming Congressional elections. Prompted by reports of a renewed Japanese counter-offensive, in late October F.D.R. finally directed the army members of the JCS 'to make sure that every possible weapon gets in that area to hold Guadalcanal . . . even though it means delay in our other commitments'.

Both King and Nimitz realized that drastic action had to be taken to relieve the unrelenting pressure on Vandegrift's Marines. For several weeks, word had been leaching out of the South Pacific to Pearl Harbor and back to Main Navy that Ghormley was unsuited for the heavy burdens of high command. Arnold visited Nouméa in September and returned to Washington convinced that the fleet in the South Pacific needed 'new leaders who know and understand modern warfare; men who are aggressive and not afraid to fight their ships'. King bore some of the responsibility for this state of affairs. His order naming Ghormley as an area commander was none too clear, and he had instructed Ghormley to run the South Pacific from Nouméa, whereas Nimitz wanted Ghormley to direct the battles at sea. Ghormley was also faulted by King and Nimitz for allowing the logistics and shipping situation in his area to reach crisis proportions. 'We are unable to control the sea in the Guadalcanal area,' Nimitz warned King, 'thus our supply of the positions will only be done at great expense to us. The situation is not hopeless, but it is certainly critical.' Nimitz grasped the nettle first, proposing to King on 17 October that Admiral Halsey replace Ghormley in the South Pacific. King hastily agreed to this step.

Owing to vastly greater American aircraft-production rates, King did not expect the Japanese to accept an air campaign of attrition in the South Pacific, but in October an analysis by Cooke demonstrated that Yamamoto had fallen into this deadly trap. Thereafter, King struggled relentlessly to ship aircraft, aircrews and spares into the lower Solomons to keep up the pressure on the enemy and prevent him from safely disengaging. And, aided by Roosevelt's increased commitment to Guadalcanal, Halsey's arrival in Nouméa on 20 October was a tonic. In short order he boosted morale, solved the logistics tangle, concentrated all his resources on holding Guadalcanal, reinforced the Marines and sent the new fast battleship *Washington* into Ironbottom Sound to prevent further enemy night-time bombardments of Henderson Field. With King's approval Halsey named Rear Admiral Thomas Kinkaid [*q.v.*], another fighter, to succeed Fletcher, and in the naval battle of Guadalcanal (13–15 November 1942) Kinkaid's strengthened air groups mauled the enemy carriers so badly that Yamamoto no longer had enough aircraft to operate his remaining three attack carriers. In spite of a brief success off Tassafaronga in December, by January 1943 Yamamoto was determined to withdraw from Guadalcanal and shore up his defences in the upper Solomons. Operation Shoestring was what King called his South Pacific gamble, and it was paying off.

The war elsewhere was not going well for the US Navy. America's entry into the war at once exposed all its warships, army troop transports and civilian cargo shipping to attacks by Axis submarines. The most immediate problem King faced was a scattered group of about ten Japanese submarines which were deployed between Hawaii and the Pacific coast during early 1942. He had to arrange for ocean escort groups to escort all Hawaii-bound and South Pacific-bound shipping, and to create a basic anti-submarine force to handle contacts in the strategic Alaska–Hawaii–Panama triangle. The navy was so short of escorts, however, that most west-coast cargo shipping could not be organized into convoys, but Japan's decision to order its submarines to attack only capital ships meant that the threat King feared to the Panama–Alaska–Hawaii line never actually developed. Having dealt with U-boats before Pearl Harbor, King predicted soon after that they would begin to operate off the east coast and in the Caribbean in early 1942. However, owing to F.D.R.'s disastrous decision to transfer the navy's anti-submarine reserve, fifty four-stack destroyers, to the British in 1940, and to Churchill's foolish strategy of wasting the Royal Navy against land-based Axis air forces in the Mediterranean, King could do little to help the British two years later when the U-boat menace erupted.

King's first major decision about the Battle of the Atlantic was that the navy's highest priority would be – as in World War One – to defend American troop shipping. The urgency of this became evident at the Arcadia Conference (December 1941–January 1942) when Churchill asked that American troops be sent to Britain. The JCS decided to send over roughly five army divisions and a large number of army air force air and ground crews. And when Pound complained in April 1942 that the Royal Navy 'simply cannot afford the scale of escort' for army troop shipping that King demanded, King was forced to accept responsibility for escorting all transatlantic troop shipping, to withdraw most of the navy's ocean escort groups from the transatlantic Lend-Lease convoys and to reorganize his ocean escort groups accordingly. This led to a host of troubles with London. The lack of reserve escorts, the need to defend Pacific shipping and the new demands for escort groups for Atlantic troop shipping meant that King had no spare destroyers or minesweepers to send to the New York-based Eastern Sea Frontier, which was responsible for defending shipping on the east coast.

'Should the enemy submarines operate off the coast,' Admiral Adolphus Andrews warned King in December 1941, 'this command has no forces available to take effective action against them, either offensive or defensive.' King's reaction was to establish an initial requirement for the sea frontiers and the Atlantic Fleet of 250 austere anti-submarine destroyer escorts which he attempted with mixed success to keep at the top of the President's production-priority list throughout 1942. Heavily defended convoys were the only way to defeat the U-boat, King realized, but the first DES would not enter the fleet for another year. In the meantime, King ordered sixty 110-foot wooden-hulled subchasers, putting this programme on a 'crash' basis in January 1942. Nevertheless, shortages of various sorts were so great that in early May the War Production Board told King that the 'production of submarine chasers has been discouragingly slow', and that 'less than half of the ships scheduled for completion by May first are actually completed'. King also tried to advance production of the 173-foot steel-hulled PC patrol craft, 350 of which eventually entered the fleet and supported the coastal and ocean escort groups. The subchasers were to make up the backbone of the sea frontier's coastal escort groups, but these delays (many of which were rooted in F.D.R.'s overly generous Lend-Lease programme and his decision to overrule King and give escort construction low priority) retarded the establishment of an effective coastal-convoy system.

None of these measures effectively insulated King from the reaction to the stunning results of the German U-boat campaign in American waters during the first half of 1942. He seemed to be helpless to stop the sinkings. Other than formations about to join the transatlantic convoys, troop shipping and a few special convoys, none of the merchant vessels or tankers steaming up and down the east coast could be taken under convoy because the Eastern Sea Frontier force simply did not have enough vessels to create new escort groups. Early in the campaign, King decided to forswear anti-submarine operations and to concentrate on establishing escort groups for a coastal-convoy system, but he was firmly opposed to instituting any convoy system until adequate coastal escorts groups were available. His reason for this was the belief that the premature adoption of poorly defended convoys would merely mass unprotected targets for the benefit of the U-boats. Since coastal traffic had to steam along established shipping lanes, it could not be defended by using evasive routes, and the army air force, bent on bombing Germany, refused to provide bombers or trained aircrews to escort convoys or for anti-submarine patrols. Yet when sinkings increased, Secretary of War Henry Stimson (who disliked the navy) criticized King and made the extraordinary demand that the navy transfer anti-submarine operations to the army. In this war of letters, King lashed back with unusual bitterness. It did little good. Not until June 1943 did the army abandon the battle and admit that the navy should be responsible for defeating the U-boat. Ultra was of little use since the German U-boats never concentrated off the east coast, and King therefore had no alternative in early 1942 but to accept fairly high merchant-ship losses for a few months until the subchaser, patrol craft and navy patrol bomber building programmes produced enough vessels and patrol planes to allow Andrews to inaugurate a fully protected convoy system. In the meantime, King was criticized by the press, the White House, Congress and the British allies.

In no other aspect of American military operations during World War Two did Roosevelt interfere so consistently, and with such disastrous results, as in the Eastern Sea Frontier in early 1942. Overly fond of small craft and blind to their unsuitability for offshore anti-submarine operations, F.D.R. directed King in February 1942 to commission thousands of civilian yachts and larger fishing craft into the Coast Guard, and ordered Andrews to organize a huge civilian coastal patrol. These wasteful measures – which King fought at every turn – had no effect on U-boat operations, subtracted manpower and weapons from other more important tasks, and delayed the inauguration of an effective coastal-convoy system. F.D.R. also bowed to Churchill's demand that the Americans put into commission some Q-ships, anti-submarine vessels disguised as unarmed merchantmen which were intended to lure U-boats into surfacing and attacking them with gunfire. F.D.R. instructed King to convert four merchantmen into Q-ships, but the entire scheme was discredited when the *U-123* sank the mystery-ship *Atik* on 26 March 1942 leaving no survivors. King, now alarmed and quite angry, demanded that F.D.R. tell Churchill that the navy intended to cancel the bizarre project.

The British also exploited the losses on the Eastern Sea Frontier to discredit the navy and persuade Roosevelt to agree to the establishment of a single Atlantic theatre under the Admiralty's control. Overlooking the other calls on the American fleet, Churchill subjected F.D.R. to a din of complaints about King's management of the Battle of the Atlantic, while Pound badgered King with gratuitous advice. One of Pound's more unusual proposals was to erect a gigantic mine, net and boom barrier which would stretch 3,000 miles along the Atlantic coast. These silly ideas undermined the Admiralty's case for a unified command, and King bluntly pointed out that the British had no record of accomplishment to which to point in making their case for an Atlantic command. Regarding the whole business as a direct affront to the Atlantic Fleet and Admirals Andrews and Ingersoll, King's reaction was unrelentingly hostile. Apparently the affront even annoyed F.D.R., for when the issue came to a head he rejected the British plan with uncharacteristic brusqueness. It was one of the few occasions in 1942 when he refused to cater to British interests.

On the other hand, the British played a vital role in hastening the establishment of coastal escort groups, by lending the Eastern Sea Frontier twenty-four converted anti-submarine trawlers. These arrived in New York in March 1942. Although this reverse Lend-Lease did not in any way begin to compensate the Atlantic Fleet for the loss of the Destroyer Deal or the large number of vessels built in the United States and given to the Royal Navy during World War Two, the trawler loan and the arrival of the first subchasers allowed King to establish a daytime convoy system from New York to Key West in April. In June there followed a full-fledged day-and-night convoy regime, called the Interlocking Convoy System, from Halifax to Key West.

'We must get every ship that sails the seas under constant close protection,' King told General Marshall in reply to an unprecedented attack on the navy by the army's Chief of Staff. During 'the first 17 days of May not one ship was lost in the Eastern Sea Frontier', Andrews reported, and during 'the 14 days that remained [in the month] only four vessels were sunk'. More U-boats operated between Halifax and Key West in June than ever before, but as the month passed losses reached new lows. King's constant faith in Adolphus Andrews, a pompous but enterprising fighter, led to the defeat of the U-boat on the Atlantic seaboard.

King took the view that the best way to defeat the U-boat was to invade France and shut down Germany's naval bases on the Bay of Biscay. Therefore, in spite of strong British objections in the spring and summer of 1942, he wholeheartedly supported Marshall's Sledgehammer plan to invade Normandy in September. No advocate of a Pacific first strategy, as the British often charged, King believed instead that 'even at the cost of taking extensive risks in the Pacific . . . we should be concentrating to the maximum on one front'. King was probably aware that the navy's First Landing Craft Programme would not produce enough LSTs to allow the Allies to execute Sledgehammer in the autumn, but he withheld this from the British. If Churchill intended to cancel the operation, then the JCS wanted him at least to agree to mount Roundup, an invasion of France in the spring of 1943. However, F.D.R. ignored the JCS, backed the British position and instructed Marshall and King to fly to London in late July and agree to Operation Torch, a British plan to invade North Africa in November. Churchill's preference for a grand strategy of dispersion and Roosevelt's vacillation thus condemned the Allies to wasteful, peripheral operations in the Mediterranean for two years. It unwittingly allowed the Soviets so to improve their position on the Eastern Front that they were ready to overrun Central Europe in 1944 when the Americans finally invaded France, and it gave the Germans at least twenty-four months to construct the formidable defences of Normandy.

The hasty Allied decision in late July 1942 to invade French North Africa in the autumn left little time to plan the complex operation. Because relations between Britain and Vichy France were acidic, Churchill wanted British troops to land under American command, and General Marshall readily agreed to King's suggestion that General Dwight D. Eisenhower, Marshall's deputy, become Supreme Commander of Operation Torch. Eisenhower then surprised King and others by naming British officers to command his air, ground and naval components. Admiral Andrew B. Cunningham [*q.v.*], whom King considered to be the Royal Navy's most able leader, became the overall Allied naval commander for Torch. Although King admired Cunningham, he disliked this arrangement, but the sea role in Torch was mostly confined to Admiral Hewitt's [*q.v.*] Western Naval Task Force which, entirely under American command, landed General George Patton's army on Morocco's coast in November 1942.

Roosevelt, Churchill and the Anglo-American CCS met at the Casablanca Conference in January 1943 to decide what to do in the European theatre after General Eisenhower's forces had evicted the Axis armies from Tripoli. Their talks set Britain's preference for a peripheral grand strategy in the Mediterranean against the American advocacy of strategic concentration and a cross-Channel invasion of France. Both Allies agreed to an increase in Lend-Lease assistance to support the Soviets, who announced that they intended to mount a counter-offensive in the summer, after they had reduced the Germans at Stalingrad. The Allies also formulated plans to conduct a Combined Bomber Offensive against German industries and cities. They were still sharply divided about where and when their armies should re-enter Europe, however. United in their opposition to Operation Roundup, the British wanted to overrun Sicily, cross the Strait of Messina and advance up the Italian peninsula to Rome and beyond to the Po Valley. This would employ forces already established in the Mediterranean, open up that sea to British shipping, drive Italy from the war and encourage the neutral Turks to turn against Germany.

King disliked Britain's Italian strategy, but he and Marshall were at odds over an alternative. Italy was a defender's paradise and an invader's nightmare, King observed; but F.D.R. was quite willing to support Churchill's position. King did not believe the shipping was available to transport Eisenhower's armies from North Africa to England. He did believe that even if it could be found, Churchill, regardless of his protestations of good faith, would never agree to Roundup in 1943. All this meant no firm decision was reached at Casablanca, but King knew when he flew back to Washington that the Americans were destined to be anchored in the Mediterranean for at least another year. Thus Germany's U-boat bases on the Bay of Biscay were immune for the time being from a landward attack and the Battle of the Atlantic again assumed an unnecessarily large role in Allied grand strategy. As a result, King and Pound persuaded their colleagues to agree to a declaration at Casablanca that 'the defeat of the U-boat must remain a first charge on the resources of the United Nations'.

The renewal of the Battle of the Atlantic in early 1943 resulted from the Allied decision to invade North Africa the previous year and the failure of the Allied air forces to provide the navies with enough bombers to establish effective air escorts to transatlantic convoys south of Greenland. King warned F.D.R. in late 1942 that losses to the transatlantic Lend-Lease convoys would increase if he accepted Churchill's plan to land in North Africa. 'The U.S., by employing every available escort vessel in the Atlantic, could not establish a new escort route without either serious effect on the movement of ships to the U.K. and elsewhere in the Atlantic or the transfer of escorting ships from the Pacific,' King cautioned. Paradoxically, Churchill's success in persuading Roosevelt to overrule the JCS and undertake Operation Torch directly resulted in reduced imports of American foodstuffs and other war goods to Britain in 1943. Torch would 'require the use of naval escorts now engaged in escorting vessels to outlying stations all over the world. The result of our thinning out of resources of this kind may bring disaster in the North Atlantic,' King declared just before Eisenhower's army landed.

The means to overcome the U-boat were already in hand, however. For one thing, by January 1943 the Americans alone were building new cargo ships faster than the Axis could sink existing ones. During the first three months of that year – allegedly the most critical period in the Battle of the Atlantic – American shipyards constructed 1.5 million tons of shipping more than the Axis sank. And, during each subsequent quarter for the rest of the war, this figure never fell below 2 million tons. This good news was offset by a nearly disastrous decision made by F.D.R. to allocate a large percentage of American shipping to the British import programme.

When the British created the first North Atlantic convoys in 1941, they simultaneously established a six-day convoy cycle which thereafter formed the basis for a large number of their vital production and rationing schedules. In the autumn of 1942, various calls on both Allied fleets and the need to provide escorts for the Torch invasion forces moved King to request Roosevelt's insistence that Churchill should agree to stretch out the convoy cycle to seven days. Churchill did agree to this disruptive step, but only after F.D.R. had promised to increase shipping allocations to Britain under Lend-Lease in 1943. King protested so loudly against this decision that F.D.R. was forced to name an *ad hoc* civilian commission (headed by his closest adviser, Harry Hopkins) to deal with the problem, thus taking it out of the hands of the JCS. However, Hopkins conceded every British point and agreed to transfer roughly twenty freighters to them each month from new American ship construction. King was furious with this result; it threatened to exhaust American shipping in short order and worse – unless U-boat losses could somehow be reduced, it would paralyse operations in the Pacific and elsewhere.

Once the Interlocking Convoy System was in place, King's next priority was to strengthen the individual Atlantic Fleet ocean escort groups and then increase their overall number. The Two-Ocean Navy Act authorized the building of hundreds of 110-foot SC coastal subchasers and 180-foot PC ocean-going patrol escort craft. These enormously successful mass-production shipbuilding programmes had already begun to meet the needs for more escort groups in the Gulf and Caribbean and Eastern Sea Frontiers. Thus King could divide new destroyer and minelayer construction between the Atlantic and Pacific Fleets, and allow Ingersoll in early 1943 to organize several new Atlantic Fleet ocean escort groups. Moreover, the first of nearly 500 destroyer escorts, which became the mainstay of the Allied ocean escort groups after 1943, entered the Atlantic Fleet in December 1942. Despite King's protests, F.D.R. had delayed destroyer escort production in early 1942 in favour of the First Landing Craft Programme. This decision significantly retarded the expansion of the ocean escort groups, since the two building programmes competed directly with one another for tools, yard space, machines, steel and various common parts such as valves. After the British had torpedoed the Sledgehammer and Roundup plans, King convinced Roosevelt to suspend the First Landing Craft Programme temporarily, in favour of destroyer escort construction. Although King transferred many of these vessels to the Royal Navy and sent some of them into the Pacific, the greatest number were dedicated to escort operations in the Atlantic.

Drawing on the experience of the Atlantic Fleet and the Eastern Sea Frontier, King also reasoned that land-based patrol planes or carrier-based escort aircraft would provide an essential second layer of protection to the transatlantic convoys. Owing to extraordinary increases in American military aircraft production, the US Navy was able not only to transfer a large number of patrol bombers and other types to the Royal Navy under Lend-Lease, but also to strengthen the Eastern, Gulf and Caribbean Sea Frontiers patrol wings. In addition, the marriage of radar to aircraft had made the anti-submarine patrol bomber an especially lethal foe of the U-boat.

By early 1943, transatlantic merchant convoys enjoyed some form of Allied air protection everywhere along the great circle route – except for one segment, known as the Greenland Air Gap. American PBY Catalinas based in Newfoundland had an operational range of 900 miles; so did Royal Air Force Coastal Command B-24 Liberators operating from the British Isles. Less capable patrol bombers could fly south about 500 miles from their bases in Greenland and Iceland. Beyond these patrol boundaries, however, lay a considerable area of the mid-Atlantic where the U-boats now concentrated. The Greenland Air Gap existed owing to the reluctance of the army air force to allow the navy to operate long-range, land-based bombers. The Royal Air Force adopted a parallel stance with respect to the Royal Navy. Only in June 1942, when the crisis in the Eastern Sea Frontier had come and gone, was King able to persuade General Marshall to instruct the 1st Bomber Command on the Atlantic Coast to respond promptly to requests from Andrews to undertake patrol missions. And it was not until March 1943 that King got Marshall and the British to divert long-range bombers to Britain's Coastal Command and the Atlantic Fleet's Patrol Force.

An additional problem in co-ordinating Allied response to Dönitz's mid-Atlantic campaign was the overly complex multi-national command structure that evolved after the 1941 Argentia Conference. Four separate naval commands shared responsibility for North Atlantic ocean escort operations: the Eastern Sea Frontier, the Canadian Coastal and Newfoundland Forces, the American Iceland Task Force and the British Western Approaches. Ingersoll's Atlantic Fleet directed most escort operations in the Central Atlantic, while Admiral Ingram's Brazil-based Fourth Fleet provided escorts for the South Atlantic convoys. Ingersoll was also responsible for the defence of all American troop convoys. Organizing and routeing the transatlantic convoys was the responsibility of Rear Admiral M. K. Metcalf, the director of Convoy and Routeing, an office that King brought under the Cominch staff in June 1942.

In mid-March 1943, King sensed that the Allies were on the verge of a great victory. The defeat of the U-boat was in fact almost at hand. Losses were high that month, but the Germans sank a large percentage of these vessels in the Greenland Air Gap where they concentrated an unexpectedly large number of U-boats. They simply could not sustain such a tempo of operations. The Allies had found evasive routeing operations especially difficult to conduct during March, owing to the high number of escorts under repair that month. This considerably diminished the strength of the ocean escort groups. King and Pound determined that this would not recur for the rest of the war. Moreover, the adoption of a new method of underway refuelling developed by the Atlantic Fleet was incomplete since there were not enough oilers to provide at least one for each ocean escort group. The situation eased when the British at long last shut down the costly north Russia convoys and thereby released nearly thirty cruisers and destroyers for the North Atlantic. The addition of more oilers to the ocean escort groups in April also allowed King and Pound to lessen their dependence on the great circle route, send some convoys further north, and increase the flexibility of evasive routeing operations. At this time, they also reached an agreement on the need to increase the size of each convoy.

The tide of the Battle of the Atlantic turned at the end of March when the Germans began to lose large numbers of U-boats. Attrition, the bearing beam of the German strategy of tonnage warfare, worked thereafter in the Allies' favour and demonstrated in short order just how feeble the entire German naval effort really was. Other factors were also in play. King knew that the Canadians wanted to withdraw their Newfoundland Force from the US Navy's Iceland Command, and there was a general agreement that an overhaul of the command arrangements was long overdue. Shifting escort responsibilities for each convoy in mid-ocean was awkward, time-consuming and confusing, not only to the convoy commodores, the masters of the merchantmen and the ocean escort group commanders, but also to the fleet commanders at sea and the various supervising commands ashore. From the British had come a proposal in September 1942 put forward by Coastal Command to create a 'single supreme control for the whole anti-U-boat war' to overcome 'the separate and often conflicting policies of the British, Canadian, and American naval and air authorities'.

King convened the March 1943 Atlantic Convoy Conference in Washington to address all of these problems at the same time. After King had bluntly dismissed the frightful concept of a unified Atlantic naval command, the conferees decided to reorganize their areas of operation. King agreed to withdraw the Atlantic Fleet's ocean escort groups from the North Atlantic convoys, leaving the British in charge of these escort operations and the Canadians in control of their own national naval forces. In return, King agreed that Admiral Ingersoll would assume responsibility for all Central Atlantic convoys and for the defence of most shipping in the Caribbean and the South Atlantic. Another decision to enlarge the size of each convoy to sixty or more ships resulted in the more rapid movement of Lend-Lease goods across the Atlantic without incurring the risk of a corresponding increase in freighter or tanker tonnage. This restructuring of the areas of operation and the reduced incidence of operating ocean escort groups with mixed national forces clearly improved the defences of the Allied shipping effort.

King also moved to streamline the Americans' anti-U-boat command by creating the Tenth Fleet. On 6 April 1943, he brought all ocean escort and anti-submarine warfare operations under his immediate control, and on 20 May he established the Tenth Fleet headquarters next door to the Cominch staff in Main Navy. Although he named himself to command this new organization, daily operations were directed by the Tenth Fleet's Chief of Staff, Rear Admiral 'Frog' Low. King believed that this arrangement called for the creation of a new command which had access to Ultra, knowledge of the availability of escorts and the whereabouts of all convoys and the authority to issue routeing orders to any element in the Central Atlantic without first getting approval for those orders from another chain of command.

The creation of the Tenth Fleet proved to be important not only to the prosecution of a more vigorous evasive routeing strategy, but also because King intended to undertake aggressive anti-submarine operations with the newly created hunter-killer *Card* and *Bogue* escort carrier formations. Ready in 1942 but occupied by the senseless North African campaign, these light carriers sprang into action in early 1943 against the U-boats and by the summer were creating havoc with Germany's strategy. King's destroyer escort programme now bore fruit – 500 DES were eventually constructed and entered the American fleet or were given to the Royal Navy – and the combination of more escorts, more powerful escorts, air coverage and offensive anti-submarine operations drove the U-boats from one hunting ground to another. The Germans abandoned the tonnage warfare strategy in 1944 and turned to guerrilla-warfare-at-sea in an attempt to obstruct Overlord, but this too failed. The Battle of the Atlantic, never the crisis that the British portrayed it to be, was unnecessarily prolonged as a result of Churchill's refusal to accept the Americans' strategy of concentration.

The defeat of the U-boat relieved the strain on Allied shipping in 1943, but King knew that only a cross-Channel invasion would bring Hitler to book. At the January 1943 Casablanca Conference, the British persuaded the Americans to continue operations in the Mediterranean for the rest of the year on the understanding that the Americans would undertake a new offensive in the Pacific. Faced with a choice of invading Sardinia or Sicily, the CCS tentatively settled on Sicily, according to King, 'because the occupation of Sicily would at the enemy's expense furnish the Allies with a useful air base at a narrow point in the Mediterranean' and 'raised the possibility of eliminating Italy from the war'. In the largest amphibious operation of the war, Admiral Hewitt's Eighth Fleet and a British task force lifted seven Allied divisions on to Sicily in August, but more of the Germans had already escaped across the straits to the Calabrian Peninsula. Churchill had then persuaded Marshall to send Eisenhower on to the Italian boot, and Hewitt's fleet lifted the newly established Fifth Army on to the beaches at Salerno. As King predicted, progress up the peninsula was slow. Heavy casualties, poor weather, wretched generalship and a bungled amphibious landing at Anzio in January 1944 led to a stalled Italian campaign that did not reach Rome until June. King was thoroughly disgusted. Italy now threatened Overlord, the codename for a 1944 cross-Channel operation. 'The British have no intention of executing a cross-channel operation unless it is a walk-over,' Admiral Cooke observed. King was willing to abandon the cross-Channel strategy at one point, on the basis that the British were merely using it as a magnet for Lend-Lease but would always find grounds to veto the actual crossing. Marshall was less despairing, and the two decided to try once again at the upcoming Big Three summit at Teheran.

At the November 1943 Teheran Conference, F.D.R. and the JCS learned for the first time that the Soviets did not believe that they could defeat Germany unless the Allies landed in northern France. Churchill and Roosevelt were chided by Stalin for not establishing a second front earlier in the war. 'It became apparent', King wrote, 'that Stalin had no real understanding of the magnitude of operations that would be involved in crossing the English Channel. Seemingly, he thought it would be very much like crossing a large river, which the Russians had done many times.' Stalin insisted 'on a fixed, early date, Churchill [was] asking for delay, and the President [was] favorably inclined toward the Soviet proposal'. In short, Russia's weakened condition led F.D.R., at long last, to support his own military leaders, assert America's primacy in the Grand Alliance and demand that the British agree to Overlord in 1944.

Once the Allies agreed to invade France, King's attention turned towards making the operation succeed. To command the American naval task force, he appointed Rear Admiral Alan G. Kirk, a veteran of several shore-to-shore landings. Admiral Stark's Twelfth Fleet supplied the operations logistic support. King also provided Overlord with a large battleship–cruiser bombardment group, and ordered that an extra month's production of LSTs be shipped to Europe to ensure that the landing forces had enough lift. Ten days after D-Day, King and Marshall arrived in London, crossed to France with Churchill and visited the front lines. King inspected the punctured Atlantic Wall – defences which had not even existed in 1942 when he and Marshall had first agreed to land on Normandy's beaches. By delaying for two years, and by shipping Lend-Lease material to the Soviets without demanding reciprocal political concessions, Roosevelt and Churchill gave the Red Army the time and the means to occupy Eastern and Central Europe at the end of the war. King was never comfortable with America's wartime alliance with Stalin, but he failed entirely to articulate his concerns until the war was almost over.

Owing to Britain's demand for a Mediterranean diversion in 1943, King turned to the Pacific that year and prepared for an all-out offensive. Admiral Thomas Kinkaid's North Pacific Force evicted the enemy from Attu and reoccupied Kiska, while Halsey marched up the Solomons. King and Marshall had quarrelled over uniting the Pacific command in 1942, with King demanding that Nimitz be given the billet and Marshall holding out for MacArthur, although Marshall knew full well that MacArthur was deranged. The resulting deadlock left MacArthur in command of the South-West Pacific theatre when Halsey's offensive moved into the Upper Solomons and fell within MacArthur's fief. Since King refused to place attack carriers under MacArthur's command, however, Halsey relied on borrowed Pacific Fleet carriers and land-based navy air forces to conduct a series of small amphibious operations that led him in early 1944 to the end of the campaign at Empress

Augusta Bay. In 1943, King decided that Rabaul was too tough a nut to crack, and he persuaded Marshall to overrule MacArthur and insist that it be surrounded and reduced but not invaded. Nevertheless, Halsey broke the Bismarck barrier, and South Pacific air forces destroyed over 10,000 front-line enemy aircraft. As a result, when the Pacific Fleet moved into the Gilberts, the Japanese could not find air groups to operate with their carriers. MacArthur had worked his way very slowly – much too slowly, King observed acidly – along the northern New Guinea coast until, in the summer of 1944, his army was within 500 miles of Mindanao, the southernmost of the Philippine Islands.

'These actions . . . were part of the delaying strategy that characterized this phase of the war,' F.D.R. told Congress in 1943, when the strategic landscape was starting to change. King, unhappy with MacArthur's 'slow pace', wanted to curtail South and South-West Pacific operations before they became too expensive. On 29 November, he told a group of reporters (with whom he met throughout the war in secret to explain American strategy) that 'once the Japanese have been expelled from Rabaul' he did not 'think it desirable to press north from Australia into the Dutch East Indies'. The 'best idea', he continued, 'is to drive straight north from Rabaul, attacking Truk in the Carolines and Guam and Saipan in the Marianas', since this would 'cut off the whole Mandated archipelago from Japan and open the way to get back into the Philippines, which in turn would cut off the Dutch East Indies and make it impossible for the Japs to hang on there'.

At Casablanca, King had outlined to the ccs the results of over three decades of navy thinking about a Pacific war. Japan was vulnerable to attack from three sides. The northern route, via the Aleutians and Russia's Maritime Provinces, was too cold for year-round naval operations, and the use of Russian bases was complicated by the 1941 Neutrality Agreement between Moscow and Tokyo. When Stalin later suggested that the Pacific Fleet operate from Petropavlovsk, King rejected the offer owing to the bad weather. Although Halsey and MacArthur were inflicting tremendous attrition on Japan's forces in the South and South-West Pacific, King pointed out that the southern flank, leading from the Solomons and New Guinea to the Philippines, was the longest road to Japan. Owing to the large number of islands which the enemy could use for his land-based air forces, it was also the most dangerous for the fleet. On the other hand, the Central Pacific seemed to him quite attractive. Between Hawaii and the Philippines, or Hawaii and Japan, there were only four well-defended enemy bastions – the Gilberts and Marshalls, the Marianas, the Carolines and Formosa. Led by the new fast *Essex*-class carriers and the *North Carolina*-class fast battleships, the fleet was perfectly configured to isolate these archipelagos one by one, land Marines or army troops trained by the navy for amphibious operations, fend off an enemy air or naval counter-attack and establish new positions from which to prepare for the next operation. At the Trident Conference in May, the ccs finally agreed to this concept. Owing to MacArthur's slow progress in New Guinea, Marshall relented in June, and the JCS soon after ordered Nimitz to open up the new Central Pacific front late in 1943.

At the end of July 1943, King met Nimitz in San Francisco for one of the most important of all the bi-monthly conferences they held during the war. King announced that Arnold was backing the Central Pacific offensive, since the army air force could conduct long-range strategic bombing of Japan with its new B-29 Superfortresses from the Marianas. He 'stressed [to Nimitz] the necessity of keeping pressure on the Japanese', something King felt had been lacking in the South-West Pacific offensive. Nimitz was to 'start one operation before another ends', so as to unbalance the enemy. King agreed to Nimitz's plan to have Spruance's [*q.v.*] new Fifth Fleet re-enter the Central Pacific in November, when Admiral Turner's newly assembled Amphibious Force would overrun Tarawa and Makin in the Gilberts. Spruance would follow this with an invasion of the Marshalls in February 1944. From the start of the war, King had believed that China's army could be used to tie down Japanese forces on Asia's mainland, spread her resources thin and so reduce resistance in the Pacific to Nimitz's offensive. At the Quebec Conference in August he was pleased to approve a British plan for a Chinese invasion of northern Burma and a simultaneous British amphibious landing on the Arakan coast of the Bay of Bengal. However, at the Cairo Conference in November the Chinese appeared and Chiang Kai-shek announced that he would not undertake the Burma offensive unless the British agreed to the Arakan Plan. Churchill was cool to this, preferring instead to land on Sumatra, and the British Chiefs of Staff wanted to abandon the entire strategy. This approach was skilfully advanced by General Alan Brooke, who was in many ways King's only intellectual rival among the Allied High Command. At one meeting, observed General Joseph Stilwell, Chiang's American Chief of Staff, 'Brooke got nasty and King got good and mean. God, was he mad. I wish he had socked him!' Brooke held firm and the Burma operation was abandoned soon after. King, never happy with British policy, was so completely infuriated that, for over an hour, he was unable even to speak.

After flying from Egypt to Teheran, meeting Stalin and agreeing to invade France the following spring, the Allied leaders returned to Cairo for a final round of talks. There they hastily approved King's plan for Pacific operations in 1944. Truk in the Carolines, the main Japanese fleet base in the Pacific, would be taken in mid-July, the Marianas in October. In the meantime, MacArthur was to continue along the New Guinea coast to the Vogelkop Peninsula in August. King was astounded when the British, who had just pleaded lack of ships in refusing to land on the Arakan coast, now proposed to send a battleship–carrier task force into the Central Pacific to participate in the major drive against Japan. He opposed this for over a year. He disliked operating combined, multi-national naval forces, distrusted Britain's political motives behind the demand and took a dim view of the Royal Navy's operational skills. F.D.R. eventually forced him in 1944 to allow a small British carrier task group to operate with the Pacific Fleet, and, as King predicted, it was relatively ineffective. King was thereafter sensitive to any British interest in Pacific strategy, which was, he declared, 'a purely American affair', but the problem never arose.

The great Central Pacific offensive was already under way. Spruance entered the Gilberts in November 1943 and overran the Marshalls in February 1944, but with news of these victories King received word of other troubles. Cooke had accompanied Marshall on a trip to the South-West Pacific following the Cairo Conference, and reported back to King in Washington that MacArthur was now claiming that the move against the Carolines and Marianas would delay a landing in the Philippines. Nimitz appeared to agree, and said as much to MacArthur's Chief of Staff during a January 1944 conference at Pearl Harbor. King's reaction when he read the minutes of this important meeting was 'indignant dismay'. The 'idea of rolling up the Japanese along the New Guinea coast . . . and up through the Philippines to Luzon, as our major strategic concept, to the exclusion of the Central Pacific . . . is to me absurd', he told Nimitz. Ever accommodating, Nimitz sent to Washington Admiral Forrest Sherman, a fine strategist whom King greatly admired, but Sherman's reception at Main Navy was cool. King 'educated' him on strategy and Sherman, doing a quick about-face, launched into a debate with MacArthur's envoys over the merits of the Central Pacific. King feared that his carefully crafted Pacific strategy was now in total disarray. Marshall pleaded in vain for MacArthur to fly to Washington, but Nimitz arrived instead, disavowed the Pearl Harbor agreement and fully backed King's concept.

Events in the field changed the picture in Washington. In February, Admiral Marc Mitscher's Fast Carrier Task Force descended on Truk in a devastating raid which ended the island's usefulness as a Japanese fleet base. King decided to bypass Truk and the Carolines altogether, and he worried that Nimitz 'seriously contemplated taking Truk by assault'. Nimitz took the hint and replied with a plan to strike directly into the Marianas in mid-summer. King approved the plan, convinced Arnold to support it and pushed it through the JCS on 5 March. The Marines landed on Saipan on 15 June, and Spruance destroyed Japan's carrier- and land-based air forces in the Philippine Sea four days later. Although many of the Pacific Fleet's air admirals complained that Spruance had tied down the fast carriers to the invasion force, King was not unhappy with the wholly one-sided result. The Battle of the Philippine Sea was a blow that 'crippled Japanese naval aviation for the remainder of the war', he observed.

The conquest of the Marianas once again left Pacific strategy up in the air. Eager to return to the Philippines, MacArthur flew to Pearl Harbor in July to discuss his plans with Roosevelt and Nimitz. By this time, King had visited Hawaii and Saipan, talked with Spruance, Turner and Nimitz and settled on a plan (which Admiral Cooke had been advancing for nearly a year) to bypass the

Philippines and invade Formosa. King 'favored a direct attack on Formosa without reference to the Philippine Islands' on the ground that Formosa 'would dominate the sea lanes by which Japan received essential supplies of oil, rice, and other commodities from her recently conquered empire'. The island had several airfields from which the army air force could mount strategic bombing operations against Japan, and a protected anchorage from which the Pacific Fleet could stage a landing on either the China coast or the Japanese island of Kyushu, under the cover of army air force land-based fighters. However, Forrest Sherman, the best strategist in the Pacific theatre, believed that the Americans did not yet possess the resources to make such a bold move and argued that King's plan was 'ridiculous and so impossible'. King was resolute. 'If we get busy and set our minds to it,' he told his Pacific commanders, 'we could do a great deal to maintain the fleet in advanced bases.' Nimitz defended the Formosa case to F.D.R. and MacArthur, but soon after told King that he did not have enough army service troops to hold the island. Roosevelt, who expressed little interest in military operations during the last year of the war and seldom met with the JCS, had gone to Hawaii as part of his re-election campaign, and he played no role in the decision. Leahy, however, supported MacArthur on purely political grounds, and this was decisive. One frustrated member of King's staff approved of the Mindanao plan since MacArthur would 'be stuck down there slogging it out for the rest of the war'.

King reluctantly agreed to instruct Halsey's Third Fleet to support MacArthur's movement from the Vogelkop Peninsula through Morotai to southern Mindanao. This was scheduled to take place on 25 October. He also agreed to MacArthur's plan to invade Leyte on 20 December, but still hoped for a descent on Formosa rather than a costly, protracted move against Luzon. To reduce Japanese land-based air strength in the Philippines in preparation for the Mindanao landings, Halsey struck north-westward from the Palaus on 10 September, assuming tactical command of the Fast Carrier Force after a series of disputes with Mitscher over the conduct of air operations. 'We had found the central Philippines a hollow shell with weak defenses and skimpy facilities,' Halsey recorded, and this prompted him to propose to Nimitz and King that the invasion of Mindanao be scrapped in favour of a movement by MacArthur to Leyte on 20 October.

Halsey's error-ridden assessment of enemy air power compelled the JCS to re-examine the problem of Pacific strategy just at the moment at which they were settling down for another major Anglo-American summit conference at Quebec. Both Nimitz and MacArthur agreed with Halsey, perhaps in part because neither of them now wanted to bypass Luzon. Both realized that the acceleration of the Philippine campaign would to a great extent undermine King's position on this issue. In the event, once he and Marshall had agreed to revise their directive to their Pacific commanders concerning the Leyte operation, King admitted that he could not hold out alone against an invasion of Luzon. On 3 October he reached a compromise with Marshall, under which MacArthur was to invade Luzon on 20 December and Nimitz was to occupy the Bonins and the Ryukyus early in 1945. Marshall and King clearly believed that MacArthur intended only to liberate key areas of Leyte and Luzon, and they never suspected that he planned to attempt to evict the Japanese from all of the Philippine Islands.

The American principals clearly understood the command arrangements for the Leyte invasion, but the hasty decision to bypass Mindanao and bring forward the date of the landing in the Central Philippines left little time for consultations among the various ground, naval and air staffs. Since King and Marshall could not agree on an overall commander for the Pacific, and because King would not put MacArthur in command of the Fast Carrier Force, the JCS told Nimitz to assign Halsey to support the landings. These were to be conducted under MacArthur's command by Vice Admiral Thomas Kinkaid's Seventh Fleet. One unintended effect of these decisions was to strip Halsey of the Third Fleet and leave him with only Mitscher's four task groups Fast Carrier Force and Vice Admiral Willis Lee's line of six fast battleships and eight heavy cruisers. Nimitz told Halsey that 'in case opportunity for destruction of major portion of enemy fleet is offered or can be created, such destruction becomes the primary task'. Neither King nor Nimitz wanted Halsey to emulate Spruance's tactical conservatism at the Battle of the Philippine Sea, when the relative strength of the opposing fleets had been somewhat less disproportionate. In the event, Kinkaid landed MacArthur's troops on Leyte. Soon after he and Halsey turned back three enemy naval thrusts against his beachhead; but Halsey was decoyed to the north to sink a handful of worthless Japanese carriers and, in so doing, exposed the landing for several hours. At first, King believed that Halsey alone had erred, but he later learned that, as in most complex operations, others were also to blame. King did not reprimand admirals who fought their ships, and both Halsey and Kinkaid were fighters. Moreover, the action in Leyte Gulf ended in an extraordinary American triumph.

The October 1944 compromise between King and Marshall – which allowed MacArthur to invade Leyte and Luzon – called for the Pacific Fleet to invade the Bonin group around January 1945 and the Ryukyus in March. Since this would outflank Japan's air forces on Formosa, Admiral King agreed to abandon his plan against that island. MacArthur's slow progress in the Philippines forced Nimitz to postpone the Bonins campaign for several weeks, however. Soon after the invasion of Leyte Gulf, King toyed with the idea of allowing Halsey to keep command of the Fast Carrier Force while placing Spruance in command of the overall invasion, but he dropped this scheme as unworkable and instead told Spruance to relieve Halsey at Ulithi at the end of January 1945. In February, Spruance directed the invasion of Iwo Jima, although the resistance there was so stiff that Nimitz persuaded King to cancel taking Miyako Jima so that the Pacific Fleet could prepare for the descent on the Ryukyus. The Okinawa campaign began on 1 April, but the heroic Japanese defence of that island meant that instead of overrunning it within a month Okinawa was not secure until June. King was now doubly impressed by the ferocity of Japan's defences, and he was more than ever convinced that invading the home islands would be very costly.

Halsey relieved Spruance during the Okinawa campaign in April, but for the second time in a row he ran the fleet across the path of a typhoon which damaged several ships and destroyed seventy-six planes. Vice Admiral John Hoover headed a court of inquiry which condemned Halsey's 'ineptness' in dealing with the typhoon, but King quietly laid aside Hoover's recommendation that Halsey be relieved. Halsey had saved the South Pacific campaign, and King refused to blacken his reputation. King also assured Admiral McCain, a talented fighter, that he would not be sent ashore. King knew that he would need Halsey and McCain for the biggest operation of the war – the invasion of Japan.

While the battle for Okinawa raged in the Pacific, victory came in Europe. After F.D.R.'s re-election in November 1944, the President had arranged for a second summit with Stalin and Churchill at Yalta in January of the following year. 'The major business . . . was done at the plenary meetings between the heads of state,' King recalled, and neither he nor General Marshall attended these sessions. The most pressing issue at the summit, however, concerned Soviet participation in the war against Japan, an issue with which the JCS were deeply involved. The Soviets, neutral in the Asian war, had told Secretary of State Hull at the Moscow Conference in October 1943 that Russia would declare war against Japan soon after Germany surrendered. King and Marshall believed their support was necessary, but how to use it created problems. Stalin offered the use of Petropavlovsk on the Kamchatka Peninsula as an advance naval base for the Pacific Fleet, but King did not take this proposal seriously since the port's primitive facility was closed by ice from November to May.

King and Marshall decided that it was best for the Red Army to tie down the large Japanese army then occupying China, so that the Americans could invade Japan, and advised F.D.R. that they preferred 'Russian entry at the earliest possible date . . . and are prepared to offer the maximum support possible without prejudice to our main effort against Japan'. MacArthur agreed that American 'strength should be reserved for use in the Japanese mainland, and that this could not be done without the assurance that the Japanese would be heavily engaged by the Russians in Manchuria'. To tempt Stalin into declaring war on Japan, F.D.R. offered the Soviets territorial concessions in China and Lend-Lease supplies to equip thirty Red Army divisions. Roosevelt had already been presented with evidence that Stalin intended to enter the Far Eastern war regardless of the outcome of his dealings with the West, however, and King felt that the other Chiefs agreed with his assessment that the 'price asked [by the Russians] was far too high'. He openly criticized the Yalta agreements in June.

King was saddened by F.D.R.'s death one month before the surrender of

Germany and Italy. He and Roosevelt had worked well together, although King thoroughly distrusted F.D.R.'s politics. The new President, Harry S. Truman, thought King to be a 'martinet' and seldom sought his advice. Following the collapse of resistance on Okinawa, the JCS faced the problem of forcing Japan to surrender. King favoured landing on the China coast, in the Chusan–Ningpo area, establishing a fleet base and staging an invasion of Japan from there. MacArthur was 'particularly emphatic against invading Japan', and spent the spring and summer clearing out the Philippines and preparing instead to invade Borneo. Nimitz vacillated between invading Japan and the China coast plan. Marshall wanted to jump directly from Guam and the Philippines to Kyushu, the southernmost Japanese island. For reasons that are not altogether clear, King abandoned the Chusan–Ningpo plan and threw his support behind Operation Olympic, the army's plan to invade Kyushu. King never claimed that a naval blockade or strategic bombing would force Japan to surrender, but he did stress the need to continue to tighten the noose around the home islands to reduce opposition to the Kyushu landings. Marshall, on the other hand, wanted to devote all American resources in the western Pacific first to the Kyushu operation, then to the invasion of Honshu, codenamed Coronet. 'Even if we wished to besiege Japan for a year or a year and a half, the capture of Kyushu would be essential,' explained James Forrestal, the new Secretary of the Navy.

Alerted to the possibility of building an atomic bomb by Albert Einstein in 1939, F.D.R. was irresponsibly slow to react, appointing a series of powerless interim committees which evolved at a glacial pace into the civilian Office of Scientific Research and Development under Massachusetts Institute of Technology Vice-President Vannevar Bush in June 1941. Bush saw OSRD as the vehicle through which he could exert his own influence over issues of military and naval policy and strategy, but he found himself locking horns with King. Bush was 'very much put out over the fact that he is not called in by King to discuss the grand strategy', recalled Admiral Julius A. Furer, who befriended both men. The navy had a much advanced atomic project when the war began, but the King–Bush feud led Bush to convince F.D.R. to assign the work to the army Corps of Engineers. Work did not get under way until late in the autumn of 1942. King had Admiral Cooke follow the project closely, and he provided the Manhattan project with considerable navy assistance in building the Oak Ridge facility.

Marshall and King could not afford to risk taking the bomb into account in their preliminary planning for the invasion of Japan. Indeed, before they even took up the issue of the invasion, they had to negotiate a new directive after liberation of the Philippines to sort out their respective commands for the final phase of the Pacific War. Marshall demanded that MacArthur be given overall charge of the Pacific theatre, while King again insisted that Admiral Nimitz rightly deserved this honour. And MacArthur surprised everyone by announcing: 'I do not recommend a single unified command for the Pacific.'

Nevertheless, the old theatre boundaries no longer made any sense, so King and Marshall agreed on 3 April that Nimitz would turn over all army forces to MacArthur, who would in turn transfer to Nimitz command of the Seventh Fleet and those Marine divisions still in the South-West Pacific. For the invasion of Japan, King allowed Marshall to designate MacArthur as the supreme commander, but Marshall agreed that Nimitz, as the overall naval and amphibious commander, could appeal any of MacArthur's decisions to the JCS. King's purpose was to prevent MacArthur from interfering with the naval aspect of the invasion. The quarrelsome but surprisingly successful system of divided command that drove the army and navy across the Pacific was to be maintained until Japan capitulated. King chose Spruance to plan and conduct Operation Olympic, the Kyushu invasion, and told Admiral Halsey to prepare his Third Fleet staff to direct the far larger and more daunting Operation Coronet, the invasion of Honshu.

As late as 17 June 1945, Truman was unaware that this compromise between King and Marshall had been reached. 'I have to decide Japanese strategy,' he wrote in his diary that night. 'Shall we invade Japan proper or shall we bomb and blockade?' King and Marshall, armed with an agreement on Olympic, if not Coronet, met with Truman at the White House the next day. Gas had been ruled out, and Lieutenant-General Ira Eaker, who represented the army air force, admitted that bombing alone would not compel the Japanese to surrender. Marshall explained the Kyushu invasion plan, ably supported by King, who told Truman that he 'was impressed with the strategic location of Kyushu, which he considered the key to the success of any siege operation' of Honshu. 'We should do Kyushu now,' King told Truman, 'after which there would be time to judge the effect of possible operations by the Russians and the Chinese.' Truman agreed, but before adjourning the meeting asked what the JCS proposed to do with the atomic bomb. A War Department targeting committee had already proposed to bomb the cities of Hiroshima, Nagasaki and Niigata. If the bomb was available, Marshall said, it should be used. Not only did King agree with Marshall, but when a suggestion was raised to demonstrate the weapon against an offshore island King joined Marshall in killing the scheme.

King had little to do with the final arrangements for dropping the bomb, other than to arrange for the heavy cruiser *Indianapolis* to carry the weapons from San Francisco to Tinian. When Truman learned at the Big Three summit at Potsdam in mid-July that the first bomb test had worked, he issued an operational order and, with Churchill, broadcast the Potsdam Declaration which called upon Japan to surrender. Since Tokyo did not respond, the bombing went ahead on schedule. Marshall and King intended the atomic bombing of Japan to appear to the Cabinet in Tokyo as a continuation of the current conventional bombing campaign and to lead the Japanese to the erroneous conclusion that the United States possessed a large stockpile of these fearsome weapons. On 6 August, Hiroshima was bombed and three days later a second atomic bomb was exploded over Nagasaki. Russia declared war on Japan that morning and the Red Army invaded Manchuria. The political shock of these events in Tokyo was overpowering – and, in Washington, altogether unexpected. On 11 August, King broadcast an historic message to the Pacific Fleet at Pearl Harbor: 'This is a peace warning.' On 2 September 1945, the battleship *Missouri*, anchored in Tokyo Bay, was the scene of Japan's surrender. That day found King at his desk in Main Navy.

By act of Congress in 1944, King was made a five-star fleet admiral on the Active List. He was never retired from the navy. In December 1945, he consolidated Cominch and CNO and turned the job over to Nimitz, his hand-picked successor, who promptly abandoned Main Navy for the army's new Pentagon building, something King had stoutly refused to do. King kept an office in the Pentagon, but he was unwanted and frustrated. The navy was his whole life, and both his career and his life were now coming to an end. He suffered a massive brain haemorrhage in 1947, but when the navy was threatened by Truman's unification plan the following year King went up to Capitol Hill to defend his service. 'Any step not good for the navy is not good for the nation,' he told Congress, and they listened. His memoirs, written with the help of a friend, came out in 1950. To this day they remain the best autobiography of an American in the High Command in World War Two. He was weighted down with honours, including a special gold medal struck by act of Congress and an honorary degree from Oxford.

King spent his last summers at the Portsmouth Naval Hospital and his winters in Washington, surrounded by friends, family and admirers. On 25 June 1956 his heart gave out and he lapsed into a coma. His only son, Commander Ernest J. King Jr, was at his side when he died the next morning, aged seventy-seven. After a ceremony in the National Cathedral, the body was placed on a horse-drawn caisson and taken down Constitution Avenue to the Capitol Rotunda to lie in state, and later laid at rest at his beloved Naval Academy.

4

Admiral of the Fleet

Isoroku Yamamoto

Commander-in-Chief Combined Fleet
Imperial Japanese Navy

1884–1943

by
Stephen Howarth

ISOROKU Yamamoto, born 4 April 1884 (sixteenth year of the Meiji era), near Nagaoka on Honshu, Japan's main 'island, son of a schoolmaster of samurai descent. Family name at birth: Takano. Graduated seventh in his class at Etajima Naval Academy, 1903; as an ensign, served in the cruiser Nisshin *during the Battle of Tsushima (27–28 May 1905) and was wounded in the right leg, also losing two fingers from his left hand. Adopted into the sonless Yamamoto family in 1914 at age thirty and took the family name. Languages officer at Harvard, 1917–19: instructor and later executive officer at Naval Air College, Kasumigaura, 1921–3. Inspection tour of USA, 1923–4; Naval Attaché in Washington DC, 1925–7. As captain, member of Japan's delegation to 1930 London Naval Conference. Promoted thereafter to rear admiral and became commander of IJN's First Air Fleet. As vice admiral (1934), senior member of Japanese delegation in London for talks preparatory to 1936 Naval Conference, where he gave the necessary two years' formal notice that Japan would withdraw from existing Naval Limitation treaties. Vice-Minister of the Navy, 1937. Opposed Japan's alignment with Germany and Italy, 1938. Commander-in-Chief Combined Fleet, August 1939. Throughout 1940 opposed Japan's entry into war. Outlined proposal for attack on Pearl Harbor, 1 February 1941.*

It seemed it could hardly have gone better. Every report was confirmed by the next until the overall picture could not be denied: under the tactical leadership of Vice Admiral Chuichi Nagumo [*q.v.*], the plan conceived and developed by the Imperial Navy's Commander-in-Chief, Admiral Isoroku Yamamoto, had been carried through without a hitch. On Sunday, 7 December 1941, surprise had been absolute, and after the double assault by aircraft from Nagumo's carriers, many of the US Navy's major vessels had been left blazing uncontrollably and sinking at their moorings in Pearl Harbor. Opened on Japanese initiative, the Pacific War had commenced with an outstanding Japanese naval victory.

It was a day to remember, and one which invigorated the entire Imperial Navy – suddenly every officer, confident of a short victorious war and fearful of being left out, was lobbying for a sea appointment. From another point of view, it was instead a day never to be forgotten – 'a date', in President Roosevelt's widely quoted phrase, 'that will live in infamy' – and, for Americans, Yamamoto's name became one spoken only with the deepest loathing. The horror and the shame of Pearl Harbor allowed no other reaction, and as the known architect of the attack Yamamoto was the obvious focus of America's hatred, an individual personification of Japanese treachery.

Yet, though he was not alone, he was one of the few Japanese who opposed what one Western ambassador called 'Japan's funeral march of aggression'. And with the news of his victory in hand, he remained gravely uncertain. 'This war will give us much trouble in the future,' he wrote to a friend. 'The fact that we have had a small success at Pearl Harbor is nothing. The fact that we have succeeded so easily has pleased people. . . . People should think things over and realize how serious the situation is.'

From his appointment in 1939 to his death in 1943, Yamamoto's actions as Commander-in-Chief of the Imperial Navy can be summarized in two sentences. Firstly, using every possible resource, he displayed a determined opposition to Japan's entry into the war. Secondly, when war became inevitable, he displayed an equally determined application of every possible resource to the war's successful prosecution.

This may sound rather like the idea behind the song, popular in nineteenth-century British music-halls, which included the lines: 'We don't want to fight, but, by jingo, if we do,/We've got the ships, we've got the men, we've got the money too.' However, it was that song which brought the word 'jingoism' – unrealistic and overblown patriotism – into the English language; and in 1940–1 the problem facing Admiral Yamamoto was Japanese jingoism. He was as patriotic as the next man, but he was also a realist, well aware, from his experiences abroad, of Japan's industrial weakness relative to Britain and (more importantly) to America. Opposing Japan's entry into the war was the act of a practical patriot; but in pre-Pearl Japan it could be, and was, interpreted as cowardly, while in post-Pearl America it was for many years forgotten or ignored.

Yamamoto was killed less than eighteen months after the assault on Pearl. His wartime career was therefore the shortest by far of all the greatest naval leaders of World War Two; yet because of Pearl it was also the one with the most individual consequence. With most of the other naval leaders of the time, it is appropriate to concentrate on their actual war careers between 1939 and 1945; their cultures and motives require little explanation. Japan in general and Yamamoto in particular are somewhat different. His pivotal personal role makes it worth studying not only his brief life in the huge war he helped begin, but also something of the history of his nation and its navy. Pre-Pearl Japan, in the 1930s until 1941, was probably a more confused society than it had ever been before. Some grasp of the long background to this confusion is essential if Yamamoto's actions and motives in the Pacific War are to be properly understood; and fortunately it can be expressed fairly simply.

Japan in 1941 was simultaneously one of the oldest and youngest nations in the world. The legendary founder of Yamato, ancient Japan, was Ninigi, grandson of the sun; in 660 BC, his grandson Jimmu became the first Emperor of Yamato. Hirohito was the 125th Emperor in direct line of descent. Yet it was only in 1868, under Hirohito's grandfather Meiji (whose name meant 'Enlightened Rule'), that Japan began to emerge from medievalism. When it did so, the nation's material progress was astonishingly fast – particularly in naval matters. Before 1868 Japan had possessed no armed fleet at all; by 1905, its Imperial Navy was the third most powerful navy in the world. With this force it had already defeated two of the world's largest empires, China and Russia, and had become the respected ally of Britain, greatest of the Great Powers. As a British ally, Japan's limited participation in World War One brought the nation disproportionate benefits – in particular, the acquisition of ex-German island groups (the Marianas, Carolines and Marshalls), which, dotting the Pacific between Japan, New Guinea and Hawaii, were of enormous strategic value.

During the early 1920s, three key naval events contributed towards a growing climate of mistrust between Japan and the other victor nations of World War One. Firstly, the white Pacific nations (particularly Australia, and to a lesser extent America) were worried by Japan's retention of the ex-German islands. Secondly, in post-war international naval disarmament talks, the '5:5:3' ratio was agreed: Britain's Royal Navy and the US Navy would be equal in size, but the Imperial Navy was limited to 60 per cent of either of the others – which seemed to many Japanese to be a deliberate insult. Thirdly, America's price for the agreement was the ending of the 1902 Anglo-Japanese Alliance. This, Britain's first full alliance with anyone for a century, had marked Japan's meteoric rise into the exclusive club of Great Powers, and was highly valued by the Japanese, if only as a symbol. To them, its abrogation by the British seemed to be confirmation that they were still viewed as a second-class nation.

On 30 May 1934, a fourth critical naval event took place: the death of Admiral Heihachiro Togo, who in 1905 had led the Imperial Navy to its annihilating victory over the Russian fleet at Tsushima. Yamamoto, who had fought there as an ensign and had been wounded, was by now a vice admiral. Togo's death signified more than just the demise of an aged hero; it marked the Imperial Navy's transition (fairly slow, but very sure) from one way of thinking to another.

In the Imperial Navy's early years, Togo and his colleagues had been trained by the Royal Navy. Yamamoto had followed much the same training – the close links between the two navies ended only when the Alliance was abandoned in 1922. Through that training, maritime traditions which were ancient in the West, but new in Japan, had been adopted into the Imperial Navy. This was done without great difficulty, partly becauase the RN was the world's premier fleet and was obviously the best one to copy; and partly because many of those traditions seemed to slot in naturally with indigenous Japanese traditions. Loyalty, hard work, conformity and discipline were characteristics expected of any armed force, on sea or land; and being central to the whole of Japanese society as well, they presented no problem.

Occasionally, superficial similarities meant a received tradition was misunderstood – for example, the Western idea that the captain of a sinking ship should be the last to leave, seemed to accord very well with the Japanese idea of honourable suicide to redeem a debt. Thus it became a Japanese naval custom that, even if there was plenty of time for the captain as well as everyone else to get away, he would nevertheless stay on board, accepting death. Because of this simple misunderstanding, the Imperial Navy lost several fine officers unnecessarily. But among the traditions which they fully understood and accepted was one which was entirely novel: the concept that a sailor fought against ships, not against the people in them. To a large extent the continuation of this custom has been rendered impossible by the twentieth century's crescendo of destructive technology. But even today the principle is still recognized, understood and, when possible, acted upon; namely that, having defeated an enemy ship, a sailor's next duty is to try and rescue enemy personnel from their common foe, the sea.

The Imperial Navy took on this custom, and followed it at least until Yamamoto's death. After that time, as total defeat approached, it did descend to atrocities, such as the machine-gunning and ramming of lifeboats. But while Yamamoto was alive the Imperial Navy's behaviour was still scrupulous; for example, hospital ships were not attacked, as British authorities noted in Ceylon. However, by accepting and following this line, the Imperial Navy immediately and inevitably set itself apart from the Imperial Army. Japan's centuries-old samurai traditions found a ready home in the army; the navy was, in comparison, a Western institution grafted on to an Eastern background. Its officers had a deep sense of the Western concept of honour; but deeper still lay their sense of the Japanese concept of honour, and the two were not always easily reconciled. This latent psychological tension existed from the start, and was made more taut by the Naval Limitation agreements. From at least 1930, when the London Naval Conference modified the 5:5:3 ratio to 10:10:7, a running political battle developed between two different schools of Japanese naval thought, the one for abrogating the treaties, the other for maintaining them. And from the time of Togo's death in 1934 to the troubled middle months of 1941, the leaders of the Imperial Army found they could exploit that internal divide.

Japan's army leaders tended (almost by definition) to be jingoists; their national traditions and training traditions made them so, not least because – unlike the navy – they did not undertake prolonged, systematic foreign tours as part of their training. Without real experience of the world beyond Japan, it was easy for them to say that men such as Admiral Yamamoto had become Westernized and were no longer truly Japanese. And since those who had travelled were, nationally, a small number, such criticisms were easy for others to believe.

The Great Depression hit Japan as badly as any other industrialized nation, providing further impetus for domestic discontent and further potential for military exploitation. Japan's rather odd constitution offered the army another seemingly profitable vein. Both the Navy and the Army Ministers had to be serving officers, with the right of direct access to the Emperor. These factors in themselves provided the forces with an immediate political influence almost unknown in the West. Moreover, if either the Navy or Army Minister resigned and was not replaced at once, the entire Cabinet had to resign. The possibilities for corrupt manipulation are self-evident, and during the 1930s the army made repeated use of them, forcing Cabinet resignations whenever foreign policies differed from what they desired.

The navy did not follow this particular abuse, largely because its leaders at the time were men who saw from their experience abroad how badly it could go wrong. But they were not blameless; it was an admiral who bombed the International Settlement at Shanghai in 1932, and through the 1930s more junior naval officers were involved on several occasions in a peculiarly Japanese habit: *gekokujo*. This term almost defies translation, but is best given as 'rule from below'. It has no direct Western parallel; the nearest equivalents are (positively) initiative and (negatively) insubordination. Initiative can be seen as *gekokujo* which succeeds; insubordination as *gekokujo* which fails. The difference between the Western and Eastern concepts is that, whether it fails or succeeds, *gekokujo* is honourable – if it is undertaken for the good of the nation.

This too offered many possibilities of manipulation which in the West would be seen as unscrupulous, and during the 1930s there were frequent occasions when – ostensibly from the best of motives – naval officers and army officers provoked extreme turmoil, often to the point of assassinating political leaders (including Prime Ministers) with whom they disagreed. As early as 1932, the US Ambassador Joseph Grew noted: 'One thing is certain, and that is that the military are distinctly running the government and no step can be taken without their approval.'

Since 1923, Yamamoto had been adamant that Japan should on no account risk war with the West, specifically with America. He had seen for himself how far American resources outstripped those of Japan, and understood clearly that if a war should ever come – and if it should be prolonged – Japan would have no prospect of ultimate victory. From that year until the beginning of 1941, therefore, he worked to restrain the army's foreign ambitions and to curb the excesses of junior officers. As he rose in seniority, so he rose in power: in 1937 he became Vice-Minister of the Navy, with Admiral Mitsumasa Yonai as Navy Minister. Their ideas were in close parallel, both positively committed to keeping Japan free from war with the West. (War with China, which began in 1937, was a rather different matter.) But in August 1939 the imminence of war in Europe altered matters in Japan. Admiral Yonai was removed from political office, and so was Yamamoto; he was made Commander-in-Chief of the Imperial Navy, a non-political post. With these two men out of political life, a strong hope for peace with the West was greatly weakened.

In January 1940, four months after the war began in Europe, Yonai returned to political power, this time as Prime Minister; but on 16 July the Army Minister resigned. The army would not replace him; Yonai and his Cabinet were consequently forced to resign too; and on 27 September 1940 Japan joined the German–Italian Axis. The country was now allied to two of the actively combatant nations of Europe. In the Pacific region, moreover, in addition to the huge political tensions generated by the undeclared war with China, Japan was simultaneously in direct economic competition with Great Britain, the Netherlands and the United States. On the day that Japan joined the Axis, the US banned the export to it of scrap iron and steel. With no common ideological ground between the two oceanic powers, it became increasingly apparent that if the trade war was not relaxed, the moment when Japan would join the shooting war as an active belligerent was likely to be only a matter of time.

When this became clear to Yamamoto, he began to consider his alternatives. If war could not be avoided, then, as he saw it, his next duty was to do his best to ensure that Japan entered the conflict on the best possible terms. That meant the prompt destruction of America's Pacific Fleet; and the example of how such an object could be achieved was offered on 11 November 1940 by the successful British attack, using aerial torpedoes, against the Italian fleet as it lay at anchor in Taranto harbour.

He first proposed the plan formally on 1 February 1941, by which time the American Ambassador Joseph Grew had already heard rumours of a 'surprise mass attack on Pearl Harbor'. Grew reported the rumours to Washington and Pearl, where they were discounted. During the summer Western economic and diplomatic sanctions increased, culminating in an international embargo on sales of oil to Japan from 26 July 1941. This was sure to cripple the country. In 1940 it had produced something over 400,000 tons of oil, but had used over 5 million tons. In 1939 its national reserves had been 51 million barrels; by the summer of 1941 that figure had dropped to 43 million, of which the navy had 21.7 million. This represented two years' needs, at best. But in the Dutch East Indies, annual oil production in 1940 exceeded 8 million tons – 60 per cent more than Japan's total needs. A simple sum promised freedom. The alternative was for industry and the armed forces to grind gradually to a halt.

By then many intelligent Japanese sincerely believed that their country faced the most serious threat in its long history, a threat deliberately created by Britain, the Netherlands and America; and in September 1941 Admiral Yamamoto was asked by the then Prime Minister, Prince Konoye, what he felt Japan's chances were in a long war. The Admiral's reply had been memorable: 'If I am told to fight regardless of the consequences, I shall run wild considerably for the first six months or a year; but I have utterly no confidence in the second and third years.'

Because of its inherent risks, the idea of attacking Pearl Harbor encountered stiff opposition, and on 20 October was accepted by the Naval Staff only after Yamamoto had threatened to resign as Commander-in-Chief. On 10 November Vice-Admiral Nagumo's [*q.v.*] force was given its orders; and it is remarkable that even at that late stage relations between the Imperial Army and the Imperial Navy were so atrocious that the new Prime Minister, General Hideki Tojo, knew neither the projected date of attack nor how much time might still be available for diplomacy.

'Further arguments pro and con will avail nothing,' Yamamoto wrote on 11 November to a friend, retired Vice Admiral Teikichi Hori. 'The only thing that can save the situation is the final Imperial decision. But how difficult that will be in view of the present situation in the country. What a strange position I find myself in now – having to make a decision diametrically opposed to my own personal opinion, with no choice but to push full speed in pursuance of that decision.' After so much effort to keep his country away from war with America, followed by so much effort to prepare for that, the Commander-in-Chief sounded distinctly weary.

Four weeks later, Pearl had happened; Yamamoto's name was known worldwide, hailed by the Axis and reviled by the Allies; but his own mood of gloomy determination had not altered at all. 'Well,' he wrote to his sister, 'war has begun at last. But in spite of all the clamour that is going on, we could still lose it. I can only do my best.'

The Pacific covers rather more than half the entire globe. Obviously the final winner in the Pacific War would be he who controlled the ocean. As far as Yamamoto was concerned, another obvious consequence of geography was that in a vast ocean dotted with small islands, naval air power would dominate. The attack on Pearl was designed to give that control, at one stroke, to Japan. As early as 1915 he had predicted that aircraft carriers would be the most important ships of the future, and from 1923 had been an increasingly outspoken proponent of naval air power. Ironically, however, at the time of his death, his fleet flagship was the 72,000-ton super-battleship *Yamato* – the largest such vessel ever built anywhere. Completed on 16 December 1941, little more than a week after Pearl Harbor, *Yamato* was already a magnificent anachronism then, and in 1945 – when Japan had no aircraft carriers left – was sunk by aerial attack alone.

But in 1941, apart from its limited oil reserves, the Imperial Navy had never been better placed to wage sea–air war. It already had four years of modern fighting experience, from the beginning of the undeclared war with China, the so-called 'China Incident' that had started in 1937. Its Mitsubishi A6M fighter aircraft – the legendary Zeros – were the best and fastest in the world. Compared to its ten commissioned aircraft carriers (six large fast ones, three light ones and an old one), the US Navy as a whole contained seven carriers (six large and one small); and, of those, only three of the large ones were in the Pacific Fleet. This disparity highlighted another Japanese advantage; since the Indian Ocean never entered greatly into its pre-war calculations, the Imperial Navy had only one ocean to think about, while America was obliged to consider the Atlantic as well as the Pacific. However, by chance, all three of the Pacific Fleet's carriers were absent from Pearl on the day of the attack, and so escaped the destruction which otherwise would certainly have come to them; and it was that, more than anything else, which was responsible for Yamamoto's gloom while the rest of Japan rejoiced, for an ocean containing three enemy carriers at large was not an ocean under his control.

He was an accurate prophet – 'I shall run wild considerably for the first six months . . .', he had said, and under his leadership in the six months following Pearl Harbor the Imperial Navy ran wild in a manner that scarcely anyone would have imagined possible. For his officers and men it was a period of sublime exhilaration; every day, the Rising Sun spread further across the seas. For their opponents, it was a terrifying sight. On Tokyo time, the calendar of conquest is still astonishing:

7 December 1941: Eighty miles south of Cape Cambodia, in Japan's first act of aggression in the Pacific War, a British Catalina flying boat is shot down by Japanese army fighter planes from Indo-China, having sighted an invasion force steaming towards the Kra isthmus.

8 December: The assault on Pearl Harbor. Hickam, Wheeler, Ford Island and Kaneohe airfields destroyed; 188 American aircraft destroyed; 300,000 tons' displacement of US naval shipping destroyed or incapacitated, including eight battleships, three cruisers, two auxiliary craft, a minelayer and a target ship; over 3,600 Americans killed or wounded, including 400 buried alive in the battleship *Arizona*. Japanese losses: twenty-nine aircraft and five midget submarines.

9 December: Airfields in Malaya, Singapore, the Philippines and Hong Kong bombed.

10 December: The British battleship *Prince of Wales* and battle-cruiser *Repulse* sunk 200 miles north-east of Singapore: the first time capital ships have succumbed to attack by aircraft alone.

14 December: Landings at Luzon in the Philippines; in Malaya, Penang falls.

16 December: Landings at Sarawak and Brunei.

20 December: Invasion of Mindanao, the second largest Philippine island, begins.

21 December: Forty-three thousand troops commence the invasion of Luzon in earnest.

23 December: After repeated attacks, Wake Island falls.

25 December: Hong Kong falls.

29 December: Attack commences on Corregidor, America's island fortress in the entrance to Manila Bay.

31 December: Japanese troops enter Manila.

The new year, 1942, opened with the fall of Manila on 2 January. By 21 January, Japanese soldiers and sailors were established throughout Malaysia, and as far south-east as the Bismarck Archipelago, where Rabaul in New Britain and Kavieng in New Ireland were taken. On 24 January in Borneo, Balikpapan fell – a major oil port – and on 30 January Amboina in the Moluccas was likewise captured. On 15 February Singapore surrendered; on 19 February Port Darwin in Australia was attacked. On 27 February the Battle of the Java Sea took place, a serious Allied defeat; in March the Indian Ocean was penetrated by the Imperial Navy with raids on Ceylon; in April Bataan fell, and in May Corregidor.

In the first three days following Pearl Harbor, the Imperial Navy snatched control of seas and oceans which stretched in an unbroken line for 6,000 miles – a quarter of the earth's circumference. In the six subsequent months it extended that control, so that by the end of June 1942 Japan was in effective, almost undisputed charge of a vast area stretching from Manchuria in the north, across to the Aleutians in the east, down to the Solomon Islands in the south, and back across through New Guinea to Burma in the west. The Japanese Empire had expanded in every direction, swelling like a balloon – a steel balloon, with a skin of ships, guns and aircraft. And, like a balloon, it was virtually empty.

Returning to the end of 1941: the Japanese then were just as much taken aback by the speed and extent of their successes as were the Allies. More rapidly than anticipated, the questions of how best to defend and exploit their new territories crowded upon their minds. Their initial targets had been astonishingly easily achieved, against opposition which, though frequently heroic, had been generally ineffective and occasionally (as at Singapore) inept. The natural resources of Malaysia, the Philippines and the Dutch East Indies – the metals, oil and rubber for which they had hungered and thirsted – were theirs, and in half the anticipated time. So what next? There had to be a second phase; if ever the enemy wished to sue for peace, it would not be yet.

In Imperial General Headquarters in Tokyo, debates on the war's next strategic phase began in the middle of January 1942. They revealed two distinct lines of thought. Basically the options were either to go on the defensive or to maintain the offensive. The army wished for two main things: continuation of the war in China and complete consolidation of the newly won territories south of Japan. This essentially defensive approach tallied with earlier thinking, and had much to recommend it; when it came, the inevitable Allied counter-attack would be conducted far from Allied bases, with long, tenuous supply lines, and with the incoming fleet subject to preliminary depredation by waiting submarines even before it entered areas securely in Japanese hands. There, of course, the Imperial Navy would be ready and waiting, with its omnipotent carriers and magnificent battleships operating in familiar waters with all necessary supplies and shore-based air support close at hand.

But the same strategy had a large drawback, which the navy now chose to magnify; namely that by waiting they would permit the enemy to build to whatever level he chose before launching his counter-attack. The strategy's original attractions now seemed unsound, partly because it handed over the initiative to the other side. Far more exciting possibilities were available. The Indian Ocean beckoned, hitherto little considered; challenging the Royal Navy's Eastern Fleet, invading Ceylon, threatening India, possibly joining with German forces in northern Africa – that was one. Or an invasion of Australia, so pre-empting its use as a launchpad for an Allied counter-attack – that was another. Or, of course, a return visit to the Hawaiian islands, entailing their seizure and the complete destruction of the Pacific Fleet – that, the third possibility, would almost certainly force America to sue for peace, and (if Germany conquered Britain and the Royal Navy fled to support America in the Atlantic) would remove much pressure from Japan.

For a proud nation and a proud fleet which, until very recently, had felt themselves to be viewed by the rest of the world as underdogs, these were all immensely stimulating projects, and to the Imperial Navy none seemed individually impossible at all. But the army's response to the Ceylon and Australia projects was simple: No Sir. They would certainly not commit large numbers of men to other plans – particularly naval ones – because, they said, they were already at full stretch. This was not completely true; their hidden agenda, just as ambitious as any naval notion, was to invade the Soviet Union. Guessing that Hitler intended to break his alliance with Stalin by attacking the Soviet Union, they were confident of his success and wished to be ready to take advantage of it.

Their refusal for other offensive action persuaded Yamamoto to order the Indian Ocean raids of March 1942. Without requiring army assistance, these offered the attractive chance of disposing of Britain's Eastern Fleet. This hastily assembled fleet consisted mostly of older ships – five old battleships, two modern carriers and an old one, two heavy and six light cruisers, and fifteen destroyers. For the raids, Vice-Admiral Nagumo led a substantial and experienced force: five of the six carriers that had attacked Pearl, three battleships, six cruisers and twenty destroyers. However, the operation was not an unqualified success. Collectively, the Nagumo Force managed to sink the two heavy cruisers and one of the light ones, the old carrier, three destroyers and a corvette, as well as four merchant ships; but the British Eastern Fleet was neither completely destroyed nor completely driven away. There were three reasons for this limited success, two of which Admiral Nagumo recognized; firstly, that ever since Pearl all Japan's naval enemies had been far more alert than before; secondly, that the British Admiral (Sir James Somerville [*q.v.*]) would not give battle against a stronger force by daylight. Somerville would have fought Nagumo by night, when British night torpedo skills (which were of a high order) would have redressed the balance somewhat, but, knowing that, Nagumo took care to avoid night action.

The third reason for the limited success was something Nagumo half guessed, but dismissed as too unlikely – that the Imperial Navy's codes had been compromised. With a confidence that would soon be fatal, naval authorities in Tokyo also dismissed the suggestion.

As far as the Indian Ocean operations were concerned, though, the two admirals' refusal to join battle except on their own terms meant that the net result was a stand-off. Most of Somerville's ships survived and, remaining at least as a fleet in being, could not be entirely dismissed from future Japanese plans. Against that, from the Allied view, the Nagumo Force was still almost unscathed; they had lost some aircraft, but no ships. Consequently, despite the Allies' urgent need for warships in the Mediterranean and Atlantic, Somerville's fleet – weak as it was – could not be withdrawn; there was no promise that the Japanese would not return.

In fact they never did. By the time Nagumo's fleet returned to Japan, two critical events had taken place – events which, only a few weeks later, would culminate in the near annihilation of the Nagumo Force.

Firstly, after studying without comment his advisers' various recommendations for the next phase of the war, Yamamoto had entered the debate with his own proposal: a variation on the Hawaiian project. His suggestion – that the next major target should be a tiny atoll named Midway, halfway across the Pacific – was met with scepticism at best and downright opposition at worst. Secondly, on 18 April 1942, Lieutenant-Colonel Jimmy Doolittle led the celebrated raid by sixteen B-25 USAF bombers on Tokyo, launched from the decks of the aircraft carriers *Enterprise* and *Hornet*. The physical damage they inflicted was slight; the mental damage was huge. The violation of Japanese airspace (particularly the proximity of the bombers to the Imperial palace) jarred everyone considerably.

That is the extent of the credit usually accorded to Doolittle's squadron: that they bolstered American morale at a time when any fillip was badly needed ('Doolittle Do'd It', said the *Los Angeles Times*), and that they gave the Japanese a nasty jolt ('inhuman, insatiable, indiscriminate bombing', said the *Asahi Shimbun*). In direct terms, the assessment is correct; but in indirect terms the effect of the Doolittle excursion was much greater, and should be credited as such.

This is because it displayed in dramatic fashion the exact problem that Yamamoto wanted to solve. Since the strike on Pearl, he had remained convinced that the Pacific Fleet's carriers must be eliminated if risks to Japan and its Imperial Navy were to be minimized. His proposed attack on Midway atoll was intended to draw out the Pacific Fleet, in which the carriers would certainly be included. He was sure the fleet would come because Midway was only 1,136 miles west-north-west of Pearl Harbor, and was moreover across the psychologically important 180° meridian, within the area of the Pacific which Americans still thought of as their own. When battle was joined he was confident that his Combined Fleet would win a decisive victory, and from that, he asserted, much would follow: the ability to threaten Hawaii and even the entire west coast at will. And with the bulk of their limited naval shipping destroyed, as undoubtedly it would be, Americans would lose the will to fight in the Pacific, and would wish to negotiate for peace.

His own staff supported the plan completely, but the Naval General Staff had several fundamental objections to it. Midway's very proximity to Hawaii offered the Americans the chance to defend it with Hawaiian-based aircraft in addition to their carrier aircraft; after Pearl, they would not be caught unawares again; and the Commander-in-Chief's judgement that the Americans would certainly emerge was a matter of opinion. If they did not, the atoll's capture would be simple, but a surprise American attack could recapture it at any time, and meanwhile (being twice as far from Japan as it was from Pearl) Midway would have to be defended by large, constant air patrols, requiring enormous quantities of supplies – particularly fuel. That in itself would be a severe drain on Imperial resources. Finally (and as the Commander-in-Chief knew perfectly well), because of the army's opposition to the grand invasion plans of Australia, a more limited campaign of consolidation in the islands towards Australia was already under way and ought to be completed before any further territorial extensions were attempted.

There was much good sense in the Naval General Staff's arguments. Yamamoto, however, was adamant; and, unwelcome as it was, the Doolittle raid won his case for him. Some rapid reference showed that no American aircraft could have flown so far across the ocean. It followed that they must have been brought by carriers; and if American carriers could penetrate so close to Japan, they must indeed be found and sunk.

That, then, was one of the indirect effects of the Doolittle raid: the firm decision, taken just before the end of April 1942, that Admiral Yamamoto's Midway plan would be put into operation. And there was a second indirect effect, of crucial importance to the Midway plan – or, as it became, the Battle of Midway. In their immediate, urgent efforts to locate and eradicate the offending USN carriers, IJN ships in home waters broadcast an abnormally large amount of signal traffic. All of it was monitored by the Pacific Fleet; much of it was comprehensible; and by its volume it provided the raw material for further comparative analysis, by which incomprehensible messages could be made clear to enemy ears.

At this point it is worth stepping aside for a moment to look more closely at what we may surmise to be the deeper reasons for Yamamoto's unswerving target, the destruction in one decisive battle of the enemy fleet. Clearly such an achievement would be highly desirable in any sea war. Just as clearly, Yamamoto was correct in his overall assessment that this was Japan's best chance of gaining a favourable negotiated peace at an early date. But the notable, even obsessional degree to which he pursued decisive battle, almost to the exclusion of other possibilities, suggests something more than the pragmatic conduct of war alone. If this is so, its source may perhaps be found in the common experience of every Imperial Japanese naval officer – the training they underwent in the academy at Etajima.

It was there, on an island in Japan's exquisite Inland Sea, that they earned their high status. It was not easily won; before graduation as ensigns, and with only seven weeks of annual holiday, officer cadets worked a full sixteen hours a day, six days a week, for four years. Nevertheless, every year each place in the academy was oversubscribed by thirty to forty times the possible number of entrants, so, from the day they began, the successful applicants knew they were special, even by Japanese standards. They had passed a stringent medical test, written examinations in twelve subjects, an oral interview, and a character and reputation check on themselves and their whole family by the police; and some who passed all those were weeded out at the last minute by a final medical check at the gates of the academy. The regime was so arduous that one in ten of those who got in had to leave before their course was over. By the end of that time, when – with a farewell from one of the Imperial princes or even from the Emperor himself – they embarked on a round-the-world training cruise, those who had survived were supremely physically fit, highly disciplined, utterly dedicated to their duty and deeply loyal to one another.

They had of course learned a great deal about their own navy, and a lot about over navies; although still young men, by then they were, for their level, thoroughly professional officers. But, however conscious they were of the strengths, skills and virtues of their training, few if any of them would have seen its inherent flaws. These were not many, but they were emphatic. From the example set by the Nelsonian tradition of the Royal Navy, their first tutors, and repeated by the example of Togo at Tsushima, the concept of the decisive battle was deeply ingrained. And, perhaps surprisingly, this was made all the stronger by four of the sports played at Etajima.

The range of energetic sports included several Western imports – competitive rowing and swimming, rugger, soccer, basketball, baseball and tennis. Given their original Royal Navy connections, one might have expected them to play cricket, that most English of sports, as well; but they did not. However, they did have four essentially Japanese sports in addition to the

Western ones: judo, sumo wrestling, kendo (a relic of samurai sword-fighting, with four-foot staves instead of swords) and *botaoshi*. All thcsc four revealed aspects of the Japanese character which affected the Imperial Navy especially deeply, and which contributed, invisibly but certainly, to its eventual downfall and the downfall of Japan.

In judo, as most people know, the strength of the opponent is used against him. In European fencing, the opponent's strength is whittled away by repeated small strikes; in kendo by contrast the objective is to land a single deadly blow – a blow that would have been deadly with a samurai sword – in any one of five designated places: the top of the head, the right arm, the neck, or either side of the body. In sumo, unlike European wrestling, the fighters never descend to grappling on the ground, but win on points – and not by *gaining* points, but by making the opponent *lose* points. Finally, *botaoshi*; this was an Etajima invention, played in the academy and nowhere else. The cadets were very proud of it, and an especially honoured visitor might be invited to watch a game.

It was very simple. The players wcrc divided into two teams, and each team was divided into attackers and defenders. Two poles, about eight feet high and topped with flags, were placed a hundred yards or so apart. The objective of the contest was merely to pull down the opponents' pole.

The defenders grouped around their pole in two tiers, the lower ones linking arms and the upper ones standing on their shoulders. On the signal of a bugle call, the attackers charged from opposite ends of the field, shrieking like maniacs. They tussled in mid-field, and those who broke through leaped bodily on to the opposition defenders, with no holds barred except scratching and biting. The first lot to pull down a pole were the winners, and the whole thing was over in three or four minutes, often with a couple of unconscious bodies being dragged out from under the scrambling heap. It was extremely vicious, incredibly exciting and swiftly finished – one quick, decisive battle.

The principles of all these distinctive sports, handed down or invented, were absorbed by every Imperial Navy officer in the most formative part of his naval career, and they were fine as sports. But, in the minds of this dedicated, loyal, elite group, their principles of sport became, consciously or unconsciously, their principles of war. Throughout its brief life, the fundamentals of Imperial Navy strategic thinking could be traced back to the games at Etajima. The seeds of thought in every naval officer's mind were there: the beliefs that they could tackle an enemy, however strong, by using his strength against him; that a single, well-calculated blow was always worth more than a dozen smaller ones; that they could always win, not by overwhelming force, but by inflicting greater losses than they sustained; and finally, that it would all be over in one fast decisive battle. This was more than a rational strategic ideal; it was an eternal conviction, deeply rooted in the psyche of every Japanese naval officer.

There was another fatal mental straitjacket traceable directly to Etajima and the culture in which it was rooted. The very dedication to duty that produced such fine professional sailors, men of unquestioning loyalty to their group, also produced a severe narrow-mindedness, an inability to improvise against the unexpected, a phobia of doing the wrong thing and a reluctance to operate without exact orders for every eventuality.

The obverse of this was that orders were always as precise and comprehensive as possible, with the intention of leaving nothing to chance. Accordingly, the naval planners worked on the complex Midway operation with their customary attention to minute detail, so that when the time came every man involved would know precisely what he had to do and when to do it. And, as they worked, the fruits of their earlier labours were being gathered over 3,000 miles south of them, in the Battle of the Coral Sea.

This was in many ways an historic encounter – the first battle ever fought solely between carriers, the first in which the opposing ships never even saw each other, and (in the context of the Pacific War) the first in which the Imperial Navy received a real setback. Nevertheless, it can be dealt with only briefly here. In summary, the operation which brought it about was Japan's intended invasions of the Solomon Islands and of Port Moresby, on the south coast of Papua, with the intention of interdicting the America–Australia supply lines. It was hoped this might before long force Australia out of the war; it was believed that Japan's hold on its new territories would be much strengthened – that the hollow interior of the steel balloon would be filled in.

But, of those objectives, only the invasion of the Solomons was attained. Expecting to achieve surprise once again, the Japanese troop convoy was escorted by the light carrier *Shoho* and four cruisers, while for the main covering force only two fleet carriers (*Shokaku* and *Zuikaku*) were used. However, their strengths and destinations were soon known to the US Navy, whose burgeoning team of cryptanalysts in Pearl Harbor was becoming daily more expert. Admiral Chester Nimitz [*q.v.*], Commander-in-Chief US Pacific Fleet, was able to deploy the carriers *Lexington* and *Yorktown* (the latter recently arrived from the Atlantic) along with a combined American–Australian cruiser force, in time to oppose the operation.

In the two-day battle (7–8 May 1942) each carrier force – uncertain of the other's location – began with a tactical error. Identifying *Shoho* and the cruisers as the main enemy group, the local American commander (Rear Admiral Frank Fletcher) launched virtually the whole of his air strength at them. *Shoho* was sunk – the first IJN carrier to be lost – but Fletcher had rendered his own carriers virtually defenceless. Fortunately for him, the Japanese did almost the same thing at the same time, misidentifying an American tanker as a carrier, and expending their striking power in sinking it and its destroyer escort. By the evening, Fletcher still did not know where his enemy was, but a Japanese scout had located him. However, out of a strike against him of twenty-seven aircraft, only four survived – some were shot down by American fighters, and most got lost in bad weather and gathering darkness. (One Japanese pilot became so confused that he tried to land on *Yorktown*.) This meant that the Japanese carriers had lost nearly one-fifth of their air strength without having actually attacked the American carriers at all.

Battle resumed the following day in a much more organized manner. Simultaneously, each side launched a strike against the other. The first, and rather curious, consequence was that on their way towards the enemy carriers the opposing fighter squadrons saw each other, and, pausing only for a brief tussle in mid-air, continued on their way. The second and more important consequence was what happened to the four carriers, then and a little later. During the battle, *Shokaku* and *Yorktown* were both heavily damaged, but managed to limp home for repairs. *Lexington* likewise was heavily damaged, and after some time suffered a series of severe internal explosions which led to her abandonment and eventual loss; and *Zuikaku*, though individually undamaged, lost the majority of her aircraft and pilots.

In another Pacific War first, the seaborne invasion of Port Moresby was called off – something which Yamamoto's fleets had never done before. However, the operation against Midway was not rescinded, nor was its timetable altered. But its scrupulously detailed plans now included a fundamental error, for in Japan *Yorktown* was reported as having been sunk. True, the damage she had sustained was so great that at home it was estimated her repairs would take ninety days, but she was certainly not sunk – and by fantastic efforts workmen at the Pearl Harbor Navy Yard had her ready again for sea in only three days.

In contrast, *Shokaku*'s repairs proceeded at a more regular pace; she was not ready for sea for a month. And because *Zuikaku*'s lost pilots could not be easily replaced, she too was temporarily out of the war. Thus, on the brink of Midway, Yamamoto was limited to only four fleet carriers instead of the six he had anticipated. But, believing there would be only one or at the most two in opposition, he proceeded, no less confident than before that the battle would be decisive.

Broadly speaking, Yamamoto divided his forces for the operation into four branches. Approaching Midway from the south-west, a host of transports would carry some 5,000 troops for the invasion of the little atoll. They would land when the Nagumo Force, approaching from the north-west, had pulverized any American defences. Far to the north, other groups of ships would perform a series of diversionary attacks on the remote Aleutian Islands; and, coming in astern of Nagumo, Yamamoto himself would lead the fleet's Main Body in his flagship, the super-battleship *Yamato*, with her sister ship *Musashi*. The atoll was believed to be but lightly defended, and would therefore fall quite easily. Either this or the Aleutian operation would bring out the Pacific Fleet. Nagumo, forewarned of its advance by a picket line of submarines, would circle round it, cutting it off from Pearl Harbor, whereupon Yamamoto and the Main Body would descend upon it and blow it from the ocean, as Togo had done to the Russians in 1905.

That was the theory, anyway. Echoing (indeed, modelled on) Hannibal's strategy at Cannae and Ludendorff's at Tannenberg, it was a typical Japanese pattern: divert, divide, tempt, trap and kill. And looking at the plan on paper, Yamamoto might have thought to echo Nelson's words before Trafalgar: 'It was singular – it was simple! It must succeed.' In fact the reality was neither singular nor simple, but multiple and complex. No one today could truthfully claim to know Yamamoto's innermost thoughts at the time; and this is a pity, because his plan was studded with inconsistencies. It gave absolutely no thought to the chance of something going wrong with the timetable. It gave absolutely no contingency arrangement to cover circumstances other than those anticipated. It assumed absolutely that Japanese intelligence was accurate and American intelligence deficient; and it placed Nagumo, with relatively little surface assistance, in a potentially very vulnerable position.

All this is puzzling. Stranger still was the way in which the war-games testing the operation were conducted. Only eight years previously, the naval author Hector Bywater had stressed that in the Imperial Navy 'manoeuvres are always conducted with as much realism as possible, and the umpires take immense pains to reach an accurate decision on every point, however insignificant'. In the first four days of May 1942, table-top manoeuvres on board *Yamato* had attempted to determine the elements of chance and probability in the operation; but when the Red team, representing the American fleet, caught Nagumo's Blue team by surprise and 'sank' two of his carriers, the hitherto scrupulously observed rules were suddenly overturned. As if the very idea of such a loss was inadmissible, one of the play carriers was allowed to pop up again in the next stage of the game, miraculously raised from the sea-bed, undamaged and fighting fit.

Yamamoto had the reputation of a gambler prepared to risk high odds. He also had the reputation of an unconventional thinker – his long-standing support of air power, his efforts to stop Japan going to war and his plan against Pearl all underlined that, and the success of the Pearl plan gave immense authority to his thinking. Yet in planning Midway he adopted a comparatively conventional formula, and in so doing considerably increased the odds against success. Over 160 vessels and over 400 aircraft – almost the whole fighting force of the Imperial Navy – were involved under his overall command. Certainly Nimitz actually had more ships and aircraft available than Yamamoto expected, but even so, the total US naval force was only twenty-five surface vessels and 351 aircraft, carrier- and shore-based. Yamamoto could have simply forged ahead: collectively, the enormous forces at his disposal could have steamrollered any possible opposition. As it was, the division of his forces brought their cutting edge, the Nagumo fleet, down to twenty-one surface vessels with 260 aircraft. Yamamoto doubted the value of the super-battleships in the first round; he judged their time would come when the Pacific Fleet's air strength had been eliminated. That was reasonable. Against that, his fleets were scattered far and wide; success depended on their clock-work co-ordination; and that in turn depended on the American fleet doing just what it was expected to do. Without wishing to criticize with the benefit of hindsight, that was not reasonable.

In the end, the battle was won and lost by naval intelligence as much as by weight of arms. On the Japanese side was a blithe acceptance – even a blind acceptance – that their estimates were correct, and that surprise would be achieved. On the American side the Pearl Harbor cryptanalysts (particularly Commander Joe Rochefort [*q.v.*]) made a superlative effort, ultimately predicting to within five minutes, five miles and five degrees of bearing the time and place that Nagumo's carriers would be found. That did not of itself ensure the decisive American victory which ensued; but it did give Nimitz a chance he would otherwise never have had.

The tactics of the Battle of Midway (3–6 June 1942) are not relevant to a study of Yamamoto, but the result of the battle certainly is. On 9 June, Rear Admiral Paul Wenneker, the German Naval Attaché in Tokyo, sent a secret telegram to his superiors in Berlin. 'Jap navy reports the following: 1) Own losses at Midway: One large carrier sunk, 2 badly damaged; American losses: 2 carriers sunk. 2) Several of the Aleutian Islands were captured.'

The previous day, he had telegrammed a complaint that 'it has been impossible to get any details on the Midway battle from the Jap navy. The army maintains that the landings were successful.' He might have been grateful for the news he received on 9 June; as he must have guessed, it was not true, but it was closer to the truth than the information publicly released in Japan. After trying to get confirmation, he reported on 10 June that 'the Jap navy has remained stubbornly silent on the subject of the strategy underlying the Battle of Midway. The following can be assembled from various utterances: the Jap fleet with transports assembled at the Marshall Islands with the intention of landing on Midway. The approach was reported prematurely by American subs and the attack was accordingly interrupted. The Americans were tenacious beyond expectation. The operation has not yet been ended, and a favourable outcome is expected.'

In fact nearly five full days before that report was sent, Admiral Yamamoto had made what must have been the most painful decision of his professional life. Broadcast to all surviving IJN ships, at five minutes to three in the morning of 6 June, Tokyo time, the Commander-in-Chief's message stated flatly: 'The Midway operation is cancelled.'

No other decision was possible. Those in Japan who knew its true results could only acknowledge that the decisive battle, which had for so long eluded them, had taken place at last, and that they had decisively lost. The American carrier *Yorktown*, ghost survivor of the Coral Sea, had truly been sunk this time. The US Navy had also lost one destroyer, over 100 aircraft and some 300 officers and men. But all four of Nagumo's fleet carriers had gone down, along with a heavy cruiser, something around 270 aircraft, and 5,000 officers and men. It was not of itself a war-winning victory for America, but it was a severely punishing defeat for Japan. The steel balloon, Japan's outer defence perimeter, had been pierced. Hollow within, no patch could completely repair it; and, although the eventual defeat of the Imperial Navy was still bitterly contested and slow, nevertheless it was, in the end, complete.

The six months of running wild were over. Yamamoto's prophecy must have haunted those who heard it, for Midway took place precisely six months after Pearl Harbor. The Commander-in-Chief Combined Fleet had been proved right, not because of any uncanny gift, but simply because he knew what he was talking about. There remained the rest of his forecast, '. . . I have utterly no confidence in the second and third years.' It was not an encouraging thought. Still, no one could say yet that the Imperial Navy had lost its war.

But on 24 August 1942 that point came markedly closer. On 7–8 August, Operation Watchtower had brought the successful American invasion of Guadalcanal in the Solomons, along with their acquisition of an airfield newly completed by the Japanese, now renamed Henderson Field. Control of the field gave a considerable degree of control over the island as a whole, offering to its possessor a base for further aggressive operations. It became, therefore, the focus of exceedingly hard fighting on land and sea for several months.

In the Battle of the eastern Solomons the opposing fleets were large: Vice Admiral Frank Fletcher led three carriers with 254 aircraft, a battleship, five heavy and two light cruisers and a dozen destroyers; Vice Admiral Nobutake Kondo also led three carriers, as well as three battleships, nine heavy and two light cruisers and twenty-three destroyers, with a total of 211 aircraft. His purpose was to land 1,500 troops, with weapons and supplies, to reinforce those on the island.

As at Midway, the Japanese plan was complicated and their strategic and tactical commands were divided; strategic command remained with Yamamoto on board *Yamato*, now at Truk. But the intelligence provided to the American commander was less startlingly brilliant than at Midway, and as a consequence partly of that the battle was tactically inconclusive. The strategic effect on the war was, however, significant. Firstly, the Japanese operation's purpose – the reinforcement of Guadalcanal – failed. Secondly, ninety more Japanese aircraft and another carrier (*Ryujo*) were lost.

At the beginning of the year, the Imperial Navy had had ten carriers, totalling just over 238,800 tons' displacement. *Ryujo* was the sixth to go down. But six others were commissioned in the course of the whole year, and it was not difficult to suppose that the supply from Japan's shipyards would keep pace with demand; once, in 1918, they had established a world record by building a 5,800-ton merchant ship in only twenty-nine days from start to finish. Yet on hearing Kondo's report Yamamoto undoubtedly knew that the picture was far bleaker than it appeared superficially. Altogether, nearly 150,000 tons of carrier shipping had been lost by then; only a little over 123,000 tons had been built. With *Ryujo* gone, there was a net loss of nearly 26,500 tons – more than 9 per cent of the original total – in the four months since *Shoho*, the first victim, went down in the Coral Sea. Moreover, the replacement ships were all conversion jobs. Two had been submarine support vessels, four had been passenger liners. With the war only nine months old, the Imperial Navy was already having to scratch around and take what it could get for carriers.

The Solomons, and specifically Guadalcanal, became the hub of the Pacific War for the rest of 1942 and the first month of 1943. It was early in February 1943, after many battles at sea and constant fighting on land, that the Japanese finally abandoned Guadalcanal. This – more than Midway, despite its apposite name – was a true turning point. On 26 March, far to the north in the Russian Komandorskiye Islands, the last major sea battle fought only with naval guns took place. It was the day after that when Yamamoto, the prophet of air power, sanctioned the beginning of a great air counter-offensive in the South-West Pacific. More than 200 carrier planes were shifted to land bases scattered throughout the Solomon Islands. Added to the 100-plus aircraft already there, this became the strongest air armada ever mustered by the Imperial Navy. Its objective was to harass, impede and with luck paralyse the build-up of American naval forces in the area. Action commenced on 7 April, and within a week considerable success was reported – 134 Allied planes shot down, twenty-five transports, two destroyers and a cruiser sunk. But as often happened with pilots' reports, from whichever nation, the figures were over-optimistic. The week's operations actually disposed of twenty-five American aircraft, two transports, one destroyer, a corvette and a tanker. Yet Admiral Yamamoto appeared to accept the claimed figures at face value, and on 16 April called the operation off, believing it to have been a considerable success.

Publicly he appeared optimistic. Privately, however, he wrote to a friend, just after the loss of Guadalcanal, and said: 'I do not know what to do next. Nor am I happy about facing my officers and men who have fought so hard without fear of death.' Nevertheless, facing them was exactly what he decided to do. He would meet as many as possible of his loyal air- and sea-warriors personally, and show them that, whatever had happened or might happen, he was still their leader, and still ready to fight.

It was an excellent idea: the personal visit to the troops by a charismatic leader has always been the best inspiration. But Yamamoto still had no inkling of the extent of American monitoring of Japanese radio messages, nor of the number of those messages they could decode. From his flagship *Yamato*, still anchored in Truk, the precise details of his itinerary were broadcast to all interested parties, so that the airbases involved could prepare for their distinguished visitor. A base which was definitely not on the list was Henderson Field in Guadalcanal, but – from eavesdropping colleagues in the Aleutians – the men there knew about Yamamoto's route, his aircraft and escorts almost as soon as did their Japanese counterparts.

Relying on his well-known habit of punctuality, the rest was rather easy. All they had to do was be in the right place at the right time with sufficient strength; and the Admiral did not let them down. At 9.33 a.m. on 18 April 1943, over the island of Bougainville, eighteen P-38 Henderson-based fighters fitted with long-range fuel tanks ambushed the flight: six Zero fighters escorting two Mitsubishi bombers, with Yamamoto's Chief of Staff, Admiral Matome Ugaki, in one, and Yamamoto himself in the other. Within two minutes, nine aircraft were spiralling towards sea and land: one P-38, and all the Japanese flight.

Yamamoto's personal plane crashed in the jungle, in flames. Colleagues found his body the following day. It had been thrown clear in the crash. Apart from his, only one other body could be identified; the rest had all been burned far beyond recognition. But Yamamoto had not been killed by the crash; it was apparent that in the attack he had been shot twice, through the shoulder and through the head, and must already have been dead when the plane hit the trees.

By the time of his death, he had espoused air power for a full twenty years. For him personally, it was an appropriate end. For Japan, however, his death was a national tragedy, kept secret until 21 May; and for America it was a corresponding national triumph, the personal conclusion of a collective revenge.

In his lifetime lay some historical imperatives – cultural and political, national and international – which may candidly be seen to have made war virtually inevitable. That Yamamoto strove against those should be placed to his credit. That he failed and subsequently fought as efficiently as he could should not be placed to his debit; he did his job, as any professional fighting man would have done. He was always a fair man, fighting hard but clean, and while he lived the Imperial Navy was the same. He was not a genius, and naturally he made mistakes, as a politician and as a naval officer. Once war had begun, of course there was no going back, and, although under certain possible but implausible circumstances things might have turned out differently, Yamamoto had the unhappy privilege of being proved a true prophet.

Posthumously created Admiral of the Fleet, 1943, by Emperor Hirohito.

5

Fleet Admiral

Chester William Nimitz
United States Navy

1885–1966

by
E. B. Potter

BORN at Fredericksburg, Texas, on 24 February 1885, of German stock. Grew up bilingual in an atmosphere at least as German as it was American. Obtained an appointment to the US Naval Academy solely to obtain an education at government expense, but there developed a dedication to the navy from which he never wavered.

Early career marked by a series of striking achievements: in 1907, given command of a destroyer, though only twenty-two years old. From 1909, commanded a series of submarines operating out of Atlantic ports. Met and married a Massachusetts girl, Catherine Freeman. His expert knowledge of submarines brought him at age twenty-seven an invitation to address the Naval War College at Newport, Rhode Island.

Campaigned for the removal of petrol engines from submarines, advocating their replacement with the new, safer diesel engine, on which he made himself an authority. Navy sent him (and his wife) to Germany to study big diesels. Back in US Nimitz supervised construction and installation of diesels in a new oiler; later, as the oiler's executive officer, joined her skipper in devising the system of underway refuelling; and during World War One employed the new technique in mid-Atlantic, refuelling American destroyers en route to European waters. Became lieutenant-commander (1918) and visited Allied shipyards and naval bases gathering ideas about designing and operating submarines. Sea duty, 1919–20; built submarine base at Pearl Harbor, 1920–2; on course at Naval War College, 1922–3. Devised circular and carrier-centred formations subsequently used in US battlefleet. During mid-1930s, in rank of captain, commanded cruiser Augusta, flagship of US Asiatic Fleet. Assistant Chief, Bureau of Navigation, 1935–8. Commander Cruiser Division Two, 1938; promoted rear admiral, July 1938; commander Battleship Division One, 1938–9. Chief of Bureau of Navigation, June 1939.

In 1941, Rear Admiral Chester Nimitz was fifty-six years old. Decisive, an excellent judge of character, robust of build and serene of temperament, widely read and experienced in his profession, he was superbly prepared to assume broad responsibilities. With flaxen hair just turning white, he had a pink complexion and blue eyes that often twinkled with mirth but could turn glacial with disapproval. He had a commanding presence without arrogance or aloofness. Ever courteous and considerate, he made and kept many friends.

On Sunday, 7 December, he was at home with his family. After a late midday dinner, he and Mrs Nimitz settled down to read. At 1500 the Admiral turned on the radio to hear a broadcast of Artur Rodzinski conducting the New York Philharmonic Orchestra. Scarcely had the music begun when the broadcast was interrupted by a flash announcement that Japanese aircraft had raided Pearl Harbor.

Nimitz leaped to his feet. He was struggling into his overcoat when the telephone rang. It was his Assistant Chief calling to say that he was driving to the Navy Department and would pick him up. As the Admiral dashed out the door, he called back, 'I won't be back till God knows when.'

Before the day was over, Nimitz knew that planes from Japanese carriers had bombed or torpedoed eighteen ships, including all eight of the battleships stationed at Pearl Harbor. They had destroyed more than 200 planes, most of them on the ground, and killed or wounded thousands of men, chiefly US Navy personnel.

Monday morning newspapers, quoting a naval communiqué, mentioned only one battleship damaged. The Navy Department had decided not to inform the Japanese, via the American press, how successful they had been and how badly the US Navy had been hurt. President Roosevelt, going before Congress, requested and was voted a declaration of war against Japan. Germany and Italy, fulfilling treaty commitments with the Japanese, soon declared war on the United States.

The Bureau of Navigation (which actually dealt with Personnel, and soon would be so named) was inundated. Survivors of the sunken ships had to be provided for. Families of those killed had to be notified and bodies brought home. Calls poured in demanding information. Nimitz and his staff worked far into the night, snatched a few hours' sleep at home and were back at their desks early next morning.

On Tuesday, 9 December, Secretary of the Navy Knox left Washington by air to make a quick inspection of Pearl Harbor and confer with officers on the scene. Back the following Monday, he held a press conference and described in more detail the damage at Pearl – not the whole grim story, of course, but only what could plainly be seen from the heights flanking Pearl Harbor and must already be known to the enemy.

That evening, in conference with the President, Knox recommended (1) immediately relieving the Commander-in-Chief of the Pacific Fleet, Admiral Husband Kimmel, whose name was now inescapably associated with catastrophe and defeat, (2) setting up a board of inquiry to determine what and who was responsible for the failure of the Pearl Harbor defences, and (3) establishing a Washington-based post, Commander-in-Chief US Fleet, vested with operational command of the entire US Navy. Roosevelt concurred with all three recommendations, and he and Knox agreed that the tough, hard-nosed Admiral Ernest J. King [*q.v.*], currently commanding the Atlantic Fleet, should be appointed to the new top command. Briefly deferring the question of who was to relieve Kimmel, they also agreed to meet the next morning to make a decision.

That morning – Tuesday, 16 December 1941 – Nimitz as usual was early at his desk. He had made a sizeable dent in the problems of the day when he got a telephone call from Knox. Would he please come at once to the Secretary's office? Nimitz trudged wearily down to the Secnav suite and was promptly waved into the inner sanctum where Knox, obviously excited, barked, 'How soon can you be ready to travel?'

Nimitz, his fatigued nerves on edge, snapped, 'It depends on where I'm going and how long I'll be away.'

'You're going to take command of the Pacific Fleet, and I think you'll be gone for a long time.'

During the next two days, Nimitz attended a series of discussions and planning sessions climaxed by a Thursday morning conference at the White House. There was plenty to discuss. The victorious Japanese seemed to be everywhere. They had landed in Malaya and were driving on Singapore. From airfields in Indo-China, their aircraft had attacked and sunk two British capital ships that sought to intervene, the battleship *Prince of Wales* and the battle-cruiser *Repulse*. They had captured Guam, invaded the Philippines and the British Gilbert Islands, bombed Cavite, Singapore and Hong Kong, and bombarded Johnston Island and Midway atoll. They had attempted to seize Wake Island. Here US Marines had hurled them back, but the atoll was under air attack from the Japanese Marshalls, evidently preliminary to a renewed invasion attempt.

In what was almost his last official act, Kimmel had sent carrier forces to rescue Wake. Now he was relieved by Vice-Admiral William S. Pye, who would serve as acting Commander-in-Chief Pacific Fleet (Cincpac) pending the arrival of Nimitz.

Knox told Nimitz that a plane was waiting to take him to Pearl Harbor. The Admiral replied that he was too tired to make a quick trip by air. He preferred, he said, to go to the West Coast by rail in order to catch up on his sleep, regain his strength and read reports.

In the afternoon of Friday, 19 December, incognito and wearing civilian clothes, Nimitz and an aide left Washington on the Capitol Limited. At Los Angeles, the Admiral and aide parted company. The latter headed back east, while Nimitz continued on by train to San Diego, where a Catalina flying boat was standing by to take him to Pearl Harbor.

Strong winds delayed his departure till the 24th. Newspapers that morning announced that Japanese had landed on Wake, but that the Marine and naval defenders continued to resist. Nimitz wondered what was holding up the relief expedition, which should have reached the atoll by that time.

Nimitz's plane was airborne at 1600. The Admiral apologized to the crew for taking them away from their families on Christmas Eve. During the night, chilled and half-deafened by the roar of the motors, he slept little. A hundred miles short of Oahu, his Catalina was met by several fighter aircraft and escorted to Pearl Harbor.

As his plane circled for a water landing that Christmas morning, Nimitz looked down through the cold drizzle at a heartrending scene. East Loch, the main anchorage, was still covered with black fuel oil, eighteen days after the assault. The battleship *Oklahoma* and the target ship *Utah* were bottoms up; a minelayer was on her side; in the distance, the battleship *Nevada*, heavily damaged, was aground in the shallows; and three more battleships – *California*, *West Virginia* and Nimitz's old flagship *Arizona* – were sunk in deeper water, only their topsides visible, with blackened and twisted masts.

At seven o'clock the Admiral's plane touched down and floated to a halt. When the door was thrown open, the horrible sights were matched by the smell – a stench of black oil, blistered paint and burned and rotting bodies. Alongside came a whaleboat, foul inside and out with oil. Nimitz, still in civilian clothes, stepped down into the filthy craft and shook hands with the three-officer reception committee. He asked the question uppermost in his mind: 'What news of the relief of Wake?' Told that the relief expedition had been recalled and that Wake had surrendered to the enemy, he remained silent for some time.

The trip to shore was miserable. The surface was choppy. The rain continued to fall. The four passengers remained precariously standing to avoid soiling their clothing. In reply to another question, Nimitz was informed that the boats moving about the harbour were fishing out the bodies of sailors, which, grotesquely bloated, were still rising to the surface.

At the submarine-base wharf Admiral Pye was waiting with the official car to take Nimitz to his quarters, a comfortable-looking dwelling, formerly the quarters of Admiral Kimmel. Presently Admiral Kimmel joined them. He was wearing two stars, replacing the four he had worn as Cincpac. A portly man, usually of imperious presence, he now appeared stooped, somehow shrunken. On 7 December, as he had powerlessly watched his fleet being demolished, a spent .50-calibre machine-gun bullet had broken through the window and struck his breast, leaving a dark spot on his white uniform. Picking up the bullet, he had said softly, as if to himself, 'It would have been merciful had it killed me.' Today, shocked at his old friend's appearance, Nimitz warmly pressed Kimmel's hand. 'You have my sympathy,' he said to the defeated Admiral. 'The same thing could have happened to anybody.'

Nimitz spent his first few days at Pearl Harbor consulting and inspecting – offices, machine shops, communication facilities, salvage operations, oil reserves. He drew two major conclusions. One was the disappointing realization that Cincpac could no longer be a sea-going command; its responsibilities were too far-flung, its contacts too numerous, for the incumbent to leave the complex communication centre at Pearl Harbor and move with the fleet. The other realization was that 'the Pearl Harbor disaster' could have been much worse. The raiding aircraft had missed the indispensable machine shops, the tank farm with its 4,500,000 barrels of fuel oil, and the Hawaii-based carriers *Enterprise* and *Lexington*, which were at sea.

On the last day of 1941 Nimitz relieved Pye as Cincpac and put on the four stars that came with the post. As a gesture to help restore morale, which had hit rock bottom with the fall of Wake, he retained Admiral Kimmel's staff.

During the first year of the Pacific War, the Japanese were on the offensive. Their basic operation consisted of two interrelated advances. The first was southward from Japan to the Dutch East Indies. The second, planned but not completed, was south-east from Rabaul in the Bismarcks, via New Guinea, the Solomons and the New Hebrides, to New Caledonia, Fiji and Samoa. All other Japanese operations in the Pacific were subsidiary to or supportive of these two advances. All US and Allied Pacific operations during that first year were in reaction to the two enemy advances or their subsidiary or supportive activities.

At this point, an outline of the background to Japanese aggression in the Pacific will be helpful. Their southward advance was in response to US refusal to sell them the oil they needed to conduct their ongoing war with China. They set out to seize another source – the Dutch East Indies, orphaned by Germany's conquest and occupation of the Netherlands. To safeguard the tankers bringing oil from the captured East Indies to Japan, they would have to conquer US and British bases flanking their route – Guam, the Philippines, Hong Kong and Singapore. Determined to control China, the Japanese recognized that these moves would bring the United States, Britain and the Dutch government-in-exile into the war as adversaries. To weaken the capacity of the US Pacific Fleet to interfere with their southward drive, Admiral Isoroku Yamamoto [*q.v.*], Commander-in-Chief of the Japanese Combined Fleet, sent his carrier force to raid Pearl Harbor. While retiring from the raid, the carriers lent support to the Japanese conquerors at Wake.

After brief upkeep in Japan, the carriers headed south to support their amphibious forces in conquering Rabaul in the Bismarcks, and Lae and Salamaua on the north coast of Papau (eastern New Guinea). The carrier force next entered the Indian Ocean and on 19 February 1942 staged a devastating raid on the Australian port of Darwin. Then, after cruising south of Java to support the Japanese invaders, in early April the carriers raided British naval bases in Ceylon and attacked British warships in the area, sinking a carrier, two cruisers and two destroyers. The remainder of the British Eastern Fleet retreated to Africa. By then, the seemingly invincible Japanese carrier force had steamed nearly 50,000 miles without any of its ships being sunk or even damaged by Allied action.

The Japanese had completed their southward drive well ahead of schedule – capturing Guam, Hong Kong and Singapore, and invading the Philippines, where they chased General Douglas MacArthur's Filipino–American army into Bataan Peninsula. Meanwhile, Japanese fleets were moving southward down the east and west coasts of Borneo. In the Battle of the Java Sea (27–28 February 1942) they destroyed the Allied defence force consisting of the small US Asiatic Fleet, to which Australian, British and Dutch ships had attached themselves.

The oilwells of Borneo, Sumatra and Java would now provide Japan with all the oil it needed. These and nearby conquered territories, which the Japanese now called their Southern Resources Area, would also provide them with ample supplies of tin, rubber, quinine and other strategic materials.

Headed south-east from Rabaul, the second Japanese advance was intended to isolate Australia. The bulk of Australia's army was in North Africa with the British, defending Egypt. What the Japanese dreaded was that the Americans would transfer armed forces to Australia, and use it as a base to recapture the adjacent Southern Resources Area and eventually to move on Japan via the Philippines. To prevent such a possibility, they hoped to establish bases on captured New Caledonia, Fiji and Samoa, from which their sea and air forces could block US–Australia communications.

With this in mind, late in April 1942, a Japanese invasion force was poised at Rabaul to take the next step in the south-eastward advance. It planned to set up a seaplane observation base at the small island of Tulagi (north of Guadalcanal in the Solomons) and to capture the Australian base of Port Moresby on the south coast of Papua. For close air support the invasion force was to be accompanied by the light carrier *Shoho*. For cover, to fend off any Allied sea force that might attempt to interfere, the Japanese carrier force (then returning from its raids on Ceylon) detached carriers *Shokaku* and *Zuikaku* and sent them to Rabaul.

Admiral King's initial orders to Admiral Nimitz were (1) to guard the Hawaiian Islands, including Midway, (2) to divert the Japanese from their southward drive into the East Indies, and (3) to protect shipping between Hawaii and the United States and between the United States and Australia. Numbers (2) and (3), if successful, would defeat the intent of the two Japanese advances.

Nimitz's assignment was complicated by orders from President Roosevelt to General MacArthur, instructing him to abandon his beleaguered army and escape from the Philippines to Australia. To solve the problem of two potential Commanders-in-Chief, the Joint Chiefs of Staff divided the Pacific theatre into four military operational areas – north, central, south and south-west. The first three were open ocean, spotted here and there with small or medium-sized islands and atolls. The fourth, the south-west area, enclosed most of the big islands – Australia, New Guinea, the Bismarcks, the East Indies and the Philippines.

Nimitz they appointed to command the north, central and south areas, which together were designated Pacific Ocean Areas. As Cincpac he continued to command US ships and sailors. As Commander-in-Chief Pacific Ocean Areas (Cincpoa), he commanded all American and Allied forces, land, sea and air, in or entering his assigned areas. They appointed MacArthur Commander-in-Chief of the South-West Pacific Area (Cincswpa), with similar overall command. The exception was the Pacific Fleet, which was to remain under Nimitz's control even if for strategic reasons it had to enter MacArthur's area.

The General raised no objection to his assignment. His South-west Pacific Area enclosed most of the terrain on which his army skills could be used to advantage, and it was the area of the Japanese advance. Hence for the present and foreseeable future it would be the main arena of the Pacific War. The long-term effect of this singular command arrangement was that the Pacific War against Japan effectively became two wars, Nimitz's war and MacArthur's war.

Besides initiating submarine warfare and organizing convoys, Nimitz believed he could best carry out King's orders (and also restore morale) by sending out carrier forces to make hit-and-run raids on Japanese bases. Vice Admiral William F. Halsey [*q.v.*], the officer commanding carriers assigned to the Pacific Fleet, led raids on the Gilberts, the Marshalls and on Wake and Marcus islands. These operations had the desired effect of bolstering American morale. Calling them 'great raids', newspapers proclaimed Pearl Harbor fully avenged, and hailed the colourful, salty-tongued Halsey as a national hero, 'Bull' Halsey, nemesis of the Japanese.

But Halsey's raids had little visible effect on the Japanese. They operated their bases as before and their southward drive continued unabated. The inherently cheerful Nimitz was discouraged. In the presence of his officers and men he maintained his usual air of serene confidence, but he was sleeping poorly. To Mrs Nimitz he wrote, 'I will be lucky to last six months. The public may demand action and results faster than I can produce.'

In April 1942, in his *Enterprise*-centred Task Force 16, Halsey escorted *Hornet* toward Japan. Lashed to *Hornet*'s flight deck were sixteen army B-25 bombers. The B-25s, with greater range than any carrier planes, could take off from the relatively short carrier deck, but they could not land back on it. On the 18th, at a point 620 miles east of the Japanese coast, *Hornet* launched the bombers. Both carriers immediately turned back and headed homeward at high speed, while the B-25s flew to Japan, dropped their bombs on Tokyo and other Japanese cities, and continued on, hoping to land on friendly airfields in China.

A couple of days after Halsey's departure for the bombing of Japan, Lieutenant-Commander Joseph Rochefort [*q.v.*] – the head of Pearl Harbor's Combat Intelligence Unit – offered two predictions based on code breaking and enemy traffic analysis. The Japanese, he said, would soon launch an operation to seize Papua, and they would follow this move with a much bigger operation in the Pacific, one involving their Combined Fleet.

The obvious target in Papua was Port Moresby on the Coral Sea. Allied bombers from there could attack Rabaul and the newly conquered Japanese positions on the Papua north coast. As for the coming Pacific Ocean operation, it seemed unlikely the Japanese would bypass Midway, the westernmost fortified US outpost in the Central Pacific.

The enemy attack force assigned to subdue and occupy Port Moresby would surely come by sea, with carrier support. Some help in reconnoitring and tracking such an approaching force could be provided by army planes in Australia and at Port Moresby, but their pilots were not trained for ship recognition or for overwater operations. If the Japanese were to be stopped at sea, the US Navy's carrier planes would have to do the stopping.

At Pearl Harbor there was hope, but no serious expectation, that Halsey with TF 16 would get back from the Tokyo Raid in time to take command and participate. Otherwise, the only naval unit Nimitz had in the Coral Sea was the *Yorktown* force, TF 17, commanded by Rear Admiral Frank Jack Fletcher, an officer not noted for audacity. Nimitz therefore sent the carrier *Lexington*'s force to join TF 17. MacArthur, now heading the South-West Pacific command, contributed a cruiser–destroyer force.

Nimitz moved rapidly. With some of his staff he flew to San Francisco for the first of a series of wartime strategy conferences with King. Returning to Pearl Harbor, he flew the 1,135 miles to lonely Midway atoll to inspect its defences. When he got back to Pearl on 3 May 1942, he learned that one of MacArthur's planes had sighted transports landing troops at Tulagi, with several Japanese warships standing by. The next day Fletcher, breaking radio silence, reported that his *Yorktown* planes had submitted Tulagi and nearby enemy ships to several hours of bombing and strafing.

Rochefort's Combat Intelligence Unit, co-operating with similar radio-traffic analysis and code-breaking units in Washington and Melbourne, had identified the detached Japanese carriers as *Shokaku* and *Zuikaku* and had traced them to Truk atoll, a Japanese base 700 miles north of Rabaul, and then to Rabaul itself. On 5 May MacArthur's scout planes observed these carriers together with two heavy cruisers passing north-east of Bougainville, evidently in response to Fletcher's raid on Tulagi. Nimitz's staff estimated that this enemy striking force would swing southward around the eastern end of the Solomons and enter the Coral Sea to hunt for TF 17, which was advancing to head off the Port Moresby invasion force.

On the morning of 6 May, bombers from Australia sighted the Japanese invasion force escorted by *Shoho* coming south from Rabaul, evidently intending to round the eastern tip of New Guinea and head for Port Moresby. The bombers attacked but made no hits. Cincpac staffers estimated that the Japanese striking force was now somewhere in the Coral Sea. After a tense afternoon anticipating contact reports that never came, they greeted the coming of darkness with relief.

Early on 7 May, a Japanese search plane over the sea reported sighting a carrier and a cruiser, and gave their bearing and distance from Rabaul. At Pearl Harbor a check on the chart of the reported position suggested that what the pilot had seen was in fact an American oiler and her escorting destroyer. A little after 0900 this surmise was confirmed when the oiler and the destroyer flashed distress signals. Several successive attacks by high-level bombers scored no hits, but a noon strike by dive bombers sank the destroyer and left the oiler a barely floating hulk.

At Cincpac headquarters concern for the oiler and destroyer and their crews was mingled with elation. Being so distant from any Japanese base, the dive bombers could only have come from carriers, which had to be *Shokaku* and *Zuikaku*. From the American point of view a dream set-up was in the making. Land-based planes – American and Japanese – reported the Japanese invasion force still coming down from the north and the American carriers coming up from the south, steadily closing the range. *Shokaku* and *Zuikaku*, whose mission it was to support their invasion force by attacking Fletcher's carriers, were off to the east bombing the oiler and destroyer. Fletcher, thus unmolested, was free to attack the invasion force.

When, after a long and tense wait, Fletcher's report reached Pearl Harbor, it gladdened all hearts there. His planes had sunk the light carrier *Shoho*, and the invasion force was in retreat. For the first time in World War Two, a Japanese advance had been turned back. The Americans had sunk their first enemy carrier, and if the Battle of the Coral Sea had ended at this point, it would have been an unqualified triumph for the US Navy.

But Nimitz knew that TF 17 was not likely to get off scot-free. The Japanese striking force was still in the Coral Sea. Its commander now knew TF 17's approximate location. He would unquestionably make every possible effort to retrieve his blunder by throwing everything he had at the American task force.

The next morning a little before noon, radio intercepts indicated that a battle was indeed in progress, apparently the first carrier battle in history – opposing ships out of sight of each other, attacking solely with aircraft. It was over in half an hour, and Fletcher made his preliminary report: 'First enemy attack completed. No vital damage our force.'

His succeeding messages were somewhat less favourable. *Yorktown*, he reported, had in fact been hit by one bomb, which had penetrated several decks. Temporarily slowed, she was now making thirty knots. *Lexington* had been struck by two torpedoes and a couple of bombs, which had done minor damage. On the other hand, one of the enemy carriers, identified as *Shokaku*, had taken at least three bomb hits and was burning briskly. Cincpac staff smiled with relief. The news could have been better; it could also have been far worse. Nimitz radioed Fletcher: 'Congratulations on your glorious accomplishment.'

But in the early evening the good cheer at Pearl Harbor was checked by an intercepted message from Fletcher to MacArthur requesting air coverage and implying that *Lexington* was having trouble. In mid-evening (still afternoon on the Coral Sea), Nimitz was stunned to learn that the 33,000-ton carrier had been abandoned and scuttled. Later information only confirmed the tragedy, with detail: petrol vapour from ruptured fuel lines had exploded deep inside her hull, setting off unquenchable fires and a series of explosions. After her crew had abandoned her, Fletcher ordered a destroyer to send her down with torpedoes.

The Japanese had taken Halsey's carrier raids far more seriously than Nimitz realized. The raid on Japan in particular was a crushing blow to Japanese pride. American bombs had fallen on Tokyo, home of the sacred Emperor, whose protection was the first duty of the Imperial armed forces. Admiral Yamamoto vowed retaliation. To complete the work of his Pearl Harbor attack, he now planned an attack on Midway. The earlier raid had sunk the American battleships; the upcoming one was intended to draw out the American carriers for destruction.

Following the Coral Sea battle, Nimitz knew enough about Yamamoto's plans to order the three available US carriers to Pearl Harbor. These were Fletcher's bomb-battered *Yorktown*, and *Enterprise* and *Hornet* of Halsey's TF 16, which had almost reached the Coral Sea when the battle there ended.

Meanwhile, working around the clock, the code breakers of Pearl Harbor's Combat Intelligence Unit were laying the groundwork for one of the all-time great feats of military intelligence. What they produced was mere scraps of deciphered enemy radio messages – fewer, in fact, than they had made available before Coral Sea. However, from the scraps and in collaboration with Lieutenant-Commander Edwin Layton, (Fleet Intelligence Officer), Rochefort worked out the Japanese plan for Midway almost completely.

The two officers learned that *Zuikaku* and *Shokaku* could not participate in the attack because in the Coral Sea battle the former had been stripped of planes, and the latter's bomb damages could not be repaired in time. Hints that transports were assembling in the southern Marianas convinced them that an invasion force would approach Midway from the south-west. It would be preceded by a carrier striking force, including four of the six carriers that raided Pearl Harbor.

At an intelligence conference late in May with Nimitz present, Layton recited all these facts and then concluded: 'The carriers will probably attack Midway on the morning of the 4th of June. They'll come in from the northwest on bearing 315 degrees, and they'll be sighted at about 175 miles from Midway, and the time will be about 0600 Midway time.'

This was a startlingly precise prediction, and it was very different from information being provided by the much larger intelligence unit in Washington and endorsed by King. Most of the Cincpac staff were inclined to believe that Rochefort, Layton and their colleagues had correctly interpreted their data, but to some of the staffers it seemed a little too complete. Might not the messages be fakes, deliberately planted to mislead the Americans? In the most daring gamble of his career, Nimitz decided to operate on the assumption that the Rochefort–Layton estimates were accurate.

On 26 May 1942, Halsey's TF 16 reached Pearl Harbor, but Halsey himself (on whom Nimitz had counted to repulse the Japanese) was suffering from severe dermatitis and required immediate hospitalization. Halsey asked to be relieved by Rear Admiral Raymond Spruance, his cruiser commander [*q.v.*]. Though Spruance was not an aviator, Nimitz consented. He was aware of Spruance's reputation for outstanding performance and had in fact requested orders for him to Cincpac as his Chief of Staff, but that new duty could wait.

The next day Fletcher's TF 17 arrived, *Yorktown* trailing an oil slick ten miles long. She was ordered directly into dry dock, where blocks were awaiting her. Before the dock had been completely drained, welding equipment, steel plate and other materials were being assembled nearby in compliance with Nimitz's fiat, 'We must have this ship back in three days.'

That evening the task force commanders and the Cincpac and task force staffs met to hammer out a battle plan. The guiding principle was that the Americans, with inferior forces but presumably better information, must achieve surprise, must get the jump on the enemy while he was in a vulnerable state.

On the morning of 28 May, Task Force 16, with Admiral Spruance in command, steamed out of Pearl Harbor in single file, assumed circular formation, took on planes and headed north-west. A little after 1100 the following morning *Yorktown* was towed out of her flooded dry dock into the harbour, where workmen continued their operations through the day and the ensuing night. On the 30th her engines started, and a loudspeaker announcement of 'all ashore that's going ashore' brought the last of the repairmen topside and into a waiting launch. Task Force 17 – *Yorktown* escorted by two heavy cruisers and two destroyers – filed out of the harbour, formed up and headed for its rendezvous with Task Force 16 at a position optimistically called Point Luck, 350 miles north-east of Midway. Here Fletcher would assume overall command.

Admiral Nimitz now could only wait. On each of the next three evenings, he retired early, banking up a little rest to help him face the busy times ahead. Dawn, 3 June, found the Admiral and his staff already at their stations. After a morning of vague radio intercepts, a solid piece of information came from Midway, which was linked to Honolulu by a segment of the old transpacific cable. The Midway cable station was relaying a report from a Catalina patrolling 700 miles to westward: 'Bearing 262, distance 700 . . . 11 ships, course 090, speed 19.'

The communication officer rushed the contact to Nimitz's office. As the Admiral read the words his expression became radiant. What the pilot had sighted was undoubtedly the Japanese invasion force – at approximately the time and location predicted by Layton. 'This will clear up all the doubters,' Nimitz said.

That night the Admiral dozed on a cot in his office. Again he and his staffers were at their stations at dawn. They knew that when first light came to Midway, Catalinas would be out to the north-west, patrolling at the edge of the nearly perpetual overcast. They were aware also that the report they were awaiting might well be the pivotal communication of the war.

Shortly after 0600 it came in plain language via the cable: 'Plane reports two carriers and main body ships bearing 320, course 135, speed 25, distance 180.' Evidently the pilot had made his report before the third and fourth carriers had come out from under the clouds. To Layton, Nimitz afterwards remarked: 'Well, you were only five miles, five degrees and five minutes off.' Never in the history of warfare had hard brainwork applied to such scanty data yielded more complete and accurate intelligence.

That day, which Americans later called the Glorious Fourth of June, was for Admiral Nimitz the most intense period of sustained tension he experienced in his entire career. He knew how much depended on the outcome of this battle, but he could not keep track of what was going on. His admirals at sea were reluctant to break radio silence, at least until they were reasonably sure of their facts, and intense static blotted out much intrafleet communication and pilot chatter. Via the cable came reports of heavy damage to Midway installations and severe loss of Midway-based planes. A Japanese search plane sighted and reported the US ships but did not for some time discern that there was a carrier among them.

Just when the battle should have been reaching a climax, Cincpac suffered a complete information blackout. Nimitz managed to look unruffled, but officers who knew him well could tell that he was deeply worried. One of them said afterwards, 'Admiral Nimitz was frantic.' Then, realizing that he had used an inappropriate word, he added, 'I mean, as frantic as I've ever seen him.'

The first news to emerge from the blackout was bad. Fletcher reported via a series of messages that his flagship *Yorktown* had been damaged by bombers, then by torpedo planes, and that she had been abandoned, but could apparently be saved. He asked Cincpac to send tugs and said that, unless directed otherwise, he would turn the tactical command over to Spruance and with Task Force 17 protect and attempt to salvage *Yorktown*.

On assuming command, Spruance reported that in a battle that morning three enemy carriers were believed to have been badly damaged. There followed several hours of long silences interspersed with reports of questionable accuracy. Nimitz wanted to hear again from Spruance, who was the type to report no facts that had not been checked and double-checked. At last – after dark, well into the Hawaiian evening – the report came. The three carriers previously attacked, said Spruance, 'were observed to the southwestward still burning', and he added that the fourth enemy carrier, plastered by bombs, was 'when last seen burning fiercely'.

When Nimitz looked up from the report, his face was glowing with one of his radiant smiles. He had a message sent to all his forces: 'You who participated in the Battle of Midway today have written a glorious page in our history. I am proud to be associated with you. I estimate that another day of all-out effort on your part will complete the defeat of the enemy.'

Before dawn all operational Japanese ships were in flight. Spruance pursued fruitlessly until 6 June, when his planes sighted two collision-damaged heavy cruisers. They sank one and heavily battered the other. That same day, a Japanese submarine found *Yorktown* under tow and fired a spread of torpedoes at her. They sank a destroyer alongside her and so damaged the carrier that she went down early on the 7th. On that day also Japanese landed on the small, barren US islands of Attu and Kiska in the western Aleutians.

The American victory at Midway was not cheaply won. It cost the United States a carrier, a destroyer, 147 planes, 307 lives and damage to base installations. But the Japanese lost four carriers and a heavy cruiser, 322 aircraft and 3,500 lives, including those of many first-line aviators whom they were never able to replace. After Midway the opposing fleets could meet on more nearly equal terms.

Shocked out of their delusions of invincibility by the defeat at Midway, the Japanese abandoned their drive to cut off Australia. The Americans had blocked their way by establishing bases at Nouméa, chief port and capital of New Caledonia, and on the islands of Efate and Espiritu Santo in the New Hebrides. The Japanese correctly surmised that these were intended not only as bars to their own advance but as springboards for an American advance in the opposite direction along the same route to recapture Rabaul.

The Japanese therefore set about tightening the defences of the points they already held. Rabaul required special attention, because it was threatened not only by the expected American advance but also by bombers from Port Moresby. Having signally failed to capture Port Moresby by sea, the Japanese now proposed to take it from the rear, by landing an army opposite it on the north coast of Papua and sending the troops against it across the 13,000-foot-high Owen Stanley Range. To block an American advance from the New Hebrides they began building a bomber base on Guadalcanal. Whoever first operated planes from this airfield would be hard to dislodge.

When cryptanalysis of Japanese radio despatches revealed these activities, the Allies snapped into action. General MacArthur took measures to block the Japanese tramontane approach to Port Moresby. Vice Admiral Robert

Ghormley, commander South Pacific Area with headquarters at Nouméa, assembled an expeditionary force of eighty-two ships, which (on 7 August 1942) entered the sound north of Guadalcanal and landed 10,000 US Marines on that island and 6,000 on nearby Tulagi. By the next day these invaders had captured both the Tulagi seaplane base and the airstrip, still unfinished, on Guadalcanal.

Before the Allied expeditionary force at Guadalcanal could complete unloading, an enemy cruiser force from Rabaul arrived at night and, firing shells and torpedoes, sank an Australian and three American heavy cruisers. Japanese failure to follow up this success with quick further action, however, enabled the Americans to complete the airstrip and have aircraft operating from it.

From this point on the Battle of Guadalcanal consisted mainly of a struggle for the airstrip. The Japanese began landing troops on the island at night, and Admiral Yamamoto based his Combined Fleet on Truk to lend support. In the fleet's first attempt at a joint operation, it lost a light carrier and a good many planes, but three of its carrier aircraft succeeded in bombing *Enterprise*. Within the next month, Japanese submarines swarming into the area sank the carrier *Wasp* and severely damaged both the carrier *Saratoga* and the new battleship *North Carolina*.

The Japanese, discovering that they lacked troops to achieve concurrent victories in Papua and on Guadalcanal, decided to assume a strong defensive posture in the former while concentrating on the latter. From Rabaul and the upper Solomons, transports – each bringing as many as 900 troops – now began arriving at Guadalcanal with such nightly regularity that the disgusted Marines called them the Tokyo Express, and as the numbers of Japanese on the island increased, the spirits at Ghormley's South Pacific headquarters sank proportionately.

Learning of the growing defeatism at Nouméa, Nimitz went south with members of his staff to investigate. They found a curious dichotomy. Ghormley and his officers were haggard with fatigue and anxiety, bogged down in detail, stymied by indecision and infected with pessimism. Flying to Guadalcanal, the Nimitz party found an entirely different spirit. Though the Marines were gaunt from fatigue and malaria and facing a growing enemy, they were determined to hold the island and convinced they could do so.

A few days after Nimitz's return to Pearl Harbor, Halsey, fully recovered, left for the South Pacific to resume his carrier command. In the meantime news from Guadalcanal of increasing gravity reached Pearl Harbor – heavy destruction of American planes, night naval bombardments of the airstrip, Japanese on the island outnumbering the Americans. When Halsey's plane reached Nouméa, he was handed a radio despatch from Nimitz: 'Immediately upon your arrival at Nouméa, you will relieve Vice Admiral Robert L. Ghormley of the duties of Commander South Pacific Area and South Pacific Force.'

Halsey, reviewing the situation at Guadalcanal, knew the price of victory at Guadalcanal would be high, but he had the nerves and courage to pay it. He sent a force with *Hornet* and the newly repaired *Enterprise* against a four-carrier enemy force. The enemy sank *Hornet* and again put *Enterprise* out of action. When Halsey had no further alternative, he sent cruisers against battleships and took heavy losses. He had *Enterprise* patched up and sent her again into battle.

At length, by adroit use of naval and land-based air power, Halsey began to inflict more damage than he was taking. Despite strenuous efforts, the Japanese did not succeed in bombing the airstrip again. When they tried to ram through to Guadalcanal a reinforcement of 13,500 soldiers in eleven transports, American aircraft sank seven of the ships. The four that reached the island under cover of darkness barely had time to discharge their troops before dawn revealed them to the Americans, whose bombers and long-range artillery quickly set all four ablaze with the supplies they had brought still on board. The Japanese garrison on Guadalcanal now had extra men to feed and otherwise provide for, without additional victuals or equipment.

It was clear to all that so far as Guadalcanal was concerned the Japanese had shot their bolt. Nimitz said to newsmen: 'Halsey's conduct of his present campaign leaves nothing to be desired.' A grateful Congress voted Halsey a fourth star.

The Pacific War had reached its real turning point. The Japanese made no further attempt to reinforce their Guacalcanal garrison. They merely held on there while they strengthened their defences in the central Solomons. In early 1943, as the Americans on Guadalcanal were about to close the pincers on the enemy positions, a score of Japanese destroyers in three high-speed night runs carried away the 12,000 half-starved survivors of their garrison – a force which, the previous November, had numbered 34,000.

While the Americans were tightening their grip on Guadalcanal, MacArthur's Australians and Americans a thousand miles to westward were also ridding Papua of the Japanese. Profiting by Japan's shift of emphasis from seizing Port Moresby to conquering Guadalcanal, the Allied troops pursued their withdrawing enemies over the Owen Stanley Mountains and in November 1942 cornered them in the Buna area. The Japanese clung to their patch of coast till late January 1943, when their defences collapsed, as much from starvation and disease as from Allied attacks.

While both Halsey and MacArthur were preparing to cap their victories with a dual advance on Rabaul, Pearl Harbor's Combat Intelligence Unit made another significant contribution. Its cryptanalysts broke a radioed schedule of Yamamoto's impending inspection tour by air of Japanese bases in the upper Solomons. After checking with Washington, Nimitz ordered Halsey: 'Get Yamamoto!'

On 18 April 1943 – a year to the day after aircraft from Halsey's task force had dropped bombs on Tokyo – long-range P-38s took off from Guadalcanal, sped 400 miles north-west out of sight of land, and met and shot down Yamamoto's plane as it approached one of the Solomon bases precisely on schedule. The consequence was twofold. The loss of Yamamoto was a severe blow to Japanese morale, particularly in the navy, where he was highly respected, not to say revered. Just as importantly, the Japanese Combined Fleet would now be commanded by Admiral Mineichi Koga, a far less able man.

At the end of June, MacArthur's South-West Pacific Forces and Halsey's South Pacific Forces began their drive on Rabaul, the former from the south-west via New Guinea and New Britain, the latter from the south-east via the Solomons. MacArthur's troops were carried to their beachheads by his small Seventh Fleet; Halsey's by his small Third Fleet, which also fought a series of night battles with Japanese surface forces.

In August, the Joint Chiefs of Staff concurred with King that Rabaul should be neutralized and bypassed rather than captured. To that end South and South-West Pacific aircraft repeatedly bombed the Japanese base, and MacArthur's forces captured the Admiralty Islands, while Halsey's captured the Green and Emirau islands, thus completing a ring of airfields around Rabaul, whence bombers kept it pounded down.

Meanwhile, a North Pacific Force under Rear Admiral Thomas Kinkaid [*q.v.*] had cleared the Japanese out of the western Aleutians. Retaking Attu required 11,000 American soldiers to dislodge the 2,600 defenders from their mountain fastness. In mid-August, supported by nearly a hundred men-of-war, transports bringing 29,000 US and 5,300 Canadian troops approached Kiska. They found the island unoccupied. In foggy weather three weeks earlier, Japanese cruisers and destroyers had slipped in and evacuated the entire garrison. Kinkaid, promoted to vice admiral, his assignment completed, went south to assume command of General MacArthur's Seventh Fleet.

Admiral Nimitz, as Cincpac, had long since developed a definite but not inflexible routine. He rose at 0645, shaved, dressed and breakfasted. Then, usually accompanied by Admiral Spruance, he walked briskly to his headquarters, which in 1943 was housed in a well-guarded white concrete, bombproof structure on Makalapa hill across the road from the Pearl Harbor Naval Base. He was usually at his desk by 0730 in his light and airy office on the first floor. He read despatches that had come in during the night and received staff members who had reports and problems requiring his immediate attention.

The Cincpac morning conference began at nine o'clock, in Nimitz's office or in a nearby conference room. Expected to attend were key staffers, visiting fleet and force commanders and senior participants in recent or forthcoming operations. Senior officers stationed or visiting on Oahu were welcome. Commander Layton opened the proceedings with his intelligence briefing. Nimitz then called on visitors from combat areas to make reports. Discussion followed under Nimitz's general guidance. Since these were informational rather than planning or decision-making meetings, the atmosphere was informal, and Admiral Nimitz might rise and close the proceedings at any time.

At eleven o'clock the Admiral received commanding officers of all ships, from lieutenants (j.g.) commanding LSTS to senior captains of battleships and carriers as they arrived at Pearl Harbor. He wanted to size them up and also let them know they had an identity with the fleet commander. He opened each meeting with a few remarks about what he was planning to do. His visitors would listen, fascinated at hearing high strategy from its source. 'Now tell me what you are doing,' he would say and look at each man he wanted to hear from. He would ask if any of them were unhappy, if there was anything he could do for any of them. When the allotted time was up, he would rise, go to the door and shake hands with the officers as they filed out.

Most afternoons were left unstructured, though there was usually plenty for Nimitz to do, including intensive planning sessions with staff members and with officers involved in forthcoming operations. It was in the planning stage that the Admiral was most thorough. He would pick drafts of war plans to pieces and send them back for revision. At planning sessions he acted like a chairman of the board, guiding and being guided by others. He made the final decisions, sometimes despite contrary advice, but he first heard the advice and weighed it carefully. He knew that World War Two was far too complex for any one man in any theatre of operations to do all the high-level thinking, keeping his own counsel and at last handing down Napoleonic decisions.

Admiral Nimitz as Cincpac undertook to do nothing that anybody else could do. He delegated as much authority to each of his subordinates as he believed he should be able to handle, reserving his own energies for decision-making and for the ceremonial and social obligations that were appropriate only for the Commander-in-Chief. His staff handled the voluminous Cincpac correspondence but kept him informed of any facts from that source that he needed to know. He personally signed answers to letters addressed to himself, including those from schoolchildren whose misguided teachers taught them that the way to do research was to write letters of inquiry to busy officials.

Nimitz's staff worked seven days a week, often well into the evenings, but there was no objection to officers knocking off work in the middle of the day to play a game of tennis. Admirals Nimitz and Spruance never hesitated to pause for exercise or relaxation when their presence at headquarters was not essential. Nimitz believed in maintaining a hard-working staff, kept as small as practical, but he also wanted a healthy, efficient staff. He expected his people to work around the clock when necessary, but when duties permitted he wanted them to keep in shape by exercising and relaxing. He could not forget the harassed look and manner of Admiral Ghormley's South Pacific staff, bogged down in detail and infecting the whole area with defeatism.

On quiet days Nimitz knocked off work at 1600 or 1630, allowing time for a long walk, often with Spruance, or a fast game of tennis, perhaps followed by a horse-shoe match, then a bath before the evening meal. Almost invariably when Nimitz did not go out to dinner, he had guests to dine with him and his housemates, who were usually his Chief of Staff and the fleet surgeon. The invitees were generally senior officers visiting or stationed on Oahu or members of his large staff. Of the latter, even the most junior could expect at some date to join one or two of his colleagues in dining with the Commander-in-Chief.

Before dinner Nimitz had cocktails served, never more than two, and had two himself, usually old-fashioneds. After dinner, which was well served and usually well worth waiting for, Nimitz joined his guests in smoking cigarettes, a nearly universal custom at that time. Sometimes he would show a movie, or (more often, and to the acute boredom of some of his guests) he would turn off the lights, throw open the blackout curtains and play records of classical music.

Nimitz went to bed at 2200. He awakened at 0300, read till 0500, and then caught another wink from 0500 till 0645. A swift reader, he consumed a good deal of material in his nightly two hours of reading – usually history or biography, preferably in military areas.

During 1943, while Halsey and MacArthur were conducting their limited offensive against Rabaul, Nimitz was assembling at Pearl Harbor forces for an all-out offensive across the Central Pacific. Since early in the century such a drive had been US strategy for relief or recapture of the Philippine Islands, should they be attacked by the Japanese. A significant modification in this time-honoured plan was now called for by MacArthur's South-West Pacific Forces, already in contact with the enemy in New Guinea. While Nimitz's Americans were advancing westward island by island across the centre, MacArthur's Seventh Fleet would carry his Americans and Australians westward beachhead by beachhead along the north coast of New Guinea.

To Pearl Harbor from American shipyards and factories came fleet carriers, fast battleships, dive bombers and torpedo planes – weapons least wanted in the European theatre, but precisely what Nimitz needed to launch his offensive. To command this growing force (later titled the US Fifth Fleet) King – on Nimitz's recommendation – appointed Raymond Spruance.

The appointment of a non-aviator to command a carrier-led armada provoked consternation and criticism among the naval aviators, but Spruance's intellectual eminence was widely recognized, and the Battle of Midway had demonstrated that he could lead carrier forces to victory. Since then, his thirteen months at Pearl Harbor as Cincpac Chief of Staff had given Nimitz adequate opportunity to size up his abilities. A Cincpac staffer remarked, 'The Admiral thinks it's all right to send Raymond out now. He's got him to the point where they think and talk just alike.'

Participation of military aircraft required another modification in the old war plan. The Central Pacific drive would begin not with an American invasion of the Marshall Islands, as originally proposed, but with occupation of the adjacent Gilbert Islands. Planes based on existing Allied airfields could reach the Gilberts for photo-reconnaissance and to provide support for the invading forces. After positions in the Gilberts had been captured, planes based on these could perform the same services for the Marshalls invasion.

In late November 1943, the Fifth Fleet commanded by Spruance (now vice admiral) invaded islands suitable for airfields in the Gilbert atolls of Makin, Tarawa and Abemama. Occupying Makin was comparatively easy and Abemama was a pushover. Interest in the Gilberts operation centres mainly on the difficult conquest of Betio Island in Tarawa atoll. The three-day battle to wrest two-mile-long Betio from its 3,000 elite defenders cost the US Marines some 3,000 casualties, including more than a thousand killed. At this harsh price the Americans learned the techniques that were to carry them across the powerfully defended beaches of the Central Pacific.

The initial targets for the Marshalls invasion were the three major islands of Kwajalein, the world's largest atoll. Profiting by the lessons of Tarawa, the Fifth Fleet and the Gilberts-based aircraft gave targets on the Marshalls such heavy and extended advanced bombing and bombardment that US soldiers took the southern island and US Marines the two northern islands without severe casualties. Since conquest of the Kwajalein targets, swiftly completed, had not required committing his corps reserve, Spruance pushed on without delay to assault Eniwetok atoll, more than 300 miles to the north-west.

Nimitz had been much involved in planning for both the Gilberts and the Marshalls. During the assaults he remained at Pearl Harbor in radio contact with elements of the Fifth Fleet, but avoided intervening in the conduct of operations. Shortly after the conquests, he arrived by plane with members of his staff to confer with the victorious officers and to study at first hand the difficulties they had overcome.

The Americans wondered why Koga's Combined Fleet had not emerged from its anchorage at Truk to contest these conquests of Japanese-held islands. The plain answer was it did not because it dared not. During their increasingly desperate defence of Rabaul and its approaches, at first sparingly and then recklessly, Yamamato and later Koga had expended their carrier planes to augment Japan's decimated land-based air force. By now, the loss of carrier pilots had so far outstripped training of replacements that the Combined Fleet was paralysed. Hence, when the Americans invaded the Marshalls, the toothless Japanese fleet hastily retreated westward to the Palau Islands. From here too it fled a few weeks later when, at MacArthur's request, the Fifth Fleet fast carrier force (Task Force 58) approached the Palaus to blast it off the flank of the General's coastal advance.

Through various intelligence sources, Nimitz kept track of the Japanese Combined Fleet. Most of it was reorganized into the carrier-centred Mobile Fleet, a carbon-copy of TF 58 but only about half as powerful. It based itself on the Tawi Tawi island group between the Philippines and Borneo, evidently to be near Borneo's oilwells – and its planes, unburdened by the weight of such lifesaving equipment as body armour and self-sealing petrol tanks, considerably outranged American carrier planes. Nimitz and MacArthur ordered submarines to the area, and these (by sinking three destroyers and half a dozen freighters) so convincingly announced their presence that the carriers remained at anchor. Their aviators, unable to practise their skills, lost their fighting edge.

Nimitz had reason to believe that when the Americans threatened the Marianas, on Japan's inner defence line, the Mobile Fleet would be obliged to fight, ready or not. His belief was correct. On 11 June 1944, when TF 58 planes began bombing the island of Saipan in preparation for an invasion, US submarines reported that the enemy fleet had left its Tawi Tawi anchorage. Subsequent submarine reports indicated that it was heading for the Marianas, apparently intent on battle.

On 19 June Pearl Harbor radio intercepts indicated that the expected battle was in progress. At dusk Admiral Spruance reported: 'Air attack on Task Force 58 commenced at 1045. . . . Over 300 enemy planes are reported destroyed by our planes and AA fire. Own aircraft losses not yet reported. Only known damage to our ships: 1 bomb hit on *South Dakota*, which does not affect her fighting efficiency.' Cincpac staff was gratified to learn of heavy enemy aircraft losses with minimum damage to TF 58, but what about the enemy carriers? Weren't any sunk? Or even damaged?

The following day the only solid information to reach Pearl Harbor was that US carrier planes had attacked the enemy fleet at sunset, with undetermined results. So far as the Americans afloat and ashore knew, not a single enemy carrier had been sunk; but in fact, three had gone down. US submarines had penetrated the Mobile Fleet on the 19th and torpedoed two carriers. A third carrier had been done in by an airborne torpedo in the sunset battle of the 20th, but as no Americans had lingered to observe the death throes of their victims, none could be certain whether the ships were still afloat.

Many US naval officers considered the slaughter of enemy planes and flyers slight compensation for the apparent fact that most, or all, of the Japanese carriers escaped destruction. In view of the American advantages, they had anticipated something like a clean sweep of the Mobile Fleet. Now the US Navy would have to fight at least one more battle to eliminate the Japanese army.

These dissatisfied officers tended to blame Spruance. They learned that Vice Admiral Marc Mitscher [q.v.], commanding TF 58, had recommended heading west towards the Mobile Fleet at 0130 on the 19th so as to have the enemy ships within reach of his planes by dawn. Spruance had rejected the proposal. He believed he was bound to remain near Saipan lest a segment of the enemy fleet, making an end-run, should get behind him and attack the amphibious shipping at the beachhead.

Thus all day on the 19th, the Mobile Fleet was able to hold off beyond reach of the American planes, while its own longer-range aircraft vainly attacked the American ships. Only when TF 58 had obviously about stripped the enemy fleet of aircraft did Spruance feel justified in heading out from the Marianas.

Uncertain in what direction the enemy was retreating, TF 58 did not locate him until late on the 20th. Hence the brief sunset battle.

Unable again to overtake the fleeing enemy, in the evening of the 21st Spruance called off the chase. The action of 19–20 June was officially titled the Battle of the Philippine Sea, but to American sailors who on the 19th had witnessed hundreds of Japanese planes falling into the sea, some like autumn leaves, others afire and streaking like comets, it would always be the 'Great Marianas Turkey Shoot'.

Both Nimitz and King (and some naval historians in later years) strongly defended Spruance's decision, but in 1944 most naval aviators insisted that Spruance had muffed the opportunity of the century. 'This', they said, 'is what comes of placing a non-aviator in command of carriers.'

The fight for the southern Marianas continued till mid-August 1944, when US forces completed their conquest of Saipan, Tinian and Guam at the cost of more than 5,000 American and nearly 60,000 Japanese lives. For both sides the effect was critical: Japan had lost its direct staging line to the Carolines; the United States had acquired logistic bases for further conquests westward and airbases from which the new, long-range B-29 bombers could reach Tokyo.

Having blocked Japan's southbound line of communications, the Americans planned to block its northbound line through the South China and East China seas, the so-called oil line. Via this route, ships carried oil and other strategic materials from the East Indies and South-East Asia to the home islands of Japan. The main choke point was the Luzon–China–Formosa triangle. The Joint Chiefs of Staff directed both Nimitz's Central Pacific and MacArthur's South-west Pacific drives towards this triangle, where bases could be set up on either Luzon or Formosa to 'plug the oil line'. The Joint Chiefs' planners estimated that one or the other of the Allied drives, or both, would reach Luzon or Formosa by the spring of 1945.

This tentative schedule called for MacArthur's forces, supported by the Central Pacific Fleet, to land on Mindanao, the large southern island of the Philippines, on 15 November 1944 and on Leyte in the central Philippines on 20 December. On Mindanao and Leyte the invading Americans were to establish airfields to neutralize and contain Japanese forces in the rest of the Philippines. Desiring to avoid another slow, island-hopping advance, King and Nimitz proposed bypassing Luzon, the northernmost and principal Philippine island. They suggested 1 March 1945 as a date when Central Pacific and South-western Pacific Forces could make a combined landing on Formosa, 375 miles closer to Japan.

MacArthur raised such strong objections to bypassing Luzon that Roosevelt joined him and Nimitz in a conference in Honolulu to discuss the move. Nimitz was persuaded by MacArthur's arguments, but King insisted on his Formosa strategy. As it turned out, the strategy was decided by neither of them, but by Admiral Halsey.

When Halsey and his force commanders completed their assignment of neutralizing Rabaul, they turned their ships over to the Fifth Fleet. The Joint Chiefs now conceived the plan of having them alternate the fleet command with Spruance and his commanders. Under Halsey it would be the US Third Fleet, with the force commands appropriately renumbered. While one team was at sea, the other would be ashore planning for the next move. This double-echelon system, unique in the history of warfare, was counted on to speed up the war.

Halsey's first new assignment was the capture of two islands in the Palau group. For that operation he left the close support to the escort carriers and the old battleships and other gunnery vessels of his amphibious force. Halsey himself in his flagship *New Jersey* joined the fast carrier force, now designated TF 38, but still headed by Mitscher, who insisted on remaining in command through the initial invasion of the Philippines. With the carrier force, Halsey moved along the Philippine coast to lend distant support to the Palau operation by raiding enemy airfields while prepared to fend off any enemy fleet that approached the Palaus to interfere.

On 12 September at Pearl Harbor, Nimitz received a startling radio message. It was from Halsey, who reported that the central Philippines, lightly defended to begin with, had been rendered practically defenceless by TF 38's raids. The islands, he said, were now wide open, and he recommended bypassing all intervening objectives and invading Leyte as soon as possible.

Nimitz was unwilling to cancel the ongoing Palau operation, but he forwarded Halsey's recommendation to the Joint Chiefs, who were then at Quebec in conference with the British Chiefs. He endorsed the Halsey proposal and offered to make available to MacArthur the 3rd Amphibious Force and an army corps. The Joint Chiefs checked with MacArthur's headquarters in New Guinea and, receiving an affirmative reply, rescheduled the Leyte operation for 20 October. In ninety minutes the timetable for the Pacific War had been advanced two months.

The temporary transfer of the 3rd Amphibious Force to MacArthur's Seventh Fleet left Halsey's command stripped down to TF 38, though it continued to be referred to as Third Fleet. In preparation for the invasion, all available Allied air power (land-based in China and New Guinea, and afloat) commenced isolating Leyte and weakening the Japanese opposition, particularly in the air. Beginning on 10 October, the Third Fleet, assigned to the northern flank, bombed airfields and hangars and other installations and shot down enemy planes over Luzon, Formosa and the Ryukyu Islands.

In the battle for Leyte Gulf (which followed MacArthur's 20 October invasion of Leyte) Halsey pursued a strategy in sharp contrast to that of Spruance in the Philippine Sea. It has been suggested that Halsey was motivated, at least in part, by the criticism he heard directed at Spruance's refusal on 21 June to advance and attack the Japanese carriers.

On 24 October, American flyers sighted two Japanese naval surface forces passing through the Philippine Islands – a powerful centre force and a much smaller southern force. They were both apparently heading to attack the Allied shipping off the Leyte Gulf beachhead after traversing, respectively, San Bernardino and Surigao Straits. Three of Halsey's carrier groups, patrolling outside San Bernardino Strait, sent bombers and torpedo planes in a series of attacks on the centre force, approaching in the Sibuyan Sea. Kinkaid ordered his Seventh Fleet gunnery ships to block Surigao Strait and waylay the approaching southern force.

At 1512 Halsey radioed his group commanders a battle plan that he proposed putting into effect, should the centre force succeed in transiting the strait. The plan listed battleships, cruisers and destroyers to be withdrawn from the Third Fleet carrier groups to form a TF 34, which was to 'engage decisively at long ranges' while the carriers kept clear of the surface fighting.

In the late afternoon, Third Fleet scout planes reported a northern force, with carriers, east of the northern tip of Luzon. At nightfall (evidently after an extended staff discussion) Halsey radioed Kinkaid, with King and Nimitz as information addressees: 'Strike reports indicate enemy force Sibuyan Sea heavily damaged. Am proceeding north with three groups to attack enemy carrier force at dawn.' The recipients of this message construed it to mean that Halsey was heading north with three *carrier* groups, leaving TF 34 behind to guard San Bernardino Strait.

Towards dawn on the 25th, Kinkaid announced by radio that his Seventh Fleet gunnery vessels, including old battleships on loan from the Third Fleet, had met the enemy southern force in Surigao Strait and virtually destroyed it. These glad tidings were swiftly followed, however, by a whole series of messages from him of a very different sort. The Japanese centre force had come through San Bernardino Strait during the night and was bombarding one of three small escort carrier units guarding the approaches to Leyte Gulf.

In despatches of increasing stridency Kinkaid called on Halsey for help. In plain English he demanded, 'Request immediate strike by fast carriers.' Then, in code, 'Fast battleships are urgently needed immediately at Leyte Gulf.' And, 'My situation is critical. Fast battleships and support by carrier strikes may be able to keep enemy from destroying escort carriers and entering Leyte.'

King's and Nimitz's headquarters were apprehensive listeners to this traffic. At Pearl Harbor, as the messages were deciphered and recorded, Captain Bernard Austin, Cincpac Assistant Chief of Staff, brought them to Nimitz in the latter's office. It was apparent that TF 34 had not been left guarding San Bernardino Strait, but Nimitz was not greatly worried. There was enough American air power in the Leyte area to hold the centre force at bay until the old battleships could arrive on the scene from their victory in Surigao Strait.

Still, Nimitz was too concerned to do useful work. He pulled a sheaf of papers over to himself. It was brief answers prepared by his staff in reply to student queries sent at the suggestion of those misguided teachers. The

Admiral was glancing over the replies and signing them when Austin brought in a shocker. It was a signal from Kinkaid telling Halsey that the Seventh Fleet's borrowed old battleships were low in ammunition.

That fact threw a different light on the situation. There was real danger that the centre force might fight its way into the gulf and do a great deal of damage. Nimitz was reluctant to intervene, however, because he considered it bad practice to interfere with a commander at the scene of action, and besides there was not much Halsey could do at a distance of 400 miles from Leyte Gulf. Knowing Halsey, Nimitz guessed correctly that he had taken all his ships north, had formed TF 34 that morning and was now in it, forging out ahead of his carrier groups to fight an old-fashioned surface battle with stragglers and with ships crippled by Mitscher's carrier planes.

Austin, observing that Nimitz was perturbed, concluded that he was wondering where TF 34 was. Trying to be helpful, he suggested, 'Admiral, why couldn't you just ask Admiral Halsey the simple question: "Where is Task Force 34?"'

Nimitz thought for a minute and then said, 'Go and write it up. That's a good idea.'

Austin supposed the question was intended as an inquiry, but Nimitz was using it as a nudge – to remind Halsey that Cincpac was listening and questioning the use he was making of TF 34.

When the message reached Halsey a little after 1000, it appeared less a nudge than a taunt. Austin's yeoman had added 'Repeat where' for emphasis, and the receiving communicator had failed to remove the after section of the fore-and-after padding that sending communicators routinely add to encoded despatches to baffle enemy cryptanalysts. The message placed in Halsey's hands read: 'WHERE IS, RPT [repeat] WHERE IS TASK FORCE THIRTY-FOUR RR THE WORLD WONDERS.'

Halsey, his nerves already in shreds from Kinkaid's persistent screaming, was stunned. His Commander-in-Chief and good friend Chester Nimitz appeared to be taunting him with heavy-handed sarcasm. The old sea-dog plucked off his cap, slammed it on to the deck and broke into sobs.

As Nimitz had guessed, Halsey was in TF 34, recently formed, including all six Third Fleet battleships, and now out ahead of TF 38. When Halsey had regained a grip on himself, he ordered TF 34 to reverse course, from due north to due south. As he passed the still northbound TF 38, he detached one of its carrier groups to provide air cover for his ships.

That morning the Japanese centre force, in attacking the escort carrier unit, had sunk one of the little carriers and damaged two others. The unit's destroyers and destroyer escorts valiantly counter-attacked, firing torpedoes. The centre force sank three of its small assailants with gunfire but fell into confusion eluding their torpedoes. Planes from all three escort carrier units and from Leyte attacked the centre force, sinking three of its cruisers and inducing the remainder of the force to retire.

Halsey, learning that the centre force was heading back towards San Bernardino Strait, shaped course to intercept it, but when he reached the vicinity of the strait a little after midnight, the only centre force ship that had not passed back through it was a destroyer that had lingered to pick up Japanese survivors. The American cruisers and destroyers darted ahead and sank the ship with gunfire and torpedoes. Halsey's six battleships had steamed 300 miles north and then 300 miles back south between the two main enemy forces without quite making contact with either.

Commanded by Mitscher, the part of Task Force 38 that had not gone south with Halsey pursued the northern force past Luzon's Cape Engaño, sinking all four of its carriers and two of its destroyers. Because the Japanese carriers attempted no counter-attack and appeared almost bare of planes, some of the American officers concluded that the northern force was a mere decoy, sent to lure Halsey away from Leyte Gulf so that the centre and southern forces could close in on the Allied shipping in the gulf. After the war the Japanese confirmed this conclusion. Unable to replace pilots lost in the Marianas Turkey Shoot, the Japanese carriers were otherwise useless.

The battle for Leyte Gulf involved more tonnage and covered a greater area than any other naval contest in history. Its outcome, despite Halsey's taking the Japanese bait, was a clear American victory. Not only had the Japanese been thwarted in their scheme to sink American shipping in Leyte Gulf, but they had lost a staggering 306,000 tons of their own ships – three battleships, four carriers, ten cruisers and nine destroyers. The Americans, at a cost of 37,000 tons of warships – one light carrier, two escort carriers, two destroyers and one destroyer escort – had won command of the Pacific Ocean and ended Japan's capacity to wage another fleet battle.

Army planes could not support US combat operations on Leyte because monsoon rains turned the island into a swamp. Army engineers were unable to extend the existing airfield or build a new one. Hence TF 38 (with Vice-Admiral John Sidney McCain replacing Vice Admiral Mitscher but with Admiral Halsey still in overall command) had to remain off the Philippines. Its carrier planes pounded the Japanese all-weather airfields on Luzon and repeatedly attacked a new Tokyo Express bringing supplies and reinforcements to Leyte.

The Japanese, seeing no way to produce adequately trained pilots, introduced the dreaded kamikazes, young men who made up in guts what they lacked in skill by hurling themselves and their planes into ships or other targets. The kamikazes inflicted severe damage on Halsey's Third Fleet, but they launched their most savage attack on Kinkaid's Seventh Fleet as it was bringing invasion forces to Luzon. In this onslaught the suicide planes damaged forty-three ships, including eighteen severely damaged and five sunk. In addition, they killed 738 men in the fleet and wounded nearly 1,400.

When the South-west Pacific forces had made good their foothold on Luzon, Halsey reported to Ulithi atoll east of the Philippines and on 27 January 1945 left his battered TF 38, which again became TF 58 as Mitscher took command. Kinkaid, after some persuasion, returned most of the ships Nimitz had lent the Seventh Fleet. These, together with TF 58 and ships newly arrived from the European theatre, formed an enlarged US Fifth Fleet with Spruance in command.

The collaboration between the South-Western Pacific and the Central Pacific forces was now at an end. MacArthur was planning a southward drive for recovery of the rest of the Philippines and of the East Indies. Nimitz was prepared to carry out his assignment: capture Iwo Jima and Okinawa. He had recently been promoted to fleet admiral. To be nearer the scene of action, he now shifted his headquarters from Pearl Harbor to Guam.

Iwo Jima, halfway between Saipan and Tokyo, is an eight-square-mile heap of lava and ashes. Major-General Curtis LeMay wanted it as a base for fighter planes to escort his Marianas-based B-29s while flying daylight missions against aircraft-engine factories in the Tokyo area. Though Iwo had 21,000 defenders, Nimitz believed the Fifth Fleet had developed sufficient power and skill to capture it in a few days.

In fact, its conquest by fleet-supported Marines required nearly a month of vicious fighting and mutual slaughter. The Japanese, having burrowed themselves behind their guns in holes and caves, had to be blasted out with grenades and satchel charges or burned out with flamethrowers and incendiary bombs. Most of the defenders were killed. In the invasion forces, ashore and afloat, more than 19,000 men were wounded, and nearly 7,000 were killed or died of their wounds. 'Among the Americans who served on Iwo Island,' said Nimitz, 'uncommon valor was a common virtue.'

Iwo Jima in American hands proved valuable as a haven for planes damaged or short of fuel, but by the time it was conquered the main reason for its conquest no longer existed. General LeMay had found what he regarded as a more efficient means of shrinking Japanese production. Instead of daytime precision bombing of factories, for which his B-29s needed Iwo-based fighter escorts, he had the big planes make night raids with incendiary bombs to set fire to the highly inflammable Japanese homes.

His most notable achievement in this type of warfare was in the night of 9 March 1945 when more than 300 B-29s, unaccompanied by fighters, dropped over 2,000 tons of fire bombs on Tokyo from low altitude. They thus burned out nearly sixteen square miles of the city, incinerating 83,000 men, women and children and burning or otherwise injuring 14,000 others.

About this time LeMay learned of a possible new dimension for his bombing plan. An officer emissary from the Joint Chiefs of Staff arrived in the Marianas to inform him, Nimitz and a few other officers that an atomic bomb was under development, expected to have an energy yield equivalent to about 20,000 tons of TNT, enough to destroy an entire city. The bomb, they were informed, should be available in the Pacific theatre about 1 August.

The recipients of this startling news, men accustomed to explosives that blasted in accordance with principles they understood, heard the message with some scepticism. 'Young man,' said Nimitz, 'this is very interesting, but August is a long time from now, and in the meantime I have a war to fight.' Then realizing that shrewd officers like the Joint Chiefs would hardly let themselves be bamboozled by some mad scientist's dream, he added, as if to himself, 'You know, I guess I was just born a few years too soon.'

The US Tenth Army, including both soldiers and Marines, began invading Okinawa on 1 April 1945. In this slim, sixty-mile-long island, just 340 miles from Japan, nearly 100,000 Japanese troops had prepared a defensive bastion like a king-size Iwo Jima, except that its holes, caves and trenches were dug not into soft lava but into solid earth and rock. When the Tenth Army reached this citadel, it slowed to the yard-by-yard sort of advance that had characterized the fighting on Iwo Jima.

To help fend off air attacks on the invading army and to protect the army's huge intake of seaborne supplies, TF 58 generally remained between Okinawa and Japan. Off the south-western end of Okinawa, to fend off air attacks from Formosa, was a British force of four carriers, two battleships, five cruisers and fifteen destroyers, now serving with the Fifth Fleet as Task Force 57. It had been invited to join the US Navy at the urging of Prime Minister Winston Churchill in order to participate visibly in the Allied victory over Japan so as to regain prestige in the Orient, where previously in the war British forces had experienced only defeat.

Every day enemy aircraft, including kamikazes, attacked ships of the amphibious or carrier forces. Among the vessels early put out of action was Admiral Spruance's flagship. On 6–7 April the Japanese launched the first of a series of massive air attacks, about 700 planes, more than half of them kamikaze.

Alarmed for his fleet and wondering why the army was making so little progress, Admiral Nimitz went to Okinawa to investigate. As his plane was landing, sirens announced Condition Red, and amid a great burst of anti-aircraft fire he saw several suicide planes hit ships. This was the only time in his life that he observed armed forces in combat.

To Lieutenant-General Simon Bolivar Buckner, Tenth Army commander, Admiral Nimitz emphasized the need to speed up operations ashore in order to release the supporting fleet. In reply, the General pointed out that this was a ground operation – implying that it was army business and something a naval officer could not be expected to comprehend. Nimitz glanced icily at Buckner. 'Yes, but ground though it may be,' he said, 'I'm losing a ship and a half a day. So if this line isn't moving within five days, we'll get someone here to move it so we can all get out from under these stupid air attacks.'

The Tenth Army picked up little momentum. Despite Nimitz's impatience, the fast carrier task force had to remain north-east of Okinawa patrolling a sixty-square-mile area for nearly three months, while its planes supported the troops ashore, combated enemy aircraft and carried out anti-submarine patrols. Six times the force moved north to attack Kyushu airfields.

The kamikazes found most of their victims among the picket destroyers and the ships off Okinawa, but the fast carrier force took its share of hits. Admiral Mitscher lost a large part of his staff and had to shift flagships twice in three days as crashing kamikazes successively put carriers *Bunker Hill* and *Enterprise* out of action. South-west of Okinawa the British carriers also came under persistent attack, but their armoured flight decks made them less vulnerable to the kamikazes than the contemporary American carriers, with wooden flight decks and armoured hangar decks.

The strain on the American senior commanders, who never left the scene of action, became almost unbearable. At last, towards the end of May, Admiral Nimitz sent in the Halsey team to relieve Spruance and his force commanders, whereupon the Fifth Fleet again became the Third Fleet and TF 58 became TF 38.

In the Okinawa campaign the Tenth Army suffered 7,600 killed and 31,800 wounded. Supporting the campaign proved the most costly naval operation in history. At least thirty US ships and craft were sunk and 368 damaged, many beyond repair. More than 4,900 sailors were killed. Many of the 4,800 listed as wounded were in fact hideously burned by the petrol fires that usually accompanied kamikaze strikes.

On 21 June 1945 the US forces declared Okinawa secured. That night the Japanese commanding General and his Chief of Staff acknowledged defeat by taking their own lives. The next day in Tokyo the Japanese Emperor announced to his Supreme War Council that Japan must find a way to end the war.

Three weeks later US code breakers intercepted a message from the Japanese Foreign Minister to his Ambassador in Moscow, directing him to ask the Soviet Union to mediate peace terms between Japan and the Allies. When the Russians took no action, the Allies responded to the Japanese peace feeler with the Potsdam Declaration of 26 July. It took the Japanese Cabinet by surprise. They had not begun preparing the armed services and the Japanese people for surrender. These would have to be assured that they could keep their Emperor, implied but not spelled out in the proclamation.

Before the Japanese could get their questions answered and their people and armed forces prepared to accept defeat, B-29s from the Marianas dropped atomic bombs on the cities of Hiroshima and Nagasaki, leaving much of the world with the firm conviction that the bombs had won the war.

On 2 September 1945 in Tokyo Bay, on board Halsey's flagship *Missouri*, General MacArthur staged the memorable surrender ceremony. After the Japanese delegates had signed the instrument of capitulation, General MacArthur signed the acceptance on behalf of all the Allied powers and Admiral Nimitz signed for the United States, followed by the signatories of the other Allied powers. When all had affixed their signatures, MacArthur addressed the assemblage: 'Let us pray that peace be now restored to the world and that God will preserve it always. These proceedings are now closed.'

At that moment the sun came from behind the clouds, and a massed flight of several hundred US planes, carrier aircraft and B-29s, swept over Tokyo Bay and the British and American ships anchored there. Some of those present thought of another massed flight of planes nearly four years earlier, that of Japanese aircraft on a less peaceful mission over Pearl Harbor.

Served as Chief of Naval Operations, the US Navy's professional head, from late 1945 to his retirement from active duty in 1947 at age sixty-two. From beginning of 1948, made himself available as a special assistant to the Secretary of the Navy and served as a roving goodwill ambassador for the United Nations (1949–51). Died 20 February 1966, four days short of his eighty-first birthday.

6

Admiral

Raymond A. Spruance
United States Navy

1886–1969

by
John F. Wukovits

RAYMOND *Ames Spruance, born in Baltimore, Maryland on 3 July 1886; entered the US Naval Academy on 2 July 1903; graduated 1906, twenty-fifth in a class of 209. Member of 'Great White Fleet', 1907–8. Commanded destroyer* Bainbridge *1913–14. Served in a variety of posts before World War Two (while steadily advancing up the command ladder, earning a reputation for 'attention to detail, poise and power of intelligent decision'. Promoted rear admiral 14 December 1940: received command of Cruiser Division Five, a unit of four heavy cruisers based out of Pearl Harbor that operated with a carrier task force led by his good friend Admiral William F. Halsey, 1941.*[1]

Spruance was eating breakfast in his cabin on board his flagship, the heavy cruiser *Northampton*, 200 miles north-west of Hawaii, when Japan struck. His flag lieutenant, William M. McCormick, called him from the bridge shortly after 0800 with the shattering news that Pearl Harbor had been attacked.

'Thank you. You know what to do,' replied a calm Spruance. McCormick immediately put into effect the orders Spruance had earlier issued covering a war situation, calling for increased alertness and battle readiness. After finishing breakfast Spruance walked to the bridge, where he remained for the next twenty-four hours.[2]

Nothing prepared him for what he saw when his force steamed into Pearl Harbor on 8 December. Considered a battleship admiral, Spruance believed

---

[1]Thomas B. Buell, *The Quiet Warrior* (Boston, 1974), pp. 3–6, 9–89; Samuel Eliot Morison, *The Two-Ocean War* (Boston, 1963), p. 334.
[2]Buell, *Warrior*, p. 96.

those mighty warships would lead his nation to a decisive naval clash with Japan. They now rested on the floor of Pearl Harbor, transformed from lethal offensive weapons into twisted metal coffins. Always a quiet man, Spruance said nothing to those around him.3

A visit later that day to Admiral Husband F. Kimmel, Commander-in-Chief Pacific Fleet, at Cincpac headquarters did nothing to lift his spirits. Kimmel appeared haggard and dishevelled. Demoralized staff members panicked at rumours that the Japanese fleet was preparing to land soldiers on Hawaii. Men whose job was to organize a navy's response to its most shattering defeat sat numbed at their desks.4

Though devastated by what he saw, Spruance contained his emotions until he reached home. There he poured out his feelings to his wife and daughter, and wept as he tried to convey the destruction at Pearl Harbor. Spruance had never before allowed his emotions to rush out in this manner, and his family would never witness it again.5

However, yearning to strike back, Spruance rebounded quickly. His enthusiasm was not shared by Kimmel's temporary replacement, Vice Admiral William S. Pye, who commanded until Admiral Chester W. Nimitz [*q.v.*] arrived in late December. Pye was reluctant to take action, so when the more aggressive Nimitz took over on 31 December Spruance was pleased as 'we commenced to go places and fight'.6

The Pacific Fleet was too shattered to organize any major operations. For the time being, Nimitz limited the offensive to quick bombardment raids against enemy-held islands, ostensibly conducted to damage Japanese installations but actually staged to boost American morale at home and in the Pacific.7

In two February 1942 raids against the Marshall Islands and Wake Island, Spruance's cruisers, and carriers under the command of Admiral William F. Halsey [*q.v.*], inflicted minor damage on the Japanese. Meagre intelligence hampered their selection of important targets, while erroneous reports from nervous lookouts about enemy submarines threw Spruance's force into disarray. Spruance was angered by the jittery reports and considered these raids failures, but typically blamed himself. 'The ships scattered in all directions,' he later said of the first raid to his new flag lieutenant, Robert J. Oliver, 'and no amount of signalling got them back. I had lost control.'8

Spruance was too hard on himself. Some damage had been done, and (more importantly) American morale rose, because the US Navy had finally retaliated after two months of war. Halsey returned a hero, and Spruance was awarded the Navy Commendation Medal.9

At times during these raids, Spruance's staff worried about his tendency to

3Ibid., p. 97; E. P. Forrestel, *Admiral Raymond A. Spruance, USN: A Study in Command* (Washington DC, 1966), p. 24.
4Buell, *Warrior*, p. 97.   5Ibid., pp. 97–8.
6Ibid., p. 98.   7Ibid., p. 99; Morison, *Two-Ocean*, p. 139.
8Buell, *Warrior*, pp. 99–107.   9Ibid., pp. 107–10; Forrestel, *Spruance*, p. 25.

remain on the open bridge (rather than retreating to the armoured conning tower) and about his refusal to wear a steel helmet or a life jacket. Spruance believed an admiral should show courage in battle, and he wanted to be out where his men could see him and he could command a better view of the action. In the Marshalls, one concerned young officer asked him, 'Admiral, don't you think you'd better get back in the conning tower?' The fifty-five-year-old Spruance replied simply, 'No, but maybe you'd better, because you have so much longer to live than I have.'[10]

For the next two months, Spruance accompanied Halsey's force as it darted back and forth across the Pacific, first delivering the men and bombers of Lieutenant-Colonel James H. Doolittle to within 700 miles of the Japanese coast for their famous raid on Tokyo, then heading to the South Pacific to assist in halting a Japanese advance in that area. Halsey's force arrived too late to participate in the Battle of the Coral Sea, the first major naval clash between aircraft carriers, but its own chance to fight was fast approaching. On 16 May, Halsey received orders to hustle back to Pearl Harbor without delay.[11]

Accompanied by Spruance, he did so, but Nimitz was shocked when he saw them – Halsey had lost twenty pounds' weight and had developed a rash covering his entire body. Obviously unable to lead Task Force 16 in the coming action, Halsey recommended that his cruiser commander, Spruance, succeed him.[12]

The proposal surprised Spruance, since he was not the most senior officer available, had never served in an aircraft carrier and was a non-aviator. In addition, his style of leadership was the direct opposite from the popular Halsey, an aggressive fighter who loved publicity. Recognition was unimportant to the methodical Spruance; doing a job correctly satisfied him. Blessed with 'a brain seemingly composed of millions of computers', Spruance was the only flag officer in the navy whom the bright Chief of Naval Operations Admiral Ernest J. King [*q.v.*] admitted was smarter than he.[13]

Nimitz explained to Spruance and to Admiral Frank Jack Fletcher that something big was in the works. Japan's most gifted naval leader, Admiral Isoroku Yamamoto [*q.v.*], Commander-in-Chief Combined Fleet, was out to destroy the American carriers missed at Pearl Harbor. He designed an intricate plan employing sixteen different groups in hopes of drawing out the American fleet in a decisive battle. His strategy focused upon Midway Island, an American base about 1,100 miles north-west of Hawaii which he believed would be too valuable for the Americans to lose. This would entice the American fleet which his powerful force (led by the Striking Force's four

[10]Buell, *Warrior*, pp. 103, 106, 113–14.   [11]Ibid., pp. 117–19.
[12]E. B. Potter, *Nimitz* (Annapolis, Maryland, 1976), p. 84; Costello, *The Pacific War*, p. 278.
[13]Walter Lord, *Incredible Victory* (New York, 1967), p. 30; Forrestel, *Spruance*, p. 3; Editors of the Navy *Times*, *Operation Victory* (New York, 1968), p. 61; Eric Larrabee, *Commander in Chief* (New York, 1987), p. 156; Thomas B. Buell, *Master of Sea Power* (Boston, 1980), p. 336.

aircraft carriers under Admiral Chuichi Nagumo [q.v.] and followed 300 miles behind by his own Main Force of battleships and a small carrier) would annihilate.[14]

Fletcher's damaged carrier *Yorktown* was rapidly being patched up for the battle. As senior officer, he would be in tactical command. Together, he and Spruance were to lie in wait north-east of Midway. Surprise was essential since the Japanese vastly outnumbered the American force, and as soon as the enemy was sighted an air attack was to be launched that would hopefully catch the Japanese carriers with half their planes away attacking Midway.[15]

According to his biographer, Thomas B. Buell, written orders directed Spruance to hold Midway, but unwritten orders specified that he was not to lose his fleet, even if it meant yielding the island, as the fleet's loss would open the entire Pacific Ocean to the Japanese. Spruance was to employ his carriers without endangering them needlessly. In a separate letter, Nimitz instructed Spruance that he was to be 'governed by the principle of calculated risk, which you shall interpret to mean the avoidance of exposure of your force without good prospect of inflicting, as a result of such exposure, greater damage to the enemy'.[16]

Spruance decided he would launch every available plane from Task Force 16, containing the two carriers *Enterprise* and *Hornet* accompanied by six cruisers and twelve destroyers, at the Japanese as soon as he knew the location of their carriers. This was a gamble, since he would be caught without his planes if the Japanese found him first, but if this calculated risk succeeded then Japan could be turned back in the Pacific.[17]

Spruance inherited Halsey's veteran staff, led by the brilliant but emotionally unstable Captain Miles R. Browning. As was his custom wherever he commanded, Spruance remained in the background while the staff went about its work, becoming involved only when necessary. He encouraged staff members to state their views at any time, believing a free exchange of opinions was 'most important to success in war planning'. To familiarize himself with Halsey's staff and to learn more about carrier operations, Spruance often invited various members to accompany him on his lengthy walks about *Enterprise*, picking their brains with each step. Even in horrendous weather Spruance could be found dashing about the decks with his latest victim.[18]

---

[14]Ronald H. Spector, *Eagle Against the Sun* (New York, 1985), pp. 166–7; Lord, *Incredible Victory*, p. 4; John Costello, *The Pacific War* (New York, 1982), p. 281.

[15]Lord, *Incredible Victory*, p. 31; Gordon W. Prange with Donald M. Goldstein and Katherine V. Dillon, *Miracle at Midway* (New York, 1983), pp. 103–4; Potter, *Nimitz*, p. 87; E. B. Potter, *Bull Halsey* (Annapolis, Maryland, 1985), pp. 79–80.

[16]Buell, *Warrior*, pp. 123–4.   [17]Ibid., pp. 123–5.

[18]Ibid., pp. 123–7; Morison, *Two-Ocean*, p. 154; Paul S. Dull, *A Battle History of the Imperial Japanese Navy (1941–1945)* (Annapolis, Maryland, 1978), p. 139; Larrabee, *Commander in Chief*, p. 390; Lord, *Incredible Victory*, p. 60.

On 2 June Fletcher, with Task Force 17 (consisting of the repaired *Yorktown*, two cruisers and six destroyers), joined Spruance at sea and assumed tactical command. The American force could now only wait and hope intelligence placed them in the best position to inflict optimum damage on the stronger Japanese fleet. Typically, Spruance issued no ringing declaration to his force before the battle, stating simply there was a chance for them to harm Japan and the 'successful conclusion of the operation now commencing will be of great value to our country'.[19]

On the morning of 4 June Nagumo stood within 200 miles of Midway Island. Optimism ran high at a pre-dawn staff meeting, since the latest intelligence reports from Tokyo indicated no evidence of an American task force anywhere in the area. At 0430 Nagumo launched the first Midway strike wave of seventy-two bombers and thirty-six fighters, retaining 126 more planes loaded with armour-piercing bombs and torpedoes to use against any American naval force that might appear. At the same time Nagumo ordered scout planes to search the area around him. He thought little of the fact that the cruiser *Tone*'s patrol plane was delayed one half-hour by mechanical problems.[20]

At 0545 Spruance learned that Japanese planes were approaching Midway from the north-west. Eighteen minutes later a search plane reported two carriers and two battleships 180 miles north-west of Midway, a mere five miles from where American intelligence had predicted they would be sighted.[21]

Fletcher ordered Spruance to proceed south-west to attack the enemy carriers while he remained behind to recover search planes. Crucial decisions regarding this important battle would thus be made by Spruance rather than by Fletcher. Spruance later explained his battle philosophy to his new flag lieutenant, Robert Oliver. A leader must go into battle with a good plan and stick with it during those times when its progress and course are clouded by quickly unfolding events. Spruance added that a commander must also understand that a battle's outcome often depends upon luck.[22]

Above all, Spruance wanted his mind free to ponder major decisions; his staff could handle other matters. Charles J. Moore, his Chief of Staff after Midway, remarked that Spruance hated being bothered with minor details and 'Unless you had something really important to talk to him about, he just wouldn't talk. He would make a nasty face and look disgusted, and if he did listen he acted as if he were bored to death.' Moore added that Spruance 'was thinking all the time, and when the time came for something to be done,

[19]Buell, *Warrior*, pp. 128–9.

[20]Costello, *The Pacific War*, pp. 286, 290; Spector, *Eagle Against the Sun*, p. 170.

[21]Lord, *Incredible Victory*, p. 95; Buell, *Warrior*, pp. 130–1; Larrabee, *Commander in Chief*, p. 361; Costello, *The Pacific War*, p. 287.

[22]John Winton, *War in the Pacific* (New York, 1978), pp. 56–7; Costello, *The Pacific War*, p. 287; Buell, *Warrior*, pp. 140–1, 260.

he usually anticipated me. He was ready to act on it before I was ready to present him with any proposals.'[23]

Spruance's first major decision was to launch his planes immediately to hit the Japanese before they hit him. When the message pinpointing the Japanese carriers came in, Spruance rose from his seat and unrolled a manoeuvring board he carried with him at all times. After plotting ranges and bearings, the Admiral estimated the Japanese were approximately 175 miles away, barely within the maximum range of his torpedo planes. Rolling up his manoeuvring board, Spruance calmly ordered Browning to 'Launch the attack', even though he knew some planes might run out of fuel before getting back to the carriers. The pilots' safety was subordinate to striking first.[24]

Spruance then took a gamble, by ordering every possible plane to attack, rather than holding back half of them for defence. Only two of the possible four or five Japanese carriers had been sighted, but Spruance trusted intelligence reports predicting that all enemy carriers would advance close together. If Nagumo's carriers were split, and the unlocated carriers found Spruance, he would be attacked with all his planes away. Spruance was willing to accept this calculated risk.[25]

He planned a co-ordinated attack in which dive bombers plunged at the Japanese from above, while torpedo planes skimmed along the surface, but slow progress in launching the *Enterprise* planes prompted him to abandon this. When the Japanese search plane from the *Tone* appeared on the horizon, indicating that Spruance's presence was known to the enemy, it became even more urgent to get his planes winging towards the Japanese carriers; so at 0745 Spruance signalled Lieutenant-Commander C. W. (Wade) McClusky, the *Enterprise* air group commander, to attack with the planes aloft. The remainder would follow after.[26]

Fletcher launched his planes at 0838. Three separate groups of American torpedo planes, dive bombers and fighters were now on their way to the Japanese carriers. As yet, not one Japanese attack plane was headed towards Spruance's force.[27]

Though he could not have realized it, Spruance's timing was perfect, for Nagumo was experiencing an excruciating ninety minutes. A second strike on Midway became necessary when the first strike failed to knock out its airfields, so Nagumo ordered his reserve planes moved below decks to switch from armour-piercing bombs and torpedoes, which were used against light-skinned ships, to high-explosive bombs appropriate for land targets. Since no American carriers had been sighted, this delay seemed safe.[28]

[23]Buell, *Warrior*, p. 260.
[24]Ibid., pp. 130–1; Morison, *Two-Ocean*, p. 154; Forrestel, *Spruance*, p. 45.
[25]Lord, *Incredible Victory*, p. 137; Buell, *Warrior*, p. 131.
[26]Larrabee, *Commander in Chief*, pp. 373–4; Buell, *Warrior*, pp. 132–3.
[27]Costello, *The Pacific War*, p. 290; Buell, *Warrior*, p. 135.
[28]Spector, *Eagle Against the Sun*, p. 171; Costello, *The Pacific War*, p. 288.

At 0728 the pilot in the tardy *Tone* search plane radioed information to Nagumo's staff that 'struck them like a bolt from the blue'. The pilot was following ten American ships, but for one hour he failed to mention if the force included a carrier. The frustrated Nagumo halted the rearming of his second Midway force until he received definite word of an American carrier, but when he finally did, the planes from his first Midway strike were circling overhead, low on fuel.[29]

He could either recover his planes and chance being attacked with crowded decks, or he could immediately launch an attack against the American carrier, forcing many of his own circling planes to ditch in the ocean. Nagumo decided he had sufficient time to recover the Midway planes first, but before the recovery and rearming were completed, Spruance's torpedo planes and dive bombers arrived to shatter the Japanese plans.[30]

American torpedo planes located Nagumo's carriers at 1000, arranged neatly in a boxlike formation surrounded by a protective screen of two battleships, three cruisers and eleven destroyers. The first three waves of torpedo attacks were easily beaten off by Japanese Zeros and anti-aircraft fire, elevating Japanese hopes for victory.[31]

But massacring the torpedo planes had drawn the protective screen of Zeros down to almost sea level, and because of their different routes many of Spruance's other planes arrived about the same time, giving him his hoped-for co-ordinated attack. Before the Zeros could regain proper altitude, McClusky's thirty-seven *Enterprise* dive bombers and Lieutenant-Commander Maxwell E. Leslie's seventeen *Yorktown* dive bombers attacked three of Nagumo's carriers. In six minutes, *Akagi*, *Kaga* and *Soryu* were blazing wrecks. Only *Hiryu*, separated from the other three carriers in manoeuvring to avoid air attacks, survived.[32]

After the war Nimitz called this air blitz 'the attack that in minutes changed the whole course of the war'. Timing and luck were everything this day. Spruance's decision to launch immediately and in an uncoordinated manner brought his planes over the enemy at precisely the most vulnerable time, while Nagumo's decision to delay an attack on Spruance's carriers to recover his Midway planes was fatal. In addition, had the *Tone* search plane not been delayed, Nagumo would have discovered the American carrier sooner, giving him more time to launch his own attack.[33]

[29]Mitsuo Fuchida and Masatake Okumiya, *Midway: The Battle That Doomed Japan* (Annapolis, Maryland, 1955), pp. 165–7; Spector, *Eagle Against the Sun*, pp. 171–2.

[30]Spector, *Eagle Against the Sun*, p. 172; Costello, *The Pacific War*, pp. 291–3; Morison, *Two-Ocean*, pp. 153–4.

[31]Buell, *Warrior*, p. 133; Morison, *Two-Ocean*, pp. 155–6.

[32]Fuchida, *Midway*, p. 177; Larrabee, *Commander in Chief*, p. 376; Spector, *Eagle Against the Sun*, pp. 174–5; Costello, *The Pacific War*, p. 295.

[33]Costello, *The Pacific War*, p. 286; E. B. Potter and Chester W. Nimitz (eds), *Triumph in the Pacific* (Englewood Cliffs, NJ, 1963), p. 20.

Spruance knew that at least one more Japanese carrier remained. At 1205 *Hiryu* dive bombers, following *Yorktown* planes to their ship, scored three hits on *Yorktown* which knocked out her radar and forced Fletcher to yield tactical control to Spruance. At 1445, after *Yorktown* had absorbed a second attack, an American search plane sighted the fourth Japanese carrier. Spruance ordered an immediate launch, and at 1700 *Enterprise* dive bombers screamed down on *Hiryu*, mortally wounding Nagumo's last carrier.34

Bold in the morning, Spruance now exercised caution in the evening. Instead of heading west after the enemy, he decided to turn east until midnight, then north for an hour before heading west for the next day's action. He later received heavy criticism from some navy leaders for this conservative move, but Spruance knew from intelligence that powerful Japanese forces were closing in from the north-west and from the Aleutians. Since none of his pilots had actually seen *Hiryu* sink, he could not discount its ominous presence in the area. He also reasoned that at night-time his carriers would be easy prey to enemy battleships and destroyers trained in night actions. With *Yorktown* badly damaged, his two carriers were all that Nimitz had left in the Pacific. Spruance no longer faced an acceptable risk.35

By doing this, Spruance avoided the trap Yamamoto set for him that night with his potent Main Force, although for a time Nimitz was not sure what his commander was doing. Commander Edwin T. Layton, Nimitz's intelligence officer, recalled, 'It was not at first clear to us why Spruance had chosen to be so cautious,' since intelligence had yet to pick up any signs of Yamamoto's Main Force. When Layton finally received indications of a powerful Japanese force west of Spruance, he realized Task Force 16 would have been gravely imperilled had it been drawn within range of Yamamoto. 'If Spruance had not exercised the caution he did,' concluded Layton, 'our victory could have been shot to pieces before dawn.' Yamamoto cancelled the Midway operation around 0300 when he saw that Spruance could not be enticed west.36

By mid-morning the next day (5 June 1942), Spruance unleashed his force on the fleeing enemy. Captain Browning developed an attack plan which pilots hotly contested as being so unrealistic in range and tonnage of bombs that few planes would have sufficient fuel to return. Wade McClusky, who had led the

---

34John Toland, *The Rising Sun* (New York, 1970), p. 421; Larrabee, *Commander in Chief*, p. 380; E. B. Potter and Chester W. Nimitz (eds), *The Great Sea War* (Englewood Cliffs, NJ, 1960), p. 238; Buell, *Warrior*, pp. 136–9; Henry H. Adams, *1942: The Year That Doomed the Axis* (New York, 1967), p. 212.

35Richard Hough, *The Longest Battle* (New York, 1986), p. 200–1; Buell, *Warrior*, pp. 139–40; Spector, *Eagle Against the Sun*, p. 175; Costello, *The Pacific War*, pp. 302–4; Lord, *Incredible Victory*, p. 256; Larrabee, *Commander in Chief*, pp. 379–80; Forrestel, *Spruance*, p. 50; Prange, *Miracle at Midway*, p. 302–3.

36Ronald Lewin, *The American Magic* (New York, 1982), p. 105; Costello, *The Pacific War*, pp. 303–4; Rear Admiral Edwin T. Layton (Ret.) with Captain Roger Pineau (Ret.) and John Costello, *And I Was There* (New York, 1985), pp. 444–5; Spector, *Eagle Against the Sun*, p. 176.

Enterprise dive bombers the day before, stormed into Spruance's flag shelter to present their case to the Admiral. Browning refused to alter his plans, and amid rising tempers one of the pilots said to Spruance, 'Admiral, we will go if *you* tell us to. But if we go, we won't be coming back.' Spruance looked at McClusky and replied, 'I will do what you pilots want.' This decision infuriated Browning, but Spruance sided with who was correct, not who carried the most rank.[37]

The planes failed to locate any part of the Japanese fleet for the remainder of the afternoon. By the time they returned to the carriers, darkness had settled in, forcing Spruance to illuminate his force to make landings safer. This action could have highlighted his ships for lurking enemy submarines, but in Spruance's mind a carrier was useless without its planes. All planes but one landed safely.[38]

Early the following day (6 June), Spruance again ordered his fleet to head after remnants of the retreating enemy. Later in the day American planes pounced on two cruisers, sinking one and badly damaging the other. Spruance steamed west until he was within 700 miles of Wake Island, when he turned back towards Pearl Harbor. He knew his pilots were exhausted from their three-day running battle and that his ships were low on fuel, but, wisely, he had also decided beforehand that he would not be drawn within the 600-mile range of Japanese land-based planes on Wake. That morning one of his staff had asked the Admiral how far he would chase Japanese remnants and Spruance responded, 'Let me answer your question by telling you what I won't do. I will not expose this force to attack by shore-based aircraft. Therefore I will not pursue within range of shore-based air power.'[39]

Once again Spruance made the proper decision. Seven Japanese cruisers and eight destroyers were then converging on him, intending to engage him in night action should he proceed far enough to the west. Spruance, who said, 'I had a feeling, an intuition perhaps, that we had pushed our luck as far to the westward as was good for us,' ended the Battle of Midway by pulling back.[40]

Spruance was criticized at the time by many naval figures for his failure to chase aggressively after the Japanese, particularly on the night of 4 June. However, these critics were not privy to intelligence which supported Spruance. Midway was a glorious triumph for the United States. Japan lost four carriers, one heavy cruiser, 3,500 sailors, 322 planes and her best pilots. Had Japan won at Midway, the entire Pacific would have been its for the taking.[41]

Captain Browning actually received most of the credit immediately after the battle, since many believed Spruance had followed his plans. In fact, all major decisions were made by Spruance, but he never contested the acclaim given to

37Buell, *Warrior*, pp. 141–2.   38Ibid., p. 143.

39Ibid., pp. 144–7; Forrestel, *Spruance*, pp. 53–4; Potter and Nimitz, *Triumph in the Pacific*, p. 23.

40Potter and Nimitz, *The Great Sea War*, p. 244; Forrestel, *Spruance*, p. 54.

41B. H. Liddell Hart, *History of the Second World War* (New York, 1970), pp. 351–2; Costello, *The Pacific War*, p. 308; Morison, *Two-Ocean*, p. 148.

Browning, since he believed a commander who sought headlines 'may subconsciously start thinking in terms of what this reputation calls for, rather than of how best to meet the action problem confronting him'. Even later in the war, when he directed enormous armadas in victorious campaigns across the Pacific, he minimized his role by telling people, 'I don't do much in this job. I have some excellent people working for me. . . . It wouldn't be right for me to sit here at the top and grab the glory.' He was content at Midway that he had commanded in a major battle, and that he had won.[42]

As time went on and a clearer picture emerged of Midway, Spruance's stature increased. His Japanese opponents lost little time in comprehending the importance of this quiet man. Captain Yasuji Watanabe, a staff officer for Yamamoto, credited Spruance with possessing an 'air admiral's best character – strong, straight thinker, not impulsive fluctuating thinker; he aims right at main point and go, no stop. That is good admiral.' Before Midway, Spruance was an unknown factor to the Japanese. Afterwards he was a man they respected and feared. The historian Samuel E. Morison summed up Spruance's actions at Midway as 'superb. Calm, collected, decisive, yet receptive to advice; keeping in his mind the picture of widely disparate forces, yet boldly seizing every opening, Raymond A. Spruance emerged from this battle one of the greatest admirals in American naval history.'[43]

On 18 June 1942, Spruance became Chief of Staff to Nimitz in Pearl Harbor, where he supervised a seventy-five-man staff and became Nimitz's main adviser. The two leaders quickly developed a close rapport, often discussing strategy and bouncing ideas off each other. Spruance admired Nimitz for his 'marvellous combination of tolerance of the opinion of others, wise judgment after he has listened and determination to carry things through'.[44]

Spruance possessed those same qualities. During the Battle of Midway, for instance, a group of naval aviators expressed their concern that their future was hopeless since the navy had no policy of relieving them. If they survived one battle, they would be thrown into another until they were killed. Spruance agreed with the pilots and persuaded Nimitz to install a rotation system which placed fresh fliers in action while sending home experienced pilots to train replacements.[45]

While working for Nimitz, Spruance received confirmation that his Midway strategy was sound. One day Layton walked into his office with captured Japanese documents proving that Spruance would have steamed directly into Yamamoto's ships had he continued west. A relieved Spruance exclaimed, 'The weight of a score of years has been lifted from my shoulders.'[46]

[42]Buell, *Warrior*, pp. 148–50, 336, 461; Spector, *Eagle Against the Sun*, pp. 176–7; Forrestel, *Spruance*, pp. 243–4.

[43]Larrabee, *Commander in Chief*, p. 393; Forrestel, *Spruance*, p. 56; Morison, *Two-Ocean*, p. 162.

[44]Buell, *Warrior*, pp. 151, 168; Potter, *Nimitz*, p. 229.

[45]Buell, *Warrior*, p. 153.　　[46]Ibid., pp. 158–9.

In August 1943, Spruance was named as Commander, Central Pacific Force and Commander, Fifth Fleet, with the responsibility of directing America's massive offensive through the Central Pacific. For the first time in his career he commanded large forces, yet rather than assembling a huge staff as many other admirals would do, Spruance kept his to a minimum. He wanted 'the smallest number of first-class men who can do the job', to whom he would give a large degree of responsibility, so he would be free to concentrate on the most important decisions. Spruance considered that some leaders 'seem to feel that to recognize and use the ideas of others is an admission of their own inferiority'. He believed that, by knowing the strengths and weaknesses of his staff and by encouraging their use of imagination tempered with common sense and reason, the staff would be highly productive. Spruance relied heavily on his staff throughout the war, often throwing them into exasperation with his refusal to consider minor details or his penchant for disappearing into the hills for lengthy hikes.[47]

Even his choice of flagship was typical. Rather than a large, new battleship he selected the twelve-year-old heavy cruiser *Indianapolis*, whose less spacious quarters would keep his staff smaller and whose presence would not be sorely missed whenever he needed to head to different parts of the battle area.[48]

His battle plans were so thorough that every subordinate commander knew to whom he reported, who reported to him and what his exact role was. Spruance commented that 'making war is a game that requires cold and careful calculation. Each operation is different and has to be analyzed and studied in order to prepare the most suitable plans for it.' Captain Emmet P. Forrestel, a member of his staff, wrote that Spruance's operations 'usually proceeded like well-planned drills', causing onlookers to admire the way his battles always seemed to unfold according to plan.[49]

Spruance considered four factors essential to success in the Central Pacific. First, it was necessary to converge on the objective with an overwhelming amount of power. Critics, particularly Vice Admiral John H. Towers, complained that Spruance sometimes used a 'sledgehammer to drive a tack', but Spruance retorted, 'That's the way to win wars.'[50]

Second, Spruance wanted to isolate his objective by achieving dominance in the air. Air admirals, again led by Towers, objected to having carriers tied down in support of a land invasion when they should be free to roam the seas, but Spruance did not agree.[51]

Spruance's biggest concern was a Japanese attack on his fleet while it was guarding invasion transports offshore. His third and fourth factors – surprise and speed – were meant to counter that threat. Obviously, surprise would hamper an effective Japanese response from its fleet or surrounding airbases,

---

47Ibid., pp. 172, 181–2, 388; Forrestel, *Spruance*, p. 70.   48Forrestel, *Spruance*, p. 81.
49Ibid., p. xiii; Buell, *Warrior*, pp. 53, 178; Potter, *Halsey*, p. 317; Potter, *Nimitz*, p. 229.
50Buell, *Warrior*, p. 154.   51Ibid., pp. 216–18; Spector, *Eagle Against the Sun*, p. 268.

and speed in landing the invasion force would free his own fleet to move into greater manoeuvring space in the ocean.52

Since he was inexperienced in amphibious warfare, Spruance chose two outstanding subordinate commanders in the field, Vice Admiral Richmond Kelly Turner [*q.v.*] and Marine Major-General Holland M. Smith [*q.v.*]. The men formed a brilliant trio which guided the American naval juggernaut as it rolled across the Pacific.53

The Central Pacific drive opened on 20 November 1943 with an assault on the Gilbert Islands, located 2,000 miles south-west of Hawaii. Separate forces from the largest amphibious operation yet unleashed in the Pacific attacked two main islands, Makin to the north and Tarawa in the south. Since this was the first large-scale amphibious operation in the Pacific, Spruance established a pattern for the remainder of the war.54

Marines and soldiers seized both islands within three days, but not before a terrible cost was exacted by entrenched Japanese defenders, particularly at Tarawa. Post-battle evaluations resulted in a number of changes for the second major Central Pacific assault against the Marshall Islands. These changes included a longer pre-invasion bombardment of the objective, use of more amphibious tractors to transport troops to the beaches and better communications systems between shore and fleet. Henceforth the systematic flattening of island installations became known as a 'Spruance haircut'. As a result, the number of casualties (which at Tarawa exceeded 1,000 dead) was proportionately reduced. For the remainder of the war, amphibious assaults, supported by carrier forces and fed by the prodigious output of American factories, rolled over Japanese strongholds until the US Navy steamed off the shores of Japan itself.55

Spruance, whose diplomacy enabled the explosive Turner and Smith to function together, received high praise for these campaigns. His flag secretary, Lieutenant Charles F. Barber, wrote to his parents during the Marshalls assault, 'If there ever was a person who was the paragon of coolness, it is Admiral Spruance ... he cannot be flustered or excited, and trusts his subordinates to handle all detail.' Nimitz compared Spruance to the Civil War General Ulysses Grant, as being 'the type who took the war to the enemy. He was bold, but not to the point of being reckless.' On 21 February 1944, Spruance was promoted to full admiral, ranking sixth in the navy and (at the age of fifty-seven) the youngest ever to be so honoured.56

For the rest of the war, Admiral Spruance shared the ships of his Fifth Fleet

52Buell, *Warrior*, p. 183.

53Ibid., pp. 166–8; Samuel Eliot Morison, *History of United States Naval Operations in World War II* vol. VII (Boston, 1947–60), p. 87.

54Hanson Baldwin, *Battles Lost and Won* (New York, 1966), p. 239; Buell, *Warrior*, p. 169; Forrestel, *Spruance*, p. xv.

55Robert Sherrod, *Tarawa* (New York, 1983), p. xii; Buell, *Warrior*, pp. 214–15, 238; Baldwin, *Battles Lost and Won*, p. 467; Editors of the Navy *Times*, p. 117; Spector, *Eagle Against the Sun*, p. 273.

56Buell, *Warrior*, pp. 223, 227; Prange, *Miracle at Midway*, pp. 82–3.

with his friend and fellow admiral William 'Bull' Halsey. In June 1944, Nimitz activated a shuttle system during which Spruance would be ashore planning his next offensive while Halsey was commanding the fleet at sea. When Halsey's offensive ended, the admirals would switch, employing the same men and the same ships.[57]

The difference between the two commanders amazed those who worked under them. One officer said that in working for Halsey 'you never knew what you were going to do in the next five minutes or how you were going to do it', while Spruance's plans 'were up to date and you did things in accordance with them'. In tense situations, Spruance maintained a quiet bridge with little yelling or dashing around,[58] and another officer admitted: 'I have never met a commander who did not prefer serving under the methodical Spruance. . . . My feeling was one of confidence when Spruance was there and one of concern when Halsey was there.'

Spruance's next objective was the Mariana Islands of Saipan, Guam and Tinian. Their possession would cut Japanese lines of communication to their outer islands while giving American B-29 Superfortresses a base from which to bombard Japan itself. Given that the Japanese fleet had not taken the offensive since Midway two years earlier, Spruance faced the possibility of a major action.[59]

Japanese naval leaders did, indeed, attack. Leading three groups consisting of five carriers, four light carriers, five battleships plus escorting cruisers and destroyers, Admiral Jisaburo Ozawa [q.v.] planned to lure Spruance to the west of Saipan into the Philippine Sea, where he could hit him with both carrier planes and land-based air power from nearby Japanese-held islands. To act as bait, Ozawa sent ahead Admiral Takeo Kurita with three light carriers and screening ships. Though he was challenging a stronger foe, Ozawa held a major advantage in that his lightly armoured planes outranged Spruance's by 100 miles. He could attack Spruance while still outside the American's range.[60]

Ozawa possessed the planes to attack Spruance, but the pilots flying them were a far cry from those skilled aviators who had dismantled the Pacific in 1941–2. One flier recalled that early in the war it was not unusual for a flight of nine dive bombers to score nine hits in practice. By Saipan the total dropped to one hit in nine. Whereas Japanese pilots barely received six months' training before being sent to war, American aviators had two years' training. This difference would prove disastrous to Ozawa.[61]

[57]Winton, *War in the Pacific*, p. 137; Morison, *Two-Ocean*, p. 326; Buell, *Warrior*, pp. 302–3.

[58]Spector, *Eagle Against the Sun*, p. 423; Larrabee, *Commander in Chief*, p. 391; Buell, *Warrior*, p. 48.

[59]Buell, *Warrior*, pp. 240, 258; Clay Blair Jr, *Silent Victory* (Philadelphia, 1975), p. 615.

[60]Winton, *War in the Pacific*, pp. 123, 126; Toland, *Rising Sun*, p. 625; Costello, *The Pacific War*, p. 479; Spector, *Eagle Against the Sun*, p. 307; Dull, *Imperial Japanese Navy*, p. 304; James H. and William M. Belote, *Titans of the Seas* (New York, 1975), pp. 299–300.

[61]Masatake Okumiya and Jiro Horikoshi with Martin Caidan, *Zero!* (Washington DC, 1979), p. 323; Spector, *Eagle Against the Sun*, p. 306; Belote, *Titans of the Seas*, p. 305.

Spruance arranged his immense fleet in a thirty-five-mile letter F, with his fifteen carriers in four groups at the points and a battleship task force at the tip of the middle bar. Spruance's main duty was to guard the invasion transports off Saipan until the Marines were firmly entrenched. He therefore wanted to avoid being drawn away by one Japanese force while another came around his flank. Since Japan had executed end-runs during every battle since the Coral Sea, and since (prior to his departure from Pearl Harbor) Spruance had read a captured Japanese document outlining such a strategy, an end-run seemed possible.[62]

Spruance removed one-half of Ozawa's striking power before the battle on Saipan began. On 11 June 1944, American carrier fighters and army bombers blasted Japanese airfields on Guam, Saipan and Tinian, while seven carriers steamed north to neutralize Iwo Jima and Chichi Jima. Having lost his land-based air support, Ozawa would now have to depend strictly on his carrier planes; yet, inexplicably, he was not informed of this destruction by the shore-based commander.[63]

As D-Day for Saipan approached, American submarine reports flooded into Spruance's command centre. On 13 June *Bowfin* sighted a powerful Japanese force entering the Sulu Sea near Borneo, while on 15 June *Flying Fish* reported a second force, including carriers, steaming west from the Philippines. The submarine *Sea Horse* sighted a third Japanese force on 16 June, 200 miles north-east of Mindanao.[64]

Spruance weighed his responsibility to guard the Saipan invasion transports, which hit the beach on 15 June, against the opportunity to engage the enemy in a major fleet action, something of which every naval commander dreams. His Chief of Staff, Charles J. Moore, recalled that during this crucial time Spruance 'was probably more quiet than ever'.[65]

Spruance ordered the carrier task force hitting Iwo Jima to rejoin Task Force 58 on the 18th, cancelled the 18 June invasion of Guam, moved a force of old battleships to patrol west of the beachhead, and conferred with Turner about his transports. He travelled over to see Turner because 'I always liked to do business by word of mouth', and learned that Turner needed his transports since the landing force was meeting stiff opposition. Spruance ordered Turner to 'get everything that you don't absolutely need out of here to the eastward, and I will join up with [Admiral Marc A.] Mitscher [q.v.] and Task Force 58 and try to keep the Japs off your neck'.[66]

[62]Costello, *The Pacific War*, p. 479; Winton, *War in the Pacific*, p. 126; Belote, *Titans of the Seas*, p. 301; Buell, *Warriors*, p. 263; Edwin P. Hoyt, *How They Won the War in the Pacific* (New York, 1970), p. 386.

[63]Hough, *The Longest Battle*, pp. 319–21.

[64]Buell, *Warrior*, pp. 260–2.   [65]Ibid., p. 260.

[66]Ibid., pp. 261–3; Morison, *Naval Operations*, vol. VIII, pp. 202–3; Potter and Nimitz, *Triumph in the Pacific*, p. 84; Walter Karig, Russell L. Harris and Frank A. Manson, *Battle Report: The End of an Empire*, (New York, 1948), p. 233.

On the morning of 17 June Spruance told Moore he would attack the Japanese fleet only if such an attack would not endanger the transports. He remembered how the Japanese Admiral Togo 'waited at Tsushima for the Russian fleet to come to him' in 1904 before annihilating it. He then issued his battle plan: 'Our air will first knock out enemy carriers as operating carriers, then will attack enemy battleships and cruisers to slow and disable them. [Rear Admiral "Ching"] Lee's battle line will destroy enemy fleet either by fleet action if the enemy elects to fight or by sinking slowed or crippled ships if enemy retreats. Action against the retreating enemy must be pushed vigorously by all hands to ensure complete destruction of his fleet.'67

Spruance erred in not issuing a clear battle order. He meant to hold his fleet near the transports and assumed the Japanese forces would move close enough for him both to guard the transports and launch an air strike, but the vague orders led some commanders, especially Mitscher, to believe they could aggressively charge the approaching enemy force. By tying himself to Saipan, Spruance also limited his range of operation. Ozawa, with his longer range, could force Spruance either to leave the transports to attack or to remain near the beachhead and absorb Ozawa's air attacks without being able to respond in kind.68

These risks were acceptable to Spruance, who believed 'if we were doing something so important that we were attracting the enemy to us, we could afford to let him come – and take care of him when he arrived'. If in the process he could smash the Japanese fleet, so much the better, but as he told Holland Smith [*q.v.*] on 16 June, while he did not count on this occurring, 'he did hope to inflict sufficient damage to put it out of action for the rest of the war'.69

Throughout 18 June Spruance received sighting reports of his opponent, but he remained unsure where his enemy lurked or whether he faced one group or a split attack. Shortly before midnight, Nimitz sent a report fixing the Japanese flagship approximately 350 miles west-south-west of Task Force 58.70

Mitscher sought permission from Spruance to head west at 0130 to be in position for a 0500 launch against this force. Even members of his own staff urged Spruance to give Mitscher this opportunity to strike first.71

But Spruance refused. He worried that the force might be a decoy to lure him away from the transports, and when a jammed submarine transmission indicated another possible Japanese force 135 miles south of the Main Force, the probability of a flanking attack appeared more likely.72

67Buell, *Warrior*, pp. 264, 268.   68Ibid., pp. 264–6; Costello, *The Pacific War*, p. 479.

69Holland M. Smith and Percy Finch, *Coral and Brass* (New York, 1987), p. 154; Karig, *End of an Empire*, p. 236.

70Buell, *Warrior*, pp. 267–72.

71Ibid., pp. 272–3; Belote, *Titans of the Seas*, pp. 302–4.

72Charles A. Lockwood and Hans Christian Adamson, *Battles of the Philippine Sea* (New York, 1967), p. 88; Buell, *Warrior*, p. 273; Spector, *Eagle Against the Sun*, p. 308.

Spruance agonized over the decision, but told men on the bridge that until he knew exactly where his enemy was, 'we must be positive that we are between his possible locations and those landing ships'. While Mitscher had only Task Force 58 to worry about, Spruance's responsibility was to the entire operation. One correspondent (William L. Worden of the *Reader's Digest*), who observed Spruance during this time, was amazed that he never showed emotion or worried about what others thought of his decision. Instead, he spent part of the night reading an English novel in his cabin. Worden wrote that Spruance was 'so unlike the popular idea of the hero. He was the schoolmaster, the naval scientist, the quiet man with little interest in public relations, only a name to the men in the fleet. How little any of us really knew about him.'73

Spruance's decision staggered those who favoured an immediate advance. Captain Arleigh Burke [*q.v.*], Mitscher's Chief of Staff, moaned that the decision 'meant that the enemy could attack us at will at dawn the next morning. We could not attack the enemy.' Many aviators in the task force grumbled that 'This is what comes of placing a non-aviator in command over aviators.'74

Four enemy waves struck in an eight-hour span on 19 June, passing first through a lethal anti-aircraft curtain thrown up by Lee's battleships, positioned fifteen miles ahead of the carriers by Spruance to blunt the enemy attack. A fantastic 426 Japanese aircraft were blasted from the sky in what American pilots called the 'Marianas Turkey Shoot'. While this massacre unfolded, American submarines silently glided towards Ozawa and sank the carriers *Shokaku* and *Taiho*. In one day, Japan lost two carriers and hundreds of irreplaceable carrier pilots.75

In mid-afternoon, Spruance signalled Mitscher to head west and hunt for the Japanese. At 1600 on 20 June, Mitscher located the enemy and launched an immediate strike which sank the carrier *Hiyo* and damaged three other carriers. At 2000 Spruance called off the chase and headed towards Saipan, thereby ending the Battle of the Philippine Sea.76

Controversy over Spruance's hesitancy in chasing after the Japanese brewed immediately after the battle, and historians have continued the debate since. Spruance realized this would happen, and his Chief of Staff Moore wrote: 'There will be a lot of kibitzing in Pearl Harbor and Washington about what we should have done, by people who don't know the circumstances and won't wait to find them out.' Mitscher's after-action report sadly concluded, 'The enemy

73William L. Worden, 'There Was a Man', *Reader's Digest* (April 1957), pp. 118–19; Karig, *End of an Empire*, p. 236; Morison, *Naval Operations*, vol. VIII, pp. 253–4.

74Potter, *Nimitz*, p. 303; Belote, *Titans of the Seas*, p. 304.

75William T. Y'Blood, *Red Sun Setting* (Annapolis, Maryland, 1981), p. 213; Dull, *Imperial Japanese Navy*, p. 305; Spector, *Eagle Against the Sun*, p. 309; Potter and Nimitz, *Triumph in the Pacific*, pp. 89–90; Costello, *The Pacific War*, pp. 480–3; Winton, *War in the Pacific*, p. 128; Theodore Taylor, *The Magnificent Mitscher* (New York, 1954), p. 227.

76Buell, *Warrior*, pp. 274–7; Spector, *Eagle Against the Sun*, p. 311.

had escaped.' Spruance's most caustic critic, Admiral Towers, strongly suggested that Spruance be fired.77

Critics assail Spruance on a number of counts. He risked his carriers rather than the more expendable transports. He allowed the Japanese to strike first. He failed to realize that carriers had drastically changed naval warfare since Tsushima. He worried about a sneak attack around his flank which scout planes would have easily detected. He could have employed old battleships and escort carriers, located nearby as part of the invasion, to guard Saipan while he attacked Ozawa. He forgot that the primary purpose of naval forces is to destroy the enemy's fleet, not to protect landing vessels. He assumed Ozawa was after his transports and reacted accordingly, rather than structuring his moves to provide for any contingency. He was, in short, a battleship admiral with a staff containing few men trained in proper use of air power.78

These criticisms may be valid, and possibly a more aggressive leader would have decisively smashed the Japanese fleet, but those thoughts belong to the realm of speculation. What is known for certain is that Ozawa emerged with the Combined Fleet to destroy Spruance's carriers; he sank none; and in the process he lost three aircraft carriers, 476 planes and 450 irreplaceable aviators.79

The next month (July 1944), King visited Spruance at Saipan and told him, 'Spruance, you did a damn fine job there. No matter what other people tell you, your decision was correct.' Japanese records released after the war revealed that Spruance had placed his force in the best position from which to inflict the maximum damage. Had he permitted Mitscher to launch an attack on 19 June, Mitscher's pilots would have had to battle their way through Kurita's van force, fly 100 miles to locate and attack Ozawa, and then return through Kurita's guns again. Mitscher would most likely have lost a substantial number of planes, reducing his effectiveness the next day when Ozawa's four waves attacked. By remaining near Saipan, Spruance still had all his planes to obliterate the Japanese. His supporters attributed this disposition of forces to Spruance's 'uncanny ability to be one thought ahead of his adversary'. Whether it was that or pure luck, Spruance made the right move.80

The calamitous losses inflicted by Spruance off Saipan neutralized enemy naval air power for the rest of the war – precisely the goal he had mentioned to Smith before heading out to battle. Though Japan retained some carriers, these held few planes and even fewer able pilots, reducing them to impotent

77Buell, *Warrior*, p. 277.

78Ibid., pp. 270–1, 277; Belote, *Titans of the Seas*, p. 361; Larrabee, *Commander in Chief*, p. 392; Potter, *Halsey*, p. 271; Y'Blood, *Red Sun Setting*, pp. 205–7; Morison, *Naval Operations*, vol. VIII, pp. 314–15.

79Y'Blood, *Red Sun Setting*, p. 213; Buell, *Warrior*, p. 280.

80Buell, *Warrior*, p. 296; Potter, *Nimitz*, pp. 303–5; Potter and Nimitz, *Triumph in the Pacific*, pp. 92–3; Larrabee, *Commander in Chief*, p. 392.

shadows of their former selves which would be used only as decoys in future operations.[81]

Ironically, Spruance's caution at Midway received praise; his caution off Saipan earned criticism. Japanese observers were kinder, calling this missed chance 'the Japanese navy's last real opportunity to destroy the enemy fleet', producing consequences 'which exceeded even our losses at Midway'. A few months later Spruance felt vindicated when Halsey was lured away from the Leyte beachhead and almost permitted a flanking Japanese force to disrupt the landings. Spruance then wrote to his wife, 'What happened during this whole Leyte action was just what I was expecting off Saipan and was trying to prevent – being drawn off to the westward while part of the Jap fleet came in around our flank and hit the amphibious force at Saipan.'[82]

Halsey relieved Spruance in late August 1944 so Spruance could plan for his next two campaigns – the assaults on Iwo Jima and Okinawa. The largest force of Marines ever assembled hit Iwo Jima's soft beaches on 19 February 1945, and slugged their way across the island in the bloodiest fighting of the Pacific War. Six weeks after landing, the island was declared secured at the cost of 6,000 dead and 25,000 wounded, the highest casualty rate in the history of the corps.[83]

While the battle raged for Iwo Jima, Spruance prepared for the 1 April invasion of Okinawa. Its seizure would yield bases for the bombing of Japan and for the severing of its shipping routes, and give Nimitz a staging area for the invasion of Japan. Spruance's 1,500 ships composed the largest fleet ever assembled, and the total assault force equalled the Normandy invasion.[84]

Okinawa would be no quick in-and-out operation for Spruance's fleet. Spruance had to provide air cover until captured airfields could support the troops ashore, and since Okinawa lay within flying distance of the Japanese home islands, he worried that his fleet would become a target for continuous air attacks. The land attack soon bogged down badly, but until those airfields were in operation he had to stay offshore. Anxious eyes searched the heavens for enemy planes.[85]

For three tortuous months the fleet sat off Okinawa, absorbing repeated death plunges by terrifying kamikazes. On 31 March, one day before the invasion, a suicide plane struck Spruance's flagship *Indianapolis*, requiring him to switch to the old battleship *New Mexico* five days later. On 12 May another kamikaze smacked into the *New Mexico*, killing fifty men and wounding over a hundred. For a few frantic moments Spruance's staff failed to locate the

[81]Hough, *The Longest Battle*, p. 325; Morison, *Naval Operations*, vol. VIII, p. 318.

[82]Mansanori Ito with Roger Pineau, *The End of the Imperial Japanese Navy* (New York, 1956), p. 107; Okumiya, *Zero!*, p. 321; Buell, *Warrior*, p. 321.

[83]Buell, *Warrior*, pp. 302–3, 317; Potter, *Nimitz*, p. 358; Costello, *The Pacific War*, p. 547; Spector, *Eagle Against the Sun*, pp. 495–6.

[84]Baldwin, *Battles Lost and Won*, p. 370; Buell, *Warrior*, p. 343.

[85]Buell, *Warrior*, pp. 343–5; Spector, *Eagle Against the Sun*, p. 536.

missing Admiral, but finally found him manning a fire hose. In those three months the Japanese sank at least thirty ships, damaged 368 more, killed 4,900 sailors and wounded another 4,800, the worst American naval losses in the entire Pacific campaign. Spruance respected the kamikazes and told staff members they were 'the opposite extreme from a lot of our Army heavy bombers, who bomb safely and ineffectively from the upper atmosphere'.[86]

Of minor concern to Spruance was the once formidable Combined Fleet. Reduced in numbers by overwhelming American might and hampered by a lack of aviators and fuel, the Combined Fleet embarked upon its last sortie on 6 April. A force of one light cruiser and eight destroyers, led by the most powerful warship ever built (*Yamato*, with her 18.1-inch guns) left Japanese home waters to battle Spruance. The ships were to inflict whatever damage they could on Spruance's fleet before beaching on Okinawa, where *Yamato*'s huge guns could hammer the American invasion force. Alerted by submarines that the Japanese navy was on the move, Spruance despatched Mitscher to counter the threat. On 7 April, 300 planes swarmed on the enemy fleet, sending to the bottom *Yamato*, the cruiser and four destroyers. For all practical purposes, the Japanese navy that Spruance had first repelled at Midway was now non-existent.[87]

In late May, Halsey relieved Spruance, even before the Okinawan campaign was complete. Spruance and his staff had been at sea for four months since Iwo Jima, much of that time dodging kamikazes, and Nimitz worried about the strain placed upon them. On 27 May, Spruance headed for Guam, where he rested and began plans for the Japanese invasion, but before he had another chance to command in action, the atom bomb ended World War Two.[88]

Post-war, relieved Nimitz as Commander-in-Chief Pacific Fleet and Pacific Ocean Areas. Served only ten weeks at the new post before receiving orders making him President of the Naval War College in Newport, Rhode Island. Retired from the navy without fanfare, a quiet man departing quietly, 1 July 1948.[89]

Served as Ambassador to the Philippines, 1952–5. Died 13 December 1969 at age eighty-three and was buried in a military cemetery overlooking San Francisco Bay, alongside Nimitz and Turner.[90]

[86]Buell, *Warrior*, pp. 349–59; Morison, *Naval Operations*, vol. XIV, p. 138; Hoyt, *How They Won the War in the Pacific*, p. 482; Baldwin, *Battles Lost and Won*, p. 380; Spector, *Eagle Against the Sun*, p. 540.
[87]Robert Leckie, *Delivered From Evil* (New York, 1987), pp. 882–3; Bernard Millot, *Divine Thunder* (New York, 1971), p. 177; Spector, *Eagle Against the Sun*, p. 538.
[88]Potter, *Halsey*, p. 333; Buell, *Warrior*, pp. 361–3.
[89]Buell, *Warrior*, pp. 379, 396–8.   [90]Ibid., pp. 401, 422, 425–8.

7

Grand Admiral

Karl Dönitz

German Navy

1891–1981

by
Peter Padfield

*K*ARL *Dönitz, born 16 September 1891. Entered the Kaiserlichen navy in 1910–*
commissioned Leutnant zur See *1913, twentieth in rank order of his year*
group. In the First War he saw much action in the cruiser Breslau *in the Black Sea,*
gaining the Iron Cross 1st class; posted to U-boats, he served through 1917 under the
'ace' Walter Forstmann in U-39. *In 1918 he commanded his own boat in the*
Mediterranean; in October he was captured while attacking a convoy. When the U-
boat arm was revived in 1935 Dönitz was appointed its first chief. He had married in
1916 and had a daughter and two sons.

In September 1939 Karl Dönitz, as Führer der U-Boote (FdU), commanded a force of fifty-seven boats. Over half were small coastal craft; of
twenty-five ocean-going boats, eighteen were the medium Type VII of some
750 tons' diplacement which with successive upgradings were to form the
majority of the force throughout the war; seven were the rather larger
Type IX. During the latter half of August all available boats had been sent
to war stations, the coastal boats to the Baltic for the coming strike against
Poland and to the North Sea in case Great Britain should honour her treaty
obligations to Poland; eighteen ocean-going boats ready for sea had been
sent into the Atlantic. They held positions to the west of the British Isles, in
the Western Approaches and the Channel, Biscay and off the Iberian
peninsula down to the Straits of Gibraltar covering – thinly – all oceanic
trade routes to the British Isles.

Despite this, Great Britain's declaration of war on the 3rd hit Dönitz like a
thunderbolt, as it hit the naval Commmander-in-Chief Raeder, who had
assured him that Hitler would prevent Britain's intervention. U-boat head-

quarters staff watched their chief pacing with the signal in his hand as if he could not grasp its meaning. It is not surprising: Hitler himself was shaken, the German people as a whole horror-struck that they had been precipitated into world war. Raeder and Dönitz had their special reasons. Planning for war against England had started only the previous year. The huge fleet-construction programme designed originally to solve the 'English question' by cutting Britain's arteries of sea trade had scarcely begun. Even that programme did not satisfy Dönitz. On 1 September – just two days earlier – he had drafted a memorandum for Raeder pointing out that the planned increases in U-boat numbers were far too gradual to allow his force to exert effective pressure on British trade within foreseeable time; it was necessary to set other considerations aside and expand the U-boat arm rapidly to a strength which would enable it to carry out its main task, 'that is to defeat England in war'.

It was a typical Dönitz paper, unequivocal, pared to essentials, narrowed to the object, 'that is to defeat England in war'. The U-boat, because of its comparative cheapness of construction, economy in materials and manpower and ability to slip beneath the otherwise decisive British naval and geographic advantages, was the ideal solution. The paper achieved peculiar force, like Dönitz, through narrowness of focus. German staff officers taking a more balanced view pointed to the Royal Navy's development of Asdic (sonar) submarine detection, and the consequent necessity to tackle escorts. Logically it was essential to develop a fleet air arm, training fliers and U-boat officers in tactical co-operation. Dönitz's paper took no account of the air, nor of any but the most obvious enemy reactions to his planned building programme. For him the U-boat would be the vital factor in the coming war, and he stated, as he had several times, that he needed ninety continuously operational boats in the North Atlantic – thus some 300 boats altogether to allow for dockyard and passage time. The inference was that with this number he could win a war against England, and it was a claim he repeated to his dying day. It was not based on operational analysis; he simply believed it. But on 3 September 1939 he had a mere eighteen ocean-going boats, allowing on average six on patrol at any given time.

'*Also wieder Krieg gegen England!*' he said – 'So it's war against England again!' He left the room without another word.

After about half an hour he returned in changed mood. The war would last a long time, he told his staff, but if each did his duty they would win. It is unlikely that he had modelled himself consciously on Nelson, yet he shared many of Nelson's qualities – absolute commitment to victory, absolute belief in his men and the force he commanded, absolute hatred of the enemy creed, indeed of the enemy, absolute commitment to his own country and creed. He was a convinced Nazi. This is not surprising since the navy had helped give birth to the party and provided the cadre of its early stormtroopers. Nor is it surprising that he hated all England stood for. Hitler aimed at agreement with Great Britain in order to secure his western frontiers while carving an empire in the east – as a first stage in world conquest – but the Imperial Navy had been created and trained to seize the trident from the Royal Navy; officers like Raeder and Dönitz, while unable consciously to plan for this between 1919 and 1938, had never doubted it was the ultimate goal.

Even deeper in Dönitz's case were personal reasons connected with the loss of his U-boat and the vilification of all things German which he experienced in the British press during his captivity in England, late in World War One. At that time U-boat officers had been singled out especially as deserving hanging for 'murdering' civilians on passenger ships, even hospital ships. Beneath a reserved and taciturn exterior he had a passionate nature – 'strong temperament and inner verve' as his commanding officer expressed it in 1930. He felt setbacks, and anything he could diagnose as personal failure, extraordinarily keenly. The British officer who had interrogated him after his capture in 1918 had reported him 'very moody and almost violent at times and it was very hard to make him talk at all'.

His beliefs in Germany and its world mission, in the Führer and the creed of National Socialism, were as fervent. On a visit to Cape Town as captain of the cruiser *Emden* in 1934 he had reported officially on the 'Jewish Mayor' of the city and agitation whipped up against Germany by 'the strongly Jewish-influenced press'. The British authorities had taken his own capacity for nationalist agitation seriously enough to forbid him visiting former German colonials in East Africa while in uniform or making speeches to them.

His commitment to his service and his U-boat arm was absolute; he had not spared himself or his young men: 'Mondays to Fridays', one officer who had joined in 1936 recalled, 'eight attack exercises under water by day and six attack exercises by night. That was the upper limit of our physical and nervous capacity.' Dönitz led from the front, inspiring each personally with his enthusiasm and absolute confidence in the weapon. After only one year as FdU the fleet commander had reported in glowing terms of his 'indefatigable work and personal instruction' and the 'military and comradely spirit' he had engendered in his force. 'Attention', he had added, 'must be paid to the point that in his burning ardour he does not demand too much from his physical strength.'

The following year a new fleet commander had reported on him as 'teacher, example and stimulus to his officers', deserving 'quite special attention' for he promised to become 'an outstanding leader in higher positions as well'. Following mutinies in the German service at the end of the Great War and afterwards, there had been a determined effort to find a less rigid, harsh, formal code of command than that in which the Imperial officers, following the Prussian military tradition, had been bred. Dönitz had adapted easily, no doubt at least in part because of his U-boat background – as he expressed it himself in a book he had brought out early in 1939 called *Die U-Bootswaffe* (The U-boat Arm): 'In the narrowness of the space mutual consideration, readiness to help and best comradeship is necessary. . . .' and 'The elder can dedicate himself to bringing up the youngster in a way that is scarcely possible in other situations . . .'

This was the spirit he brought to the task of working up his infant arm; another of his superiors had reported that he had 'an extremely warm heart for the needs and cares of officers and men; cordial, candid and pithy character, always ready to help . . .'. He had taught his men to believe themselves an elite; they were convinced of it. He was probably the most inspired leader in the higher ranks of the navy; his officers were equivalent in their faith in their arm, in their chief and in their cause to Nelson's 'Band of Brothers'.

There, probably, the comparison ends. Nelson was raised in a tradition of victory, Dönitz in the very different, prickly ethos of a young service that had still to prove itself – not only against the numerically superior Royal Navy, but also against the naval blindness of the German generals and people, and recently against the terrible humiliation of mutiny, surrender and fleet internment. His was of necessity a harder, more ruthless, even vengeful brand of leadership. And in a personal sense, while Nelson was loved probably as much for his human failings as for his zeal and warm heart, Dönitz appeared to lack weaknesses of the flesh. He was a popular messmate, but too deeply conscious of himself, too sensitive, driven by too hard an ambition and probably too insecure – as will appear – to allow himself human frailties. The wife of a close year-group comrade described him as a 'duty-man [*Pflicht-Mensch*] who lived for his work' and devoted so much time to his 'task' that his married life suffered – not simply from his absences but from moods born of overtiredness and frustration. It is probably significant that as a captain and later an admiral, he remained so slim that he was able still to wear his midshipman's uniform. He held himself ramrod straight and was usually described in reports as tall – also as '*straffe*' which can be translated as taut, stern or very upright; all fitted. His lips were rather thin and often tightly compressed; his young-looking face was dominated by his eyes, which were direct and mirrored the deep passions within. His gaze compelled.

All in all he was, as his fleet chief reported, 'an excellent officer of iron will-power, goal-oriented certainty and unwearying toughness . . .'. As a front leader he was potentially the most dangerous naval opponent Great Britain faced; but, in the free-for-all that passed for co-ordination in Hitler's armed services, he was to be betrayed by his own qualities.

The U-boats Dönitz deployed in 1939 were hardly changed from the boats of the Great War – submersibles rather than true submarines. The Type VII had a top speed on the surface under diesels of sixteen knots, seventeen in later marks, but submerged could make no more than eight knots, and that only for a limited time. This made manoeuvring into a favourable torpedo-attack position difficult or impossible in daylight, so Dönitz had trained his force in the torpedo-boat tactic of gaining and holding touch with a target at extreme range by day, closing on the surface at dusk – when the U-boat's low silhouette gave it the advantage – and working into position ahead on the surface either for submerged attack if the moon were full or surface attack in darkness or in the period of the hunter's moon. He had also taken advantage of developments in wireless to perfect group tactics pioneered in the final stages of the Great War. He had begun this training for action against warships but, directly planning had started for war against Great Britain, had switched easily to the idea of deploying groups against merchant convoys, and in the artificial conditions of pre-war exercises he had achieved annihilating success. The need for a 'concentration' of U-boats against a 'concentration' of ships in a convoy became the theme of his arguments for a rapid build-up of the U-boat arm. In September 1939 he envisaged a two-tier command structure: the groups would be ordered to their reconnaissance patrol lines by wireless from U-boat headquarters, but once in contact with the enemy the senior commander on the spot would take over local tactical control – again by wireless. In the exigencies of real action, this was to prove an unnecessary complication and the concept of group leaders was eventually dropped.

There were scarcely enough boats for group tactics at the outbreak of war – although a 'flotilla leader' had been sent out with the Atlantic boats – nor were there as yet any convoys to attack. The boats were each allotted a separate patrol area and each commander carried instructions to operate under the internationally agreed Prize Rules. These stipulated stopping and searching merchantmen and, before sinking them, ensuring that the crew were in lifeboats and near to land. The rules effectively nullified the U-boat's advantages of stealth and surprise and made it vulnerable to counter-action – as was intended by the British who had promoted them. Raeder, Dönitz and the U-boat staff were clear that it would be necessary to go over to 'unrestricted' U-boat war if they were to achieve results, but in the meantime Hitler had no intention of stirring up the kind of feelings against Germany that the Great War passenger-liner sinkings had generated. He still hoped to woo England back to the negotiating table after he had smashed Poland and he did not want to antagonize the neutrals who supplied England by sea, above all the United States.

It was a shock, therefore, when on the evening of 3 September the commander of *U-30*, waiting in the steamer lane some 250 miles north-west of Ireland, sank the passenger liner *Athenia*. Not only did he torpedo her from a submerged position without warning, but also she was carrying some 300 US citizens among her passengers. Why he so blatantly disregarded orders will never be known; no doubt with such a large ship in his periscope sights his ardour to strike a blow against England overwhelmed his judgement. Goebbels went into action to throw a smokescreen over the incident, accusing the British Admiralty of sinking the liner to create another *Lusitania* to bring the United States into the war, and claiming 'it is established beyond doubt that not a single German warship is near the Hebrides . . .'. But Dönitz knew that *U-30* was precisely in the area. The following day he sent a signal to all boats calling attention to the instructions for operating against merchant shipping under the Prize Rules, and that night passed on an order from Hitler that no passenger ships were to be sunk even if in convoy. When *U-30* returned home towards the end of the month the commander was not disciplined; he and his crew were merely sworn to secrecy about the *Athenia*, and both the U-boat's log and U-boat headquarters war diary were doctored to conceal the 'illegal' sinking.

This might suggest that Dönitz took the first step in integrating himself and his arm of the service in the Nazi system from the first day of war; in truth he and Raeder and the service had already long been integrated. The U-boat arm had been started up under cover of deception; the tonnage of Raeder's armoured ships had been grossly under-represented to conform with international limitation rules, a naval treaty with Great Britian had been signed with the most cynical of motives and there were plans to escalate the war on trade into an 'unrestricted' U-boat campaign directly Hitler gave permission under the pretext that the British were arming merchantmen.

These were not merely deceptions forced on the weaker naval power, they were inherent in the Prusso-German thought system which the Nazis inherited and took to extremes. Where the state was concerned, normal personal codes of morality did not apply. War was the ultimate expression and testing ground of the state and subsumed all morality. In this sense there was no break between Bismarck's Germany and the Third Reich, nor any abrupt moral crisis for those officers of Hitler's Kriegsmarine who had been brought up in the Kaiser's navy; that only came later to some like Dönitz.

On 5 September, Dönitz rang Raeder's Chief of Staff in Berlin to press for the creation of a U-boat department which would be responsible for planning and implementing large-scale U-boat construction – an idea he had put to Raeder on the 3rd – and to suggest himself as its chief. He admitted it was wrong in principle for the FdU, who had trained the officers and ratings, knew them and was known by them, to be removed just as the training was about to be put to the test. 'On the other hand,' he explained, 'it is a fact that the operational activities of the branch will soon be practically non-existent (because of the small number of boats) and control of it superfluous unless we succeed in building up quickly a numerically strong and effective U-boat arm. . . .'

This had to be regarded, he went on, as the most important task for the future of the arm, and it was therefore right that it should be entrusted to the most experienced officer who knew the operational requirements – himself. Raeder decided he could not be spared from the front. On the 7th Dönitz visited Berlin. Raeder was with Hitler, but Dönitz succeeded in bringing the Chiefs of Staff around to his point of view and insisted that Raeder should see him before making an appointment. The stratagem failed: the following day he was called by telephone and informed that Raeder did not wish him to come to Berlin – he had appointed an officer to head the new U-boat department and Dönitz was to remain at his post.

The first sighting report of a convoy came in from *U-31* off the Bristol Channel on 15 September. Dönitz had recalled the more distant boats from Iberian waters, Biscay and those further out in the Atlantic the previous week in order to prevent all boats coming in at the same time when their fuel ran out and so leaving a long period without any boats at sea. There were, however, three besides *U-31* still on station in the Western Approaches and off southern Ireland, and Dönitz ordered these towards the convoy. In the war diary, he noted: 'They may have luck. I have hammered it into the commanders again and again they must not let such chances pass. . . . If only there were more boats at sea now! The disposition of the next series of boats which *must* destroy a convoy is under constant consideration. . . .'

Here he might be accused of allowing his enthusiasm and frustration to run away with him by showing the enemy his hand – his new group tactics – before he could bring a decisive concentration to bear and while he was still restricted by Hitler's orders not to antagonize neutrals. However, in order to convince Raeder and Hitler of the correctness of his views on U-boats as the decisive arm against England, he may have wanted a success such as he had achieved in his peace exercises. The correctness of his view was something he was always at pains to stress. In the event the group missed the convoy. Elsewhere, though, individual boats were sinking many independently routed merchantmen, and on the 18th *U-29* sank the British aircraft carrier *Courageous*, subsequently evading pursuit by her escort. 'A glorious success,' Dönitz wrote, 'and further confirmation of the fact that English counter-measures [Asdic] are not as effective as they maintain.'

Towards the end of the month Raeder brought Hitler, fresh from Polish triumphs, to the single-storey timber barrack hut at Wilhelmshaven that served as U-boat headquarters. Dönitz was on his briskest, most optimistic and persuasive form, telling his Führer it was not true that the English had found a technical device to nullify U-boats; operational experience showed that English anti-U-boat measures were less effective than they claimed. Moreover, there had been enormous advances in U-boat communications and it was now possible to concentrate all boats in a given area on to a convoy. He was convinced that U-boats provided a means of inflicting decisive damage on England at its weakest point. Here he succumbed to thought patterns enshrined in the German language – the *Entscheidungsschlacht*, decisive battle, and for all 'questions' an *Endlösung*, a final solution. In order to settle the English question he needed 300 boats, Dönitz went on, so to cover losses a far larger number had to be built. 'If this number of boats is available, I believe that the U-boat arm can achieve decisive success.'

The Führer was impressed; he was equally impressed afterwards when he was taken to the U-boat officers' mess. Confident and combative in their youth, the elite band that he met had returned from the front line proud of their successes – approaching the respectable total of 150,000 tons of shipping sunk by that date. Hitler's naval adjutant recorded that the Führer 'carried back to

Berlin an excellent impression of the leadership of the U-boat arm, as well as the liveliness and spirit of the crews'.

On 1 October Dönitz was promoted to rear admiral. The same day he committed to his war diary his considerations on the deployment of those boats which had returned and would soon be ready for sea again. The aim, he wrote, had to be to intercept convoys and destroy them with the few available boats. This meant operating as a group in areas of traffic convergence – either the Western Approaches to the Channel or the Gibraltar area. The latter had the disadvantage of a longer route out, but this was counterbalanced by better weather, greater density of shipping and less risk of air patrols. He decided on the Gibraltar area – where as a lieutenant in *U-39* in 1917 he had assisted Forstmann to achieve spectacular hauls of shipping. Success, he went on, would depend on the boats making a surprise appearance together. Since they would not all be ready to sail together, he decided to concentrate them south-west of Ireland, where the majority of sinkings had been made so far, and where they should make more; then when all were gathered, he would order them south to the straits under a group leader. Here, in only the second month of the war, are all the principles to which his opponents in 'anti-submarine operations' were soon to become accustomed: concentration and surprise, probing for the enemy's weak points, disconcerting and dispersing the defence.

Meanwhile he had begun planning a strike at the British battlefleet. Specially commissioned aerial photographs had revealed a seventeen-metre-wide passage between blockships sunk across the eastern entrance to the fleet base at Scapa Flow in the Orkneys. He selected one of his favourites, a tough and fanatically Nazi commander named Prien [*q.v.*] and outlined a scheme for penetrating the Flow on the surface by night at slack water. The ensuing successful attack (detailed by Dan van der Vat in Chapter 19) was a damaging psychological blow against Britain. In immediate operational terms mines laid by U-boats in Loch Ewe and the Forth probably accomplished more, when the modern battleship *Nelson* and the new heavy cruiser *Belfast* fell victim and were crippled for some time, but it was the triumph in Scapa Flow that caught German imagination, not least Hitler's.

When news of the Prien's success was intercepted, Hitler – who had been briefed on the mission beforehand – boasted to everyone he saw that it was the work of a U-boat. Dönitz was elevated from Führer to Befehlshaber-(C-in-C) der U-Boote (BdU). When Prien and his men returned, they were greeted by a band and cheering crowds, and Raeder and Dönitz awaited them on the quay. Flown to Berlin, they were paraded through ecstatic crowds to the Kaiserhof Hotel as the Führer's guests, and from there taken to the Chancellery, where Hitler decorated Prien with the Knight's Cross. Dönitz could not have dreamed of a more spectacular success, nor more popular adulation for his arm.

Nevertheless, the great convoy success continued to elude him. He was well served by the wireless intelligence service, B-Dienst, which had cracked British naval codes, but he had too few boats to cover the vast areas of the Atlantic where evasive routeing was practised. In the first eight weeks of the war, seven boats had failed to return and they had not been replaced by new ones coming into service. From the fact that many of the crew members were in British prisoner-of-war camps, Dönitz assumed that their boats had been surprised on the surface, and issued orders that ships were not to be boarded when they had been stopped; examination was to be of their papers only, and they were to be sunk by torpedo, not gunfire. On 30 October, however, he noted that torpedo failures were his 'most urgent problem'; 'at least 30 per cent of torpedoes are duds. Either they do not detonate or they detonate in the wrong place. The commanders must be losing confidence in their torpedoes. In the end their fighting spirit must suffer. . . .'

His own fighting spirit was conveyed in fiery aphorisms to his commanders before they sailed, and at the tough debriefing to which he submitted each on return from the front. Its tone is caught in his standing orders. Order number 151, probably issued in November 1939, began: 'a) In the first line attack, always keep attacking; do not allow yourself to be shaken off; should the boat be forced away or under water for a time, search again in the general direction of the convoy to regain touch, advance again, attack!'

Number 154 likewise enjoined commanders 'to attack with stubborn will until the destructive end is really accomplished'. From his own experience he knew the isolation of the commander at the periscope. Alone in his knowledge of the target's aspect and any dangers from escorts or aircraft, he could attack or give up as he chose, without his officers or crew being able to gauge his will or courage, or lack of either:

There are situations in attack when one could have grounds for giving up. These moments or feelings must be overcome.

Never give in to self-delusion: I will not attack now or I will not stick stubbornly to it now because I hope, later, somewhere else to find something else. What one has, one has! Spare no fuel on such grounds!

From October 1939 Hitler gave permission progressively for easing the Prize Law regulations. With the lessons of World War One in mind, the aim was to reach an 'unrestricted' campaign without announcing it as such. The 'siege of England' was felt to be a more acceptable concept and a propaganda campaign was aimed at the neutrals to discourage them from trading with Great Britain, suggesting that ships and crews ran into mortal danger there. On 24 November it was spelled out in an official warning that 'the safety of neutral ships can no longer be taken for granted' in the waters around Britain and France. Enormous care still had to be taken with ships flying the Stars and Stripes. Dönitz's standing orders stipulated that outside the official 'danger zone', extending to 20 degrees west in the Atlantic – thus some 400 miles west of Ireland – US ships were to be handled with more than ordinary care; if the ship had to be sunk passengers and crew were to be brought to safety in lifeboats in exact observation of Article 74. 'The USA propaganda of hate should be given no occasion for the kindling of new sources of hate.' By the end of November it is clear from Dönitz's orders that inside the danger zone the Prize Rules had been abandoned: 'Rescue no one and take no one with you. Have no care for the ship's boats. . . . Care only for your own boat and strive to achieve the next success as soon as possible! We must be hard in this war. The enemy started the war in order to destroy us, therefore nothing else matters.'

It was not of course Dönitz's decision to go over to virtually unrestricted U-boat warfare – although still not in the case of passenger ships – without announcing it as such, or to attempt to terrorize neutral sailors; he was simply the front commander carrying out the policy. But he had pressed for it, chiefly it seems from his war diary comments on grounds of the dangers his commanders faced on the surface when stopping and examining ships. There were fewer U-boats lost over the next months, but there were fewer of them at sea and fewer ships sunk; it was not until February 1940 that the monthly sinking figure returned to that of the first month of the war. By then, after six months, 199 Allied and neutral ships of a total 703,000 tons had been destroyed by U-boats – excluding those sunk by U-boat-laid mines – for the loss of fifteen boats, or rather over a quarter of the force.

This was the end of the first round of the Atlantic battle, for in March 1940 Dönitz was ordered to move his boats to northern waters to cover an impending attack on Norway. Had he taken stock of results to date, he would undoubtedly have been satisfied with the training and potential of his force and the calibre of individual commanders, now vying with each other as in World War One for the honour of highest-scoring 'ace'. That position was held by Schultze, who towards the end of February had brought *U-48* home after her fourth war cruise flying four pennants denoting ships of a total 35,000 tons. This had brought his personal aggregate to 114,000 tons for which he was awarded the Knight's Cross.

In other respects Dönitz was filled with frustration. He had fewer boats at his disposal than at the start of the war; they had a limited time in the chief operational area to the west of the British Isles because a mine barrage across the Straits of Dover had proved too hazardous to negotiate and they had to be routed around the north of Scotland. No convoys had been caught by a group, indeed only seven ships had been sunk from escorted convoys; the vast majority had been sunk while sailing independently; many had been neutrals. And though there were individual high-scoring 'aces', the average exchange rate of thirteen ships or some 47,000 tons for each U-boat lost was, with the present U-boat building rate, quite inadequate to achieve the decisive success he craved. On top of this the Torpedo Inspectorate had not diagnosed the fault in the detonating pistols and he could still not rely on the torpedoes provided. The Norwegian campaign finally proved this. On 19 April 1940 he recorded: 'Of twenty-two shots fired in the last few days at least nine have been premature detonations, which have in turn caused other torpedoes fired at the same time to explode prematurely or to miss. . . .'

When Prien recorded failures at 900 yards against the battleship *Warspite* on the night of the 19th–20th, Dönitz refused to hazard his boats any longer. He recalled the entire force and rang Raeder in Berlin demanding action. Raeder set up a full board of inquiry next day. The findings, reported to Dönitz in mid-May, showed that before the war the detonating pistols had been proved by only two shots, and that those had not been perfect. He poured out his feelings in his war diary: 'Such methods of working can only be described as criminal. . . . It is true that a splashless discharge has been developed, but otherwise there is *nothing right with our torpedoes*. I do not believe that ever in the history of war men have been sent against the enemy with such useless weapons. . . .'

Thus the first nine months of his war ended in despair. He had fewer boats than at the start and their main armament was so unreliable as to prevent deployment.

The prospects for U-boat warfare were transformed by the fall of France in June 1940. Dönitz lost no time in touring the Biscay ports to choose bases which would allow his boats to reach their Atlantic hunting grounds without making the long journey around Scotland. Choosing Lorient as his main base, he requisitioned for his headquarters a small château on the water's edge at Kerneval, towards the mouth of the river serving the port. In the meantime he sent out a boat to test a simple percussion pistol on torpedoes, and when this proved effective despatched thirteen boats in two groups named after their senior officers who would take over tactical control if necessary – 'Prien' and 'Rösing'. He positioned them across the courses of two homeward convoys whose routeing instructions had been decoded by B-Dienst. Each boat was some forty miles from its neighbour, with one in the group sufficiently far behind the centre of the line to be able to catch the convoy, wherever sighted. In this way he hoped that at least two boats of each group would succeed in making contact. They were ordered to keep radio silence and attack nothing – unless an especially valuable target – in order not to disclose their presence.

Both convoys missed the lines, but sufficient independently routed ships were caught afterwards to produce a record sinking tally for June, fifty-eight ships of 284,000 tons; no boats were lost. A further 300,000 tons of shipping was destroyed by surface commerce raiders, Luftwaffe, *Schnell*-(E-)boats and mines in coastal waters, bringing the month's total to almost 600,000 tons – potentially a fatal rate of attrition, could it be maintained. The British responded by re-routeing Atlantic convoys by way of the North Channel north of Ireland, instead of using the south-western approaches. The change was soon detected and Dönitz positioned his next groups in this area in north–south patrol lines across the trend of traffic. The number of deployable British escorts and aircraft was restricted by the need to keep large forces on the south and east coasts against the threat of German invasion – Operation Sea Lion. Nevertheless, air patrols of Coastal Command so harassed the U-boats off the

North Channel that Dönitz was forced to move them further into the Atlantic. Deploying them in east–west lines, he accepted the smaller angle of interception with the traffic lanes 'for the sake [as he put it in the war diary] of giving them greater freedom of action' to move westwards. Thus began the struggle between aircraft and U-boats which was to drive Dönitz to form his lines ever further west. At this juncture the aircraft could do little more than force the boats under water, for no aerial depth charge had been developed, nor an efficient aiming device for the bombs carried – omissions quite as heinous as the lapses which had resulted in Dönitz's torpedo failures.

In mid-August 1940, under the guise of blockade, Hitler sanctioned the official announcement of unrestricted warfare; neutrals were warned formally that any ships entering the 'blockade zone' around the British Isles were liable to destruction without warning. Meanwhile, Dönitz's boats off the north-western approaches at last found convoys and, in September, achieved the successes he sought, using night surface attacks and pack tactics. The first convoy to suffer was SC-2 from Canada. B-Dienst decrypts provided its course and speed and the position it was due to reach on 6 September. Dönitz positioned one boat at this point, with the rest of the group diagonally, in quarter line astern along the course line. All were instructed to keep radio silence except for convoy reports. 'It is to be expected', he noted in the war diary, 'that unless the convoy deviates from the route all boats will be able to attack.' Despite bad weather, the convoy was found, shadowed and reported by the touch-keeping boat in exemplary fashion, and five ships were sunk. There was a still more convincing demonstration towards the end of the month, as Dönitz described in the war diary:

> This inward convoy was attacked by a total of five boats which were originally up to 350 miles away from the point of first sighting. Thirteen ships were sunk. This success is thanks to 1) early interception of the convoy from the west while the escort was still weak [that is, before it had been reinforced by additional escorts from England to take it through the danger zone] 2) correct tactical procedure of boats as shadowers . . . (3) fair weather. . . .
>
> Actions in the last few days have shown that the principles established in peacetime for the use of radio in sight of the enemy and the training of U-boats for attacks on convoys were correct.

His belief was reinforced the following month: on 16 October *U-48* sighted an inward-bound convoy, reported its position, course and speed, held contact and attacked that night on the surface, sinking two ships before being forced under by the escort and losing touch. The convoy was found next day by *U-38* and was again reported, shadowed and attacked by night, losing another ship before the boat was forced under. Dönitz, meanwhile, had positioned another five boats across the course as reported and the convoy ran on to this line in the evening of the 19th. The moon was nearly full; eight columns of ships stood out brightly as the pack, dropping behind two escorts ahead, closed from either side and began picking off vessel after vessel in a wild mêlée, soon lit by flames from burning tankers and bursts of starshell from the outnumbered escorts, which tried in vain to catch the surfaced boats. By accident or design, one of the latest 'aces', Kretschmer [q.v.], found himself inside the columns and notched another seven ships to augment his reputation as the 'tonnage king'.

Two other convoys savaged during the same period brought the claims of sinkings reaching U-boat headquarters to forty-seven ships of 310,000 tons in three days. This was an exaggeration, but even so the actual toll fully justified Dönitz's war diary comment – 'A colossal success!' He continued:

> The operations prove that the development of U-boat tactics since 1935, and the training based on the principle of countering the concentration of ships in a convoy by a concentration of U-boats attacking was correct. . . . Further, if there were more U-boats the English supply routes would not be left free even after such attacks just because, as happens today, nearly all boats have to return after using all their torpedoes. . . .

He tempered these comments with the thoughts that 'Fog, bad weather and other conditions could nullify prospects from time to time', and 'the main factor will always be the ability of the commander'. In the flush of victory, he did not foresee either technical or organizational responses by the enemy having more effect than the weather. Perhaps he would have been more than human if he had, for no boats had been lost in September, only one boat was lost in October and the monthly sinking figure had risen to over 350,000 tons. Moreover, he had never had more than a dozen boats, and usually a far smaller number, in the operational area.

This was the first 'Happy Time'; for Dönitz it was a period of great fulfilment, success apparently almost within grasp – if only he could get more boats. He continued to lead in his vivid personal style, making time to attend as many U-boat departures and arrivals as his busy schedule allowed, relentlessly probing each commander back from the front, in order to draw out anything the commander might be reluctant to report. Those found wanting were transferred to less demanding posts; those who satisfied him emerged glowing with his approval. He had a retentive memory, and concerned himself with personal and family affairs of officers and men in what he clearly felt to be the great family of the U-boat camaraderie. Important news, such as a birth, was signalled to boats at sea. He impressed on his staff that they were the servants of the men on operations; if instructions were misunderstood, he blamed them – the staff – not the recipients. His two nicknames, *der Löwe* (the lion) and *Onkel Karl*, indicate the mixed awe and affection in which he was held.

Expecting 100 per cent from his crews while at sea, he did his utmost for them when they returned. Rest camps – 'U-boat pastures' – were established at holiday resorts on the Biscay coast, where the men lived a high life on U-boat allowances which practically doubled their pay. Luxury hotels were requisitioned where officers could release the tremendous strain of patrols, and for those going back to Germany there was either a private express train, the so-called 'BdU-Zug' via Nantes and Paris, or special flights home. There they found themselves glorified in press and radio; successful convoy battles, or the return of boats with a high tally of sinkings, were the subject of special announcements; the names of 'aces' were on everyone's lips. To British interrogators, captured U-boat officers appeared to have gained an exaggerated idea of themselves: 'these inflated opinions were no doubt due to the extraordinary degree of public adulation to which they had become accustomed. Special aeroplanes and bouquets of flowers at railway stations had long since become part of their daily lives when ashore.' These interrogation reports on captured crews reveal another side of the high morale of the arm: 'The prisoners were all fanatical Nazis and hated the British intensely.... German successes during 1940 appear to have established Hitler in their minds not merely as a God but as their only God. ...'

Such was the spirit of the U-boat men at this high point in Germany's fortunes – not only of the U-boat men, of course; the mood was shared by the greater part of the nation, especially young Germany. Undoubtedly it was shared by Dönitz, *der Löwe*.

The almost tangible prospect of defeating England by throttling her sea supply lines was snatched away in 1941 by Hitler's assault on Russia. The centre of gravity of the war effort shifted east; with it went the resources and any hope of the co-ordinated attention vital if the Atlantic battle were to be won. For already in the summer and autumn of 1940 the scale of U-boat successes had concentrated minds in London and also in Washington. Although the United States remained formally neutral, President Roosevelt had recognized the danger if England were defeated and had pledged all aid short of war, placing the huge industrial and shipbuilding resources of America and a series of distinctly unneutral measures in the scales against Dönitz's campaign of attrition. By mid-April 1941, US naval escort groups were patrolling a so-called American Defence Zone, extending over 2,000 miles into the Atlantic, and in September the US Navy began escorting convoys from American ports as far as Iceland.

Meanwhile the Royal Navy, Coastal Command and British scientists had combined to produce answers to night surface attack and the *Rudel* (or pack) tactic. The chief weapon was radar; the primitive early models were being fitted in escorts and aircraft as early as October 1940. Equally important were the training of special escort groups and the tactical integration of the aircraft of Coastal Command, which by the spring of 1941 were being supplied with effective depth charges. The weak link in group tactics – the U-boats' slow submerged speed – was now shown up. For a threatened convoy to escape, it was only necessary for escorts or aircraft to force shadowing boats below the surface and keep them there. Radar and a powerful searchlight fitted to Coastal Command aircraft allowed them to accomplish this even in darkness.

Another weakness of the group was the need for the touch-holding boat to report by wireless. By the summer of 1941, convoy escorts were being fitted with direction-finders enabling them to home on to these signals. In addition, the British Government Code and Cipher School at Bletchley Park broke into the naval code intermittently from March 1941 and continuously from June. This information, passed to the central submarine tracking room in London under the top-secret designation 'Ultra', enabled convoys to be routed around Dönitz's patrol lines. It is possible that the importance of Ultra has been exaggerated since, despite B-Dienst's excellent code breaking, Dönitz was complaining as early as December 1940 that 'in all cases the first contact with the convoy was a matter of chance'.

In contrast to the strides made by the British, which forced Dönitz to deploy his patrol lines further and further west in the Atlantic outside the range of Coastal Command aircraft and strengthened escorts – by June the boats were operating off Newfoundland – he was unable to gain Luftwaffe co-operation in finding targets. This was not his fault, nor was it for want of trying. It was a result of several factors: the uncoordinated service command structure under Hitler; Göring's determination to control everything that flew; and, no doubt, the lack of an extreme stimulus such as had forced the British services to co-operative effort. It was also due to shortage of suitable aircraft and the needs of the east. Dönitz did manage to arrange reconnaissance flights with the local air commander, but they proved spasmodic and unproductive, showing only that the pilots had not been trained for the task. On 6 May 1941, he noted: 'In no case has it been possible with their aid [Luftwaffe] to guide U-boats on to the enemy.' An Italian U-boat flotilla which he had been operating out of Bordeaux since the previous October proved equally disappointing. All attempts to train the officers in his methods failed. He noted in May: 'They sight nothing, report nothing, or report too late, and their tactical knowledge is practically nil.' Putting this down to national character ('they are not sufficiently hard and tough for this type of warfare'), he assigned them patrol areas in the Eastern Atlantic where they would not affect his own operations, but if sighted might divert convoy traffic towards his groups.

The decisive failure, however, was in technology. While the British were developing radar-equipped aircraft and escorts which could surprise and attack surfaced U-boats, no comparable advance took place in the design or arming of the boats. They were eventually equipped with a receiver called 'Metox', developed from a device presented to Dönitz by the French Admiral Darlan. This detected radar transmissions and so gave time to dive. But it was purely defensive, and did nothing to regain the initiative. Again, Dönitz was not directly to blame. A prototype submarine with a revolutionary fuel and hull shape had achieved an underwater speed of twenty-eight knots in tests in 1940, and its inventor, Professor Walter, had designed an ocean-going type. This was shelved as too futuristic when Hitler made tanks, guns and aircraft for the east his top priority. Similarly Führer decisions held back development work on radar. Here again Dönitz's arm was a victim of the Russian campaign and Hitler's genius. It was also a victim of the German warrior and racial ethic in which civilians like scientists and production engineers were a class below fighting men and were directed by them, and in which heroism and the quality of the blood counted for more than technical innovation.

Of course, Dönitz himself was a part of this ethos. He thrashed across the Breton fields on post-prandial walks with his dog Wolf and one or two of his young staff officers, trying to tease out operational problems, or stared at his great wall chart of the Atlantic marked with convoys and U-boat patrol lines, puzzling if his enemy were discovering his dispositions by means of spies or radio direction-finding. In fact, his boats were simply outdistanced technologically, and his commanders were forced to fight an ever grimmer, more dangerous mid-Atlantic battle. The 'Happy Time' was over; it had really ended in March 1941 when he lost three of his favourite 'aces', Schepke, Prien, Kretschmer, to the new, trained escort groups.

Hitler's declaration of war on the United States in December 1941 gave Dönitz another opportunity against soft targets. The US Navy had been escorting convoys in the Western Atlantic for some months, but merchant ships still proceeded independently on the American east coast with undimmed lights along marked routes, and they continued to do so after Hitler's declaration. Dönitz saw a chance to repeat the successes of the early months of the war against unprotected single ships, and determined to make a quick, concentrated strike. Gathering as many of the longer-range Type IX boats as he could, he sent them to positions along the eastern seaboard of the United States with instructions not to reveal themselves until he gave the codeword *Paukenschlag* – Drum Beat. This he did when all were on station on 13 January 1942, and the boats achieved immediate success. After debriefing the first commander to return, he noted: 'The expectation of coming across much single-ship traffic, clumsy handling of ships, few and unpractised sea and air patrols and defences was so greatly fulfilled that the conditions have to be described as almost of peacetime standards. . . .' Typically he added, 'The single disposition of boats was therefore correct.'

Thus began the second 'Happy Time'. US naval command took unexpectedly long to respond. It was six months before an effective convoy system had been organized on the east coast, and during this time Dönitz's commanders, roaming as far south as the Caribbean and Gulf of Mexico, beat all previous sinking records. As well as inexpert defence, there were more U-boats. They were coming from the yards at about seventeen a month and by May, when the sinking figure topped 600,000 tons, Dönitz had over 300 boats. This was not the magic number he had always stipulated since many were on trials or used for training, but at any one time that spring and early summer he had at his disposal between 120 and 170 operational boats. Now his principal frustration was Hitler, who insisted on keeping a flotilla off Norway and sending others to the Mediterranean. Dönitz argued vehemently against this dispersal of forces, expressing his creed in this war diary entry for 15 April 1942:

> The enemy powers' shipping is one large whole. It is therefore immaterial where a ship is sunk – in the end it must still be replaced by a new ship. The decisive question for the long term lies in the race between sinking and new construction. However, the centre of the enemy's new construction and armaments is in the United States. . . . I am therefore grasping the evil at the root if I attack supplies, especially oil at this centre. Every ship which is sunk here counts not only as a ship sunk but at the same time damages the enemy shipbuilding and armament at its inception. . . .

The US coast, he went on, was also the area where ships could be sunk most expeditiously and cheaply in terms of losses. It followed that he had to concentrate there: 'it is incomparably more important to sink than to reduce sinkings by making them in a prescribed area'. Here he was answering those of the naval staff who advocated specifically cutting supplies to England (the 'supply war') rather than sinking ships anywhere (the 'tonnage war') that he always advocated.

The figure he was now keeping under constant observation was what he termed the 'potential' of his boats – the tonnage sunk per boat per day at sea, days which of course included getting to and from the operations area. This rose from 209 in January 1942 to 409 in March and remained over 400 for the next three months. The high figure was achieved by single U-boats against single, unescorted ships – not by packs against convoys, as in the legend he and his supporters sought to foster after the war. (In fact, over the war as a whole, 80 per cent of U-boat sinkings were of single, independently routed ships.) For by this date the *Rudel* tactic, as practised by the current type of U-boat, had been defeated in principle; only the Allies' largely self-imposed shortage of aircraft and an 'Air Gap' in the central Atlantic beyond the range of shore-based planes allowed the possibility of continuing it. This was clearly perceived at Anti-submarine operations in London, where the monthly report for April 1942 stated: 'with an adequate and efficient air escort wolf-pack tactics on a convoy should be impossible. . . . we hope to achieve this beyond the reach of land-based aircraft by auxiliary carriers with the convoys.'

All the signs were there for Dönitz and his staff as well. Before the windfall off the US coast, his packs had been forced ever further into mid-ocean by air patrols; it should not have been difficult to foresee that, if this monthly sinking rate ever threatened to achieve the 'decisive' success he aimed for, his enemies would take steps to close the Air Gap – as indeed they were doing already. Yet he remained transfixed by numbers of boats and the monthly 'potential'. When the demands of the Eastern Front again cut into naval building, he suggested dropping the larger Type IX boats. Two Type VII could be built for one

Type IX and it was *numbers* he would need, for reconnaissance lines to find convoys when he had to return to the Atlantic shipping lanes. Already Dönitz's 'iron will-power, goal-oriented certainty and unwearying toughness' can be seen betraying him and his beloved U-boat arm.

By September 1942 it had become plain that the U-boat campaign faced defeat. Organization of convoys along the US coast had forced Dönitz back to mid-Atlantic as he had anticipated, but the Air Gap where success could be achieved had been narrowed by longer-range aircraft. Moreover, the British had command of the air over Biscay, and boats on passage in and out were forced down or destroyed by day or night; beginning in July the loss rate had risen to over ten boats a month. Crews – now including many conscript replacements – lived under constant tension from the moment they sailed; those fortunate enough to be rescued after the loss of their boat told their interrogators how they loathed service in the U-boat arm, 'which they find very different from what propaganda had led them to expect'. Meanwhile, the naval staff had revised estimates of the new tonnage being made available by the US emergency shipbuilding programme, and concluded that to reduce Allied shipping capacity no less than 1.3 million tons must be sunk every month. This was almost a million tons over the September sinking figure as estimated by U-boat command.

Dönitz's war diary entries revealed bitter despair – although of course this did not show in his public face, rather the reverse – and he sent urgent pleas for long-range aircraft to contest enemy air command over Biscay and the Atlantic. He also asked for the rockets under development at Peenemünde to be adapted for U-boats to enable them to fight escorts and aircraft. It was, of course, too late. There were insufficient aircraft even to protect Germany, whose cities were being subjected to massed Allied 'terror' raids.

It was at this time that he issued two new and unusually imprecise standing orders to his boats which probably brought him close to the gallows after the war at Nuremberg. Since at least the beginning of the year Hitler had been calling for the destruction of survivors from ships sunk; the aims, as he rationalized them, were firstly to terrorize merchant sailors, secondly to reduce their numbers so that the huge quantity of ships built under the US programme could not be manned. What evidence there is of Raeder's and Dönitz's response suggests that both rejected the idea as likely to lead to retaliation. On 17 September, however, after US Liberators had attacked *U-156*, which was displaying red crosses while towing lifeboats carrying mainly Italian prisoners-of-war from the British troop transport *Laconia*, which she had sunk, Dönitz sent a signal to all boats reiterating his previous orders not to rescue survivors, and adding: 'Rescue contradicts the most fundamental [*primitivisten*] demands of war for the annihilation of enemy ships and crews. . . . Be hard. Think of the fact that the enemy in his bombing attacks on German towns has no regard for women and children.'

The British prosecution at Nuremberg argued and certainly believed that the words 'annihilation of enemy ships and crews' – and an even more suggestive phrase in another signal sent out at about the same time stressing the desirability of sinking so-called 'Rescue ships' attached to convoys 'in view of the desired annihilation of ships' crews' – were intended as secret, unattributable licence for U-boat commanders to kill survivors. Yet, though there was one proven case of this by the commander and officers of *U-852* in 1943, the Court did not accept the argument.

Early in 1943 Dönitz's superior, Grand Admiral Raeder, resigned. As possible successors, he submitted the names of Generaladmiral Carls, a senior and safe choice, and Dönitz.

Dönitz was riding high at this point, the dismay of the summer almost forgotten. New sinking records had been set in recent months, partly by the exploitation of more distant soft targets off South Africa and in the Indian Ocean, chiefly because the Allies had diverted escorts and aircraft from the North Atlantic to protect the invasion fleet for the North African landings in November. In that month the U-boats had sunk, by estimate, 900,000 tons. This was actually some 160,000 tons too high; but, filled with almost manic confidence that he could reach the necessary 1.3 million tons if only he had the support of other arms and other departments, Dönitz had fired off peremptory demands to Raeder, who had eventually been obliged to forbid him from meddling in technical matters, and told him to confine himself to operations. Temperamentally the two were poles apart: Raeder regarded Dönitz's pushiness, and his inflated ego after the U-boat successes, as insufferable. A dangerous breach had opened between the two, yet Raeder never seems to have doubted the worth of his over-ardent junior – even at the height of their quarrel that November, he penned a generous tribute to Dönitz's unfailing good judgement in the conduct of the U-boat war, ending: 'If the U-boat war proves able to bring about in essentials – as I am satisfied it will – the decision of the war, this will be primarily to the credit of the Admiral Dönitz.' This was appended to the annual report on Dönitz by his fleet chief, Schniewind. Like all earlier reports by his commanding officers it stressed his 'superior intellectual gifts and special leadership qualities', his 'energetic and indefatigably tough' style of command. 'The BdU sphere has been welded together by him into a tight, war-sworn community', wrote Schniewind, judging Dönitz 'in my opinion suitable in personality to rise to the highest positions of leadership'.

The uniformly good opinions of Dönitz's handling of the U-boat arm reveal that the naval High Command as a whole was little aware of the Allies' technological lead, or indeed of the technological nature of the war. This must call into question the criticism that Dönitz individually lacked foresight. He was part of a service that, by the nature of the Führer system and the fight for its own allocations, strategies, indeed its very existence, had turned inwards, and was as divorced from reality and wedded to the Aryan myth as the Führer himself. Personally Dönitz was both victim and exemplar of the myth. Undoubtedly this was a chief ingredient of his success: his superiors admired him for it; his young officers expected these iron qualities; and one of his longest-serving staff officers recollected after the war that 'Dönitz very seldom "ordered". He convinced, and because all that he wanted was very precisely considered, he really convinced.' It would almost certainly be as true to say that he inspired by the will and undaunted optimism which they looked for in their leader.

Because of this, and because the recent U-boat successes were the only remaining gleams of light now that the war had turned against Germany, it was inevitable that Hitler should choose him over the more obvious successor, Carls. On 30 January 1943, Dönitz took over as Supreme Commander of the navy with the rank of Grossadmiral (Grand Admiral) and a present of 300,000 marks to remind him where his loyalties lay.

He needed no such inducement. Undoubtedly he enjoyed his new lifestyle as one of the top leadership of the Reich – now he had his own special train, an ss guard and escort wherever he went, a grand villa in Berlin-Dahlem with other top Nazis, an art collection, and soon his own quarters in the Führer headquarters complex, Wolfschanze, the Wolf's lair. But the springs of his loyalty came from deeper sources. As his own young officers needed to believe in *der Löwe*, so he needed to believe – and did believe – in Hitler as the man of German destiny. Hitler sensed this and played up to the expected part, addressing Dönitz as 'Herr Grossadmiral', bowing always to his professional judgement, but educating him in the wider spheres of statecraft, grand strategy and the *Weltanschauung*. Thus began one of the most influential partnerships of the second half of the war, for just as Dönitz needed Hitler as focus for his inner drives, Hitler needed Dönitz's optimism and devotion to lift him from the increasing gloom outside. Hitler, now a stooped, greying figure, smitten with an uncontrollable shake in his left hand and arm, became Dönitz's war father.

A chief cause of Raeder's resignation had been an order by Hitler to scrap the big ships. At first Dönitz seems to have agreed. Thus his first directive to the naval staffs in Berlin: 'The sea war is the U-boat war. . . . All has to be subordinated to this main goal. . . .' He retired or moved senior officers associated with Raeder's policies to backwaters and promoted much needed young blood to the top commands, but he remained BdU himself and moved U-boat headquarters to Berlin-Charlottenberg so that he could retain personal control. Nevertheless, he was soon convinced by the staff that to get rid of the big ships would not only hand the enemy the cheapest of victories, but would release huge enemy forces at present tied up guarding against their break-out. It was the classic argument of the 'fleet in being'. Moreover, the resources it would release for U-boat construction were minimal. He set about persuading Hitler of this and, during the course of three conferences in February 1943, he succeeded. He had to promise to send the *Tirpitz* and

Scharnhorst against the supply convoys to Russia as soon as opportunity offered, but there is little doubt that he would have wanted to do this anyway – as British naval intelligence had predicted, directly he took over.

This was but the first example of the dexterity with which Dönitz handled Hitler in all matters where his service was concerned. He did it by his narrow focus on the goal, rather than the difficulties the enemy might put in the way; by his ability to pare problems down to essentials – strictly from his own point of view; by his optimism, which was precisely what the dictator needed; and by his transparent devotion and commitment. His first directive as Supreme Commander ran: 'Our life belongs to the state. Our honour lies in our fulfilment of duty and our readiness for action. None of us has the right to private life. The question for us is winning the war. We have to pursue this goal with fanatical devotion and the most ruthless determination to win.'

Rommel had retreated, and the Allies had landed in North Africa; the Axis partner, Italy, was in the grip of defeatism; German armies had surrendered to the Russians at Stalingrad, and defeatism was even apparent in sections of the German population. But by example and rhetoric, Dönitz joined himself to the exponents of 'total war', Goebbels, Himmler and Speer in particular. By doing so and pursuing the goal of victory, in his own words, 'with fanatical devotion and the most ruthless determination' even after it disappeared from rational view, he integrated the navy into the National Socialist state. It was for this as much as his U-boat successes that Hitler had chosen him.

Both Himmler and Speer courted him as an ally from the beginning. By 24 February 1943 – that is, within a fortnight of his takeover – Himmler had instigated a meeting aboard the flagship of U-boat command to analyse the prospects of increasing the underwater speed of the boats. Himmler was insinuating himself into all areas of the war economy at this time by virtue of his concentration-camp workforce and the opportunities it presented to carry out development work under conditions of absolute secrecy. It is interesting that he at least evidently understood one of the crucial weaknesses of the existing U-boats before their final defeat in the Atlantic battle.

Meanwhile, Dönitz was discussing with Speer plans for the construction of a literally fantastic fleet of existing types of U-boats and small craft. Speer was trying to persuade him to place all naval building under his own Ministry of Armaments. Raeder had always refused to part with responsibility for naval construction, but Dönitz saw the advantages of a central allocation of scarce materials and labour in place of the current inter- service rivalry and came to an agreement by which Speer, in return for taking naval building under his wing, undertook to produce the craft at the rate stipulated in the programme. Dönitz had to fight this through in the teeth of opposition from his own departments. His arguments were that Germany was engaged in an *economic* war with the sea powers, and that the difficulties which had ruined all Raeder's efforts to build up a balanced fleet would actually increase. His new, more ambitious programme was possible only with Speer's co-operation: '*without* him meant *against* him'.

Here again he showed his skill in tackling essentials. Again, however, they were essentials within the narrowest focus. His own staff pointed to the desperate need for aircraft over the Reich, and the navy's own need for an air arm. Yet his programme as eventually worked out called for forty U-boats a month over five years – a total of 2,400 boats with which to cover the Atlantic. Together with other small craft deemed essential, it required 50,000 tons of steel a month more than the navy's quota, nearly 150,000 extra shipyard workers and three times the annual intake of recruits to man the craft. In Germany's situation it was fantasy. Yet it was a fantasy shared by Speer, who had far greater knowledge of the manpower and material problems facing them; it was a part of the group fantasy of 'total war'. Subscribing to it, Dönitz was both its victim and a considerable driving force.

Before the final agreement with Speer, Dönitz was forced to call off the Atlantic battle. The signs had been apparent almost from the time he took over as Supreme Commander, determined to make the U-boat war the focus of effort. In February 1943 a record total of nineteen boats had been lost, and there were many reports of surprise attacks undetected by the 'Metox' receivers. The rate of losses continued in March. 'We cannot tell whether this is due to improved location gear or more suitable types of aircraft. . . .' ran the war diary comment. In fact it was the former, in the shape of a new, more powerful 'centimetric' radar. Towards the end of the month there was a surge in confidence after the most successful pack attack ever. Boats from three patrol lines named by Dönitz himself, in typical style, *Raubgraf* (Robber baron), *Stürmer* (Daredevil) and *Dränger* (Harrier) caught two convoys in mid-Atlantic and hung on for four days of desperate attack and counter-attack by escorts and – as the convoy moved out of the Air Gap – long-range aircraft. U-boat command war diary recorded: 'Altogether thirty-two ships totalling 186,000 tons and one destroyer were sunk, and nine others hit. This is so far the best result obtained in a convoy battle. . . .'

By this date Dönitz had 423 boats in total, of which an average of 116 were at sea each day. During April, fifteen boats were lost – many surprised on passage through Biscay. This was two less than deliveries from the yards, so by the end of the month he had 425 boats; 240 were operational and on average 111 were at sea each day. However, when averaged out over the few months of the year, the 'potential' of each had dropped to under 160 tons per sea day, and fell to 127 in the month of April. Together with evidence from all recent convoy battles of the steps the Allies were taking to close the Air Gap (by using long-range Liberators and auxiliary carriers with escort groups), these figures revealed that with the existing type of boat the 'tonnage war' was unwinnable. Over the period needed (even on Speer's increased production schedule) to fill the Atlantic with enough boats to sink a million tons a month given the present 'potential' – an extrapolation of the monthly loss rate pointed up the disastrous scale of human loss to be expected. Dönitz had frequently noted that success in U-boat warfare was largely dependent on the training and above all the quality of commanders. Recent war diary conclusions blamed lack of success not simply on enemy air cover but on 'inexperienced' commanders. To continue the Atlantic battle meant the certain loss of hundreds of commanders and officers, not to mention trained crews; yet Dönitz was determined to fight on.

There can be no excuses. He was waging a war which would be decided on figures and he was studying the figures which told him the battle was lost. Whether viewed from outside or inside the group, it is plain that his goal-oriented certainty and optimism had become negative qualities; he was sending his young men – including his own son Peter, serving as watchkeeping lieutenant in *U-954* – to their deaths in obsolescent boats in a hopeless struggle under conditions of enemy superiority, which neither he nor any other submariner of the Great War had experienced.

In 1930, one of Dönitz's pre-war commanding officers, the legendary Admiral Canaris, had suggested in his annual report that Dönitz was, for his age, unbalanced and must be 'brought to take things more calmly and not set exaggerated demands, above all on himself'. During the Battle of the Atlantic's most critical period, early May 1943, Dönitz's performance reveals the accuracy of this assessment. The first half of that month saw the loss rate double; *U-954*, his son's boat, was one of those failing to report – news which Dönitz took without visible sign of emotion. The reasons for the dramatic increase were set out clearly in U-boat command war diary:

'Enemy radar location is the worst enemy of our U-boats. . . . The enemy air forces are already able to take over convoy escort duty in almost the whole North Atlantic area, and it must be expected that the only remaining gaps will be closed in a reasonable period. . . . Air escort . . . has always forced our U-boats to lag hopelessly behind a convoy and prevented them achieving any successes. . . .

Nevertheless, he did not alter his convictions. After trying (and failing) to persuade Hitler that the Iberian peninsula should be occupied in order to widen the base for U-boat operations, Dönitz addressed a message to commanders of Atlantic boats. They had been directed to a convoy discovered by B-Dienst, and he told them:

If there is anyone who thinks that fighting convoys is no longer possible, he is a weakling and no U-boat commander. The Battle of the Atlantic gets harder, but it is the decisive campaign of the war. Be aware of your high responsibility and be clear you must answer for your actions. . . . Be hard, draw ahead and attack. I believe in you. C-in-C.

Arriving in the vicinity of the convoy on 21 May, the U-boats found two escort carriers and a support group as well as the normal escort. When they tried to obey orders to draw ahead on the surface, the boats were forced under or destroyed, and before the operation was called off on the morning of 23 May, five were sunk. Then at last Dönitz gave in: losses, he noted, had reached an intolerable level without corresponding successes. He disguised defeat, however, as a 'temporary shift to areas less endangered by aircraft'; the battle would be resumed directly the boats were equipped with the necessary weapons to fight aircraft.

The scientific–technological nature of Dönitz's defeat is underlined by the US Navy's opposite result in the Pacific. There, American submarines equipped with radar achieved decisive victory over Japanese shipping whose escorts lacked radar. Try as he might to achieve mastery over aircraft by equipping his boats with multiple AA guns, or mastery over surface escorts by using acoustic torpedoes, all Dönitz's efforts failed. Finally he had to await the production of new classes, designated Types XXI and XXIII. These had a streamlined hull shape (taken from Walter's design) and an enormously increased battery capacity, boosting their underwater speed to eighteen knots. They had emerged as an alternative to the Walter boat, which could be produced with existing technology and without development time – indeed Speer's technical director proposed prefabricating sections in factories and transporting them to the dockyards to be welded together, much as the Americans were mass-producing merchant ships. It was estimated that this would halve building time and prevent enemy disruption, since the sections could be built out of range of Allied bombers. Dönitz took the considerable risk of sanctioning this radical departure and further broke tradition by calling for series production without testing a prototype. In this case he was proved correct; the first Type XXIs passed trials in early 1945 and were prevented from operating only by the collapse and capitulation of the Reich.

In the meantime, their promise enabled Dönitz to make confident predictions to Hitler about the renewal of the tonnage war, for, once in service, they would render 'all former enemy striving for counter-measures ineffective since the construction of escort vessels is based on the low speed of U-boats under water . . .'.

To his adjutant he was wont to say, 'We'll get them!' He meant the British. 'We'll get them in the end! But first we must have the new boats.'

This was the hope on which he based his continuing support for Hitler and his strategy. No doubt other secret 'miracle weapons' like the V-rockets, jet fighters and jet 'flying wing' bombers under development or production by Himmler's slave-labour forces played their parts, as did the belief shared by all members of the leadership that the eastern and western sides of the enemy coalition must break apart, but as the overall situation deteriorated, it was the prospect of resuming U-boat warfare with the new boats that Dönitz held constantly before Hitler's eyes. That at least was his rationalization. The record of his fanatic support for Hitler's strategy of no retreat anywhere reveals it as merely rationalization. First in Tunisia, next in Sicily, then in the Crimea, East Prussia and Kurland – in each case, against the studied opinions not only of the General Staff but of his own naval staff – Dönitz backed his Führer's resolve to stand fast at all costs. An extraordinary note which he appended to a war diary entry composed by an officer who did not share Hitler's views shows his utter devotion:

> The huge force the Führer radiates, his unshakeable confidence, his far-sighted judgement of the situation in Italy have made it plain during these days what very poor little fry [*Würstchen*] we all are by comparison with the Führer, and that our knowledge, our vision of things outside our limited sphere is fragmentary. Anyone who thinks he can do better than the Führer is foolish.

Dönitz constantly disregarded the opinions of his operations staff; finally he reduced them to a mere rubber stamp for his own blood-reasoning. The truth is he had lost touch with any reality except the Nazi ideal, where logic was derived from the *Weltanschauung* and the group psychology. Himmler's interest in U-boat development has been mentioned; another sign of Dönitz's relationship with him from the beginning of his period as Supreme Commander of the navy is contained in a document sent to Himmler by the ss-Obergruppenführer responsible for the valuables taken from Jews before their deaths in the extermination camps. Dated 13 May 1943, it proposed immediate distribution of 3,000 men's watches and 2,000 fountain pens to the U-boat arm. It is known from testimony that cases of second-hand watches *were* distributed to boats returning from operations, and outside the Waffen-ss the U-boat arm was the only branch of the services to be chosen for such treatment. Dönitz was BdU as well as Supreme Commander; it is inconceivable that this occurred without his knowledge and concurrence.

Towards the end of 1943 Himmler revealed the secret of the genocide policy to selected groups of high officers of the party, the ss and Wehrmacht. On one of these occasions, a Gauleiter conference on 6 October, 1943, Dönitz and Speer were among the guest speakers. When it came to Himmler's turn at the end they heard him explain why it had been necessary to kill women and children as well as male Jews; he had not felt himself justified in exterminating the men and allowing children to grow up as their avengers, he told them. 'The difficult resolution must be taken – to cause this people to disappear from the earth.'

Two months later Dönitz invited Himmler to speak at a conference of senior naval officers at Weimar; again Himmler explained why it was necessary for him to kill the women and children of 'Partisans and Jewish Commissars' in the east; he did not mention genocide but implied it, by saying that he would be a weakling and a criminal were he to allow the 'hate-filled sons of these subhumans [*Untermenschen*] executed in the battle of human against sub-human to grow up'.

The following day Dönitz addressed the conference and spent some time stressing the need for the ideological training of officers and men: it was necessary to train the sailor 'uniformly and comprehensively to adjust him ideologically to our Germany' – National Socialist Germany – because 'every dualism, every dissension in this training, every divergence or unreadiness implies a weakness . . .'. They had to put their full weight behind the state from 'deepest conviction'. The Russians did so, and the Germans could only hold their own in the struggle if they followed their own ideological path 'with holy ardour, with complete fanaticism'.

Turning then to review the war situation and the navy, he said that if conditions arose for the battle group to strike he would 'under all circum-stances go at the enemy'. He repeated this to Hitler two days later (19 December 1943) at Führer headquarters. It is possible that time was running out in the bargain he had struck about the employment of his big ships – more probable that he was determined to offer his Führer a proof of the navy's commitment and, he hoped, a success. Whichever it was, his chance came within days: a convoy for Russia was sighted heading up towards northern Norway. U-boats were ordered to take station across its course; surface vessels comprising Battle Group North – reduced by repairs to the battle-cruiser *Scharnhorst* and her destroyer escort – were ordered to prepare to sortie, and air reconnaissance was requested in order to locate a possible 'distant heavy escort group'. Such a group was not found, but the weather had prevented a full search, and meanwhile radio signals had been plotted from 200 miles astern (west) of the convoy. It was assumed at Arctic Command (Narvik) that this was the position of the British heavy escort. Such was the uncertainty, however, that Dönitz broke off a planned Christmas visit to his U-boat bases in France and returned to his headquarters complex (known as Koralle), arriving early in the afternoon of Christmas Day. By this time, *Scharnhorst* had received preliminary sailing orders. Dönitz set about putting his personal stamp to the operational instructions for the force commander: 'Fight not to be ended with half-success. Opportunities seized to be pressed home. . . . I trust in your offensive spirit. *Heil und Sieg!*'

The shore commander of Battle Group North at Kiel (Dönitz's former superior, Schniewind) had already expressed his opinion that, in view of the bad weather and uncertainty about the enemy covering force, the stakes were high and success unlikely. Now came an appalling weather forecast: gale-force winds, heavy swell, rain, overcast and snow in the Barents Sea, 'visibility only occasionally ten miles'. This nullified the advantage expected from *Scharn-horst*'s long-range guns and played into the hands of any British heavy covering force – if one were in the vicinity – since British gunnery radar was known to be superior. Nevertheless Dönitz had his revised orders sent. Narvik Command meanwhile requested Kiel to break off the operation. Schniewind rang Koralle to inform Dönitz and to tell him that the air commander had ruled out reconnaissance on account of the weather. Still Dönitz resolved not to break off. Schniewind then took the courageous step of sending him a strongly argued message expressing his own grave doubts about the operation. It did not change Dönitz's determination.

As it turned out, the radio signals from 200 miles astern of the convoy had been from a British heavy group headed by the battleship *Duke of York*. *Scharnhorst*, unwilling to use her radar lest she give away her presence, was caught by the British flagship at close range with her guns fore and aft. She ran, but was slowed by the British radar-directed fire and finally, after heroic resistance, was overwhelmed. Her last message was, 'We shall fight to the last shell. *Heil* Hitler!' And as the British closed to rescue survivors, hurrahs and shouts of '*Heil* our Führer!' sounded amid the wreckage.

Dönitz felt the disaster keenly – yet he was unable to accept even a measure of personal responsibility. In his report to Hitler, he advanced tactical errors by the force commander – which were indeed made – as the whole cause of the loss. Before long he had convinced himself that 'the idea of using *Scharnhorst* during the Arctic night was basically correct'. Taken with other indications – his tendency to try and impress young officers with his collections of paintings or with his closeness to the Führer – Dönitz's inability to admit the slightest degree of error suggests that beneath his taut, spare, diamond-hard exterior he was very unsure of himself. This was no doubt why he needed the Führer, and the Nazi creed. On 1 January 1944, he addressed a characteristic New Year message to the navy: 'The Führer shows us the way and the goal. We follow him with body and soul to a great German future. *Heil* our Führer!'

By this time he and Himmler were the only leaders of fighting services who still enjoyed Hitler's confidence. Göring had failed, the generals (so Hitler believed) were disloyal as a caste. And when, in March 1944, Hitler retired to his mountain eyrie for rest and medical treatment, he gave Dönitz the signal honour of speaking in his stead at the annual heroes' day parade. The speech Dönitz made might have come from the lips of Goebbels or Himmler; it was a pure expression of National Socialism and the Hitler cult. Where would the nation have been without the Führer? Had they still been 'permeated with the disintegrating poison of Jewry' and vulnerable to it because they lacked 'the protection of our present uncompromising ideology', how would they have survived the war years?

Invasion of the continent by the Western Powers was imminent, and was naturally at the forefront of Dönitz's attention during this period. He believed the assault could be thrown back and that this would be the turning point of the war, allowing German troops held in the west to be transferred east to throw back the Russians. He had commissioned a particularly ardent and inventive admiral, Heye, to build a force of midget submersibles, manned torpedoes and the like to contest the inshore waters off the invasion beaches, and he held the U-boat flotillas in their French and southern Norwegian bases ready to sortie against the Allied fleet directly it was reported. Towards the end of March he began issuing a series of orders stressing that, since the coming battle for the beaches would determine the future of the German *Volk*, normal considerations of risk were not valid. He enjoined his U-boat commanders to have only one goal before their eyes and in their hearts: '*Angriff – ran – versenken!*' (Attack – forward – sink!). To the men of all units he addressed an order entitled 'Reckless Attack!' in which he demanded complete commitment without regard for the preservation of the boat or the force relationship, and he warned that he would disgrace and destroy any man who did not fulfil his duty to the utmost. In view of the enemy's total air command, improved radar, Asdic and depth charges and the numbers of escorts which would undoubtedly be deployed to protect the invasion fleet, these were suicide orders. Against the counter-measures the enemy had developed, the U-boats' one advance was the *Schnorchel*, a device which could be raised above the water to allow the diesel engines to suck in air while the boat was submerged. With skilled depth-keeping it did enable a boat to maintain speed under water, but it was a most difficult and taxing method under any but ideal conditions. As for Heye's small craft, they were extraordinarily primitive weapons.

It might be said that Dönitz, convinced that Germany's survival was at stake, had no alternative to such orders. Yet once again he was disregarding the arithmetic of battle, the evidence of enemy technological superiority and the economic nature of the war. He was thinking with his blood; his premises and the slogans he employed were those of Hitler and the Führer's close circle. The basic error was the belief that fanaticism could triumph over material superiority; this had been disproved too many times in the previous year for it to have been a rational response. In the event the Allies achieved such complete strategic and tactical surprise that when the invasion force reached Normandy, Dönitz was on holiday. The U-boats were ordered to sortie, but it was too late. So great was the Allied air and surface cover that only three boats reached the Channel within a week; one reached the Cherbourg peninsula some days later and sank a single US landing craft before starting its perilous return voyage. Dönitz's light forces made equally little impact; Heye's midget craft were not yet ready.

Dönitz had said this was the decisive battle for the Reich. Logic should have dictated that once the Allies had established themselves ashore with uninterrupted supply lines from England and undisputed air command, Germany's war was lost. The generals – with a very few exceptions – soon came to this view; Dönitz never did. On 20 July 1944, when Hitler survived the bomb attempt on his life Dönitz issued a proclamation to the navy expressing 'Holy wrath and bitter rage towards our criminal enemies and their hirelings'. In a second proclamation the following day, he explained what would have happened had the 'criminal attempt' succeeded: 'The extermination of our people, the enslaving of our men, hunger and nameless misery would have resulted. Our *Volk* would have experienced an unspeakable time of endless misfortune, much crueller and harder than the present war can bring. . . .'

This was indeed the fate that Goebbels and Himmler had conjured from the Allies' announced intention to partition Germany and the 'Morgenthau plan', designed to destroy Germany's industrial base and reduce her to a primarily agricultural nation. It was this threat, together with the idea that the enemy coalition would break apart, and the promise of the secret 'miracle weapons' under development, including of course the Types XXI and XXIII U-boats, that enabled Dönitz to rationalize his continuing devotion to the Führer, though the borders of the Reich were being squeezed ever inwards and its cities reduced to deserts of rubble. His reports to the Führer became caricatures of his earlier goal-oriented optimism. After expressing outrageous confidence in Heye's midget submarines, a few days later he reported the total failure of a sortie of these craft as having the greatest value since 'all the teething troubles which might never have shown up under test in the Baltic have shown up in the severe conditions . . .'. On New Year's Day 1945, he distributed an article from *Picture Post* which suggested weak construction in mass-produced US merchant ships.

There was another side to the picture. Military and political observers at the Führer conferences were invariably impressed by Dönitz's calm bearing and reasoned manner. One young army officer, who laid out maps for Hitler's inspection in the wrong order, recalled that amid the general reproval 'only Grossadmiral Dönitz smiled at me, lifted the pile of maps and requested me with a nod to lay them out again'.

Dönitz was always ready to assume responsibility and extemporize practical solutions, and no difficulties discouraged him; he looked only for answers, giving always the same impression of energy, reliability and quiet conviction that finally they would achieve victory. In the circumstances this must have taken all his will. If this outer poise is contrasted with the absurd optimism of the reports he delivered in his terse style to the Führer, or with the scale of disaster outside Führer headquarters, his attitude might be described as going down with his ship in the best traditions of the service. This was indeed very much in his mind, as can be seen in a decree he promulgated on 11 April: 'No one thinks of giving up his ship. Rather go down in honour. . . . The Kriegsmarine will fight to the end. Some day its bearing in the severest crisis of this war will be judged by posterity. The same goes for each individual. . . .' Like all senior naval officers, he was determined that the naval mutinies which were supposed to have started the collapse of Imperial Germany in 1918 would never be repeated. He offered his sailors to Himmler and Hitler for the defence of Berlin partly in order to keep the young men busy – and also partly from fanatic devotion. A secret decree he issued on 7 April 1945, ran: 'We fighting men of the Kriegsmarine know how we have to act. . . . Any scoundrel who does not behave so must be hanged and have a placard fastened to him,

"Here hangs a traitor who by his low cowardice allows German women and children to die instead of protecting them like a man."' He had borrowed the idea from Himmler's summary Court Martial teams and his naval police, responding to this injunction fanatically, earned an equal reputation.

In the end Hitler rewarded his supreme loyalty by appointing him his successor. Dönitz was conducting a huge naval operation to rescue troops and German civilians from East Prussia when he received this stunning news, followed shortly by the still more stunning news of Hitler's death below the ruins of Berlin. He attempted to buy time to continue his rescue of Germans from the east by capitulating to the Western Powers alone, but was soon made to realize that surrender had to be unconditional to all the Allies. Even as his plenipotentiary was signing these terms he began the task – carried on later by others – of separating the navy and the other fighting services from the Nazi regime, and laying the odium of criminality solely on his erstwhile ally Himmler and the ss. Several believed he would succeed: even as he formally dismissed Himmler, Goebbels, Bormann and Ribbentrop from his government on 6 May, two days before the capitulation came into effect, some of the more notorious ss leaders (including the chief of the Concentration Camp Inspectorate and the former Commandant of Auschwitz) donned naval uniform and adopted new identities as humble ratings in the Kriegsmarine.

Taken into custody on 23 May 1945, and charged with other surviving German leaders at the first Nuremberg War Crimes Trial. Found guilty of 'waging aggressive war' and of 'war crimes', but it was held that the evidence did not establish with the certainty required that he deliberately ordered the killing of shipwrecked survivors. Sentenced to ten years in prison, serving eleven years, six months as the time before the judgement was disallowed. Afterwards he wrote three books of memoirs which form the basis of his legend; they should be treated with caution. He became a devout Christian. Died in his sleep in January 1981, honoured by his former officers, and was buried alongside his wife under a large carving of Christ crucified.

8

Admiral of the Fleet

Viscount Cunningham
of Hyndhope
KT, GCB, OM, DSO**
Royal Navy

1883–1963
by
John Winton

*B*ORN *Dublin, 7 January 1883. Went to* HMS *Britannia at Dartmouth as a cadet, January 1897. As a midshipman he served with the Naval Brigade in the Boer War in 1900. First command, Torpedo Boat No. 14. Commanded new destroyer* Scorpion *1911–18, winning the* DSO *in the Dardanelles in 1915. Won a bar to his* DSO *in* Termagant *in the Dover Patrol, 1919, and a second bar a year later in* Seafire *in the Baltic.*

In 1920, as a captain, in charge of the Naval Inter-Allied Commission of Control supervising the demolition of the fortifications on the island of Heligoland. Returned to destroyers, being captain (D) of the 6th and 1st Flotillas, and captain in charge of the destroyer base at Port Edgar, Firth of Forth. In 1927 he was flag captain and chief staff officer to Vice Admiral Sir Walter Cowan, C-in-C North America & West Indies.

Met Miss Nona Byatt in the West Indies and married her in December 1929. The same year he was appointed in command of the battleship Rodney. *In 1932 he was Commodore Royal Naval Barracks Chatham. Rear Admiral Destroyers, Mediterranean, December 1933.*

Promoted vice admiral, July 1936; became second-in-command of the Mediterranean Fleet. Also commanded the Battle Cruiser Squadron, flying his flag in Hood. *Deputy Chief of the Naval Staff, December 1938. Appointed C-in-C Mediterranean in the summer of 1939.*

'I felt a great joy in being at sea again,' he said, 'steaming at high speed in perfect weather to what I have always considered is the finest appointment the Royal Navy has to offer.' It was 2 June 1939, and Andrew Browne

Cunningham (A.B.C., as he was always known in the navy), was on board the cruiser *Penelope* en route from Marseilles to Alexandria.

While on passage, A.B.C. read some of the hundreds of letters of congratulation he had received. Their writers were all confident he was the man for the job, and A.B.C. himself shared that confidence. He was fifty-six years old and had been forty-two years in the navy, spending more than ten of those years in the Mediterranean, in eight different ships. He knew the Mediterranean better than any other serving naval officer. He knew its seas, its climate, its geography, its harbours and coasts from Gibraltar to Gallipoli and from Sfax to Split, and its people, from the King of Greece to the Maltese dghaisamen of Grand Harbour. He was personally acquainted with many of the senior officers of other Mediterranean navies, some of whom were shortly to become his enemies. 'It has always seemed to me', Admiral Sir William James wrote later, 'that A.B.C. was a gift from the gods to us at that moment in history. . . .'

A.B.C. was a small man, although nobody noticed his height, but broadshouldered with a red face and a permanently aggressive manner, as though he was always just about to put his fists up; indeed, as a cadet in *Britannia*, he was noted for fighting. He had bright blue eyes, with distinctive red-rimmed lids, which gave him a rather alarming appearance. He was a hard driver of men, with a rough tongue: in 1911, when he had just joined *Scorpion*, he was officially warned by Their Lordships as to his future conduct after he had used intemperate and exasperating language towards a leading signalman. He would not tolerate fools, expected the highest standards (of himself as much as others) and speedily rid himself of anyone who disappointed him; one officer, who later rose to flag rank, claimed to be *Scorpion*'s thirteenth first lieutenant.

Yet A.B.C. had an almost feminine sympathy for anybody ill or in pain, and would go to endless trouble for the wounded or the bereaved. He was a modest man but, in spite of his protests, he secretly loved having his photograph taken or his picture painted. He had a very keen sense of humour and relished jokes, especially bawdy ones. He played tennis and golf well, enjoyed party games and dancing, especially Scottish reels, and was passionately fond of gardening and fishing.

He was not an intellectual. He was, if anything, rather proud that he had never had any staff training. A stickler for the correct dress, for the proper routine, for everything being done according to tradition, A.B.C. was very conservative and in some ways slow to react to technological change in the navy. He was a late convert to the virtues of air power at sea; it took strenuous efforts by the Regia Aeronautica and the Luftwaffe to complete, belatedly, his education on this aspect of naval warfare.

Like many great naval commanders, A.B.C. had the knack of inspiring anecdotes about himself, which kept him in the minds' eyes of his sailors when he himself was not there. He inspired fanatical loyalty among those who served under him, particularly among his personal staff. Above all, A.B.C. inspired a sublime confidence in his fleet. His sailors genuinely believed, and with good reason, that nothing could possibly go wrong so long as he was there.

A.B.C. took over the staff of his predecessor, Sir Dudley Pound [*q.v.*], almost to a man. They were, as he said, 'a very happy party in the dining room' and most of them were to serve him for the next four years. The one exception was an officer who, as his successor said, 'argued, lost his temper and was fired'.

The Chief of Staff was Commodore 'Algie' Willis, known as 'Com', a prickly, sombre, humourless little man whose wife had left him. But he was an excellent staff officer, and he and A.B.C. made a good team. 'Quite different to Pound,' Willis wrote. 'A.B.C. well understood how to use a staff and I personally found everything much easier.'

The only newcomer was the Staff Officer (Operations), Commander Manley Power, known as 'Lofty' as much for his manner as for his height. He quickly learned the art of survival. 'A.B.C. was a bully,' he said. 'If he was not stood up to he could become unbearable. Fortunately very early I had a couple of showdowns with him and hence the pattern of a long, fruitful and stormy relationship founded on mutual respect.'

A.B.C., his staff and his fleet prepared for the war they all knew was coming, but when it did come they had nothing to do. A.B.C. was actually standing with Willis on top of 'A' turret in the battleship *Malaya*, watching the fleet regatta races in Alexandria harbour, when the signal was handed up to him that Great Britain was at war with Germany. 'I never expected to find myself in the position, when war was declared,' A.B.C. wrote to an aunt at home, 'to have nothing to do but to go ashore and have tea with [his wife] Nona. But so it happened. What a senseless business!'

Within a few weeks A.B.C.'s highly trained fleet had been dispersed to other war theatres. However, he was sure that the Mediterranean would not remain 'an area of complete calm' for long. When he said goodbye to his flagship *Warspite*, in November 1939, he told her ship's company he would see them back in the spring.

He was right: *Warspite* was back in the Mediterranean in May 1940. A.B.C. had always supposed that Italy would enter the war as soon as Mussolini decided that the war was going well enough for the Axis. By May 1940 this moment could not be far off. A.B.C. firmly believed that 'our only policy against Italy was to cut off her supplies, interfere with her communications, bombard her ports, destroy her submarines, and later on, when our military build-up was complete, to conquer Libya and the Italian colonies in East Africa'.

He was therefore amazed and angered when Churchill, who had just become Prime Minister, said he thought A.B.C.'s statement of policy on 23 May 1940 was 'defensive'. A.B.C. resented the imputation. 'Nothing was further from our thoughts,' he said. It was Pound who acted as mediator, convincing Churchill he was mistaken, and mollifying an outraged Cunningham.

Certainly, A.B.C. waged an aggressive naval campaign from the moment the Italians declared war on 10 June 1940. He took his ships to sea whenever there was the faintest chance of action. Good intelligence and keen counter-attacking resulted in quick successes against Italian submarines, who were never able to exert the strategic influence they ought to have done in the Mediterranean.

After the collapse of France in June 1940, A.B.C. was called upon to show a quite unexpected talent for diplomacy. Churchill was bent on showing the world, and especially the Americans, that even if France had surrendered, Great Britain was still determined to go on with the war.

The main units of the French navy were at Dakar, Casablanca and Sfax, with two sizeable fleets at Mers-el-Kebir (the naval base at Oran) and at Alexandria. It was essential to prevent French ships joining the Axis. Orders were given to neutralize the French fleet, either by immobilizing the ships, or by steaming them to British or neutral ports, or by destroying them. It was to be done with French co-operation if possible but, if not, then by force.

The task of dealing with the French at Oran fell to A.B.C.'s old friend and *Britannia* term-mate, Admiral Sir James Somerville [*q.v.*]. There, as is tragically well known, negotiations broke down, ships were sunk and many lives lost, causing a lasting national bitterness. But at Alexandria A.B.C. played the French Admiral Godfroy with the skill of a fisherman. Very ably assisted by his staff, and especially his Staff Officer (Plans) Commander Royer Dick, who spoke fluent and idiomatic French, A.B.C. set out to persuade Godfroy to immobilize his ships without bloodshed.

Despite Godfroy's changes of mind, and the impact on him of the terrible news from Oran, and in spite of badgering, insensitive and unhelpful signals and directives from London which A.B.C. ignored, Cunningham succeeded by appealing to Godfroy's sense of honour (and also, let it be said, by telling the French sailors over Godfroy's head that the terms offered by the British government were the best they could hope for). Godfroy agreed to defuel and de-ammunition his ships. Those who wanted to be repatriated to France could go. Godfroy, who stayed at Alexandria, became and remained A.B.C.'s friend.

A.B.C.'s staff had always regarded their chief affectionately but warily, as though he were a bulky little bear, furry and cuddly to a degree, but capable of a ferocious and deadly hug. This unsuspected talent for diplomacy therefore came as a complete surprise to them. 'A.B.C.'s moral courage and width of view over this period', wrote Royer Dick, 'is the moment when one first realized his qualities of greatness. Of course we knew him as a fine dashing leader, but his handling of the French problem was masterly and one wonders how many others would have had the breadth of mind, let alone the moral "guts", to disregard his instructions [from London]. That was truly Nelsonic.'

One crisis was succeeded by another, in which A.B.C.'s firmness and confidence had a major effect upon strategy. With France out of the war and Italy in, the balance of power had changed so much to Britain's disadvantage that Pound, whose main concern was quite rightly the Atlantic, began to consider the abandonment of the Eastern Mediterranean if the worst should come to the worst.

A.B.C. prepared the necessary plans, as bidden, although his whole spirit rebelled against the proposal. He stressed the importance of Malta, the catastrophic effect on Britain's prestige of a withdrawal from the Mediterranean, and his confidence that he and his fleet could win through. Such confidence impressed the War Cabinet and Churchill, who also bristled at any suggestion of retreat. The project was abandoned. 'I do not know how near we came to abandoning the Eastern Mediterranean,' A.B.C. said, 'but if it had come to pass it would have been a major disaster, nothing less.'

As the war in the Mediterranean developed, both sides ran convoys – the Axis convoys north–south to and from Italy and Libya, the Allied convoys east–west to and from Gibraltar and Alexandria. The point where the two routes crossed was Malta. The island's relief and supply soon became one of A.B.C.'s most pressing and continuing concerns.

On 7 July 1940 he took his fleet to sea to cover two convoys, a 'fast' and a 'slow', from Malta to Alexandria. The Italian fleet was also at sea, with two battleships, covering a convoy from Naples to Benghazi. At 3.08 p.m. on 9 July, off the coast of Calabria in southern Italy, the cruiser *Neptune* made the signal 'Enemy battle fleet in sight' – the first time this signal had been made by a British fleet in the Mediterranean since Nelson's ships sighted de Brueys' fleet at the Nile in 1798.

A.B.C. took the calculated risk of continuing to close the Italian coast. He had three aged and slow battleships, *Warspite, Royal Sovereign* and *Barham*, and a veteran aircraft carrier *Eagle*, small and slow, against an enemy who had a larger, faster fleet at sea, with two fast modern battleships and a powerful shore-based air force only a few minutes' flying time away. But A.B.C. had shrewdly and accurately summed up the mettle of the Italian navy. He was rewarded at 4 p.m. when *Warspite* obtained a 15-inch shell hit upon the battleship *Giulio Cesare*, the Italian flagship, at the prodigious range of over 26,000 yards.

With his traditional scepticism towards the gunnery branch, A.B.C. said that that hit might 'perhaps be described as a lucky one' but it did some damage to *Giulio Cesare*, causing casualties, putting some of her secondary armament and four boiler rooms out of action, and reducing her speed from twenty-seven knots to eighteen.

The main damage was not physical but psychological. The Italians at once turned away behind a smoke screen and broke off the action, and henceforward were very reluctant to face the fire of a British capital ship.

Characteristically, A.B.C. was disappointed with that sole hit. 'The brush with the Italian fleet', he told Pound, 'was most irritating and disappointing. But there is no doubt that it was a carefully set trap. I walked into the trap with my eyes open. . . . Their battleships and 8-inch cruisers straddled us comfortably at 26,000 yards. . . . I must have one more ship that can shoot at a good range. . . . There is one thing on the bright side. I do not think we need expect anything very dashing from the Italian fleet.'

Italian radio and newspapers claimed a great victory. 'British dominion of the Mediterranean is at an end,' they proclaimed. This was nonsense. Nevertheless, as A.B.C., his staff and his ships had been made painfully aware, the Regia Aeronautica was not so negligible and inefficient a force as was so publicly and derisively claimed in Britain. A.B.C.'s ships were being spotted and bombed as soon as they put to sea and, as the moon climbed towards the full, even in Alexandria harbour.

The Italian bombing was unpleasantly prolonged and accurate – off Calabria, the cruiser *Gloucester* was hit and damaged, *Warspite* more than once had to fight off six air attacks in an afternoon, while *Royal Sovereign* survived eighty close and near misses in one bombing raid. These constant air attacks eventually affected the morale of some ships' companies, especially in the destroyers, who began to 'look askance' at the prospect of going to sea yet again to endure even more attacks.

A.B.C. and his fleet were therefore relieved and delighted to welcome, in August 1940, the new aircraft carrier *Illustrious* with her armoured flight deck and her thirty aircraft, including Fairey Fulmar fighters. These had an immediate effect and the fleet were able to cheer the sight of some of their tormentors being shot down. Meanwhile, in July and August, Malta-based Swordfish attacked shipping at Augusta in Sicily, at Tobruk and at Bomba, west of Tobruk.

With *Illustrious* and *Eagle*, and the addition of the old but modernized (including radar) battleship *Valiant*, A.B.C. had a balanced fleet of carriers and capital ships, which ranged freely from Rhodes in the east to Sfax in the west, covering convoys east and west and carrying out shore bombardments, while its aircraft bombed airfields and harbours, laid mines in coastal waters and strafed road and railway traffic. It was a supremely confident demonstration of naval air power, which reached its climax with a stunning feat of arms in November 1940.

A Fleet Air Arm strike at the great naval base of Taranto, on the 'toe' of Italy, had been discussed and planned in the Mediterranean Fleet for some years before the war. With the Italian battlefleet in Taranto and apparently reluctant to leave it, it seemed the perfect time to carry out the strike.

After photo-reconnaissance by Maryland bombers from Malta had shown that the Italian capital ships were in harbour, *Illustrious* took departure from the rest of the fleet on the evening of 11 November and with an escort of cruisers and destroyers headed for the flying-off point some 170 miles south-east of Taranto.

The Swordfish, which included some from *Eagle*'s squadrons, were armed with torpedoes, or bombs and flares. They took off in two strikes, the first (of twelve aircraft) at 9 p.m. and the second (of nine aircraft) some twenty minutes later. The torpedo bombers were briefed to attack the battleships lying in the outer harbour, the Mar Grande, while the bombers attacked cruisers and destroyers in the inner harbour, the Mar Piccolo.

By the light of the drifting flares and the waving searchlights and a hail of anti-aircraft fire laced with red, green and white tracer, the Swordfish dived to thirty feet above the water to drop their torpedoes. The bombers jinked and swerved at masthead height into the inner harbour, where their crews could actually smell the acrid stink of incendiary bullets and their ears were deafened by the combined roar of flak batteries on ship and shore. The second strike flew in through a renewed storm of fire to drop torpedoes, and bomb ships and oil tanks beside the inner harbour.

The results went far beyond anyone's wildest expectations. The battleship *Littorio* had three torpedo hits, which put her out of action for nearly a year. The older battleship *Caio Diulio* suffered one torpedo hit and was flooded so badly she had to be beached to stop her foundering. A third battleship *Conte de Cavour* also had one torpedo hit and sank in shallow water; she was raised but took no further part in the war. The heavy cruiser *Trento* had one bomb hit and damage was done to destroyers and oil storage tanks in the inner harbour. Two Swordfish were lost, the crew of one being taken prisoner.

Three Italian battleships were incapacitated and the remaining three were soon moved to Naples. Thus a major threat to the Allied convoys was removed. The capital-ship balance in the Mediterranean had decisively shifted in the Allies' favour literally overnight. It was a famous victory and should have been celebrated as such. For instance, there was a strong case for awarding both strike leaders the Victoria Cross.

Instead, A.B.C.'s leadership faltered. The first awards were so meagre and appeared so grudging that angry sailors in *Illustrious* were reported to have ripped the lists off the notice-boards in disgust. A further list followed months later, but the golden moment had been fumbled. As guest of honour at a Taranto Night Dinner after the war, A.B.C. confessed 'that it was some time before I realized what a tremendous stroke it was'.

But Taranto had one very ominous consequence. Fliegerkorps X, the Luftwaffe's anti-shipping specialists, began to arrive at airfields in Sicily and southern Italy early in 1941. On 10 January, they caught *Illustrious* at sea off Malta when she was giving air cover to another convoy.

A.B.C. himself was a reluctant spectator. 'One was too interested in this new form of dive-bombing attack really to be frightened,' he said, 'and there was no doubt we were watching complete experts. Formed roughly in a large circle over the fleet they peeled off one by one when reaching the attacking position. We could not but admire the skill and precision of it all. The attacks were pressed home to point blank range. . . .'

Illustrious was hit by six large bombs and limped back to Malta where, under fierce daily attack by the Luftwaffe, she was patched up and sailed on the 23rd for repairs in America. A.B.C.'s fleet was once more without its own air cover until the arrival of *Illustrious*'s sister ship *Formidable* in March.

Towards the end of March 1941, decrypts of Italian diplomatic radio traffic revealed that the Italian navy was at last about to respond to German urgings to disrupt the flow of British convoys taking troops and supplies to Greece. On 27 March an RAF Sunderland flying boat reported three cruisers and a destroyer at sea, steaming towards Crete.

A.B.C. was anxious to conceal the departure of his own ships from Alexandria for as long as possible. A dinner was arranged in *Warspite* that evening. A.B.C. himself went ashore to play golf, where he could be seen by another keen golfer, the Japanese Consul in Alexandria. A.B.C. took with him an ostentatiously large suitcase as though intending to spend the night ashore.

After dark, A.B.C. returned on board, the dinner was cancelled, steam was raised, awnings were furled and *Warspite* sailed with *Valiant*, *Barham*, *Formidable* and nine destroyers. A.B.C. was not convinced the enemy would come out and bet Power ten shillings that nothing would be seen.

In fact, the Italian fleet was out and in strength, with the new 35,000-ton 15-inch-gun battleship *Vittorio Veneto*, wearing the flag of the fleet commander Admiral Iachino, six 10,000-ton 8-inch-gun and two 8,000-ton 6-inch-gun cruisers, and thirteen large destroyers.

A.B.C. had ordered Vice Admiral Pridham-Wippell, who was already at sea with a force of cruisers and destroyers, to rendezvous with him south of Crete at dawn on 28 March. At the appointed time, A.B.C.'s ships were some 150 miles to the south-east of the island, steaming north-west at twenty knots. Dawn flights from *Formidable* sighted two groups of Italian cruisers and destroyers. One group was sighted soon after 8 a.m. by Pridham-Wippell's ships, who at once steered south-east hoping, in the classical cruiser tradition, to draw the enemy towards A.B.C.'s battlefleet.

After a brief gun action Pridham-Wippell noticed that the enemy was no longer following, so he turned back to the westward, hoping again to lure the enemy on.

This time the bait was taken rather too enthusiastically. At 11 a.m. a lookout in Pridham-Wippell's flagship, the cruiser *Orion*, reported an unknown ship to the north. It was the fighting top of a battleship. Soon Pridham-Wippell's ships were being pursued and under fire from *Vittorio Veneto* on their port quarter and three 10,000-ton heavy cruisers on their starboard.

Matters might have gone hard for them had not Albacores from *Formidable* attacked *Vittorio Veneto* with torpedoes, while Swordfish from Maleme in Crete attacked the three heavy cruisers. No hits were scored but Iachino broke off the action and turned away. *Vittorio Veneto* was also bombed by RAF Blenheims from Greece at this time, adding to Iachino's sense of grievance. Later, he complained bitterly that while his ships were sighted, reported and attacked by various Allied aircraft, he himself was denied proper reports of the enemy and his ships were left totally undefended by German or Italian fighters.

Pridham-Wippell's urgent signals to his ships, to make smoke, turn together, proceed at utmost speed, were intercepted in *Warspite*. A.B.C.'s staff pondered on their import. But A.B.C. took one look at them and said, 'Don't be so damned silly. . . . He's sighted the enemy battlefleet. Put the enemy battlefleet in at visibility distance to the north of him.' The signal confirming this arrived a few minutes later. On *Warspite*'s flag bridge, ten shillings changed hands.

At the prospect of meeting the enemy, as Captain Geoffrey Barnard, the Fleet Gunnery Officer, said, 'A.B.C.'s burning desire to get at them and utterly destroy them would at once become evident. . . . He would pace one side of the Admiral's bridge, always the side nearest the enemy. . . . This mood was known colloquially among the staff as "the caged tiger act". . . .'

Unknown to Iachino, A.B.C. was now only forty-five miles astern of him. But the Italian ships were so much faster that A.B.C.'s battleships had no chance of catching up. However, that afternoon RAF Blenheims scored a near miss on *Vittorio Veneto* while Fulmars from *Formidable* strafed her upper decks, distracting her gunners and allowing Albacores to close and score one torpedo hit port-side aft.

Thousands of tons of water flooded in. *Vittorio Veneto* stopped, listing to port and noticeably settling by the stern. It seemed that A.B.C.'s heart's desire was about to be granted. But *Vittorio Veneto* got under way again and eventually managed to work up her speed to nineteen knots.

Throughout the afternoon A.B.C. had confusing reports of the enemy's position, course and speed. At 5.45 p.m. one of *Warspite*'s Swordfish was launched, with a very senior and experienced observer, Lieutenant-Commander 'Ben' Bolt, on board. Bolt found the enemy, and his reports over the next hour were models of clarity and precision – even Iachino admired them. A second Albacore strike had been flown off from *Formidable*, joined by two Swordfish from Maleme. They attacked the Italian fleet after dark. The heavy cruiser *Pola* was hit by one torpedo and stopped dead in the water.

Iachino still had no idea that A.B.C.'s battlefleet was anywhere near him. The nearest reported British ships, which Iachino assumed were cruisers and/or destroyers, were seventy-five miles away. It could be argued, with hindsight, that with the information he did receive during the day Iachino might at least have considered the possibility that they were battleships. But he detached *Zara* and *Fiume*, *Pola*'s sister ships, with four destroyers, to go back and assist her.

A.B.C. now had to make up his mind and issue his night instructions. Pridham-Wippell, somewhere up ahead, had reported two unknown ships. It was known that one large Italian ship had been hit by a torpedo. But the Italian fleet was making disappointingly good progress for home. At the present rate it would take A.B.C.'s ships six or seven hours to overhaul them.

The question was, should A.B.C. pursue his enemy into an unknown situation, in the dark, with the danger of his heavy ships becoming involved in a destroyer mêlée? Some of A.B.C.'s staff counselled caution. However, as Barnard recalled, 'The well-known steely blue look was in A.B.C.'s eye. "You're a pack of yellow-livered skunks," he said. "I'll go and have my supper now and see after supper if my morale isn't higher than yours."'

When A.B.C. returned, his mind was made up: pursue. Once again, his boldness was rewarded. At 10.03 p.m. *Valiant*'s radar detected a large ship to the south-west, stopped, eight to nine miles on the port bow. This could be *Vittorio Veneto*.

At 10.25, the new Chief of Staff designate, Commodore Edelsten, who had taken Willis' place for this trip, calmly reported two cruisers with a smaller one ahead of them, crossing the bows of the battlefleet, from starboard to port. A.B.C. put his binoculars up, and there they were. Power, 'an abnormal expert at recognizing the silhouettes of enemy ships', said they were two *Zara*-class cruisers with a smaller cruiser ahead. They were, of course, *Zara*, *Fiume* and the destroyers, coming back to assist *Valiant*'s stationary radar contact, *Pola*.

At 10.28 the destroyer *Greyhound* switched on her searchlight, to illuminate a row of beautiful silver ships, all with their gun turrets trained fore and aft. The range was about 4,000 yards – point blank. The three battleships opened fire. The enemy ships were helplessly shattered before they could put up any resistance. *Zara* and *Fiume* were overwhelmed and sunk by the combined fire of *Warspite*, *Barham* and *Valiant*. In what A.B.C. called 'a wild night', the destroyers found and despatched *Pola*. For good measure, two Italian destroyers, *Alfieri* and *Carducci*, were also sunk.

Five of *Warspite*'s first salvo of six were seen to hit an enemy cruiser along the water-line and burst in splashes of brilliant flame. At this Captain Douglas Fisher, *Warspite*'s Captain and a gunnery officer of note, was heard to say in a voice of 'wondering surprise', 'Good Lord, we've hit her!' A.B.C. ordered the remark to be recorded in case he ever needed to pull the legs of the RN gunnery school at Whale Island.

In the morning, the destroyers rescued some 900 Italian survivors before a German aircraft appeared and the rescue work had to stop. The ships were well within range of German airbases. But A.B.C. magnanimously had a signal made in plain language to the Chief of the Italian Naval Staff, giving the position of the two or three hundred remaining survivors. An Italian hospital ship came out and picked them up.

The one disappointment came just after the main battle, when A.B.C. made what he later called 'an ill-considered' signal, ordering all ships not engaged in sinking the enemy to withdraw to the north-east. A.B.C. meant merely to clear the scene so as to give his destroyers a free hand. But the signal had the quite unforeseen effect of causing Pridham-Wippell, who was then some thirty miles from *Vittorio Veneto*, to break off the pursuit.

Typically, A.B.C. commented in his report that 'The result of the action cannot be viewed with entire satisfaction, since the damaged *Vittorio Veneto* was allowed to escape.' Nevertheless, this victory off Cape Matapan was, as John Jervis said of his own in an earlier campaign, 'very essential to England at this moment'.

Like his fleet, A.B.C. had no time to rest on his laurels after Matapan. The ships were soon at sea again, while A.B.C. grappled with a host of problems. There was the continuing need to supply Malta and later Tobruk. There was an exchange of thunderous signals with Mr Churchill, ever pressing for yet more action to cut the Axis supply line to Tripoli, even to the extent of sacrificing *Barham* and most of her people in an attempt to block Tripoli harbour – a scheme which A.B.C. strenuously opposed and eventually defeated.

There were problems of morale: one cruiser captain had to be replaced and some other officers showed signs of 'cracking up'. There was the army in Greece to be supplied and, when that campaign collapsed in April 1941, to be evacuated. Some 50,000 personnel were taken off, almost all by night and most over open beaches, in seven days, for the loss of two destroyers and four transports to air attack.

A.B.C. confided his concern privately in his letters to Pound but publicly he remained cheerful and imperturbably optimistic. He and Nona entertained generously. Their house in Alexandria was always full of guests, whose ships had been damaged or sunk. James Munn, commanding the destroyer *Hereward*, had been A.B.C.'s flag lieutenant in *Hood* before the war and could therefore compare A.B.C. past and present. A.B.C., he said, had mellowed slightly but 'he was always in good form and after dinner made us all lie down on the floor and throw ping-pong balls into the electric light bowl hanging from the ceiling. I wrote home to my family saying I felt certain we would win the war.'

Such optimism was to seem misplaced in the next few weeks. The battle in Greece was hardly over before the battle in Crete began. A.B.C.'s ships bloodily repelled German attempts to send troops to Crete by sea, but after German paratroopers had established themselves on the vital airfield of Maleme the battle on land turned against the Allies. Before long A.B.C.'s ships were called upon to evacuate the army a second time.

After recent operations, including the passage of the Tiger convoy to Alexandria, *Formidable* had only four serviceable aircraft. On 26 May, she was bombed and severely damaged by Stukas and followed *Illustrious*'s melancholy path to the United States for repairs. Without air cover, A.B.C.'s ships suffered a prolonged ordeal under ferocious air attack. Three battleships (*Warspite*, *Valiant* and *Barham*), four cruisers (*Orion*, *Dido*, *Naiad* and *Perth*) and four destroyers (*Nubian*, *Nizam*, *Napier* and *Kelvin*) were badly damaged; two cruisers (*Gloucester* and *Fiji*) and six destroyers (*Greyhound*, *Juno*, *Kelly*, *Kashmir*, *Imperial* and *Hereward*) were sunk; and James Munn, recently so optimistic, became a prisoner-of-war.

A.B.C. had decided that, for once, he could better direct affairs from shore. The feeling in the fleet was that some of the ships would not have been sunk if A.B.C. himself had been at sea. But whatever the day's disasters, which piled upon each other until eventually even A.B.C. admitted that he winced every time a telephone rang, outwardly he remained unshakeably firm. 'Stick it out,' he signalled to his ships on 22 May, a particularly bad day, 'Navy must not let the Army down.'

Some sailors, feeling that A.B.C. was driving them unreasonably hard, called him 'The Butcher'. His barge was catcalled and jeered at as he passed one ship in Alexandria. A.B.C. visited that ship next day and there was no more jeering.

Even Lofty Power began to feel that enough was enough. It often fell to him to be the bearer of bad news. When he went in to report the loss of *Gloucester*, one of A.B.C.'s favourite ships, A.B.C. said, 'It's no use looking like a bloody undertaker.' Power said he did not think they were going to achieve anything to justify losses on the present scale and they had better withdraw.

Using his favourite expression for anyone who counselled caution, A.B.C. retorted: 'You're a pusillanimous bugger – what the hell's the matter with you?' Power said that if you went on knocking your head against a brick wall you'd get knocked right out. Typically, A.B.C. replied, 'Maybe, but you may also loosen a brick!'

Captain Lees, commanding the anti-aircraft cruiser *Calcutta*, outraged that his ship was being sent to sea again when his sailors were out on their feet, burst into the staff offices and berated the staff. A.B.C. overheard, called Lees into his own office and talked to him gently. *Calcutta* went to sea that night as ordered.

On 31 May, General Wavell, the Army C-in-C in the Middle East, flew to Alexandria to thank A.B.C. for what he and his ships had done and to tell him that the army did not expect any more. He would absolve A.B.C. from any further responsibility.

Wavell 'saw the faces of A.B.C.'s staff light up with relief'. But A.B.C. said to Wavell, as he had said more than once to his staff, that he meant to go on. He would not let the army down. There was a tradition to be upheld. It took three years to build a ship, he said. It would take three hundred to rebuild a tradition.

Next day, 1 June, *Calcutta* was bombed and sunk. Her survivors were picked up by her sister ship *Coventry*. A.B.C. was waiting on the jetty when *Coventry* returned to harbour and came on board as soon as she had secured. A.B.C. felt the loss of every ship deeply but *Calcutta* was special to him. He had commanded her himself before the war and she had served him well in war. 'As we walked up and down the quarterdeck,' said Lees, 'A.B.C. was in tears.'

By 2 June some 16,500 troops had been evacuated from Crete, at a cost to the navy of 1,828 men killed and 183 wounded. But A.B.C. was fully justified. The soldiers never doubted that the ships would be there to take them off. 'With a torch we flashed an SOS,' said one New Zealander, 'and, to our tremendous relief, we received an answer. It was the Navy on the job – the Navy for which we had been hoping and praying all along the route.'

From time to time A.B.C. was pressed to move his headquarters to Cairo. This would have been much more convenient for Wavell and Sir Arthur

Longmore, the Air OC-in-C, and their staffs. But A.B.C. insisted on remaining with his fleet, although he did move his office ashore when *Warspite* left in June 1941. This made life slightly easier for his staff.

A.B.C. prided himself on having a small staff, a handful of hand-picked officers, as compared with the 'thousand and one brigadiers' in Cairo. A.B.C.'s staff were always hard-pressed, carrying out one operation, planning for the next and writing up the reports of the last, while also dealing with the myriad administrative affairs of the fleet, on board a flagship often at sea and in action, keeping radio silence.

In the summer of 1941 the 'Lords of the Middle East', as Willis called them, broke up, leaving A.B.C. the sole survivor. Longmore went home in May and did not return. There was the suspicion he was the scapegoat for the RAF's shortcomings in Crete. He was replaced by his deputy, Tedder. This was 'replacing a first-class mind with a second-class' in A.B.C.'s opinion. Relations between the navy and the RAF were never as close under Tedder. Nor were navy–army relations ever as close under Claude Auchinleck, Wavell's replacement from July 1941. A.B.C. liked, admired and trusted Wavell and 'was desperately sorry to see him go'. By contrast, he found Auchinleck a remote, somewhat aloof personality, one of the 'heaven-born' from the Indian Army in whose order of precedence naval officers, even the Commander-in-Chief, came well below the salt. Auchinleck, A.B.C. told Willis, was 'wooden-headed and self-opinionated . . . [he] knows damn-all about the navy, but doesn't know that he doesn't'.

Despite many more setbacks, and the loss of many more ships and men, A.B.C. established such an ascendancy over his opponents in the Mediterranean that when he was relieved, in April 1942, he was smuggled away, in plain clothes, and his departure was kept secret, lest it bring comfort to the enemy.

His next appointment was in Washington DC, as head of the British Admiralty Delegation. After winning a fierce fight over status and salary with the Prime Minister and the Treasury, who at first proposed to pay him less than the Naval Attaché, he flew to America at the end of June 1942, quietly marvelling at the fact that one could now cross the Atlantic in one flight – twenty-six hours in a flying boat without touching down.

Washington was a new experience for A.B.C. and for Nona. There were problems over the intense summer heat, American cooking, relations between British and American domestic staff, driving a large eight-cylinder Buick on the right (that is, wrong) side of the road, the shortage of accommodation, the high cost of living, the frenetic diplomatic entertaining, the endless conferences and the sheer unreality of A.B.C.'s job: 'an interesting but amazing job this', he wrote. 'You haven't anything at all under your command and all you do is to sit out on deck and on committees.'

But the biggest problem was the US Navy's Commander-in-Chief, Admiral King [*q.v.*]. A rabidly Anglophobic Irish–American, 'Ernie' King was difficult, obstinate, unhelpful and discourteous to the point of disbelief. After his first formal call, A.B.C. asked for an interview to discuss naval affairs, and was brusquely told that King's diary was full for the next five days. When they did meet their encounters were always stormy. They clashed violently over every kind of topic, from the number of submarines in the Mediterranean to the question of US warships coming under British command (which King, of course, flatly and adamantly opposed).

King soon recognized that in A.B.C. he had met a personality as strong as himself. He acknowledged his own rudeness, but thought that A.B.C. was 'needling' him. 'I was very rough with him,' King said. However, he came to respect A.B.C. 'They got a *man*,' he said. 'A fighter. He would fight like hell. When I had something to say against the British he would stand up and say, "I don't like that."'

For his part, A.B.C. was much less complimentary about King. 'He was abominably rude,' he wrote to Pound, 'and I had to be quite firm with him and I told him that the remarks he made got us no further in winning the war. . . . At the last Chief of Staff's meeting, King was quite impossible and just objected to everything, his cry being that it was contrary to what had been agreed to in London.' This, A.B.C. wrote, 'might affect Torch. I am sure King is dead against it.'

Operation Torch (the Allied landings in North Africa planned for November 1942) was uppermost in everybody's mind at that time. Significantly, the Americans asked – indeed they demanded – that A.B.C. be appointed Naval Commander-in-Chief, Allied Expeditionary Force, North Africa and Mediterranean. So high had A.B.C.'s standing risen that even King agreed, not just to the US Navy Task Force coming under A.B.C.'s command but to A.B.C. sending home any American flag officer he thought incompetent because he (King) 'would know that Cunningham was right'.

A.B.C. himself said he had no objections whatever to serving under an American Supreme Allied Commander for Torch, although he had private reservations about 'Supreme Command', which went to the heart of his own beliefs about the nature of leadership. A.B.C. conceded that 'Supreme Command' was probably necessary among Allies, but he strenuously opposed it where forces of his own country were concerned. He believed that matters were better organized by three commanders-in-chief, among themselves – as in the Middle East.

The Supreme Commander for Torch was Lieutenant-General Dwight D. Eisenhower. A.B.C. took to 'Ike' at once. They became friends for life; yet it might not have been so. A.B.C. was a war celebrity. Matapan had made him as internationally famous as Nelson after the Nile. He was one of the very few Allied commanders at that stage of the war with victories to his credit.

Eisenhower, on the other hand, had no battle experience. He had not served in Europe in the Great War. In fact, he had never commanded troops in the field before Torch. He was unknown to the British army and not much better known in his own. But A.B.C. supported Eisenhower from the start. If he had done nothing else in the war, the Allies would still owe him gratitude for the generous and wholehearted way he backed Eisenhower.

Pound, for one, realized A.B.C.'s achievement. At the end of the year he wrote to say 'how thankful we all are that you are where you are, not only because we feel we are in safe hands with you in charge but also because it is evident you have obtained Eisenhower's confidence, which means so much'.

A.B.C. had been confirmed in the rank of admiral on 3 January 1941 (he had become C-in-C in the acting rank), was made GCB on 11 March 1941 and a baronet in the Birthday Honours of June 1942. On 21 January 1943 he became an admiral of the fleet, a promotion which roused more excitement among others than it did in him (although he brightened when his secretary told him that admirals of the fleet never retired).

On 20 February 1943 A.B.C. was appointed C-in-C Mediterranean again, only the second officer in naval history to hold the office twice. Now the Allies were on the offensive. In May 1943, when the North Africa campaign was drawing to a close and there was a chance the Axis might attempt a 'Dunkirk' from Africa to Italy, A.B.C. launched the aptly named Operation Retribution with the signal to his destroyers: 'Sink, burn and destroy. Let Nothing Pass.'

On 11 September 1943, A.B.C. had the great satisfaction of sending the Admiralty an even more dramatic signal (actually drafted by Royer Dick): 'Be pleased to inform Their Lordships that the Italian battlefleet now lies at anchor under the guns of the fortress of Malta.' There had been more than three years of hard fighting, with some bitter losses in ships and men, but this was a sweet ending.

Admiral of the Fleet Sir Dudley Pound, the First Sea Lord, was suffering from a tumour which was growing in his brain. He had worn himself out in the service of his country and the navy. He had more than once asked A.B.C. whether he should resign and allow A.B.C. to succeed him. A.B.C. had always urged him to stay on. Now, Pound's failing health made resignation inevitable. Churchill's first choice for his successor was Bruce Fraser [*q.v.*], but Fraser himself demurred and suggested Cunningham, because Cunningham would have the confidence of the whole navy. A.B.C. had a message from the Prime Minister on 28 September asking him to come home for consultations about Pound's successor. A.B.C. and Nona went to Chequers on 3 October. There, Churchill asked A.B.C. if he would take Pound's place. Cunningham accepted. He felt it was his duty.

It has been said that Churchill did not want so strong a character as A.B.C. as First Sea Lord in close proximity in the Admiralty. This could well be true. But it is also possible that Churchill genuinely believed that Fraser would have been a better First Sea Lord.

In unexpected contrast to his powerful leadership at sea, A.B.C. was a curiously passive First Sea Lord. In the Mediterranean he had been the master of events and of men. He had made things happen. In Whitehall he let things happen to him. By his own testimony, there were Chiefs of Staff meetings at which he made no contribution, or remained neutral on a particular subject because in his opinion it did not concern the navy. But there is the suspicion that A.B.C. was not quite the intellectual equal of his fellow Chiefs of Staff, the Chief of the Imperial General Staff General Sir Alan Brooke, and Air Chief Marshal Sir Charles Portal, the Air Chief of Staff.

A.B.C. admitted that the office desk was not his strong suit. This was true: as one of his staff said, A.B.C. had 'a blank spot' for administration. His only previous experience of the Admiralty had been a few months as Deputy Chief of the Naval Staff in 1938–9. But when he joined on 16 October 1943 he found, as he said, a well-oiled machine, although he felt it might be too inclined to run in a groove. All the disasters, difficulties and disappointments of earlier years had been borne and surmounted by Pound. The Atlantic U-boat was still dangerous but was not the mortal peril of the spring of 1943. Victory was not yet in sight but it was only just below the horizon.

The war certainly looked different when seen from a Whitehall desk. As somebody who had always thought of nothing but how to inflict further damage upon the enemy, A.B.C. found the Admiralty tempo very slow. Accustomed to taking and acting upon his own decisions at once, he was appalled by the number of departments and people who had to be consulted before any action could take place. For A.B.C. the war had been literally a matter of life and death. Here, it was more a matter of daily routine.

For A.B.C., that routine became a matter of meetings and paperwork and social functions. He confessed that the countless official luncheons, receptions and cocktail parties to meet this personage or that, the mass of papers and dockets flooding into his in-tray and the endless stream of people coming to see him made it physically impossible to give proper attention to all the matters brought before him. He had to delegate much to his staff and accept their opinions.

Some of his visitors were very welcome. Vice Admiral Sir Bernard Rawlings came in one morning, before he left for the Far East, and they had a long chat about past days in the Mediterranean. The Mediterranean was always in A.B.C.'s thoughts. 'My heart remains in the Mediterranean,' he once wrote to Willis. 'I was told the other day that Nelson once said "Waking or sleeping, Malta is always in my thoughts" and that exactly describes my case.'

Certainly A.B.C. was always drawing comparisons with the old days in the Mediterranean. When he saw the 'gadgets' needed for the Normandy landings, every one of them 'essential', he began to wonder how 'we had ever succeeded in any of our enterprises in the Mediterranean with our poor, austerity standards of assault equipment'. Again, when considering the number of ships required for the Fleet Train in the Pacific, 'to the mind of one accustomed to the austere standards of the Mediterranean some of the ships demanded appeared at first redundant . . .'.

To many in the Admiralty, A.B.C. must have appeared to have somewhat reactionary views. He criticized the new large destroyers being built, saying they had become 'carriers of radar and radar ratings' and, while they detect any enemy at any range, they could do nothing about it because they lacked the guns. He disapproved of ships being provided with 'American' amenities such as cafeteria messing, laundries and soda fountains, on the grounds that the navy had done very well without them for hundreds of years. He felt that RNVR medical officers in escort carriers were too ready to pronounce aircrews unfit for flying duty. He was sceptical about trooping to the Far East by air and not by ship, viewing it as 'partially a method of keeping up the number of the RAF after the German war'.

A.B.C. could sometimes misread events. For instance, he believed the Admiralty were too cautious about the enemy's air power which, in his opinion, was not the force it had been in the first three years of the war. Norway, Greece and Crete, he said, seemed to have left their scars on the navy. Yet at the very time he became First Sea Lord the Royal Navy was actually embroiled in a disastrous little campaign in the Aegean in which six destroyers were sunk, and two cruisers and two destroyers damaged, precisely because of lack of air cover.

It is not clear when A.B.C. found out that Fraser had been Churchill's first choice as First Sea Lord, but find out he did and he seems to have been mortally affronted. Ever afterwards there was a sour note in his references to Fraser. He attributed Fraser's reluctance to carry out another Tungsten strike on the *Tirpitz* (a proposed repetition of the April 1944 attack against that ship) to the fact that Fraser 'resented very much being practically bludgeoned into Tungsten originally and is determined to resist further pressure'.

When Fraser came to lunch, A.B.C. thought he looked 'very fat and rather soft and wants a little warm weather to fine him down'. In November 1944, Fraser wrote what A.B.C. called 'an unpleasant letter' about his misgivings as to his future as C-in-C British Pacific Fleet. A.B.C. commented: 'I am in doubt myself if he is the man for the job the way he has behaved lately. He seems to think that he has only to put something forward and the Admiralty must agree. I decline to accept this idea of how things should work.'

Later in November Fraser wrote again to say that there would be a delay because Admiral Chester Nimitz [*q.v.*] wanted the oil refineries at Palembang attacked and this could not be done in December (1944). 'I confess I do not understand Fraser,' A.B.C. confided to his diary. 'There is no urgent desire to get to the scene of the action. It may be the climate but there has been dilatoriness in all his dealings, particularly changing the carriers over to Avenger squadrons, since he has been in command of the Eastern Fleet.'

Even A.B.C.'s approval of Fraser was qualified. 'A very good signal from Fraser giving results of his meeting with Nimitz,' he noted in December 1944. 'He is of course bitten with the US logistics bug.' This somewhat acid reference to the 'logistics bug' shows that A.B.C. never really came to terms with the sheer global scale of the war in the Pacific.

However, he did believe, and argued strongly, that the British fleet should take part in the main war in the Central Pacific under Nimitz and not be side-tracked into apparently peripheral operations in the South-West Pacific under MacArthur. Our final stake in the Pacific, he said, was fully the equal of the Americans'. A.B.C. stuck to this view even under pressure from Churchill, who, for some reason A.B.C. admitted he could never understand, preferred that the British effort in the Far East be centred in the Indian Ocean, being directed at the recovery of British colonies in the area and the forcing of the Malacca Strait. Even after he had agreed to the Central Pacific strategy Churchill still tended to hark back to his former enthusiasms.

A.B.C. was therefore delighted when, at the Quebec Conference in September 1944, Churchill offered President Roosevelt the main British fleet for operations against Japan in the Central Pacific in co-operation with the American fleet, and Roosevelt said at once, 'No sooner offered than accepted.'

That seemed to settle the matter. But next day, when the Joint Chiefs of Staff met, Admiral King disputed the decision and tried to persuade the meeting that the President's acceptance did not mean what had been said. With the other American Chiefs of Staff ranged against him, King eventually gave way but, as A.B.C. said, with a very bad grace.

King remained implacably hostile to the presence of a British fleet in the Pacific and made his feelings evident again and again in a series of other irritating unilateral decisions, always seeking to remove American forces from under British command. Such were the difficulties King continued to create that Captain Stephen Roskill, then serving in the British Mission in Washington, was sent back to London to explain the situation. A.B.C. heard him out and then said, 'Roskill, we'd get on better if you'd shoot Ernie King!' To which Roskill, who knew A.B.C. well, replied, 'Is that just a suggestion, sir, or an order?' whereupon A.B.C. 'good-humouredly turned me out of his office'.

A.B.C. kept a sharp eye on the navy's doings worldwide and was quick to punish incompetence. On 8 August 1944, the floating dock in Trincomalee, the large harbour in the north of Ceylon (Sri Lanka), suddenly collapsed with the battleship *Valiant* inside it. *Valiant* was badly damaged and had to go home round the Cape of Good Hope for refit. She took no further part in the war.

The officers to blame were to have received Their Lordships' displeasure in varying degrees. This was not enough for an enraged A.B.C. 'Here is a valuable capital ship put out of action for many months and a valuable floating dock completely lost through the gross neglects and omissions of various officials. . . . It is indeed a mercy that the neglect of these officers did not result in a much greater disaster, i.e. the total loss of the *Valiant* and a large number of her ship's company.'

A.B.C. ordered the Constructor Captain responsible to be relieved forthwith and stripped of the acting rank of chief constructor. The Constructor Commander involved was to revert to his proper rank of inspector of shipwrights and the Captain of the Dockyard merited Their Lordships' displeasure.

A contrasting aspect of A.B.C.'s character, and one which he never lost, was his mischievous sense of humour. After the Quebec Conference the Chief of the Canadian Air Staff lent his aircraft to fly A.B.C. to New York, there to embark in the *Queen Mary*, accompanied by Captain Guy Grantham and the Admiralty and War Cabinet secretaries. While waiting to take off, A.B.C. told the girls they were sure to be sick, and began ostentatiously feeling below his seat. When asked if he were looking for something, he said he was 'looking for that damned paper bag to be sick into!' The thoughtful silence which followed was broken when he added: 'Grantham, when I was a young lieutenant I was in the Sail Training Squadron. Do you know what the sailors had to do if they felt sick when they were out on a yard?' Grantham tried to avoid replying but eventually had to say, 'No, sir?' 'They had to be sick into their caps and put them back on their heads again!' That, Grantham said, finished the girls off.

Unlike Pound, A.B.C. made sure he had proper rest and recuperation. He was in bed most nights by 11 p.m., or as soon as possible after the end of a Chiefs of Staff meeting. The only man who could keep A.B.C. up later was Mr Churchill. A.B.C. and Nona had a flat in the Admiralty, at the top of Mall House. It had once been the First Sea Lord's official residence. They spent their weeks there, although their nights were often disturbed from the summer of 1944 onwards by the V-1 flying bombs or 'doodlebugs'. The V-1s, which flew regardless of bad weather or the moon or darkness, were so persistent and menacing that they eventually affected Londoners' morale more than the Blitz earlier in the war.

A.B.C. and Nona spent every weekend they could at Palace House, the house they had bought at Bishop's Waltham in Hampshire. Although there was a 'scrambler' telephone, installed on Mr Churchill's orders, A.B.C. was able to relax from the cares of the war. He and Nona worked industriously in the garden. So, too, did any guests. Visiting Cunningham relatives and even admirals and generals were put to work clearing nettles and brambles and stoking up the bonfire.

A.B.C. was sure Japan would have surrendered without either invasion or atomic bombs. He thought it a pity and a mistake that the bombs were dropped. But the end of the war found A.B.C. supremely thankful although mentally tired out, after years of exertion with no proper holiday. He compared himself most touchingly to Collingwood, who had to serve on in the Mediterranean for five years after Trafalgar, while longing for his home in Northumberland; but as he said, he and his colleagues soon found that it was easier to make war than to reorganize for peace. There were changes in the government after the general election, and changes in the Board of Admiralty. Fraser was not chosen to relieve A.B.C. Instead, Sir John Cunningham (no relation) was selected.

A.B.C. retired on 6 June 1946, leaving the Admiralty for the last time and driving down to Bishop's Waltham. He was back in London on the 8th for the Victory March and took his seat, with Brooke and Portal, to the right of the royal saluting base in the Mall. Two days later the three of them went in state landaus to the Guildhall to receive the Freedom of the City of London.

Looking back on his fifty years of naval service, A.B.C. wrote, 'I have little to regret. Fortune favoured me at every turn. How else could one of such limited attainments have reached so far? . . . I have no profound philosophy of life to propound. . . . I have always been inclined to rebel and to speak out against decisions that I felt to be wrong. Otherwise I think I have usually taken things as I found them, and tried to make the best of them.' He quoted some lines of Graham, Marquis of Montrose, which hung over his desk for many years:

> He either fears his fate too much
> Or his deserts are small,
> That dares not put it to the touch,
> To gain or lose it all.

Finally, said A.B.C., 'to the end of my life, I shall remain convinced that there is no service or profession to compare with the Royal Navy'.

The Freedom of London was only one of the honours such as A.B.C. 'never dreamed of' which poured in upon him: Knight of the Thistle, New Year's Honours List, 1945; baron, Churchill's Resignation Honours List, August 1945; viscount, New Year's Honours List, 1946; Order of Merit, 1946 Birthday Honours List; US Navy's Distinguished Service Medal (he already had the US Army's Distinguished Conduct Medal); French Médaille Militaire (he was already a Commander of the Legion of Honour); Chief Commander of the US Order of Merit; Grand Cordon of the Order of Nichan-Iftikhan (Tunisia); a Grand Officer of the Order of Quissan Alaouite (Morocco); Knight Grand Cross of the Order of George I (Greece); Special Grand Cordon of the Order of the Cloud and Banner (China); Knight Grand Cross of the Order of the Netherlands Lion; twice Mentioned in Despatches. Still more honours followed, and in 1951 he published his memoirs A Sailor's Odyssey. *A.B.C. died suddenly in London (in a taxi on his way to the House of Lords) on 12 June 1963, aged eighty. He was buried at sea off Portsmouth.*

PART TWO

The Air Admirals

9

Fleet Admiral

William F. Halsey Jr
United States Navy

1882–1959

by
James M. Merrill

*W*ILLIAM *Frederick Halsey Jr, born 30 October 1882, in Elizabeth, New Jersey. Spent his childhood as a navy junior, attending prep schools in California, Pennsylvania and Maryland before entering the Naval Academy in 1900.*

When a young ensign, his ship Kansas *steamed around the world as part of President Roosevelt's White Fleet. Halsey rose rapidly in rank and, in December 1909, married Frances Cooke Grandy in Old Christ Church, Norfolk, Virginia.*

Soon after the United States entered World War One, Halsey joined the American Destroyer Force based at Queenstown, Ireland, taking command of the Benham, *then the* Shaw. *Halsey took command of the new destroyer* Yarnall, *1918, and with her worked with the Pacific Fleet for a year. Halsey, then a commander, was ordered to Washington for duty in the Office of Naval Intelligence, and was appointed Naval Attaché at the American Embassy in Berlin.*

Commanded Dale, *1924, and later* Osborne, *two of six American destroyers still operating in European waters, before service as Executive Officer in* Wyoming. *Promoted captain, 1927.*

Following duty at the Naval Academy, Halsey took command of a squadron of destroyers operating in both the Atlantic and the Pacific. Qualifying as a pilot in 1935, he was ordered to command the carrier Saratoga. *In 1937 transferred to the naval station at Pensacola, Florida, as commandant, and was promoted to rear admiral. Received command of Carrier Division Two, 1938. When carrier divisions and their commanders were reshuffled, Halsey was made Commander Carrier Division One with his flag in* Saratoga.

In the spring of 1940, Halsey was detached from Carrier Division One and

designated Commander Aircraft Battle Force with the rank of vice admiral. He now
commanded all the carriers in the Pacific Fleet and their air groups.

When the Japanese struck Pearl Harbor on 7 December 1941, Admiral
William F. Halsey Jr, commanding Aircraft Battle Force in the Pacific Ocean,
was on board his flagship, the carrier *Enterprise*, roughly 150 miles west of
Honolulu. Receiving despatches and frantic radio reports, *Enterprise* and her
escorts swerved northward to search for the enemy fleet, but to no avail.

On Christmas Day, Admiral Chester Nimitz [*q.v.*] (the new Commander-
in-Chief, Pacific Fleet) arrived in Pearl Harbor. Over the strong objections of
his conservative staffers, Nimitz decided to despatch a carrier force to strike
the Japanese where it would hurt – in their Marshall island bases in the Central
Pacific.

But after frustrating patrols in search of enemy submarines, Halsey, a risk-
taker, welcomed the hazardous mission of running his task force into enemy
territory. For years he had been an apostle of naval air power, touting its
importance, its effectiveness and its flexibility. In the kind of war that the vast
expanses of the Pacific dictated, strong, fast carrier forces could strike with
surprise at long range. 'We do the unexpected,' said Halsey. '. . . We expose
ourselves to shore-based planes. We don't stay behind the battle with our
carriers. But . . . whatever we do, we do fast.'

Early on 1 February 1942, Halsey's planes streaked towards Kwajalein, Roi
and Jaluit, while cruisers bombarded Wotje atoll. Although the raid yielded
meagre results, American pilots gained valuable combat experience and their
overly optimistic reports of the damage inflicted had a symbolic importance.
Hitting the heart of the Japanese defences in the Central Pacific, Halsey was
thrust into the limelight and acclaimed the nation's first naval hero of World
War Two. In Washington, President Franklin D. Roosevelt awarded him the
Distinguished Service Medal.

After a one-week respite at Pearl Harbor, Halsey's ships slipped their
moorings and moved down channel. Halsey then raised Marcus Island, 1,000
miles from Tokyo. In this attack, for the first time, he relied on radar to locate
his own aircraft on their way to and from their objectives and to correct their
navigation.

By April 1942 Washington established the command structure in the
Pacific, giving Nimitz direct control over the North and Central Pacific Areas.
In accordance with the Joint Chiefs of Staff instructions, he appointed a
subordinate as Commander of the South Pacific Area, Admiral Robert
L. Ghormley, with headquarters at Nouméa, New Caledonia.

A few days after Halsey had returned from Marcus, Nimitz called him to
Fleet Headquarters for a conference with Rear Admiral Donald Duncan, just
arrived from Washington. Duncan related that a top-secret operation was
under way. Colonel James H. Doolittle, USAF, had trained sixteen army
aircrews in Florida to take B-25s off a carrier's deck, and the navy had

promised to launch them against Tokyo. The stakes were too high for a strike by navy planes, but an attack on Tokyo from carriers by army bombers flying on to Chinese airfields would not only retaliate for Pearl Harbor, but was intended to provide planes for China. This would be Halsey's boldest raid to date. Its main purpose was psychological – to raise American spirits and to dumbfound the Japanese. On both counts, it succeeded.

At a meeting with Doolittle in San Francisco, Halsey reported that his force would consist of two carriers, four cruisers, eight destroyers and two tankers. The B-25s would be hoisted on board the *Hornet* (Captain Marc A. Mitscher [*q.v.*] commanding), then in San Francisco harbour. Escorted by half the task force, *Hornet* would rendezvous in mid-Pacific with the *Enterprise* group from Pearl Harbor. If the group escaped detection, the carriers would make a high-speed run to within 400 miles of the Japanese coast. The plan suited Doolittle. The two men shook hands and Halsey wished Doolittle luck.

In April the *Enterprise* and *Hornet* units got under way and on the 13th merged at a point between Midway Island and the western Aleutians. Five days later, at 0800, the blinker lights flashed from *Enterprise*: 'LAUNCH PLANES. TO COL. DOOLITTLE AND HIS GALLANT COMMAND GOOD LUCK AND GOD BLESS YOU.'

Later, Halsey learned that thirteen of Doolittle's B-25s had bombed Tokyo, Nagoya, Osaka and Kobe, and, inflicting only minor damage, had flown on towards China, where the planes, short of fuel, had crash-landed or their crews had parachuted out. Eight men landed in enemy territory and, of these, three were executed for bombing Japanese residential areas.

When Halsey returned to Pearl Harbor he learned that the South Pacific Area was warming up. Nimitz ordered him to the South Pacific to reinforce Task Force 17. On 7 May, while Halsey's group was under way, American naval forces in the South Pacific fought the Battle of the Coral Sea – the first battle of carriers against carriers. Tactically the Japanese won, sinking the American carrier *Lexington*, but it was a strategic victory for America. The enemy's planned invasion of Allied-held Port Moresby, New Guinea, collapsed and the Japanese ships retired to Rabaul. Nimitz ordered Halsey's force to return to Pearl Harbor.

Working under stress in the heat and humidity, Halsey had developed a skin disease. His sweat glands had become irritated and swollen and he had a fine pebble-like rash on his waist, neck, chest, back and armpits, accompanied by intolerable itching. When he went to Fleet Headquarters, Nimitz immediately ordered him into hospital, and placed Admiral Raymond Spruance [*q.v.*] – a good friend of Halsey's – in command of the task force. Thus, while the critical Battle of Midway was fought on 4–6 June 1942, while US marines stormed on to the beaches of Guadalcanal and Tulagi on 7 August, and while the US Navy suffered its devastating defeat at Savo Island, on the night of 8–9 August, 'Bull' Halsey lay frustrated and impatient in hospital. First he was treated at Pearl, then at Richmond, Virginia; and two agonizing months passed before he was again certified fit for duty. At last, early in September 1942, he was able to return to San Francisco to confer with Nimitz and Admiral Ernest J. King [*q.v.*], Commander-in-Chief, United States Fleet, and their advisers to discuss the Pacific strategy.

At one of the meetings, after Halsey had stepped out of the room, Nimitz and King discussed the deteriorating situation at Guadalcanal. The overall responsibility for the Savo Island defeat fell upon Nimitz's deputy, Admiral Ghormley, Commander of the South Pacific Force. King and Nimitz decided to strengthen the South Pacific Force by sending Halsey down as task force commander, a subordinate to Ghormley. Until Halsey organized his staff he was placed on temporary duty.

Leaving California, Nimitz and members of his staff stopped at Pearl Harbor before flying out on an inspection tour of the South Pacific. On 28 September at Nouméa Habour, New Caledonia, they boarded Admiral Ghormley's flagship. After meetings and on site inspections, Nimitz flew back to Pearl. Distressed by the morale problem in the South Pacific, and by Ghormley's inadequate performance, Nimitz sent a letter to him announcing that Halsey would soon be arriving in Nouméa. Halsey was to take command of Task Force 16, and be under Ghormley's operational control as long as he was in the South Pacific.

On 18 October a navy Coronado arrived in Nouméa's lagoon. As Halsey emerged from the plane's wide-flung hatch, a whaleboat came alongside with Ghormley's flag lieutenant, who saluted and handed Halsey a sealed envelope marked 'secret'. It contained Nimitz's orders for him to take immediate command of the South Pacific Area and its forces, replacing Admiral Ghormley.

Halsey's arrival in the South Pacific lifted naval and national morale. The press was delighted with the appointment: as the *New York Times* proclaimed, 'Shift to Offensive Is Seen in Selection of "Fighting" Admiral Halsey as Commander in the South Pacific'.

Halsey's bellicose slogan was 'Kill Japs, Kill Japs, Kill more Japs.' His 'bloodthirstiness' was not just a put-on to gain headlines. He strongly believed that by denigrating the enemy he was counteracting the myth of Japanese martial superiority which had developed in the wake of Pearl Harbor and the early Japanese victories in the Pacific. Halsey's racial slurs made him a symbol of combative leadership, a vocal Japanese-hater. He was outspoken because he believed that the vast majority of the soldiers and sailors in his command, motivated by hatred of the Japanese, were fortified by his disparagement of the enemy; and he was probably right.

Halsey was not an intellectual. His official reports were written in commonplace language. His speeches and private correspondence reveal that he often thought in clichés, that his vocabulary was narrow and that he had difficulty with syntax. His letters confirm his contempt for the Japanese in locker-room jargon. But intellect is not always necessary in service life, or in war, and despite his shortcomings Halsey had the knack of appointing extremely intelligent officers to his staff upon whom he relied for decision-making. On only rare occasions did he overrule them. 'Admiral Halsey's strongest point', wrote a staff officer, 'was his superb leadership. While always the true professional and exacting professional performance from all subordinates, he had the charismatic effect on them which was like being touched by a magic wand. Anyone so touched was determined to excel.'

The battle ashore on Guadalcanal continued to intensify. As Halsey analysed the problem, the island was the key to the entire campaign. The Japanese poured in reinforcements almost nightly. They also possessed a powerful armada. To counter them, Halsey had his South Pacific Force.

The Battle of Santa Cruz, 26 October, was a carrier duel. The Japanese jumped Halsey's forces by launching planes twenty minutes before the Americans did. The enemy concentrated on the carrier *Hornet*. Five bombs hit her flight deck, several dropping into the hull before exploding. Torpedoes ripped in and exploded in her engine spaces. Dead in the water, *Hornet* was ablaze and listing. Far to the north-west, her planes broke through enemy air patrols to pummel a cruiser, and knocked the carrier *Shokaku* out of commission.

The crippled *Hornet*, left without air cover, became the primary target of repeated air strikes. As the blazing carrier listed dangerously, the Japanese force approached her, but were unable to take her in tow and sent her to the bottom.

In the Battle of Santa Cruz, the American forces received the heaviest blows, but lost only seventy-four planes to the Japanese loss of one hundred. To Halsey this meant the four air groups on the Japanese carriers had been cut to pieces, and that the enemy's naval forces would be unable to provide effective support for their troops on Guadalcanal.

He was right. In early November, he and his staff became aware that the enemy was mounting another offensive; but because of the actions of Halsey's surface forces and planes, this Japanese attempt to retake Guadalcanal ended in failure. After these futile offensives, the Japanese risked no more capital ships in the Solomons campaign.

At Pearl Harbor Nimitz asserted that the 'victory surpassed anything of the kind that the United States Navy had done before in its history', and that 'the United States had eliminated the immediate danger to our hold on Guadalcanal so that now we can begin the reinforcement, consolidation, and onward offensives'.

Washington promptly promoted Halsey to four stars. The Secretary of the Navy termed him 'One of the few great naval leaders of history'.

In Washington Admiral King clarified naval organization by numbering the fleets. Halsey's South Pacific Force became the Third Fleet; the Central Pacific Force, based at Pearl Harbor, the Fifth Fleet; and MacArthur's South-West Pacific Force, the Seventh Fleet.

Meanwhile the Joint Chiefs of Staff outlined broad terms for the strategy for the South Pacific and South-West Pacific campaigns. They directed the capture of the remaining Solomon Islands and of Lae and Salamaua, and other points on the coast of New Guinea. The forces of both Halsey and MacArthur were to attack Rabaul, the Japanese bastion on New Britain Island in the Bismarck Archipelago. Bristling with warships and aircraft, this stronghold threatened the line of communications from the United States to Australia, and blocked any Allied advance along the north coast of New Guinea to the Philippines. The reduction of Rabaul became the primary mission of both the South Pacific and South-West Pacific Forces.

In Nouméa, Halsey and his staff looked on Munda Point (on the south-west corner of New Georgia Island, in the central Solomons) as the most likely first objective for his forces. New Georgia is the name of a large group of islands in the central Solomons, which include Vella Lavella, Kolombangara, New Georgia (the main island of the group) and Rendova.

On 30 June 1943, in preparation for an assault against the Munda airfield, 6,000 amphibious troops eliminated the small force of Japanese on Rendova Island, five miles to the south of New Georgia beaches, where the main landing was planned. After securing Rendova, the Americans waded ashore on New Georgia under friendly artillery cover for the push against the Japanese airfield.

Supported by air and ship bombardment, the American advance inched forward, gaining momentum, until troops secured the island on 31 July 1943. Construction battalions started the work of widening, resurfacing and regrading the airfield on Munda.

As a result of the New Georgia campaign, the Americans forced the enemy to abandon his naval base in the Kahili–Buin–Shortlands area of southern Bougainville, gained airbases for the neutralization of Japanese airfields on Bougainville, and brought Rabaul into range.

Simultaneously with Halsey's invasion of New Georgia, MacArthur's South-West Pacific Forces captured the Japanese fortress at Lae on the mainland of New Guinea.

During the New Georgia campaign, Halsey and his staff saw the difficulty of rooting out the enemy from powerful defensive positions. Several staff members argued that American forces might have 'hard sledding' if they attempted to invade Kolombangara, the next island north of New Georgia. Assured by intelligence that the Japanese were consolidating their position on Kolombangara, the staff unanimously decided to leap over this island and hit Vella Lavella, the next island up the line, forty miles closer to Bougainville. In principle, this technique of bypassing or leapfrogging strongholds was simple. Jump over the enemy's fortified points, blockade them and leave them to stagnate. The concept was not new in the Pacific, but Halsey's staff refined it, and eventually MacArthur's and Nimitz's forces employed this strategy both in New Guinea and in the Central Pacific.

On 13 August 1943 American troops assaulted Vella Lavella. Construction units began work on the airfield. The first US plane landed on 24 September and within two months after the invasion the field accommodated 100 aircraft.

Rabaul, the last remaining threat to the America–Australia–New Zealand lifeline, now confronted Halsey and his staff. They realized that the fortress must be taken or neutralized before the Allies could move towards the Philippines or operate unharassed in the South Pacific. Thus the invasion of Bougainville in the northern Solomons became the campaign to contain Rabaul: on Bougainville, the largest of the Solomon Islands, there were 35,000 Japanese troops. The island lay close to Rabaul and other subsidiary bases within easy reach of the enemy fleet at Truk.

Submarines, planes and PT boats put reconnaissance teams ashore at several points on Bougainville. These units reported that Cape Torokina in Empress Augusta Bay, halfway up the south-western coast, was the best possible landing site.

D-Day for Cape Torokina was 1 November 1943. Boatloads of Marines waded ashore at 0726 and, by 1100, they held Cape Torokina.

On 4 November American planes reported an enemy armada steaming towards Rabaul from Truk. At Nouméa Halsey and his staff estimated that the enemy would refuel at Rabaul, then move towards Empress Augusta Bay to shell the Marines' beachhead. The Admiral therefore decided to despatch carriers and hit Rabaul from the air, hoping to cripple the warships.

At 0900 on 5 November, the carriers *Princeton* and *Saratoga* reached their launching positions in the Solomon Sea, at a point fifty-seven miles south-west of Cape Torokina and 230 miles south-east of Rabaul. Ninety-seven planes lifted off the carriers. Evading severe ack-ack fire from the guns at Rabaul, they sneaked through the enemy's fighter screen, shot down twenty-five enemy planes, and bombed and damaged five cruisers and two destroyers anchored in the harbour. The attack's effect was precisely as desired: the Japanese pulled their heavy cruisers back to Truk, and the threat to Empress Augusta Bay was ended.

One officer close to Halsey later described the carrier assault on Rabaul as 'The major turning point in the South Pacific campaign', explaining that 'By this bold strike the Bougainville operation was . . . secured and as a result Rabaul became eventually no longer a major threat to our forces.' Later, planes from airfields on New Georgia, Bougainville and other islands, stepped up raids on Rabaul to immobilize it completely.

The war in the South Pacific was changing dramatically in pattern and scope. Less than two years earlier, the Japanese had swept down from their homeland and mandated islands and conquered millions of square miles of territory that they felt destined to exploit. Forced to fight defensively, the Allies eventually halted the enemy and pushed him back from Guadalcanal, back from New Georgia, back from Bougainville.

In December 1943 Halsey and his staff returned to Pearl Harbor for talks with Nimitz on the developing situation. Flying on to San Francisco, Halsey met with Admirals King and Nimitz for intensive discussions involving the objectives in the Central Pacific campaign. To control the seas and secure a route from Hawaii westward, King and Nimitz advocated continued leapfrogging of enemy bases, which were unnecessary to the Allied strategy.

After a brief visit to Los Angeles, Halsey went on to Washington, where Secretary Knox awarded him a Gold Star in lieu of a second Distinguished Service Medal. Halsey learned that in January and February 1944 Americans had secured Kwajalein and Eniwetok in the Central Pacific. These actions and the neutralization of Truk were accelerated by Spruance's Fifth Fleet.

In February, Halsey journeyed back to Nouméa via Pearl Harbor. Later he met with King and Nimitz in San Francisco, then flew to Los Angeles for a news conference. 'The only good Jap is a Jap who's been dead six months,' he told reporters. 'When we get to Tokyo, where we're bound to get eventually, we'll have a little celebration where Tokyo was.' In April he enthusiastically welcomed the news of MacArthur's invasion of Hollandia in central New Guinea, the first direct move in the South-West Pacific Forces' advance towards the Philippines. In May 1944 Halsey once again flew to San Francisco for a further conference with Admirals King and Nimitz. The navy's war in the South Pacific had ended. Halsey had fought himself out of a job. He would continue as Commander, Third Fleet, but in June was relieved as Commander, South Pacific Area. The Pacific Fleet was divided into two teams: Spruance's Fifth Fleet and Halsey's Third Fleet. One group could plan, train and be resupplied, while the other fought, reducing the time between operations. When Halsey and his staff arrived in Pearl Harbor, they immediately began work on plans for the invasion of the Philippines. The Joint Chiefs of Staff's timetable set 20 December as the date for D-Day on Mindanao.

Preparations completed, Halsey's flagship, the battleship *New Jersey*, left Pearl Harbor with her escorts and set a course westward. Meanwhile, the core of the Third Fleet – Admiral Mitscher's fast carriers, Task Force 38 – pounded Iwo Jima, then moved south to the Palaus, before hitting weakly defended Mindanao, the southernmost of the Philippine Islands. *New Jersey* and her escorts dropped anchor in the harbour at Manus Island. Several days later Admiral Kinkaid [*q.v.*], commanding MacArthur's Seventh Fleet, and his aides came on board the battleship to co-ordinate plans for the coming operations with Halsey and his staff. On 5 September *New Jersey* departed from Manus to rendezvous with Mitscher's fast carriers. Six days later they met, and on 12 September the carrier groups launched devastating strikes on Leyte, Cebu and Negros. Caught completely off guard, the Japanese had their airfields crowded with planes which became 'sitting ducks to the fighters that suddenly swept in'. Further carrier strikes over the following two days destroyed enemy installations 'far and wide', severely weakening enemy air power.

After an American pilot, who had spent a day and a night on Leyte in friendly guerrilla hands before being rescued, reported the limited number of Japanese on that island, Halsey called a staff meeting on board *New Jersey*. He and his aides agreed that, commencing with Mindanao, the proposed stepping-stone campaign up the Philippines should be scrapped and the invasion of Leyte itself should commence months ahead of schedule. Nimitz, however, refused to cancel the invasion of Palau.

After numerous messages, the Joint Chiefs of Staff ordered MacArthur and Nimitz to cancel the Mindanao operation. MacArthur told the Joint Chiefs that their decision about Leyte would make it possible for his forces to land on Luzon on 20 December, two months ahead of the earliest date previously contemplated.

On 15 September, as scheduled, units of the 1st Marine Division landed on the beaches of Peleliu, an island in the southern Palaus. One of Halsey's carrier groups rendered air support. The troops moved forward, slowly but steadily, and on 30 September Halsey's task force commander announced that the southern Palaus had been secured. The Admiral had been correct in his assessment of the Palau campaign. Those islands should have been bypassed when the decision was made to strike Leyte.

While MacArthur's invasion troops assembled at Manus and Hollandia for the Leyte assault, Halsey launched air strikes to neutralize the island.

The only weakness, but a major one, in the American plan for the Leyte invasion was the absence of a unified command, a handicap which was to plague the entire campaign. The task of transporting, landing and covering MacArthur's amphibious force (the Sixth Army) was the direct responsibility of Admiral Kinkaid's Seventh Fleet. In this venture, Kinkaid was supported by Halsey's Third Fleet, operating by agreement with MacArthur, but still under Nimitz's command. The Third Fleet was, essentially, Mitscher's fast carriers (Task Force 38), over which Halsey exercised direct tactical command. These ships were organized into four strong groups of equal strength. Halsey's mission was to support the landings themselves, by striking the Central Philippines immediately before and during the landing operations. He was also responsible for destroying any enemy naval and air elements that might threaten the beachheads.

His operational order, which was written by him and approved by Nimitz, emphasized that, if the chance to knock out a 'major portion' of the enemy fleet was 'offered or could be created', this would become the Third Fleet's 'primary task'.

During the early October operations, Nimitz wrote to Halsey:

You are always free to make local decisions in connection with handling of the forces under your command. Often, it will be necessary for you to take action not previously contemplated, because of local situations, which may develop quickly, and in the light of information which has come to you, and which may not yet be available to me. My only requirement in such cases is that I be informed, as fully and as early as the situation permits.

The Philippine campaign was a new challenge to Halsey for neither he nor any of his staff had participated in the great carrier duels of the Pacific War – Coral Sea, Midway, the Philippine Sea. Halsey intended to knock out Japanese carriers at the first opportunity.

Making the destruction of the enemy fleet a higher priority than that of protecting the landing at Leyte represented a drastic change in doctrine. Up to October 1944, the primary task of any fleet supporting an invasion had been to protect and assist the amphibious forces. Since MacArthur had no authority over Halsey, the Admiral intended to manoeuvre his fleet as he chose.

In the early hours of 20 October 1944, combat ships, troopships, command ships and landing ships moved into Leyte Gulf. At once, with intervals of only a few seconds, battleships of Kinkaid's Seventh Fleet began to volley tons of shells into the dense tropical jungle. Cruisers and destroyers ranged beside them, peppering the shore. Now and then the naval fire stopped, and planes from Halsey's Task Force 38 and Kinkaid's Seventh Fleet flew overhead, bombing towns, installations, trenches, pillboxes and supply dumps. Although Japanese air offered only token resistance, Halsey's planes the next day struck the Central Philippines to neutralize enemy air activity there. By 21 October, Halsey calculated that in eleven days his aircraft had sunk 141 ships, damaged 249 others and shot down or destroyed on the ground 1,225 planes. Ninety-five aircraft had been lost, but a large number of their pilots and crewmen were saved through intensive air–sea rescue forces, lifeguard submarines and Filipino guerrillas.

To counter this massive assault, Admiral Soemu Toyoda at Japanese naval headquarters ordered the Combined Fleet to carry out Sho-1 – a plan which, if successful, would keep open Japan's lifeline to the East Indies. By now, the shortage of land-based planes was so acute that in order to execute Sho-1 almost all the Japanese carriers' remaining aircraft had to be sent to land bases in Luzon. In a three-pronged attack against Leyte Gulf, their Northern Force (Admiral Jisaburo Ozawa [*q.v.*]) was to act as a decoy, attempting to lure Halsey's Third Fleet northward, away from the American beachhead at Leyte. This unit was composed of six almost empty carriers – together they had only 116 planes – screened by cruisers and destroyers.

The Centre Force (Admiral Takeo Kurita) was built around the world's two largest and most powerful super-battleships, *Yamato* and *Musashi*, accompanied by three older battleships, ten heavy cruisers, two light cruisers and nineteen destroyers. These ships were to steam through the San Bernardino Strait, which separates Samar and Luzon, and descend upon Leyte Gulf. A Southern Force (Admiral Shoji Nishimura) was to manoeuvre through the Surigao Strait, to the south of Leyte, complete a pincer movement on the amphibious and fire support ships at Leyte Gulf, and thereby destroy them.

At 0016 on 23 October in the Palawan Passage, the American submarines *Dace* and *Darter* detected the Centre Force, long before it was anywhere near the San Bernadino Strait. The *Darter* got a message off to Admiral Ralph W. Christie, Commander Submarines South-West Pacific, who relayed the message to Halsey.

To intercept the Japanese Southern Force, Admiral Kinkaid deployed almost all his ships, which had supported the Leyte landings, to the Surigao Strait. Contact was made in the early hours of 25 October. The American ships defeated the Japanese force, which withdrew. After dawn carrier planes chased the retreating enemy ships, sinking most of them.

Meanwhile, Admiral Kurita's massive Centre Force of battleships and cruisers, first detected and attacked in the Palawan Passage by submarines, slowed down and was damaged by Halsey's carrier bombers. Employing Ozawa's carriers as decoys, Kurita sought to lure Halsey's ships north so that Kurita's fleet could enter Leyte Gulf.

Overestimating the damage his planes had inflicted upon Kurita's force, and bent on destroying the Japanese carriers, Halsey left the San Bernardino Strait unguarded after his search planes had located the Japanese carriers.

Halsey and his staff assumed that by heading north they were pursuing the more powerful unit of the enemy's naval forces; in reality they let the stronger Centre Force move unseen and unchallenged through San Bernardino Strait, towards the entrance to Leyte Gulf. 'It's not my job', Halsey said, 'to protect the Seventh Fleet.' Later he wrote, 'I felt Kinkaid was amply strong enough to handle this situation.' Off Samar, early on the morning of 25 October, the Japanese were intercepted by Rear Admiral Clifton Sprague's small group of six escort carriers. In a bloody confrontation, the American force suffered severe casualties against the superior number of Japanese ships. In the uneven encounter, Sprague's only advantage was the absence of enemy air support. Eventually Kurita halted the action and retreated.

Meanwhile Halsey's flat-tops were moving northward. Admiral Ozawa, commanding the Northern Force, said later, 'We expected complete destruction.' He could well expect defeat, as sixty-four ships were hunting his nineteen – and if the disparity in numbers of planes was great, the disparity in quality of pilots was still greater.

A little after 0200 on 25 October, Halsey's search planes, scouting ahead, made radar contact with two separate Japanese surface units of the Northern Force. At dawn that day American carriers launched 180 bombers, fighters and torpedo planes. 'Our next few hours were the most anxious of all,' recalled Halsey. 'God, what a wait it was!'

In the Battle of Cape Engaño, Halsey's planes arrived in sight of Ozawa's force and promptly destroyed a dozen approaching enemy fighters. They swiftly sank a destroyer and hit one heavy cruiser, and a second attack widely scattered the enemy ships, leaving a carrier ablaze and listing. At 1055, flash reports indicated that the Japanese force had been seriously damaged and partly sunk.

Halsey radioed Nimitz: 'JAPANESE NAVY HAS BEEN BEATEN AND ROUTED BY THE THIRD AND SEVENTH FLEETS.'

The three-part battle for Leyte Gulf left the United States Navy in complete control of Philippine waters; never again would the Japanese navy offer a genuine threat.

In Washington, having analysed all the battle reports of the Leyte Gulf action, Admiral King concluded: 'Apart from all questions of relative importance in Halsey's mission of covering the Seventh Fleet as against creating an opportunity for the destruction of a major portion of the enemy fleet . . . [I] was never able to fathom why planes from the Seventh Fleet escort carriers had not adequately scouted the area of San Bernardino Strait from the Sibuyan Sea to the eastward before dawn on the morning of 25 October, and thus detected Kurita's approach.'

After the Battle of Leyte Gulf, the Third Fleet remained in Philippine waters to cover MacArthur's troops and to harass Japanese airfields and shipping. One of the more successful attacks was against Luzon on 5–6 November. Aircraft shot down 105 enemy planes and destroyed 321 on the ground. They struck installations, destroyed a railroad locomotive, five tank cars, and sank or heavily damaged seventeen transports, fifty cargo ships, ten oilers, two cruisers, fifteen destroyers and twenty-six small craft. American losses were minimal.

In mid-December, the Third Fleet withdrew to refuel. Threatening weather, however, obliged Halsey to stop fuelling. On the morning of the 18th, a typhoon, which aerologists failed to detect, lashed the Third Fleet. The destroyers *Hull*, *Monaghan* and *Spence* capsized and sank. The typhoon heavily damaged seven other ships. Planes were blown or pushed overboard but not before several collided and burned. When the storm abated Halsey's force returned to Ulithi.

Admiral Nimitz, who had arrived in Ulithi on an inspection tour, ordered a court of inquiry to investigate the loss of *Hull*, *Monaghan* and *Spence*. After questioning numerous witnesses, the court placed the blame for the tragedy on Halsey and said that the 'mistakes, errors and faults' were 'errors in judgment under stress of war operations'.

Nimitz approved the findings of the court. The evidence brought forward indicated to him that the responsibility for the storm damage and losses rested with Halsey. 'However,' he wrote, 'the convening authority is of the firm opinion that no question of negligence is involved, but rather, that the mistakes made were errors in judgment committed under stress of war operations. . . . No further action is contemplated or recommended.'

While workmen laboured to repair the damaged ships, Halsey and his staff worked out combat plans which called for strikes on Formosa, Okinawa and Luzon to support General MacArthur's amphibious forces, which were scheduled to invade Lingayen Gulf (western Luzon) in January 1945.

On 30 December 1944 the repaired Third Fleet moved out of Ulithi and headed towards the Philippines. After refuelling, Task Force 38's aircraft pummelled Formosa. Intelligence reported that B-29s had sighted elements of the Japanese heavy fleet at sea off Kyushu and *Ise* and *Hyuga* in Camranh Bay on the coast of Indo-China. Further reports indicated that MacArthur's troops at Lingayen Gulf had landed on schedule. Eager to attack the remnants of the Japanese fleet, the Third Fleet entered the South China Sea.

At dawn on 12 January 1945, it launched heavy air strikes ranging up and down the Indo-China coast from Saigon to Quinhom. Aircraft located no heavy surface units in Camranh Bay – the Imperial Navy had already departed. However, American aircraft found ample merchant shipping to attack, and Japanese opposition was slight.

From Washington, Admiral King directed the Third Fleet to position itself to intercept enemy forces approaching the Lingayen Gulf area from either the north or the south.

On 15 January Halsey's main strength zeroed in on Formosa, while fighters swept across the Hongkong–Canton–Amoy area. On the following day, American planes struck the China coast and the coastal areas between these points.

Five days later, after sneaking through the Balingtang Channel between Luzon and Formosa, the Third Fleet entered the Philippine Sea. At dawn on the 21st its carriers launched fighter sweeps to neutralize airbases in Formosa and the Pescadores. Enemy planes retaliated. Bombs hit the *Langley*, kamikazes tore into the *Ticonderoga*, a fighter crashed into the *Maddox*. On board the *Hancock* a bomb exploded in one of her own planes.

Despite these casualties, the Third Fleet struck Okinawa the following day. The fleet then headed for Ulithi for a well-earned rest, and here Halsey turned over the fleet to Admiral Spruance.

Leaving *New Jersey*, Halsey and his staff departed for Pearl Harbor and the States for recuperation and briefing. During March, while on temporary duty in Washington, Admiral Halsey was summoned to the White House. There, President Roosevelt awarded him a further Gold Star in lieu of a third Distinguished Service Medal.

On 1 April, 50,000 American amphibious forces went ashore at Okinawa, supported by Spruance's ships and planes. Japanese resistance stiffened and kamikazes struck the fleet continually, taking a heavy toll of men and ships. Naturally Spruance wanted to retaliate against the kamikaze airfields and installations, but he could not: his planes were needed to support ground troops advancing against the strongly entrenched Japanese, and the Fifth Fleet had to be held at Okinawa.

Halsey arrived back at Pearl Harbor in early April. After a detailed study of American objectives in the Pacific, he and several staffers flew to Guam to meet with Nimitz, who had transferred his headquarters to that island.

At Guam Halsey hoisted his flag in the battleship *Missouri*, since *New Jersey* was undergoing repairs. On 18 May, accompanied by escorts, *Missouri* headed for Okinawa, where Halsey once more took command of the Third Fleet.

Unhappy as he was playing a defensive role, Halsey had no alternative but to continue supporting the troops at Okinawa. He urged that American air power based on the island be strengthened so that his fast carriers could be relieved of supplying air cover for the operation.

In June the build-up of air power on Okinawa, and the successes of the B-29s operating against Kyushu out of China and Saipan, permitted Halsey's fleet to leave Okinawan waters and head for his ultimate target. On 2–3 June aircraft from his carriers struck southern Kyushu: now Japan itself was under attack.

The fleet was receiving reports of tropical weather disturbances forming far to the south and east. Studying these, the fleet's aerologist reported the ships to be out of danger. But after their disastrous experience the previous December, Halsey refused to discount the warnings, and issued a typhoon alert to all ships. This was fortunate, because the weather rapidly deteriorated. As swiftly as the barometer fell, waves increased savagely in height and strength. As one captain reported, 'Seas were phenomenal; with extremely heavy sprays, the sea and ceiling appeared to merge.'

After numerous course changes to avoid the typhoon, the storm took a sudden turn right into the fleet. Nevertheless, by 1000 on 5 June the Third Fleet had cleared the storm. Twenty-six ships reported minor damage; eight others reported major damage. But this time, none was sunk.

The fleet fuelled, and planes conducted support missions over Okinawa on the 6th and 7th. The Okinawa campaign was now over. On the night of the 10th, the Third Fleet turned south towards the new fleet base at Leyte for repairs.

For the second time, a court of inquiry held Halsey primarily responsible for the typhoon damage sustained. The court also recommended that 'serious consideration' be given to assigning Halsey to other duties. In Washington, Secretary James Forrestal was ready to retire Halsey on the spot. He was dissuaded on the grounds that Halsey was a popular hero, and that any such action would lower fleet morale. Halsey himself adamantly believed that the major blame for the disasters rested with the weather-reporting service.

Repaired and replenished, the Third Fleet moved out of San Pedro Harbour, Leyte, to carry out Nimitz's Operational Plan 4-45. This gave Halsey the task of attacking Japanese naval and air forces, shipyards and coastal objectives. Now that organized enemy resistance on Okinawa had ceased, Halsey was free to hit Japan from within its home waters.

In July American planes struck the Tokyo area and other targets, while surface units pounded coastal areas. The enemy's failure to retaliate indicated to Halsey's staff that the Japanese were hoarding their meagre air power against an expected invasion of the home islands. The air strikes of the 24th and 28th were among the heaviest of the war. At Kure and Kobe, aircraft sank fifty-three merchant ships and badly damaged twenty-two warships, totalling 250,000 tons. These included the battleships *Haruna*, *Hyuga* and *Ise*, two heavy cruisers, two destroyers, several transports, cargo ships and oilers. Bombing and strafing, planes ripped apart the flight decks of the *Amagi* and *Katsuragi*. The Kure naval yard 'ceased to exist'.

On 6 August the atom bomb destroyed Hiroshima and, three days later, another was dropped on Nagasaki. To Halsey, 'it was a mistake ever to drop it. Why reveal a weapon like that to the world when it wasn't necessary? The Japanese were utterly defeated . . . before the atomic bomb was ever used.'

At 1055, 15 August 1945 Halsey received a despatch from Nimitz: 'CEASE OFFENSIVE OPERATIONS AGAINST JAPANESE FORCES. . . .'

The war had ended. On 2 September 1945, in Tokyo Bay, Halsey's flagship *Missouri* was the scene of the formal surrender of the Japanese. With the ceremony completed, all Allied representatives went to Halsey's cabin. For many years, no US warships had been allowed to carry alcohol and now, for once, the Admiral regretted it. Later on, he said wryly: 'If ever a day demanded champagne, this was it – but I could serve them only coffee and doughnuts.'

Less than two weeks after the surrender, Admiral Spruance relieved Halsey, who with his staff immediately departed by air for Pearl Harbor. He had already sent in his request for retirement from active service. In Hawaii, he formed Task Force 30 and, on the morning of 9 October, headed for the west coast. On their way, the various task groups within TF 30 separated and proceeded independently to their assigned ports. TG 30.2 – which included Halsey's new flagship *South Dakota*, three other battleships, a cruiser, destroyers and submarines – set a course for San Francisco. Soon they sighted the Golden Gate, the most welcome thing they had seen in four terrible years; and as they passed beneath the great bridge, bands hailed them and their victorious Admiral with a perfectly chosen fanfare – 'There'll Be a Hot Time in the Old Town Tonight!'

Turned over the command of his fleet to Rear Admiral Howard Kingman, November 1945. Promoted to fleet admiral of the United States Navy, five stars, December 1945. Subsequently chairman of the University of Virginia's Development Fund. Goodwill tour of South America, summer 1946, where he received the Order of Liberator (Venezuela); Order of Ayacucho (Peru); Grand Cross of Legion of Merit (Chile); National Order of the Southern Cross (Brazil).

Placed on the Retired List, 1 March 1947.

During the 1950s Halsey toured Europe and Australia, looked after his business interests and resigned his board chairmanships. On 1 August 1959, he died of a heart attack at Fishers Island, Long Island Sound. His body lay in state in the Washington National Cathedral for two days before the funeral services were held on 21 August. Burial with full military honours followed at Arlington National Cemetery.

10

Admiral

Marc A. Mitscher
United States Navy

1887–1947

by
Clark G. Reynolds

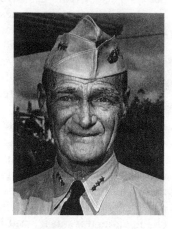

MARC *Andrew Mitscher, born Hillsborough, Wisconsin, 26 January 1887; raised in Oklahoma and Washington DC. Physically short and slight, he spent six years at the US Naval Academy, 1904–10, two longer than normal because of rambunctious conduct. This behaviour, along with only average grades, placed him well down in his class standing. Nicknamed 'Pete' by his classmates, he was quiet, rugged and wizened throughout his life.*

Following duty on eight different US warships, Mitscher underwent flight training at Naval Air Station Pensacola, Florida (1915–16) to earn his 'golden wings' as Naval Aviator No. 33. Commanded three naval air stations in rapid succession during World War One and was one of two pilots of the NC-1 flying boat in its abortive attempt to fly the Atlantic in 1919 (though the NC-4 made it). A brilliant flyer, he excelled as an early gunfire spotter for battleships (1919–21) and as an international air racer (1922 and 1923).

A pioneer in carrier aviation, Mitscher served as air officer and executive officer of both aircraft carriers Langley *and* Saratoga *during the tactical exercises which first demonstrated their offensive capabilities during the 1920s and 1930s. He performed equally well in seaplanes as chief of staff to the Base Force air commander, executive officer and captain of the seaplane tender* Wright, *and commander of Patrol Wing One at San Diego, California. Several tours of duty at the Bureau of Aeronautics in Washington culminated in his posting as Assistant Chief of Bureau, 1939–41, in the rank of captain.*

Captain 'Pete' Mitscher and Commander George R. Henderson, US Navy, had just completed a round of golf at the Norfolk Yacht Club and were having lunch in the clubhouse when a sombre ensign handed the Captain a message.

It was from the duty officer of his ship. 'Pearl Harbor has been bombed,' Mitscher read the note to Henderson, 'we're at war with Japan.' The date was 7 December 1941.[1]

The two men hastened back aboard their ship, the brand-new 19,800-ton aircraft carrier *Hornet*, commissioned less than two months before and still in the midst of shakedown training out of the great Virginia naval base. The inevitable had finally occurred, long before the navy had hoped, and Mitscher must now hasten with his green crew and air group to the Pacific to reinforce the fleet, whose main arm, the battleships, lay sunk or crippled at Pearl Harbor, Hawaii.

The small fraternity of the navy's aviators had only recently been freed from lean pre-war Congressional appropriations in the frantic race to strengthen the nation's defences after the fall of France in mid-1940. The mobilization and training of a wartime naval air force had been the task of the Chief of the Bureau of Aeronautics, Rear Admiral John H. Towers, and his Assistant Chief, Captain Mitscher, until Mitscher's transfer to the uncompleted *Hornet* in the summer of 1941. They had had to delay production of newer planes and equipment in order to build a pilot training programme for a fleet of newly authorized 27,100-ton *Essex*-class carriers. Since neither pilots, carriers nor advanced aerial weapons were expected 'to begin entering the fleet until mid-1943, the blow at Pearl Harbor forced the navy and its air arm to fight Japan on a proverbial shoestring until that time.

One crucial weapon American naval aviation did not lack, however, was leadership. The accession of Towers – since 1912 the senior career navy airman – to the helm and the promotion of career pilots like Mitscher to the grade of captain on the eve of World War Two gave the US Navy a cadre of senior aviation experts at the opportune moment. Furthermore, the projected armada of carriers and naval aircraft guaranteed the advancement of the best of these men to positions of wartime leadership. For example, Towers was immensely pleased to congratulate Mitscher on his selection for rear admiral only seven weeks after the Pearl Harbor attack. The promotion would not take effect, however, until another flag billet became available, several months hence.[2]

Naval aviation had evolved as a team effort, and this spirit of teamwork – honed over three decades of trials, errors and fatal crashes – was nowhere better exemplified than in Mitscher's *Hornet*. Mitscher had selected George Henderson as his 'exec' because of Henderson's long experience in carriers, overlooking the fact that he had been a World War One Naval Reserve pilot rather than a Naval Academy graduate. The air officer, Commander Apollo Soucek, had Academy and wide carrier and flying credentials, while

---

[1] Theodore Taylor, *The Magnificent Mitscher* (New York, 1954), pp. 104–5.

[2] Towers to Mitscher, 30 January 1942 (M. A. Mitscher papers, Naval Historical Foundation, Library of Congress, Washington DC): 'I knew you would make it.'

Commander Frank Akers, the navigator, had pioneered in aviation electronics as the first pilot to land on a carrier using instruments alone. Like Nelson's Band of Brothers, these men thought and fought as a team. And if Mitscher was anything, he was a team player.3

With only seven 'fast' carriers (thirty-plus knots) in the navy at the outbreak of war – *Saratoga, Lexington, Ranger, Yorktown, Enterprise, Wasp* and *Hornet*4 – the career aviators harboured great misgivings about the ability of men who had entered flight training late in their naval careers to lead carriers with genuine expertise. Like Towers, Mitscher disparaged these so-called JCLs (Johnny-Come-Latelies) for exploiting the fleet's need for senior aviation officers to enhance their own promotions. Rather than mere jealousy, the resentment stemmed from very real fears by the career airmen that such latecomers lacked the knowledge and experience to be effective carrier leaders; the risk was to lose not only naval battles but the precious few carriers in the process. Worse, most of the admirals then commanding carrier forces in the Pacific were not even JCLs; they were non-aviators altogether, battleship men selected for their seniority and overall abilities in the surface line. Neither group was part of the well-honed aviation team.5

Before Mitscher was even ready to take his ship to the Pacific, however, he was told to undertake an unusual experiment – launching two army air force B-25 twin-engine bombers from *Hornet*. Though these were landplanes, Mitscher figured he could do it and handily accomplished the feat off Norfolk early in February 1942. No one confided to him the purpose of the exercise, but he and his officers guessed what it portended. Fresh sailing orders simply instructed him to depart with *Hornet* for the west coast at the beginning of March. Soon after the ship arrived at San Diego, Captain Donald B. Duncan, another career aviator, came aboard for a top-secret conversation with Mitscher. Said Duncan, 'Pete, you're going to take Jimmy Doolittle and fifteen army bombers to hit Tokyo.' Mitscher, always a man of few words and masked emotions, replied, 'That's fine.'6

Lieutenant-Colonel James H. Doolittle, an old friend of Mitscher's as a counterpart in the army's aviation team, would lead the momentous attack. Immediately upon *Hornet*'s arrival at Alameda, San Francisco Bay, on 31

3Taylor, *The Magnificent Mitscher*, pp. 103–4. Henderson had spent one year at the University of Maine, earned his wings at Pensacola in August 1918, and transferred into the regular navy in 1922.

4The navy's first carrier, the *Langley*, had been converted into a seaplane tender. The *Ranger* remained in the Atlantic. The US Navy also had one escort carrier, the *Long Island*, largely for experimental purposes.

5Admiral A. A. Burke recalled that Mitscher 'used to ridicule Admiral [E. J.] King, Admiral [J. S.] McCain and Admiral [A. W.] Fitch and all the other johnny-come-latelies ...'. Quoted in Vice Admiral M. W. Cagle, 'Arleigh Burke – Naval Aviator', *Naval Aviation Museum Foundation*, vol. II, no. 2 (September 1981), p. 8.

6Taylor, *The Magnificent Mitscher*, pp. 111–16; Alexander R. Griffin, *A Ship to Remember: The Saga of the Hornet* (New York, 1943), pp. 45–9; Carroll V. Glines, *The Doolittle Raid* (New York, 1988), pp. 21–2.

March, sixteen B-25s were hoisted aboard by crane. Two days later the ship, with escorting cruisers and destroyers, sortied for a direct voyage to the target, joined en route by Vice Admiral William F. Halsey Jr [*q.v.*] with *Enterprise* and more escorts out of Pearl Harbor. With the B-25s crowding *Hornet*'s flight deck, the 'Big E' had to provide all fighter and scouting services for this Task Force 16. Morale in *Hornet* ran up to a fever pitch from the moment Mitscher announced their destination.[7]

Mitscher performed his part of the Halsey–Doolittle raid without a hitch, using his own team to counsel the B-25 crews for the mission. Early on 18 April the force unexpectedly encountered Japanese patrol vessels (the one in view was sunk by cruiser fire) and had to launch immediately in hope that the element of surprise should not be lost. Mitscher's and Doolittle's crews had rehearsed the launching procedures so well that in spite of heavy seas they were able to get all sixteen B-25s into the air in fifty-nine minutes for the 668-mile flight to Tokyo and three other Japanese cities. As the ships then turned eastward for home, Mitscher had planes of the *Hornet* air group brought up from the hangar to resume the carrier's own defence: F4F Wildcat fighters, SBD Dauntless scout/ dive bombers, and TBD Devastator torpedo bombers. The Doolittle raiders accomplished their task with great skill and only minimal losses, going on to crashland in China. As far as Mitscher was concerned (and as he recommended to the navy) more such raids should be undertaken without delay, 'to keep up morale and action exhilaration'.[8]

It was not to be, for the singular air-raid on the Japanese homeland was only one aspect of the US Navy's strategy of a fleet in being. In the stratagem practised in 1690 by Admiral Lord Torrington against the superior French navy, the American Pacific Fleet was carrying out hit-and-run raids against Japanese island outposts in order to keep the enemy off-balance until the fleet was strong enough to assume the offensive. This included strengthening Allied island airbases in the South Pacific and concentrating available carrier strength to contest Japanese fleet movements. *Hornet* and *Enterprise* combined both missions in early May 1942 by ferrying Marine Corps fighters to the New Hebrides Islands and, en route, racing towards the Coral Sea to join *Yorktown* and *Lexington* in stopping a Japanese invasion force moving into these waters. They arrived too late, though the latter carriers stopped the Japanese in the Battle of the Coral Sea, but at the cost of *Lexington*. After launching the Marine planes to Nouméa, Mitscher sped *Hornet* back to Hawaii.[9]

7Glines, *The Doolittle Raid*, p. 50; Samuel Eliot Morison, *History of United States Naval Operations in World War II* (Boston, 1957), vol. III, p. 391. The extra plane was to have been launched as a demonstration for the other army pilots, but it was retained instead for the mission once the ship was at sea.

8Morison, *History of United States Naval Operations*, vol. III, pp. 394–8; Griffin, *The Doolittle Raid*, pp. 65–8; Taylor, *The Magnificent Mitscher*, p. 121.

9Griffin, *The Doolittle Raid*, pp. 72–80; [E. T. Stover] (Clark G. Reynolds (ed.)), *The Saga of Smokey Stover* (Charleston, 1978), p. 28.

Captain Mitscher's disappointment at not being able to engage enemy forces proved short-lived. Soon after arriving at Pearl, he learned of his advancement to rear admiral, effective 31 May. But he was prevented from relinquishing *Hornet* to his relief because the main Japanese fleet was reported advancing towards Midway Island in the western Hawaiian group with a view to capturing it. A turnover of ship command required at least a few days, and before that could happen *Hornet* sortied for battle on the 28th.[10]

Her unblooded ship's company and pilots went into the Battle of Midway with full confidence in the only skipper the ship had ever known. They respected his obvious professionalism and no-nonsense way of doing things – 'Mitscher was a guy you didn't fool with,' one sailor remarked over a petty incident at the time. He knew how to whip his men into a fighting spirit, keeping them informed as events unfolded and sneering with them at the hated foe: 'Let's get a few more yellowtails,' he said as *Hornet* waded into the epic battle. He engaged in some lighthearted tomfoolery with his officers to help ease the pre-battle tension and conveyed to his flyers the sincere impression that, as a former pilot himself, he would go to any reasonable lengths to protect them or to rescue them if necessary.[11]

Hornet and *Enterprise* still comprised the striking power of Task Force 16, now commanded by Rear Admiral Raymond A. Spruance [*q.v.*], Halsey having been hospitalized with a severe skin ailment. Though a non-aviator without carrier experience, Spruance had led Halsey's cruiser screen in the early raids and retained Halsey's air staff. Admiral Chester W. Nimitz [*q.v.*], Commander-in-Chief Pacific Fleet, directed the American forces in general from Pearl Harbor, and Rear Admiral Frank Jack Fletcher, another non-aviator, led the task force centred on *Yorktown*. The Japanese fleet had four carriers to Nimitz's three.

Shortly after dawn on 4 June, *Hornet*, steaming north of Midway with *Enterprise*, received word of Japanese carrier air strikes on the island, along with orders to launch a full deckload strike in the presumed direction of the enemy carrier force. The five strike leaders of the *Hornet* air group raced up to the Captain's bridge for a final word from Mitscher. Most concerned about the TBD torpedo planes – short-ranged (175 miles), sluggish and always vulnerable to fighters and anti-aircraft fire – Mitscher gave a final pat on the shoulder of the skipper of Torpedo Squadron 8, Lieutenant-Commander J. C. 'Jack' Waldron. The fighters took off first, ten Wildcats for escort, then thirty-four SBD scout-bombers, and finally all fifteen torpedo planes. They headed to the south-west. Afterwards, all that Mitscher and his shipmates could do was wait.[12]

---

[10]Griffin, *The Doolittle Raid*, pp. 100–1; Taylor, *The Magnificent Mitscher*, pp. 122, 126; Gordon W. Prange, *Miracle at Midway* (New York, 1982), p. 111.

[11]Walter Lord, *Incredible Victory* (New York, 1967), pp. 32, 59; Taylor, *The Magnificent Mitscher*, pp. 127–8. See Stover, *The Saga of Smokey Stover*, p. 19, for Mitscher's berating sentries who left their posts.

[12]Taylor, *The Magnificent Mitscher*, pp. 130–1; Griffin, *The Doolittle Raid*, pp. 126–8; Morison, *History of United States Naval Operations*, vol. IV (1949), pp. 113–14; Prange, *Miracle at Midway*, p. 242.

Mitscher had worked out the plan of attack with his air group commander, Lieutenant-Commander Stanhope C. Ring. Covered by the Wildcats of Fighting 8 high aloft at 19,000 feet, the dive bombers of Bombing 8 and Scouting 8 would make high-angle drops in a co-ordinated attack with Torpedo 8, coming in at masthead level, below 1,000 feet. Unfortunately, this mission was a search-strike, and when the air group arrived at the expected enemy position the placid Pacific below them lay devoid of ships. Equally bad, an increasingly overcast sky caused the four squadrons to lose sight of one another and become separated – with doctrinal radio silence frustrating any possible rendezvous. Then, instead of flying in an expanding search square, which would have consumed too much of the precious aviation fuel for a return flight, Stan Ring elected to press straight ahead for fifty miles. At that point, Ring split up his bombers and fighters to look for *Hornet* in order to land aboard and refuel. Ring found the ship and brought twenty-one SBDs aboard, the other bombers going on to Midway. But all ten fighters got lost and ditched in the sea, out of fuel.[13]

Meanwhile, Jack Waldron – unaware that his escorting comrades were no longer above the overhead clouds – used his aviation knowhow to reason that the enemy fleet had probably begun to withdraw after launching its attack planes. He therefore headed north-west with Torpedo 8, exercising the individual initiative that was the hallmark of aggressive aviation tactics. That he was correct had already been confirmed in *Hornet*, for Mitscher had received intelligence that the four Japanese carriers had done just that. But because of the requirement to maintain radio silence, Mitscher did not have this crucial intelligence relayed to his flyers. It was the worst mistake of Mitscher's career, and he probably knew it after the battle. Waldron had made a correct estimate of the tactical situation, whereas Ring had not.[14]

For now the fifteen defenceless TBDs flew on alone, doomed if they tried to engage the Japanese fleet singlehandedly, but still ignorant of the whereabouts of their mates or of the *Enterprise* and *Yorktown* air groups. Before long, according to one account, Waldron's voice crackled over *Hornet*'s radio saying that he had spotted columns of smoke – obviously from already damaged enemy ships over the horizon – and requested permission 'to withdraw from action to refuel'. As it was, his planes probably lacked sufficient fuel to make it back, depending on the position of the ship. But Mitscher and his officers knew the opportunity was a golden one, especially if other squadrons were in the vicinity to support Waldron. 'Attack at once!' they ordered him.[15]

Waldron did. Torpedo 8 lined up for its torpedo runs – the mandatory straight, low approach necessary for a proper altitude, angle and speed of release. But this formation also made the TBDs sitting ducks for the defending Japanese Zero fighters which began to pounce on them from above. One by

[13]Prange, *Miracle at Midway*, pp. 243–5; Stover, *The Saga of Smokey Stover*, p. 30; Lord, *Incredible Victory*, p. 141.
[14]Prange, *Miracle at Midway*, pp. 244–5; Taylor, *The Magnificent Mitscher*, p. 132.
[15]Griffin, *The Doolittle Raid*, p. 130.

one the hapless Devastators were shot down, and eight miles from the Japanese carriers the surviving American planes came under anti-aircraft fire from the enemy ships as well. All fifteen TBDS were thus destroyed, without scoring a hit, and only one pilot survived to be rescued later.

But Waldron's sacrifice was not without its reward. The enemy Zeros and ships, preoccupied with this slaughter, failed utterly to notice the arrival, high above, of dive bombers from *Enterprise* and *Yorktown*. These came screaming down to drop their bombs squarely on to the decks of three of the Japanese carriers, which erupted in explosions and flames. Over the horizon to the south, one of *Hornet*'s fighter pilots spotted the smoke billowing skyward just as he ditched into the sea out of petrol.[16]

The fog of battle, complicated greatly by the mandatory radio silence, only gradually yielded the true tactical situation to the US fleet. For Mitscher, it was sickening: Torpedo 8 annihilated; his bombers had missed the fight; and ten of his fighters had disappeared (most were rescued eventually). He kept defensive fighters airborne and quickly despatched them to help repel a bombing attack on *Yorktown* by planes from the fourth enemy carrier. But it was too late; *Yorktown* was stricken and would later sink. One of that carrier's planes sought refuge on *Hornet* but crashlanded on the deck, its machine-guns being triggered, killing or wounding twenty-five crewmen. The ship sent off its own dive bombers in a late-afternoon strike but failed to hit two enemy cruisers after *Enterprise* bombers had mortally damaged the fourth Japanese carrier. Mitscher lighted up his flight deck to assist his pilots – unskilled in night landings – in coming aboard. He repeated this bold action – in defiance of lurking enemy submarines – the next night after strikes on the retiring Japanese fleet.[17]

During the night of the main action (4–5 June), Admiral Spruance had his carriers retire to the eastward, a decision which frustrated the aggressive Mitscher, especially in light of the great victory. All four Japanese carriers had been sunk, and active pursuit could well have enabled the American bombers to finish off the enemy's gun ships. Given the uncertain condition of the crippled *Yorktown*, however, Spruance preferred not to risk *Hornet* and *Enterprise* unduly. Mitscher also told his officers that Spruance had erred in not keeping all three American carriers concentrated within visual contact during the battle in order to enhance their mutual protection. Spruance, however, resumed his westward course at daylight, and on 6 June *Hornet* and *Enterprise* SBDS made low bombing drops on two Japanese heavy cruisers, sinking one and seriously damaging another. Mitscher could take pride in that.[18]

[16]Morison, *History of United States Naval Operations*, vol. IV, pp. 116–20; Stover, *The Saga of Smokey Stover*, pp. 30–1; Lord, *Incredible Victory*, pp. 142–3.

[17]Taylor, *The Magnificent Mitscher*, pp. 132–5; Prange, *Miracle at Midway*, p. 291; Lord, *Incredible Victory*, p. 269.

[18]Taylor, *The Magnificent Mitscher*, pp. 135–6; Thomas B. Buell, *The Quiet Warrior: A Biography of Admiral Raymond A. Spruance* (Boston, 1974), pp. 139–43; Morison, *History of United States Naval Operations*, vol. IV, pp. 149–50.

The epic Battle of Midway was over – the island was not invaded, and the striking power of Japan's carrier force had been decimated. But Mitscher was not happy; he had lost many friends and comrades, and the performance of his team had been questionable. The normally uncritical Spruance shared this view by blaming Ring's failure to locate the enemy carriers with *Hornet*'s bombers for the loss of *Yorktown*. If *Hornet*'s SBDs had made contact, the fourth enemy carrier could have been sunk rather than attacking *Yorktown*. Furthermore, *Hornet* had disobeyed Spruance's orders to arm with 500-pound bombs on 5 June by partly using 1,000-pounders. Despite the clear victory, the confused battle generated acrimony and debate which would continue for many years.[19]

Within a week of the battle, Admiral Nimitz ordered Admiral Mitscher to retain his flag on *Hornet* for possible action, but in July transferred him ashore as Commander Patrol Wing Two in Hawaii. Mitscher's long pre-war experience in patrol aviation suited him well for handling PBY Catalina seaplanes in Hawaiian waters, and he was due for a respite from further combat afloat. But he chafed at going ashore, convinced he had fallen into disfavour – an unlikely surmise, for Mitscher had been one of six career aviators of thirty-nine admirals and admiral-selectees that Admiral Towers at the Navy Department in March had recommended to Admiral Ernest J. King [*q.v.*], Commander-in-Chief US Fleet, as the officers best suited for high command. This was part of Towers' campaign to place career airmen in the crucial aviation commands, an insistence that led to Towers' premature transfer out of Washington in October. But Towers also reported to Hawaii, shore-based as administrative commander of the Pacific Fleet's air forces. One of Towers' first recommendations to Admiral Nimitz was, on Mitscher's advice, to transfer Mitscher's patrol bombers – and Mitscher himself – from their idle training chores in Hawaii to advanced bases in the embattled South Pacific.[20]

Not only planes but knowledgeable leaders were in great demand, for American and Allied forces had invaded Guadalcanal in the Solomon Islands in August and for many weeks fought off determined Japanese counterattacks. Finally, at the end of December 1942, Mitscher followed several of his PBY squadrons to the South Pacific theatre as Commander Fleet Air at Nouméa. There he forged a team of trusted associates into an efficient staff, selected for their ability, ideas and willingness to challenge their boss. Commander Stan Ring soon arrived to be Chief of Staff. Commander W. A.

---

[19]Prange, *Miracle at Midway*, pp. 244–5, 248; Taylor, *The Magnificent Mitscher*, p. 138; Buell, *The Quiet Warrior*, pp. 143, 149.

[20]Morison, *History of United States Naval Operations*, vol. IV, p. 257; Clerk G. Reynolds, *Admiral John H. Towers: The Struggle for Naval Air Supremacy* (Annapolis, 1991), pp. 384–5; Taylor, *The Magnificent Mitscher*, pp. 139–40. The other five picked by Towers – in consultation with career airmen Captains D. C. Ramsey, A. W. Radford, R. E. Davison and Forrest P. Sherman – were Towers himself, P. N. L. Bellinger, C. A. Pownall, C. P. Mason and Ramsey.

'Gus' Read, a World War One naval aviator and peacetime banker whose administrative skills Mitscher had witnessed at the Bureau, became an operational planner. The irrepressible, unorthodox Commander Luis de Florez, a renowned civilian inventor and pilot, rotated between the Bureau and Mitscher's staff to test new techniques and aeronautical devices against the enemy. These and other talented officers would remain at Mitscher's side for significant periods of their Admiral's wartime service.[21]

Mitscher's pragmatic brand of leadership yielded handsome results as the Japanese quit Guadalcanal in February 1943 and began to reel from growing Allied air power in the South Pacific. The Japanese focused their air attacks on Guadalcanal, a furious and extended assault that caused the local air commander at that base to break under the pressure. The theatre commander, Admiral Halsey, had no doubt who should step in to become Commander Air Solomons and lead the fight: 'That's why I sent Pete Mitscher up there,' said Halsey later. 'Pete was a fighting fool and I knew it.'[22]

Mitscher directed US Navy, Army and Marine Corps and Royal New Zealand Air Force planes in the defence of Guadalcanal and the assault on New Georgia Island in the central Solomons from April until July 1943. Since it was a combined-service command, air doctrines and personalities often conflicted. Furthermore, his Chief of Staff was a Marine, Brigadier-General Field Harris, assisted however by Ring and Read. But in no time the flyers were welded into the inevitable team that was a Mitscher trademark, as they learned to appreciate his patience, determination and genius at command. The tide of battle inexorably turned towards the Allies in the South Pacific, while Mitscher cast covetous eyes on the new *Essex*-class carriers then entering the fleet. He wanted to join them, but malaria soon added to his growing exhaustion, and he had to be sent home in late summer to rest and recuperate for more important commands. His detachment from his important work however frustrated both Admirals Halsey and Towers; 'his combat experience afloat and ashore is very badly needed', wrote the former to the latter.[23]

A haggard Pete Mitscher reported to San Diego as Commander Fleet Air West Coast in August 1943. Towers had instructed Mitscher's new Chief of Staff, Captain John Perry, to indulge him in his favourite passions of fishing and hunting in order to 'get him back in shape as soon as possible'. He could also spend some time with his wife of thirty years, Frances (they had no children). The respite proved to be an elixir, with Mitscher doing little more on the job than signing official papers for training the new carrier air groups prior to their being deployed for combat with the Pacific Fleet. Within a month of

[21]Taylor, *The Magnificent Mitscher*, pp. 141–3, 146.
[22]Halsey quoted in Taylor, ibid., pp. 144–5. Mitscher relieved Rear Admiral Charles P. Mason, the officer who had relieved him as captain of the *Hornet* after Midway.
[23]Taylor, *The Magnificent Mitscher*, pp. 145ff; Halsey to Towers, 10 June 1943 (William F. Halsey Jr papers, Naval Historical Foundation, Library of Congress); Towers to Rear Admiral J. S. McCain, 2 May 1943 (Naval Historical Center).

assuming this relaxing schedule, Mitscher became impatient and wrote to Towers to say, 'I am feeling great now. When do I get out of here [?]'[24]

Towers knew that one month was hardly enough time to recuperate, but in any case no job existed for Mitscher in the post-Pearl Harbor fleet of new warships gathering in Hawaii for the counter-offensive against Japan. The Central Pacific Force, formed in August under the command of Vice Admiral Spruance, had received no fewer than eleven fast (thirty-three-knot) carriers by mid-November when it assaulted the Japanese-held Gilbert Islands. The senior carrier division commander, Rear Admiral Charles A. Pownall, a Naval Academy classmate of Mitscher's, was made Commander Fast Carrier Forces Pacific Fleet and undertook several raids against enemy island outposts before the Gilberts operation. Pownall's performance in these raids and at the Gilberts, however, was lacklustre, culminating in downright ineptness during a carrier raid on Kwajalein in the Marshall Islands early in December.

On Christmas Day, Admiral Nimitz asked Vice Admiral Towers' advice for a possible replacement for Pownall. Mitscher headed Towers' list: 'A quiet, hard-working officer, of great strength of character. He is tough and aggressive. Has always turned in a splendid job. Particular attention is invited to his recent performance of duty as ComAirSols [at Guadalcanal]. I regard him as tops for carrier task force command.'[25]

There could be no question in Nimitz's mind that his Pacific Fleet required an aggressive leader of the new carriers, which, it had by now finally become obvious, would spearhead the American offensive. Such a leader must seek out and defeat the Japanese fleet, cover and support the many planned amphibious assaults all the way to Japan, and neutralize formidable enemy land-based air forces. Nimitz decided to accept the advice of Towers and appointed Mitscher as the new fast carrier commander. Nimitz had the support of Admirals King and Halsey but not that of his trusted overall commander afloat, Spruance. The latter liked the mild-mannered Pownall and had not forgotten the failure of Mitscher's *Hornet* bombers to locate the Japanese fleet at Midway. Nimitz also overlooked Spruance's resentment of the outspoken aviators by elevating Towers to be his own deputy Pacific Fleet commander. The Pacific War had become an air war, and Mitscher assumed command of the main US naval striking arm early in January 1944.[26]

The Fast Carrier Task Force, now designated Task Force 58, belonged to Spruance's Fifth Fleet, still based in Hawaii. Mitscher spent his first week there living and working with Towers as they outlined the role of the carriers in the offensive. He selected as his flagship the new *Yorktown* because of its

---

[24]Mitscher to Towers, 13 September 1943 (Mitscher papers); Taylor, *The Magnificent Mitscher*, pp. 163–6. Towers did not reply.

[25]Clark G. Reynolds, *The Fast Carriers: The Forging of an Air Navy* (Annapolis, 1992), pp. 91ff; Towers to Nimitz, 27 December 1943 (Naval Historical Center); John H. Towers diary, entry of 25 December 1943 (Towers papers, Naval Historical Foundation, Library of Congress).

[26]Reynolds, *The Fast Carriers*, pp. 121–3; Buell, *The Quiet Warrior*, p. 216.

outstanding combat performance to date under the hard-driving part-Cherokee Indian Captain J. J. 'Jocko' Clark. Mitscher retained Pownall's staff, notably the excellent Chief of Staff, Captain Truman J. Hedding. TF 58 was divided into four task groups of three carriers each, with fast battleships, cruisers and destroyers arranged in concentric defensive cruising dispositions about the flat-tops. All four task group commanders were experienced air rear admirals whose judgement Mitscher trusted: 'I tell them *what* I want done. Not *how*!'[27]

Mitscher led the fast carriers to sea in mid-January to provide support for the infantry assaulting Kwajalein and Eniwetok atolls in the Marshall Islands. The air battles of late 1943 had decimated Japan's air forces in the region, and the fleet's new Grumman F6F Hellcat fighters had no trouble eliminating the few planes and inferior pilots which contested the invasion on the very first attack day, 29 January 1944. Like his superiors, Mitscher hoped that the operation would lure the Japanese Combined Fleet out of its anchorage at Truk in the eastern Carolines. When this did not occur, the carriers spent the week providing close air support for the successful Marine Corps and army assault troops. Majuro atoll and its vast lagoon was also taken, giving the fleet an invaluable forward anchorage, thereby enhancing its mobility and eliminating the necessity of returning to Hawaii.[28]

The relative ease of this quick victory caused Admiral Nimitz to order an immediate carrier strike against the much feared bastion of Truk, hoping to catch the enemy fleet there. This was music to Mitscher's ears, for it meant that the fast carriers could demonstrate their offensive mobility and power. Any fears over Truk's defences proved unfounded when (on 16 February) Hellcats from nine carriers swept in on Truk and obliterated the defending 250 airborne and grounded planes, though Japanese anti-aircraft fire was more deadly than before. The enemy fleet had escaped some days earlier, but in the space of forty-eight hours Mitscher's bombers sank some 200,000 tons of merchant shipping, while Spruance's gun ships sank a fleeing cruiser and destroyer.

The success at Truk was so complete that Nimitz released Mitscher with six carriers to head further west to test the defences of the Mariana Islands. Now in independent command, Mitscher pressed ahead, undeterred even when a Japanese patrol plane detected TF 58 during its final night-time run-in to the target on 21–22 February. 'We have been sighted by the enemy,' announced Mitscher to the force. 'We will fight our way in!' His skilful anti-aircraft gunners repelled several enemy bombers, and just before dawn he sent off his planes against Saipan, Guam and Tinian. There they destroyed 168 Japanese

[27]Quoted in Taylor, *The Magnificent Mitscher*, p. 171. Recalled Clark of Mitscher: 'A thin, wiry little man, completely bald, with sharp blue eyes, he would scarcely talk above a whisper. I had to learn to read his lips to understand him. . . .' Admiral J. J. Clark, with Clark G. Reynolds, *Carrier Admiral* (New York, 1967), p. 143.
[28]Reynolds, *The Fast Carriers*, pp. 134–5.

aircraft (against six planes lost) and sank several transports, assisted by American submarines. TF 58 returned to Majuro flushed with victory.[29]

Mitscher's dramatic achievements with the carriers not only won him promotion to vice admiral in March, but also enabled Allied strategic planners to decide to bypass Truk rather than assault it, thus accelerating the Pacific offensive timetable. Mitscher was now able to choose the best staff officers, task group commanders and ship captains for TF 58 – with one exception. Admiral King had ruled that all non-aviator admirals should have aviators as deputies or chiefs of staff – hence Towers' elevation to be Nimitz's deputy. This would better integrate aviation into the top commands of the air-oriented fleet. But the reverse was also ordered: air admirals like Mitscher would have non-aviators assigned as their chief advisers. So outraged was Mitscher by this directive that he let Captain Hedding select the man: Captain Arleigh A. 'Thirty-One-Knot Burke' [*q.v.*], a celebrated destroyer leader in the Solomons. Burke reported late in March, equally disgruntled at being yanked from his beloved destroyers. The two men barely spoke to one another for weeks, but the frostiness melted away as they learned mutual respect for the other's talents. Soon they became inseparable and would remain so for the rest of Mitscher's life.[30]

In preparation for the next major invasion – Saipan in the Marianas in June 1944 – Mitscher and TF 58 were charged with raiding Japanese island aerodromes further west to weaken the defences of the Marianas and to support the assault on Hollandia, New Guinea by General Douglas MacArthur's forces. Hoisting his flag in the new *Lexington*, Mitscher again brushed off Japanese 'snoopers' on the final run-in to the Palau group of the western Carolines on 30–31 March and unleashed his planes against aircraft and merchant shipping targets with devastating effect. Returning briefly to Majuro, the fast carriers then struck northern New Guinea's defences 21–23 April but found that US Army Air Forces had already cleared the way for MacArthur at Hollandia. During the retirement, Mitscher received orders to revisit Truk, recently reinforced by Japanese aircraft. So the task force pummelled the place again on 29–30 April, finally rendering the once mighty bastion impotent as an aerodrome. 'I can go anywhere and nobody can stop me,' Mitscher remarked to Luis de Florez. 'If I go in and destroy all their aircraft, their damned island is no good to them anyhow.'[31]

This could sound like over-confidence, but Mitscher's first four months at the helm of the most powerful naval striking force the world had ever known had enabled him to hone his command skills to near perfection. In spite of

[29]Ibid., pp. 136–41; Mitscher quoted in Taylor, *The Magnificent Mitscher*, pp. 186, 188–9. For a detailed account of these operations as undertaken by Mitscher's flagship, see Clark G. Reynolds, *The Fighting Lady: The New Yorktown in the Pacific War* (Missoula, Montana, 1986), pp. 94–108.

[30]Taylor, *The Magnificent Mitscher*, pp. 189–94; Oliver Jensen, *Carrier War* (New York, 1945), p. 19. Burke became Chief of Naval Operations in 1955 for six years.

[31]Quoted in Taylor, *The Magnificent Mitscher*, p. 189.

Admiral Spruance's overall seniority, Mitscher had usually exercised tactical control, and had won the confidence of his pilots and crews – especially for employing submarines as 'lifeguards' for downed aviators. He shared Admiral Towers' opinions of the officers best suited to be his task group commanders and carrier skippers, summarily relieving two of the former and one of the latter who did not measure up. He preferred aggressive fighters such as Rear Admirals Alfred E. Montgomery, Frederick C. 'Ted' Sherman and J. W. 'Black Jack' Reeves Jr, who erred on the side of commission rather than omission, though he might disagree and argue with them; and he settled upon the equally tough Rear Admiral Jocko Clark to be his premier task group leader for the duration.

In aircraft, the F6F Hellcat had beaten the Zero fighter in nearly every dogfight; the TBF Avenger had become the reliable anti-ship torpedo bomber; and the big though difficult SB2C Helldiver gradually replaced the SBD dive bomber. Mitscher kept four night fighters – Hellcats and F4U Corsairs – on each large carrier but rarely employed them because they deprived his deck crews of much needed sleep and risked dangerous deck crashes. The Corsair would later join the Hellcat as a regular day carrier fighter, flown by Marines as well as navy pilots.[32]

On 6 June 1944 – D-Day in Europe – Mitscher sortied with the fifteen fast carriers and their 900 planes for the invasion of the Marianas. This truly promised to test the staying power of ships and aircraft. Mitscher expected to face the concentrated land-based air power of Japan's island base network as well as the new carriers of the Mobile Fleet – stronger than ever since Midway two years before. With the Marine Corps and army assault at Saipan set for the 15th, Mitscher planned to work over the target island and the airfields on adjacent Tinian, Guam and Rota with air strikes over the preceding three days. En route, however, he changed his mind. Remembering the inevitable night-time air searches and attacks by Japanese planes as soon as the carriers were in their range, he decided to launch an unprecedented late-afternoon fighter sweep on the 11th, hoping to catch the enemy off guard. These flexible tactics worked admirably; the 211 attacking Hellcats eliminated all 150 aircraft in the Marianas, leaving the next three days for other missions.[33]

While the planes bombed and strafed all four islands, US intelligence learned that the Japanese were indeed going to contest the invasion with all their available power. Large numbers of land-based planes were flying down from Japan to Chichi Jima and Iwo Jima for staging south to the Marianas. And the Japanese fleet threatened to disgorge from the Philippines to engage TF 58; its accurately estimated strength was nine carriers mounting some 450

---

[32]Reynolds, *The Fast Carriers*, pp. 146–55. Mitscher replaced Rear Admiral S. P. Ginder after Palau, Captain Miles R. Browning for general incompetence and Rear Admiral W. K. Harrill during the Marianas in July. So keen was he on Clark that he kept him in the Pacific in February rather than letting him be rotated Stateside for the usual breaking in as a new flag officer.

[33]Ibid., pp. 156–62, 169–74; Taylor, *The Magnificent Mitscher*, pp. 208–11.

aircraft. The immediate threat was the former, whereupon Spruance ordered Mitscher to detach two of the four fast carrier task groups to head north and eliminate the Japanese air reinforcements at the 'Jimas'. As the two groups set their course late on 14 June, Spruance learned from American submarines that the Japanese fleet was on the move. He instructed Mitscher to recall his Jimas-bound carriers after only one instead of two days of strikes in order that they could participate in the anticipated fleet action. The aggressive Jocko Clark, however, raced ahead of schedule to get in the two days of strikes which decimated the Japanese planes in those islands on the 15th and 16th.34

Mitscher relished the prospect of finally facing the Japanese with the full weight of TF 58. As fresh intelligence arrived, he plotted the Mobile Fleet's reported positions with his key advisers – Captains Burke [*q.v.*] and Hedding and the new operations officer, veteran bomber and fighter pilot Commander W. J. 'Gus' Widhelm. On the 17th, Mitscher received Spruance's battle plan: TF 58, its screen reinforced by more cruisers and destroyers from the amphibious bombardment force off Saipan, would steam west to attack the Japanese fleet in a carrier battle, possibly on the 18th. The amphibious shipping would retire to safety 200 miles to the east, leaving the bombardment force – principally seven pre-war battleships and eight new but smaller escort carriers – twenty-five miles west of Saipan. Mitscher was instructed to detach the seven fast battleships from the carrier task group screens to form a battle line fifteen miles ahead of the carriers under the tactical battleship commander, Vice Admiral W. A. 'Ching' Lee. Although Spruance hoped for a traditional gunnery duel, this battle line would also provide a heavy anti-aircraft barrage against incoming enemy planes and enhance the freedom of the carriers to manoeuvre in and out of the wind to launch and recover aircraft during the battle. Mitscher asked Spruance his plans for the night, and Spruance replied that Mitscher should 'proceed at your discretion', thus implying that Mitscher retained tactical command.35

Welcoming the return of the two task groups from the Jimas foray early on 18 June, Mitscher headed west with his fifteen fast carriers and escorts and Lee's battle line. While his long-legged Hellcat fighters searched 350 miles ahead, Mitscher asked Lee if his battleships could engage the enemy surface units in a night action, leaving the carriers to launch massive strikes at dawn on the 19th to finish the job. But Lee declined, his crews untrained for such a task after months of inaction with their main batteries. This disappointed Mitscher, for it meant that TF 58 might have to retire eastward again; American wartime pilots had generally neglected night training and operations. Lee's reluctance also fouled Spruance's battle plan, Spruance now agreeing to a night retirement. This defensive attitude mystified Mitscher, his staff and his carrier admirals, for it meant that TF 58 would be tied to the beach by dawn on the 19th, when Japanese carrier strikes could be expected to attack in force. And

34Reynolds, *The Fast Carriers*, pp. 174–9.
35Ibid., pp. 179–81; Buell, *The Quiet Warrior*, pp. 264–6.

since Mitscher's carriers would have to head into the wind – eastward – in order to launch planes, they would not be able to steam westward to attack the Japanese fleet during the day.

Furthermore, fresh intelligence on the 18th indicated two new developments. First, the Japanese fleet seemed to be split into two groups – to the west and south-west. This old Japanese ploy suggested an end-run by one part to fall on the Saipan beaches. What Spruance, the non-aviator, failed to grasp was what Mitscher and the aviation team took for granted: surface ships could not outflank a carrier force whose planes patrolled out to 250 miles. Mitscher's staff believed that any secondary force would inflict heavy damage at Saipan only (in Burke's words) with 'an inordinate amount of luck'. Any such force was therefore unlikely to undertake an attempt of that nature, for it would surely be annihilated.

Apparently confirming this belief, the Japanese fleet seemed to be slowing down. It looked as if it intended to stay beyond the range of Mitscher's carrier planes but to launch long, 400-mile one-way strikes on TF 58 on the 19th. The aircraft could land on Guam to refuel, then shuttle back to the fleet. A message from Admiral Nimitz's staff, written by Towers, had so forewarned Spruance on the 16th. Spruance paid little heed, however, and took the safer course of retiring during the night to be certain of protecting the Saipan beachhead (although the transports had moved 200 miles to the east, out of any danger). Spruance's battle plan had failed to account for either eventuality – the end-run or one-way shuttle strikes – and at sunset he succumbed to caution and turned TF 58 eastward.[36]

Mitscher was not happy. By turning the back of the Fast Carrier Task Force to the enemy, Spruance had assumed tactical command. As the night of 18–19 June wore on, an enemy radio transmission placed the Mobile Fleet Main Force 355 miles to the west-south-west. If TF 58 reversed course in that direction just after midnight, the carriers would be within 200 miles of the enemy at dawn – optimum range for a full deckload strike by over 400 planes at that moment. 'It might be a hell of a battle for a while,' Mitscher remarked to his staff, 'but I think we can win it.' He radioed his recommendation to Spruance, but the latter demurred, still fearing the so-called end-run. Mitscher and the staff were dumbfounded. Spruance had revealed himself to be a formalist in the tradition of conservative fleet tacticians of the pre-Rodney era. Mitscher, by contrast, was a mêléeist of the Nelson mould – aggressive, flexible, accustomed to seizing the initiative by careful timing.[37]

Shortly after sun-up on 19 June 1944, Japanese planes began attacking

[36]Reynolds, *The Fast Carriers*, pp. 181–7; Taylor, *The Magnificent Mitscher*, pp. 217ff; Buell, *The Quiet Warrior*, pp. 268–70; Towers diary, 13–15 June 1944; A. A. Burke transcribed interview, 'The First Battle of the Philippine Sea: Decision Not to Force an Action on the Night of 18–19 June' [1944] (1945) (US Naval Academy Library, Annapolis, Maryland), pp. 4–5.

[37]Reynolds, *The Fast Carriers*, pp. 163–9, 187–90; Burke, 'The First Battle of the Philippine Sea', p. 10; Buell, *The Quiet Warrior*, pp. 270–3; Taylor, *The Magnificent Mitscher*, pp. 220–2.

TF 58 – from Guam and from the Mobile Fleet. The Battle of the Philippine Sea was on. But it would be dubbed the 'Marianas Turkey Shoot', for the Japanese pilots – most of them inferior and undertrained – ran into a veritable wall of 450 defensive Hellcat fighters flown by highly trained combat veterans. The waves of attackers continued most of the day, until some 400 had been destroyed in the air or on Guam, trying to refuel – at the cost of only twenty-five US planes. What was more, the submarines which had been stalking the nine Japanese carriers attacked and sank two of them. With their aircraft expended, the seven surviving Japanese flat-tops turned tail for home, but the cautious Spruance still did not release Mitscher and TF 58 to pursue until well after sundown.

All next day (the 20th) Mitscher's planes searched westward, finally making contact in mid-afternoon. Mitscher sent off a strike of 215 planes, knowing his short-legged bombers might run out of fuel on the return flight. They caught up with the Mobile Fleet for a wild, uncoordinated attack in the last glow of sunset but sank only one carrier with aerial torpedoes. Mitscher and his task group commanders lighted up the force to assist the night recoveries, an audacious action, given the possibility of lurking enemy subs. Fortunately none appeared. Water landings contributed to the 100 American planes lost in the desperate gamble; nevertheless all but sixteen pilots and thirty-three aircrew-men were rescued.[38]

Even so, Mitscher remained unsatisfied. 'The enemy had escaped,' he wrote in his action report of the battle. 'His fleet was not sunk.' Six Japanese carriers had survived to fight again, and controversy over Spruance's tactics would rage from that day on.

Whatever the verdict, no one could dispute the fact that the aircraft carrier – and its admirals – had changed the character of naval warfare; but Mitscher knew that through no fault of his own he had missed the chance of a lifetime.[39]

From late June to mid-August Mitscher kept TF 58 in the Marianas supporting the invasions and conquest of Saipan, Guam and Tinian. His almost unbroken combat leadership had lasted seven months, making him due for a rest. Admiral King had devised a two-platoon arrangement whereby Spruance and Mitscher would go ashore and be replaced by Halsey and Vice Admiral John Sidney McCain respectively, both late-comer aviators. King also wanted Mitscher to return to Washington to lead the navy's fight against a growing movement to unify the armed forces. If successful, this unification could lose the navy's air arm to an independent air force. But since Halsey

[38]Reynolds, *The Fast Carriers*, pp. 190–204; Taylor, *The Magnificent Mitscher*, pp. 224ff. For the flight and recovery of Air Group 16 planes from Mitscher's flagship *Lexington*, see Joseph Bryan III and Philip Read, *Mission Beyond Darkness* (New York, 1945).

[39]Mitscher (CTF 58) Action Report, 11 September 1944 (authored by Burke and the staff) (Naval Historical Center). On the controversy, see Taylor, *The Magnificent Mitscher*, pp. 238–40; Reynolds, *The Fast Carriers*, pp. 204–10; Buell, *The Quiet Warrior*, pp. 277–80; and William T. Y'Blood, *Red Sun Setting: The Battle of the Philippine Sea* (Annapolis, Maryland, 1981), pp. 203–11.

lacked experience with the new carrier armada, and because none of the senior admirals had confidence in McCain (a King favourite), King agreed to keep Mitscher in task force command until both Halsey and McCain were broken in to their new responsibilities. Mitscher (who was anyway inarticulate in military politics and unskilled for the Washington post) would then go home on leave and assist Spruance in planning subsequent operations that both men would again lead. Thus in August, Mitscher's title changed from Commander Fast Carrier Force Pacific Fleet to Commander 1st Fast Carrier Task Force, with McCain in command of the Second.[40]

During early September, preliminary to the liberation of the Philippines, Mitscher's redesignated Task Force 38 struck the Jimas and supported the Marines at Peleliu in the western Carolines. The Mitscher team centred on Commodore Burke (Chief of Staff) and the new operations officer, the superb fighter tactician Commander J. H. 'Jimmy' Flatley Jr. Task group leaders were Admirals McCain, Sherman, Gerald F. Bogan and Ralph E. Davison, the latter two career pilots and veteran carrier leaders. Such superior leadership guaranteed optimum performance of the sixteen fast carriers, bearing over 1,000 aircraft. Unfortunately, as events were to prove, Mitscher would find the airman Halsey exercising tactical command, for what had become the Third Fleet was little more than TF 38; the amphibious forces belonged to the Seventh Fleet under Vice-Admiral Thomas C. Kinkaid [q.v.]. Worse, Halsey and Mitscher reported to Nimitz, Commander-in-Chief Pacific Fleet, whereas Kinkaid was subordinate to General MacArthur, Commander-in-Chief South-West Pacific theatre – a violation of unity of command due largely to inter-service rivalry.

With Halsey running the show, for two weeks in October 1944 the fast carriers neutralized Japanese land-based air forces between the Philippines and southern Japan, including Okinawa and Formosa (Taiwan). This enabled Kinkaid to land MacArthur's army at Leyte in the central Philippines on the 20th. While the carriers were covering the beachhead, the Japanese fleet launched a masterful counter-stroke: two battleship forces penetrated Philippine waters from the west on the 24th, while land-based planes from Luzon attacked TF 38. Mitscher's aircraft struck both gun forces with mixed results and fended off the Luzon attackers, except for one which dropped a bomb on to the light carrier *Princeton*; the flames spread until Mitscher had to order her scuttled. Then, in late afternoon, a search flight located four Japanese carriers 190 miles north of the task force, retiring at high speed. Here was an opportunity to finish off once and for all the carriers which had escaped from the Battle of the Philippine Sea.

---

[40]King–Nimitz conference notes, San Francisco, 4–7 May 1944 (Naval Historical Center); Reynolds, *The Fast Carriers*, pp. 216–18, 232–3, 238–9. Mitscher's choice for his own relief was Rear Admiral F. C. 'Ted' Sherman, also Halsey's preference, but King prevailed. Sherman had been Captain of the old *Lexington* at the Coral Sea and a carrier task group commander throughout much of 1943 and early 1944.

But Mitscher's hands were tied again, as Halsey directed the carriers' role in this Battle of Leyte Gulf. Halsey issued a preparatory battle plan to detach four of Ching Lee's six fast battleships to guard San Bernardino Strait, lest the main force of Japanese gun ships try to penetrate it during the night of 24–25 October and attack Kinkaid's assault ships at Leyte. Lee's other two battlewagons would accompany the carriers north to destroy the enemy carriers. But that was all that Mitscher was told. Instead, Halsey kept all of Lee's ships with TF 38 as it raced north; his failure to articulate his movements – even to Mitscher, let alone Kinkaid – was then compounded by tedious manoeuvring en route. Mitscher, Burke and Flatley believed that Lee's battleships should be left to guard the Strait, but Mitscher was not about to subject himself to another rebuff like the one Spruance had given him off Saipan by recommending it to Halsey. 'If he wants my advice,' Mitscher told Flatley, 'he'll ask for it.' Lo and behold, having penetrated the Strait during the night, at dawn the main Japanese gun force appeared off Leyte and began sinking Kinkaid's ships. Halsey had Mitscher's planes sink the four planeless carriers which had lured him away from Leyte, then raced back to the strait but too late to prevent the escape of the Japanese force through it.[41]

Although the Americans won the Battle of Leyte Gulf and preserved MacArthur's beachhead, and the Japanese carrier fleet had finally been neutralized, Pete Mitscher had been thwarted again from directing the battle by a less knowledgeable superior. On 30 October he relinquished command of TF 38 to McCain, who with Halsey did not perform in the subsequent Philippine campaign nearly as ably as had Mitscher, even taking the Third Fleet into a devastating typhoon. By now, Mitscher was the measure against whom any combat admiral was measured by the men of the Pacific Fleet, a respect echoed by the renowned war correspondent Ernie Pyle when he got to know Mitscher: 'From now on, Mitscher is one of my gods.'[42]

To complete the air–sea blockade of the Japanese homeland, Spruance and Mitscher relieved Halsey and McCain at the end of January 1945. While Spruance used the amphibious component of Fifth Fleet to invade Iwo Jima in February and Okinawa in April, Mitscher and the redesignated TF 58 provided tactical close air support at the beaches and strategic support by attacking enemy aerodromes in the Ryukyu Islands, Formosa and Japan itself. It was a gruelling four-month-long campaign, virtually without respite, for the enemy had introduced the deadly suicide kamikaze corps – piloted planes that crashed into carriers and their radar picket destroyers. But Mitscher had as his lieutenants the very best task group commanders available – Jocko Clark, Ralph Davison, Ted Sherman and Arthur W. Radford, as well as M. B. Gardner leading two carriers solely for night opera-

[41]Reynolds, *The Fast Carriers*, pp. 253–84; Taylor, *The Magnificent Mitscher*, pp. 253–66; E. B. Potter, *Bull Halsey* (Annapolis, Maryland, 1985), pp. 297–9.
[42]Quoted in Taylor, *The Magnificent Mitscher*, p. 272.

tions. Four British carriers joined as TF 57 under Rear Admiral Sir Philip Vian [*q.v.*]; they conformed to Mitscher's tactical authority.

With his flag in *Bunker Hill*, Mitscher in mid-February 1945 led TF 58 in the first carrier raid on Tokyo since he had sent Doolittle's raiders there nearly three years before. One by one, however, the carriers received bomb and kamikaze hits, especially because they had to be virtually tied down off Okinawa in round-the-clock support operations. None was sunk, but several, like *Franklin*, had to withdraw for weeks or even months of repairs. Mitscher had no choice but to remain on station, much as he hated to, and his planes even sank the 72,000-ton super-battleship *Yamato* south of Japan in April. But Mitscher grew exhausted and remained in his cabin for days at a time while his staff ran the show. During the equally rigorous fighting on Guadalcanal in early 1943, rumour had had it that he had suffered two unreported heart attacks. Now Arleigh Burke was convinced that Mitscher had another one off Okinawa. On 11 May a kamikaze slammed into the flagship *Bunker Hill*, killing thirteen men of the staff and many others. Mitscher shifted his flag to *Enterprise*, only to abandon it three days later after another deadly kamikaze hit that ship. He then moved to *Randolph*, but the campaign was nearly over.[43]

On 28 May 1945, Mitscher relinquished command of the fast carriers for the last time – to McCain and Halsey, who would direct them to the final victory. All that remained was the invasion of Japan, ultimately rendered unnecessary largely because of the air–sea battles which had been led by Mitscher in destroying Japan's navy and air forces. After two weeks of fishing in California, he returned to Washington in mid-June as Deputy Chief of Naval Operations for Air, the top aviation post in the navy. Miserable behind a desk, he had only two months to wait until Japan surrendered.

The advent of the atomic bomb and guided missiles meant that the carrier battles of the type Mitscher had fought were already a thing of the past. In their brief day, World War Two, Pete Mitscher had been the master warrior – as leader and tactician. No man in any navy had been his equal in the art and science of naval air warfare.

Promoted to full admiral early 1946 and given command of the Eighth Fleet. That September Mitscher became Commander-in-Chief, Atlantic Fleet, but died on active duty, 3 February 1947.

[43]Reynolds, *The Fast Carriers*, pp. 331–46; Taylor, *The Magnificent Mitscher*, pp. 160, 275–99; author's conversation with Burke in 1966.

11

Vice Admiral

Chuichi Nagumo
Imperial Japanese Navy

1887–1944

by Kyoshi Ikeda
Translated by Richard Harrison

CHUICHI *Nagumo, born Shinobu-machi, Yomezawa City, Yamagata Prefecture, Japan, 25 March 1887. Graduated from Etajima Naval Academy and took up posting as naval cadet on the* Soya, *November 1908; became midshipman, October 1910; graduated from the Torpedo School (Senior Class), November 1914; took command of the destroyer* Kisaragi *after serving on the destroyer* Sugi *and battle-cruiser* Hirado, *December 1917. Graduated from the Naval Staff College (lieutenant-commander, thirty-three years old) and took command of the destroyer* Momi, *December 1920; became staff officer of 1st Torpedo Squadron, November 1921; became staff officer of Naval General Staff Office, November 1922. Promoted commander (thirty-seven years old), November 1924. Instructor at the Naval Staff College, November 1927. Took command of light cruiser* Naka *(captain, forty-two years old), November 1929; commander of the 1st Destroyer Flotilla, December 1930. Staff officer at the Naval General Staff Office, October 1931; took command of the battle-cruiser* Takao, *November 1933. Took command of the battleship* Yamashiro, *November 1934; became commander of the 1st Torpedo Squadron (rear admiral, forty-eight years old), November 1935; commander of the 8th Squadron, December, 1936. Principal of the Torpedo School (vice admiral, fifty years old), November 1937; Commander-in-Chief of the 1st Carrier Division, April 1941; entered the Pacific War, 8 December 1941 (Tokyo dates).*

Pearl Harbor

Chuichi Nagumo was a respected figure in the techiques of torpedo warfare in the Japanese navy, having graduated from both Naval Academy and Naval Staff College. However, until he was given the post as Commander-in-Chief of the 1st Carrier Division he had virtually no knowledge or experience of airborne warfare. The final tragic episode of his life began when he took up the post of Commander-in-Chief of the airborne fleet, an area in which he did not have the necessary expertise. Mitsuo Fuchida (commander of the Flying Corps) who served under Nagumo at the time of the Pearl Harbor attack evaluates his credentials as a commander thus:

> Nagumo's leadership as a commander was extremely conservative and he would never take the initiative. In the end he would always agree with the Staff Officer's opinion and just give a short 'I see . . . very well' when taking decisions. The credentials of a commander are the ability to foresee the development of a battle and calculate accordingly. These qualities were lacking in Commander-in-Chief Nagumo.

At the time the Pacific War broke out, Nagumo displayed great understanding of and sympathy for the men under his command, but he had lost both his vitality and his fighting spirit and had begun to appear quite neurotic. The following is an illustration of his psychological condition immediately prior to the attack on Pearl Harbor.

The 1st Carrier Fleet, which had finally left Hitokappu Bay at 0630 on 26 November 1941 bound for Pearl Harbor, was steaming towards a holding position (north 42°, west 170°) 200 miles north of Oahu Island. Operating under complete radio silence, the fleet was concentrating on monitoring broadcasts from Tokyo Naval General Staff and Seto Inland Sea Allied Command Fleet flagship *Nagato* as well as broadcasts from Honolulu. On the morning of the 27th Admiral Nagumo, who had come on to the bridge, whispered to Vice Admiral Kusaka, who was the Chief Staff Officer: 'Chief Staff Officer. . . . What do you think? Do you think I should have been a little more forceful? . . . Well, we're on our way now [to Pearl Harbor] but do you think we will be able to pull it off? . . .' Kusaka was shocked to hear such an indecisive statement from someone with a reputation like Nagumo's.

Admiral Isoroku Yamamoto [*q.v.*], Commander-in-Chief of the Japanese Combined Fleet, was the main figure in urging the use of a surprise attack on Pearl Harbor. However, this was at first opposed by the General Naval Staff Office as it was a very risky strategy, and they were focusing on an invasion strategy in an area to the south of Japan rich with mineral deposits. Nevertheless, Yamamoto was adamant in proposing the attack on Pearl Harbor for two reasons. Firstly, it would come as a great shock to the US Navy and, he believed, would knock the fighting spirit out of them. Secondly, while the US Navy was based at Hawaii, Japanese plans to invade the southern mineral areas would be in jeopardy. On 19 October 1941, Admiral Osami Nagano (Secretary-General of the General Staff), who was aware of Admiral Yamamoto's determination, gave approval for an attack on Pearl Harbor using six large aircraft carriers. This decision gives some indication of Yamamoto's powerful character, and the influence it had on the Japanese navy.

With the decision made, events began to move quickly. Yamamoto's orders to Nagumo were simple – destroy the US fleet at Hawaii by a surprise attack. To execute this order, Nagumo had a fleet of thirty-three warships. Central to it was the carrier force of six aircraft carriers: *Akagi, Kaga, Hiryu, Soryu, Shokaku,* and *Zuikaku* (382 aircraft). Supporting them were two battleships, *Hiei* and *Kirishima,* and two heavy cruisers, *Tone* and *Chikuma.* Guarding them was the light cruiser, *Abukuma,* accompanied by nine destroyers. Logistical support was provided by eight ships including *Kyokutomaru.* In addition, there was a patrol force of three submarines and the 'Midway Gunboat Force' of two destroyers. The holding position was at the halfway mark from Hitokappu Bay.

At 2000 on 2 December 1941, orders came by telegraph from Commander-in-Chief of the Combined Fleet Yamamoto that 'It has been decided to commence war on 8 December.' At Pearl Harbor, on the other side of the International Date Line, that would be 7 December. 'Carry out the attack as planned.' The mobile force had reached a position 230 nautical miles north of Oahu, and the first attack force of 123 aircraft, as well as the second attack force of 170 aircraft lying at a position 200 nautical miles from Oahu, were despatched. The commander of the airborne forces was Commander Mitsuo Fuchida.

At this time the US Navy had stationed nine of its fleets in the Pacific Ocean and eight in the Atlantic Ocean. These included three aircraft carriers in the Pacific and three in the Atlantic. Commander-in-Chief of the Pacific Fleet was Admiral Husband E. Kimmel, stationed at the land-based General Staff Office in Pearl Harbor as he was also serving as Commander-in-Chief of the US Navy.

The attack on Pearl Harbor was a total success. Both the primary target of ships stationed at Pearl and the secondary target of aircraft bases took heavy losses. Of the eight battleships there, the *Arizona, Oklahoma, West Virginia* and *California* were sunk and the 'remaining four damaged. The US flagship *Pennsylvania* was in dock and received a direct hit from only one bomb, thereby escaping major damage. The six aircraft bases on Oahu lost 231 army aircraft and 80 naval aircraft. This left a mere seventy-nine aircraft that were operational after the Japanese attack.

However, a stroke of good fortune for the US forces was that none of the Pacific Fleet aircraft carriers was at Pearl Harbor at the time of the attack. The *Saratoga* was at San Diego, the *Lexington* was delivering aircraft to Midway Island and the *Enterprise* was on its way back to Pearl from Wake Island where it too had been delivering aircraft. This was to prove a great factor in the subsequent plans and failure by Nagumo's forces in the Battle of Midway Island.

Damage to Nagumo's aircraft forces totalled a mere twenty-nine aircraft, which was far lower than had been estimated. All aircraft were retrieved by 1350 (Hawaii time) on 7 December (Japanese time 0920 on the 8th) at a position approximately 250 nautical miles north of Oahu. Although there was more than enough fighting strength and margin for a secondary attack, and there had been no retaliation from the US forces, Nagumo's forces made a rapid exit from the battle area, heading away from the airborne security zone and onward back to Japan.

As far as the surprise attack went, Nagumo's achievements were substantial. However, there were two errors on his part. The first was that he did not carry through the attack to its conclusion. When he received a telegraph from the airborne force informing him that the attack had been successful, Staff Officer Minoru Genda strongly recommended to Nagumo and Chief Staff Officer Kusaka, that a second attack should take place at once. Commander Mitsuo Fuchida (general commander of the airborne attack) who was the last to return to the ship, emphasized this, telling Nagumo: 'We must carry out another attack as there are still factories and destroyers that are undamaged.' There was a disagreement between Genda and Fuchida on the one side, who argued that there should be a secondary attack to improve the results of the first, and Chief Staff Officer Kusaka and Staff Officer Oishi on the other, who were worried that there could be heavier losses if a secondary attack was carried out. It was left to Nagumo himself to make the decision. He decided to take Staff Officer Kusaka's advice and call off a secondary attack. From the outset he had not had much confidence in the success of the Pearl Harbor plan and had led the attack timidly, retreating as quickly as possible to an area outside the range of the US aircraft. Of course there was strong dissatisfaction at the General Staff at the incompleteness of Nagumo's attack. Admiral Matome Ugaki, Chief Staff Officer of the Combined Fleet, criticized Nagumo, saying, 'He was like a robber fleeing the scene, happy with small booty.'

Nagumo's second error was that the attack concentrated almost exclusively on ships, especially battleships, and left facilities such as oil dumps and factories unscathed. This mistake was not made by him alone. The strategic concept of the entire Japanese navy up to the opening of the Pacific War was based on the idea that naval conflicts were won by fleets, and that big ships and big guns were the key to victory. However, as a result of leaving the manufacturing facilities, which could provide the capability to rebuild strength, unscathed, almost all of the ships left on the bottom of Pearl Harbor after the attack were later refloated and were able to take part in the fighting from the middle stages of the war.

Meanwhile the campaign in the south was progressing smoothly. Java was invaded on 9 March and Sumatra was virtually secured at the end of the month. The Andaman Islands was also invaded around that time. The General Staff Office estimated that the British naval fighting strength in the Indian Ocean consisted of two aircraft carriers, three heavy cruisers, four to seven light cruisers, several destroyers and 300 or so British aircraft deployed at bases around the Indian coast. On 9 March, Admiral Yamamoto issued orders for a campaign in the Indian Ocean with the intention of destroying the British fleet there through a joint operation with land forces operating in

Burma. Nagumo's force (1st Carrier Division, 3rd Squadron, 1st Torpedo Squadron and others), which had set out from Stirling Harbour on 5 March 1940, formed the main force in the Indian Ocean campaign. On 5 April they attacked Colombo and inflicted heavy losses on ships and land-based facilities, destroying over twenty Hurricane fighters. They also discovered the heavy cruisers *Dorset* and *Cornwall* escaping to the south and sank both ships in a mere twenty minutes, using twenty aircraft in a secondary attack. On the following day, the 9th, the force attacked Trincomalee naval port on the east coast of Ceylon, sinking two light cruisers, several destroyers and ten freighters. Around the same time, they discovered the undefended British aircraft carrier *Hermes*, a destroyer and a large merchant vessel to the south of Ceylon's east coast, and in just fifteen minutes sank all three. They returned to Japan on 22 April, without encountering any enemy vessels.

However, the Indian Ocean campaign could have inflicted greater damage. It turned out to be an 'expensive excursion'. During the six months after the Hawaii campaign, the fighting strength of the Nagumo force had reached its limit in terms of both men and materials. Nagumo and his force had certainly taken control of the seas and skies from the Western Pacific to the Indian Ocean and had rightly earned a reputation as an 'invincible fleet'. But lurking in the shadows of these triumphs was a feeling of tiredness, both physical and mental, which could not be hidden, and even more obvious was an air of over-confidence and boastfulness. Unrecognized at the time, it was a potentially fatal combination, which the Japanese later sadly described as 'the victory disease'.

Battle of Midway

On the morning of 5 June 1942 (Japanese time) the Nagumo Force was sailing unhindered. However, by that evening his fleet would be totally defeated. In the turbulent history of naval warfare in the Pacific there has been no greater or dramatic turn-around of fortunes than that seen at the Battle of Midway.

The Midway campaign was a concept born from Yamamoto's wish for a quick decisive battle, similar to the one carried out at Pearl Harbor. Convinced that the key to the Pacific War was the US fleet, especially their aircraft carriers, he planned to draw the US fleet into action by attacking Midway Island. He envisaged that if the enemy fleet did not take the bait, he would then be able to secure patrol bases in the Eastern Pacific by invading and capturing Midway and the Aleutian Islands. At first the General Staff Office opposed this strategy. They argued that even if they captured Midway it would be a difficult place to keep supplied. They also pointed out that if US forces later launched an attack to retake Midway, Japanese forces might not be able to carry out a counter-attack. Not only the General Staff Office, but also Admiral Nagumo's forces – which were to form the core of this campaign – argued against it in this way. The forces were drained both physically and mentally

Men of War

from the campaigns since the start of the war and there was a dire need to take rest and replenish supplies. But Yamamoto was steadfast, and on 5 April 1942 Admiral Osami Nagano, General Commander of the General Staff Office, adopted the strategy put forward for the Midway campaign. Yamamoto had by this time earned such a charismatic reputation that no one could gainsay him, either within the Combined Fleet or within the General Staff Office. Admiral Kusaka, Chief Staff Officer in Nagumo's Forces, recalls that time:

> Commander Minoru Genda and Admiral Tamon Yamaguchi, Commander of the 1st Airborne Squadron, protested violently; but the Combined Fleet General Staff Office ignored their complaints as though it had been decided already. I resigned myself to the situation allowing myself to think that although it might be risky, once they set off they would be able to pull off a victory.

Admiral Nagumo was as strong in his criticism as Kusaka but it was to no avail. The strategy of the Midway campaign was decided by Yamamoto's forcefulness.

At 0600 on 27 May, Nagumo's forces left the port of Hashira Jima in the Seto Inland Sea, heading for Midway Island. Following them were the other forces which were to take part in the battle. It was a huge armada – 127 warships altogether. The Main Force, under Yamamoto, included eight battleships (*Yamato*, (flagship); *Musashi*, *Nagato*, *Mutsu*, *Ise*, *Hiuga*, *Fuso*, *Yamashiro*), one aircraft carrier (*Hosho*), three light cruisers (*Kitakami*, *Oi*, *Sendai*), twenty-one destroyers and six auxiliary vessels and supply vessels. The First Force, under Nagumo, included four aircraft carriers (*Akagi* (flagship); *Kaga*, *Soryu*, *Hiryu*). Between them they carried 261 aircraft – eighty-four naval bombers, ninety-three naval attack planes, eighty- four naval fighters – together with thirty-six fighters of land-based airborne forces. Added to these were two battleships (*Kirishima*, *Haruna*) two heavy cruisers (*Tone*, *Chikuma*), one light cruiser (*Nagara*) and twelve destroyers, along with eight large tankers. The Invasion Force, the armada's third element, included two battleships (*Kongo*, *Hiei*), eight heavy cruisers (*Atago*, *Chokai*, *Myoko*, *Haguro*, *Kumano*, *Suzuya*, *Mogami*, *Mikuma*), two light cruisers (*Yura*, *Shinzu*), seventeen destroyers, one aircraft carrier (*Zuiho*), two amphibious carriers (*Chitose*, *Kamikawamaru*) and twelve supply vessels. These last carried no less than 3,000 men of Army Itinokishi Force and 2,800 men of Naval 2nd Combined Special Marines – Landing Force. Ahead of them in the Advance Force were fifteen submarines (deployed between Hawaii and Midway) and a land-based airborne squadron, as well as the 24th Airborne Squadron, composed of seventy-two land-based fighters, seventy-two fighters and sixteen flying boats (deployed at bases throughout the South Pacific).

Yamamoto also formed a Northern Force for a planned simultaneous diversionary attack on the Aleutian Islands of Attu and Kiska. The commander of the Northern Force was Admiral Kakuji Kakuta, who commanded a secondary force centred around the two aircraft carriers *Ryujho* and *Shoho*.

The Japanese navy had committed all its forces, even more than had been deployed at Pearl Harbor. Yamamoto's Main Force left the Seto Inland Sea on 29 May, following Nagumo's forces, and commanded the campaign from an area between Midway and Junyo.

Yamamoto was convinced that an attack on Midway would draw out the US fleet, especially the aircraft carriers, by using Midway as the bait. But it can now be seen in retrospect that the Japanese navy at that time did not have enough information or capability to evaluate the situation. There was little possibility of the US aircraft carriers entering a battle at Midway and even if they had it would have been after the invasion was over. This was a fatal miscalculation on the part of the Japanese forces. Added to that, around 10 May, Admiral Nimitz (Commander-in-Chief of the US Pacific Fleet) learned of the Japanese navy's plan to attack Midway, and grouped his forces for this attack by calling Admiral Halsey's force back to Hawaii for 17 May. The US Navy had a clear advantage in terms of intelligence and code breaking.

Admiral Spruance's [*q.v.*] aircraft carriers *Enterprise* and *Hornet* were ordered to leave Pearl Harbor, and on 1 June the forces led by Admiral Fletcher's *Yorktown* headed for Midway. Defences on Midway were also strengthened directly by putting a total of 121 land-based aircraft on standby and deploying submarine patrols. This meant that, to the north-east of Midway and outside the zone of detection of the Japanese land-based airborne forces, three US aircraft carriers which did not enter into Japanese calculations were lying in ambush for Nagumo's force.

Nagumo had no idea that any American ships, let alone the three aircraft carriers, were waiting for him when his force took up a position north-west of Midway Island on the morning of 5 June. At 0130 (Japanese time) the first attack group, led by Lieutenant Tomonaga, set off from a point 210 nautical miles from Midway Island to carry out an attack on land bases.

At the same time Nagumo sent out seven reconnaissance planes to check out the area from the south of Midway to the north. If the reconnaissance plane sent out by the heavy cruiser *Tone* had flown the fourth reconnaissance line smoothly, it would have spotted the US aircraft carrier fleet. However, there was trouble with the plane and it failed to spot the ships in time.

Meanwhile, Lieutenant Tomonaga's attack force were ambushed by a US navy fighter squadron and were drawn into a fierce aerial conflict. Virtually all the US ground-based planes had taken off, nullifying most of the damage done to the runways. Lieutenant Tomonaga contacted Nagumo, saying, 'We must send in the second attack force.' On Nagumo's four aircraft carriers they were preparing the second attack force after they had sent the first off. This group had been armed with torpedoes, to enable them to attack the US fleet should it be discovered.

Nagumo, who had wrongly believed that there were no US aircraft carriers in the area, made up his mind to send the second attack force to attack Midway and at 0415 ordered the torpedoes to be changed for bombs. While this order was being carried out his fleet came under attack from US land-based fighters. There was very little damage, but much worse was to follow. At 0428, spotter plane from *Tone* at last saw the US aircraft carriers for the first time and at 0520 reported that 'the enemy are to the rear, accompanied by what look like aircraft carriers'.

At 0445 Nagumo decided that there were aircraft carriers among the enemy fleet and ordered the planes to change their weapons from bombs back to torpedoes in order to attack the new enemy. The first attack wave finally returned from Midway, and the aircraft carriers were frantically trying to cope with getting the planes back on board. Around that time they came under attack from the fighters from the US aircraft carriers and a fierce mid-air battle took place. The changeover of weapons (from bombs to torpedoes) of the second attack force had not yet been completed. This was to prove a fatal error.

Around 0723, US Navy dive bombers attacked Nagumo's aircraft carriers and hit *Akagi*, *Kaga* and *Soryu* with two to four hits each. Large fires broke out on all three carriers. Weapons being prepared for battle exploded all around, rendering all three vessels inoperative. Shortly after, they all sank.

The one remaining aircraft carrier, *Hiryu*, sent out an attack force and inflicted a large amount of damage on *Yorktown* but at 1403 it took four direct hits from US fighters and sank. All four of Nagumo's carriers had now been destroyed.

As soon as he learned the full measure of this disaster, Yamamoto took command of the rest of the fleet and pursued the US fleet. At one stage he decided to go into night combat and take Midway, but changed his mind when he learned of the strength of the US aircraft carriers. At 2350 he gave the order to cease the assault on Midway.

Meanwhile, Japanese Marine forces had taken the islands of Kiska and Attu, and *Yorktown*, which was damaged and drifting, was attacked and sunk by submarine on the morning of the 7th.

The Japanese navy had been completely outstripped by the US fleet at Midway and the 'invincible' Nagumo Force had been wiped out. The greatest blame for this defeat should probably rest with Commander-in-Chief of the Combined Fleet Yamamoto and his staff, who crushed any resistance to his plans. However, by itself this is not a fair apportioning of criticism, if one does not take into account the several errors of leadership and tactics on the part of Admiral Nagumo, who actually directed operations at sea. His two biggest errors were as follows.

Firstly there was a failure to search properly for the enemy. The aim of the Midway attack, as planned by Admiral Yamamoto, was to draw the US fleet into a confrontation by using Midway as the bait. But Nagumo and his General Staff did not understand fully the implications of this and concentrated simply on the invasion itself. As a result, they failed to search for the enemy thoroughly at sea and the reconnaissance planes, which would have spotted the enemy quickly, were sent out only when the first attack forces were sent off. On top of that, the number of reconnaissance planes was small. It could also be said that a separate reason why Nagumo did not take the search for enemy forces seriously was that he was certain – mistakenly as it turned out – that there were no enemy aircraft carriers in the vicinity. This could be attributed to his over-confidence, the result of the 'invincible' tag he gained in the campaign at Hawaii. However, the General Staff Office too should bear some of the responsibility for this error. They did not make enough effort to gather information about the US fleet around the area between Hawaii and Midway. Also the flagship *Yamato* intercepted a signal from something that resembled a US aircraft carrier on the night of the 4th to the north of Midway, immediately before the battle began. Yamamoto instructed Staff Officer Kurosima to inform *Akagi* immediately but Kurosima thought that *Akagi* must have been able to pick up the signal itself. In the end, therefore, he did not pass on the information, and since *Akagi* had not intercepted the original American signal, there was nothing to contradict Nagumo's belief that no American carriers were close. This could be said to have been a major factor in the eventual defeat of the Japanese forces.

The second of Nagumo's errors was his lack of decisiveness and foresight in the midst of the battle. After receiving a report from Tomonaga (commanding the first attack force) that 'We must carry out a second attack' he changed the weapons on the aircraft from torpedoes to bombs. Later, when he then learned from a reconnaissance plane from *Tone* that there were US aircraft carriers in the area, he issued a new command to change the weapons back to torpedoes. Rear Admiral Yamaguchi, commanding the second attack force, also advised him that 'We must attack at once.' That is to say, he meant 'Leave the bombs on and attack immediately, as speed is of the essence.' However, Nagumo did not take his advice and ordered the weapons to be changed back to torpedoes. In retrospect, he should have sent out the planes armed with bombs, as even they would have inflicted a considerable amount of damage on the flight decks of the aircraft carriers. But Nagumo was restricted in his decision-making by his rigid understanding that 'Ships are to be attacked by torpedoes, land bases by bombs.' It was while they were recovering aircraft from the first attack force and switching weapons on the aircraft of the second attack force that attack aircraft from the US carriers struck.

Guadalcanal

The Japanese navy suffered heavy losses in the Battle of Midway. Now four carriers were down, the General Staff changed the fleet's formation for the first time since the war began. This was a drastic alteration, attempting to make good the losses suffered at Midway. The main points of the change were the dismantling of the 1st Carrier Division and the formation of a new 3rd Carrier Division and 8th Division.

The 8th Carrier Division, which was to take part in operations in the Solomon waters, was formed of a total of thirteen ships – heavy cruisers, light cruisers and destroyers headed by the flagship *Chokai*. The commander was Vice Admiral Mikawa.

The 3rd Carrier Division was a new force formed after Midway, led by Admiral Nagumo and Staff Officer Kusaka. The formation of this new force (twenty-nine ships) was as follows:

1st Carrier Squadron	*Shokaku, Zuikaku, Zuiho*
2nd Carrier Squadron	*Hio, Junyo, Ryujo*
7th Squadron	(heavy cruisers) *Kumano, Suzuya*
8th Squadron	(heavy cruisers) *Tone, Chikuma*
10th Squadron	(light cruiser) *Nagara*, sixteen destroyers
12th Squadron	(battleships) *Hiei, Kirishima*

This new formation reversed the roles of aircraft carriers and battleships, so that the aircraft carriers had more protection. This had the effect of taking away some of the effectiveness of the big battleships like the *Yamato* and *Musashi*, with some officer dubbing the *Yamato* the *Hotel Yamato*, because it could not move out of Truk Island.

On 7 August 1942, US armed forces landed on Guadalcanal to begin the turn-around in the Pacific War. Heavy fighting continued on the Solomon Islands until around the end of the following year, 1943. The special characteristic of this conflict was that it became a tactical war of production, supplies and intelligence-gathering. In terms of military tactics, it developed into a war for securing aerial supremacy. Yamamoto, who had been watching the US advance on to Guadalcanal closely, ordered the 3rd Carrier Division led by Admiral Nagumo and the 2nd Division led by Vice Admiral Nobutake Kondo to head out for Rabaul. The orders given to Admiral Nagumo were to support the landing force under the command of Vice Admiral Kondo which was to land on Guadalcanal on 25 August.

At 0400 on 24 August, Nagumo headed south for Guadalcanal sending *Ryujo* ahead with the 8th Carrier Division. They were at a point 250 nautical miles north of Guadalcanal when a patrol craft from a US force (the carriers *Saratoga*, *Enterprise* and *Wasp* commanded by Admiral Fletcher) which was 150 miles to the east of Guadalcanal spotted *Ryujo*. Admiral Fletcher was not able to join *Wasp*, which was heading to the south to refuel, and so decided to carry out an air strike on *Ryujo*. He launched an aerial assault with his full complement of F4F Wildcats and in the early afternoon launched another attack on the *Ryujo* with thirty bombers and eight torpedo planes. The *Ryujo* had just sent off fifteen planes to attack Henderson airbase. Immediately prior to this, the flagship *Shokaku* had come under attack from two US dive bombers but had not been damaged. Also around that time, reconnaissance planes from the forward-placed *Chikuma* reported that they had spotted the US fleet, at a position near Shituwal Island and that the strength was 'two aircraft carriers, two battleships, two cruisers and sixteen destroyers'.

Admiral Nagumo ordered an 'immediate attack'. He despatched a total of seventy-three aircraft, twenty-seven naval bombers and ten fighters in the first attack force and twenty-seven naval bombers and nine fighters in the second attack force. Fletcher could see the Japanese attack from the north on radar and shot down six Japanese planes with fighters commanded by Vice-Admiral Kinkaid (*Enterprise*).

The Japanese attack force did not notice *Saratoga*, though she was only ten miles further away, and concentrated their attack solely on *Enterprise*. There was a tremendous amount of anti-aircraft fire from the US gunners which meant the torpedo planes could not get within range to let their torpedoes go, and only some of the bombers were able to attack the ship. However, three determined bombers got through the anti-aircraft fire and put three direct hits on the flight deck of *Enterprise*. These killed seventy-four crewmen, damaged two elevators and opened up a gaping hole in the side of the ship. This was all in the space of just six minutes of fighting. The second attack force could not find the US force because of cloud and turned back.

Kondo considered attacking the US fleet in a night attack but called off a chase due to lack of fuel and headed off to the north. This is how the 2nd Solomon Battle (known as the East Solomon Battle by the US Navy) finished. Nagumo's fleet had inflicted a great deal of damage on *Enterprise* but she was able to recover all her aircraft and change course to the south one hour later at twenty-four knots with only a slight list. The US armed forces had lost only fifteen aircraft, whereas the Japanese navy had lost the aircraft carrier *Ryujo*, the destroyer *Mutsuki* and ninety aircraft. One could say that the failure of Nagumo's forces to carry through their attack on the US forces invited failure for the first rescue force landing on Guadalcanal; but that responsibility should also be shared by Vice Admiral Kondo.

On 4 August Japanese forces landed 4,000 men on Guadalcanal and carried out a second all-out offensive on the 14th, but again this failed. The 'fight to the death' between the US and Japanese forces over Guadalcanal grew ever fiercer after that September. On 3 October the army landed the 2nd Division (Sendai) on the island and began attacks to regain Henderson airbase. But this attack ground to a halt when it came under counter-attack from US forces. The war became a defensive battle to supply Guadalcanal, bringing increased losses of aircraft and ships to both US and Japanese forces.

The US Navy were attacked by Japanese submarines and on 31 August the aircraft carrier *Saratoga* was holed by the submarine *I-26* and the aircraft carrier *Wasp* was sunk by the submarine *I-19* on 19 August. The waters around this area were at that time covered by twelve I-class Japanese submarines.

At the same time, the Japanese also suffered huge losses. On 11 October a destroyer and three cruisers of the 6th Squadron (which was conveying armed forces to Guadalcanal) were caught up in a night-time conflict with three heavy cruisers and five destroyers eight miles west off Savo Island. The ships *Furutaka* and *Fubuki* were lost and the *Aoba* was damaged amidships. The US forces suffered heavy damage to just one heavy cruiser. The night raids, which had been a specialist feature of the Japanese navy for many years were now easily countered by the US Navy, which had new technology in the form of radar. Using radar for the first time in this conflict (known as the Battle of Cape Esperance in the US), rather than conventional spotlights, the US ships rained down direct hits on the Japanese ships from the first shot.

At 1600 on 25 October, Nagumo's forces went south from a point 500 miles north-east of Guadalcanal Island at a speed of twenty knots. At 0445 the next morning (26th) a plane from *Shokaku* which had headed off to the south-east reported a sighting of 'Enemy aircraft carrier(s) heading north-west'. In fact it was a large advance group consisting of three groups, ten to fifteen miles apart. The first group was twelve ships headed by *Enterprise*, the second was eleven ships headed by *Hornet* and the third was eleven ships headed by *Washington*.

Twenty miles ahead of the aircraft carrier group, Nagumo's fleet sent out a scout party of *Hiei*, *Kirishima* and *Chikuma*. *Tone* and a destroyer were also lying 200 miles to the south-east looking for distant enemy forces. The US forces spotted Nagumo's force at almost the same time and the first attack forces from each side squared up against each other.

It was 0515 when Nagumo ordered the first attack force of sixty-seven aircraft (eighteen naval attack aircraft, twenty-two naval bombers and twenty-seven fighters) to take off. The attack force concentrated on *Hornet*, ten miles away from *Enterprise*. Five bombs hit the flight deck to be followed by several hits which went through the armour plating and exploded inside the ship. Two torpedoes hit the engine room. It became inoperative and the carrier was sunk twelve hours later by torpedoes from the destroyers *Akigumo* and *Makigumo*.

The second attack force of forty-eight aircraft (naval attack planes, naval bombers and fighters) was sent out an hour later bound for the group headed by *Enterprise*. *Enterprise* suffered three hits to her flight deck but was able to escape to the south-east. Nagumo was swift in sending out the second attack force this time after the lesson he had learned at Midway.

At 0600, immediately after he had sent out the second attack force, Nagumo changed course to the south-east, increasing speed, and took up position for an aerial conflict. The first wave of the US attack force came upon the 11th Squadron and *Chikuma* was struck by a single hit. Bombers from *Hornet* broke through the Japanese aerial defences and scored four hits on the flagship *Shokaku* giving rise to a huge fire on board. As *Shokaku* had become inoperative, Nagumo transferred to *Arashi* of the 4th Squadron and handed command over to Captain Tameteru Nomoto commanding the aircraft carrier *Zuikaku*. *Shokaku*, which was ordered to return to Truk, as she had been severely damaged, was unable to take any part in the war for several months after, *Arashi*, with Nagumo on board, headed south and joined up with *Zuikaku* the next morning (the 27th). They continued to search for enemy vessels but were ordered to return to Truk after these attempts proved unsuccessful.

In the South Pacific battle (known as the Battle of Santa Cruz in the US), Nagumo's fleet won a strategic victory over the fleet led by Admiral Kinkaid. The reason Nagumo's losses were small was that he sent out his second attack force early and that a scout party absorbed some of the attack from the first US attack wave. However, looked at over a longer period of time, it could be said that it was a strategic triumph for the US forces. While Nagumo's fleet lost sixty-nine aircraft in action and a further twenty-three which ran out of fuel before being able to land, the US fleet (Kinkaid) lost only seventy-four. When considering the difference in aircraft production and pilot training in the US and Japanese forces the outcome of the Pacific War was already clear.

A more important point is that the forces led by Nagumo failed to keep control of the skies, and therefore had no option but to relinquish control of Guadalcanal. The US forces were able to secure Henderson airbase and the second Japanese all-out assault on Guadalcanal was halted on the 26th.

Back to the Mid-Pacific as Commander-in-Chief of the Fleet

The US push, which began with the landing at Guadalcanal, exceeded all expectations in terms of speed and scale. The islands in the South Pacific fell one after another to American forces. On 18 April 1943 Commander-in-Chief of the Combined Fleet Yamamoto was killed when a plane taking him up to the front line was ambushed by US fighters, after American intelligence had broken Japanese navy coded messages. Admiral Mineichi Koga, who took over from Yamamoto, carried on with Yamamoto's strategies and increased defences in the south-east to check the American advance.

The US advance quickly changed direction from the South-East Pacific to the Mid-Pacific. In November 1943 there was fighting in the Gilbert Islands, which spread to the Marshall Islands on 5 December. Losses to the Japanese navy increased rapidly, particularly in terms of aircraft, crew and ships. On 17 February 1944, American forces attacked Truk with around 450 aircraft and inflicted huge damage on Japanese aircraft, ships and boats stationed there. Truk was the Japanese navy's largest base in the Pacific Ocean, and (after the US push from the South Pacific) had been used both as the headquarters of the General Staff and as the home of the major seaborne forces, including *Yamato* and *Musashi*. Commander-in-Chief Koga, who was aware of the dangerous situation, ordered a pull-back of the main forces to the Home Island and Palau.

Going along with recommendations from headquarters back in Japan, he then switched to a strongly defensive strategy in response to the deteriorating situation, to hold the defensive line. This involved pulling back the fleet from the Marshall Islands to the west Caroline Islands and switching the land-based airbases to aircraft carriers. Both he and headquarters knew that if the line from the Marianas to the west Carolines was broken by the Americans the war would be lost. However, on 31 March 1944 Koga was killed in an air crash while moving between Palau and Davao. He was replaced by Admiral Soemu Toyoda on 3 April. Before his death Koga had changed the formation of the fleet to create a new Mid-Pacific Fleet for the defence of the Marianas and the Caroline Islands. Nagumo handed over as commander of the Third Fleet in December 1943 to Admiral Jisaburo Ozawa, and, after temporary positions at Saseno and Kure dockyards and as commander of the First Fleet, was appointed to the command of this newly formed Mid-Pacific Fleet. His new fleet (the Fourth Fleet) included the light cruisers *Natori* and *Isuzu*, five destroyers, various land forces and the 14th Carrier Division with 490 aircraft. The 1st Carrier Division (commanded by Vice-Admiral Kanji Kakuta) was also deployed to support Nagumo's fleet in the islands of Iwo Jima, Palau, Guam, Truk and around Tinian, which had an airbase with 1,644 aircraft. To repulse the anticipated invasion, around 120,000 troops were positioned on these islands under Nagumo's command, but the leadership of the campaign against the US landings was given to Lieutenant-General Hideo Obata of the 31st Army.

As soon became apparent, the defence of the Mariana Islands was inadequate, in terms of both the Marine forces and the preparation of the soldiers. In particular, the defensive force positioned on Saipan by the Marines General Staff added up to the paltry total of 31,629 men – 25,469 infantry and 6,160 Marines. The US attack force on Saipan, the 51st Allied Strike Advance Force (commanded by Vice Admiral R. Turner [*q.v.*]) numbered 66,779, just under twice the number of the Japanese forces. The orders given to Vice-Admiral Nagumo were to hold the Mariana Islands as long as possible by taking up a defensive formation and to draw out the US attack forces. This would form the core of the General Staff plan 'A'. While Nagumo's forces were holding up the US advance, the force led by Ozawa would challenge and destroy the US fleet. This meant that the defence of Saipan and the other Mariana Islands rested on the ability of Ozawa's forces to destroy the US fleet.

On 11 June Task Force 58, led by Admiral Spruance, appeared to the east of Saipan. For three days, from the 12th, air-raids continued incessantly on all the bases in the Marianas with particularly heavy losses on Saipan and Tinian. Eventually, on the 15th, the first assault wave (consisting of the 2nd and 4th Marines Divisions, and the 27th Infantry Division, commanded by Marine Major-General H. Smith [*q.v.*]) landed on Saipan in around thirty LST carriers. Commander-in-Chief of the Combined Fleet Toyoda issued the command to put plan 'A' into action. But by this time the bases of the airborne force of the 1st Carrier Division (under Vice Admiral Kakuta) which were meant to support both the Nagumo and Ozawa forces had been wiped out. Ozawa's forces went to Saipan on the 18th but were defeated by the TF 58 led by Admiral Spruance in a battle on the 19th–20th. Ozawa's forces lost the *Taiho*, *Shokaku* and *Hio* and were forced to retreat.

Admiral Nagumo and Lieutenant-General Obata in command of the 31st Army waited for the Combined Fleet to come to their rescue. But the resounding defeat of the airborne fleet and Kakuta's forces left them with no hope. All that was left was to put up a defensive fight with the land- based forces. The US landing forces became ever stronger and on 4 July invaded the east coast, advancing through the central mountainous area to the north where the General Staff of Nagumo's Forces and the army were.

On that day the divisional commander of the 43rd Division, Yoshiji Saito, who was in command of the army forces, decided on an all-out final attack and received acknowledgement from Nagumo. On the next day, the 5th, Nagumo sent a telegraph message to the General Commander of the General Staff, Shigetaro Shimada, in Tokyo, informing him of the command for this final assault.

At 1000 on 6 July, Saito committed suicide in a cave, using a military sword. Nagumo was in another cave a short distance away. He addressed the Saipan defence squad, saying, 'Let us be buried here together in Saipan! Carry on. . . .' We are beaten, his words meant, but shall die here with honour. These were his last words: he then took his pistol and committed suicide.

That night a force of 4,000 people, including civilians, gathered on the coast and launched a final suicidal attack on the US lines at 0510 on the 17th. All 4,000 perished.

12

Vice Admiral

Jisaburo Ozawa
Imperial Japanese Navy

1886–1966

by Kiyoshi Ikeda
Translated by Colin Jones

J₁SABURO Ozawa, born in the town of Takanabe in Miyazaki Prefecture, in 1886. Graduated from the Imperial Naval Academy at Etajima, November 1909. Assigned to warship Soya, *graduated from Navy Torpedo School advanced course, December 1917; assigned to torpedo boat* Kamome, *then commanded* Shirataka. *Saw action as a lieutenant in destroyer* Hinoki *escorting British convoys in the Mediterranean, November 1918. Lieutenant-commander, 1921; commanded destroyer* Take. *Joined the staff of the strategic port of Makung, 1922. Commander, 1926; Staff officer for the First Fleet and the Combined Fleet. Captain, 1930. In America and Europe to research the Battle of Jutland, March–November 1930. Commander of the 4th Destroyer Squadron, January 1931. In October of the same year, became commander of the 11th Destroyer Squadron for a period of two months, after which he was assigned to the Naval Academy as an instructor. Captain of cruiser* Maya, *1934, and of battleship* Haruna, *1935. Again posted to the Naval Academy as an instructor, lecturing on tactics, 1936. Promoted rear admiral. Became Chief of Staff for the Combined Fleet, February 1937; commander of the 8th Naval Division. Commanded the landing operation at Bayas Bay, October 1938. As a rear admiral, commanded the 1st Carrier Division and in 1940 became commander of the 3rd Division. Assigned as commander of the Southern Expeditionary Fleet, October 1941. In this capacity he faced the start of the Pacific War.*

Jisaburo Ozawa was a taciturn man with a deliberate, though independent, personality. He was also a battle-hardened and unfrivolous admiral who provided apt and concise leadership. Neither attractive nor stylish in appearance, he was nicknamed 'the Gargoyle'.

A former torpedo tactics specialist, who had particularly espoused the importance of night attacks by torpedo squadrons, in the 1930s he became a proponent of the primacy of naval air power. It was from his proposal that the First Air Fleet was formed, placing all air units of the Combined Fleet under a single, unified command, in March 1941. At this time, Japanese naval strategic and tactical thought was firmly based on the traditional concept of the primacy of heavy surface units (that is, battleships). In this sense, in his advocacy of the formation of an 'air fleet', Ozawa's strategic and tactical insight was epochal. In December 1941, it was the First Air Fleet that became the centre of the task force, led by Admiral Chuichi Nagumo [*q.v.*], which attacked Pearl Harbor.

The Southern Campaign

On 18 October 1941, in an atmosphere of increasingly tense Japanese–American relations, General Tojo was appointed Prime Minister of Japan and formed his first Cabinet. On the same day, by Imperial decree, Admiral Ozawa was made commander of the Southern Expeditionary Fleet, and on 24 October he arrived for duty aboard his flagship, *Kashii*, anchored in Saigon. When hostilities commenced on 8 December (Tokyo time), the Japanese navy had been organized into seven fleets, which were standing by in their various areas of operation. The seven fleets and their positions on 8 December were: the Main Body (commander: Admiral Isoroku Yamamoto [*q.v.*]), based in Japan's Inland Sea and whose duty it was to provide support for all other operations; the Pearl Harbor Attack Task Force (commander: Vice Admiral Chuichi Nagumo), which was halfway between Hawaii and Hitokappu Bay in the Kurile Islands; the Scout Force (commander: Vice Admiral Mitsumi Shimizu) which was engaged in surveillance within 300 nautical miles of Oahu, and poised to surprise and attack American units around Hawaii; the Southern Force (commander: Vice Admiral Nobutake Kondo), waiting in Makung to support the Southern operations; the South Sea Force (commander: Vice-Admiral Shigemi Inoue), based in Truk and charged with guarding the South Pacific Islands (as well as with the invasion of Guam and Wake); the Northern Force (commander: Vice Admiral Moshiro Hosogaya), based in Oominato and charged with patrolling and defending Eastern Honshu; and the China Area Fleet (commander: Admiral Mineichi Koga), based near Shanghai and charged with patrolling the Chinese coast and supporting the attack on Hong Kong.

The Southern Expeditionary Force (which Ozawa himself commanded) was a part of Admiral Kondo's Southern Force, whose duties were to escort and support the army landings at Kota Bharu on the Malayan Peninsula, and also to destroy British air and sea power in the area. The Southern Expeditionary Force was composed of a Main Force (consisting of Ozawa's flagship, the heavy cruiser *Chokai* and one destroyer), and an escort force of four heavy cruisers (*Kumano*, *Suzuya*, *Mikuma* and *Mogami*), the light cruiser *Sendai*, one other cruiser (*Kashii*), the sea defence ship *Shumushu* and sixteen destroyers. There was also a reconnaissance force made up of the light cruisers *Kinu* and *Yura*, sixteen submarines, one torpedo boat and a special-duty ship. Finally there was the air element, made up from parts of the Eleventh Air Fleet (commander: Vice Admiral Nishizo Tsukahara) with a total of 191 aircraft and four special-duty ships.

The Malayan operation was the key to the whole southern campaign, and Ozawa was insistent upon the vital nature of the Kota Bharu landings. Although the army had demanded that the landings take place at Kuantan, in the end it was decided that they would be made at Kota Bharu as Ozawa had demanded. However, the success of the landings would depend upon the movements of the British fleet based in Singapore. Reconnaissance of Singapore Harbour on the afternoon of 8 December had confirmed the presence of a battleship, a battle-cruiser, two cruisers and four destroyers. The battleship was the powerful new *Prince of Wales* (35,000 tons) and the battle-cruiser the high-speed *Repulse*.

The commander of the British force, Admiral Tom Phillips, first received reports of the Japanese Malayan landings early on the morning of 8 December. By 1900 of the same day he and his ships had left port and were heading north to attack their transports. At 1710 on 9 December, Phillips' two ships were spotted by a patrolling Japanese submarine, *I-65*. The transports at the landing area immediately fled at full speed towards the Gulf of Siam, and Admiral Ozawa's Malay Force (which had been returning to Camranh Bay from the landing site) immediately reversed course and headed towards the area of the enemy sighting. But, set upon by a squall, the Japanese lost the British force.

At 1140 on the 10th, a Japanese navy reconnaissance plane resighted the enemy warships, heading south about forty nautical miles east of Kuantan. From bases around Saigon, eighty-five medium bombers from the 22nd Squadron attacked the British ships from 1245 to 1450. *Repulse* sank first, hit by one bomb and five torpedoes, followed by *Prince of Wales*, which sank into the sea near Malaysia at 1450 after taking hits from two bombs and no fewer than seven torpedoes. Admiral Phillips shared the fates of his ships. With the battle finished, and after his force had returned to Camranh Bay, Admiral Ozawa remarked to one of his subordinates: 'One of these days, I think I too will meet with the same fate as Admiral Phillips.'

After sinking *Prince of Wales* and *Repulse*, Ozawa's ships supported the February 1942 landings at Java by the Sixteenth Army (under Lieutenant-General Hitoshi Imamura) and the March landings on Sumatra by the Twenty-fifth Army (under Lieutenant-General Tomoyuki Yamashita). Following this, Ozawa's forces invaded the Andaman Islands at the end of March, eventually reaching the east coast of Burma. In April, Admiral Nagumo's task force drove into the Indian Ocean and launched a surprise attack on Colombo. Acting in concert with this attack, Ozawa's units carried out a series of hit-and-run attacks in the Bay of Bengal, sinking twenty Allied transports and seriously damaging another nine. As a result of these activities,

Japan's supply lines between Singapore and Burma were secured, greatly simplifying the army's Burmese campaign.

In July 1942 Admiral Ozawa left his command of the Southern Expeditionary Force and returned to Tokyo, where he was attached to the Naval Staff. However, a month before, on 5 June, Admiral Nagumo's task force had been shattered in the Battle of Midway. Having lost the carriers *Kaga*, *Akagi*, *Soryu* and *Hiryu*, as well as scores of its best pilots, the navy was in a state of ruin, making strategic planning noticeably more difficult. A new task force, the Third Fleet (again commanded by Nagumo), was organized on 14 July.

The Americans began their counter-attack in earnest with their landing on Guadalcanal on 7 August 1942. Admiral Yamamoto, Commander-in-Chief of the Combined Fleet, immediately ordered Nagumo's Third Fleet and Kondo's Second Fleet to advance to Rabaul. The land-based air units of the Eleventh Air Fleet were also advanced into Rabaul, and the headquarters of the Combined Fleet moved to Truk. In this way the struggle for the Solomon Islands – the campaign which determined the course of the Pacific War – started to unfold. A characteristic of this series of battles was that they were a contest of productive capacities, of supply and of information. A further characteristic was that they were centred on aerial battles for control of the sky. From the Battle of Savo Island on 8 August 1942 to the air battle for Bougainville on 3 December the following year, there were no fewer than seventeen major air and sea battles in the Solomon Islands area. In these battles, involving severe attrition of air power, Nagumo's task force was gradually losing its fighting strength. It is at this point that Ozawa entered the scene, as Nagumo's replacement.

The Air and Sea Battles of the Solomon Islands

On 2 February 1942, by Imperial decree, Ozawa was made commander of the Third Fleet as Nagumo's successor, and on the 14th of the same month he boarded his flagship, the carrier *Zuikaku*, anchored in the Inland Sea. The forces which he inherited when he took command of the Third Fleet are as follows:

1st Carrier Division:	*Zuikaku, Shokaku, Zuiho*
2nd Carrier Division:	*Jinou, Tsuou*
3rd Battleship Division:	*Kongo, Haruna*
7th Cruiser Division:	*Kumano, Suzuya*
8th Cruiser Division:	*Tone, Chikuma*
10th Escort Division:	*Agano*
50th Carrier Division:	*Hosho, Ryuho, Yukaze*

4th, 10th, 16th, 17th and 61st Destroyer Divisions, plus the naval air forces based in Kanoya and Chikujo. The cruiser *Oyodo* was also attached.

Ozawa's Third Fleet sortied from the Inland Sea on 18 January 1943, arriving at the Japanese navy's advanced base in Truk on the 23rd of that month. At this time most of the fighting was taking place around the Solomon Islands. The Japanese evacuated their forces from Guadalcanal in February, and a vicious war of attrition was being enacted over control of supply lines. Admiral Yamamoto (flagged on *Yamato*, later *Musashi*) had also moved the headquarters of the Combined Fleet to Truk, from where he directed the southern operations. Under orders from Yamamoto, Admiral Ozawa advanced the air component of the Third Fleet into the south-eastern area, and along with the air component from the Eleventh Air Fleet, an element of Admiral Kusaka Jinichi's South-eastern Force, commenced a series of aerial campaigns. To command this operation (codenamed I-go), Ozawa flew out to Rabaul. A total of 419 aircraft (195 from the Third Fleet, and 224 from the Eleventh Fleet) were thrown into the I-go campaign and they achieved significant results, but also suffered heavy casualties. The greatest loss to the Japanese navy was, however, the loss of Admiral Yamamoto, who was shot down on 18 April by US fighters over Bougainville, while on an inspection tour of the front lines.

On 25 April Admiral Mineichi Koga arrived on board *Musashi* to take Yamamoto's place as commander of the Combined Fleet. On 3 May the 1st Carrier Division (led by Ozawa) left Truk Harbour and headed for the Japanese mainland to rebuild its air units, which had been seriously depleted in the I-go campaign. The remaining units of the Third Fleet also returned to Japan in order to prepare for action in the northern campaign, but when the relief of Japanese forces on Attu was declared to be hopeless, the campaign was called off.

Thus, on 15 July Ozawa's Third Fleet returned to Truk in preparation for an attack by the US fleet, which was expected to come from the Marshall Islands. But the predicted attack never materialized. Ozawa thereupon advanced with his air units to Rabaul (for the Ro-go campaign) on 1 November and, in the first half of that month, the repeated actions of the air battle of Bougainville took place. In this campaign the air component of the Third Fleet suffered serious casualties, caused primarily as a result of the development by the Americans of the proximity fuse, which greatly increased their anti-aircraft firepower. Out of a total of 178 aircraft (eighty-seven fighters, forty-five carrier bombers, forty torpedo bombers and six reconnaissance planes, with a total of 728 aircrew) 121 machines were lost – 68 per cent of the fleet's aircraft and 45 per cent of their crews. This amounted to crippling damage to the Third Fleet, and Admiral Koga was forced to order an end to the Ro-go campaign.

Having been defeated in the Solomon and Marshall Islands, the Japanese navy was forced to pull its forward base back from Truk atoll to the Palau and Singapore areas. This was done in order to maintain distance from the American forces, to buy time for the rebuilding of air units, and to ease fleet refuelling. Following its return to Japan to replenish its air units after Ro-go, the Third Fleet (with Ozawa flagged on board *Shokaku*) arrived in Singapore on 13 February 1944. Admiral Koga was having to face some unpleasant realities: the tremendous attrition of Japanese air power, and the ever increasing American fighting strength in the Central Pacific. Thus by the end of 1943 he had had to request that Imperial Headquarters contract the battle front, and readjust overall strategy. This would now have to be of a primarily defensive nature; the line where the 'decisive fleet battle' should take place would be pulled in from the current front line at the Marshall Islands back to a line connecting the Marianas and western Caroline Islands. Here Japan's numerous island airbases could take the place of aircraft carriers. It was thought that the only possible defensive strategy left to the Combined Fleet was to maximize the use of land-based air power. This change in the course of the navy's strategy owes a great deal to the report submitted by Admiral Ozawa. Imperial Headquarters were nevertheless unenthusiastic about the creation and provisioning of land airbases, and while waiting orders at Truk Ozawa was even forced to use men from the Third Fleet as labourers in order to develop an airfield on Kaede Island.

The Battle of the Marianas

With the beginning of 1944, the situation in the Central Pacific was becoming urgent: in February, American forces took the atolls of Kwajalein, Eniwetok and Majuro in the Marshalls, and from February to March US task forces launched air-raids on Truk, Palau and the Marianas. Around the time of the Palau air-raid, Admiral Koga was killed in a flying-boat accident en route to Davao in the Philippines to direct operations. Imperial orders dated 3 April made Admiral Soemu Toyoda the new commander of the Combined Fleet.

In accordance with Imperial Headquarters' Current Plan of Operation (Naval Order 373, dated 3 May), Admiral Toyoda drafted plans for Operation A-go. This would involve the concentration of a large portion of the forces the navy was hoarding for a decisive battle, and the subsequent utilization of these forces in the areas of American advance. Out of these forces Toyoda superintended four fleets:

The First Air Fleet, commanded by Vice Admiral Kakuji Kakuta with its headquarters in Tinian. Kakuta's forces consisted of numerous land-based air units whose installations were spread over the Marianas and the western Carolines. As of 15 May, the total air strength of these was 653 aircraft. However, the level of training of the aircrews was generally low, and many of these were ill from overwork. Furthermore, the defences of these airbases were insufficient, as were their stocks of fuel and ammunition.

The Sixth Fleet, commanded by Vice Admiral Takagi Takeo, with its headquarters in Saipan. This consisted of fifty submarines scattered over a wide area, and was primarily occupied with the reconnaissance of the activities of US forces.

The Central Pacific Fleet, also based in Saipan, and led by Vice Admiral Chuichi Nagumo. Nagumo was also unified commander of the various army and navy defence battalions throughout the islands of the Central Pacific.

The First Mobile Fleet, commanded by Ozawa on his flagship, the carrier *Taiho*. This fleet was the product of the unification of the Second and Third Fleets in order to create (as Ozawa had been advising Admiral Koga to do since the close of the previous year) a mobile surface force formidable enough for a decisive engagement against the advancing Americans. Admiral Toyoda's plan was that any American advance and subsequent landing operations would be met by the full strength of Ozawa's carrier planes as well as Kakuta's land-based aircraft, whose primary goal would be the destruction of the enemy task force. Ozawa's fleet was composed as follows:

Main Force (previously the Third Fleet), commanded directly by Ozawa

  1st Carrier Division: *Taiho, Shokaku, Zuikaku*, plus the 601st Squadron with 225 aircraft (eighty-one fighters, eighty-one bombers, fifty-four torpedo bombers, nine reconnaissance).

  2nd Carrier Division: *Jino, Hio, Ryuho*, plus the 652nd Squadron with 135 aircraft (eighty-one fighters, thirty-six bombers, eighteen torpedo bombers).

  3rd Carrier Division: *Chitose, Chiyoda, Zuiho*, plus the 653rd Squadron with ninety aircraft (eighteen fighters, forty-five fighter bombers, twenty-seven torpedo bombers).

  10th Cruiser Division: *Agano, Yahagi* and fourteen destroyers.

  The heavy cruiser *Mogami* was also attached.

Advance Force (Second Fleet)

  1st Battleship Division: *Yamato, Musashi* and *Nagato*

  3rd Battleship Division: *Kongo* and *Haruna*

  4th Cruiser Division: *Atago, Takao, Chokai* and *Maya* (on board which the author was an officer)

  5th Cruiser Division: *Myoko* and *Haguro*

  7th Cruiser Division: *Kumano, Suzuya, Tone* and *Chikuma*

  2nd Destroyer Division, with the light cruiser *Noshiro* and fifteen destroyers.

All told, therefore, Ozawa's First Mobile Fleet included fifty-seven ships and 450 aircraft. On the other side, Admiral Raymond Spruance [*q.v.*] commanded the Fifth Fleet of the US forces, tasked with landing on Saipan. Taking part in this operation was Task Force 58 (commander: Vice Admiral R. K. Turner [*q.v.*]), which was divided into four carrier groups with a total strength of fifteen carriers, and five groups of surface units (all under the command of Vice Admiral 'Ching' Lee) with a total strength of seven battleships, three heavy cruisers and fourteen destroyers. Altogether the task force had ninety-three ships and 902 aircraft.

Starting from 11 June a US Navy task force under Admiral Marc Mitscher [*q.v.*] launched savage air-raids throughout the Marianas and from 13 June, Saipan and Tinian were subject to bombardment by Lee's battleship groups. Early on the morning of the 15th, the landing operations were commenced. On this same day at 0717, Admiral Toyoda ordered the beginning of Operation A-go. By this time, however, the land-based air units of the First Air Fleet had already suffered considerable losses, and were incapable of even keeping Ozawa's First Mobile Fleet informed, let alone providing him with effective support. Thus, by 18 June, the only air power available to help Ozawa in a decisive action had been reduced to a mere 156 planes.

The First Mobile Fleet left their anchorage at Linga, and on 14 May arrived in Tawi Tawi. There they awaited an opportunity to engage the enemy in a decisive battle. Upon receiving the orders which set A-go in motion, Ozawa's force had passed through the San Bernardino Strait by the evening of 15 June and were headed east, directly for Saipan. At 1700 on 16 June, they joined the *Yamato* force and spent the night in refuelling, finishing at 0300 on the 17th. Early on the morning of the 18th, Ozawa commenced search operations and stole a march on the Americans when, at 1430, his search planes spotted an American task force. It was divided into three groups, included six carriers, and was 380 nautical miles to the north-east. However, the distance being too great, Ozawa decided against launching an attack that day; instead he chose to wait until early the next morning, by which time the enemy task force would have closed to 300 nautical miles, and then launch an attack with all his available forces.

At 2000 Ozawa ordered his Advance Force (the Second Fleet) to detach and advance 100 nautical miles ahead of the main body (the Third Fleet), thus stationing his forces in depth as a precaution against air attacks. Unfortunately, although there was tactical logic in this disposition in that it would initially allow the Advance Force to absorb the brunt of enemy air attacks, it also created a situation in which, with his ships widely scattered, Ozawa's carriers lacked sufficient escorts to provide protection against enemy submarines.

At 0300 on 19 June, Ozawa's fleet changed its compass bearing to 50°. At 0330, as his ships bore down upon the American task force, Ozawa launched the first of three waves of search planes (totalling forty-three aircraft). Just over three hours later, at 0634, one of these search planes sighted the US task force off Saipan. This enemy force was further identified as being divided into four groups. At 0730, Ozawa ordered the first attack wave launched.

Spruance was aware that a Japanese fleet was drawing near, but did not know of its exact location. At 0619 he had ordered his ships to reverse course and endeavoured to station them for defence against an air attack. At 1000, radar picked up Japanese aircraft (the Third Squadron), composed of forty-six dive bombers, eight torpedo bombers and fourteen Zero fighters) closing from the east at a distance of 150 nautical miles. Task Force 58 launched its total fighter strength of 450 aircraft. After the war, Fleet Admiral Nimitz and Professor E. B. Potter described this action:

As the first wave of Japanese attackers were re-forming themselves at a point about 70 miles away from Task Force 58, the incredible capabilities of the Combat Information Centre (CIC) sprang into action, guiding the Hellcats over the enemy's compass position, and instructing them to wait there at high altitude. Swooping down on the poorly trained Japanese formations, the fighters immediately shot down 25 enemy. A few of the enemy planes were able to break through the American defensive perimeter and reach the fleet line of battle, but there they were blown to bits by antiaircraft shells equipped with the formidable VT proximity fuse. One plane which was able to pass through this defensive wall of steel dropped a near miss on the heavy cruiser *Minneapolis*, while another hit the *South Dakota* with a bomb which caused many casualties, but no serious damage to the ship itself.

Afterwards, only 27 Japanese aircraft returned to their carriers, while all American planes but one landed safely.

The second attack of 129 aircraft from Ozawa's main force were intercepted and their numbers cut in half by Hellcats about fifty miles in front of the US task force. Of those Japanese planes which survived this onslaught, the only results achieved were a suicide plunge into the side of the battleship *Indiana*, and two other hits which set *Bunker Hill* afire. Only thirty aircraft from this wave made it back to their carriers. Of the forty-nine aircraft of the third wave, most were unable even to find the US task force, and ended up dropping their bombs in the ocean and heading for airfields on Guam, where thirty of them were shot down by Hellcats waiting in ambush. Of the eighty-two planes of the second attack force which had been launched at 1003, approximately half were able to find their way to the American task force, but inflicted only light damage with a few near misses. Only eleven returned to their carriers.

In this way, on the first day of the attack Ozawa had already lost 193 aircraft, in return for which seventeen enemy planes had been shot down, and light damage caused to the battleship *South Dakota* and five other ships. Even more calamitous was that at 0810 on that day Ozawa's flagship, *Taiho*, had been hit by a torpedo from the US submarine *Albacore*. At 1600, it sank after gas fumes, which had been filling its compartments as a result of this attack, ignited in a tremendous explosion. Prior to this, at 1400, the veteran carrier *Shokaku* was hit and sunk by three torpedoes from the submarine *Cavella*. Moving his flag to *Haguro* and then to *Zuikaku*, Ozawa pulled his forces back to plan a second attempt. His air strength had been reduced to a mere 100 planes.

On the following day, 20 June 1944, Mitscher set out in pursuit. But he misjudged Ozawa's position and thus advanced south and did not discover Ozawa's fleet until 1600. With the order 'Launch all aircraft for attack', 216 aircraft (eighty-five fighters, seventy-seven dive bombers, fifty-four torpedo bombers) were sent towards it. To defend against these Ozawa launched his remaining fighters, which shot down twenty enemy craft. Nevertheless, the Americans hit and sank the carrier *Hiyo* with a torpedo, and also damaged the carriers *Chiyoda*, *Zuikaku*, *Junyo* and *Ryuho*, the battleship *Haruna* and the cruiser *Maya*. By the end of the battle on this day, Ozawa was left with only sixty-one aircraft.

Nevertheless, still full of fighting spirit, he ordered Kurita's Advance Force to prepare for a night attack. But this was countermanded by Admiral Toyoda. Recognizing defeat, he ordered Ozawa to withdraw. Although he believed then and later that this was a mistake, Ozawa obeyed, calling off the night attack planned for 2100, and ordering all his forces to pull back towards the north-west. After the war he remarked: 'If I had been the commander of the Combined Fleet, I would probably have gone through and carried out the night attack.' However, given the disparity in fighting strength between the Japanese and US forces, and the fuel situation on the Japanese side, it is more likely that the Japanese fleet would have been annihilated.

The Battle of the Philippine Sea was a devastating loss for the Japanese navy. What lay behind the crushing defeat of Ozawa's force, the largest Japanese fleet to be assembled since the start of the Pacific War? One reason is that the copies of plans for Z-go (A-go's forerunner) had fallen into American hands, and thus Spruance knew almost the entire composition of the Japanese involved, as well as their plan of attack. Moreover, the Japanese had wrongly predicted that the primary target of an American landing would be Palau; so one could say that even before battle began, Japan had lost the war of information. A second reason is simply that American weapons and tactics were superior to those used by the Japanese Navy: the Grumman F6 was far superior to its Japanese counterpart, the Zero, in both quality and quantity; in aerial combat they were guided by the US carrier's Combat Information Centre; and the destructive power of their anti-aircraft shells was hugely increased by the proximity fuse, of whose existence the Japanese were not even aware until after the war. A third reason lies in Ozawa's strategy of trying to outrange the enemy. Utilizing the superior range of his aircraft, he had hoped to launch a forestalling attack from a range of over 350 nautical miles while their carriers were still out of the Americans' range. However, this strategy became feasible only if it was carried out by well-trained and superior flight crews, whereas the level of training of Japanese navy flight crews at this point in the war was generally low, and the level of Ozawa's crews was especially poor. His carriers had been berthed at Tawi Tawi for over a month and new aircrews had had little chance to train sufficiently.

Thus in reality Ozawa's task force had fighting strength of neither the quality nor the quantity necessary to challenge successfully the American task force in a decisive battle. Realistically it would probably have been more effective for Ozawa to have chosen the time and the place more subjectively, and struck at the Americans with a series of surprise attacks.

The Battle of Leyte Gulf

After the loss of the Marianas, Imperial Headquarters drew up plans for Sho-go – Operation Victory. The plan was this: without relying on carriers, but under the protection of land-based air power, the entire surface force of the Combined Fleet would sortie to annihilate the American landing armada, wherever it chose to strike next. Operation Sho-go was subdivided into numerous contingency plans, depending upon where the Americans attacked: Sho-1 (the Philippines), Sho-2 (Taiwan/Okinawa), Sho-3 (southern Japan: Honshu, Shikoku and Kyushu) and Sho-4 (northern Japan: Hokkaido and the Chichijima Island chain).

On the morning of 18 October 1944, American forces commenced landing operations on Leyte Island, and at 1730 on the same day Admiral Toyoda gave orders for Sho-1 to be put into operation. At the time the three units of the Combined Fleet were comprised as follows:

> The First Flying Column (commander: Vice Admiral Takeo Kurita)
>   First Force (directly led by Admiral Kurita)
>   1st Battleship Division: *Yamato, Musashi, Nagato*
>   4th Cruiser Division: *Atago, Takao, Chokai, Maya*
>   5th Cruiser Division: *Myoko, Haguru*
>   2nd Destroyer Division: *Noshiro*, nine destroyers
>   Second Force (commander: Vice Admiral Yoshio Suzuki)
>   3rd Battleship Division: *Kongo, Haruna*
>   7th Cruiser Division: *Kumano, Suzuya, Tone, Chikuma*
>   10th Destroyer Division: *Yahagi*, six destroyers
>   Third Force (commander: Vice Admiral Shoji Nishimura)
>   2nd Battleship Division: *Yamashiro, Fuso, Mogami*, four destroyers

The First Flying Column was to be the Main Force of Operation Sho-1. Admiral Kurita was to lead his First and Second Forces north along the west coast of Palawan Island, through the Sibuyan Sea and the San Bernadino Straits and from there, on the morning of the 25th, attack the landing forces in Leyte Gulf. At the same time, Admiral Nishimura would lead the Third Force through the Sulu Sea and the Strait of Surigao, and also charge into Leyte Gulf on the morning of the 25th. Setting sail from its berths in Linga the First Flying Column arrived in the Gulf of Brunei at 1200 on the 20th, and after refuelling set sail again at 0800 on the 22nd, headed for Leyte Gulf.

> The Second Flying Column (commander: Vice Admiral Kiyohide Shima)
>   21st Cruiser Squadron: *Nachi, Ashigara*
>   1st Destroyer Division: *Abukuma*, seven destroyers

Shima's little fleet sortied out from the Japanese mainland on 15 October, and after passing Amami Oshima Island, and going through the Sulu Sea and the Surigao Strait, it was to dash into Leyte Gulf after Nishimura's force.

Task Force (commander: Vice Admiral Jisaburo Ozawa,
3rd Carrier Division: *Zuiho, Chiyoda, Chitose, Zuikaku*
4th Carrier Division: *Ise, Hiuga*
31st Cruiser Division: *Isuzu, Ohyodo, Tama*, eight destroyers

This task force had lost all but 119 of its aircraft in a series of air battles off Formosa in early September. Accordingly, the duty of Ozawa's 'task force' was not that of a primary attacking force, but that of a decoy to lure the American task force north and away from Leyte, thus leaving the American transport fleet prey to the forces of Kurita, Nishimura and Shima. On 20 October at 1700, Ozawa's ships left the Bungo Channel and headed south. Thus, in total, four separate Japanese naval units were advancing simultaneously on Leyte. The success of this complicated plan depended upon well-organized, concerted action and on perfect timing, yet the exchange of information between the various units participating was quite insufficient.

Meanwhile, the attacking US Navy forces in the gulf were positioned in a multi-tiered arrangement. First, both inside and outside Leyte Gulf was the Seventh Fleet in formation and commanded by Vice Admiral Thomas Kinkaid [*q.v.*], Rear Admiral Jesse Oldendorf's Bombardment Force (six old battleships, four heavy cruisers, four light cruisers, twenty-one destroyers) and Rear Admiral Clifton Sprague's three groups of escort carriers (sixteen escort carriers, nine destroyers, twelve escorts). Also in the area were the submarines of Rear Admiral Ralph Christie's submarine fleet. Kinkaid was on board his flagship *Wasach* and the Supreme Commander of the South-West Pacific Area, General Douglas MacArthur, was on board the cruiser *Nashville*. Furthermore, on the ocean to the east of Luzon was stationed Admiral William Halsey's Third Fleet, comprised of four groups of fast carriers, with an imposing total strength of sixteen carriers, six battleships, six heavy cruisers, nine light cruisers and fifty-eight destroyers. Halsey, on board his flagship *New Jersey*, awaited the approach of the Japanese fleet.

As a whole, the Battle for Leyte Gulf contained four separate battles – the Battle of the Sibuyan Sea, the Battle of the Surigao Strait, the Battle of Samar Island and the Battle off Cape Engaño. The first three do not directly concern the subject of this chapter, and need not be described in detail here. But the fourth, the Battle off Cape Engaño, was fought directly between Admiral Halsey's forces and those of Admiral Ozawa.

The Air and Sea Battles off Cape Engaño

At around 0200 on 25 October, an hour or so before Kurita's fleet turned south-east after its passage through the San Bernadino Strait, search planes from Halsey's fleet (Task Force 34) caught two groups of surface units in their radar. It was Ozawa's Advance Force. Mitscher launched a dawn attack force of 180 planes. At 0600, in response to their attack, Ozawa recombined his two groups into one and launched his remaining few Zeros. At 0815, he sent off a wireless message – 'Currently engaged in combat with 80 American aeroplanes' – but as had been the case with many others like it, this message was received by no one. As a result Kurita knew absolutely nothing of Ozawa's situation. By the end of the day, Ozawa's ships had been attacked six times by a total of 527 aircraft, and as night drew in they were set upon by Halsey's light cruiser squadron. The Japanese task force had lost four of its six carriers, as well as the light cruiser *Tama* and two destroyers. When Ozawa, his flag moved from *Zuikaku* to the cruiser *Ohyodo*, heard that there were enemy surface forces in pursuit, he temporarily ordered his ships to reverse course and considered executing a night attack, but it was never carried out.

On the other side, it was at 0800 that Halsey received a desperate message requesting aid from Sprague, who was being battered by Kurita's forces. Almost immediately afterwards, Halsey received another message, this one uncoded and from Kinkaid, requesting air support from the fast carriers. Having already made the destruction of Ozawa's ships his first priority, Halsey continued with his northward advance, but also sent orders to a subordinate carrier group, which was at that moment refuelling in the south-east, commanding them to proceed at full speed and rescue Sprague's escort carriers.

At this point, it seems that Admiral Nimitz at Pearl Harbor, watching over the whole sequence of battle and listening to transmissions from all units involved, decided that it was necessary for him to take some control of the situation and, at just after 1000, he sent to Halsey the following urgent message: 'WHERE IS, REPEAT WHERE IS, TASK FORCE 34? THE WORLD WONDERS.' Halsey was furious, but nevertheless ordered a 180° change of course, from due north to due south. This turn was made at a point only forty-two miles south of Ozawa's fleet, which was nursing along two seriously damaged warships. As a decoy, Ozawa had been a total success, although at the cost of the almost complete destruction of his forces.

At 1100, about the same time that Halsey's ships began to head south, Kurita had regrouped and was charging towards Leyte Gulf again. His forces had been whittled down to four battleships, two heavy cruisers, two light cruisers and eight destroyers. Attacked by American planes seven times since morning and unaware that Halsey's task force was far to the north and until recently closing on Ozawa at full speed, Kurita was mistakenly convinced that he had been surrounded by Halsey's forces. At 1226, a little over an hour since he had resumed it, Kurita called off the second charge into Leyte Gulf and turned north. His aim was to attack an American carrier group that had been reported to be 115 nautical miles at 5° from the lighthouse on Suluan Island. However, this enemy carrier group proved to be no more than a phantom. Moving on false information, Kurita had abandoned his supreme mission, that of penetrating Leyte Gulf and attacking the US forces within. By 2135 on the

25th, he and his ships were once again retreating west through the San Bernardino Strait towards Colon Bay. The enormous sacrifice made by Ozawa, who had risked the total annihilation of his forces and succeeded in luring Halsey to the north, had been in vain.

As Last Naval Supreme Commander and Last Commander of the Combined Fleet

After Japan's defeat in the Battle of Leyte Gulf, Ozawa became the Dean of the Naval Academy on 11 November 1944, and was at the same time made Vice-Chief of the Naval General Staff. The Chief of the General Staff was Admiral Koshiro Oikawa. On becoming Vice-Chief, Ozawa thought it would be best to defend Taiwan, the Philippines and Iwo Jima only with the forces already available in these areas, and to use all other remaining fighting strength to counter the Allied invasion of Okinawa, which it was anticipated would take place in March or April 1945. That way, it seemed possible that enough casualties could be inflicted upon the Americans to induce them into a peace settlement. The Allied landings began on 1 April 1945 and, despite suicide attacks by the land, sea and air forces of the Japanese army and navy (Operation Ten-go), by 23 June the invasion of Okinawa was successfully completed. The last of Japanese naval surface strength, led by Vice Admiral Seichi Ito and consisting of his flagship, the super-battleship *Yamato*, the light cruiser *Yahagi* and eight destroyers, were also thrown into Operation Ten-go. This force was, however, almost totally wiped out by over 300 American carrier planes on the afternoon of 7 April, with *Yamato*'s sinking representing the effective end of the Japanese navy. After the war Ozawa acknowledged that 'As Vice-Chief of Staff at the time, I must bear responsibility for the *Yamato*'s suicide attack.'

With the opening of 1945, Japan's political and strategic situation was rapidly crumbling. Air-raids on the Japanese mainland from American carrier task forces and from bases in the Marianas grew in intensity, and the destruction of shipping by American submarines was also increasing greatly. Air-raids had destroyed 40 per cent of Japan's industrial capacity and fuel reserves were almost totally depleted. Even the quantity of ammunition produced, let alone that of ships or aircraft, had dropped severely. On 7 April, the same day that *Yamato* was sunk, Prime Minister Suzuki, Navy Minister Mitsumasa Yonai and Foreign Minister Shigenori Togo began taking secret steps towards ending the war. Nevertheless, Army Minister Korechika Anami and the Japanese army were insisting upon a fight to the finish, and were busily making preparations for the 'decisive battle' which was supposed to take place on the Japanese mainland.

On 29 May, Ozawa was ordered to replace Admiral Soemu Toyoda and thus became the last Commander of the Combined Fleet, as well as Supreme Commander of the Japanese navy. He owed these appointments to his popularity within the navy and the control he was able to maintain over his subordinates; Navy Minister Yonai, secretly planning for peace, calculated that

Ozawa's prestige would provide enough security against the disorder and possible rebellion which he predicted would occur within the navy at the end of the war. But the Japanese navy had in reality ceased to exist. All that remained to it were a few aircraft. Ozawa made plans for a series of suicide surprise attacks on US air installations on Tinian, Guam and Saipan (Operation Ken), but the war ended (15 August) while these plans were still in a preparatory stage.

After the war Ozawa felt acute responsibility for Japan's defeat; he refused to participate in public gatherings and consistently said nothing about the war. He died peacefully in his home in Setagaya, Tokyo, on 9 November 1966.

PART THREE

The Amphibious Admirals

13

Admiral

Richard L. Conolly
United States Navy

1892–1962

by
Jeffrey G. Barlow

RICHARD Lansing Conolly, born in Waukegan, Illinois, 26 April 1892. Graduated US Naval Academy, Annapolis, 1914. Served in destroyer Smith May 1916– November 1918, including convoy escort duty; awarded Navy Cross. Postgraduate degree in electrical engineering, Columbia University, 1922. Assistant Engineering Officer, USS New York, 1924–5; on Naval Academy Staff, 1925–7; Engineering Officer, USS Concord, 1927–9. Commanded USS Case and Dupont, 1929–30. On course at Naval War College, 1930–1; on staff at College, 1931–3. Aide and Flag Secretary to Commander Cruisers, Scouting Force, 1933–5; Navigator, USS Tennessee, 1935–6; instructor at Naval Academy, 1936–9; Commander, Destroyer Division 7, 1939–41; Commander, Destroyer Squadron 6, 1941.

On 7 December 1941, the nine destroyers of Destroyer Squadron (DesRon) 6 were about 230 miles west of Pearl Harbor when they got the despatch reading, 'Air attack on Pearl Harbor. This is no drill.'* The squadron commander, Captain Richard L. Conolly, was in flag plot on his flagship *Balch* when the message was handed to him. His ships had been at sea for ten days, escorting Vice Admiral William F. Halsey Jr's [*q.v.*] Fast Carrier Task Force, built around *Enterprise*, which was returning to Pearl having delivered a Marine fighter squadron to Wake Island.[1] The ships and aircraft of the task force spent the next

*The author would like to thank the Oral History Office, Columbia University and the US Naval Institute for allowing him to quote from oral histories in their collections. He also would like to thank Mike Walker of the Naval Historical Center's Operational Archives for his help in connection with this chapter.

[1] Richard L. Conolly, Interviews by Donald F. Shaughnessy, 1958 and 1959, transcript, Oral History Research Office, Columbia University, New York, NY, p. 94.

hours fruitlessly searching for the Japanese fleet, before entering Pearl Harbor to refuel during the afternoon and early evening of 8 December.

By December 1941, Conolly had been in the battlefleet for some twenty-two months, first as a destroyer division commander and then as a squadron commander. A bluff, outgoing Irishman, Dick Conolly was an old destroyer hand whose service in these ships dated back to escort duty aboard *Smith* (DD 17) in European waters during World War One. An electrical engineering PG (postgraduate), he prided himself on analytical skills honed during scientific training at Columbia University and on his advocacy of wide-ranging professional training.[2] He was known for his thorough, methodical approach to problem solving and his enjoyment of the challenges and responsibilities which came with new assignments.

In the first few months of the war in the Pacific, Conolly and his squadron were busily engaged as part of Halsey's force in carrying the war to the enemy, as best they could under the circumstances. In late January 1942, after covering the convoying of US troops to Australia, Halsey's ships were ordered to attack the Japanese-held Marshall Islands, at the same time as a Southern Force under Rear Admiral Frank Jack Fletcher attacked the Gilbert Islands. Halsey divided his task force in order to attack the several targets simultaneously. *Balch*, with Dick Conolly on board, and another of DesRon 6's destroyers were assigned with the cruiser *Chester* to bombard Taroa Island, Maloelap atoll. The bombardment group was under the command of Captain Thomas M. Shock, the Captain of *Chester*.[3]

On 1 February 1942, the operation went off as planned. However, the attack on Taroa proved more perfunctory than the aggressive DesRon commander would have liked. Conolly wanted to demolish the target, but *Chester*'s skipper apparently was too concerned about the safety of his ship to remain in the area long enough to accomplish such an extensive bombardment. As Admiral Conolly later recalled:

> I was very much disappointed in the bombardment, because I wanted to go in closer to the island, steam across the end of it, and put the airfield out of commission. We could have steamed across the end of it at high speed about five or six thousand yards away, and could have knocked that airfield practically off the island, with the eight-inch battery the cruiser had and my two destroyers. But the fellow on the cruiser didn't want to.[4]

Conolly and his destroyer squadron were also part of Halsey's force when, in order to create military diversions, it launched hit-and-run raids against Wake Island (24 February) and Marcus Island (4 March). Although these attacks provided a valuable boost to Allied morale, they did not result in significant destruc-

[2]Ibid., pp. 48, 63.

[3]Samuel Eliot Morison, *History of United States Naval Operations in World War II, vol. III: The Rising Sun in the Pacific 1931–April 1942* (Boston, 1948), pp. 261–3.

[4]Conolly oral history, Columbia University, pp. 108–9.

tion to Japanese forces. During the raid against Wake Island, for example, the bombarding cruisers and destroyers remained 14,000 to 16,000 yards offshore, in order to stay outside the range of the island's shore batteries.5 Such long-distance shooting did little to increase the bombardment's destructiveness.

DesRon 6 was with Admiral Halsey too on the famous Doolittle Tokyo Raid. However, the destroyers and the accompanying oilers were dropped behind to refuel on 17 April and thereby missed the excitement the following morning, when Task Force 16 encountered Japanese picket boats and was forced to launch Doolittle's B-25 bombers some hours earlier than planned. Conolly later commented that he regretted that Halsey had not waited for his destroyers. He thought that if DesRon 6 had been with the task force the next morning, it might have been able to sink the Japanese vessels before they had recognized Halsey's force and alerted Japanese authorities to the presence of the American navy some 600 miles from Japan.6

Two days after Task Force 16 had returned to Pearl Harbor from the Doolittle Raid, Captain Conolly was detached from command of DesRon 6 and ordered to duty in the Office of the Chief of Naval Operations (CNO) in Washington.7 He reported in at the end of May 1942. On 8 July, he moved from the Office of the Chief of Naval Operations to Headquarters, Commander-in-Chief, US Fleet (Cominch) – the central headquarters of the operational navy – to become the Assistant Planning Officer. Working for Admiral Ernest J. King [*q.v.*], Cominch and (from March 1942) CNO, proved a difficult but rewarding task.8 Dick Conolly later recalled his interview with Admiral King when he was given the planning job. King asked Conolly, 'Now, just what background have you got to be my assistant planning officer?' When Conolly replied that he had had war experience, King said to him, 'Well, that's fine. I want that. But that's not enough.' The Admiral then asked the Captain if he had been at the Naval War College. Conolly carefully refrained from telling the Admiral that he had been on the staff of the War College when King was there as a student. Instead, he remarked that he had been there at the same time that King had and that he also had served on the staff. Admiral King concluded the interview by commenting to Conolly: 'Well, I'd have liked to have someone with war planning experience, but they can't be found, and yours adds up.'9

As Cominch's Assistant Planning Officer, Conolly served with his army

5Morison, *Rising Sun in the Pacific*, p. 268.

6Conolly oral history, Columbia University, pp. 109–10.

7Admiral Richard L. Conolly's Official Biography, 16 March 1962, p. 2; 'CONOLLY, RICHARD L. ADM' Folder, Box 122, Officer Bio Collection, Operational Archives, Naval Historical Center, Washington DC (hereafter cited as OA).

8For information on King's personality and work habits as CNO/Cominch, see Thomas B. Buell, *Master of Sea Power: A Biography of Fleet Admiral Ernest J. King* (Boston, 1980), pp. 226–39 ff; and Robert W. Love Jr., 'Ernest Joseph King 26 March 1942–15 December 1945', in *The Chiefs Of Naval Operations*, ed. Robert W. Love Jr (Annapolis, Maryland, 1980), pp. 137–79 and this volume.

9Conolly oral history, Columbia University, pp. 114–15.

and army air forces (AAF) counterparts, Brigadier-Generals Albert Wedemeyer and Orvil Anderson, on the Joint Staff Planners (JPS) of the Joint Chiefs of Staff. This responsibility required that Conolly and the others thrash out many of the disagreements which could not be resolved at the Joint Chiefs' level. Another JPS duty was to meet on occasion with the British planners and, functioning as a combined planning staff, to work out Allied priorities. This proved burdensome to Dick Conolly, from time to time, since the British were very intent on seeing that the overwhelming operational and logistic effort continue to be concentrated on the European war, while his own interest was oriented towards the war in the Pacific.[10] During his time in Washington, Conolly felt that he worked well with Albert Wedemeyer. His relationshp with his AAF counterpart was something else again. Dick Conolly continued to have personal and professional disagreements with Orvil Anderson throughout his tour on the Joint Staff Planners. The two men's differing conceptions of the proper role for the army air forces undoubtedly was one major reason for these clashes. Conolly stressed the AAF's importance as a supporting arm for the army in the land campaign, while Anderson argued strongly that it must assume an independent role in national strategy.

During his time at Cominch headquarters, Dick Conolly was involved in the planning for several pivotal operations, including the invasion of Guadalcanal and Operation Torch (the invasion of North Africa). With regard to the latter operation, Conolly remembered being called in to see Rear Admiral Charles M. ('Savvy') Cooke Jr, King's chief planner, after the Joint Chiefs of Staff had come back from London with the outline plan for Torch. Conolly noted: 'Admiral Cooke called me in and said, "Now, you've read this over, Dick. What do you think of it?" I said, "I think it will succeed." He said, "You and I and Admiral King are the only ones who think it will. Everybody in the Army is against it – the whole General Staff."'[11]

Although Dick Conolly remained on Cominch's staff for only about seven months, he left that duty assignment believing that it was the best possible education he could have had for seeing the war as a whole. In February 1943, Conolly, with his replacement on hand at Cominch headquarters,[12] was ready for sea duty. He had already received orders to go out to the South Pacific to command the battleship *Washington*. However, something else suddenly intervened. At that time, Admiral King had a policy that no one could be promoted to flag rank unless he had had a major ship command (a cruiser, a battleship or an aircraft carrier). The *Washington* was to have been Dick Conolly's major ship command. However, the planned build-up for Operation Husky – the invasion of Sicily – changed everything for Conolly. Within hours of the time that he was to leave for the west coast, his orders were cancelled. Savvy Cooke informed him that it was Admiral King's decision that

[10]Ibid., pp. 115–16.   [11]Ibid., p. 117.
[12]Bernard H. Bieri, whom Conolly had relieved in 1942, was brought back as his replacement.

he be promoted to rear admiral without having commanded a major ship and that he be sent to the Mediterranean, to an amphibious command.[13]

Before Conolly left for a tour of base sites in the Mediterranean, he managed to select a chief of staff. Captain (later Vice Admiral) George C. Dyer, the intelligence officer on King's planning staff, had just received Cominch's permission to go back to sea. While awaiting word of his new command, he was visited by Dick Conolly. As Dyer remembered, the question and answer were supremely simple. Conolly 'said, "I'm about to be promoted to flag rank and go over to the Mediterranean,"' then added: '"We're going to do the invasion of Sicily. Wouldn't you like to go along as my Chief of Staff?" I said, "Nothing would please me more." So, I went along as his Chief of Staff.'[14]

Rear Admiral Conolly's new command was an administrative command, not an operational one. He was named Commander of Landing Craft and Bases, North-West African Waters – a title which Admiral King humorously abbreviated ComLanCrabNaw. The purpose of the newly established command was to set up amphibious bases along the North African coast in preparation for the Sicilian landings and to organize and train the landing craft that were arriving from the States for use in Husky. The decision to establish Conolly's command had been made in Washington, without consultation with some of the navy commanders on the scene in the Mediterranean. The new amphibious force commander there, Rear Admiral John L. Hall Jr, was one who was not consulted, and he was not happy about it. As he later recalled:

> [T]hey had somebody in Admiral King's office in Washington arranging to set up bases in all these little ports on the north coast of Africa, with machine tools. All I wanted was two or three repair ships. I didn't want these fixed bases, but I had nothing to do with it. . . . First thing I knew, Rear Admiral Richard M. [*sic*] Conolly, of the class below me at the Naval Academy, came over and reported to me to command . . . [the] landing craft and bases of my command.[15]

The new command was a tremendous responsibility for a newly promoted rear admiral. In February 1943, a large number of the landing craft destined for use in Operation Husky set out across the Atlantic, in convoys shepherded by regular navy ships, headed for the Mediterranean. Many of the crews of the LSTS (landing ship, tank) had never been at sea before.[16] The responsibility for organizing these vessels and training their crews, once they arrived in the Mediterranean, was all Conolly's. It was one, however, that he had no trouble in meeting.

[13]Conolly oral history, Columbia University, pp. 119–22.

[14]George C. Dyer, Interviews by John T. Mason Jr, April 1969–May 1971, transcript, Oral History Program, US Naval Institute, Annapolis, Maryland, pp. 7–261.

[15]John Lesslie Hall Jr, Interviews by John T. Mason Jr, 1963, transcript, Oral History Research Office, Columbia University, New York, NY, pp. 128–9.

[16]H. Kent Hewitt, Interviews by John T. Mason Jr and another, unnamed interviewer, 1961, transcript, Oral History Research Office, Columbia University, New York, NY, pp. 20–9.

Rear Admiral Conolly assumed his duties as ComLanCrabNaw on 16 March 1943,[17] and wasted no time in acquainting his staff with the magnitude of the job to be done. Dick Conolly had no problem in delegating authority to his subordinates.[18] His approach to command was to sketch out his thinking on the major issues and then allow his staff to work out the details. As his first wartime Chief of Staff, George Dyer, explained: 'Admiral Conolly made, with no problem at all, all the big decisions. He didn't pay any attention to the details. The Chief of Staff handled all the details.'[19] Conolly was extremely successful in motivating the people who worked for him. He accomplished this by maintaining frequent personal contact with people at the different levels and by imbuing them with his own enthusiasm for the tasks at hand. As his second Chief of Staff, Captain (later Vice-Admiral) Charles Wellborn Jr, recalled:

At the beginning of the day, maybe at breakfast or maybe at a quick conference . . . he would get his staff going on the lines that he wanted to pursue for that day. Then he'd be off to circulate around with the various people who comprised the force. He had personal contact with them. He had great enthusiasm himself and I think he transferred a lot of this enthusiasm to the various people who comprised his force.[20]

In order to accommodate the large number of landing craft expected, LanCrabNaw was soon opening and utilizing almost every available port of at least the minimum necessary size from the Spanish Moroccan frontier to a point just east of Algiers. The headquarters was established at Arzeu, located east of Oran, close to where General Eisenhower had already set up an army amphibious training command under Major-General Michael O'Daniel. Other bases under Conolly's command eventually included – from west to east – Port Lyautey (French Morocco), Nemours, Beni-Saf, Mostaganem (across the bay from Arzeu), Cherchel and Tenes (all in Algeria). Following the defeat of the Axis forces in Tunisia, the ports of Bizerte and Tunis were also acquired.[21]

After spending his first days in Oran, Conolly moved with his staff to Arzeu, in order to be close to the army amphibious training camp at Port au Poule.

[17]Rear Admiral Richard L. Conolly's Official Biography, 17 August 1944, p. 3; 'CONOLLY, RICHARD L. ADM' Folder, Box 122, Officer Bio Collection, OA.

[18]As Admiral H. Kent Hewitt, Commander Naval Forces North-west African Waters and Commander Eighth Fleet, expressed it, 'a commander can't do all the thinking for himself. The commander has to make the decisions, but let his staff do some of the thinking for him, and present the situation to him for decision.' Hewitt oral history, Columbia University, pp. 24–38.

[19]Dyer oral history, US Naval Institute, pp. 10–369.

[20]Charles Wellborn Jr, Interviews by John T. Mason Jr, November 1971–May 1972, transcript, Oral History Program, US Naval Institute, Annapolis, Maryland, pp. 6–214.

[21]Hewitt oral history, Columbia University; and Dyer oral history, US Naval Institute, pp. 7–264.

There Conolly worked closely with General O'Daniel, assisting in the setting up of the training establishment that was used to provide the army troops with the fundamentals of amphibious warfare. Dick Conolly got along well with the practical but forceful O'Daniel, whom he considered a fine officer in every way. Conolly recalled, 'We had a fight every day, I guess, but they all turned out to be inconsequential in the end.'[22]

At this time, many of the practical aspects of getting the troops and equipment ashore still had not been satisfactorily worked out. As Vice Admiral H. Kent Hewitt [*q.v.*], Commander Naval Forces, North-West African Waters (Com-NavNaw) and Commander Eighth Fleet, recalled, 'This was the first big operation in which these landing craft had ever been employed. There were still a number of problems to work out in that connection. . . . '[23] Indeed, the US Army, which had not been satisfied with the navy's handling of the landings during Torch, wanted to use rubber pontoons as assault craft to ferry the troops ashore. Admiral Hewitt thought such a proposal was absurd. As he commented on an army training paper which advocated this plan, 'Rubber boats might be serviceable as life preservers. Might have some value for a raider landing. But for the assault!! . . . I wouldn't guarantee they'd paddle straight in formation for even 100 yards in the dark.'[24] The upshot of this disagreement was a meeting at Port au Poule at which Lieutenant-General George Patton and Vice Admiral Hewitt presided. Admiral Conolly remembered that after a heated exchange on the issue, General Patton got up and said to the army representatives, 'Once and for all, the navy is responsible for getting you ashore and they can put you ashore in any damned thing they want to.'[25] The next day, General O'Daniel called Admiral Conolly into his office and said, 'Well, of course, you're going ahead with rubber boats, aren't you?' Conolly replied in the negative, and when O'Daniel questioned him again, he replied, 'No, we're not going to use rubber boats. They're completely out. From now on, we'll train in LCVP's [landing craft, vehicle, personnel].'[26]

Another problem that was worrying the planners was how to enable the LSTs to discharge their cargoes safely on to the Sicilian beaches. Most of the Sicilian beaches were fronted by 'false beaches' – sand bars covered by a few feet of water which would prevent the LSTs from passing over them – behind which were 'runnels' (lagoons deep enough to drown tanks and other vehicles attempting to wade ashore).[27] Without some way of bridging the distance

[22]Conolly oral history, Columbia University, p. 125.

[23]Hewitt oral history, Columbia University, pp. 12–15.

[24]'ARMY'S RUBBER BOAT PROPOSAL', n.d. – typed notes taken from an April 1943 document, ComNavNaw files; 'HUSKY – PLANNING, TRAINING AND EXECUTION OF 1943–1953' Folder, Box 51, Papers of Samuel E. Morison, OA. These papers consist of the office files compiled by Morison and his staff for use in the writing of Morison's fifteen-volume history of US naval operations in World War Two.

[25]Conolly oral history, Columbia University, p. 140.   [26]Ibid.

[27]Samuel E. Morison, *History of United States Naval Operations in World War II*, vol. IX: *Sicily–Salerno–Anzio January 1943–June 1944* (Boston, 1954), pp. 30–1.

covered by the runnels, the LSTS would be unable to get their cargoes safely on to the beaches.

British and American planners had been working on a solution for some time, with only partial success. Finally, a joint effort by Admiral Conolly and his people and planners on Admiral Hall's 8th Amphibious Force staff paid off. It was determined that pontoon causeways could be hinged to the sides of LSTS, to be lowered, hooked together and attached to the bows, once the ships had grounded on the false beaches.[28]

The concept worked successfully in a number of tests. The most important test occurred during a visit to Arzeu by General Sir Harold Alexander, the ground forces commander. Lieutenant-General Mark Clark had invited him to witness the army's solution for crossing the runnels. Its answer was to drag the tanks and other vehicles from the LSTS through the water of the runnels to shore and then attempt to dry them out. Admiral Conolly, who was present for this test, recalled that while the army was demonstrating its concept, the LST which had been tested with the pontoon causeways arrived, towing them behind it. Conolly noted: 'All the time as Alexander was watching this test of the drowned-out [army] equipment, he kept casting his eye up the beach. And finally there came a tractor out from the bow of the LST and fished the ramp on the end of these two causeways which they'd finally got harnessed up. Then it went over the ramp and landed on the beach.'[29] By this time, the navy's LST had stolen General Alexander's complete attention. When a medium tank made its way to the beach over the pontoon causeway, Dick Conolly recalled, General Alexander went running up the beach to see the operation at close range. Alexander was obviously very impressed with what he saw. His first question to Admiral Conolly was 'How long have you had this working?'[30]

When Conolly had first arrived in the Mediterranean, he had requested that Admiral Hewitt allow him to command one of the landing forces for the Sicilian invasion. At that time Hewitt had assured him that he would be given one of the coveted commands. In early April 1943, Hewitt honoured his promise. ComNavNaw wrote to Major-General Geoffrey Keyes, Deputy Commander Task Force 343, on 9 April, 'I now propose that Rear Admiral Conolly, Commander Landing Craft and Bases, be assigned to ENSA [the US 3rd Infantry Division, commanded by Major-General Lucian Truscott Jr], as the craft engaged will be entirely landing craft. . . . '[31] The pairing of Conolly and Truscott was to prove highly beneficial to the success of Husky. From the first, Dick Conolly's attitude was that it was the navy's job to do what it could to make sure the 3rd Infantry Division's landings were successful. The relationship between the two headquarters was so cordial that a British

[28]Just who deserves the majority of the credit for the idea remains in dispute.
[29]Conolly oral history, p. 136.   [30]Ibid.
[31]Typed extracts from a memorandum from VADM Hewitt to MGEN Keyes, 9 April 1943, ComNavNaw Files; 'HUSKY – PLANNING, TRAINING AND EXECUTION OF 1943–1953' Folder, Box 51, Morison Papers, OA.

observer with the assault force, designated Joss Force, praised it highly. He reported:

Coming from London last April, it was most refreshing to meet the Naval Staff of Admiral Connolly's [*sic*] headquarters in North Africa. The attitude there was not one of educating the army to an understanding of Naval limitations . . . it was rather a complete and generous appreciation that the Army had the 'sticky end' of the job, and that somehow or other the Navy would find ways of seeing them through and of implementing *any* landing plan dictated by the tactical needs of the military tasks. . . . In fact, however monstrous the military demands, I can recall no single instance where they were flatly rejected, the most unpromising response being 'I very much doubt its practicability, but we'll try it out and see.'[32]

During the final weeks of training before the invasion of Sicily, Joss Force polished its amphibious proficiency at the new advanced base at Bizerte.[33] This hard work paid off during the actual landings on 10 July 1943. Despite the heavy swell in the offshore anchorages and the heavy surf on the beaches astride the port of Licata, the Joss Force landings took place almost completely as planned, and by noon on D-Day Licata was in American hands.[34]

It was at Licata that Admiral Conolly got his first chance to employ naval gunfire in support of ground troops, an aspect of his responsibility as an amphibious commander which was to assume an increasing importance for him in subsequent operations. He recalled that at one point during the operation General Truscott became concerned about the fire his troops were receiving from some enemy artillery batteries. Conolly ordered the cruiser *Brooklyn* to fire on these targets for five minutes, and then, for good measure, he ordered an additional five minutes of firing. It was then, according to Conolly, that his Chief of Staff turned to him and said, 'My God, Admiral, do you know how many rounds of ammunition those guns will fire in five minutes?'[35] Not unexpectedly, after ten minutes of gunfire from *Brooklyn*'s six-inch guns, the enemy batteries failed to resume their firing.

With Sicily over, Conolly and his staff returned to Bizerte to prepare for the

[32]Emphasis in original. COHQ [Combined Operations Headquarters] Bulletin No. Y/1, 'NOTES ON THE PLANNING AND ASSAULT PHASES OF THE SICILIAN CAMPAIGN by a Military Observer [Colonel R. D. Q. Henriques, a British Combined Operations staff officer]', October 1943; 'THE SICILIAN CAMPAIGN Notes on Planning & Assault Phases 1943' Folder, Box 56, Morison Papers, OA.

[33]It should be remembered that Conolly was responsible for preparing, organizing and equipping not only his own force of landing craft, but those of Rear Admirals Hall (DIME Force) and Alan G. Kirk (CENT Force), as well.

[34]See the comments in S. W. Roskill, *The War at Sea 1939–45*, vol. III: *The Offensive Part I 1st June 1943–31st May 1944* (London, 1960), p. 136; and Morison, *Sicily–Salerno–Anzio*, pp. 90–1.

[35]Conolly oral history, Columbia University, p. 157. For an account of *Brooklyn*'s participation in the invasion of Sicily, see 'U.S.S. BROOKLYN CL40 Action Report Of The "Husky" Operation [10–14 July 1943]', Serial 008, 25 July 1943; Box 867, World War II Action Reports File, OA.

invasion of Italy. The month of August 1943 was busy with planning, and with the staging and concentrating of the necessary landing craft for the invasion. Although Conolly had his training responsibilities as ComLanCrabNaw, he was not scheduled to take part as an amphibious commander for the upcoming Operation Avalanche, the landings at Salerno. The Southern Attack Force was to be commanded by Admiral Hall, and the Northern Attack Force was to be under Commodore G. N. Oliver, Royal Navy. The plans called for using almost all of the landing craft under Conolly's administrative command and for his Chief of Staff, Captain George Dyer, to serve as an amphibious group commander under Oliver to land the British 46th Division.

Dick Conolly, undeterred by this gloomy scenario, was determined to participate in the operation, even though it would mean serving under Oliver, his junior in rank. Accordingly, he received Admiral Hewitt's permission to approach Admiral Andrew Cunningham [*q.v.*], Commander-in-Chief, Mediterranean. Admiral Conolly commented: 'I told . . . [Admiral Cunningham] I wanted to command this task group, and that the ships were all mine and I had successfully commanded the task force at Sicily and I didn't want to be left out of this one. He said, "Well, are you willing to serve under Oliver?" I said, "Certainly." He said, "Well, all right then."'36

The landings at Salerno taught Conolly the lesson that even the best-planned amphibious operations could be thrown off by unexpected occurrences. On one of his two beaches (Red Beach), the assault went exactly according to plan and with almost perfect timing. On the other one (Green Beach), however, an LCT(R) (landing craft, tank (rocket)), supporting the landings, fired its rockets on to the wrong section of the beach. This, in turn, resulted in the assault waves being guided into that section of beach rather than the portion where they were supposed to land. Confusion and heavy casualties resulted from this change in plans, and, as a result, nothing could be unloaded on that beach during D-Day.37

Admiral Conolly maintained his eager, aggressive outlook throughout his participation at Salerno. For example, on the morning of D-Day, when he was unable to communicate with the destroyers on gunfire-support duty (which had reverted to Oliver's command), Conolly took his flagship *Biscayne* in to fire on German shore batteries south of Salerno. *Biscayne* fired twelve rounds of five-inch/38-calibre ammunition before the enemy guns ceased firing.38

36Conolly oral history, ibid., p. 172; and Richard L. Conolly, 'THE LANDING AT SALERNO IN WORLD WAR II An Address Before THE NAVAL HISTORICAL FOUNDATION May 14, 1957', p. 4; 'CONOLLY, RICHARD L. Adm USN "The Landing at Salerno in World War II"' Folder, Box labelled 'WW II CF INDIV. PERS. CELPHANE – COMSTOCK', Indiv. Pers. Files, World War II Command File, OA.

37Roskill, *The Offensive Part I*, p. 171; and 'ACTION REPORT COMMANDER TASK GROUP 85.1 OPERATION AVALANCHE – ADDITIONAL REPORT OF', Serial 0562, 21 November 1943, pp. 37, 39; Box 302, World War II Action Reports File, OA.

38Conolly oral history, Columbia University, pp. 178, 191–2; and 'ACTION REPORT OPERATION AVALANCHE', p. 6.

The biggest German threat to the amphibious shipping off Salerno was the radio-controlled bomb, which was launched against major targets by high-altitude bombers. Dick Conolly found he could counter both the high-altitude bombers and the lower-altitude fighter bombers by laying smoke over the anchorage – something he had tried first during the invasion of Sicily – and not allowing the anchored ships to fire back at the German aircraft unless they were being directly threatened with attack. As he remarked:

> In my anchorage we had smoke generators on our small ships (sub-chasers and YMS's), and then we put smoke generators ashore . . . and when we'd get a red alert, we'd start the smoke generators and smother the whole anchorage with smoke during the bombing attack. We knew it was effective, because we could intercept the conversation[s] in German between the commander of the flight and his squadron commanders.39

The use of smoke to protect amphibious shipping against air attack was a tactic that Admiral Conolly advocated strongly in operations thereafter. Eventually, it was adopted by (then) Vice Admiral (later Admiral) Richmond Kelly Turner [*q.v.*] for regular use in amphibious operations in the Pacific.

On 18 September 1943, during his participation in Avalanche, Admiral Conolly was detached as ComLanCrabNaw and ordered to duty as an amphibious commander in the Pacific Fleet.40 Years later, he recalled wryly: 'The idea was for me to take the lessons learned in the Mediterranean out to Pearl Harbor to be used in the Central Pacific offensive, then about to start. In plain English, this meant I was to go out to try to tell Kelly Turner how to run his business. This was for me, literally, out of the frying pan into the fire.'41 He took with him his new Chief of Staff, Captain Charles Wellborn, and several other officers from his staff. His previous Chief of Staff, George Dyer, had been struck in the leg by a spent twenty-millimetre shell during a German air attack on 15 September and was resting in a hospital with a badly broken leg.

After spending a few days with his family in Washington DC, Admiral Conolly headed to the west coast. His destination was San Diego, close to Camp Pendleton, California, where the recently activated 4th Marine Division was in training in preparation for its participation in Operation Flintlock – the invasion of Kwajalein.42 No sooner had Conolly arrived in San Diego (reporting in as Commander Group Three, 5th Amphibious Force on 23

39Conolly oral history, ibid., pp. 194–5; and 'ACTION REPORT OPERATION AVALANCHE', pp. 41–2.

40Rear Admiral Conolly's Official Biography, 17 August 1944, p. 3; 'CONOLLY, RICHARD L. ADM' Folder, Box 122, Officer Bio Collection, OA. Because of a delay in obtaining a relief, he was not relieved until 25 September. Conolly oral history, Columbia University, pp. 204, 207.

41Conolly, 'THE LANDING AT SALERNO', p. 8.

42Conolly's original orders had been issued with the intention that he mount the landing of the 2nd Marine Division at Tarawa, but he was delayed too long at Salerno. Conolly oral history, Columbia University, pp. 210–11.

October) than he was ordered to Pearl Harbor for temporary duty, to attend a conference with the Pacific Fleet's senior amphibious commanders, Rear Admiral Kelly Turner and Major-General Holland M. Smith USMC [*q.v.*].43 It was during the discussion with Turner and Smith over the Kwajalein operation that Dick Conolly displayed a bit of his temper. He recalled:

> I remember they had the outline plan, and Turner said to me, 'Now, as a result of the experience we've had at Tarawa, I want to make sure that we use enough gunfire on getting this island ready.'
>
> He nettled me a little, and I said, 'Admiral, I'm going to sink that God-damn island. There won't be any place for the Marines to land!'
>
> Everybody looked aghast and looked at Admiral Turner, and Admiral Turner's face lit up, and he said, 'That's the way to talk, boy!'44

Upon their return to the United States, Conolly and Major-General Harry Schmidt, the 4th Marine Division's Commanding General, set about whipping their untried forces into shape. Conolly had asked for and received a headquarters located on Camp Pendleton, which allowed him to work closely with his Marine counterpart. During November and December 1943, Conolly's staff was assembled and the ships and craft assigned to Group Three reported. Plans and amphibious training were handled as joint matters, with all action taken having the agreement of both Admiral Conolly and General Schmidt, as the respective attack force and landing force commanders. During this time each Regimental Combat Team of the 4th Marine Division was given a two-week period of ship-to-shore training from transports.45

In December, a firm decision was received that Amphibious Group Three would lift the 4th Marine Division and attack the northern part of the Kwajalein atoll – the primary targets being the islands of Roi and Namur.46 A rehearsal for the attack on the Northern Islands was held at San Clemente Island on 2–3 January 1944. Most of the ships which had been assigned fire-support duties for the landings were present and fired on targets located on San Clemente. The rehearsal revealed problems – particularly with the inexperienced amphibian tractor crews and some almost equally inexperienced LST crews – which were to recur at Roi and Namur.47 Three days later,

---

43He arrived at Pearl Harbor to find that Kelly Turner had suffered a relapse of malaria. For a few days, Conolly stood by in case he had to take Turner's place in the Makin operation.

44Conolly oral history, Columbia University, p. 213.

45'COMMANDER TASK FORCE 53 (COMMANDER FIFTH AMPHIBIOUS FORCE, GROUP 3) REPORT OF AMPHIBIOUS OPERATIONS FOR THE CAPTURE OF ROI AND NAMUR ISLANDS (FLINTLOCK)', Serial 0028, 23 February 1944, p. 1; Box 197, World War II Action Reports File, OA.

46The overall plan for Flintlock envisioned assaults on Kwajalein by three attack forces – Conolly's Northern Attack Force (Roi and Namur Islands), Kelly Turner's Southern Attack Force (Kwajalein Island), and Rear Admiral Harry W. Hill's Sundance Attack Force (Majuro atoll). Turner, as Commander Fifth Amphibious Force, was also the Joint Expeditionary Force Commander, while Major-General Holland Smith was the Commander Expeditionary Troops.

47Conolly oral history, Columbia University, pp. 215–17; and Jeter A. Isely and Philip Y. Crowl, *The U.S. Marines and Amphibious War: Its Theory and its Practice in the Pacific* (Princeton, 1951), pp. 268–9.

Amphibious Group Three's LSTS, loaded with most of the amphibian tractors, departed San Diego for Hawaii, en route to Kwajalein. The main body of Group Three departed from San Diego on 13 January.

The actual attack, which began on 31 January 1944, proved both better and worse than had been anticipated. The landings (directed against four outlying islands) by the LVTS (Landing Vehicle, Tracked) on D-Day were slow and laborious. Those the following day against Roi and Namur started out chaotically but were finally put right when Admiral Conolly (after consultation with General Schmidt) ordered the Namur assault to begin, even though not all of the assault elements were in position. Vice Admiral Raymond Spruance [*q.v.*], Commander Fifth Fleet, who was watching the assault on board *Indianapolis*, turned to one of his staff after Conolly had restored order out of the chaos and remarked: 'Seeing this proves that you can put complete faith in the men you have selected to do a job.'[48] Admiral Conolly later faulted the complexity of the landing plan for magnifying the weaknesses of untried crews. One particular bright spot in the attack, however, was the effectiveness of the naval bombardment in destroying Japanese defence positions and installations on Roi–Namur. During the planning period for Flintlock, Conolly's staff had determined that it would be necessary to use accurate close-range fire from major-calibre guns to destroy reinforced concrete pillboxes and other strong points on the island.[49] During the operation, this was accomplished methodically and with great skill. In fact, at one point, when several of the heavy gunfire-support ships seemed hesitant about closing with the Japanese shore batteries, Dick Conolly personally manned the voice radio (TBS) circuit and said forcefully, 'When I say close in, I mean *close in*, under two thousand yards!' It was this incident which earned the Admiral the admiring Marine nickname 'Close-In' Conolly. As the Admiral later remarked: 'There was ever present the shadow of Tarawa over this operation, and I think it was reassuring to our troops to know that we were going to give them everything we had in the way of gunfire.'[50]

Following the successful attacks at Kwajalein, Conolly found himself somewhat at a loss as to what his next operation would be. He was a forceful individual with his own ideas of how best to mount an amphibious assault, and after having conducted successful landings in three major amphibious operations, he was clearly one of the most experienced amphibious commanders in the navy. While it cannot be proven, it is likely that Kelly Turner saw Dick Conolly as a possible rival. That may be the reason that Conolly was not employed as effectively as he could have been in the final months of the war. Commenting on why he felt that Conolly and Turner didn't get along well together, Conolly's Chief of Staff, Charles Wellborn, said:

[48]Quoted in Thomas B. Buell, *The Quiet Warrior: A Biography of Admiral Raymond A. Spruance* (Boston, 1974), p. 223.
[49]See 'AMPHIBIOUS OPERATIONS FOR THE CAPTURE OF ROI AND NAMUR', p. 40.
[50]Conolly oral history, Columbia University, p. 217.

They were two very strong, very able leaders. I think Kelly Turner tended to, maybe subconsciously, feel that in Admiral Connoly [*sic*] he had a possible competitor, and I think he tended not to give Admiral Connoly [*sic*] any very tremendous opportunities to distinguish himself for this reason. In this respect . . . [Conolly] may also . . . have tended to – antagonize is too strong a word, but tended to make Admiral Turner kind of stand off from him a little bit.[51]

After several months of waiting, Conolly asked Turner what his next assignment might be. The next day, Turner called him into his office and said, 'I find you operate independently very well, and I don't want you with me. You and I won't get along. But I'd like to have you do these independent operations, and I'm thinking of asking them to give you the Guam operation.'[52]

The invasion of Guam proved to be the culmination of Dick Conolly's many months of experience as an amphibious commander. To facilitate joint planning between his amphibious group and the troops of Major-General Roy S. Geiger's 3rd Amphibious Corps, he flew to Guadalcanal in April 1944 and set up a temporary headquarters near the Corps' 3rd Marine Division. Staying there for some ten days, until the arrival of their flagship *Appalachian*, the naval officers of Amphibious Group Three got a taste of 'camping out' with the troops.[53]

With the two planning groups working smoothly together, the plans for Stevedore – the codename for Guam – rapidly began taking shape. The excellent working relationship between Conolly and Geiger guaranteed that differences of opinion were resolved without animosity. In fact, on one occasion, Admiral Conolly was overheard telling General Geiger, 'my aim is to get the troops ashore standing up. You tell me what you want done to accomplish this and we'll do it.'[54]

Admiral Conolly was determined that nothing would be left to chance as far as training was concerned. He instituted what he called pre-rehearsal training, where the separate parts of the Third Amphibious Group were trained individually – the naval gunfire support group, the transport groups, the mine-sweepers and so on. Thus, when the operation's rehearsal was held the separate parts of the force would be fully ready to accomplish their missions.[55] By late May 1944, everything was in readiness for the recapture of Guam.

One of the final but most important aspects of the plan was the question of the pre-invasion bombardment. Admiral Conolly wanted to make certain that

51Wellborn oral history, US Naval Institute, p. 215.

52Conolly oral history, Columbia University, p. 226.

53Major O. R. Lodge, USMC, *The Recapture of Guam* (Washington, 1954), pp. 19–20. Conolly had come to Guadalcanal with his staff to stay with the Marines during the planning phase at Geiger's request. Conolly oral history, pp. 231–2.

54Quoted in Lodge, *The Recapture of Guam*, p. 21n.

55Conolly oral history, Columbia University, p. 232.

Guam was properly softened up before the troops were landed. The sticking point was Admiral Spruance's concern over an indiscriminate bombardment which would endanger the island's native population. Conolly recalled his discussion with Turner: 'I said, "Well, this wouldn't be indiscriminate. I'd plan it all out." He said, "Who'd conduct it?" I said, "I don't know. I suppose a lot of people could." He said no, he didn't think so. I said, "Let me think it over."'[56] Within a few minutes, Conolly returned to Admiral Turner's cabin. He said to Turner, 'I just wanted to tell you that I thought of the fellow to conduct the bombardment.' When Turner asked who it was, Conolly replied, 'Conolly.'[57] The answer satisfied Kelly Turner; Conolly was allowed to conduct his bombardment; and the final result was what the Admiral later described as 'the most prolonged directed bombardment of the war'. The actual softening-up process began on 8 July 1944, fourteen days prior to the landings. The gunfire-support ships involved included a number of old battleships (OBBS), including *New Mexico, Pennsylvania, Idaho* and *Tennessee*. By W-Day – 21 July, the date of the landings – these and other ships in the force had fired many thousands of major-calibre rounds into carefully selected Japanese targets on Guam. As just one example, from 12 July until W-Day, *Pennsylvania* fired more than 1,300 fourteen-inch/45-calibre bombardment shells and more than twice that number of five-inch/38-calibre shells at targets on Guam.[58] Close co-ordination of naval gunfire and air support was handled by a special board of officers, which prepared a daily target list to guide the ships and aircraft in their bombardment missions. As particular targets were knocked out, they were taken off the list, while new targets were added as they were discovered. Admiral Conolly noted, 'We bombarded, stripped off the camouflage as the bombardment progressed, and then every morning took pictures of the objectives. Every night we made out a new bombardment schedule, both by gunfire and by air.'[59] The end result was a significant reduction in American casualties during the invasion. On 10 August, General Geiger sent a message to Conolly which read in part:

NAVAL GUNFIRE CONTRIBUTED LARGELY IN KEEPING LOSSES OF THE LANDING FORCES TO A MINIMUM AND IN BRINGING THE GUAM CAMPAIGN TO AN EARLY AND SUCCESSFUL CLOSE X IT IS BELIEVED THAT THIS CAMPAIGN HAS SET A NEW MARK FOR THE EMPLOYMENT OF THE FIRE POWER OF OUR SHIPS AND IT IS HOPED THAT IN FUTURE OPERATIONS OF THIS FORCE NAVAL GUNFIRE MAY DO AS MUCH FOR US.[60]

---

[56]Ibid., p. 239.   [57]Ibid.

[58]'USS PENNSYLVANIA BB 38 ACTION REPORT FOR THE BOMBARDMENT OF GUAM ISLAND', Serial 063, 8 August 1944, pp. 12–13; Box 311, World War II Action Reports File, OA.

[59]Conolly oral history, Columbia University, p. 238; and Lodge, *The Recapture of Guam*, p. 34.

[60]Message from Commanding General 3rd Amphibious Corps to Commander Task Force 53, 101413K (10 August 1944); 'Correspondence May–Dec 1944' Folder, Box 1, Papers of Richmond Kelly Turner, OA.

Despite his outstanding success at Guam, during the last year of the war Dick Conolly found himself under-employed as an amphibious group commander. In the autumn of 1944 his services were lent to Vice Admiral T. S. Wilkinson, Commander 3rd Amphibious Force, for the landings in the Philippines. In October 1944, his Group landed the 7th Infantry Division at Leyte, but Conolly was relegated to a minor role after the initial landings. He wrote to Admiral Turner on 28 October, 'I do not know what employment is planned for me here. I am very much an also-ran down here and, from the looks of things, likely to stay so. I hope that I will not lose out when things begin to cook up again in the Central Pacific. Please keep me informed of prospects.'[61] Turner sent Conolly a pessimistic reply, noting that he was going to have to stay in the South-West Pacific for the M-1 (Luzon) operation and therefore could not participate in Iceberg – the invasion of the Ryukyu Islands.[62]

In January 1945, Dick Conolly, the man Kelly Turner later called 'about the best and most experienced amphibious commander we have', was shepherding the Luzon Attack Force Reserve – bringing up the first reinforcement echelon for Luzon landings.[63] In February, Major-General A. V. Arnold, Commander 7th Infantry Division, wrote to Admiral Turner, praising the job which Admiral Conolly had done in landing the division at Leyte and expressing the hope that Conolly could be made available for its next operation. Kelly Turner wrote back:

> Due to his participation in the Luzon Operation, and the fact that he has had more than a solid year of successive adventures (four major attacks during that period), I have taken the opportunity to send him and his staff home for a short period of relaxation.
>
> Therefore, though I shall very much miss him, he will not be available for your next operation.[64]

When Dick Conolly arrived back at Pearl Harbor, following his service in the Lingayen Gulf, he told Admiral Turner that he wanted to get into one of the other operations. Turner told him to take a month's leave. Conolly recalled: 'He said I needed some leave. I told him I didn't want any leave, I wanted to be employed in one of the operations.'[65] During his leave in Washington DC in February 1945, all Dick Conolly could think about was that the war was coming to a close and he was missing out on these operations.

[61]Letter from Rear Admiral Richard L. Conolly to Vice-Admiral Richmond Kelly Turner, 28 October 1944; ibid.

[62]Letter from Vice-Admiral Richmond Kelly Turner to Rear Admiral Richard L. Conolly, n.d. [November 1944]; ibid.

[63]See Samuel Eliot Morison, *History of United States Naval Operations in World War II*, vol. XIII: *The Liberation of the Philippines, Luzon, Mindanao, the Visayes 1944–1945* (Boston, 1959), pp. 97, 130, 144–5 ff.

[64]Letter from Vice-Admiral Richmond Kelly Turner to Major-General A. V. Arnold, 15 February 1945; 'Correspondence 1945' Folder, Box 1, Turner Papers, OA.

[65]Conolly oral history, Columbia University, p. 266.

Admiral Conolly was destined to remain disappointed in his hopes for further combat. Although he was involved in the planning for several subsequent operations, including that for the invasion of the Japanese home island of Kyushu, none of them came to fruition. Meanwhile, in early 1945, Fleet Admiral Chester Nimitz [*q.v.*] asked Kelly Turner for his recommendation as to who should succeed him as Commander 5th Amphibious Force, specifying that his relief should be one of three people – William H. P. Blandy, Dick Conolly or Harry W. Hill. Turner recommended Hill.[66] Turner's response was similar when, some weeks later, Nimitz asked his advice as to who should be appointed as ComDesPac (Commander Destroyers Pacific Fleet). The same three names were suggested by Nimitz. Turner replied:

> I believe any one of them would be satisfactory. If you accept the nomination of Hill as Com5thPhibFor, that will put him outside of consideration. Conolly would do well, but he is essentially a man of action, and about the best and most experienced amphibious group commander that we have. While Blandy is doing exceptionally well in his present duty, he is a most able administrator, and I believe he would make the best ComDesPac of the three.[67]

Turner's attitude meant that Conolly would have to wait until after the war for his chance to advance to a position of higher responsibility in the US Navy.

Richard L. Conolly's wartime career was distinctive even during a period when the fortunes of senior officers most often rose and fell on the question of competence. An outstanding leader, who was described by his Chief of Staff as having probably the best perception of what the role of a commander was of anyone he had served with, Dick Conolly was an individual who at the same time combined a highly analytical mind with a love for action. One of his most engaging characteristics as a wartime commander was his unreserved willingness to co-operate fully with other commanders, in order to further the common goal – victory for the Allied Powers. Though he was never in a position to become known to the public at large, Admiral Conolly handled faithfully and with great competence whatever responsibilities were entrusted to him. His reward was the respect in which he was held not only by his own service but by others. Indeed, to the US Marines, Dick Conolly was probably the most admired naval officer to emerge from the Pacific War.[68] There is little more that a dedicated officer could ask for his years of service.

After being Deputy cno (Operations), from 1945–6, Conolly was Deputy cno (Administration) during 1946. Other posts, 1946–50, included Naval Adviser to

---

[66]Harry W. Hill, Interviews by John T. Mason Jr, 1966–7, transcript, Oral History Research Office, Columbia University, New York, NY, p. 632.

[67]Letter from Vice-Admiral Richmond Kelly Turner to Fleet Admiral Chester W. Nimitz, 17 April 1945; 'Correspondence 1945' Folder, Box 1, Turner Papers, OA.

[68]Isely and Crowl, *Marines and Amphibious War*, p. 260.

Secretary of State; Commander US Naval Forces Europe; Commander US Naval Forces Eastern Atlantic and Mediterranean; Commander-in-Chief US Naval Forces Eastern Atlantic and Mediterranean; President, Naval War College. Retired from the navy, 1953. Killed in an airline crash at Idlewild Airport, New York City, 1 March 1962, a few weeks short of his seventieth birthday.

14

Admiral

H. Kent Hewitt
United States Navy

1887–1972

by
Thaddeus V. Tuleja

*H*ENRY *Kent Hewitt, born Hackensack, New Jersey, 11 February 1887. Entered the US Naval Academy 1903. Divisional officer in the battleship* Florida, *1912. Married Floride Hunt, 1913; two daughters, Floride (1915) and Mary Kent (1923), both of whom married naval officers.*

Promoted lieutenant-commander, 1917; awarded Navy Cross as the commanding officer of the destroyer Cummings *for carrying out his duties in an 'exacting and hazardous' situation. Promoted to commander, 1922, and a decade later, after extensive sea duty, to captain. His command, the cruiser* Indianapolis, *was chosen to bring newly elected President Franklin D. Roosevelt to the Pan-American Conference in Buenos Aires.*

Promoted to rear admiral, 1939, and later became Commander, Cruiser Division 8. Roosevelt's policy of 'all aid to Britain short of war' quickly drew Hewitt into the neutrality patrols. With Pearl Harbor only half a year away, Hewitt would soon steam to the very edge of battle.

Admiral Henry Kent Hewitt, who preferred to be known among his colleagues as 'Kent', was one of the most professionally competent and dauntless American flag officers to emerge from the havoc of World War Two, for he carried out his duties with unerring precision and he was imperturbable under fire. A tolerant and modest man who shunned public clamour, he was ever generous in his praise of others. He justly earned a reputation for fairmindedness among those under his command; and despite his calm demeanour, he managed throughout his naval career – as sailors say – 'to run a taut ship', and he did it without bluster.

The neutrality patrols, to which Hewitt was assigned, had been launched early in 1941 under the banner of the US Atlantic Fleet. It had been agreed between the US Navy and the British Admiralty that American escort vessels were to take over eastbound convoys from the Canadian navy off the coast of Newfoundland, then escort them over the 1,500 sea miles of dreary ocean to Reykjavik, from whence the Royal Navy would shield them to the Western Approaches. Hewitt, now in command of the Atlantic Fleet's Cruiser Force, was responsible for patrols covering a vast oceanic area reaching to the Azores.

There was a brief interlude in the wearisome neutrality patrols that foreshadowed Hewitt's future. American and British naval strategists knew that in the growing global conflict, costly invasions would have to be made on enemy beaches. So both navies, aware of history's demanding lessons, had been studying the inevitable problem of amphibious warfare with all its inherent uncertainties. During the first week of August 1941, Admiral Ernest J. King [*q.v.*], Commander-in-Chief of the US Atlantic Fleet, ordered all available flag officers attached to his command to proceed forthwith to the beaches of North Carolina, where the 1st Marine and 1st Army Divisions, under the command of Major-General Holland M. Smith [q.v.], were to assault the coast in a mock invasion. Hewitt observed the landings from an aircraft. Later, he told Smith that he had found the exercises 'interesting', an understandably bland remark from a sailor whose professional sea-going life had been spent in preparation for some great sea battle across blue water. Hewitt was ready for another Jutland, but he did not yet know in which direction Neptune would point his trident. The tempo of the war, however, would lift him into commands compatible with his talents, as it would sweep others less endowed into the backwaters.

By the autumn of 1941, the Battle of Britain – that deadly air war that will forever illuminate the pages of history for the dogged defiance of a gallant people – was turning sharply against the Luftwaffe, whose losses were becoming insupportable. Moreover, some months earlier Hitler had rashly committed millions of troops to a massive and doomed invasion of the Soviet Union. What aircraft he had left after his degrading defeat by the Royal Air Force were all desperately needed in the east to support his Napoleonic illusions of conquest.

For Great Britain, the growing U-boat challenge was the most grievous problem at hand, and for that reason Admiral Hewitt and other force commanders continued to lend their anti-submarine protection to those Allied and neutral merchantmen who were attempting to follow the North Atlantic convoy routes drafted by the British between Canada and Great Britain. It was a nascent time of trial and error; of painful lessons learned; of cherished schemes discarded, before the intricate Allied convoy routes were finally spun, like a great web, across the war-ridden oceans of the world. Like other convoy guardians, Hewitt was a pioneer in the tactical control of large numbers of merchant ships, but the violence of the war would, in time, reorder his sea-going career. His last peacetime convoy, the delivery of a Canadian division to replace a British one in the home islands, ended in a mishap when his flagship (the light cruiser *Philadelphia*) touched a submerged rock and had to proceed to Boston for repairs. Hewitt was there when Japanese carrier pilots, skimming over Oahu's Diamond Head, made a funeral pyre out of most of the Pacific Fleet moored at Pearl Harbor.

Suddenly on 7 December 1941, during a quiet Hawaiian morning, the United States' quasi-war with U-boats in the Atlantic became a matter of total involvement. New war plans were shaped, and late in the month, Hewitt, flying his flag again from the repaired *Philadelphia*, was joined by a naval improvisation – the CVE, a dwarfish aircraft carrier built on a merchant ship's hull. Hewitt's 'jeep carrier', the first of a numerous and varied fleet, was the 7,886-ton, 492-foot *Long Island*, capable of mounting more than twenty-one war planes. In the course of the long war, the CVE (carrier vessel, escort), with its invaluable airborne eyes, would participate in the protection of hundreds of convoys.

Just after Christmas, Hewitt sailed his new escort force (now called Task Force 26) to the fog-shrouded port of Argentia, Newfoundland, where, after weathering the tumultuous North Atlantic seas, he dropped anchor on New Year's Day 1942. For the next few months he continued his plodding convoy escort duties between Argentia and Iceland, now under full war conditions.

Meanwhile, the indefatigable Admiral Ernest J. King had released plans for the establishment of an amphibious force, Atlantic Fleet. The art of invasion from the sea had seen many technological changes since William defeated Harold at Hastings in 1066, but there were then, as now, two changeless features of all assaults from the open sea: the enemy's strength on the hostile shore, and the capricious mood of the surf. For modern warfare, an abundant armada of assault ships of all sizes had to be built to carry troops and tanks, vehicles and supplies. It was quite clear that the construction mission now awaiting Allied shipyards would be Herculean. And more landing craft would be needed in the Pacific when the 'island-hopping' campaigns got under way.

Admiral Hewitt, at this time, was remote from amphibious warfare, but a twist of fate would bring him into its very midst. Admiral King's chessboard bore the names of many capable naval officers to command his announced amphibious force. King decided, finally, that the entire command – its operational training and its detailed planning – should be under one commander, and for this duty he chose Rear Admiral Roland E. Brainard, who hastened to the Naval Base in Norfolk, Virginia, to take on his gigantic task.

Hewitt's senior in northern waters was Vice-Admiral Arthur L. Bristol, who remained at his exhausting post in Argentia, manoeuvring the increasing flow of inbound and outbound convoys that came under his command. In April, while Hewitt was covering a southbound convoy from Iceland, Bristol suddenly died of heart failure. There was time only for a deserved salute; none for prolonged grief. Admiral King had to shift his chess pieces. Admiral Brainard was recalled from Norfolk to take over Bristol's command at

Argentia; and Hewitt, his naval future decided as quickly as the snap of a finger, was relieved of his command of Cruisers, Atlantic Fleet, and ordered to become Commander, Amphibious Forces, Atlantic Fleet – or simply Com-PhibLant, to use his truncated title. He noted in his unpublished memoirs: 'This was the quickest change of duty I ever made.'

Even Admiral King had become a chess piece in the game of war. At the end of 1941 he had been named Chief of Naval Operations; and a few months later he was given command of the US Atlantic Fleet, the only man to possess both titles at the same time. Hewitt's naval future, then, depended not only on his own proven competence but upon King's trust in him.

Before Hewitt went to sea again he had to learn, in those inchoate days, all that he could about amphibious warfare. His headquarters in Little Creek, Virginia, was a cramped building of small size for himself and his staff. Hewitt, in his new and unfamiliar role, was fortunate to have had, even briefly, the good counsel of an experienced amphibious warrior, Marine Major-General Holland M. Smith, who had worked closely with him when both were sea-going officers in the US Pacific Fleet in the early 1930s. But General Smith, an Amphibious Corps Commander, had little left to command, for the Marine 1st Division was bound for the Pacific, and the 1st Army Division had been sent to the British Isles. And Admiral Hewitt would soon bid farewell to General Smith, also Pacific-bound. Fortunately, the 9th Army Division, stationed at Fort Bragg, North Carolina, under the command of Major-General M. S. Eddy, was assigned to Hewitt, providing him with enough troops to play out the strategy and tactics of modern amphibious warfare.

Hewitt's first task was to devise training programmes for the inexperienced crews who were to man the assault transports and the diverse invasion vessels then sliding down the ways of countless Allied shipyards: LSTs (landing ship, tanks); LCIs (landing craft, infantry), and LCVs (landing craft, vehicle), which represented only a few of the fifty-odd vessel types of the Allies' extraordinary landing fleet then being born.

Since Hewitt had lost the trained Marines to the Pacific theatre, he had to indoctrinate green recruits in the embarking and unloading of amphibious transports, and the precise combat-loading of attack ships, a principle of assault neglected in so cavalier a manner at Gallipoli in 1915. Hewitt had the unenviable job of teaching the rudiments of amphibious warfare, while he himself had just become a student of the very same subject. He arose early, donning his khaki work uniform, and pursued his duties each day with the imagination and thoroughness that had been, and would remain, the outstanding qualities of his naval leadership.

Early in June, Admiral King summoned Hewitt to his Washington office, permitting no delay. Without changing his dusty uniform, Hewitt took the first flight he could find and was ushered into a private luncheon to meet Vice-Admiral Lord Louis Mountbatten, who wished to co-ordinate Anglo-American amphibious doctrine. Mountbatten, a man of great courage and charisma, who deserved a better death than the absurd and cruel one fate gave him, had just been designated to head British Combined Operations, a command that was in many ways similar to Hewitt's own Amphibious Forces. King's introduction of Hewitt to Mountbatten was direct: 'Here's your admiral,' he said. These words were both a tribute and a challenge, and Admiral King would never regret that he spoke them.

Hewitt gladly accepted Mountbatten's invitation to visit England, where he arrived on 19 June. During a stay of two weeks, he was shown all that the British had worked out for amphibious landings, including top-secret plans for an exploratory raid on Dieppe, a coastal town some fifty miles to the north-east of Le Havre. The meeting yielded another unforeseen benefit: both men got along like old friends, assuring the closest possible alliance between the Royal Navy's Combined Operations and the US Navy's Amphibious Forces.

The future of Hewitt's amphibious command had, in fact, been decided in a strategic debate between the American Joint Chiefs of Staff and their British counterparts, the former demanding, as was Stalin with merciless insistence, that the summer of 1942 was the proper time to open a 'second front'. Such an operation meant the early landing of Allied troops on the German-controlled French coast, an operation dubbed Sledgehammer. This was a bold enough risk, like the tossing of a gauntlet at the feet of an armoured knight. Roosevelt, at first, gave his support to the plan. The British Chiefs sided with Churchill's 'peripheral' scheme, and proposed that an invasion be mounted at the western end of North Africa to threaten from behind Erwin Rommel's Afrika Korps, whose tanks were then grinding towards the delta of the Nile. There was a military impasse: the Americans adamantly in favour of Sledgehammer; the British just as forcefully opposed to it.

By mid-August 1942, the British argument – that German coastal defences were still impenetrable – was painfully proved by the long-planned Dieppe raid that Admiral Hewitt, through Mountbatten's courtesy, had been privileged to witness earlier in its full-dress rehearsal. Some 5,000 Anglo-Canadian amphibious troops, supported by tanks, stormed the beaches of Dieppe on 19 August. It was a forlorn disaster. The loss of landing craft and tanks was a minimal price for a hard-learned military lesson: priceless, though, was the sacrifice of more than 3,000 soldiers – the large majority Canadian – left dead or wounded on the beaches of Dieppe. And it was ironic that Roosevelt, weeks before the doomed Dieppe raid, had come round to accepting Churchill's strategic instincts. For once, Roosevelt overruled his own military advisers and agreed that an Anglo-American strike against Hitler in 1942 would have to be in North Africa.

And so it came about – with firm resolve on the British side and averse acquiescence on the American – that Operation Torch was drafted. The Anglo-American coalition, unique in military history for its constancy, endured its genial grumbling and difference of strategic opinion. Both English-speaking allies agreed that even though the war was being brought to

Germany with day and night bomber raids, and that the German juggernaut into Russia was losing its stamina before the defiant gates of Stalingrad, there was as yet no good reason to believe that cracks were beginning to show along the Nazi edifice. Dieppe had become a symbolic warning.

Admiral Hewitt, drilling his forces through countless simulated landings, was informed of the probability of an invasion of North Africa and that he would be involved in the gamble. The coastal targets of Torch were three major ports in North Africa, selected because they were beyond the range of the Luftwaffe – Casablanca on the Atlantic side, and Oran and Algiers inside the Mediterranean. The Combined Chiefs of Staff were able to determine how many troops and transports were needed for Torch; how many escorts; how many front-line fighting ships. It was a game of numbers that, in the end, provided some clear answers. But there were some imponderables. Would the French forces in North Africa resist the invasion? How would the German High Command react? And what would be the mood of wind and wave on the landing beaches so late in the year?

Hewitt had only one way to find out: try it and see. To carry Torch through, an unusual (and very effective) command system was adopted. Leadership of Allied naval forces was in the capable hands of Admiral Sir Andrew Cunningham [*q.v.*], Britain's ubiquitous sea-dog of the Mediterranean. The all-American invasion fleet, assigned to capture Casablanca and named the Western Task Force, was placed under the command of Admiral Hewitt. The assault troops – 35,000 strong, embarked in twenty-nine transports – were under the command of the flamboyant Major-General George S. Patton Jr. And controlling them all, the Supreme Allied Commander for the North African expedition was Lieutenant-General Dwight D. Eisenhower, then in command of US troops in Great Britain.

Even on its own, Hewitt's part in the mammoth operation was quite sufficiently complex. His orders were to land troops at three separate places: Mehedia, sixty miles north of Casablanca, close to Port Lyautey's airfield; Fedhala, less than twenty miles north of Casablanca, at the extreme range of Casablanca's batteries; and Safi, about one hundred miles south of the primary target. The separate Anglo-American forces assembled in Great Britain to capture Oran and Algiers were scheduled to reach their invasion points simultaneously with Hewitt's landings.

Flying his flag from Admiral King's former flagship, the heavy cruiser USS *Augusta* – the only command ship available with adequate communication facilities – Hewitt oversaw the departure of the vessels under his command in a grand nautical ballet that he had choreographed. The Northern and Southern Attack Groups (Mehedia and Safi) left Hampton Roads, Virginia, on 23 October on a deceptively south-easterly track that shifted in mid-course; the Centre Group, with Hewitt in *Augusta*, headed directly for Casablanca; and a Covering Group, bearing Hewitt's heavy guns in the battleship *Massachusetts* and the cruisers *Witchita* and *Tuscaloosa*, steamed out of Casco Bay, Maine.

The Admiral's Air Support Group, carriers *Ranger* and *Suwanee*, left Bermuda in time to rendezvous with the main force on 25 October, just 500 miles south of Cape Race, Newfoundland. When Hewitt's converging fleet finally gathered under his flag, it covered a sea area of hundreds of square miles, and he could keep in touch with his ships only by relays of flashing light, for radio silence was imperative. Considering the throng of U-boats at sea, it was great seamanship and good luck that not a single enemy submarine sighted Hewitt's invasion fleet, even though the German High Command had had wind of a big operation under way in the Atlantic. But the Germans were also frustrated by the high-frequency direction-finder (Huff-Duff in naval jargon) that enabled Hewitt to plot the positions of patrolling U-boats as they surfaced each night to report their whereabouts and simply avoid them by altering course.

The other forces of Torch were a mixture of Anglo-American fighting men, launched from Great Britain to take Oran and Algiers, inside the Mediterranean. They passed under the hunched shoulder of Gibraltar on schedule and arrived off their respective beaches on 8 November, just as Hewitt's three-pronged fleet arrived off the north-western Moroccan coast. The force that landed at Oran faced some spirited resistance from the shore, but the struggle was brief. The other force, after encircling Algiers, accepted surrender just two days later.

Though it was quite hard enough, Torch might have become a much more arduous affair had it not been for a tumble of chance that would alter the flow of everything. At the precise time that the landings were taking place, Vichyite Admiral Jean Darlan was taken into custody while visiting his sick son in Algiers. Within a few days, his capture would shape strategy.

As Hewitt approached North Africa, the earlier imponderables were still weighing on his shoulders. Even though the United States, in a calculated gamble, had chosen not to break off relations with Vichy, and several clandestine efforts had been made to persuade the French in North Africa to hold their fire as the Allied invasion forces landed, the Allies had received no positive assurances from the French, who were themselves agonizing over divided loyalties that had become a moral dilemma. Hewitt, therefore, while approaching the shores of Morocco, still faced the unresolved question: would the French fight? He would not have to wait long for his answer.

Weather was also one of the Admiral's unsparing thoughts. Just two days' steaming from his landing beaches, he received dismal reports from Washington and London, forecasting waves of fifteen feet rolling along the Moroccan coast. In the event of dirty weather, he and Patton were to steam for Gibraltar and land their forces inside the Mediterranean. Hewitt sought the advice of his staff aerologist, Lieutenant-Commander Richard C. Steere, who had been monitoring the winds for several days. The day before the invasion, Steere climbed to *Augusta*'s flag bridge at night, carrying a smudged weather map and a flashlight and awakened Admiral Hewitt, who had been trying to get some sleep on a cot set up for him at his command post. Steere predicted that the worst of the storm would soon be spent and that sea conditions would be moderate enough for the landings to take place. Hewitt now faced his moment of truth: he could accept the official weather warnings received earlier, or trust the judgement of his aerologist. He chose to go along with Steere, whose forecast, fortunately, was not far off the mark.

Just before midnight on 7 November, the eve of the assault, Hewitt signalled 'Stop!' The night was black as pitch. Landing craft from Hewitt's central fleet of fifteen transports were lowered to the moderate swells, gently tumbling over the beaches north of Casablanca. Fully packed troops climbed down draped cargo nets, filling the bobbing launches. All went well. *Augusta* stood to the right of the troop transports, facing shoreward; the cruiser *Brooklyn* stood to the left, with ten control destroyers ready to lead each landing wave to the beaches.

Dawn had not yet broken when Hewitt arrived at his rendezvous. The black shore was silent; it promised to be an untroubled landing. Slowly, though, Hewitt's magic spell was broken. An unexpected current pushed several troop transports out of position; and the young, untrained coxswains, steering blindly for an obscure shore, collided in the dark night, or turned into the ground-swells and capsized. Then the French, catching the sound of the landing craft, manned their guns and fired at ill-defined targets. The firing had begun in the early moments of the mid-watch, and Hewitt now knew that the French would fight.

He launched the second and third waves of landing craft. By the time the first blush of dawn tinged the eastern sky, there were 3,500 troops ashore with advance units pushing into Fedhala. Fifteen miles south-west of the landing beaches was Casablanca with its own coastal batteries resting behind El Hank lighthouse; and inside the harbour was the French cruiser *Primauguet* and a small force of destroyers and submarines. Also moored in Casablanca, and most menacing of all, was the unfinished battleship *Jean Bart* with one of her two forward turrets operable. Her four 15-inch guns could easily ravage Hewitt's landing forces and do grave damage to his Covering Group – battleship *Massachusetts* and cruisers *Witchita* and *Tuscaloosa*, all patrolling at action stations within shooting range of Casablanca.

Against an opaque early sky, while Hewitt continued to direct the landings from *Augusta*, a sporadic gun duel broke out between the cruiser *Brooklyn* and the French shore batteries. Aircraft from the carrier *Ranger* attacked grounded planes at several French airfields and dive-bombed the submarine base at Casablanca. At 0700 the 8-inch shore guns behind El Hank lighthouse at Casablanca opened against Hewitt's Covering Group and were joined by the big guns of *Jean Bart*'s operable turret, but *Massachusetts* swiftly turned her 16-inchers on the French battleship and crippled her with several salvoes.

At 0800, with the sky fully brightened, Vice Admiral F. C. Michelier, in command of French naval forces at Casablanca, ordered his seven destroyers, the cruiser *Primauguet* and eight surviving submarines, to steam north under a smoke screen and attack Hewitt's assailable troop transports anchored off Fedhala. Although the sudden French sortie scored a few minor hits, American gunfire was more intense and accurate and the French assault never reached Hewitt's transports, still disembarking troops. Two French destroyers were sunk by gunfire, two more succumbed to dive-bombing attacks, and *Primauguet*, already torn badly by shots from Hewitt's flagship and *Brooklyn*, died in a welter of bomb hits. The one-sided battle ended just before noon with *Witchita* taking a hit from El Hank's shore guns. And still the landings went on throughout the day. By late afternoon Hewitt had put nearly 8,000 troops ashore.

The slow unloading of transports continued through 9 November as Hewitt's carrier-based aircraft pounded shore batteries. On the 10th, with most of his troops and equipment ashore, General Patton planned a full assault on Casablanca for the following day. By this time, aircraft from carriers *Ranger* and *Suwanee* had won command of the air, and when *Jean Bart* fired her repaired turret at Hewitt's flagship, *Ranger*'s dive bombers quickly silenced her. Nevertheless, a proud Michelier was not ready to yield Casablanca without a last stand. His heroic wish was denied him by distant events.

Admiral Darlan, a powerful figure in Pétain's Vichy government, had been named head of the French armed forces and High Commissioner in French North Africa. After his capture in Algiers, he reversed sides and arranged an armistice with the Americans, who, in turn, accepted him as head of the French government. Before noon on 10 November, he ordered an end to hostilities between the Allies and French forces in North Africa. Since there could be no guarantee that the order would be obeyed, General Patton approached Casablanca ready for battle. But whatever his personal feelings, Michelier did obey, and the invaders were greeted not with bullets but with a flag of truce. The brief Franco-American war was over.

The British, who preferred the unsullied and imperious Charles de Gaulle as head of state, deplored the 'Darlan deal', and a public outcry in both the United States and Great Britain denounced the deference given to a marked collaborator. But the furore did not last long. Admiral Darlan was assassinated on Christmas Eve by (of all people) a French monarchist, an event which did little to unravel the tangled skeins of French politics.

On the 11th (the day Darlan's ceasefire order reached Patton north of Casablanca) Hewitt's invasion force of fifteen transports and cargo vessels was still anchored outside the cluttered harbour of Fedhala, protected on one side by a minefield and on the other by patrolling destroyers. In spite of this shield, a daring U-boat captain glided past the defences, sinking one transport and damaging a tanker and destroyer. Later, a second U-boat sent three of Hewitt's transports to the bottom. These were his major losses in the assault, save for the countless landing craft strewn along the Moroccan beaches like so much discarded debris of war.

Taking into account Admiral Hewitt's limited equipment (no LSTs were ready for Torch) and his inexperienced forces, he performed his first landing operation with unruffled composure and commendable judgement, even though Darlan's *volte face* eased his travail. During the next few days, he moved some ships to sea and sent others into Casablanca harbour to avoid any further luckless losses. He also met with a cordial and proper Admiral Michelier to agree to an armistice which, for the French, involved no surrender but merely a desire once again to embrace an old ally. US Naval Operating Bases were soon established in French North Africa, and General Patton, his military destiny still awaiting him, set up headquarters in the heart of Casablanca.

Hewitt sent his task force back to the United States in separate convoys. On the 20th, twelve days after the landings, he boarded the *Augusta* for a speedy return home. On the day of his departure, he received two despatches. One came from Eisenhower:

> With successful completion of your task under Allied Headquarters and your return to normal American command, I want to express my grateful appreciation of the splendid service you and the forces under your command have rendered. I am making immediate official report to Washington . . . but in the meantime I hope it is proper for a soldier to say to a sailor 'Well done.'

The other despatch came from Admiral Cunningham:

> . . . I send you my congratulations on a fine job well done. The problems faced were in many ways the most difficult and I have admired the energy and resolution with which you and all under your command have tackled them. I send very good wishes to your forces for a speedy passage and good landfall.

Hewitt returned safely to the United States, as did his convoys. He was again Commander Amphibious Forces, Atlantic Fleet, but now with the third star of a vice-admiral flying over his headquarters.

Still, the war went on and Hewitt would be swept into it again. A few days before the Torch landings, British General Bernard Montgomery had inflicted a grave defeat upon Rommel's forces at El Alamein, a victory that probably saved the Suez Canal for the Allies, but did not put a stop to the see-saw war along the North African coast. Hitler reacted to Torch by flying German and Italian troops into Tunisia to strengthen Rommel in the midst of the Anglo-American pincer. And at the same time his troops overwhelmed unoccupied France, thus sweeping away the anomalous government of Vichy. The French fleet moored at Toulon, unable to raise steam in time to avoid capture, scuttled itself rather than fall into enemy hands.

Following the landings in North Africa, most US warships left the Mediterranean. The US Navy operated the Moroccan Sea Frontier, with headquarters at Casablanca, as well as the port of Oran and Mers-el-Kebir.

The rest of the Allied occupied coast remained under the control of the Royal Navy. Meanwhile, Admiral Hewitt, who emerged as a new Viking, soon received 'for exceptionally meritorious service' the army's Distinguished Service Medal from the hands of Secretary of War, Henry L. Stimson, and the navy's Distinguished Service Medal from Secretary of the Navy, Frank Knox.

As the New Year (1943) began, most of North Africa was in Allied hands, save for Tunisia, whose Cape Bon was just ninety miles from the Sicilian coast. American forces under Patton pushed eastward out of Algeria, while a weary Rommel moved westward across northern Libya with Montgomery snapping at his heels. Towards the end of January, the dusty armies faced one another in Tunisia. The Americans were badly blooded at Kasserine Pass, but in the end Rommel's strategy came apart; and by mid-May American, British and French forces brought Axis resistance to an end as enemy troops surrendered by the thousands.

There was a strategic logic that flowed from Hewitt's Torch landings of November 1942. In January 1943, therefore, months before the Tunisian war was won, Roosevelt and Churchill, along with the Combined Chiefs of Staff, met in Casablanca to discuss, among other things, the invasion of Sicily, an undertaking that it was hoped would topple Mussolini, ease German pressure on the Russian Front and make safer the lines of communication in the Mediterranean. In February, Admiral Hewitt was relieved of his amphibious command in Virginia and named Commander United States Forces North-west African Waters, a cumbersome title that was later changed to US Eighth Fleet.

The Sicilian operation, codenamed Husky, was set for early July 1943, and envisioned an American invasion launched from numerous ports in North Africa under Hewitt's command, and a British force, staged from the Eastern Mediterranean under Vice Admiral Sir Bertram Ramsay [*q.v.*]. Hewitt set up his headquarters in Algiers on 17 March, sharing a suite of offices in the St Georges Hotel with his British naval senior, Admiral Sir Andrew Cunningham, who had recently been promoted to the rank of admiral of the fleet. Hewitt's unfeigned honesty won for him Cunningham's enduring respect. The two men pored over the initial plans of Husky shoulder to shoulder and agreed on how sea power ought to be used in the Sicilian assault. Echoing Lord Nelson's campaigns in the same sea 140 years previously, Cunningham would remember after the war that during those days of historic moment Hewitt and he had 'worked together like brothers'.

Most of the senior officers who had been involved in the North African and Tunisian campaigns were again on call for Husky. General Eisenhower, now wearing a fourth star, was put in command of the invasion. General Sir Harold Alexander commanded the ground troops; Cunningham, as before, the sea forces; and British Air Chief Marshal Sir Arthur Tedder, Allied air power.

Planning for the Sicilian campaign was more thorough than for Torch. The large LSTs, so painfully absent in the North African landings, were in place for Husky. It was an enormous Anglo-American undertaking; the numbers of ships and troops involved, plus the length of the landing beaches, stretching for more than one hundred miles, actually exceeded the celebrated assault on Normandy that was to take place a year later. Nearly half a million American and British troops were mustered for the capture of Sicily. Admiral Ramsay, with a force of 800 vessels, was to cover the broad Gulf of Noto, just south of Syracuse. Admiral Hewitt was to assault a wide beach front on Sicily's southern shore, from Licata eastward to Scoglitti. Under his command were nearly 600 ships and more than 1,000 landing craft berthed along the North African ports won in the recent fighting.

By mid-June, the small island of Pantelleria, a mere seventy miles from Sicily, was captured by a British assault force. General Patton, given command of the US Seventh Army, rode with Admiral Hewitt in USS *Monrovia*, a troop transport hastily converted into an amphibious flagship. Admiral Ramsay, carrying Montgomery's Eighth Army, steamed westward towards the Sicilian coast. Tedder's Allied air forces for weeks had been flying bombing raids against Axis airfields in Sardinia, Italy and Greece, and concentrating especially on Sicilian airbases.

On the enemy side was General Alfredo Guzzoni's Italian Sixth Army, made up of twelve Italian and two German divisions. Field Marshal Albert Kesselring, German commander for the Mediterranean area, anticipating (among other things) a landing at Gela, remained confident that the Allies would be crushed on the beaches. Guzzoni entertained no such hope.

By 9 July 1943, all ships were at sea, steaming towards Sicily. Admiral Hewitt directed his invasion fleet towards three separate targets, each about fifteen miles distant from one another. Hewitt's western force (Task Force 86) veered westward to flank Licata on the left; his centre force (Task Force 81) continued to Gela in the middle of the broad bay that bears its name; and his eastern force (Task Force 85) broke off towards the right and headed for the beaches of Scoglitti. These landings under Hewitt's command, and those of Admiral Ramsay around the corner of the island, were to establish beachheads for Patton and Montgomery from which they were to drive towards the northern ports of Palermo and Messina.

The day before the landings, Admiral Hewitt, a tall and stocky man, sat hunched in the admiral's chair on *Monrovia*'s flag bridge. He had much on his mind: he could expect some Allied air cover from recently captured Pantelleria and from Malta, but the inter-service planning that he had repeatedly urged was ignored by Allied air commanders, who held the tightest control of all their aircraft. This absence of co-operation was to lead to a tragic blunder, as will be seen.

In the early afternoon Hewitt felt a change in the sea as the winds sharpened from the west. From *Monrovia*'s bridge some LCI(L)s were visible, loaded with troops and pitching badly in the mounting seas. Eisenhower and Cunningham at their posts on Malta were equally concerned about the weather and even considered calling off the operation, for a failed amphibious landing would have led to an irreparable disaster. But Hewitt's aerologist, Lieutenant-Commander Richard C. Steere, the weather prophet during Torch, predicted that the strong winds would fade before midnight and that the landings, set for 0245 on the 10th, would encounter only moderate swells of 3–4 feet. Such a surf would not be a serious challenge to an experienced coxswain of a landing craft. What Steere could not predict was the effect of the increasing wind and mounting white-capped waves during the passage of Hewitt's invasion fleet from the North African coast to the Sicilian beaches. The surface winds, driving hard from the north-west, reached thirty-seven knots, and the groups of landing craft, trying to hold station with their cargoes of desperately seasick soldiers, were scattered by the storm. It was the discipline that Admiral Hewitt had demanded of his amphibious forces that held the fleet together. His force commanders, following his drill, gathered in the wayward ships and led them to the Sicilian beaches, where, as Steere had promised, the surf was not violent.

Exactly on time, Task Force 86 (Rear Admiral R. L. Conolly [*q.v.*]) flanked Licata at several points, and the troops under Major-General L. J. Truscott Jr rushed inland. They faced slight resistance and were covered at first light by gunfire from cruisers *Brooklyn* and *Birmingham*. By midday, Truscott had set up a command post in Licata itself as Italian soldiers, weary of the war, surrendered in large numbers.

Rear Admiral J. L. Hall's Task Force 81 also arrived on schedule at the beaches of Gela, supposedly sighted in ancient times by Virgil's Aeneas. The landing of troops under Major-General Terry Allen was carried out with precision under the cover of night, but at daybreak, with the beaches abrim with supplies, the enemy began their air attacks, throwing everything into a shambles. Since the tactical flagship air support that Admiral Hewitt had requested was virtually absent, he ordered float planes from his cruisers to search for enemy targets. One aircraft spotted two columns of Italian tanks grinding towards the landing site, but they were stopped literally in their tracks by gunfire from the cruiser *USS Boise* and two destroyers. On the following day, firing her six-inch guns with a vengeance, *Boise* demolished a column of some sixty German Panzer tanks. For the rest of the day, Hewitt's naval guns punctured the staging grounds of the enemy.

Rear Admiral A. G. Kirk's Task Force 85 had already landed Lieutenant-General Omar N. Bradley and his staff of II Corps, and Major-General T. H. Middleton's troops, on the beaches of the small fishing village of Scoglitti, close to the airfields of Biscari and Comiso. Although there was minimal opposition from the shore, the groundswells in that part of the bay made landings hazardous, causing many casualties among the landing craft. Erratic bombing attacks failed to halt the frantic flow of troops and supplies to the beaches, and by the 11th Scoglitti was in Allied hands.

But it was at this time (the night of 11–12 July) that the air force planned a parachute drop from 144 transport aircraft and gliders. Admiral Hewitt was not informed of this intention and was unable to warn his force commanders. The aircraft flew directly over his invasion force, whose anti-aircraft guns were still hot from repelling a recent enemy air-raid. The gunners instinctively opened fire, shooting down many of their own planes – the saddest episode of Husky. It was no consolation to the American gunners that a similar misfortune happened in the British sector for the same reason. Hewitt, who rarely lost his composure, was quick to blame the disaster on the air force's fatuous refusal to join in inter-service planning.

Admiral Ramsay, with the benefit of a lee shore, had less trouble landing Montgomery's army, although he had his share of air attacks. Even so, in the space of just two days, he and Hewitt together had put some 80,000 troops ashore, plus thousands of guns, tanks and vehicles, with more to come.

General Patton's Seventh Army swept through western Sicily like a whirlwind, captured Palermo on the 22nd, and then turned eastward towards Messina. To aid him in his spectacular drive, Admiral Hewitt assembled some destroyers, minesweepers and other craft. This diversified squadron was put under the command of Rear Admiral Lyal A. Davidson, whose flagship cruiser *Philadelphia* and her consort the light cruiser *Savannah*, added greatly to the gunfire of the force and enabled Patton to 'leapfrog' his way along the northern coast of Sicily. The force became known unofficially as 'Patton's Navy', for it guarded his coastal flank and gave him gun support whenever he asked for it, which was often.

Montgomery's Eighth Army, working northward through stiff German resistance, entered Messina on 17 August, just two hours after Patton's forces had arrived. The objectives had been reached and taken in remarkably short time; but, unfortunately, neither army commander had reached Messina in time to prevent the massive evacuation of over 100,000 Axis troops and all of their equipment, even including a few mules.

Prime Minister Churchill, elated over the grand success of Husky, sent a congratulatory message to Eisenhower, asking that his compliments be sent to Admiral Hewitt because the bad weather 'gave occasion, according to reports by the Admiralty, for a magnificent display of American seamanship'. It was recognition well deserved, for Hewitt's amphibious forces carried out their landing operations with skill, fortitude and resourcefulness. Sicily was won: the Italian campaign, next on the agenda, was about to begin.

On 24 July, Mussolini was toppled from power and the government placed in the hands of Marshal Pietro Badoglio. In public, Badoglio vowed to continue the war; secretly, however, through agents in Lisbon, he sent out feelers for an armistice. The possible withdrawal of Italy from the war was bound to influence Allied strategic thinking on the imminent Italian campaign because it would force Hitler to replace defecting Italian troops by German soldiers – and that meant not only in Italy, Greece and

Yugoslavia, but essentially in France, so vital to the defence of Hitler's southern flank.

American and British strategists were not able to agree on a common plan, so a compromise was reached, out of which emerged Operation Avalanche. Montgomery's Eighth Army was to cross the Messina Strait and land on the Calabrian Peninsula, as a diversionary thrust. The major landings were aimed at Salerno for 9 September, led by Lieutenant-General Mark M. Clark, whose ultimate target was Naples, just thirty-five miles away. The amphibious forces were divided into a Northern Attack Force (British) and a Southern Attack Force (American), each made up of two divisions embarked in twenty-six troop transports. They were to land in the Bay of Salerno with more than one hundred tank-carrying LSTS. Behind these forces were numerous cruisers, destroyers and small craft to support the landings, as well as a British Covering Force of four battleships and two carriers.

Admiral Hewitt, recognized as *primus inter pares* among amphibious tacticians, was called upon to command all Allied amphibious forces. He had had to confront troubled seas during both Torch and Husky. Weather reports from Avalanche promised a calm surf on Salerno's beaches, a gift from the gods for which a price would be exacted. During the first week of September, Hewitt ordered some of his ships to leave their North African ports in staggered order and rendezvous with other ships of his command, which were then getting up steam in northern ports of Sicily. He flew his flag from the *Ancon*, a converted passenger ship which, unlike the ill-suited *Monrovia* of Husky, was well equipped with radar and communication gear.

General Clark and an air force team came on board and Hewitt left Algiers on the 6th to lead his forces to the beaches of Salerno. While at sea, Hewitt received word that Italy had surrendered, a defection that seemed to promise some advantages for the Allies; but none materialized. The Germans promptly disarmed all Italian soldiers and took over all centres of communication. It was now clear that Hewitt would have to make his landings against disciplined German troops. Nor could he soften up the beaches with a naval bombardment because the army, as they had done in Sicily, insisted upon 'surprise'.

At 0330 on 9 September 1943, Hewitt's Southern Attack Force approached the beaches south of the Sele river that flows into the Bay of Salerno. Dawn was breaking as the first invasion wave waded ashore. Suddenly they were met with a barrage of tank, machine-gun and rifle fire. Casualties mounted quickly, but still the Americans poured in, landing tanks and mortars. Then the beaches were bombed and strafed by German planes, adding to the pandemonium. Some troops finally encircled the German shore guns, and by noon the Americans had gained a shaky claim to their sector.

Hewitt's Northern Attack Force faced the same fierce resistance and likewise suffered heavy casualties. His cruisers and destroyers concentrated an unremitting bombardment on German gun emplacements, tank formations and infantry; but, by the 12th, Clark's Fifth Army had only a precarious hold on the assigned beachheads, while Kesselring rushed more guns, troops and tanks to Salerno. Two days later, Clark's position seemed untenable, while Hewitt kept up his incessant gunfire, aided by air and ground spotters. The battered Fifth Army held its ground. On the 14th, the British battleships *Valiant* and *Warspite*, on Admiral Cunningham's orders, joined Hewitt's invasion force to add their thunder to the American naval bombardment.

Two days later, the vanguard of Montgomery's Eighth Army touched the southern fringe of Clark's Fifth. It was now 16 September. On the same day, realizing that he was paying too dear a price in trying to crush the Salerno beachhead, Kesselring pulled his troops out. Later, he noted in his memoirs that it was the 'effective shelling' by Allied warships that had convinced him to disengage. Salerno vindicated Admiral Hewitt in his uncompromising argument that heavy naval bombardment of an enemy shore must precede the landing of troops and must continue to support the invading soldiers once they were ashore.

General Clark, now with a firm base, began his march northward and (on 1 October) entered a sadly demolished Naples. A few days later, he was joined by Montgomery at the Volturno river, north of Naples, where the retreating Germans stopped briefly before withdrawing about forty miles north of Naples to dig in along their 'Winter Line'. Clark and Montgomery were to fight a bitter war in Italy, helped little by the nominal invasion of Anzio in late January 1944, months before Rome finally fell in June.

Immediately after the Salerno landings, Hewitt's great amphibious armada was pulled apart. The upgraded naval campaign in the Pacific demanded more LSTs; the planned invasion of southern France, to be led by Hewitt, required more; and Overlord, the grand opera of amphibious deeds, needed every landing craft that it could requisition or steal. Yet, in spite of round-the-clock construction in both American and British shipyards, there were simply never enough invasion craft to go around in the war-churned oceans of the world. Less than two months before the Normandy invasion, Winston Churchill wired General Marshall: 'How is it that plans of two great [nations] should be so much hamstrung and limited by a hundred or two of these particular vessels will never be understood by history.'

Hewitt, meanwhile, moved to Palermo, then to Algiers, where he would find little escape from the drudgery of administrative work. In October he was genuinely saddened to learn of the impending departure of his British naval chief, Admiral Cunningham, a man he sincerely admired and with whom he shared a warm friendship. Cunningham, London-bound, was to be installed as First Sea Lord – the equivalent of CNO – following the retirement through ill-health of Admiral of the Fleet Sir Dudley Pound [*q.v.*]. But before he left, he and Hewitt shared one last pleasant association: they were both made Honorary Members of the Seventh Spahis, a corps of native Algerian cavalrymen in the French army serving in North Africa, and each was draped with one of the regiment's distinctive white-lined red woollen cloaks. It was a touching token of respect from their French allies.

For the next several months, Hewitt worked over plans for Operation Dragoon (originally named Anvil) to take place in mid-August against southern France, along the Côte d'Azur between Toulon and Cannes. Dragoon's primary purpose was to protect the southern flank of Overlord, whose defiant curtain would finally be raised on 6 June 1944, with bright media spotlights focused on the Normandy stage. Hewitt had just two months to prepare his forces for the assault on southern France. In mid-March USS *Catoctin*, a merchantman converted into an amphibious command ship, arrived in Algiers to become Hewitt's flagship.

By now, Admiral Hewitt – who, earlier in the war, had been thrown by chance into amphibious warfare and had quickly become its master – had had much time to contemplate the errors of earlier tactics that had affected the three previous invasions that he had led in North Africa, Sicily and Salerno. His repeated requests for daylight landings, heavy naval bombardment before launch and massive air cover of the invasion beaches were denied him. This time, Admiral Hewitt (always in favour of daylight landings) again argued his case before the army brass as forcefully as he could. This time he won his point. Because the devastating effect of naval bombardment in earlier landings had proved its worth, the Allied air forces acquiesced: Hewitt had won his military argument. It was agreed that Dragoon would be executed in daylight and preceded by an intensive naval bombardment of the invasion beaches, so that Lieutenant-General Alexander Patch, who was to lead the US Seventh Army to the hostile shore, would not have to grope around in the darkness. And although bombers of the Mediterranean Allied Air Forces for many days had pounded a long stretch of the coast of southern France, Hewitt called for, and received, air power that would be under his control. His force was soon increased with nine CVES, four from his own navy and five from the Royal Navy. For the first (and last) time he had things the way he wanted them.

Dragoon provided for four landing sites along a fifty-mile stretch of beach, reaching from Iles d'Hyères, near Toulon, to Calanque d'Anthéor, just south of Cannes. Hewitt's large invasion fleet of transports and landing craft, backed up by battleships, aircraft carriers, cruisers, destroyers, minesweepers and anti-submarine forces, was scheduled to arrive off the launching areas just before dawn on 15 August 1944, thus allowing for two hours of early-daylight aerial bombardment. This time, communications between flight commanders and the flagship were perfect, much to Hewitt's belated satisfaction. As dawn broke, his forces approached the French beaches. At 0600, as he watched from the *Catoctin*'s bridge, more than a thousand Allied bombers pounded the entire area, virtually destroying all opposition from the shore. At 0730, with the shoreline clear under a brightening sun, Hewitt ordered 'open fire', and a powerful force of battleships and many cruisers ripped the coastline with broadsides.

Admiral Hewitt commanded the invasion from his flagship as landing craft churned over a tranquil sea towards their designated points of attack. Patch's Seventh Army went first, followed by a newly formed First French Army under General Jean de Lattre de Tassigny, a landing that for the invading French soldiers must have been a moment of exultation.

Tassigny moved westward upon Toulon and Marseilles, while paratroopers glided down upon Nice and Cannes, and the Americans pressed northward inside southern France. By the end of August, Tassigny had captured his objectives, and General Patch's troops were racing up the Rhône Valley in pursuit of the retreating enemy. The expulsion of all German forces from France was under way.

Dragoon had been carried out as Hewitt had wanted it to be. He left the area knowing that this, his last grand assault from the sea, had been the best. The US Army thought so too, for they awarded him an Oak Leaf Cluster in lieu of a second Distinguished Service Medal.

In April 1945, one month before Germany surrendered, Hewitt received his fourth star, a tribute bestowed upon him for his superb mastery of amphibious warfare. With the European war over, he returned briefly to the United States. Then, on 1 August, he took command of US naval forces in Europe just two weeks before Japan accepted defeat, bringing World War Two to an end.

After his detachment from his European duty, Admiral Hewitt reported to the US Naval War College in Newport, Rhode Island, during the autumn of 1946, where he lectured to senior naval officers on his experiences during his numerous amphibious campaigns in the Mediterranean.

From 1947 until his retirement in 1949 at age sixty-two, Admiral Hewitt was the US Naval Representative on the United Nations Military Staff Committee.

Upon retirement after forty-six years of continuous naval service, Admiral Hewitt bought a home in Orwell, Vermont, which he nostalgically named 'Foretop'.

He earned many awards from Brazil, Ecuador, Tunis, Italy, Greece, Belgium and the Netherlands. His proudest honours were the Navy Cross in World War One; the British Knight Commander of the Bath; the Russian Order of Kutuzov; and the Legion of Honour and the Croix de Guerre of France.

He died in September 1972, aged eighty-five, and was buried (as he had wished) at the Naval Academy, Annapolis, Maryland. His wife, Floride, with whom he shared most of his naval career, died one year later and rests beside him.

15

Admiral

Thomas C. Kinkaid
United States Navy

1888–1972

by
Gerald E. Wheeler

*T*HOMAS *Cassin Kinkaid, born Hanover, New Hampshire, 3 April 1888.*
Graduated, US Naval Academy, passed midshipman, June 1908; USS
Nebraska, *July 1908–August 1910; USS* Minnesota, *October 1910–September*
1913. Married to Helen Sherburne Ross, Philadelphia, 24 April 1911. Postgraduate
education in ordnance (USS Machias, *April 1914–January 1915), September*
1913–June 1916; USS Pennsylvania, *USS* Arizona, *July 1916–July 1919.*
Promoted lieutenant-commander, 14 April 1918; staff, Commander, US Naval
Forces in Turkey, June 1922–July 1924; USS Isherwood *(commanding officer),*
November 1924–June 1925. Promoted commander, 4 June 1926; staff, Comman-
der-in-Chief, US Fleet, November 1927–May 1929; Senior Course, Naval War
College, July 1929–May 1930; Secretary, General Board, Navy Department, June
1930–January 1933; USS Colorado *(executive officer), January 1933–October*
1934. Promoted captain, 1 January 1937; USS Indianapolis *(commanding officer),*
January 1937–August 1938; Naval Attaché, Rome, November 1938–March 1941;
Commander, Destroyer Squadron 8, June 1941–December 1941.

On the day the Japanese opened the Pacific War with the United States and
Great Britain, Rear Admiral Kinkaid was en route to San Francisco for further
transfer to Pearl Harbor. He had been promoted to rear admiral a few weeks
earlier and ordered to take command of Cruiser Division 6 (CruDiv 6) in
the Pacific Fleet. When he arrived at the Pacific Fleet's main base on 12
December, evidence of the Japanese surprise attack filled his eyes. He later
recalled what he had seen from his window in the Pan American seaplane as it
circled to land: 'Pearl Harbor, with ships listed and resting on the bottom,
some with wreckage hanging over the sides and other capsized and showing

their bottoms above the surface, everything covered with black fuel oil, was not a pretty sight from the air. It was a shocking sight. . . . '

Clearly the most important tasks for the remaining Pacific Fleet were those associated with defending the Hawaiian Islands. Were the navy to be driven from the islands, the road to victory over Japan would be infinitely longer. From war's beginning the Chief of Naval Operations (CNO), Admiral Harold R. Stark [*q.v.*], called on the Commander-in-Chief, Pacific Fleet (Cincpac), Admiral H. E. Kimmel, to concentrate on the defence of Hawaii and its supporting outlying bases at Midway, Johnston, Palmyra and Wake Islands. Kimmel was also to reinforce the American base in Samoa and provide for the defence of the lines of communication from the mainland to Samoa, the New Hebrides and New Caledonia, and on to the east coast of Australia. As the Japanese descended on the Philippines, Malaya and eventually the Dutch East Indies, planners in Washington and London could see that the defence of the 'Malay Barrier' might well be anchored in Australia. Finally, because the navy had four carriers in the Pacific, the CNO believed they could be used to defend the Hawaii line, but also offensively to raid Japanese lines of communication and bases in the Marshall and Caroline Islands, the so-called Mandated Islands. The grand strategy, agreed upon in early 1941 with the British, called for standing on the defensive in the Pacific until Germany and Italy were defeated, but such a stance did not preclude jabbing at the Japanese when possible to do so.

During Kinkaid's first four months in the Pacific Fleet he took part in two minor operations. Starting 15 December, he spent two weeks as an observer with the abortive expedition to relieve Wake Island's garrison. On 17 December, inevitably though perhaps unfairly, Admiral Kimmel was relieved of his command at Pearl Harbor, to be replaced by Admiral Chester Nimitz [*q.v.*]. Upon return to Pearl Harbor, Kinkaid too relieved Rear Admiral Frank Jack Fletcher, taking command of CruDiv 6, and on 31 December joined Vice Admiral Wilson Brown's Task Force 11 for a raiding operation in the south-west Pacific. Off Bougainville, on 21 February 1942, he experienced his first bombing attack against his ships. Two weeks later he stood by with his cruisers in the Gulf of Papua as squadrons from *Lexington* and *Yorktown* crossed New Guinea and attacked an enemy invasion force at Lae and Salamaua on the north coast. These operations taught Kinkaid a good deal about operating cruisers with carrier task forces and about the mobility and striking power of such forces.

After a quick return to Pearl Harbor for reprovisioning, TF 11 on 15 April 1942 sortied again for the South Pacific. Rear Admiral Aubrey Fitch, a naval aviator, now commanded and Kinkaid continued in command of the cruiser screen. TF 11's mission was to join Admiral Fletcher near the Fiji Islands and then the combined task force would move into the Coral Sea. Here, it was anticipated, Fletcher's carriers would confront a Japanese move to capture Port Moresby. These orders from Admiral Nimitz were largely based on the output of his radio communications intelligence (code-breaking) unit in Pearl Harbor.

Once in the Coral Sea, Fletcher's carriers did not have long to wait before the Japanese showed their hand. On 3 May, TF 17 received word that a B-17 had sighted a Japanese invasion force in Tulagi Harbour off Florida Island. It was seizing an Australian seaplane base just a few miles across from Guadalcanal. Leaving TF 11 to refuel, Fletcher took TF 17 and the next day attacked the Japanese at Tulagi. While the Americans did considerable damage, they did not force the enemy to evacuate his foothold in the southern Solomons. The action, though, was a confirmation of the intelligence estimate provided by Cincpac's code breakers. The Japanese were on the move.

Operation MO, the Japanese scheme for the capture of Port Moresby, involved five different naval forces, all under the command of Vice Admiral Shigeyoshi Inouye with his headquarters in Rabaul. One force was to capture Tulagi; three of the forces, under the command of Rear Admiral Aritomo Goto, focused on taking Port Moresby; and the fifth group, a carrier striking force, was commanded by Rear Admiral Takeo Takagi. The Striking Force included two fleet carriers, *Shokaku* and *Zuikaku*. After rounding the Solomon Islands from the east, the Striking Force's mission was to engage the American carriers by a flanking attack.

Following his attack on Tulagi, Fletcher's TF 17 joined with Fitch's TF 11, fuelled and then combined into TF 17 and moved towards the Louisiades. At dawn on 7 May, TF 17 was approximately 115 miles south of Rossel Island, the easternmost of the Louisiades, which lies about 210 miles east of the tip of New Guinea. The Japanese invasion, support and covering forces were then about 125 miles north-west of Rossel Island. The Striking Force, with its two carriers, bore almost due east of TF 17, distance 210 miles. About 0730 scouts from *Yorktown* located the Japanese invasion force, which included the light carrier *Shoho*. At about the same time, scouts from the Striking Force sighted TF 17's oiler *Neosho*, to the south, with its escorting destroyer *Sims*. The Japanese scouts reported them as a carrier and a cruiser, thus triggering deck-load strikes from the carriers. Fletcher held his squadrons on deck while TF 17 closed Admiral Goto's invasion forces. Finally, at 0926 *Lexington* began launching, followed soon after by *Yorktown*. The hapless *Shoho* was overwhelmed and quickly sunk. The Japanese squadrons rapidly disposed of *Sims* and turned *Neosho* into a shambles, but the empty oiler had too much buoyancy to be sunk.

Both admirals, Fletcher and Takagi, recognized that they hadn't come to grips with the main enemy carrier force. Fletcher, however, kept his attention directed to the north; his mission was to prevent the invasion of Port Moresby. In this he had already been successful. The Japanese decided to pull back towards Rabaul until the issue of sea control was settled. The two commanders considered making night surface searches towards one another in order to engage in night surface battle; but both really preferred to wait until daylight and then seek action. And so they waited.

Morning searches from the American and Japanese carriers were both successful in locating their foes. At 0900 *Yorktown* commenced launching its squadrons for attack and *Lexington* followed immediately. The Striking Force was 175 miles to the north-east. Squadrons from TF 17 and the Striking Force passed one another en route to their targets, but their aircraft did not engage. The Americans reached their targets first at 1057 and immediately pounced on *Shokaku*; her twin sister, *Zuikaku*, was almost ignored. Hit by three half-ton bombs, *Shokaku* was heavily damaged but survived. The principal damage to *Zuikaku* came from the decimation of her squadrons in attacking the Americans.

The Japanese began attacking TF 17 about 1115 and Kinkaid had a ringside seat for the action. At first concentrated for defence, the two carriers separated and took their circle of defenders with them. Kinkaid now controlled heavy cruisers *Minneapolis* and *New Orleans*, plus four destroyers, for protection of *Lexington*. Compared with later carrier actions, this screen was a bit anaemic. Damage to Kinkaid's ships was comparatively light and so were personnel casualties, but not in the carriers. The concentrated attention of the Japanese resulted in mortal damage to *Lexington* and internal damage to *Yorktown*. After appearing to have her damage under control, *Lexington* suffered a massive petrol explosion that finally resulted in the loss of the carrier. *Yorktown*'s damage, while serious, was reparable once she reached Pearl Harbor.

In the interval until *Lexington*'s situation became terminal, Fletcher took *Yorktown* and its screen to a covering position and left the wounded carrier in Kinkaid's hands. He was to provide fire-fighting assistance and protection if needed; and if the flat-top had to be abandoned, he was to manage the rescue of the crew. By 1700 the situation was hopeless and Captain Frederick Sherman ordered his ship abandoned. Working quickly and efficiently, the destroyers picked up 2,685 men and distributed some of them among the cruisers. Finally, Kinkaid ordered the destroyer *Phelps* to sink the furiously burning carrier with torpedoes. With that the Admiral joined Fletcher and all shaped course for Nouméa and eventually Pearl Harbor.

Once in port, Kinkaid quickly learned that the Japanese were again on the move and Midway was the target. Nimitz's code breakers had performed magnificently. This time they had turned up Admiral Yamamoto's [*q.v.*] operation order for taking Midway. It would be a major effort involving an invasion force, a covering fleet which would include battleships, and a four-carrier striking force. The plan also included a diversionary attack on Dutch Harbor, Alaska and occupation of Attu and Kiska Islands in the Aleutian chain. If the Americans chose to oppose them, Yamamoto anticipated that he would have enough power available to annihilate them. With the loss of their Pacific Fleet, he predicted the United States would seek a negotiated settlement of the war.

Nimitz's plan to oppose the Japanese was fairly simple. He would continue to build up the defences of Midway; and he would have his PBY Catalinas searching 700-mile sectors from Midway trying to get an early fix on the enemy. Finally, he planned to set an ambush by placing his three aircraft carriers to the north-east of Midway in a position to attack the Japanese on their flank as they approached from the north-west.

To block the Japanese, Nimitz had just three carriers, distributed into two task forces. Vice Admiral William Halsey [*q.v.*] would normally have taken TF 16 (*Enterprise, Hornet*) to sea, but he was too ill to do so. Instead, Rear Admiral Raymond Spruance [*q.v.*] would take command. The cruisers of TF 16 were again to be commanded by Rear Admiral Kinkaid. If the carriers separated, then the Admiral would take three cruisers and four destroyers and form a protective circle around *Hornet*. The remaining three cruisers and five destroyers would work with *Enterprise*. TF 17, centred on *Yorktown*, had two cruisers and six destroyers commanded by Rear Admiral Fletcher, who also would be officer in tactical command (OTC) of the two task forces.

TF 16 sortied on 28 May, followed two days later by Fletcher's *Yorktown* force. On 2 June the two task forces rendezvoused and began the tense wait for the Japanese. In the afternoon of 3 June, the situation clarified. A searching Catalina discovered the invasion fleet 700 miles due west of Midway. That evening Fletcher brought his task forces to the south-west so that at morning they would be in a flanking position if the Japanese followed their comprom-ized operation plan and made their approach from the north-west.

The ambush worked perfectly and pilots from the three carrier air groups sank four Japanese fleet carriers: *Kaga, Akagi, Soryu* and *Hiryu*. American losses, particularly in the three torpedo squadrons, were catastrophic. Also lost, two days after the 4 June battle, was the heavily damaged carrier *Yorktown* and destroyer *Hammann*. During the counter-attacks against the American task forces on the 4th, *Hornet* never came under attack and thus Kinkaid's cruisers never opened fire. His role at the Battle of Midway, arguably the most important US Navy action of World War Two, was that of an interested observer. On the other hand, in terms of his future, the past operations he had participated in had given him a solid grounding in carrier task force operations.

Upon returning to Pearl Harbor on 13 June, Kinkaid found that Admiral E. J. King [*q.v.*], the Commander-in-Chief, US Fleet (Cominch) and new CNO had decided that an 'offensive–defensive' operation was needed in the South Pacific. He believed that seizing positions in the lower Solomon Islands, at Tulagi and Guadalcanal, would enhance the defence of US bases in New Caledonia (Nouméa) and the New Hebrides Islands (Espiritu Santo, Efate) and would be first steps towards recapture of Rabaul and the Philippines. Following negotiations with General Douglas MacArthur in Australia, Nimitz ordered Vice Admiral R. L. Ghormley, Commander South Pacific Area (Comsopac), to develop plans for landings on 7 August. The date was earlier than desired by anyone, but recent photo-intelligence and code breaking revealed that the Japanese were already preparing an airfield on Guadalcanal.

Code named Operation Watchtower, the Solomons Expeditionary Force (TF 61) would be commanded by Vice Admiral Fletcher. The landing force (TF 61.2) was to be led by Rear Admiral R. K. Turner [*q.v.*] and the air support forces (TF 61.1) by Rear Admiral Leigh Noyes. The air support forces consisted of three carrier task forces: TF 11 (*Saratoga*) under Fletcher's personal command; TF 18 (*Wasp*) commanded by Noyes, and TF 16 (*Enterprise*) commanded by Kinkaid. Because Admiral Nimitz wanted to use Rear Admiral Spruance as his Chief of Staff, and Vice Admiral Halsey was not ready for sea duty as yet, Nimitz decided to assign Kinkaid to command the *Enterprise* force. He would continue to use Halsey's staff, which contained three senior naval aviators. Though non-aviators, Fletcher and Spruance had both been successful carrier task force commanders; there was no reason why Kinkaid should not be used as such.

Given the short preparation period and minimum rehearsal, Operation Watchtower went off fairly smoothly. On 7 August the carriers began launching their squadrons at dawn and in a few minutes rained bombs down on the few targets available without interference. It was clear that tactical surprise had been achieved. The Marines stormed ashore with minimum resistance from the Japanese. Yet everyone knew there would be a counter-attack once the Japanese headquarters in Rabaul and Truk received word that the Americans had invaded the Solomons.

Afternoon attacks followed for two days that cost the Japanese forty planes and crews. In return, the carriers lost twenty-one Wildcats, a 21 per cent reduction in defence capability for the force. Lacking a flow of replacement aircraft, a war of aircraft attrition with the Japanese was unacceptable to Fletcher. Given this situation, plus the fact that his force was very low on fuel, Comsopac authorized Fletcher to withdraw his carriers in the early hours of 9 August. Admiral Turner was forced to follow with his invasion force shipping and escorts. The Marines were now on their own until Fletcher and the carriers could return.

Fortunately for the Americans, the Japanese were unable to put together a reinforcement group for a couple of weeks. On 20 August Comsopac ordered Fletcher to bring his carriers back to Guadalcanal to be in position to counter expected Japanese moves. On the 23rd, Kinkaid's TF 16 and the others were positioned about 100 miles south-east of the Solomon Islands awaiting further information. Informed that the Japanese carriers were north of Truk, Fletcher decided it was safe to release Admiral Noyes' *Wasp* force for refuelling, a decision he was greatly to regret. In fact, the Japanese were coming in four different groups: a Guadalcanal Reinforcement Force consisting of transports and escorts; a covering force of battleships (*Hiei* and *Kirishima*), cruisers and destroyers; a small carrier task group built around *Ryujo*; and a striking force consisting of fleet carriers *Shokaku* and *Zuikaku* and their escorts. On the 24th Kinkaid's scouts located the *Ryujo* task force first and then the covering group. *Saratoga* responded with a deckload strike against the light carrier *Ryujo* and she was quickly put under. Meantime, *Enterprise* scouts turned up the Striking Force with its two carriers. With *Saratoga*'s planes atacking *Ryujo* and *Enterprise*'s doing the searches, there was little to send against them. A strike was cobbled together from the two American carriers, but it proved ineffective. The planes could not find the Japanese carriers, though they did manage to get damaging near misses on the seaplane carrier *Chitose*, a part of the covering force.

The inevitable Japanese counter-attack soon illuminated the radars in TF 16. At 1711 *Enterprise* became the target of two waves of attackers. Fletcher in *Saratoga* could only watch, though his Wildcats did help fight off the Japanese. Of the thirty or so Vals that dived on the 'Big E', three hit the carrier and three obtained destructive near misses. Only four or five Vals escaped. None of the torpedo planes managed to penetrate the fighter screen and gunfire wall surrounding TF 16. For the first time in the war, Kinkaid felt enemy bombs rock his flagship. Damaged, with two elevators jammed in the raised position, *Enterprise* could recover most of her aircraft, but she was not a very efficient carrier. Informed that the flat-top could not operate against the enemy without repairs, Cincpac ordered the 'Big E' back to Pearl Harbor.

The Battle of the eastern Solomons earned Kinkaid a second Distinguished Service Medal. The Japanese had lost a carrier and more airmen than they could possibly spare, and had not been allowed to reinforce their embattled troops on Guadalcanal. Kinkaid had learned a great deal about managing a carrier task force in combat. In his action report, he urged that better anti-aircraft weapons be installed on the ships and that the carriers be assigned larger fighting squadrons. He knew that the best defence for a carrier is to engage the enemy many miles from the airspace above the ships. He also knew that better-trained fighter director officers were needed so that the Wildcats would meet the enemy at the proper altitude and far from the task force.

During the month that TF 16 was in Pearl Harbor, Cincpac's code breakers again uncovered the next Japanese moves. They predicted the Japanese would send a large reinforcement to Guadalcanal around 23 October. Before an attempt to land the troops was made, the enemy would try to eliminate the airfield and aircraft on the island through surface bombardment. To cover the reinforcement convoy, there would be a substantial surface force which would include carriers. So informed, Nimitz prepared a response for the Japanese, somewhat similar to the Midway ambush. The key was the carrier task force, but here Cincpac's resources were severely limited. Hard times had fallen on Fletcher's carriers. During September, *Saratoga* had been torpedoed and severely damaged; *Wasp* had been hit by three torpedoes and sunk; and *North Carolina* had been torpedoed and damaged. The Pacific Fleet now had only *Enterprise* and *Hornet* to face this new Japanese challenge.

Cincpac again had to decide who would take TF 16 to sea. Admiral Halsey was ready, but Nimitz had other plans for him; so once again he turned to Kinkaid. He had done well at the eastern Solomons battle; he would now get a further opportunity. The *Hornet* task force (TF 17) was given to Rear Admiral George Murray, a former skipper of *Enterprise*. The plan was to have Halsey go to Nouméa and evaluate Comsopac's operation for Nimitz. When finished he would relieve Kinkaid of TF 16 and the latter would relieve Murray of TF 17. Halsey would command both task forces for operations. But all of this changed on 18 October (Nouméa date) when Nimitz ordered Halsey to relieve Ghormley as Comsopac. Kinkaid would stay with the *Enterprise* force and command both task forces, as Task Force 61.

The Japanese did not arrive on the 23rd, but tender-based Catalinas did locate a carrier force in the afternoon of the 25th. Kinkaid launched a strike from *Enterprise*, but it failed to locate the enemy. The next day, 26 October, Kinkaid's carriers came to grips with the enemy. Strikes from *Hornet* and the 'Big E' found three Japanese carriers and inflicted severe damage on two of them, *Zuiho* and *Shokaku*. A third fleet carrier, *Zuikaku*, was not hit, and *Junyo*, a light carrier, was never located. As at the eastern Solomons, Japanese strikes hit the American carriers while their planes were attacking the Japanese. *Hornet* was severely damaged and eventually sank; *Enterprise* was again hit by three bombs and her forward elevator was immobilized in the raised position. The flat-top was able to recover planes from both carriers, but she was too crowded for effective operations. Once *Hornet*'s situation was determined to be hopeless, Kinkaid arranged for the rescue of the crew and then left the field of battle. He could not afford to risk the last operational (though limited) carrier available to Comsopac. The Japanese also had had enough and they too turned away.

This, the Battle of the Santa Cruz Islands, had been a costly one to both sides. The Japanese lost the use of two carriers and a cruiser for an extended period. Kinkaid's task force lost a carrier and a destroyer and had a battleship, an anti-aircraft cruiser and a destroyer damaged. By losing almost 100 aircraft and pilots, the Japanese were so grievously hurt that they were unable to use their carrier task forces for more than a year. This was particularly serious since 1943 was the year that new American carriers began to flood into the Pacific Fleet.

Although *Enterprise* was badly damaged, Admiral Halsey kept TF 16 in the South Pacific. He knew the Japanese were planning a new effort to reinforce Guadalcanal and he needed the help of TF 16 to frustrate this move. For three days, 13–15 November, American and Japanese surface forces slugged it out around Guadalcanal. Losses were heavy on both sides. Kinkaid's TF 16 lent assistance by having its planes operate from Guadalcanal's Henderson Field. With no Japanese carriers to interfere, the 'Big E's' pilots, and the Marine and Air Corps pilots on the island, demolished the Japanese reinforcement fleet. Of 13,000 troops destined for the island, probably no more than 2,000 made it ashore.

After 15 November, Kinkaid knew his days in the South Pacific were drawing to a close. In his personal correspondence with his wife, and in some reports, the Admiral left little doubt that his duty in *Enterprise* was the most exciting and most interesting of his wartime career. By the time he met the Japanese in battle on 26 October, at the Santa Cruz Islands, he had had the necessary foundation experiences, of a cruiser division and a carrier task force, to allow him to fight TF 61 effectively. The mission of stopping the Japanese reinforcement of Guadalcanal had been accomplished. His airmen had also knocked out of action the remnants of Japan's carrier fleet. In leading TF 61, Kinkaid demonstrated a characteristic that was appreciated by Admirals Halsey, Nimitz and King: he did the best he could with what he was given.

Upon arrival at Pearl Harbor on 2 December, Kinkaid discovered that he had been selected to relieve Rear Admiral R. A. Theobald as Commander, North Pacific Force (Comnorpacfor). After five months of tempestuous relations with the army and Air Corps, Theobald had exhausted the patience of Admiral King and General Marshall, and Nimitz had been asked to find a replacement. What was needed was someone who could manage the drive to eliminate the Japanese in the Aleutians, and who could do so without engaging in almost open warfare with his opposite numbers. Having just left the *Enterprise* task force, Kinkaid was 'available'.

From Hawaii, Kinkaid travelled with Nimitz to his bi-monthly meeting in San Francisco with Admiral King. Here he obtained the views of both Cincpac and Cominch concerning the importance of the work he would be undertaking. What he learned was that the Aleutians had a rather low priority in the plans of Cominch and the Joint Chiefs of Staff (JCS). They did not want the Japanese to expand their holdings, but the JCS did not want to invest very much in removing them from American soil. The key problem for everyone was shipping, particularly attack transports (APAS) and attack cargo vessels (AKAS). There simply were not enough of these ships in the Pacific to meet the needs of General MacArthur (Comswpa), Admiral Halsey (Comsopac) and Kinkaid as they planned operations for 1943.

In San Francisco, Kinkaid found the army (personified in Lieutenant-General John L. DeWitt, Commander, Western Defence Command) eager to open operations in the Alaskan theatre. Plans were already under way to seize Amchitka Island, about sixty miles south-east of Kiska. Because the Japanese had been displaying some interest in this island, pre-emptive action was needed. Occupation would then make it possible to step up bombing of Kiska and Attu and to intensify an aerial blockade. Also, once Amchitka was taken, it would be possible to move against Kiska with air cover from the neighbouring island. The Amchitka occupation took place on 12 January 1943 and army engineers immediately began construction of an airfield. Because of stormy seas, the operation cost the navy a destroyer and an attack transport.

While construction of the Amchitka airfield went forward, Kinkaid's staff had to complete plans for the assault on Kiska. With more than 5,000 estimated to be in the Japanese garrison, a difficult campaign was anticipated. In early March, following the transfer of ten AKAS and APAS to the Atlantic, Kinkaid suggested to Nimitz the substitution of Attu for Kiska in their planning. Anticipating that Attu was more lightly garrisoned than Kiska, the Admiral argued that it could be attacked with fewer troops and thus fewer cargo and transport vessels would be required. Nimitz quickly accepted the proposal. He set an invasion date (D-Day) for 7 May 1943.

With the opening of spring, Kinkaid moved his headquarters from Kodiak Island to Adak in the Aleutians. He was now 1,000 miles closer to the war and better able to deal with his commanders at first hand. Because Major-General S. B. Buckner (Commander, Alaskan Defence Command) and Brigadier-General W. C. Butler (Commander, 11th Air Force) also moved their headquarters to Adak, Kinkaid and Buckner established a joint mess. Now meeting daily over meals, Kinkaid and Buckner became fast friends, and their staffs found it increasingly easier to work out problems quickly and amicably. This daily relationship provided the Admiral with a valuable education concerning how the army operated, an education that would be put to good use in the future.

Despite controlling the sea and air around and above Attu, the assault (code named Landcrab) proved much more difficult than planned. Instead of an estimated 500 to 1,800 Japanese troops on Attu, there were 2,380. When the army drive stalled, with over 11,000 troops ashore, Kinkaid – fearing that the commanding General was digging in for a long campaign – replaced him. In this action he had the full support of Generals DeWitt and Buckner, but he intensely disliked doing it. Kinkaid's impatience stemmed from his concern that the Japanese were planning to send a major surface force to attack the beachhead. He wanted his fighting ships, particularly the battleships and cruisers, released from close support duties and resupplied with ammunition before the enemy arrived. By 30 May Attu was completely in American hands and engineering troops were sent to Shemya, a neighbouring island, to begin runway construction there. Kiska could now be pounded by bombers from Adak, Amchitka and Attu.

The successful campaign against the Japanese on Attu earned Kinkaid his first national attention, promotion to vice admiral and a third Distinguished Service Medal. More importantly for him, Admirals Nimitz and King were pleased with the results. Kinkaid had proved to be a careful planner and a firm leader.

The victory at Attu made the planning for Kiska much easier. King, Nimitz and DeWitt were eager to finish the Aleutians campaign with the retaking of Kiska. Once the Combined Chiefs of Staff and the JCS fell into line, Kinkaid was told to move ahead with a target date of 15 August 1943. In the interim Kinkaid stepped up the pressure on Kiska. Daily bombing raids were supplemented by frequent bombardments from his ships. A tight blockade was maintained, but it was not impenetrable. The planning, which had actually begun the previous November, called for about 30,000 American troops, plus a Canadian brigade of 4,800. No one knew how many Japanese were in the Kiska garrison, but for planning a figure of 9,000 to 10,000 was used.

The assault of 15 August went off smoothly. Several weeks of intensive aerial and surface bombardments had pulverized the beaches and Japanese cantonments, and when the troops landed, no resistance was met. Not surprisingly, because the island was empty. The Japanese had evacuated; in fact they had left two weeks earlier. Aerial reconnaissance had not revealed their departure, and bomber-pilot reports of light anti-aircraft fire had led Kinkaid and Butler's intelligence staffs to believe that the Japanese were simply keeping their heads down. Though disappointed that so many (5,200) had escaped through the fog, a collective sigh of relief was expressed at not having to take a large number of casualties. The operation had been a very large and expensive amphibious rehearsal. A bit embarrassing for Kinkaid and Buckner, but no personal damage to their careers resulted. The Admiral wrote to his wife: 'Our objective of ridding the Aleutians of the Japs has been accomplished. The stratagem of taking Attu in order to weaken their hold on Kiska succeeded beyond all expectations and Kiska fell of its own weight.'

In late September, Kinkaid received orders to Washington for consultations and then leave. Following a month of well-earned relaxation, the Admiral reported to Admiral King and learned that he had a new, possibly portentous assignment. In the South-West Pacific Area (SWPA), General MacArthur was preparing to open a major campaign to clear the Japanese from New Guinea, the Bismarck Archipelago and the Admiralty Islands and he wanted a new naval commander for his Seventh Fleet. The incumbent, Vice Admiral A. S. Carpender, had been too cautious for the General. King knew he needed an aggressive, battle-experienced admiral who had demonstrated ability to work with the army. Given his record in the Aleutians, Kinkaid appeared to fill the bill nicely.

MacArthur warmly welcomed the Admiral on 23 November, and quickly set him to work. In serving the Commander, South-West Pacific Area (Comswpa), Kinkaid would wear two hats. As Commander, Naval Forces, SWPA he would command naval units of Australia, New Zealand and the Netherlands East Indies; and he would be Commander Seventh Fleet ('MacArthur's Navy') with an amphibious force, plus a variety of cruisers and destroyers. He was to receive his orders from General MacArthur, but he would receive his ships and personnel from Admiral King. On occasions he would request from Cincpac additional naval vessels for certain operations.

While his first contacts with the General were pleasant and reassuring, Kinkaid could do very little to relieve an underlying tension that suffused the General's business. Given the priorities of early 1944, as the Allies prepared to invade France, MacArthur simply could not command the resources he desired for the campaigns he was planning. While somewhat understanding the needs of the European theatre, the General was particularly galled by the siphoning of naval resources for Admiral Nimitz's Central Pacific campaign. In its simplest form, the current strategy called for an approach to the Philippines and the China coast along two lines of advance. One axis of movement was to be through the Solomons and the New Guinea coast to drive the Japanese from Rabaul in the Bismarcks and then from Mindanao and the rest of the Philippines. MacArthur and Halsey were already moving ahead along this line. The other axis was a drive through the Central Pacific islands that would require seizing the Gilberts and Marshalls, the Marianas, the Palaus and then perhaps the Philippines or Formosa. Because the navy would be moving against Japanese airbases in the islands, carrier task forces were constantly in demand to cover the amphibious landings. MacArthur felt a few could be spared for his command; but basically he believed the Central Pacific thrust was unnecessary.

Starting with the landing at Arawe on New Britain in mid-December 1943, Kinkaid's amphibious commander, Rear Admiral Daniel E. Barbey, worked steadily at his craft for the next eighteen months. An excellent planner and inspirational leader, Barbey saw to it that MacArthur's amphibious operations went smoothly. Kinkaid recognized that his amphibious leader worked best under a loose rein and rarely interfered in his operations. Barbey actually commanded more than fourteen landings before Leyte (20 October) and thirty-two afterwards.

Despite having his headquarters in Brisbane, Kinkaid spent as much time as possible 'at the front', as he called it. Though 250 miles from the fighting along New Guinea's north coast, Kinkaid and MacArthur spent long stretches of time at Port Moresby, where a secondary headquarters was established. With Milne Bay, at the tip of New Guinea, serving as a naval base for the Seventh Fleet, the Admiral could regularly visit his forces from Port Moresby. Later, in April 1944, after the assaults at Humboldt and Tanemerah Bays and Aitape, MacArthur (and Kinkaid later) moved his permanent headquarters from Brisbane to a hill overlooking Lake Sentani above the harbour at Humboldt Bay. Here army and navy planners worked out future moves west along the north New Guinea coast and the jump to the Philippines.

By the first of September 1944, MacArthur was poised to seize Morotai in the Halmahera Islands and then wheel north for the return to the Philippines at Sarangani Bay in southern Mindanao. This operation would be preceded by a Pacific Fleet assault in the Palau Islands. These plans were all scrapped following Third Fleet carrier raids against Morotai, the Palaus, Yap, Mindanao and the Visayan Islands (including Leyte) in the Central Philippines. To Halsey the Japanese response seemed unexpectedly weak. He then advised Nimitz, who informed Admiral King and the JCS, that current plans should be altered. He recommended that Leyte be invaded as soon as possible. Nimitz agreed, but insisted that plans to take the Palaus not be altered. Interestingly the Combined Chiefs of Staff had been meeting with President Roosevelt and Prime Minister Churchill and thus agreement to the switch in plans could be achieved at the highest levels immediately.

With a proposed assault date of 20 October facing them, army and navy planners accelerated their efforts. To avoid placing experienced Third Fleet amphibious commanders under Rear Admiral Barbey, Admiral King insisted that Kinkaid personally command the Central Philippines Attack Force (TF 77) with two subordinate task force commanders, Barbey (TF 78) and Vice-Admiral T. S. Wilkinson (TF 79) from the Third Fleet. Each task force commander would manage the landing of two divisions on the east side of Leyte between Tacloban and Dulag. Within the first two days, more than 200,000 troops would be put ashore to face an estimated 21,000 Japanese. To support the landings, Cincpac had sent six reconditioned old battleships, survivors of the Pearl Harbor attack, commanded by Rear Admiral J. B. Oldendorf, four light and three heavy cruisers, and twenty-one destroyers. Nimitz also provided sixteen escort carriers and twenty-one destroyers to furnish anti-submarine protection and close-support missions for the troops ashore. For distant cover and support, there would be Halsey's Third Fleet with its extremely powerful TF 38 containing four fast carrier task groups and a total of seventeen carriers, six fast battleships, fifteen cruisers and fifty-eight destroyers. Halsey's basic mission was to prevent any Japanese naval interference with the Leyte landings and to keep enemy aircraft suppressed. Also included in Halsey's orders from Nimitz was the proviso: 'In case opportunity for destruction of major portion of the enemy fleet is offered or can be created, such destruction becomes the primary task.' Missing from Operation King II was the designation of a supreme commander to whom Kinkaid and Halsey would report. The former, of course, was responsible to General MacArthur, the latter to Admiral Nimitz. Their instructions called for consultation and collaboration.

The 20 October landings went smoothly, a tribute to the careful planning at Lake Sentani. MacArthur waded ashore in the early afternoon and announced: 'People of the Philippines, I have returned. By the grace of Almighty God our forces stand again on Philippine soil.' Three days later, in a ceremony at Tacloban, the General restored civil self-government to the Filipinos by declaring President Sergio Osmeña again President of the Commonwealth. Kinkaid was there, but very restless. Recent despatches had indicated the Japanese navy was coming their way.

Between submarine contacts, aircraft sightings and code breaking, it was clear the Japanese had planned a great pincer movement against Leyte Gulf. A very large force, commanded by Vice Admiral Takeo Kurita and consisting of five battleships, twelve cruisers and sixteen destroyers, was approaching by way of the Sibuyan Sea and was expected to exit the islands at San Bernardino Strait between Luzon and Samar. After passing south along the coast of Samar, this Central Force would obviously enter Leyte Gulf from the east. A second group, considerably smaller and commanded by Vice Admiral Shoji Nishimura, included two battleships, a cruiser and four destroyers. It was to be joined by three cruisers and seven destroyers led by Vice Admiral Kiyohide Shima. Designated the Southern Force by Kinkaid's staff, it was expected to enter Leyte Gulf from the south, from the Mindanao Sea by way of the Surigao Strait, and join Admiral Kurita's Central Force.

In the morning of 24 October pilots from Halsey's carriers, now standing off Samar, located Kurita's and Nishimura's forces and commenced aerial attacks. The Southern Force was lightly damaged and continued undeterred. Kurita's Central Force suffered the loss of the super-battleship *Musashi* and the disabling of a cruiser, but the pilots left with the impression that they had dealt even heavier damage and that the enemy was retreating westward. Later that same day, searchers from the carriers located a Northern Force of four carriers, two hermaphrodite battleship–carriers, several cruisers and escorting destroyers. Led by Vice-Admiral Jisaburo Ozawa [*q.v.*], the Northern Force was a decoy designed to pull Halsey's carriers away from the Leyte Gulf area as the Central and Southern Forces fell on the Americans in the gulf.

With the movements of the Japanese Central and Southern Forces clear, Kinkaid at noon on the 24th made his preparations to meet the enemy. Admiral Oldendorf would block the Surigao Strait with his six old battleships, eight cruisers and twenty-six destroyers. They would be assisted by thirty-nine motor torpedo boats. These ships were expected to engage Nishimura's ships in the early morning of the 25th. Rear Admiral T. L. Sprague's CVES (TF 77.4) were disposed about fifty miles east of the gulf entrance, in three groups, and were expected to keep the area clear of Japanese aircraft and submarines and to be ready to attack enemy naval vessels if called upon to do so. Once his dispositions were made, Kinkaid let Halsey know by radio that the Seventh Fleet could handle the Southern Force and that he expected the Third Fleet to stop the Central Force.

To meet the contingency of a possible surface engagement with Kurita's Central Force, Halsey (in a 'preparatory despatch') created a surface battle force from TF 38. To be led by Vice Admiral W. A. Lee, TF 34 would consist of four fast battleships with supporting cruisers and destroyers and would be formed only if specifically so ordered by Halsey. Kinkaid's staff intercepted the preparatory signal and later assumed that it had missed the 'execute' signal. In other words, the staff believed that TF 34 had deployed and was guarding San Bernardino Strait. Later in the afternoon Halsey radioed Kinkaid: 'Central Force heavily damaged according to strike reports. Am proceeding north with three groups to attack carrier force at dawn.' Here is where the confusion began. Kinkaid assumed that the 'three groups' were carrier task groups and that TF 34 had been left behind to block San Bernardino Strait.

Admiral Oldendorf's night engagement with the Nishimura–Shima Southern Force (Battle of Surigao Strait) was a blazing success. Two battleships, a cruiser and three destroyers were sunk in the main battle and pursuit; two more cruisers, under Shima's command, were destroyed by air attack a few days later. During the battle, and the previous evening as well, Kinkaid and his staff remained with their command ship, *Wasatch*, in Leyte Gulf. As the evening progressed, the Admiral ordered night and dawn searches of the San Bernardino Strait area by tender-based patrol planes and scouts from the escort carriers. Finally, having spent the night together, Kinkaid asked his staff if anything had been overlooked. His operations officer suggested that Halsey be asked directly if he were guarding San Bernardino Strait. Kinkaid agreed and a query was sent at 0412 on the 25th. Due to delays among Halsey's communicators, the reply came too late to be useful.

At 0647 a plane from the escort carrier *Kadashan Bay* reported that he was being fired on by a Japanese fleet. He had flushed Kurita's Central Force, now well south of San Bernardino Strait. There followed a desperate fight between the six CVEs of Task Unit 77.4.3. ('Taffy-3'), commanded by Rear Admiral C. A. F. Sprague, and the Japanese. In this battle off Samar the carriers *Gambier Bay* and *St Lô* were sunk as were the destroyers *Johnson* and *Hoel* and the destroyer escort *Samuel B. Roberts*. While this battle was being fought, Kinkaid ordered Oldendorf to bring his battleships to the entrance of Leyte Gulf to meet Kurita's force if he tried to enter. Fortunately for all Americans involved, Admiral Kurita's nerve broke and he retreated back to the straits, snatching defeat from the jaws of victory. At about the same time that Kurita flinched, a deeply irritated Halsey responded to Kinkaid's calls for assistance by sending his battleships south, but he really felt that he had more important work for them at hand.

While Kurita's big ships were holding reveille for Sprague's 'Taffy-3', Halsey's squadrons were demolishing Ozawa's decoy force. The four enemy carriers, with no protecting aircraft, were easily sunk. The old hermaphrodites were tougher and managed to escape. While an important victory, because it just about finished off the remaining Japanese carrriers, the battle off Cape Engaño had almost led to a serious débâcle in Leyte Gulf. With shortages in their armour-piercing shells after the shoot-out in the Surigao Strait, it was not certain that Oldendorf's old battleships could have stopped the Japanese, had there been a challenge. But a fifth battle did not eventuate. Pounded in the Sibuyan Sea, the Surigao Strait, off Samar and off Cape Engaño, and with no significant assistance from land-based squadrons, the Japanese had had enough, and Kurita retreated through San Bernardino Strait before Halsey's TF 38 could get within striking distance.

With the repulse of the Imperial Navy in the Battle of Leyte Gulf, MacArthur could now turn his attention to the elimination of the Japanese from the Philippines. His timetable called for the seizure of Mindoro Island on 5 December and then a huge landing at Lingayen Gulf, in north-west Luzon, on 20 December. Mindoro was to be taken to provide airbases for planes to cover the Lingayen attack force. As the time approached when the Mindoro expedition had to depart from Leyte Gulf, Kinkaid became convinced that a delay was imperative. Because of soaking rains and sodden terrain, the Air Corps had been unable to build a sufficient number of airfields to handle the fighter squadrons needed to protect the Mindoro force. The Admiral was forced to confront General MacArthur and insist on an extra ten days. When the General discovered that Halsey's carrier task forces had to be rested, and thus could not engage in air suppression attacks for a 5 December landing on Mindoro, he caved in. Mindoro was rescheduled for 15 December and Lingayen for 9 January 1945. Much to Kinkaid's relief, the Mindoro attack, led by one of Barbey's amphibious commanders, Rear Admiral A. D. Struble, went quite well. Within five days army engineers had constructed airfields and the Air Corps was at work protecting the route from Leyte.

The plans and execution of the Lingayen Gulf landings were quite similar to the Leyte operation. Four divisions from two army corps would be landed by Vice-Admirals Barbey and Wilkinson. Vice Admiral Oldendorf would again bring six old battleships, six cruisers and eighteen destroyers to provide gunfire support. Rear Admiral C. T. Durgin now commanded the eighteen escort carriers that Nimitz provided. Unlike at Leyte, Admiral Halsey's Third Fleet was not tied to the operation, but it was assumed that it would lend assistance if called upon. What was different, Kinkaid quickly learned, was the extreme danger posed by the Japanese special attack squadrons, the kamikazes ('divine wind'). En route to Lingayen, the cve *Ommaney Bay* was sunk and *Manila Bay* damaged, as was Oldendorf's flagship *Louisville* and another cruiser, plus three lighter vessels. On 6 January, as Oldendorf brought his bombardment and fire support group (TF 77.2) into the gulf, the kamikazes struck with an awesome intensity. Two battleships, three cruisers and nine lighter vessels were hit. On board the battleship *New Mexico*, Rear Admiral T. E. Chandler was killed. On 8 January, the day before the landings, two more escort carriers were heavily damaged, and the heavy cruiser *Australia* received its third and fourth hits, yet it remained on station. Again, as at Leyte, Kinkaid remained personally in the thick of the action and in great personal danger. From the day he left the anchorage off Tacloban until 14 January in Lingayen Gulf, *Wasatch*'s war diary reported air attacks on Kinkaid's flagship and those around him, but his luck held. *Wasatch* was never struck by bombs, torpedoes or kamikazes.

After the Lingayen operation, Kinkaid's headquarters were established at Tolosa in Leyte Gulf until a final move to Manila in early July. From Tolosa he commanded the mop-up operations of the Seventh Fleet. With Barbey leading, the Seventh Fleet Amphibious Corps made twenty-seven assaults throughout the Philippines and three in Borneo. Kinkaid's own involvement with these operations was minimal since they came on orders from MacArthur and Barbey's staff did the planning. It was while at Tolosa, on 6 April, that Kinkaid received his final promotion, to admiral. He now joined as junior member a very select circle of three fleet admirals and nine admirals who stood at the top of the navy's High Command. By coincidence his effective date of rank and fifty-seventh birthday were the same, 3 April.

With promotion, Kinkaid was ordered to Washington for consultations and then a well-earned lengthy leave. Between visits with Fleet Admirals King in Washington and Nimitz, now in Guam, Kinkaid learned about future operations designed to bring the Pacific War to a close. While the naval commander for the invasion of Japan had not been selected, it was clear that he would take some important part in what would be gigantic amphibious operations. But the atomic bombing of Hiroshima and Nagasaki dramatically precluded the need for the final assault from the sea. As it turned out, the Seventh Fleet was destined to transport troops for the occupation of Korea and certain North China areas. Kinkaid missed the surrender ceremonies in Tokyo Bay on 2 September because he was at sea, en route to Korea. Finally, on 19 November 1945, Admiral Kinkaid's wartime career came to a close when Vice Admiral Barbey relieved him of command of the Seventh Fleet. He would now enter the peacetime world as Commander, Eastern Sea Frontier, and Commander, Atlantic Reserve Fleet, with headquarters in New York City and a comfortable old home in the Brooklyn Navy Yard.

Admiral Kinkaid's wartime years as a flag officer can be divided into two separate and distinct types of service. During 1942, as a rear admiral, he commanded cruiser screens as part of carrier task forces until the close of the Midway campaign and then he became a carrier task force commander. As a screen commander, there was little opportunity for initiative or a display of strong leadership. His outstanding achievement was the management of the rescue operation for the survivors from the sinking of the carrier *Lexington*. It was this effort which won him his first Distinguished Service Medal. After Midway, he took command of TF 16, the *Enterprise* force, and led it through the invasion of Guadalcanal and the Battle of the eastern Solomons. Though a task force commander, he continued to serve under the leadership of Vice Admiral Frank Jack Fletcher. Yet, while brigaded with two other task forces into TF 61, Kinkaid's aggressiveness came through. His flagship was punished, but he concentrated on the mission of stopping the enemy reinforcement of Guadalcanal. Again he was awarded a DSM for 'His keen leadership, determined action and outstanding resourcefulness . . .'.

Once he moved to the Aleutians, Kinkaid became the Commander, North Pacific Force and controlled navy, army and Air Corps units. Leadership now equated with management of those who led his units in the field. He worked to infuse his unit commanders with the spirit of the offensive so that his campaign to eliminate the Japanese from the islands would be concluded in a timely manner. For his operations there he received a third DSM, with the citation: 'Exercising his command . . . with sound judgment and tact, he conducted a determined and successful offensive . . . which resulted . . . in the final expulsion of the Japanese from the Aleutians.' With the successful Leyte campaign came a fourth DSM. Focusing on the period October to December 1944, the citation called particular attention to the Battle of Surigao Strait: 'As a result of his aggressive leadership and brilliant over-all strategic control, two major task forces of the Japanese fleet were repulsed and decisively defeated.' Again, management of the gigantic Leyte invasion was Kinkaid's real assignment. When the Japanese challenge arrived, the Admiral made his dispositions and his subordinates came to grips with the enemy. In writing the citation for the award, Admiral Nimitz summed up the Admiral's headership at Leyte: 'A master of naval warfare, Admiral Kinkaid planned and carried out the naval phases of this operation which made possible the liberation of the Philippines.' From the viewpoints of General MacArthur and Admiral Nimitz, Kinkaid had delivered the goods.

Commander, Eastern Sea Frontier, and Commander, Reserve Fleet, Atlantic, January 1946–May 1950. Retired to home, Washington DC, 1 May 1950. Recall to active duty. Member, National Security Training Commission, July 1951–March 1953. Died Washington DC, 17 November 1972.

Select Bibliography

PERSONAL MANUSCRIPTS: Thomas C. Kinkaid MSS, Naval Historical Center (NHC), Washington DC; William F. Halsey MSS, Library of Congress (LC), Washington DC; Ernest J. King MSS, NHC; Chester W. Nimitz MSS, NHC.

OFFICIAL MANUSCRIPT RECORDS: War diaries of ships and commands, after-action reports, fleet records, task force records, are all available at Navy Operations Archives, Navy Yard, Washington DC. 'Command Summary' (war diary) for Pacific Fleet, December 1941–August 1945, is particularly useful.

BOOKS AND ARTICLES: Two series particularly useful are: *The United States Army in World War II*, published by the Office of the Chief of Military History; Samuel Eliot Morison, *The History of United States Naval Operations in World War II*. Important autobiographies and memoirs include: Daniel E. Barbey, *MacArthur's Amphibious Navy: Seventh Amphibious Force Operations, 1943–1945* (1969); William F. Halsey and J. Bryan, *Admiral Halsey's Story* (1947); Ernest J. King and Walter Muir Whitehill, *Fleet Admiral King: A Naval Record* (1952); Douglas MacArthur, *Reminiscences* (1964); Jesse B. Oldendorf, as told to Hawthorne Daniel, 'The Battle of Surigao Strait', *Blue Book Magazine* (March 1949) and 'Lingayen Landing', (April 1949). Important biographies include: Thomas B. Buell, *Master of Sea Power: A Biography of Fleet Admiral Ernest J. King* (1980); D. Clayton James, *The Years of MacArthur*, vol. II: *1941–1945* (1975); E. B. Potter, *Bull Halsey* (1985) and *Nimitz* (1976). See also: Gerald E. Wheeler, 'Thomas C. Kinkaid: MacArthur's Master of Naval Warfare', in William M. Leary (ed.), *We Shall Return! MacArthur's Commanders and the Defeat of Japan* (1988); Hanson W. Baldwin, 'The Sho Plan: The Battle for Leyte Gulf, 1944', in *Sea Fights and Shipwrecks* (1955); Eric Hammell, *Guadalcanal: The Carrier Battles* (1987); Edwin B. Hoyt, *The Battle of Leyte Gulf: The Death Knell of the Japanese Fleet* (1972); C. Vann Woodward, *The Battle for Leyte Gulf* (1947).

16

Admiral

Sir Bertram Ramsay
KCB, KBE, MVO
Royal Navy

1883–1945

by

W. J. R. Gardner

*B*ERTRAM *Ramsay, born January 1883, third son of an old and distinguished Scots family with a strong military tradition; his father, a cavalryman, rose to the rank of brigadier-general. Joined Royal Navy and went to* Britannia *January 1898, just before his fifteenth birthday. Conventional early career, spent mostly in cruisers and battleships. Before World War One there were two signs his promise had already been recognized: he was appointed bridge watchkeeper in* HMS Dreadnought *during her first commission, and subsequently received several appointments as flag lieutenant, obtaining more exposure to flag officers than average. During World War One, commanded monitor* M25 *and was promoted to rank of commander.* CO *of destroyer* Broke; *promoted to rank of captain in 1923, at age forty. Other commands included the cruisers* Weymouth, Danae *and* Kent, *and the battleship* Royal Sovereign. *In all his ships he required and gained the highest possible standards of efficiency and appearance, strict demands which were balanced by a strong sense of fairness and an appreciation of his subordinates' limitations. From his earliest days in the navy he received unusually frequent appointments to staff courses as student or teacher; these gave him a very 'modern' outlook on the nature of command. In 1935 (when he was promoted to rear admiral) this led in turn to what appeared to be the end of his career. In August 1935 he took up an appointment as Chief of Staff to his old friend Admiral Sir Roger Backhouse, C-in-C Home Fleet: in December, despite their friendship, he requested to be relieved, citing Backhouse's (old-fashioned) habit of acting as his own Chief of Staff as the cause. He was placed on half-pay without further appointment, and, at the beginning of 1939, placed on the Retired List in the rank of vice admiral.*

Admiral Sir Bertram Ramsay is one of the least known of this select band of officers. He never commanded any of the major fleets such as the Home Fleet, or one of the significant formations of capital ships. He never served in the Admiralty, except for a few months as a junior officer. If these apparent disqualifications were insufficient, he deliberately asked to be relieved from his first flag appointment after only a few months and spent four years virtually without employment before being retired at the beginning of the year in which war broke out. Yet he belongs without doubt in the first rank of British naval leaders of World War Two.

From the seemingly chance appointment as Flag Officer Dover, he moved on to plan and command a series of naval events which amounts to a catalogue of all the significant amphibious operations in the Mediterranean and Western European theatres. These ranged from the magnificent retreat at Dunkirk, through the triumphal re-entry into Europe at Normandy in 1944 and culminated in the hard-fought battle for Walcheren. He died on active service, if not actually as a direct result of enemy action, in the opening days of 1945. For a twentieth-century RN officer of his rank – then an admiral on the Active List – this was an unusual, possibly unique, occurrence.

Oddly enough, for most of Ramsay's war service, he served as a flag officer on the Retired List. As a result, in almost ten years from his first advancement to admiral's rank until his death, he spent only just over a year filling flag posts while on the Active List.

Despite his retirement, Ramsay had been nominated for the appointment of Flag Officer Dover, and he assumed this post on 24 August 1939. It was fortunate that he had filled the same position briefly in 1938 during the Munich crisis; during this period he had made the unpleasant discovery that the war headquarters was in a deleterious condition. Ramsay's recommendations were to be responsible for improving on this poor standard in the intervening period prior to the outbreak of war.

There were two events of great note during his tenure, which was to last some two and a half years. These were the evacuation of the British Expeditionary Force (BEF) from Dunkirk and the passage of the *Scharnhorst* and *Gniesenau* through the Channel. Before turning to these actions, it is worthwhile considering his period at Dover in more general terms. Prior to Dunkirk, the main task of the Dover command was to ensure the passage of Allied shipping, both military and economic, while denying the use of the straits to enemy traffic, most particularly in the case of submarines. The latter was accomplished largely by the use of mines, and was done so well that the passage was effectively prohibited to German submarines for the whole of the war.

The evacuation of many British troops of the BEF from France and the Low Countries was carried out over several weeks and is now remembered best by a single location – Dunkirk – but it should be remembered that demolition and withdrawal operations took place in several locales from Ijmuiden in the north to St Jean de Luz in the south.

For a number of very good reasons, however, Dunkirk is properly regarded as the *chef-d'oeuvre* of evacuation operations. This is mainly because it was responsible for the extraction of a very large number of troops in a relatively short period of time. The forces concerned were obtained and organized on an improvised basis, giving the lie to any thought that Ramsay, a master of planning, might be incapable of dealing with fast-moving, highly dynamic operations in which there was a paucity of correct and relevant information. It has been argued that the success of Dunkirk owes as much to Hitler's reluctance to pursue the BEF to extinction as to any British maritime skill. However, his all-important Panzers had not only run themselves virtually to a standstill, but had also outstripped the German infantry. Whatever the reasons which limited the German advance on the Channel, the British ability to exploit a port and coastline, and their command of the neighbouring sea, allowed the avoidance of an encirclement on a grand scale similar to that executed by the Germans a year later at Smolensk.

The great German military achievement of reaching the Channel only a fortnight after the beginning of their invasion of the Low Countries meant that there was very little time for the British commanders, and for Ramsay in particular, to lay plans and gather the necessary suitable forces for the great evacuation from Dunkirk. Ramsay's experience quickly led him to appreciate the peculiar problems which he was going to face: the limitations of the one port in the area, the alternative beaches and their nature, and the likely effect of enemy action on these operations. A further difficulty was introduced by the problems of communicating with such a large and varied force, of which significant numbers were not warships.

The order to start Dynamo, as the operation had been named, was given on the evening of Sunday, 26 May. By this time, Ramsay had already ordered the sailing of several small passenger ships. In broad terms, these were to be one of the main types of vessel employed on the operation, the others being destroyers and the various 'little ships'. The government anticipated that some 45,000 troops might be retrieved during the entire evacuation but, as will be seen, this number was greatly exceeded. At the same time, Ramsay's staff was augmented to deal with the vast amount of work involved; this encompassed route planning to allow for varying degrees of enemy attention, balances having to be struck between quick but hazardous and relatively safe albeit longer passages.

This point was brought home from the outset when one of the first of the passenger ships returned to Dover having suffered bombing, strafing and bombardment from the enemy-held shore. The difficulties of using Dunkirk harbour, and the comparatively small numbers brought off from the port, together with the ever present risk that intensity of attack or sunken ships could close it altogether, led to the early appreciation that there was a requirement to use the French beaches as well. For this task, smaller craft would be needed, not so much to carry troops all the way across the Channel as to ferry the soldiers to larger ships waiting offshore. A very considerable effort had to be made to requisition and prepare these craft, in locations ranging from Westminster Pier in the heart of London around the coast as far west as Portsmouth. The new alternative routes needed surveying and minesweeping and, once troops in appreciable numbers started arriving in Dover, arrangements had to be made for their reception and dispersal into the country.

As late as the morning of 28 May, insufficient numbers of small craft were available to permit speedy beach evacuation, so the risk of sending passenger ships back into the harbour was deliberately taken, although by this time extensive use of the mole was necessary. This led to further sinkings, but the rate of embarkation was improved. Attempts were also made to maximize the number of men embarked by night to cut down on the dangers of attack from the air, but these were hampered to some extent by the limitations of communications equipment. By this stage, every available destroyer in Western Approaches and Portsmouth Commands was ordered to join Ramsay. At the same time, many fighter sorties were being flown in support of the operation. Although a notable controversy was to be aired after the operation was completed about the adequacy of this support, many of the most effective actions were carried out well away from the embarkation beaches, giving rise to the army accusation that there was little help from the RAF because aircraft were not actually seen over the beaches.

The 29th saw a considerable increase in the number of ships sunk or damaged but, more importantly, a very significant improvement in the number evacuated. Some 47,000 were taken off, over twice the sum of the previous two days' total and well over the first estimate of the grand total recoverable. These successes probably went a long way to stiffening the morale and therefore the resistance of the remaining troops; in turn, this led to a more ordered drawing in of the perimeter, thereby increasing the ultimate numbers recovered.

The succeeding days were to see further increases in the numbers of troops evacuated, reaching a peak on 31 May, when 68,014 were brought off; the cumulative total was now little short of 200,000. The strain on both ships and men was becoming very great indeed. As well as the perils of enemy action, the vessels had very demanding seamanship and navigational tasks imposed on them. Ships were turned around virtually straightaway, and Ramsay had to make difficult judgements as to which needed to be stood down for a few precious hours, to allow them sufficient rest to carry on with their work. Although not all were subjected to fire, Ramsay's ever expanding staff were also worked very hard, both in Dover and ashore in Dunkirk. Ramsay himself was relieved periodically by Vice Admiral James Somerville [*q.v.*], the soundness of Ramsay's organization being demonstrated by the efficacy of this arrangement. Somerville himself was a man of considerable strength of character, and yet this system, which would have been anathema to the older style of flag officer, worked extremely well.

Much of the ability to evacuate large numbers came about through gross overloading of the ships concerned; on one occasion, a Solent steamer took 2,700 and destroyers about 1,000 each. Meanwhile, as more and more troops were withdrawn, the defensive perimeter was contracted, further limiting the choice of embarkation points. The pressure of airborne attack was maintained and in many cases soldiers evacuated by one ship were rescued by a second before their safe return to Dover. There were, inevitably, casualties but the availability of speedy rescue meant that these losses were relatively small. By late on 2 June, Captain Tennant, the naval officer in charge at Dunkirk, was able to report that the BEF had been evacuated.

The British forces had managed to leave in such numbers because the remaining territory was held by French troops. Despite the shipping casualties sustained and the exhaustion of the remaining crews, it was decided to continue the operation to embark as many of the French as possible. Operation Dynamo was finally completed some two days later, when a total of 338,226 troops had been evacuated. The immediate military significance of this force was negligible. It was exhausted and had lost much of its heavy equipment. On the other hand, the German army was not prepared either mentally or materially for an immediate assault on Britain. More importantly, the British troops were to form a nucleus of experienced men, to continue even the limited land campaigns that could be fought until the vastly superior American resources could be brought to bear on the war. Perhaps the most significant point was the much needed fillip given to British morale, at one of the lowest points of the war. It was a triumphant vindication of the additional strategic options available to a nation which understood and practised the difficult art of sea-power, and produced leaders such as Ramsay. For his part in the operation he was created a Knight Commander of the Bath.

After Dunkirk, and until Hitler's switch to the east with the invasion of Russia in June 1941, the emphasis changed to the prevention of invasion. All these various tasks were well conducted, and the Dover command was very much at the centre of attention while the risk of invasion was considered to be high. Co-operation with Alan Brooke, now Commander-in-Chief Home Forces, was re-established, and a new army relationship was formed with the commander of XII Corps, Bernard Montgomery.

Early in the following year, there occurred one of the few less happy events in the period that Ramsay spent at Dover. The battlecruisers *Scharnhorst* and *Gneisenau*, together with the cruiser *Prinz Eugen*, were all at Brest, and it was anticipated that this force would attempt to return to Germany by way of the Channel. The operation was successfully executed on 12 and 13 February 1942. Despite considerable British efforts the ships all reached Germany, although *Gneisenau* suffered very severe mine damage at a late stage.

The failure to engage the group effectively was attributable to a number of factors. None of the intelligence assets deployed against the ships was able to do more than give a general suggestion that the force might be about to sail.

This deficiency was made worse by reconnaissance failures, which deprived commands of the essential information that the ships had left Brest. A further point of importance was that it was assessed that they would attempt to transit the Dover Straits, considered to be the most dangerous part of the passage, by night. Instead, the Germans achieved tactical surprise by planning their passage so as to pass the straits by day. By the time it was appreciated that they had sailed, it was almost too late to implement the various measures planned to attack them during their transit. Although attacked by light craft, destroyers, shore guns and most famously by the Swordfish torpedo bombers of Lieutenant-Commander Eugene Esmonde's 825 Naval Air Squadron, the force suffered no check in Ramsay's area.

The 'Channel dash' was a considerable tactical success for the Germans, but in strategic terms it was a retreat back to safer, less operationally relevant areas. Such an appreciation might have balanced the failure to stop the force, but the problem was a much wider one, in both area and forces, than could have been addressed solely within the Dover command. Shortly after the action, Ramsay was appointed to take charge of the naval plans for the first large Allied amphibious landings.

By the middle of 1942 it had become clear that, barring any catastrophic reverses, an Axis victory was becoming increasingly unlikely. There were certainly areas of very deep concern such as the Japanese advance in the Pacific, the titanic land war in Russia and the activities of the U-boats in the Atlantic, but the entry of the USA into the war at the turn of the year had refired a sense of optimism and provided the means to effect an eventual return to the European mainland. It would, however, take time to train the necessary large number of troops and provide them with their equipment; and the still desperate condition of the USSR created enormous pressure, both from Stalin and from the Allies themselves to open a 'second front' as soon as possible.

In the complex debate over the location for this operation, only one thing was clear to all concerned: namely that wherever the landing might occur, it could be mounted only from the sea. No such operation on any significant scale had been carried out during the war so far, and the Royal Navy's previous experience in World War One had hardly been an unqualified success. This deficiency had been partly corrected early in the war with the establishment of Combined Operations, although their efforts were biased towards raiding rather than the lasting establishment of a large, balanced and well-supported army on the continent.

By the middle of 1942, the Americans had been persuaded (against their own wishes) to substitute a North African operation, codenamed Torch, for one against Europe. Torch was to take place in the autumn of that year, leaving Ramsay a mere three months to make the necessary plans. Much had to be done; the operation was planned to take place under the command of General Eisenhower, and would involve both British and American troops landing simultaneously on both Atlantic and Mediterranean coasts. Although it was hoped that the landings would be unopposed, the reaction of the Vichy French could not be predicted with confidence, and it was necessary to plan for this contingency.

The scale of the operation was very much greater than any undertaken before in the war and involved some 70,000 troops in 350 transport and landing ships supported by 200 warships. Assaults were to take place in three locations at the same time, adding a further degree of complexity to the operation. The long sea passages involved a considerable degree of risk, not least from U-boats in the Atlantic, and this factor was to cause a great deal of concern, but assurances from intelligence indicated that strategic surprise was being maintained. Although Ramsay had been involved in the planning of the operation from the outset, it was decided that the naval command should be given not to him, but to Sir Andrew Cunningham [*q.v.*]. Such a change was brought about partly because of Cunningham's experience in working with the Americans, but also because Ramsay was still on the Retired List and his rank of admiral was only an acting one. Nevertheless, he served as a very willing and co-operative deputy to Cunningham. On 8 November, the assaults were made and despite some stiff naval resistance from the French, particularly at Oran, troops were quickly landed and they rapidly established themselves with minimal losses.

Although the military side of Torch was very satisfactory and led a few months later to the expulsion of Axis forces from North Africa, it should not be assumed that it was either effortless or carried out without continuing support from the sea. The latter point is important as Ramsay, remaining in London as Cunningham's deputy, had to resist strongly the twin demands of further 'sideshows' inspired by Torch's apparently easy success, and for the return of shipping to other tasks. It would be convenient to view the Admiral's war at this stage as episodic – Torch followed by Husky, before the next step on to Neptune – but this would seriously misrepresent the degree of follow-up work involved in all these operations.

In any case the last enemy forces in Africa fell into Allied hands in May 1943. In January of that year the Casablanca Conference considered Sicily as the next objective. This operation (Husky) was once more to be under the overall command of Eisenhower with Cunningham again as his naval deputy. There were to be two task forces, the western being American, and the eastern British and Canadian under Ramsay's command. The time was quickly filled with the planning, the assembly of forces and the very necessary training of the sailors and troops.

A relatively late train of decisions made the planning of the operation difficult. The Combined Chiefs of Staffs endorsed the strategy of Sicily being the target as late as 7 April, a bare three months before the operation. Such a schedule made the organizing task difficult, but by no means impossible; however, a further complication was produced by a change in the strategy on the ground. The original notion of conducting the assault close to Palermo in the west was set aside after some debate for a policy of landing on the south-eastern part of the island. This was done largely at the insistence of Montgomery, who introduced a further layer of difficulty by asking for an extra division to be included in the plan. The new plan was not approved until 13 May, and although this timing might appear to be perfectly adequate for an operation in July, it should be realized that the first ships, troop transports from the USA, had to sail by the end of May to meet the timetable. Husky was to establish several precedents. Although Torch had experienced some local and largely limited resistance from Vichy French forces, Husky was likely to be conducted against much stronger and more determined opposition. New techniques, too, were to be practised: for example, Torch had used only large transports from which all troops were ferried to the shore in smaller craft; in Husky, some specialized landing craft were to take a portion of the troops all the way, obviating the necessity for the time-consuming and potentially hazardous transfer between ships. As well as this, fully amphibious vehicles – DUKWS – were also to be used for the first time. The plan called for some 180,000 British Empire and American troops to land.

On 10 July, the operation went ahead, an unexpected but welcome degree of surprise being achieved because of the previous weather being bad, and the defenders believing that this would ensure immunity from invasion. Ramsay had been responsible for making the final recommendation that the assault should continue, despite the conditions being poor, a precursor of the situation almost eleven months later. The anticipated degree of resistance on the ground did not materialize, and the Allied troops quickly established themselves: within a month the Axis forces were conducting their own version of Dunkirk across the Messina Straits. Ramsay, meanwhile, was back in Britain, becoming involved in the greatest amphibious operation of all – Overlord.

By the autumn Ramsay was confirmed in his appointment as the Naval Commander-in-Chief for the invasion of France. At the end of 1943, Eisenhower was again given the supreme command. The planning meanwhile had continued apace; although great experience had by now been gained in amphibious operations, there was considerable apprehension about Overlord.

Although it had been anticipated that the assault on Sicily would have been opposed, there was no doubt whatsoever that this would occur in the case of Normandy. Further, although Italian troops had been of variable quality, resistance from the German army was likely to be of a completely different order; an extra problem was posed by the enemy's efforts over a considerable period of time to render landing difficult along a significant length of the French coast.

Ramsay and his staff went to work on these problems with great energy. The naval operation, called Neptune, was to be on the largest scale yet, the initial landing involving five divisions. These forces would require organizing to enable them to reach their assault areas, without suffering attack, in a suitable condition for immediate combat. Such a stringent requirement involved measures against enemy aircraft, ships, submarines, coastal artillery and even the humble but effective mine. These preparations would need to be conducted in such a way that the activities would not in themselves serve to alert the Germans to the existence, objectives or timing of the operation. The aim was to ensure the maximum degree of security for the invasion force, without sacrificing the essential requirement for strategic surprise. For this reason, an exceptionally complex and well-co-ordinated series of measures for deception was set in train. Some idea of the extent of these can be gauged by a reference to one of these measures – the setting up of a 'ghost' army group in south-east England 'commanded' by General Patton, complete with dummy landing craft, vehicles, camps and even communications.

Ramsay appreciated that it would be difficult to gain tactical surprise and concentrated on being able to assure the delivery of troops to beaches in the most efficient manner possible: such an aim could be ensured only by concentration on two main facets, planning and training.

Plans involved a great deal more than producing the orders for the ships taking part in Neptune. It was necessary to determine the proper types of shipping for the operation. In some cases, this involved the further development of the rapidly maturing genus of amphibious ships; these diversified into such types as different varieties of tank landing craft and ships, and specialized vessels for inshore fire support, among others. Ramsay was also involved in superintending the training of these forces, realizing that if it did not perform properly on the day required, there was little point in assembling all this material. Many other matters required attention, such as navigation, virtually all the way to the beaches. Such innovative solutions as midget submarines acting as beacons were adopted to ensure that the necessary accuracy was achieved. A further aspect of the operation was the need to make a rapid build-up of forces, and the material to support them.

Here, even more revolutionary methods were required. The problem of supply could be met only by the relatively early acquisition of an intact port, but the area selected made this an unlikely prospect. Two novel expedients were adopted to meet this need, Mulberry harbours and Pluto. The first were a series of large concrete caissons, which in conjunction with blockships were joined up to make artificial harbours, and used for landing vehicles and solid stores. The second was a long flexible pipeline laid under the Channel which supplied fuel in the large quantities required.

The success of all these plans, both those which matured on 6 June 1944 – D-Day – and the later measures, is best indicated by the simple statistic that little more than a week later some half-a-million soldiers and 77,000 vehicles had been landed. Although some forces, particularly the Americans, had encountered stiff initial resistance they quickly became well established, and were more than adequately supplied, permitting their subsequent advance into the European hinterland.

The success of the Normandy landings was to be reflected in the relative rapidity of the advance northwards to liberate France and then the Low Countries, but this was not without its own difficulties. Firstly there was a very considerable debate between Montgomery and Eisenhower over whether a narrow- or broad-based advance should be the preferred strategy. Ramsay was not directly involved in this dispute, but he was very much concerned in sorting out its consequences.

In early September the important port of Antwerp had been captured with its facilities intact. However, it was not usable as its approaches, the banks of the Scheldt, were still in German hands. As a result, the Mulberry harbours, intended only as a temporary solution, were becoming somewhat weather-beaten; perhaps more significantly, the Allied armies were daily extending their logistic tail, thus degrading their offensive efficiency. The Montgomery strategy apparently did not need this port, and it was not until the offensive for the short cut into Germany – Arnhem – failed so dramatically that attention was turned to the Scheldt. By this time, not only had the Germans prepared themselves well on land, but they had also mined the river. The land battle – something of a misnomer as the Germans had made extensive use of the old and natural enemy of flooding – was again mounted from the sea under Ramsay's overall control. In many ways this proved to be a much harder-fought struggle than Normandy, albeit on a smaller scale. Different challenges, too, were met with new techniques: one example was a squadron of small gunships which provided naval gunfire support by day, and defence against E-boats by night. The planned degree of air co-operation could not be achieved because of the weather, and the assault, largely made up of Royal Marines and Canadians, rapidly developed into that most euphemistically termed struggle – a soldier's battle. Put more directly, there were many casualties, but unlike an earlier British adventure on Walcheren some centuries before, the outcome was successful; another triumph for the Ramsay method. By the end of November, Antwerp was functioning fully as a supply port.

Ramsay continued his work, organizing the maritime support of the army, but Walcheren was to be the last major operation under his command. On 2 January 1945, accompanied by several of his staff, his aircraft crashed killing all on board.

Such is an account of Bertram Ramsay's life and career. It makes by any reckoning a distinguished enough story, but it also deserves further study for two reasons: firstly, because of his undoubted mastery of the art of amphibious warfare, a vital component of the Allies' war-winning strategy; and secondly, because he represented an interesting combination of old and new styles in naval leadership, at a time of great changes in both equipment and techniques. At the outset, it is perhaps important to consider the matter of what is commonly called luck, that is the role which fortune might appear to play. It might be argued, for instance, that it was Ramsay's good luck to have the command at Dover at the time of Dunkirk. It was indeed the fortunate occasion which proved to be a turning point of his career, but the episode could have served equally well as the end of his employment in the service, had it not turned out so well. In other words, by making his own 'luck', he opened the door to his later successes.

What therefore were the qualities which enabled him to capitalize on this opportunity? And how had he learned from his experiences in such a way that he was able to help turn the event from a rout into that most beloved of British military operations, the well-conducted retreat?

Firstly, it is important to consider Ramsay's reputation as a disciplinarian. There is no doubt that he possessed this trait in abundance. As early as his time as a junior officer, he was extremely concerned that everything should be properly done, and this approach was carried forward into his later career. This trait was also very obvious to his subordinates; he was almost certainly more respected than liked by his juniors.

An example of his attitudes was demonstrated when he took over command of the famous *Broke*, and recorded a sufficiently large number of faults to fill more than two pages. Most of the points he made were summed up by 'discipline – bad'. There is every indication, too, that Ramsay was well aware that his concern with discipline was out of the ordinary, and was recognized as such by both his ship's companies and his superiors.

This characteristic was to have two important consequences, one specific-ally applying to him, and the other to the large formations of ships, with their valuable military cargoes, with which his various commands were entrusted.

As far as the Admiral was concerned, the external interest in propriety spoke of a deep internal concern for an ordered world. It is probable that this trait in a lesser man would manifest itself in a concern for detail and little else, but in Ramsay's case it was allied to an ability to think in very much broader terms as well. Thus the sense of discipline was there to serve a purpose, not merely for its own sake. This is perhaps best illustrated by reference to a leader in earlier times, the Duke of Wellington, who was said to have defined genius as the infinite capacity for taking pains.

Externally, this approach was particularly applicable to amphibious opera-tions, where many very disparate components have to be brought together in such a way as to produce a coherent, and thus effective, fighting entity. Churchill described this well by deploying the analogy of the intricate jewelled bracelet. It is only by unremitting attention to the multifarious details that such an operation can even be mounted, far less successfully concluded.

It has already been suggested that Ramsay's breadth of thought provided the essential leavening of his character, which might otherwise have resulted in his being merely a martinet. It is relatively easy to chronicle some of the occasions on which this quality was demonstrated. At least as early as his time as a flag lieutenant, he was capable of thinking well beyond his years and previous service experience. His decision to apply for one of the first War Staff courses was another indicator of the direction he saw as that which the Royal Navy should be taking. In the era of *Dreadnought*'s pre-eminence and the consequent stress laid on material matters, this was a far-sighted decision for a relatively young officer to take. His appointments in staff work between the wars served to provide further expansion of his horizons, giving him more acquaintance not only with rising officers of the other two services, but also with senior civil servants.

All these experiences served to sharpen further Ramsay's capacity for logical, incisive analysis, which always remained grounded in common sense. He was therefore able to plan operations of a type and scale never before attempted, with the powerful combination of innovative but methodical thinking allied to an instinctive realization of the areas where problems were most likely to occur.

During the war, he prepared the draft of a lecture for the Royal United Services Institute on the subject of combined operations. Sadly, he was denied permission to deliver it, but the draft still exists, and it is both an excellent analysis of amphibious warfare and a very workable planning guide. Interestingly, its principles are sufficiently robust to serve as a modern text, with a minimum of changes. It covers such essential features as the provision of shipping, port supply and air cover. The importance of the administrative plan is not ignored, but it is made plain that its requirements should always be subordinated to the operational plan. There is a very clear appreciation of the salient features of the three environments involved: sea, land and air; their differing characteristics and the consequences of these on operations. Carried through into the natures of the respective services Ramsay, the Admiral from army stock, notes the predilection of the army for rigid plans, as against the navy's understanding of the need for flexibility brought about by the vagaries of the elements, among other factors. A clear and witty exposition of this point is made by writing of the 'uncertain character of the elements and marine internal combustion engines'.

Another undelivered piece of writing is an accurate and hard-hitting response to an article on the Dieppe raid which appeared in *The Times* in 1944. He points out that many of the 'lessons' supposedly learned on that operation had previously been recognized and were being acted on at the time of Dieppe, but were not being applied during that operation. In his last paragraph he demonstrates an unusual burst of passion, which may be why he never sent the letter: 'Dieppe was a tragedy and the cause may be attributed to the fact that it was planned by inexperienced enthusiasts.'

By setting high standards for his staff, he was able to transmit these qualities to his subordinates. Such an ability was important because he recognized that it would not be possible for him to plan and superintend every detail of such a large undertaking. This passing on of the Ramsay method resulted in the justifiable compliment on the subject of his instructions for Neptune from

Commander-in-Chief Portsmouth: 'Your orders for the operation have of necessity been voluminous but if I may presume to say so, so explicit that their successful implementation was assured.'

A further point which springs from this is the rare ability to delegate authority to allow such work to be efficiently carried out. Such a philosophy was a deeply embedded article of Ramsay's professional faith. It played an important part in the Backhouse affair, but it is of sufficient importance to merit some expansion.

Ramsay, at an early stage in his life and career, formed the conclusion that success in running a warship, a fleet or an operation was founded on two important principles. The first was that the commander's subordinates should be in no doubt as to what was required of them in either general terms – their discipline and conduct – or their particular role, in which training was all-important. Once these points were established, it was then necessary to encourage the use of initiative to deal with the inevitable appearance of the unexpected. Under these circumstances, it was often not possible or convenient to refer the matter to a superior for decision. Having therefore established the aim of the commander; provided plans to cater for most reasonable contingencies, and cultivated the ability to cope with the unreasonable ones; and lastly supplied the confidence in technique which training and rehearsal bring, the operation stood the best possible chance of success.

There was another important aspect to extensive delegation; it provided the time and mental space for the officer in command to concentrate on essentials, and to be able to comprehend the whole picture, instead of being overwhelmed with detail. This had always been a tenet of Ramsay's thinking; eventually it served him well in the conduct of the massive operation that was Neptune, but it was also at the root of his divergence from Backhouse. It was probable, too, that Backhouse, although famed for being a centralizer, was not markedly worse than many other senior officers of his era, so it might be argued that Ramsay was ahead of his time in his predilection for decentralization. It can also be suggested that, without the ability to deploy this technique, such operations as Neptune (and therefore Overlord) could not have been carried out at all, or at least not with the success that they achieved. The great strength of this method was also vividly demonstrated, in a parallel rather than vertical sense, by his ability to let James Somerville take over from him for periods during Operation Dynamo.

There are also two, more private aspects of Ramsay which have a major bearing on his character and life: his concern for personal appearance, and his family. It is clear that Ramsay maintained a most correct and smart personal appearance throughout his career. His photographs always suggest this strongly, and the sideways look which one of his chiefs of staff received when making a first appearance in an unsuitable civilian hat confirms that he applied these standards to others. On the other hand, this trait stopped well short of a vanity which would suggest an ego well on the way to being out of control. One does not need to look too far among Ramsay's colleagues at high levels to find disturbing signs, such as the wearing of more than one beret badge and an inordinate interest in the obtaining of medals and other insignia, to realize that personal vanity was quite foreign to Ramsay.

His wife and two sons provided him with an enormous stock of inner strength during the war. He corresponded regularly with the former, often at the end of a long and gruelling day. These letters doubtless reinforced his already keen sense of what the war was being fought for, and it is very clear that he longed for the brief periods that he could spend at home. He was also likely to have anticipated a longer spell in retirement there at the end of the war, an ambition never realized.

It may smack of cliché to say that Ramsay stood at the crossroads between the battleship navy of the early twentieth century and the modern navy of electronics and guided missiles, but clichés are often a powerful, concise and truthful method of expression. Perhaps in Ramsay's case, the metaphor is all the more striking because his methods also stood midway between those of the post-Victorian autocrat and those of the modern managerial admiral. Alternatively, this may be just another way of saying that although his skills were best applied during a specific period of conflict, his qualities are timeless.

17

Admiral

Richmond K. Turner
United States Navy

1885–1961

by
Paolo E. Coletta

*R*ICHMOND *Kelly Turner, born in Portland, Oregon, 27 May 1885. Entered the Naval Academy in 1904 and graduated with distinction, the fifth out of the 297 men in the class of 1908. Promoted to ensign in June 1910, on 3 August of that year he married Harriet Sterling, his high-school love.*

Destroyer executive officer, then postgraduate student of ordnance engineering at Annapolis, Maryland, 1913. During World War One he served in battleships, mostly as a gunnery officer. After ten years with big-ship guns and command of a destroyer, in 1927, at the age of forty-two years he qualified as a pilot at Pensacola and served for five years in aviation. As a captain he took the Naval War College course and remained in Newport for a year as head of the Strategic Section. Emphasizing carrier and amphibious warfare, he was rated as the best teacher of naval strategy since Mahan.[1] He then commanded the heavy cruiser Astoria. *As head of the War Plans Division in Admiral Harold R. Stark's Office of Chief of Naval Operations (*CNO*) and as Assistant Chief of Staff to the Commander in Chief, US Fleet, Admiral Ernest J. King, after December 1941, he helped plan the navy's areas of operations and basic strategy for World War Two.[2]*

*

[1] Thomas A. Buell, *The Quiet Warrior: A Biography of Raymond A. Spruance* (Boston, 1974), pp. 72, 81–2.

[2] Thomas A. Buell, *Master of Naval Strategy: A Biography of Fleet Admiral Ernest J. King* (Boston, 1980), pp. 130n, 174; Fleet Admiral Ernest J. King and Walter Muir Whitehead, *Fleet Admiral King: A Naval Record* (New York, 1952), pp. 327–8, 331–7, 360–4; Edwin P. Hoyt, *How They Won the War in the Pacific: Nimitz and His Admirals* (New York, 1970), pp. 136–7; Vice-Admiral George F. Dyer USN (Ret.), *The Amphibians Came to Conquer: The Story of Admiral Richmond Kelly Turner*, 2 vols (Washington DC, 1971), vol. I, pp. 160–2; Eric Larrabee, *Commander in Chief: Franklin Delano Roosevelt, His Lieutenants and Their War* (New York, 1987), pp. 48–50, 76, 186–7, 210, 216–17, 224–47; Samuel E.

Commander Edwin T. Layton, intelligence officer at Pearl Harbor, saw him as many others did: 'Lean and quick-acting and over six feet tall, he cut an imposing figure, with lantern jaw and beetling black brow that gave him a Mephistophelean aspect. Turner was intimidating both in appearance and personality.' Subordinates found him 'rasping as a file', and 'few of those who worked closely with him . . . could forget – or forgive – his stormy temper, overbearing ego, and celebrated bouts with the bottle'. However, the CNO, Admiral Harold Stark [*q.v.*] held him to be 'invaluable' because he relieved him of memorandum writing and details of staff work. He was respected as a master of his profession.3

Turner continued as the Plans Officer for Admiral Ernest J. King [*q.v.*], who in late December 1941 became Commander-in-Chief, US Fleet (Cominch) and then the CNO as well. Although the navy had but twenty-six amphibious ships,4 Turner got King to establish an Amphibious Warfare desk in his Cominch office and called for advance base units to build and operate main and secondary bases at Bora Bora (Society Islands), Guadalcanal (in the Solomons), and Espiritu Santo and Efate in the New Hebrides.5 Turner also sat with King, the Army Chief of Staff, and their deputies on the Joint Army and Navy Board. His reputed failure to have kept the Commander-in-Chief, Pacific Fleet, informed of Japanese intentions and his 'goddamning' of his army colleagues on the Joint Board determined King to employ him elsewhere.6

Morison, *The Battle of the Atlantic, September 1939–May 1943* (Boston, 1947), pp. 145–7; Louis Morton, 'Germany First: The Basic Concept of Allied Strategy in World War II', in Kent Roberts Greenfield (ed.), *Command Decisions* (Washington DC, 1960), pp. 1–48; Maurice Matloff, 'Prewar Military Plans and Preparations, 1939–1941', United States Naval Institute *Proceedings*, 79 (July 1953), pp. 741–8 (hereafter cited as USNIP).

3Rear Admiral Edwin T. Layton, USN (Ret.), *'And I Was There': Pearl Harbor and Midway – Breaking the Secrets* (New York, 1985), pp. 19, 20, 96; John Toland, *The Rising Sun: The Decline and Fall of the Japanese Empire* (New York, 1970), p. 400; Robert Leckie, *Challenge for the Pacific: Guadalcanal, The Turning Point of the War* (Garden City, NY, 1965), pp. 54–5; H. M. Smith and Percy Finch, *Coral and Brass* (New York, 1949), pp. 109–10; Joseph Driscoll, *Pacific Victory* (Philadelphia, 1945), pp. 58–60.

4King and Whitehill, *Fleet Admiral King*, pp. 381–2; Larrabee, *Commander in Chief*, pp. 200–1. For the status of the navy at the beginning of World War Two, see Merle Armitage, *The United States Navy* (New York, 1940), and Walton L. Robinson, 'Naval Actions, 1939–1941', USNIP, 68 (August 1942), pp. 1125–33.

5Dyer, *Turner*, vol. I, pp. 169, 175–7, 208–11, 421–33; King and Whitehill, *Fleet Admiral King*, pp. 381–2; Larrabee, *Commander in Chief*, pp. 200–1; Dalibor W. Kralovec, 'A Naval History of Espiritu Santo, New Hebrides', 2 vols, Shore Establishment, 1945. Washington: Command File World War II, Naval Historical Center, Operational Archives Branch (hereafter NHC: OA).

6Turner believed that all the information available in the Department was being sent to both the Commander-in-Chief, Pacific, and to Commander, Asiatic Fleet. Turner to Admiral H. R. Stark, 21 December 1944, Admiral Richmond Kelly Turner Papers, NHC: OA; Buell, *King*, pp. 158–9; Layton, *'And I Was There'*, pp. 20–2, 97–100, 329, 367; 'The Reminiscences of Rear Admiral Arthur H. McCollum, USN (Ret.)', transcript of oral interview by John T. Mason, 2 vols, US Naval Institute, 1971; Toland, *Rising Sun*, pp. 220–1; Gordon W. Prange, in collaboration with Donald M. Goldstein and Katherine V. Dillon, *At Dawn We Slept: The Untold Story of Pearl Harbor* (New York, 1981), pp. 45, 87–8, 440, 447–8, 455, 457–8, 527, 585, 735; Buell, *King*, pp. 158–9.

Following the battles of the Coral Sea and of Midway, although the Atlantic still had top priority, King urged the Joint Chiefs of Staff (JCS), to approve an offensive–defensive to be led by Vice Admiral Robert L. Ghormley, Commander, South Pacific Force and Area, and alerted Turner to expect a command in the Pacific.[7] On 25 June 1942 King called for an assault on the Japanese at Tulagi, in the lower Solomons, and the pre-emptive taking of the Santa Cruz Islands. Turner briefed Ghormley on the build-up of his forces for the operation.[8]

With orders from King dated 20 May, Turner left Washington to assume command of Ghormley's amphibious force. He had little training in amphibious warfare, but he had studied the landing manual, Fleet Tactical Publication 167, and reports on amphibious exercises held in the 1930s.[9] On 4 July he conferred in San Francisco with King and Admiral Chester W. Nimitz [*q.v.*], the latter being Commander-in-Chief, Pacific Fleet and, as Commander, Pacific Ocean Areas, in control of all army, navy and Marine Corps forces in that theatre. Turner had been chosen for his first amphibious assignment because Nimitz knew that he had planned it and, like King 'was brilliant, caustic, arrogant, and tactless' – just the man for the job.[10] When Turner complained that he knew little about amphibious warfare, King replied, 'You'll learn.'[11] During 5–8 July Turner conferred about his plans at Pearl Harbor with, among others, Admiral Frank J. Fletcher, who had no amphibious experience. He then left for Auckland, New Zealand, arriving on 15 July, thence for Wellington where on the 17th he boarded his flagship, the transport *McCawley*, and began work.

Among Turner's qualities were a brain that could hold more details about an operation than his staff could, great courage, relentless drive – the will to win, and the ability to make decisions quickly. His original doctrine called for choosing an undefended site at which landing craft could beach while aircraft and naval gunfire isolated the battle area. After a logistic line of communications was established, supporting forces would be released for other tasks. When the Marines had obtained a secure lodgment, the army would take over.[12]

As the JCS directed, Ghormley's first step would be to seize the Santa Cruz

[7]Buell, *King*, p. 202; Ernest J. King, *Navy at War: Official Report to the Secretary of the Navy* (Washington DC, 1946), p. 49.

[8]COMINCH: Memorandum, 'Limited Amphibious Offensive in South and South-West Pacific', 5 July 1942, Turner Papers; Dyer, *Turner*, vol. I, pp. 249, 252–3, 259–62.

[9]Ibid., pp. 224–5.

[10]Buell, *King*, p. 202; John Costello, *The Pacific War* (New York, 1981), p. 315; Dyer, *Turner*, vol. I, pp. 263–76; King and Whitehill, *Fleet Admiral King*, p. 642. While Nimitz was chief of the Bureau of Personnel, he had asked Turner if he could see the war plans. Turner replied, 'We will tell you what you need to know.' Nimitz had never served with him, but upon obtaining command of the Pacific Fleet he asked that he serve as his Chief of Staff. He was turned down. Dyer, *Turner*, vol. I, p. 279.

[11]Jeter A. Isely and Philip A. Crowl, *The U.S. Marines and Amphibious Warfare: Its Theory and Its Practice in the Pacific* (Princeton, NJ, 1951), pp. 87–8; Dyer, *Turner*, vol. I, pp. ix, xx, xxi, 114, 143, 453. The quotation is from Buell, *King*, p. 202.

[12]Dyer interview with Turner, 1960. In Dyer, *Turner*, vol. I, pp. 224–5.

Islands, the harbour at Tulagi the Japanese had occupied in May, and adjacent areas. Ghormley would exercise strategic control of Operation Watchtower; Fletcher would be the Expeditionary (carrier) Force commander; Turner would command the Amphibious Force; and Major-General Alexander A. Vandegrift, USMC, could command the 1st Marine Division, the assault force. Confining himself to his carriers, Fletcher by default let Turner handle all other matters. The discovery on 5 July that the Japanese were building an airfield on Guadalcanal caused President Roosevelt to direct King to include it in the plan. At Ghormley's request, D-Day, set for 2 July, was postponed until 7 August.

Turner learned some vital lessons during his first campaign. He commanded ships that had never manoeuvred together and a staff he had never seen before, but it helped that he had gunnery and aviation experience. He was dismayed when Ghormley disregarded orders to assume personal strategic charge of the operation and remained at Nouméa, New Caledonia. By never discussing plans with his top commanders, Turner failed to secure unity of command. Second, because he was late in arriving in New Zealand, he had to accept tactical and logistic plans Vandegrift had already made. Third, Fletcher (whose carrier planes should have isolated the battle area for the five days Turner said were needed to protect the landing of men and supplies) said that the operation would fail, and that he could not support Watchtower after the second day. 'This left us bare arse,' said Turner.[13] Moreover, Fletcher held Turner responsible for launching the operation and criticized his planning and lack of fighting experience. From rehearsals held off the Fijis late in July, Turner saw that ships smaller than cruisers and destroyers were needed for boat control and bemoaned the lack of aerial reconnaissance needed to permit effective naval gunfire, ground observers to direct aircraft call fire, shore parties, amphibious tractors and boats with bow ramps. What would he do if the Japanese defeated him?, Fletcher asked. Turner replied: 'I am just going to stay there and take my licking.' Fletcher admitted that 'Kelly was tough, a brain, and a son-of-a-bitch and that's just what he did.'[14]

On 8 August Ghormley directed Turner to keep in the forward area a sixty-day level of supplies of ammunition and ninety days of building materials. In addition he must build airfields, seaplane bases, radio stations, harbours, hospitals and underwater defences. Being 6,000 miles from the United States, and having only fifteen logistic support ships, he found this very difficult to do.[15]

[13]'Rough Notes by the Admiral on First Rehearsal', 28 July 1942; Turner Papers; John T. Foster, *Guadalcanal General: The Story of A. A. Vandegrift, USMC* (New York, 1966), pp. 44–6; Larrabee, *Commander in Chief*, p. 274; A. A. Vandegrift, as told to Robert Asprey, *Once a Marine: The Memoirs of General Alexander A. Vandegrift* (New York, 1964), pp. 111, 119, 120.

[14]Dyer, *Turner*, vol. I, pp. 262, 299–302; Samuel B. Griffith, *The Battle for Guadalcanal* (Philadelphia, 1963), pp. 44–6; Larrabee, *Commander in Chief*, p. 265; Robert Leckie, *Challenge for the Pacific: Guadalcanal, The Turning Point of the War* (Garden City, NY, 1965), pp. 55–6.

[15]Rear Admiral Worrall Reed Carter, *Beans, Bullets and Black Oil: The Story of Fleet Logistics in World War II* (Washington DC, 1953), pp. 24, 28; Dyer, *Turner*, vol. I, pp. 317; Isely and Crowl, *U.S. Marines and Amphibious Warfare*, p. 108; John Miller Jr, *Guadalcanal: The First Offensive. United States Army in World War II*, vol. 2, part 3 (Washington DC, 1949), pp. 27–8, 40–1.

His attention to logistic details served to mark him as the greatest of all amphibious commanders.

While a northern group seized Tulagi, a southern one landed Marines on Guadalcanal who seized what would become Henderson Field by the evening of 8 August. However, the rest of Watchtower could not be implemented. Air attacks seriously slowed the unloading of Turner's transports and moving supplies inland from the beachhead. Tenacious Turner nevertheless decided to remain for at least two days, to 9 August, when intelligence came that a Japanese surface force was approaching Guadalcanal via 'the Slot' through the Solomons. There ensued his bad defeat in the Battle of Savo Island, but his transports remained untouched because the Japanese commander violated his orders and did not attack them – or his amphibious craft or supplies on the beach. Timid, tired after eight months of continuous operations, and refusing to endanger his three carriers, Fletcher withdrew twelve hours earlier than he said he would, at 1807 on 8 August. Since he had no reinforcements or systematic resupply, the 17,000 troops Turner had landed were exposed to the enemy and brought to the verge of disaster after 9 August, when, as he put it, he and his remaining ships 'hauled awrse' to Nouméa.[16]

Turner received severe criticism for his defeat in the Battle of Savo Island, in which his warships had been deployed by his second-in-command, Rear Admiral Victor A. C. Crutchley, RN.[17] Rather than blaming Crutchley or anyone else for the débâcle, however, he gave as its primary cause 'inadequate and faulty air reconnaissance', adding that 'Whatever responsibility for the defeat is mine, I accept.' King and Nimitz upheld him, an investigation conducted by Rear Admiral Arthur Hepburn concluded that the blame was too evenly distributed for any one officer to be censured, and President Roosevelt awarded him a Navy Cross.[18]

[16]Dyer, *Turner*, vol. I, pp. 355–402; King, *Official Report*, p. 53; Samuel E. Morison, *Struggle for Guadalcanal, August 1942–February 1943* (Boston, 1950), pp. 17–35; Vandegrift, *Memoirs*, pp. 124–289; John L. Zimmerman, *Guadalcanal Campaign, August 1942–February 1943* (Washington DC, 1949).

[17]Among others, see COMAMPHIBFORSOPAC [Turner], War Diary, 8 August 1942, NHC: OA, WWII Command File; War College, Battle Analysis Series, Training Commands. 'The Battle of Savo Island, August 9, 1942.' 1950; Buell, *King*, pp. 205–9; Richard F. Newcomb, *Savo Island: The Incredible Naval Debacle off Guadalcanal* (New York, 1961); Stan Smith, *The Battle of Savo* (New York, 1962); Larrabee, *Commander in Chief*, pp. 271–3, 281; Captain H. L. Merillat, *The Island* (Boston, 1944); Miller, *Guadalcanal*, pp. 78–81, 119–25, 174–7, 180, 220; E. B. Potter, *Nimitz* (Annapolis, Maryland, 1976), p. 181; Charles Bell, 'Shootout at Savo', *American History Illustrated*, 8 (January 1975), pp. 28–38.

[18]COMPHIBFORPACFLT, War Diaries, June–December 1942, Turner Papers; COMSOPAC [Ghormley] Action Report, NHC: OA; Dyer interview with Turner, 1960. In Dyer, *Turner*, vol. I, pp. 357; Admiral A. J. Hepburn, 'Report of Informal Inquiry into Circumstances Attending Loss of USS. *Vincennes*. . . . August 9, 1942, in Vicinity of Savo Island, 13 May 1943', NHC: OA: 'Solomons Islands Campaign II and III'. . . . Office of Naval Intelligence, 1 October 1943. Copy in Turner Papers; Driscoll, *Pacific Victory*, pp. 61–2; Toland, *Rising Sun*, p. 408. On 12 August, Turner sent Crutchley 'a summary of what I can reconstruct from the disastrous battle of SAVO ISLAND . . . '. On the next day Crutchley replied that two main points stood out: (1) fatigue of personnel that caused lack of warning, and (2) lack of practice in night fighting. As for the battle, Turner took the attitude that 'I have been

Turner was also criticized for failing to understand the tactical situation ashore. Substituting a baton for a sextant, he demanded that he rather than Vandegrift control troops after they had been landed. Yet he did a superb job for the next four months in sending more supplies, troops, aircraft and Seabees to Guadalcanal than the Japanese could.[19] Moreover, he had helped to dispel the myth of Japanese invincibility; he had developed tactics that were adopted as doctrine throughout the war; and he had seasoned young leaders, who would strike at the Japanese thereafter.[20] After being relieved of tactical operational control there, his twenty-hour days, a bout with malaria and a mild coronary attack put him under medical care for a spell. He nevertheless hoped that a Central Pacific drive would soon start and that he could engage in it.[21] His wish was granted.

Turner's primary concerns now were to reduce the unloading times of ships and to ensure that continuous air and naval surface cover were provided for landing areas. As it was, his performance at Guadalcanal was enough to have it said that 'If you want something tough done, call Turner.'[22]

The situation in the South Pacific improved after Fletcher was relieved of command and Ghormley was succeeded on 18 October 1942 by Vice Admiral William F. Halsey [*q.v.*]. Halsey, who had missed the Battle of Midway because of illness, promised to return to the Pacific and 'have a crack at those yellow-bellied sons-of-bitches and their carriers'. He cancelled the Ndeni venture and diverted troops destined for it to Guadalcanal, consolidated at Nouméa the staff Ghormley had divided between there and Auckland, and greatly pleased Vandegrift by directing that the latter, as the General ashore, have parallel rather than subordinate authority with Turner. Moreover, in the battles of the eastern Solomons in September, of Cape Esperance and Santa

---

thoroughly bitched in many ways on the Guadalcanal operation of August 7, 1942, and I do not intend to do anything about it whatsoever either now or after the war.' Turner to Captain George H. Bowdey, 9 April 1944, Turner Papers.

[19]Hoyt, *Nimitz and His Admirals*, p. 30; Vandegrift, *Memoirs*, pp. 169–71, 183–5. See also Foster, *Guadalcanal General*, pp. 63, 122–3; Griffith, *Battle for Guadalcanal*, pp. 141–2; Bill D. Ross, *Iwo Jima: Legacy of Valor* (New York, 1985), pp. 29, 214; Larrabee, *Commander in Chief*, pp. 283, 288, 295; J. Robert Moskin, *The Marine Corps Story*, rev. edn (New York, 1982), p. 257.

[20]Fifth Amphibious Force, South Pacific Force. 'Action Report Covering Reinforcement of Guadalcanal Island by Seventh Marines'. 27 September 1942. Turner Papers; Griffith, *Battle for Guadalcanal*, pp. 127–8; Larrabee, *Commander in Chief*, pp. 283, 295; Leckie, *Guadalcanal*, pp. ix, 184–5, 189, 231, 321, 325–6; Vandegrift, *Memoirs*, pp. 153, 175.

[21]Costello, *Pacific War*, p. 347; Dyer, *Turner*, vol. I, pp. 402–10, 455–6; Frank O. Hough, Verle E. Ludwig and Henry I. Shaw, *Pearl Harbor to Guadalcanal: History of the U.S. Marine Corps in World War II* (Washington DC, 1963), vol. I, pp. 240–1, 256–7, 261–2; Isely and Crowl, *U.S. Marines and Amphibious Warfare*, pp. 153–6; Larrabee, *Commander in Chief*, pp. 288–9; Toland, *Rising Sun*, pp. 444–5.

[22]Turner to Colonel James W. Webb, USMC. 20 August 1942, and to General A. A. Vandegrift, 23 August 1942, Turner Papers; Paolo E. Coletta, 'Daniel E. Barbey: Amphibious Warfare Expert', in John Leary (ed.), *We Shall Return!: MacArthur's Commanders and the Defeat of Japan* (Lexington, 1988), pp. 211, 215; Dyer, *Turner*, vol. I, pp. 402–10; Isely and Crowl, *U.S. Marines and Amphibious Warfare*, pp. 153–6; *New York Times*, 14 February 1961, 37:1.

Cruz in October, and of Guadalcanal and of Tassafaronga in November, Americans so wounded the Japanese navy that Turner could outspeed the 'Tokyo Express' in feeding men and supplies into Guadalcanal. Using lessons learned, he won approval from Halsey and Nimitz to make certain changes in the amphibious bible, FTP 167.[23]

Halsey (now Commander, Third Fleet) determined to establish two fighter strips and radar-warning installations on the Russell Islands, sixty miles north-north-west of Henderson Field, to help protect Guadalcanal and also as a first step up the Solomons ladder towards Rabaul. On 21 February, Turner's joint command transported army and Marine troops that easily occupied the islands and secured its 4,700-foot airstrip.[24] Halsey's next objectives were enemy airfields in the central Solomons. Turner drafted the operations plans himself, letting subordinates fill in details.[25] As for Kolombangara, Halsey bypassed it and left its defenders to starve. He would then attack Bougainville. Meanwhile Turner created a Joint Logistic Board to keep Washington informed of his supply needs. After a week's suffering with malaria and dengue fever, he sailed from Nouméa to Koli Point, Guadalcanal.[26]

On 30 June, Turner landed on Rendova Island 6,000 army and Marine troops which wiped out the enemy garrison, turned American guns on Munda and covered troops being ferried to the invasion site. On this occasion he almost lost his life when an enemy plane fell only 200 yards from his flagship, and again when a Japanese aerial torpedo seriously damaged it. He transferred to the destroyer *Farenholt*, and almost all of his crew was rescued. Unfortunately, mistaking *McCawley* as enemy, an American PT boat sank her.[27] Thereafter Turner prohibited PT boats from being near a landing area. On 15 July 1943 he was relieved by Rear Admiral Theodore S. Wilkinson and reported for duty to Nimitz as Commander, Amphibious Forces, Pacific Fleet.

[23]Vice Admiral Robert L. Ghormley, 'South Pacific Command: Events Leading Up to U.S. Attack on Solomons Islands.' Forces, 1943. 23pp. Washington: NHC: OA. The Admiral apparently prepared these pages to accompany several motion-picture films. A much more extended account is his 'South Pacific Command History: Early Period,' Forces, 1943. 150pp., ibid. See also Buell, *Spruance*, p. 157; Dyer, *Turner*, vol. I, p. 443; Griffith, *Battle for Guadalcanal*, pp. 163–4; Larrabee, *Commander in Chief*, p. 295; Leckie, *Guadalcanal*, pp. 300–1; Toland, *Rising Sun*, pp. 452–3.

[24]Russell Islands Naval Base, 'First Narrative of the Russell Island Naval Command.' Shore Establishment, 1945. Washington: NHC, OA, Command File World War II; 'Russell Islands. COMPHIBSFORPAC, Report of Occupation of Russell Islands, 21 April 1943', ibid; Costello, *Pacific War*, pp. 401–4; Fleet Admiral William F. Halsey and J. Bryan III, *Admiral Halsey's Story* (New York, 1947), p. 157; Eric Hammel, *Guadalcanal: The Carrier Battles and Operations in the Solomons, August–October 1942* (New York, 1987); Isely and Crowl, *U.S. Marines and Amphibious Warfare*, pp. 156–9; Miller, *Guadalcanal*, pp. 351–6; Samuel E. Morison, *Breaking the Bismarck Barrier, 22 July 1942–1 May 1944* (Boston, 1950), pp. 97–100.

[25]For Turner's planning and briefing of war correspondents, see Driscoll, *Pacific Victory*, pp. 63–8.

[26]Dyer, *Turner*, vol. I, pp. 458–74, 498–9.

[27]Ibid., pp. 542–62; Morison, *Breaking the Bismarcks Barrier*, pp. 147–53. Upon reaching the *Farenholt*, Turner exclaimed to a newspaper correspondent, 'Didn't I tell you that there was going to be a great story here?' Driscoll, *Pacific Victory*, p. 56.

As his flagship captain recalled, the only exercise he got during the last six months was in walking to and from a private drinking room in Nouméa. There he chain-smoked and 'he and his staff drank heavily and relaxed. . . . Turner was lots of fun and forgot his problems here.'[28]

By the summer of 1943, American productive capacity gave a Central Pacific Force fast new battleships, heavy and light carriers, and cruisers and destroyers that could isolate a battle area and defend amphibious forces. Also, a top-priority billion-dollar programme of 1942 for amphibious craft provided such 'miracle ships' as the LST (landing ship, tank), LCI (landing craft, infantry), LSD (landing ship, dock), LCM (landing craft, mechanized), LCI(R) (landing craft, rocket), LCT (ramp bowed craft), and LVT (tracked landing vehicles like the Alligator and Water Buffalo that could travel over land, through water and over reefs much as could the army's two-and-a-half-ton amphibious truck, the DUKW).[29]

On 8 August 1943, Raymond A. Spruance [*q.v.*], promoted to vice admiral, assumed command of the Fifth Fleet. Spruance had served with Turner in *Pennsylvania* during World War One and again at the Naval War College, 1935–8. With King's blessing he named him to command his amphibious forces, the second most important billet in his fleet. Turner reported for this duty at Pearl Harbor, where he worked closely with Major-General Holland M. Smith, USMC [*q.v.*], who was responsible for training all Nimitz's amphibious troops.[30] Smith was as blunt, tactless, strong-willed and stubborn as Turner, yet Turner had asked King to order him out. It took Nimitz and King to arrange it so that Turner remained in command during training manoeuvres and landing operations while Smith did the planning and commanded landed troops. Meanwhile, on 24 August 1943, Turner was designated Commander, 5th Amphibious Forces, Pacific, with the 3rd and 5th Amphibious Forces as components. He assembled a new staff and won permission to establish an administrative command ashore that would free him to fight. In addition, in conjunction with the type commander for Pacific cruisers and destroyers, in September he established a training school in Hawaii for naval gunfire ships and shore fire-control parties. With no amphibious-force flagship yet available, he rode the battleship *Pennsylvania* (BB-38).

To avoid a battle of attrition by relying upon air strikes and the siting of artillery near Betio (the main target on Tarawa, in the Gilbert Islands, because it had an airfield), a direct assault had to be made, with Turner's warships engaging before his transports and cargo ships went in. Turner wanted carriers to serve defensively in close air support, but Nimitz overruled him,

---

[28]Driscoll, *Pacific Victory*, pp. 58–9; Dyer, *Turner*, vol. I, p. 593.

[29]George E. Mowry, 'Landing Craft and the War Production Board: April 1942 to May 1944'. 8 March 1946. Washington: NHC: OA., Command File World War II.

[30]Turner to Lieutenant-General T. H. Holcomb [Commandant of the Marine Corps], 13 October 1943, Turner Papers; Buell, *Spruance*, pp. 177–8; Dyer, *Turner*, vol. II, pp. 599–601, 616–18; Isely and Crowl, *U.S. Marines and Amphibious Warfare*, p. 202; Smith, *Coral and Brass*, p. 117.

saying that carriers must remain mobile.[31] However, the number of amphibian tractors available could not carry all the assault troops, and landing craft needed at least four feet of water over the reefs. Oft-told has been the story of the exceptional neap tide that forced the invaders to wade a long distance to the beaches under enfilade fire that caused 50 per cent casualties.[32]

Turning tactical control at Tarawa over to Rear Admiral Harry Hill, Turner and Holland Smith accompanied the Makin expedition, because Makin was closer to the Marshalls than Tarawa and therefore the more dangerous target. When Turner would not use amtracs, Holland Smith bluntly told him, 'No amtracs, no operation.' Amtracs were used. Moreover, Americans had to face entrenched defenders rather than operate in a jungle environment. On 18 November, Turner's landing parties made short work of lightly defended Makin while men landed from the submarine *Nautilus* took Apamama.[33] Tarawa, however, would provide the testing ground for techniques that gradually carried Americans to the shores of Japan. Among the most important studies of the operations were those issued by Hill and Turner. In brief, it was learned that hydrographic intelligence must be obtained prior to a landing; underwater demolition teams were needed; point fire (high angle plunging trajectory with armour-piercing shells) as well as neutralization naval gunfire should be used; a greater number of armed and faster tracked landing vehicles were needed; and precise timing based upon the movement of men towards shore must be arranged among all co-operating arms. It was vital that men should be able to form an organization after they had landed, and that they should have their own demolition men rather than depend upon combat engineers. In addition to communications ships, radios must be improved and made waterproof, and communications themselves must be bettered. Pilots needed training in close air support, and beachhead logistics must be improved. Turner forwarded his plans for the Marshall Islands to Spruance, who directed him to confer with Nimitz at Pearl Harbor.[34]

[31]Clark G. Reynolds, *The Fast Carriers: The Forging of an Air Navy*, rev. edn (Huntington, NY, 1978), pp. 89, 92–3.

[32]Patrick L. McKiernan, 'Tarawa: The Tide that Failed', USNIP, 88 (July 1962), pp. 38–49.

[33]Buell, *Spruance*, pp. 307–8; Susan H. Godson, 'The Development of Amphibious Warfare in World War II as Reflected in the Campaigns of John Lesslie Hall, Jr., USN', PhD diss. American University, 1979; Ann Arbor, Michigan: University Microfilms International, 1979, pp. 275–8; Dyer, *Turner*, vol. II, pp. 646–7, 651–4, 657–82; Dick Hanna, *Tarawa: The Toughest Battle in Marine Corps History* (New York, 1944); Isely and Crowl, *U.S. Marines and Amphibious Warfare*, pp. 229, 262; Samuel E. Morison, *Aleutians, Gilberts, and Marshalls, June 1942–April 1944* (Boston, 1951), pp. 121–350, H. M. Smith, *Coral and Brass*, pp. 118–19; James R. Stockman. *The Battle for Tarawa* (Washington DC, 1947); Rear Admiral Carl J. Moore, 'Assault on Tarawa and Apamama', in John T. Mason Jr, *The Pacific War Remembered: An Oral History Collection* (Annapolis, Maryland, 1986), pp. 172–7; Rear Admiral William D. Irvin, 'Trial of the *Nautilus*', in ibid., pp. 178–91.

[34]COMFIFTHPHIBFOR, 'Report of GALVANIC Operation, Ser. 00165 of 4 Dec. 1943', 'Statement on National Broadcast Concerning Iwo Jima Operation, 27 Feb. 1945' and 'Statement on Cessation of Resistance on Iwo Jima, 8 Mar. 1945', Turner Papers. The 21 February radio broadcast of Tokyo's 'Home and Empire' programme said that Turner's name was associated with the alligator, 'which lives

The textbook developed from Tarawa was put to excellent use at the Marshalls. Spruance, Turner and Holland Smith argued unavailingly when Nimitz decided to bypass many of the eastern Marshalls.[35] However, when Turner opposed his plan for three assaults, the number was reduced on 1 February 1944 to two, Majuro and Kwajalein.[36] When Turner strenuously objected to Kwajalein as 'being reckless and dangerous', Nimitz said that he should obey orders; he could find a replacement for him and asked, 'Do you want to do it or not?' – and gave him five minutes to decide. Turner smiled and said, 'Sure I want to do it.'[37] From USS *Rocky Mount*, one of his two new headquarters communications ships, he had his force lift 85,000 combat, garrison and construction personnel. Dividing his force into three groups, he kept tactical control over the entire expedition and over the group destined for Kwajalein. He also convinced Nimitz to transfer command of Air Support Control Units now aboard from Commander Air, Pacific. Harry Hill would take Majuro and Rear Admiral Richard L. 'Close-In' Conolly [*q.v.*], newly arrived from the Mediterranean, Roi–Namur.[38] A great help was the fact that there were few coral heads in Kwajalein's lagoon to impede amphibious boat traffic. Also, the acceptance of Turner's recommendation that the operation be postponed by two weeks resulted in the receipt of a large number of additional amphibious tractors.

More than three times the quantity of ammunition used at Tarawa was used at Kwajalein, and air strikes were delivered for several days. Turner's plans for creating and training of Underwater Demolition Teams (UDTs), beginning in mid-1943, also saw light. Helpful also were pallets that speeded logistic loading and unloading and the arming of infantry landing craft with machine guns and rockets. Undefended Majuro was taken quickly on 30–31 January 1944, and Americans landed on Kwajalein standing up. Namur was overrun on 2 February, Kwajalein on the 5th and Eniwetok on the 7th. Twenty-seven

---

both on land and in the water. Also . . . once he bites into something he will not let go. This man Turner, who has been responsible for the death of so many of our precious men, shall not return home alive. He must not, and will not.' When Turner heard about the broadcast, he signalled Spruance one of the few jokes of his life, saying, 'Maybe you'd better send a few Marines to protect me.' Ross, *Iwo Jima*, p. 152; Toland, *Rising sun*, p. 740.

35Edwin P. Hoyt, *To the Marianas: War in the Central Pacific* (New York, 1980), pp. 16–18.

36Buell, *Spruance*, pp. 209–12; Larrabee, *Commander in Chief*, p. 389; Reynolds, *Fast Carriers*, pp. 114–15, 350; H. M. Smith, *Coral and Brass*, pp. 141–2.

37Dyer, *Turner*, vol. II, pp. 738–42.

38Conolly had served as Commander Landing Craft and Bases in North-West Africa under Admiral H. Kent Hewitt and commanded a major task force in the Sicilian campaign. At their first meeting, he remarked about his experience in the Mediterranean. Turner replied: 'If you stay around here, you and I are goin' to fight.' However, 'they respected each other and got along famously'. Morison, *Aleutians, Gilberts and Marshalls*, p. 232, n. 2. During the Okinawa campaign Turner evaluated Conolly as 'about the best and most experienced amphibious commander we have'. Turner to Fleet Admiral C. W. Nimitz, 17 April 1945, Turner Papers.

Japanese died for each American.39 Such success was made possible not only by the lessons learned from Tarawa but by the usc of tracked landing vehicles, repair stations for small amphibious craft established ashore or in ships, use of LSTs as temporary hospital ships, improved ship-to-shore movement, employment of naval star shells, and the fact that forward logistics ships kept warships operating unless they had to return to rear areas to repair serious damage.

Their accomplishments at the Marshalls caused Nimitz to recommend promotion for Spruance, Turner and Smith. Secretary of the Navy James V. Forrestal, who was present at the taking of Roi–Namur and Kwajalein, quickly approved. Although Turner's actions at Savo Island and the loss of life at Tarawa were questioned, and *Time* in its cover story of 6 February 1944 called him a 'mean son-of-a-bitch', the Senate confirmed him to be a vice admiral.40 The occupation of the Marshalls also had important strategic repercussions, for the Japanese evacuated the Carolines including Truk and retreated behind the Philippines–Netherlands East Indies–New Guinea barrier. Nimitz therefore advanced the date for assaulting the Marianas by twenty weeks. But would Nimitz or General Douglas MacArthur, Commander, South-West Pacific, command the next line of advance and obtain forces from the South Pacific, now in garrison status? MacArthur wanted to move from New Guinea via the Palaus to the Philippines; King and Nimitz preferred to continue the Central Pacific drive; Turner would bypass all islands and land on the Tokyo Plain but lacked strength to do so. It was decided (in large part because they could be used for advance naval and air bases and B-29s could hit Japan from them) that Nimitz would assault the Marianas in June. MacArthur would assault Mindanao, in the Philippines, in November, with the two drives being mutually supporting. Leyte was soon substituted for Mindanao, with D-Day set for 20 October 1944. In the division of the South Pacific forces, Nimitz fared better than MacArthur. In June 1944, Turner had six amphibious groups; in September, fourteen – more than he could employ. By this time, too, as Samuel E. Morison put it, 'He had learned more about this specialized brand of warfare than anyone else ever had, or probably ever would.'41

39'COM V PHIB Report on Operation "Flintlock", 25 February 1944', Turner Papers, Series IV; Commander in Chief, US Pacific Fleet, 'Administrative History of The ComMarGils Area', 6 vols. Washington: Navy Department Library; Dyer, *Turner*, vol. II, pp. 619, 636–43, 762–851; Lieutenant-Colonel Robert D. Heinl Jr, USMC, and Lieutenant-Colonel John A. Crown, USMC, *The Marshalls: Increasing the Tempo* (Washington DC, 1954); Samuel L. A. Marshall, *Island Victory: The Battle of Kwajalein Atoll* (Washington DC, 1944); H. M. Smith, *Coral and Brass*, pp. 144–5, 147–51.

40*Time*, 7 February 1944, p. 19; Robert Greenhalgh Albion and Robert Howe Connery, *Forrestal and the Navy*, (New York and London, 1967), p. 22. The *Time* correspondent on Kwajalein criticized the harshness of the magazine's cover story on Turner, saying in part that his impression was of a 'warm, witty, caustic gentleman, who while warily respected is at the same time whole-heartedly loved'. William H. Chickering to David Hulburd, 9 February 1944. Copy in Turner Papers.

41Buell, *Spruance*, pp. 255, 267–72; Dyer, *Turner*, vol. II, p. 853; Emmet P. Forrestel, *Admiral*

After the Marshalls operation, Turner said, 'I was dead tired. I stayed dead tired for the rest of the war.' If he drank a lot, he was nevertheless clear-headed every morning. When Nimitz queried him on the matter, Spruance assured him that he could handle Turner.[42]

Because it was 100 miles closer to Japan and had airfields, Turner recommended taking Saipan first. Nimitz and Spruance agreed to seize it and Tinian first, then Guam. Under Spruance, Turner would command the Joint Expeditionary Force. For the purpose he was given every amphibious ship in the Pacific. In his operation plan of 6 May 1944, he retained command of a Northern Attack Force for Saipan and Tinian; Conolly would command a Southern Attack Force for Guam; and released a happy Holland Smith to operate independently.

In conference at Eniwetok on 8 June, Spruance and Turner agreed that the pre-invasion bombing of Tinian, Saipan, Rota and Guam would begin on 11 June with carrier air strikes. With UDTs and minesweepers clearing channels, Turner's and Conolly's warships bombarded the invasion beaches on Saipan for two days and then provided call fire including star shells. The landings that began on the 15th were so well executed that 8,000 men were ashore in twenty minutes, and with the landing of artillery the beachhead was secured. Stiff resistance determined Holland Smith to land the army's 27th Infantry Division, and by the 19th the first phase of the operation was completed. Upon learning of the approach of a Japanese fleet, Spruance conferred with Turner, gave him eight cruisers and twenty-one destroyers to aid in defending the beachhead, and left for battle. In turn, Turner gave Admiral Marc A. Mitscher [*q.v.*], commanding the fast carriers, seven cruisers and eleven destroyers. In the Battle of the Philippine Sea, Americans shot down 476 Japanese aircraft and sank three carriers and two tankers, thus freeing the troops ashore from danger.[43]

On 20 June, Smith sent his troops northward. When the 27th Division, which he distrusted intensely, could not keep pace with Marines to its left and right, on 24 June, without consulting Nimitz, he requested and received approval from Spruance and Turner to relieve Major-General Ralph Smith of his command.[44] At 1800 on 9 July, Turner radioed Spruance that Holland

---

Raymond A. Spruance: A Study in Command (Washington DC, 1966), pp. 135, 144; Hoyt, *To the Marianas*, pp. 98, 112, 140, 142, 144; Samuel E. Morison, *New Guinea and the Marianas, May 1944–August 1944* (Boston, 1953), p. 159; Reynolds, *Fast Carriers*, pp. 180–1.

[42]Buell, *Spruance*, p. 255; Dyer, *Turner*, vol. II, p. 853; Hoyt, *To the Marianas*, p. 112.

[43]Joseph Clark, 'The Marianas Turkey Shoot', *American History Illustrated*, 8 (October 1967), pp. 26ff; Rear Admiral Draper Kauffman, 'The UDTs Came of Age at Saipan', in Mason, *The Pacific War Remembered*, pp. 236–45; Vice Admiral Bernard Strean, 'A High Score and Close Call in the Philippine Sea', in ibid., pp. 216–21.

[44]'Smith vs. Smith folder', Turner Papers; Buell, *Spruance*, pp. 281–7; Hoyt, *To the Marianas*, pp. 186–7, 189, 199–210; Carl W. Hoffman, *Saipan: The Beginning of the End* (Washington DC 1950);

Smith had declared Saipan secure. On 12 July, Lieutenant-General Robert C. Richardson (the senior army General in the Pacific) distributed medals to army troops ashore that were outside his jurisdiction. When he called on him, Turner vented blazing wrath upon him for his 'high-handed and irregular actions'.[45]

The assault on Tinian was simplified because artillery from Saipan could reach its northern sector, its smaller beaches received extended naval and air bombardment, supplies could be delivered from shore to shore from Saipan, and intelligence about it obtained on Saipan was quite complete. At Holland Smith's suggestion, Turner had beaches scouted and chose the northern ones. Although they were very narrow, rearrangements in landing doctrine resulted in what Spruance called one of the best landings in history.[46]

After Harry Hill relieved him as commander of the naval attack force, Turner proceeded to Pearl Harbor to help plan for the attack on Guam. For that operation it would again be the Spruance–Turner–Smith team. Spruance set D-Day for 18 June. As for Saipan, the invasion troops had been sent away during the Battle of the Philippine Sea,[47] so the landings did not occur unil 21 July. In the interim, however, for two weeks Turner carried out the heaviest preliminary bombardment yet delivered by the navy in the Pacific, with wonderful results. He declared Guam secure on 9 July. Within three months, B-29s were winging their way over Japan.[48]

Rather than Amoy or Formosa, Nimitz's next objectives were Iwo Jima and Okinawa. Iwo was some 660 miles from Tokyo and from the southern Marianas, Okinawa on southern Japan's doorstep. Turner planned for both campaigns

Captain Edmund G. Love, *The 27th Infantry Division in World War II* (Washington DC, 1949), p. 247; Moskin, *Marine Corps Story*, pp. 326–7; H. M. Smith, *Coral and Brass*, pp. 163–4, 168–76, and, with Percy Finch, 'My Trouble with the Army on Saipan', *Saturday Evening Post*, 231 (13 November 1948), pp. 32ff.

45CTF 51 [Turner] to COM 5th Fleet [Spruance], S: 'Reporting unwarranted assumption of command authority by LtGen. R. C. Richardson, Jr., USA'. 16 July 1944, Turner Papers; Buell, *Spruance*, pp. 295–6; Carter, *Beans, Bullets, and Black Oil*, pp. 158–62; Forrestel, *Spruance*, pp. 152, 156; H. M. Smith, *Coral and Brass*, pp. 176–8; Toland, *Rising Sun*, pp. 574–5; Vandegrift, *Memoirs*, p. 264. On 25 August 1944, Turner's force included 90 transports and supply ships, 11 LSDS, 24 APDS (fast destroyer transports), 189 LSTS, 239 LCIS and 386 LCTS. 'Memorandum: Chief of Staff, Commander in Chief, Pacific Fleet. 25 Aug. 1944', Turner Papers.

46Amphibious Forces, Pacific, 'Report of Amphibious Operations, Marianas Islands, 25 Aug. 1944', Turner Papers. Carl W. Hoffman, *The Seizure of Tinian* (Washington DC, 1951); H. M. Smith, *Coral and Brass*, pp. 163–4, 168–76; Admiral Harry Hill, 'A Perfect Amphibious Assault', in Mason, *The Pacific War Remembered*, pp. 236–45; Louis Morton, 'The Marianas', *Military Review*, 47 (July 1967), pp. 71–82.

47Dyer, *Turner*, vol. II, pp. 852–968; H. P. Willmott, *June 1944*, (Poole, Dorset, 1984), pp. 192–3; Thomas B. Buell, 'Battle of the Philippine Sea', USNIP, 100 (July 1974), pp. 64–79.

48Commander in Chief, US Pacific Fleet, 'Administrative History of Forward Area, CenPac and the Marianas Area. 1946', Washington: Naval Department Library; Philip A. Crowl, *Campaign in the Marianas* (Washington DC, 1960); Major O. R. Lodge, USMC, *The Recapture of Guam* (Washington DC, 1954); Morison, *New Guinea and the Marianas*.

concurrently. Iwo was needed for airstrips from which fighters could escort B-29s to Japan and as a haven for returning cripples. For this vast and complex operation, the Spruance–Turner–Smith team exercised strategic rather than tactical control. At Guadalcanal, Turner had had 51 ships; at Iwo, 495. He also controlled supporting aircraft. While he was again ill with a virus that threatened pneumonia and wore a brace to ease back pain, Rear Admiral W. H. P. Blandy, heading Amphibious Group One, served as Commander, Amphibious Support Force – that is, he integrated all naval gunfire, minesweeping, underwater demolition and air support during the period prior to the beach assault. Soon after it was reported that President Roosevelt had nominated both Spruance and Turner for promotion, on 19 February Blandy turned his task over to a recovered Turner, now in *Eldorado* (AGC-11). Turner delegated his tactical duties to Harry Hill, his second-in-command.49

Nimitz's staff had recommended eight days of preliminary bombardment. Pressed by the needs to counter possible surface action, to undertake three days of air strikes against Japan in which capital ships accompanied the fast carriers, and to prepare for landing on Okinawa prior to the commencement of the typhoon season, Turner reduced requests by the tactical Marine commander (Major-General Harry Schmidt, USMC) for ten days of pre-bombardment to three, arguing that the concentration of fire by thirteen capital ships during those days would hurl more shells at Iwo than during the ten days asked for. He thus missed the point that what was needed was slow, deliberate destructive fire at blank range. When Schmidt asked for four days, he deferred to Spruance, who rejected the request but told Turner that he could add a fourth day and could use some battleships and cruisers returned from the Tokyo Raid. Turner decided not to do so and also rejected Schmidt's request for fire only on preferred landing beaches and nearby areas, in favour of full coverage of the island. The best excuse that can be offered is that, while Spruance considered the carrier strikes at Japan as cover for Iwo, Turner pondered the entire strategic situation and favoured Okinawa over Iwo.50 The result, however, was that although 30 per cent more ammunition was expended on Iwo than at Saipan, a large number of Japanese defences remained unscathed and wreaked destruction upon beach personnel, landing craft and ships. To lift troops, lend strategic support and reinforce the assault, Turner's 800 vessels lifted 220,000 men. Instead of lasting a few days, the operation would continue from 19 February to the end of March. Because early casualty rates rose to 75 per cent and more, Turner had to forward replacements. During the operation he provided close air support and naval

---

49Commander Amphibious Forces, US Pacific Fleet, to Commander in Chief, US Pacific Fleet, S: 'Support Aircraft Command – Organization of, 10 June 1944', Turner Papers; *New York Times*, 11 February 1944, 7:3; Ross, *Iwo Jima*, pp. 44–5.

50Lieutenant-Colonel Whitman S. Bartley USMC, *Iwo Jima: Amphibious Epic* (Washington DC, 1954), p. 40; Buell, *Spruance*, pp. 327–35, 339; Ross, *Iwo Jima*, pp. 52–4; H. M. Smith, *Coral and Brass*, pp. 244–7.

gunfire support, supplies and medical care. The average daily expenditure of artillery ammunition alone being 231,000 rounds, only his emergency logistic plans saved the Americans on Iwo.[51] Further, he lost the support of the fast carriers while they struck Japan. On 9 March he turned command over to Hill and left for Pearl Harbor, to help plan for the invasion of Okinawa, only seventeen days away – an operation he predicted would be '*really* tough'.[52]

Okinawa, only 350 miles from Kyushu, was needed to establish airfields and staging areas for a possible invasion of Japan. Nimitz assigned Spruance to command an operation equivalent in magnitude to the invasion of Normandy, and Turner to command the Joint Expeditionary Force. Instead of a Marine, Lieutenant-General Simon B. Buckner of the US Army would command the troops. All forces of the Pacific Ocean Areas were assigned supporting tasks. Exclusive of Task Force 58, the ships and craft used to make and supply the landing numbered 1,400; the troops, 541,866. D-Day was 1 April 1945. A huge naval gunfire and support force would bombard Okinawa for seven days and then support the expeditionary troops. Army bombers would bombard both Japan and Okinawa. Denied his request to seize islands to the north upon which to establish early-warning radars, he directed (in one of the most difficult decisions he ever made) that radar picket destroyers and even smaller craft patrol stations be located from fifteen to a hundred miles about Okinawa. With the amphibious phase completed, the battle raged for eighty-one days between ships and kamikazes and the troops ashore.[53]

After the troops he had landed met no resistance for a week, on 8 April Turner confidently – and wrongly – radioed Nimitz: 'I may be crazy but it looks like the Japs have quit the war, at least in this section.'[54] Knowing that he could not oppose Turner's amphibious assault at the beach – a tribute to how well Turner had developed amphibious operations – Lieutenant-General Mitsuru Ushijima had decided to defend Okinawa in depth in its southern part, in what Turner called a 'Cassino-type operation'. Even so, Okinawa brought army, navy and Marine Corps air power within reach of the China coast, Korea and Japan's home islands and would have been very useful had the projected invasion of Japan been necessary.[55]

[51]'Ammunition of all types sufficient to fill 480 freight cars was unloaded across the beach, plus food enough to feed Columbus, Ohio, for 30 days, and fuel to form a train of tank cars several miles in length, with 10,000 gallons per car.' Isely and Crowl, *U.S. Marines and Amphibious Warfare*, p. 517.

[52]'COMPHIBSPAC (CTF 51), 'Iwo Jima Report, 19 May, 1945', and Turner to Frank M. Folson, Radio Corporation of America, 31 March 1945, Turner Papers; Arthur J. Barker, *Suicide Weapons: Japanese Kamikaze Forces in World War II* (New York, 1961); Dyer, *Turner*, vol. II, pp. 969–1041; Godson, 'Hall', pp. 279–80.

[53]Turner to Admiral C. W. Nimitz, 16 April 1945, Turner Papers; Walter F. Karig, Russell L. Harris and Frank R. Manson, *Battle Report*, vol. V: *Victory in the Pacific* (New York, 1949), pp. 387, 389, 412.

[54]Toland, *Rising Sun*, pp. 788–9; Samuel E. Morison, *Victory in the Pacific, 1945* (Boston, 1960).

[55]COMPHIBSPAC Okinawa Gunto Report, 25 July 1945, 31 July 1945, and Turner to Secretary of

Deciding that Turner had served long enough in continuous combat, Nimitz had Hill relieve him on 17 May, and ordered him and Spruance to plan for the invasion of Kyushu. Turner did his planning in *Eldorado*, in Manila Bay, until the fighting ended on 13 August.

It has been said that Turner was 'amphibious warfare's unchallenged master'. It is better to say that he was the unchallenged master of 'aero-amphibious warfare'.[56] Holland M. Smith, who had perpetually argued with him, wrote to him following the Kwajalein operation declaring that 'this Corps takes pride in serving under the Force, and with it behind us we would storm the very gates of hell'. Smith later stated that 'We [the Marines] would rather go to sea with him in command than any other admiral under whom we have served.'[57] Employing lessons learned at Guadalcanal and especially Tarawa, amphibious assault provided a main key to success and ranked with carrier air power and submarines in defeating Japan. For his earliest landings, as at Guadalcanal and Tarawa, Turner lacked sufficient naval gunfire support, adequate landing craft and logistic support ships. By mid-1943 these deficiencies had been overcome in large part both in quantity and in quality. In addition, amphibious doctrine had been refined by the better co-ordination of supporting arms, close air support and naval gunfire support, the creation and employment of UDTs, and the use of forward naval gunfire and air observers. In pre-bombardment, pinpoint and close-in firing was added to neutralization fire. Turner credited his success, in order of priority, to 'people' – failing to note that he had instructed many of them – organization and close air support. He lauded the separation of operational from administrative command, for separating out the latter freed him for fighting. Third, amphibious landings had been greatly aided by the co-ordination of the air support of all the services.[58] Spruance praised him as the acme of a fighter with a creative mind.[59]

After attending the Japanese surrender ceremonies on 2 September, Turner on 14 October 1945 was relieved by Rear Admiral John L. Hall, who had commanded an assault force at Okinawa, and returned home for a month's leave.

---

the Navy [James V. Forrestal], 16 May 1945, Turner Papers; Dyer, *Turner*, vol. II, pp. 1053–111; James H. Belote and William M. Belote, *Typhoon of Steel: The Battle of Okinawa* (New York, 1970); Benis M. Frank, *Okinawa: Capstone to Victory* (New York, 1970); Ian Gow, *Okinawa: 1945: Gateway to Japan* (Garden City, NY, 1985); Charles S. Nichols and Henry I. Shaw, *Okinawa: Victory in the Pacific* (Washington DC, 1955); Denis Warner et al., *The Sacred Warriors: Japan's Suicide Legions* (New York, 1982).

[56]Aviation History Unit, Office of CNO, 'Inter-Service Cooperation in Aeronautics', CNO, 1948, copy in Washington: NHC: OA; Logan C. Ramsey, 'The Aero-Amphibious Phase of the War', USNIP, 69 (May 1943), pp. 695–701.

[57]Smith cited in Larrabee, *Commander in Chief*, pp. 201–2.

[58]Dyer, *Turner*, vol. II, pp. 1054–8.

[59]Buell, *Spruance*, p. 385.

Post-war, Turner was ordered to serve on the General Board. In December 1945 he was detailed to the UN Security Council Military Staff Committee. In the spring of 1946 he went to London to attend the first meeting of the UN General Assembly. The Russians blocked all attempts by Turner's committee to provide for the organization and use of UN forces. He firmly supported restoring Germany and Japan to the family of nations.

Retired on 15 July 1947, aged sixty-two, he relocated at Monterey. The tough master strategist, pedant, planner and logistician deteriorated rapidly in part because of his alcoholism, in part because for four years before his death he constantly attended his wife Harriet, an invalid. They had celebrated their golden wedding anniversary in 1960. Six weeks after her death, on 13 February 1961, he died of a coronary occlusion. He was buried at Golden Gate National Cemetery because Harriet was there. Later, Spruance and Nimitz were also buried there.[60]

[60]*New York Times*, 14 February 1961, 37:1; Buell, *Spruance*, pp. 425, 428.

PART FOUR

The Submariners

18

Admiral

Otto Kretschmer
German Navy

1912–

by
Bodo Herzog
Translated by Marianne Howarth

OTTO Wilhelm August Kretschmer, born 1 May 1912 in Ober-Heidau (Kreis Liegnitz), son of the schoolmaster and precentor Wilhelm Otto Kretschmer and his wife, Alice (née Herbig). Attended his father's primary school, 1918–21 and then, until 1929, the Staatliche Bildungsanstalt (State Educational Institution) in the former monastery at Wahlstatt. Took Abitur examinations before the age of seventeen. Being too young to join the Reichsmarine, he applied to join 'Crew 30', the class that would begin in 1930, and for a time travelled and studied in England, France and Italy. Accepted into the Reichsmarine against stiff competition, he did basic training at Stralsund on the Baltic coast. Rated sea cadet 9 October 1930 and joined the sail training ship Niobe before joining the training cruiser Emden on a voyage to the Far East. Rated petty officer 1 January 1932 and served in pocket battleship Deutschland and light cruiser Emden. Commissioned Leutnant (sub-lieutenant/lieutenant (j.g.) 1 October 1934. Posted to U-boat Command May 1936. Lieutenant, 1 June 1936; posted to Second U-boat Flotilla. Watch Officer in U-35, 1935–6, in Spanish waters during Spanish Civil War. Given command of the small U-23 in 1937, aged twenty-five. Lieutenant-Commander, 1 June 1939.

Lieutenant-Commander Otto Kretschmer was twenty-seven years old when war began in September 1939. By then he had commanded *U-23* for two years, and knew the boat extremely well. 'For his age,' said a contemporary official report,

> he is an unusually quiet, well-formed character, yet with inner strength.
> Very likeable, unassuming, well mannered in behaviour and demeanour.
> He never seeks to give himself airs and graces. He is well groomed and his

general appearance is good. Socially, he is reserved but poised. Good intellectual ability, many varied interests, well read and stimulating in discussion once he has overcome a certain shyness and reserve. He tends to be a loner and to work everything out on his own, despite the fact that he is popular with his colleagues because of his basically cheerful and particularly comradely manner as well as his dry humour. In two years of peacetime, he has already discharged his function as a U-boat commander in an exemplary manner; he trained and led his crew well and piloted his boat well in every regard. His quite exceptional ability as a sailor was very noticeable. As a navigator, sensible and safe. On exercise he displayed good tactical qualities and understanding. Kretschmer has acquitted himself exceptionally well in several wartime expeditions.

This was true. In the six months from the beginning of the war to the end of February 1940, he took *U-23* on eight separate expeditions, including a minelaying operation in Cromarty Firth (during which no torpedoes were carried on board), and the support of Nordmark, an operation (18–20 February 1940) of the pocket battleships *Scharnhorst* and *Gneisenau* against convoys between the UK and Scandinavia. His areas of operation were the North Sea and the eastern coast of Britain including Flamborough Head, Firth of Forth, Firth of Tay, Stonehaven, Montrose, the Shetland Islands, the Orkneys and Ingeness Bay (Kirkwall). During this period Kretschmer succeeded in sinking six merchant ships, totalling 20,939 GRT, as well as the destroyer HMS *Daring* (Commander Sidney Alan Cooper). For these achievements he had been awarded the Iron Cross 2nd Class and (in December 1939), the Iron Cross 1st Class.

The official report continued:

His operations against the enemy were distinguished by the untroubled, calm, resolute and very able way in which he conducted them. He is a U-boat commander who, because of the qualities listed above, is especially suited to undertake difficult tasks. Physically he is still fresh and not yet over-stretched, so his future career can be expected to be a successful one. Kretschmer would be especially suitable as the commander of a large U-boat next. In the longer term, when the appropriate service age has been reached, it would be more sensible to use him as a fleet commander or as a referent or as admiral's staff officer. He will discharge any responsible position given to him to the full and merits attention for the future. . . .

The Fleet Commander's report agreed, assessing Kretschmer as:

an extremely quiet, reserved yet hard-working and energetic officer. Talented and clear-thinking, thoughtful and confident about the objectives he sets for himself, he has shown excellent traits of character for his official position. Kretschmer is very popular with his men and his fellow officers, who are quick to look beyond his reserve and recognize his true value. I have been able to endorse fully my predecessor's very positive view of Kretschmer's professional achievements. In three further successful war operations Kretschmer pursued the enemy indefatigably, giving maximum performance himself and getting the same from his men. He kept coming up with new ways of reducing the time spent in port and to increase the number of torpedoes to be taken on board. . . . Lieutenant Kretschmer is exceptionally well suited to be the commander of a large U-boat.

These eight operations in the latter part of 1939 and beginning of 1940 may be summarized thus. The first, which began before war broke out, involved eleven days at sea (25 August to 4 September) and was followed by four days of refit. The second, of thirteen days (9–21 September), was followed by seven days' refit and two days' transit; the third, of sixteen days (1–16 October), brought the first successful hit – a merchant ship of 876 GRT – and was followed by fifteen days' refit. The fourth voyage, of nine days (1–9 November), was the minelaying operation off Cromarty Firth, during which no torpedoes were used. Twenty-five days' refit followed before the fifth operation, of eleven days (5–15 December). This brought one more sinking (2,400 GRT) and necessitated twenty-three days' refit. The sixth, although only eight days long (8–15 January), resulted in two sinkings totalling 11,667 GRT, after which only two days' refit were required. The seventh operation, of twelve days (18–29 January) found another victim – a merchantman of 1,000 GRT – and was followed by ten days' refit in dock; while the eighth, of seventeen days (9–25 February) added two more sinkings (one of 4,996 GRT, the other of 1,375 ts) to Kretschmer's growing list.

During the six-month period, *U-23* had spent ninety-seven days at sea and eighty-eight in port. There had been six successful hits, totalling 20,939 GRT, or a tonnage sinking quotient of 215.87 GRT per day of active service. But of the twenty-three torpedoes that had been fired, fifteen had produced no result. This was the fault of the torpedoes rather than the commander. Recalling the situation he then faced, Kretschmer has recently explained that many torpedoes detonated prematurely. When that happened, ships sometimes switched on their side lights, believing they had entered a minefield. On one such occasion, Kretschmer was so frustrated that he decided to test his weapons properly. With his boat on the surface, he subjected the ship to a 20-mm artillery bombardment, forcing the crew to disembark. When they were all off, he fired a torpedo at the beam of the stopped ship at short range, to find out what the torpedo, which was set to go off, was doing. The result showed him their weakness: 'The magnetic firing mechanism had to be reset every time we entered a new zone.'

He has no complaints about his boat: 'As a Type II-B boat, *U-23* was particularly good for entering narrow waters such as Ingeness Bay in the Orkneys and the Shetland fjords (Busta Voe, Sullom Voe, Yell Sound etc.), where the British Northern Patrol was present.' But concerning the torpedoes, he adds simply: 'In my view, the failure rate was fifty per cent.'

In addition to these professional disappointments, Kretschmer suffered a personal tragedy at this time. His younger brother, Hans-Joachim (known as Achim), born in 1916, was a lieutenant in the Luftwaffe and commander of a long-range reconnaissance aircraft; in October 1939, when the war was only a few weeks old, he was killed in an air battle over the sea near the Firth of Forth.

On the professional front, Kretschmer's ability was rated very highly, as indicated by the reports cited above. But he had as yet no prominent public profile; most people outside the Reichsmarine remained unaware of his exploits. This situation was soon to change. For some eight months (to be precise, from 3 August 1940 – the date of his first mention in an OKW report – to 25 April 1941, when the loss of his U-boat was announced), Kretschmer, labelled 'the wolf in the Atlantic', was national headline news in Germany. To become a household name in this way was somewhat ironic, given that previously, his characteristic reserve had earned him the nickname 'Silent Otto'. It was obvious that he could be a very useful tool for the Nazi propaganda machine; even today, his influence on naval history is still felt. Yet though other U-boat commanders, such as Prien [*q.v.*], Hartmann, Hardegen, Metzler, Korth, Schepke and Lüth, were willing to oblige, Kretschmer steadfastly refused to write the hoped-for propaganda book, aimed at young people and based on his great deeds. Similarly, he would not make propaganda speeches the way Bleichrodt, Hartmann, Hardegen, Lüth, Schepke and many others were prepared to do. Unlike them, he would not let himself be knowingly exploited. To have behaved otherwise would have been against his nature. This is a trait which, in conversation with him, is visible to this day. Kretschmer takes this view.

> The Weimar constitution placed a binding obligation on the Reichswehr to be non-political. Both active and passive voting rights were in abeyance. I regarded this clause in the constitution as absolutely correct for the armed forces of the Reich in the Weimar period. . . . But that did not stop some officers from recording their singularly loyal allegiance to the National Socialist leadership.

Even then, he was perfectly willing to make his own views known. During May Day ceremonies in Kiel in 1936, when he was still a sub-lieutenant, there seemed to him to be 'an excess of bowing and scraping on the part of senior naval officers'. He complained to the Commander of the Submarine School, and the complaint was 'a success!' The events which gave rise to it did not recur in later years.

Almost two years previously, just after the death of President von Hindenburg, a similar but altogether more dramatic event had taken place. Still wondering whether he was the only one present actually to notice, Kretschmer describes this as:

the most spectacular break with the Weimar constitution, a break which had set in train the erosion of a state based on the rule of law. The Wehrmacht swore a personal oath, a 'sacred oath', of allegiance to the Führer, Adolf Hitler. In constitutional terms, we had already sworn allegiance to the Weimar constitution. At that time I was a leading petty officer on the cruiser *Köln*. The swearing-in took place in the stern to the call of 'All hands on deck'; we were wearing our working clothes and there had been no prior notification, so actually we were taken by surprise. . . . Apart from me, nobody on board seemed very bothered by it.

In April 1940 Lieutenant-Commander Kretschmer took into service *U-99*, a Type VII-B boat. After a short period of training, it was attached to the 7th U-Boat Flotilla. In June 1940 he left Kiel for the first operation. This had to be aborted because the boat was mistakenly damaged by a naval aircraft from the German battleship *Scharnhorst*. During *U-99*'s second operation (June–July 1940), Kretschmer's activities in the North Channel and off Cape Finisterre resulted in seven merchant ships sunk, totalling 22,719 GRT. His return on this occasion was not to Germany but to the French base of Lorient – now, since the fall of France, German property – and here *U-99* was permanently attached to the 2nd U-Boat Flotilla.

On 3 August 1940 Kretschmer's achievements were first mentioned in a brief OKW report. 'In one long-distance voyage,' it said, 'a U-boat, captained by Lieutenant-Commander Kretschmer, sank seven armed enemy merchant ships, including three escort tankers, totalling 56,118 GRT. To date, this boat has sunk a total of 117,367 GRT as well as the British destroyer *Daring*.' Two days later, *U-99* returned again to Lorient from her third operation with yet more victories. Another four merchant vessels, totalling 32,345 GRT, had been sunk, and her twenty-eight-year-old commander was awarded the Ritterkreuz (Knight's Cross) of the Iron Cross, presented personally by the Commander-in-Chief of the Kriegsmarine, Grand Admiral Erich Raeder [*q.v.*]. As another source observed, Kretschmer 'owes his particular success, achieved in a very short space of time with his new boat, to his excellent ability, his unshakeable calm and his readiness to do battle. He also knows how to imbue his men with these qualities very quickly. A man above criticism, a rounded personality, able to make clear, independent decisions. Very quiet and reserved but an excellent and popular fellow officer.' In an interview, one of his men confirmed this, saying: 'His sang-froid . . . gave the entire crew on board a feeling of absolute security.'

Next month (September 1940) *U-99*'s fourth operation took place. Success followed success: Kretschmer's boat sank six ships, totalling 24,145 GRT. The operation was particularly notable because *U-99* was part of the first successful wolf-pack operation of World War Two, targeted against the convoys SC2 (fifty-three ships) and HX72 (forty-one ships).

On the basis of his experience at the front, Kretschmer was soon to develop his own, somewhat unorthodox methods – not always to the approval of his superiors. U-boat commanders had initially been instructed that the best torpedo range was 3,000 metres, and that torpedoes should be fired in fan-shaped salvoes to maximize the chances of hitting. However, combining a certain doggedness with outstanding tactical insight, Kretschmer developed completely novel ideas, though not necessarily with the blessing of the U-boat Commander-in-Chief, Admiral Karl Dönitz [*q.v.*]. Kretschmer was the first commander to surface his U-boat at night while shadowing a convoy escort. Penetrating the convoy itself, he waited until then to fire his torpedoes. He did not fire them from a distance safe for himself; he did not go in for firing fan-shaped spreads of torpedoes. Instead he fired them at the shortest range possible, and was guided by the maxim: 'One torpedo – one ship'. The technique was risky but extremely successful, and, as British authorities later acknowledged, extremely difficult to counter.

October 1940 brought *U-99*'s fifth operation. Working in the North Atlantic, to the west of the Hebrides on the Rockall Bank, it was no less a success than before: six ships, totalling 27,396 GRT, were sunk. The targets were in convoys SC7 (thirty ships) and HX79 (forty-nine ships). German weekly cinema newsreels filmed the triumphant return of *U-99* in company with *U-47* (Prien) and *U-100* (Schepke). The OKW report published three days prior to the release of the film reads: 'German U-boats sank . . . 31 enemy merchant ships with a total of 173,650 GRT. Of these, 26 ships were shot out of heavily defended convoys. Lieutenant-Commander Kretschmer's U-boat's share of these successes . . . was seven ships totalling 45,000 GRT.'

It will be noted that the figures of ships and tonnages do not tally – a point to which we shall return. *U-99*'s sixth operation was relatively short, lasting only from 30 October to 8 November 1940, but it was enormously successful: four large vessels were sunk, totalling 42,407 GRT. Two of the vessels were British armed merchant cruisers, *Laurentic* (18,724 GRT) and *Patroclus* (11,314 GRT). In this very tenacious attack Kretschmer used ten torpedoes, but, if he fell short of his own ideal of 'One torpedo – one ship', his superiors were not disappointed, and the operation became known as 'the oak-leaf trip'. The OKW report declared that 'with this success Lieutenant-Commander Kretschmer has achieved a total of 217,198 GRT sunk, and is thus the second U-boat captain to destroy more than 200,000 GRT'; the weekly newsreel again filmed the return of *U-99*; and on 13 November, in the Chancellery in Berlin, Hitler himself presented Kretschmer with the sixth oak leaf to the Ritterkreuz of the Iron Cross. In this context it is also worth mentioning that on 5 November

1940 Kretschmer's coxswain, Petersen, was the first non-officer in the navy to receive the Ritterkreuz.

With the approach of winter in November 1940, *U-99* was engaged in heavy weather conditions against convoys HX90, SC13 and OB252. The result was four ships sunk, with a total of 34,291 GRT. This, her seventh and penultimate operation, took place to the west of the North Channel. On 2 December 1940, using five torpedoes, Kretschmer sank the British armed merchant cruiser *Forfar* (16,402 GRT). He remains 'particularly proud' of this.

'I had to submerge in the face of an advancing destroyer,' he recalls, 'but I still continued to fire, having previously cleared the bridge. I got away across the enemy's bow, because I always set the firing pin on the nose of the torpedo in view of the unreliability of the firing mechanisms. The situation was similar to my single shot from *U-23* at HMS *Daring*. Here too I was operating on the "one torpedo, one ship" principle, though this time the distance was quite large and the target was only recognizable as a shadow in the pitch-black night.' *U-99*'s war log shows that the range was 3,600 metres – 'a huge distance at night', comments Kretschmer – and that Type G 7a torpedo, Number 6814 hit its target in two minutes fifty-nine seconds. At first Kretschmer thought he had missed, 'and was astonished when the destroyer did not attack me and when there was the noise of a detonation soon after. When I surfaced I realized that my torpedo really had scored a hit and that the target was an armed merchant cruiser whose engine had been put out of action by the hit. It had to be sunk before help from a destroyer arrived.'

'This officer', said the subsequent OKW report, 'has now sunk a total of 252,100 GRT and is the first submarine commander to sink more than 250,000 GRT.'

At that time, there were some very substantial differences between the OKW figures for success and the actual results. For some years now, interesting details about British counter-measures in radio and signals have been available. From time to time the Royal Navy was able to read and decode signals from the U-boat commanders. Out of the 329 pages in *U-99*'s war log, 191 list a total of over 1,500 signals, of which only about one hundred were transmitted from *U-99*. Kretschmer had a deep-seated dislike of sending signals (and, as a result, got into trouble with his superiors on more than one occasion). This dislike dated from 1932, when, as a young petty officer at naval college, he read Hector Bywater's book *Strange Intelligence*, a volume then little known in Germany, which indicated how one's own transmissions could be used against oneself by an enemy. Kretschmer was also unconvinced of the security of the German signals code M (Enigma), and suspected that his assessment of British abilities in this regard was more accurate than was that of the German naval leadership. He says himself, 'I thought that far too many signals were sent in the U-boat war.'

On 22 February 1941, after a long period in dock, *U-99* left Lorient for her eighth operation. It would be her last, and was, for the BdU, a major disaster. In a notable coincidence, Prien's boat (*U-47*) and Schepke's boat (*U-100*) were both lost in similar circumstances, that is, on the first voyage following lengthy repair work. When *U-99*'s fatal voyage began, all her officers, with the exception of the Leading Engineer and two petty officers, were new on board. But at first all went exceptionally well, even by *U-99*'s own standards. The boat attacked convoys OB290, OB292, OB293 and HX112 to the north-west of the North Channel and scored the best result of her career, sinking seven vessels with a total of 61,711 GRT. Then the disaster began to take shape. On 8 March, *U-47* was sunk with all hands – and her commander was the ace U-boat captain Günther Prien, with twenty-eight sinkings to his credit. Before then *U-47* and *U-99* had been in sight and speech contact; and nine days later, south-east of Iceland at approxi-mately 61°N 12°W, at 0334 on 17 March, *U-99* herself was sunk near convoy HX112.

She was sunk by a depth-charge attack carried out by the destroyer HMS *Walker* (Commander Donald Macintyre), which, only half an hour earlier, had sunk Schepke's *U-100*. *Walker* had located *U-99* through an over-hasty alarm submersion manoeuvre begun by a miscalculation of the situation by the U-boat's bridge watch. At the end of a highly dramatic action, marked on both sides by supremely professional seamanship, *Walker* was able to rescue *U-99*'s entire crew, with the exception of three men.

It is not surprising that Kretschmer still recalls these events vividly. 'The stern had already once sunk down because of leaking stern diving chambers, where the depth charges had hit, with the result that when the artillery attack ended, those members of the crew standing on the after deck (following my command of "All men out of the boat") were washed overboard – with the exception of Seaman No. 1, Boatsman Thoenes, who was tightening up the galley hatch and then held on tight to the net cutter even though he then went down with it as a result.' From the bridge, Kretschmer ordered an immediate Abandon Ship. Two officers 'were hauled on to the bridge through the green sea which was streaming into the boat through the tower hatch'. One had destroyed secret documents below deck; the other, who had been checking the engines, had quickly pumped air into diving chamber no. 1, which made the stern come up again. Kretschmer sent a message to HMS *Walker* in morse code: 'Captain to Captain: Please save my men drifting in your direction. I am sinking.' As Kretschmer remembers, 'Macintyre gave the order to turn on the backboard signal lights, to shine on the people in the water and took them on board over his scrambling net. Macintyre then came alongside to windward and we could see that he was making ready to lower a boat. In other words, there was the danger we might be boarded! Even though the water in the central part was well above the floorboards, we had to speed up the sinking of *U-99* by means of explosives.'

But the explosives store was jammed shut. An officer suggested that the air in diving chamber no. 1 should be vented again – only a small turn on a wheel would be needed. Kretschmer agreed; but the officer opened the vent more than necessary. As the stern began to sink rapidly, Kretschmer called him back. He did not reappear.

Kretschmer was now alone on the bridge with the waters rising around him. The boat sank away from under his feet. He did not swim directly to *Walker*; instead, first, he made sure there were none of his men left in the water. This was almost his undoing, because when he reached the scrambling net, the destroyer was starting to move ahead, and he was so chilled he was about to lose his grip. But his own bosun saw him from the British deck, and, with a British seaman, climbed down and pulled him on board.

Many U-boat officers, trained to regard themselves as an elite, were ardent Nazis, and Kretschmer's captors expected him to be one himself. Moreover, to maintain their authority in the very confined quarters of a U-boat, commanders – necessarily isolated in their role, yet in constant close contact with all their crew – often developed a habit of overweening arrogance. Yet Admiralty records of Kretschmer's interrogation show British surprise: 'The crew of *U-99* gave the impression of having attained a higher degree of efficiency than any other U-boat crew interrogated so far. For the first time there was no criticism of officers. On the contrary, a marked degree of loyalty and admiration for their captain was expressed by the men. He was less of a Nazi than had been assumed.' Recent conversations with British witnesses confirm this; he was seen as 'a young and obviously self-confident naval commander who bore himself, in the difficult conditions of recent captivity, with self-respect, modesty and courtesy'.

As an officer, Kretschmer himself 'consciously felt in the old Prussian tradition'. He had no fundamental objection to the swastika symbol,

> because, as a historian, I knew its original meaning, which had absolutely nothing to do with anti-Semitism. I also knew it as the symbol of the Finnish Air Force after the First World War. All the same, it annoyed me that, after 1933 [when Hitler came to power] you found it everywhere and anywhere, however inappropriate. And I regarded the swastika on the Iron Cross as particularly inappropriate. In the 1950s, when I was a member of the Honours Commission of the Federal Republic, I immediately argued for the oak leaf to be restored to the front of the Iron Cross and that is what happened. . . .

In wartime Germany, news of the loss of Prien, 'the bull of Scapa Flow' and one of the navy's most willing propagandists, was suppressed at first; but the loss of so many aces in such a short space of time could not be kept secret. 'The capture of Kretschmer and loss of *U-99*', said the British Admiralty interrogators, ' . . . is a serious blow to German morale and propaganda and an important victory for Britain over the U-boats.' So it was; and when the news broke in Germany that not only Schepke but also Kretschmer – the war's highest-scoring U-boat commander – had been lost, German papers responded with passionate flights of rhetoric, urging their readers to follow the example of the lost commanders. 'With sadness and pride, the nation kneels before these brave men of the U-boat arm, these men who have not returned from their mission against the enemy. The deployment of men demands sacrifices, brave deeds and burning heroism. . . . ' 'We know that every hole this war tears in our ranks is immediately closed, that other men are there to continue the fight against England with the same readiness for action. . . . ' 'No loss will prevent Germany from finishing the work started by men like Kretschmer and Schepke with ever greater vigour. . . . '

Much more was printed in the same bombastic vein. But to repeat it in detail would do Kretschmer a disservice; he never lent himself to the propaganda machine, and today the outpourings sound so overblown that they actually obscure the supreme calibre of his achievements. In the sixteen missions carried out by his two boats over the first eighteen months of the war, he spent 224 days at sea and sank the 1,375-ton destroyer HMS *Daring*, and forty-four merchant ships totalling 265,953 GRT. This gave him an average of 1,187.3 GRT sunk per day at sea. In both world wars only one man (Vice Admiral Lothar von Arnauld de la Perière, who did not fight at sea during the second war and died in February 1941) achieved a higher daily average; and even though Kretschmer's capture suddenly curtailed his U-boat career, no other U-boat commander in World War Two ever beat his record.

Kretschmer remained a captive for the rest of the war, held in Bowmanville Camp, Ontario. Even so, as far as the Naval High Command was concerned, he was still on the active list, and on 26 December 1941 he became the first U-boat commander to receive a fifth oak leaf 'with swords' – a notable added distinction – to his Knight's Cross. Despite his imprisonment, he too considered himself still firmly on the active list, and while in Bowmanville he devised a system, circumventing camp censorship, of transmitting intelligence back to Germany. This became so refined that he was able to arrange for a U- boat to rendezvous at the mouth of the St Lawrence river to pick up escaped prisoners. In the event, the prisoners were recaptured before they were picked up, but the U-boat did appear punctually. In both aspects, the episode was an appropriate conclusion to an outstanding wartime career.

Released from prison, 1947. Married Luise-Charlotte Mohnsen-Hinrichs, née Bruns (Doctor of Medicine), 1948. First President of the newly founded German Marine-Bund (Navy Federation); joined the Bundesmarine, 1955. Kapitän zur See, 1958; service in the USA, France, Britain, Belgium, Denmark, Norway, Greece, Portugal, the Netherlands and Turkey. Frau Dr Kretschmer launched U-1, first U-boat of the Bundesmarine, 1962. Kretschmer was promoted flotilla admiral in 1965 and from then until 1970 was Chief of NATO Staff to the Chief of Staff, Allied Naval Forces, Baltic Approaches. In 1966 the first reunion of the surviving crew members of U-99 took place; HMS Walker old hands were included later. In 1970, and at his own request, Admiral Kretschmer retired.

19

Commander

Günther Prien

German Navy

1908–1941

by
Dan van der Vat

GÜNTHER Prien, born near Leipzig to middle-class parents on 16 January 1908. Prien went to sea as a Merchant Navy cadet on a sailing ship, duly became an officer and took his master's ticket in January 1932. Unable to find work in the Depression, he drifted into the Nazi Party. He joined the navy as an officer-candidate in January 1933.

Prien went to the secretly resurgent submarine-arm and served as First Officer on U-26 off Spain during the Civil War. In autumn 1938 he was given command of U-47 and soon promoted to Kapitänleutnant. Thus when war came he had spent a year working up his boat and his all-volunteer crew into a skilled fighting unit.

The salient feature of the short but outstanding career of Günther Prien as a German submarine commander was his uncanny knack of always being in the forefront. He opened the war on Britain's seaborne commerce as the first skipper to sink a cargo-ship, and under Prize Rules at that. He was of course the first and only raider to penetrate Scapa Flow and thanks to that the first submariner to receive the Knight's Cross of the Iron Cross for sinking the battleship *Royal Oak*. He went on to be the first to qualify as an ace, the first to complain formally about the unreliability of German torpedoes, the first to sink five ships from a single convoy, the first to publish his 'memoirs'. And, when the end came, he was the first of the three aces caught in March 1941 in the earliest palpable victory of the Royal Navy against the U-boats. Finally he was the first and only submarine captain whose death the Supreme Command of the Wehrmacht suppressed for fear of demoralizing the German people.

These remarkable milestones in a wartime career of just eighteen months were not matched even by Otto Kretschmer [*q.v.*], in tonnage terms the leading ace of World War Two. And from what little is known for certain about Prien's character it seems more than likely that he would not have wished to be in the shoes of Fritz-Julius Lemp on the first day of the war at sea. The latter fired the first torpedo of World War Two from *U-30* – only to sink the passenger-liner RMS *Athenia* with heavy loss of life, in contravention of strict orders. He thus presented Germany with a reprise of the *Lusitania* crisis of 1917 on 3 September 1939, the opening day of hostilities against Britain.

The question of Prien's character is more complicated than his appalling 'memoir', *Mein Weg nach Scapa Flow* (Berlin, 1941, uncritically translated into English after the war as *I Sank the Royal Oak*), might lead us to believe. This is an issue which can usefully be addressed first. Richard Humble, for example, writes in *Undersea Warfare* that 'Prien was an enthusiastic Nazi, unlike most of his comrades.' But the indefatigable H. J. Weaver traced the ghostwriter of Prien's hastily produced, best-selling memoir while researching his *Nightmare at Scapa Flow*, a painstaking investigation of the anomalies in the various accounts of the sinking of HMS *Royal Oak*. Weaver concludes that Paul Weymar, the author conscripted to write *Mein Weg* on the strength of a few hours with Prien and his own hyperactive imagination, made 'a liar and a braggart' out of his subject. Weymar was horrified when he heard that his spatchcocked text, as severally embellished by the Wehrmacht Supreme Command and Goebbels' Propaganda Ministry, was being published un-altered and unannotated, complete with swastika on the cover, in England ten years after the war. He tried hard but failed to obstruct this event.

Prien's widow said he was very angry about his 'autobiography' and made many deletions and alterations which were simply ignored. She also said he loathed the circus atmosphere which surrounded him after the raid on Scapa. Weymar quoted Prien as saying about one of his sinkings: 'When I first saw the burning tanker in front of me and . . . the wretched hundreds of men perishing in this dome of flames, I felt like a murderer before the scene of his crime' (Weaver, Chapter IX). Neither this observation nor any other serious hint of doubt, remorse or mercy found its way into *Mein Weg*, a volume its real author described as intended for schoolboys.

On the other hand Prien did join the Nazis, like many another embittered, young, jobless German men, some months before they came to power; and he clearly managed to overcome his distaste for being lionized by the Nazi propaganda machine sufficiently to co-operate with it whenever required, even though he was to prove quite capable of challenging authority, even in Hitler's wartime Germany. His main value to the Nazi cause was arguably as a propaganda asset – at home, where his exploits were played up to bolster public morale, and abroad as a unique scourge upon the enemy. His role as underwater Teutonic knight, the 'Red Baron' of the North Atlantic, far outweighed the strategic worth of the superannuated battleship and thirty-one merchantmen he sent to the bottom in his brief but spectacularly destructive stewardship of *U-47*. We may therefore both take *Mein Weg nach Scapa Flow* with liberal pinches of salt and also agree that Prien was not untypical of his service, man for man and mark for mark by far the most successful arm of the Wehrmacht – ruthless, patriotic, but not the slavering Nazi the Royal Navy wrongly expected to find when it captured Kretschmer. There can be no doubting Prien's unsurpassed popularity among the German public – a fact which was to have bizarre consequences after his death, as will be seen.

Unterseeboot-47 was one of thirty-nine German boats which took up stations round the British Isles in the last two weeks of August 1939. *U-47* was a Type VII-B, constructed at the Germaniawerft in Kiel and commissioned in 1938, displacing 753 tons (857 submerged) and capable of 17.2 knots surfaced or eight underwater. The two dozen VII-B boats were slightly superior to the VII-C, soon to become the workhorse of the Atlantic campaign, in several respects. They had the edge in speed and could carry fourteen rather than eleven torpedoes for their five 21-inch tubes, four in the bow and one in the stern. *U-47* was 218 feet long, just over 20 feet across and drew 15 feet 5 inches surfaced (31 feet submerged). Her 108 tonnes of oil gave her an endurance of 6,500 nautical miles at twelve knots; underwater her batteries allowed ninety miles at four knots before recharging. Her other armament was one 8.8cm gun and one 2cm Flak. She carried a crew of forty-four officers and men under Kapitänleutnant (lieutenant-commander) Prien as captain and Oberleutnant-zur-See (lieutenant) Engelbert Endrass (later an ace himself in command of *U-48*) as first officer (first lieutenant or executive officer). *U-47* was ordered to patrol off the northern coast of Spain.

At breakfast-time on Tuesday, 5 September 1939, Prien himself sighted, in indifferent weather north-west of Spain, a small ship zigzagging on the horizon on an approaching course. *U-47* dived to await developments and was soon able to identify the vessel as the British steamer *Bosnia* (2,407 tons), sporting the black-tipped, red funnel of the Cunard Line. Surfacing astern and to one side of her, *U-47* fired a shot across her bows. *Bosnia* (Captain Walter Poole, RNR) put about and tried to run for it, drawing a second shot very close across the bow. The German wireless operator reported that the British cargo-ship was transmitting the 'sss' message saying she was under submarine attack, as prescribed by the Admiralty. Prien ordered a live round fired into the freighter amidships. *Bosnia* stoutly sailed on, stopping only after five more German shells had torn into her hull. A huge, thick column of bluish-yellow smoke poured up from the stricken ship's cargo of noxious sulphur. The British seamen began to take to their boats as the German lookouts sighted a wisp of smoke to the north-west. Keeping a sharp eye out for the oncoming second ship, the Germans began to rescue the crew of *Bosnia*. This was in full conformity with Prize Rules, which the U-boats were at this stage under strict orders to observe, Lemp notwithstanding: the regulations included ensuring the safety of passengers and crew before sinking their ship, which rather blunted the submarine's main weapon – surprise.

Prien gave one distressed British seaman a glass of brandy. The master meanwhile remained aboard the vessel, still punctiliously following Admiralty instructions on what to do in the presence of an enemy raider by burning his ship's papers even as she did her best to save him the trouble – by this time the unfortunate *Bosnia* was an inferno. Poole, a veteran of 'Q-ships' (disguised submarine-hunters) in World War One, finally dived over the side. When the approaching ship turned out to be the still neutral Norwegian SS *Eidanger*, Prien asked her captain to take on the British crew (of whom one had died, probably of exhaustion). *U-47* finally despatched *Bosnia* with a single torpedo, removing the evidence of her first attack, the first British cargo-ship sunk in the war. It had been a model encounter on both sides; sadly chivalry very soon became the exception rather than the rule. Prien and his crew sank SS *Rio Claro* (4,086 tons) on the 6th and SS *Gartavon* (1,777 tons) on the 7th, both British freighters, under Prize Rules in the same general area. The rest of *U-47*'s first war patrol was generally uneventful and the boat returned to Kiel on 15 September for replenishment and a minor refit.

As was to be the case with so many German moves on the various fronts of World War Two in Europe, the German commanders' first thought was to 'correct' the results of the great conflict of 1914–18. Commodore Karl Dönitz [*q.v.*], the Commander, Submarines, was no exception. Günther Prien divided his time ashore in Kiel between his young family (his wife Ingeborg and their two daughters) and attending to his boat and crew. Calling in at the submarine officers' mess on Sunday, 1 October, he was told that Dönitz wanted to see him at once. Like most people in such circumstances he wondered what he might have done wrong; his chief was a stern taskmaster who took an intense, almost intrusive interest in all his men and personally debriefed every skipper on his return from patrol. Prien found Dönitz in his 'plot' room poring over a chart of Scapa Flow, principal anchorage of the British Fleet in World War Two as it had been in the first war. There the Kaiser's interned High Seas Fleet scuttled itself at mid-summer 1919, because its admiral had been led to believe that hostilities were about to resume. There also, in November 1914 (Henning) and again in November 1918 (Emsmann), German submarines had been lost trying to penetrate the enemy's main base.

Like Admiral Erich Raeder [*q.v.*], the naval C-in-C, Dönitz, who would have liked 300 boats for a war against Britain, had been told that no such eventuality would arise before 1944. In September 1939 Germany had just fifty-seven operational U-boats and Dönitz was not having much success in the scramble for resources involving the army, the Luftwaffe and the rest of the navy now that war had broken out. The spectacular sinking of the aircraft carrier HMS *Courageous* by Otto Schuhart in *U-29* on 17 September brought praise, but neither the British nor the Germans could foresee the potential of carriers in the coming maritime struggle, and *Courageous* was the enemy's oldest. Thus the dashing coup had not brought the service the material reward its chief thought it deserved and knew it urgently needed. Dönitz was determined to avenge the frustrated navy he had served in 1914–18 and to seize Hitler's attention at the same time. He decided to risk one boat, and his favourite skipper, on a mission which, if successful, could yield a harvest in influence, morale and resources out of all proportion to such a small investment. He spelt out the hazards exhaustively to Günther Prien and gave him forty-eight hours to say yes or no, as he chose. Prien was back in twenty-four hours with a ringing yes, cheerfully volunteering his entire crew without giving them the choice that he had himself enjoyed.

U-47 slipped out of Kiel westward along the Kaiser Wilhelm Canal, linking the Baltic and the North Sea, at 10.00 a.m. on Sunday, 8 October. The boat passed out of the Elbe estuary into the open sea, submerging by day and surfacing only by night. Prien's plan, endorsed by Dönitz, was to make his attack on the night of Friday, 13 October, when there would be no moon and the fiendishly complex pattern of tides and currents around Scapa Flow would favour entry at about 11.30 p.m. GMT via the route carefully chosen by Dönitz.

Before the Churchill Causeway was built down the eastern side of the Flow later in the war in belated response to Prien's exploit, there were seven entrances to Scapa: one from the north-west between the islands of Mainland and Hoy, two from the Pentland Firth to the south and four from the east through a chain of islands and islets. The bulk of Mainland lies to the north. The gaps were defended by a ramshackle collection of blockships, patrol vessels, chains and cables, booms, nets and mines, much of it left over from the first war. Since then, little had been done to stiffen the defences, despite urgent recommendations to the Admiralty in the last months of peace. Air and anti-aircraft cover were abject; ships in the anchorage were expected to use their usually inadequate ack-ack not just to protect themselves, but also to cover targets on shore. Such was the main repository of His Majesty's Navy, guardian against invasion and chief instrument of British power, at the start of the second war with Germany in a quarter of a century.

Aerial reconnaissance ordered by Dönitz in the last days of September revealed that the northernmost entrance on the eastern side, Kirk Sound, between the mainland and the islet of Holm, was not fully barred by blockships and offered the best chance. The U-boat chief ordered further reconnaissance flights on 11 and 12 October; the latter reported the presence in the main fleet anchorage, north of Flotta Island and east of Cava and Fara, of one aircraft carrier, five capital ships and ten cruisers. The German Submarine Command war diary attributes the subsequent departure of most of these ships to the reconnaissance on two successive days, perhaps portending in British eyes a major bombing attack. The diary regrets the unintentional alerting of the enemy, which seemed to Dönitz almost to have gratuitously aborted Prien's dangerous mission in advance.

In fact the guilty party was the German naval command. Uninformed of Dönitz's initiative and itself not bothering to inform him, the Seekriegsleitung in Berlin had decided to trail its coat in the North Sea. This was mainly intended to divert attention from the pocket-battleships *Deutschland* and *Graf Spee* in the Atlantic, but also to lure the British Home Fleet into a trap. The formidable battle-cruiser *Gneisenau*, the light cruiser *Cöln* and nine fleet destroyers were ordered to sortie towards Norway on 7 October, just twenty-four hours before Prien sailed. If the British fell for it, they were to be attacked by air and with submarines directly controlled by the High Command (Dönitz was not in charge of all German boats). The Home Fleet duly left Scapa on the 8th in response to a sighting report from RAF Coastal Command.

The Home Fleet C-in-C, Admiral Sir Charles Forbes, was already known below decks as 'Wrong-Way Charlie' for having failed to sight the main units of the German fleet, let alone bring them to action, in six weeks of war. He upheld this unfair reputation on this occasion; but he had the sense to worry about the patchy security of his principal base and decided to disperse his force after the abortive hunt for the German group. Both sides had withdrawn by the evening of the 9th. Forbes sent some of his ships to Loch Ewe on the west coast of Scotland and others briefly to Scapa, which they reached on the 11th. Among them was *Royal Oak*, whose slow maximum speed of 21.5 knots had forced her to play 'tail-end Charlie' to the fleet in the brief hunt. She returned to her customary spot at the southern end of Scapa Bay in the north-eastern corner of the Flow, whence her guns could cover a radar station ashore. Due north of her as usual lay *Pegasus*, a 1914 seaplane-carrier of 6,900 tons. After the German reconnaissance on the 12th, the battle-cruiser *Repulse* left for dry dock at Rosyth, the carrier *Furious* for Loch Ewe and three cruisers for the Northern Patrol, covering the Atlantic exit of the North Sea. By the afternoon of the 13th the brand-new cruiser *Belfast* was the only other large operational ship in the entire Flow.

Before surfacing on the evening of the 12th to get an exact bearing from shore, Prien exhibited a touch of gallows humour when he gave his crew, puzzled by the elaborate circumspection of the voyage so far, their first intimation of the boat's mission. Anyone who did not wish to come along, he said, was free to leave now. His war diary (narrative log) proudly notes that the visual bearing showed his dead reckoning to have been less than two miles out. At 4.37 a.m. GMT on the 13th *U-47* once again eased gently some 300 feet to the bottom and Prien allowed most of his men to rest all day until 4 p.m. Then after 'breakfast', preparations for the raid continued, not forgetting the explosive charges placed round the boat in case it became necessary to scuttle. Another meal was served after surfacing at 7.15 pm, whereupon the stealthy approach to Kirk Sound began.

In the historic present too often favoured by less gifted exponents of the German language for special occasions, Prien noted in his log:

> Everything goes according to plan until [11.07 p.m. GMT] when we have to dive for a steamer just before Rose Ness . . . Surfaced again at [11.31] and run into Holm Sound. Current running inward. . . . It now

pays off that I have thoroughly learned the chart beforehand as the passage [of Kirk Sound] proceeds at an incredible speed. . . . The next moment the boat is seized by the current and turned to starboard. Simultaneously the anchor-chain of the northerly blockship is recognized ahead at an angle of forty-five degrees. . . . the boat turns very slowly, touches bottom. The previously flooded diving-tanks are blown, the boat turns, turns further. The stern still nudges the anchor-chain, [the] boat is free, is wrenched around to port and lets herself be brought back on course only by hard, swift measures but: we are in Scapa Flow!!!

According to the log it was now 0027 on the morning of 14 October.

The unpredictable Northern Lights (*aurora borealis*) more than made up for the lack of moonlight. They enabled Prien to see that the main anchorage to his south-west was apparently devoid of worthwhile targets. He therefore turned to run northward up the eastern side of the Flow, close to the islands. To the north he thought he discerned two capital ships: the battleship *Royal Oak* and behind her the battle-cruiser *Repulse* (32,000 tons – actually *Pegasus*, whose high side, flat aircraft-deck and seaplane-hoist must have been confused with the long nose and forward turret of the *Repulse*-class. By the time Prien fired his torpedoes, the Northern Lights had gone out). He ordered all four forward tubes fired in succession at 3,000 metres; number four jammed. One of the three launched exploded after about 210 seconds. He turned and fired his single stern tube (to no discernible effect) while the three operable forward tubes were reloaded; all three of his final salvo exploded mightily in quick succession after less than three minutes.

As it is not controversial, we may quote the following purple passage from *Mein Weg nach Scapa Flow*:

Then there occurs something that nobody [could] imagine, which nobody who had seen it would ever forget as long as he lived. Over there, a curtain of water rises. It is as if the sea is suddenly standing up. Dull thumps sound rapidly in succession, like an artillery barrage in a battle, and grow together into a single, earsplitting crash – bursts of flame surge up, blue, yellow, red. The sky vanishes behind this hellish firework [display]. Black shadows fly like giant birds through the flames, falling with a splash into the water. Fountains metres high spring up where they fall. They are huge fragments from the masts, the bridge, the funnels. We must have made a direct hit on a magazine and this time the death-dealing ammunition tore up the body of its own ship. . . .

I call below: 'She's finished!'

Seconds of silence. And then a yelling, a single, animal cry in which the frightful tension of the past twenty-four hours released itself. A cry as if the boat, this great steel beast, were itself screaming. 'Silence!' I yelled – and the boat was still.

The Germans got out the same way as they had come in, undetected and unaffected by the British search which eventually got under way (and was not given up until the 22nd). *U-47* was well clear within an hour of the last explosion.

The first torpedo to detonate struck *Royal Oak* on the starboard bow, blowing a hole some fifty feet wide and three plates deep above the waterline and starting one more plate below. A dull, hollow crump rocked the 29,150-ton ship, a veteran of the Battle of Jutland in 1916, at about 1.04 a.m. and her anchor-chains ran out with a roar. There was no injury and no panic. Captain William Benn RN eventually concluded after an inspection that there had been a spontaneous explosion in the inflammable store forward and ordered damage-control measures. The wound looked far worse than it was. Some members of the 1,257 men aboard thought it was an aerial bomb and took shelter below the old battleship's armoured deck, a fact which tragically increased the eventual loss of life.

The three torpedoes which struck the ship's vitals in quick succession at 1.16 set off a main magazine and tore her apart. She turned turtle and sank in thirteen minutes. Captain Benn was blown overboard and survived. Rear Admiral H. E. C. Blagrove, the divisional flag officer, refused a lifebelt and helped others to safety before going down with the ship. A total of 424 men were saved; the final death toll was 833. A Board of Inquiry chaired by Admiral the Hon. Sir Reginald Aylmer Ranfurly Plunkett-Ernle-Erle-Drax, KCB, DSO, RN, sat at Thurso from 18 to 24 October and came to the unexceptionable conclusion that *Royal Oak* had been sunk by submarine torpedo attack. It recommended that the gaps in the defences be closed forthwith. Ironically the elderly SS *Neuchatel* crept into the Flow on the night of 14–15 October, just when Prien had surfaced to report 'mission accomplished as ordered': her role was to close the gap in Kirk Sound in conformity with an order several weeks old. Admiral Sir Wilfred French, commanding Orkney and Shetland, was made scapegoat and transferred. As First Lord of the Admiralty, Churchill had the grace to describe Prien's devastatingly embarrassing stroke to Parliament as a 'remarkable exploit of professional skill and daring'. It was the greatest naval tweak of the lion's tail since the Dutch Admiral de Ruyter stole Charles II's flagship from the River Medway in 1667. Such was its significance, no more and no less.

U-47 arrived unscathed at Wilhelmshaven, the main German North Sea base, at 11.44 a.m. on 17 October. Raeder and Dönitz (the latter already promoted rear admiral on the strength of Prien's success) were on the quay to award Prien the Iron Cross 1st Class and his entire crew the 2nd Class. They went on to Kiel for fresh uniforms and were then flown to Berlin to meet Hitler, who had already ordered an immediate escalation of the submarine war (but without as yet willing the means). The men of *U-47* were driven triumphally in open cars through wildly cheering crowds along the streets of Berlin to the Chancellery, where Hitler invested Prien with the Knight's

Cross. The associated radio interview and press conference were notable for the restraint shown by Prien, the instant national hero. For him a tumultuous day ended in a visit to the theatre with Dr Goebbels, already revelling in the propaganda harvest from *U-47*'s exploit.

Between the Scapa raid and the Norwegian campaign of spring 1940 *U-47*, still sporting the now famous charging bull on her conning-tower (Prien was henceforward known as 'the Bull of Scapa Flow'), sank just four ships in outer British waters. The U-boats were redeployed to cover the German seizure of Denmark and Norway. In mid-April Prien saw 'a wall of ships' – British men-of-war and transports – through his periscope, fired four torpedoes while submerged and missed the biggest target he ever saw. So he surfaced and fired four more, which also missed; one hit a distant rock and exploded, forcing him to withdraw. While doing so he sighted the battleship *Warspite* and fired two more at her. One went off too soon, the other too late and destroyers hunted *U-47* for hours. The great German torpedo crisis had come to a head.

It was to be two years before Germany had a fully reliable torpedo. Meanwhile staff officers arrogantly blamed nervous or inexperienced commanders for failing to follow proper firing procedure. Such Germans were as unable to accept that their equipment could be faulty as they were incapable of imagining that their ciphers could be broken: human error was the only possibility. This did not wash with someone of Prien's repute and he wrote a blistering report to Dönitz on his hair-raising Norwegian experience which ended with the words: 'I cannot again be expected to fight with a dummy rifle.' Dönitz gloomily wrote in his war diary: 'The boats are thus practically without a weapon.' He immediately launched an inquiry and eventually a vice admiral and two other officers were court-martialled, sentenced to six months each – and then allowed to return to armament work, merciful indeed in Hitler's Reich. The story of Prien's verbal torpedo reached a surprisingly wide audience by word of mouth.

None of this prevented Prien from claiming early in July 1940 a total of 66,600 tons sunk, thanks largely to a patrol unprecedented for its destructiveness in the war thus far. Among the eight victims, however, was SS *Arandora Star*, a British liner of 15,501 tons. Prien expended the last torpedo of his patrol on her on 2 July 1940 and made off without waiting to register the full effect. The days of warning shots and Prize Rules were already long gone. She was carrying 1,250 enemy aliens, mostly Italian though some were German, from Britain to internment in Canada, as well as 254 army guards and 174 crew; 821 people died. Prien's reaction on learning what he had done apparently went unrecorded. He was awarded the oak leaves to his Knight's Cross for thus becoming the first ace of the war, with more than 50,000 tons to his name.

By the end of February, *U-47* under her only captain had accounted for 173,961 gross registered tons (post-war corrected figure) of merchant shipping sunk, 11,179 tons shared with other submarines and 8,106 damaged – plus *Royal Oak*.

On her last patrol in February/March 1941, *U-47* damaged one and sank four ships of convoy OB290, heading west to the south of Iceland. Prien was in the van once again, opening Dönitz's spring offensive; and soon after attacking OB290 he sighted and reported OB293, asking for reinforcements to join him in a wolf-pack assault. Three boats came and a fierce battle, unlike any in the war hitherto, developed round the convoy as Allied escorts trained to new standards of teamwork took on a pack of Germany's finest submariners – and won.

Senior Officer, Escort, was Commander James Rowland RN in HMS *Wolverine*, supported by another destroyer, *Verity*, and two corvettes. They had trained as a group and when their convoy came under skilled and fierce attack, two submarines were soon detected and relentlessly depth charged for five hours; one was sunk. During the night of 7–8 March in a rainstorm, Prien was still doggedly in pursuit, undeterred by the aggressiveness of the escort; he even called for more reinforcements to continue harrying OB293. Just before 1 a.m., *Wolverine* spotted *U-47* only yards away: Rowland could hear her engines and smell the diesel fumes of her exhaust. As the boat dived, *Verity* fired a starshell and the two destroyers dropped patterns of ten depth charges. Three minutes later, oil came to the surface; then a hydrophone operator heard from underwater 'a loud clattering sound like crockery breaking'. Almost at once *U-47* briefly surfaced close by *Wolverine* and as quickly vanished, as if out of control. The destroyer turned sharply and dropped one more pattern – with an effect unmatched before or since. Those on *Wolverine*'s heaving deck and bridge looked down and saw an unearthly orange fireball in the deep; some swore it burned for ten seconds, others that the flames briefly broke the surface. Though the British did not then know their victim's name, it was a truly Wagnerian end for one of Dönitz's 'grey wolves'. In all, the Royal Navy destroyed five boats in the North Atlantic in fifteen days, three commanded by aces, in the greatest counter-blow against the U-boats so far.

It was the German habit not to announce for some time that U-boats were missing. They observed wireless silence whenever they could, for a week at a time or even longer in quiet periods. But it was five weeks before the High Command admitted on 25 April to the loss of the boats commanded by the aces Joachim Schepke (killed) and Kretschmer (captured). Prien's death however was suppressed for eleven weeks. The SD, the security and intelligence branch of the SS, took regular, secret soundings of German opinion and reported on 28 April that people were worried about the absence of Prien's name for so long from the daily Wehrmacht bulletin. It was only on 23 May that his presumed loss was finally announced.

But for many ordinary Germans Prien lived on. A story went the rounds to the effect that he and his entire crew had been spirited away to a concentration camp for insubordination, a rumour embellished by the true tale of Prien's torpedo revolt and word of a political mutiny on *U-47* (false). The rumours outlived the war. Liberated prisoners claimed to have sighted Prien in their concentration camp at Torgau on the Elbe early in 1945 and even to have seen the record of a court-martial of him and his crew. It was all without foundation. It amounted to the secular canonization of a popular war-hero without equal in the bleak and bloody history of the Third Reich.

Select Bibliography

File ADM 199/158, Public Record Office, Kew, Richmond, Surrey: Board of Enquiry into the Loss of HMS *Royal Oak*.

Böddeker, Günter, *Die Boote im Netz* (Bergisch Gladbach, 1983).

Gröner, Erich, *Die Schiffe der deutschen Kriegsmarine und Luftwaffe 1939–45 und ihr Verbleib*, 8th edn (Munich, 1976).

Humble, Richard, *Undersea Warfare* (Birmingham, 1981).

Lenton, H. T. and Colledge, J. J., *Warships of World War II* 2nd edn (1973, reprinted London, 1980).

Prien, Günther, *Mein Weg nach Scapa Flow* (Berlin, 1941). Translated as *I Sank the Royal Oak* (London 1954).

Rohwer, Jürgen, *Axis Submarine Successes, 1939–1945* (Cambridge, 1983).

van der Vat, Dan, *The Atlantic Campaign* (London, 1988).

Weaver, H. J., *Nightmare at Scapa Flow* (Malvern, Worcester, 1980).

Wistrich, Robert, *Wer war Wer im Dritten Reich* (Munich, 1983).

20

Admiral

Charles Andrews Lockwood Jr
United States Navy

1890–1967

by
Edward L. Beach

*B*ORN *in Virginia, USA, 6 May 1890; graduated US Naval Academy, 1912.
Served in USS* Arkansas *(BB-33) until 1914, thence ordered to Manila in
the Philippines for duty in Asiatic Fleet, where entered submarine service. 'Detail
card' thenceforth held by 'submarine desk' in Bureau of Navigation (later Bureau
of Personnel), and sea duty assignments were associated with submarines. Commanded antique submarines A-2, B-1, G-1 and after World War One ex-
German U-boat* UC-97. *His experience in these old boats combined with his own
propensities as he gained seniority, and he became known as a 'submariner's
submariner', full of innovative ideas. Then came World War Two.*

'Those splendid ships – lost in the first scrap ... and after all the warnings
that have gone out!! We just stand around in groups and mourn.' On 8
December 1941, the day after hearing the dreadful news of Pearl Harbor,
Captain Charles Lockwood, US Naval Attaché in London, wrote these
lamenting words to his wife, herself a 'navy junior' well acquainted, through
father and husband, with those very ships and many of their personnel. His
main interest, however, was in the undersea battle then going on. During
the previous decade, while new war clouds were gathering once again over
Europe, Lockwood had been prominent among the American submarine
officers campaigning for long-range boats suitable for Pacific Ocean service, and for increased appreciation of submarine potential in general. Of
all people, these were the least surprised when for the second time in two
decades World War Two saw Great Britain – the United States' primary
ally in Europe, the nation holding most of America's ties of blood and
history – again at the mercy of German U-boats. Once again, the entire

island nation of millions of people lay prostrate before a few thousand submariners.

As US Naval Attaché in London, Lockwood's duties included passing along full and accurate information of the effect of the German submarine campaign upon England. He also served as one of the conduits by which President Roosevelt and Prime Minister Churchill maintained their voluminous correspondence during those terrible days. He had arrived there early in 1941, and there he sat in December on the sidelines as the war for which he had been training all his adult life went suddenly into full swing. Decorously, in all the ways open to him, he began begging for duty with the submarine combat forces, but it was months before anyone heeded his increasingly desperate pleas.

A year later, however, and for the remainder of World War Two, Lockwood was ComSubPac – Commander Submarine Force Pacific Fleet – in charge of the major portion of America's submarine war against Japan. His was the responsibility for sending those young men in their 'fleet submarines' to invade Japanese waters, for providing them with sustenance, weapons, instructions, intelligence, everything they might need in the desperate war they were waging. The responsibility included selection of the men, especially their officers, and most particularly the young submarine skippers. This duty he performed with kindness and generosity of spirit, exercising command in a gentle way so that everyone in the submarine force knew he was one of them, felt for them, was doing everything he knew how to do to help them fight the war better, would watch out for them and fight their rearguard actions for them. Often he complained about the timing of fate that put him behind a desk in a bureaucratic position while younger men, with better submarines than he had grown up with (new submarines that he had helped conceive and design), fought the war for which he had been trained. To the men of the US Submarine Force he will always be remembered simply as 'Uncle Charlie'.

Even today, the world of submarines and submariners is a secluded world, visited by most people only in imagination. I am proud to have been a member of it, and it was my good fortune and privilege to have had some of my time overlap with Charles Lockwood: I was able to count him not only as a respected and admired senior officer, but also, even then, and to a continually increasing degree as we both grew in years, as a valued personal friend. For all these reasons I think it is worthwhile in this chapter to go back long before Pearl Harbor to trace Uncle Charlie's earlier life in some detail. Perhaps this will help it become clear why we US submarine officers of World War Two held him in such high regard. He fought, and won, vital battles on our behalf; not against the Japanese, but against a hidebound naval bureaucracy in Washington DC. This he was able to do because, from his own long experience in submarines, he knew so personally the problems we were facing. We knew that he knew, for, best of all, he was one of us. Of that there was never any doubt.

Like nearly all US naval officers of his time, Charles Lockwood attended the US Naval Academy at Annapolis, Maryland, from which my father and I also graduated, and all three of us claim a place in the ranks of the men in blue uniforms who have fought our country's battles on the sea. The navy was small in the old days. It is much bigger now, with more sweeping responsibilities, but at heart it is still a grand brotherhood, fired by love of country and common contest against the vagaries of the sea and the violence of the enemy. There were only 155 new ensigns in 1912, all of them new graduates of Annapolis, and Charlie Lockwood knew all his classmates well. (My father's class graduated thirty-five members in 1888, and both he and Lockwood had a great advantage over me, for fifty-one years later mine had 581. Another half century, and today's graduating classes number more than a thousand.)

I share another distinction with Lockwood, in that although submarine duty has always been a volunteer service, he and I were both drafted into it against our will, tried unsuccessfully to avoid the orders and discovered after a very short time 'in the boats' that we loved it. In his case, two years after graduation from Annapolis he applied for duty in the Asiatic Fleet, travelled to the headquarters in Manila, and found himself ordered without ceremony as the only officer, and in command, of the ten-year-old but already long-outmoded submarine *A-2*. As implied by its name, the *A-2* was the second submarine of that class in service in the US Navy. (She was actually our navy's fourth submarine, the first two being the 1900 *Holland* herself, named after her inventor, and her improved but less successful successor, the *Fulton*, named after an even earlier submarine inventor.) Sixty-four feet in length and slightly over 100 tons total displacement, built by the Holland Torpedo Boat Company, *A-1* and six sister submarines had been brought to Manila as deck cargo on board freighters. These primitive '*A*-boats' were classed as 'harbour defence vessels', had crews of seven men and one officer, and had a cruising range of only a few hundred miles. In practice, therefore, they confined their operations to Manila Bay and its vicinity. Except for the submarine *Holland* that he had visited as a midshipman, Lockwood had never before set foot aboard such a craft. Now he was skipper of the *A-2*, and his first duty was to qualify himself for the job. Wholeheartedly he threw himself into the effort, and in the process another feature of his character came forward.

In his own personal make-up, Lockwood loved the physical challenges of the outdoors: hunting, fishing, hiking. The undersea was as different from this as it could possibly be, and it was probably psychologically apt that the very dissimilar characteristics of the mountainous country of the Philippines should have posed a powerful attraction for him. Being cramped up with a few others in a tiny submersible boat, at great risk all the time, was to him every bit as fascinating as (and by far a greater challenge than) the wide open out-of-doors. Yet, spending much of each day cooped up in that eggshell of a boat, both physically and mentally he and like-oriented submariners found an irresistible compensatory lure in the wilderness. His tales of those early days contain many references to the joys of camping out in the cool green mountains surrounding hot and humid Manila.

At the same time, as with all submariners, the boats became his life. He became adept, for example, at paying more than usual attention to some of his less used senses. That of smell is an example. Petrol vapour anaesthetizes the sense of smell before it does anything else. This means that even a tiny petrol leak in a confined space can build to an explosive gaseous mixture without detection.

The *A-2* carried a petrol engine for use while surfaced, and with the engine running and the ventilation system rigged and operating, petrol vapour could not normally accumulate to dangerous levels. But with the boat sealed for submergence, a few teaspoons of petrol leaking in an unnoticed spot could be menacing. After eliminating the natural warning of smell, the vapours insidiously become intoxicating, destroying one's natural cautionary instincts at the same time as they build up to an acute fire hazard. By far the greatest number of early submarine accidents had petrol vapour as the root cause. Thus all early submariners learned that inability to smell normal odours must be taken as an important danger signal, for soon a crew's normal discipline will also disappear and an electric spark, as from a carelessly handled motor rheostat, will produce a disastrous explosion.

Another sense Lockwood developed was an acute feeling of pitch, as distinguished from roll. Surface ships operate in only two planes. Pitching in a seaway is rarely dangerous to them, while rolling heavily from side to side may become a matter of concern. The opposite is true of submarines; being very low in the water, rolling from side to side is not a frequent problem, but undue inclination of only a few degrees by bow or stern may be the precursor of radical difficulty in fore-and-aft trim. (Excessive fluids seeking the low point may cause a submerged submarine literally to upend. During the US Civil War, it was insufficient understanding of this that sank the Confederate submarine *Hunley* three times during her trials.)

Submariners of the early years of the twentieth century developed a special sense of the right and wrong about how their particular sub behaved under all circumstances, and it is still a proud boast, occasionally heard, that a true submariner 'could dive and surface the boat while sound asleep in his bunk' – by which was meant that he would subconsciously check off each of the many noises and phenomena (like slightly increased air pressure) that take place during such evolutions. Anything out of the ordinary sequence would be cause for alarm.

One of the desirable features of a small organization, as the US Navy and its Submarine Force were in 1914, is the intimate familiarity that develops among its members. Admiral Lockwood's memoirs, published in 1967, are studded with names and descriptions of nearly all the submariners of these early days, most of whom served with distinction in World War Two and are still recalled with pride and nostalgia. Foremost among them was Lieutenant Chester W.

Nimitz [*q.v.*], later one of the principal architects of the defeat of Japan. As this is written, fifty years after the close of that awful conflict, the name 'Nimitz' graces one of our first-line aircraft carriers and still evokes reverence for the man. But there were other submariners, too, and to this small fraternity who followed Nimitz, and later Lockwood, fell much of the prosecution of the greatest naval war in history.

Two years out of the US Naval Academy, aged twenty-four years and commander of the old submarine *A-2*, Lockwood gained experience rapidly. As his reminiscences show, the 'old navy', especially the US Asiatic Fleet, had more than its share of interesting, sometimes hilarious, occurrences, usually due to its ancient ships and antiquated equipment. Submarines and aircraft were the new things, however, and despite battle-line die-hards who still prepared for – and in a nearly religious way expected – the climactic fleet action between two columns of great ships, naval aviators were beginning to realize they could reach much further and more accurately with a bomb, and that as a result, no matter how powerful or how well served the battleship's main battery, its big guns were no longer relevant.

In a similar way, submariners knew that a torpedo below the waterline could sink any ship. Although Lockwood's 'boat' was already a museum piece because of the leaps being made in submarine development, he and all the other submariners were filled with the heady knowledge that they, like the aviators, were the spearpoints of naval advance. Even the ancient and crude *A-2* could have had a decisive effect on any naval battle fought in history to that date. The much revered Admiral Dewey himself reportedly said that had there been a single submarine in the Spanish fleet, only sixteen years earlier, he could not have risked the Battle of Manila Bay. Ensign Charles Lockwood and his comrades gloried in their awareness that this was so.

Under the impetus of World War One, which began in Europe the same year Lockwood became commander of the *A-2*, ferment and change reached new peaks so far as submarines were concerned, and submarine potential as a result became indelibly fixed in the thinking of all navies. The war was hardly a month old when Germany's *U-9*, displacing 450 tons and with a crew of only twenty-six men, in the space of an hour and a half sank three great 12,000-ton British cruisers and cost England the lives of 1,400 crewmen. During the course of that war – and in spite of the acknowledged power of the British navy – German submarines (30,000 men altogether and comprising at most about fifty effective boats at any one time) nearly defeated Great Britain. The unpalatable effectiveness of the submarine was lost on no one.

Lockwood, now promoted to junior-grade lieutenant, was skipper of several different submarines during this period. For a time he was division commander of his group of antiques in Manila, and shortly after US entry in the war was ordered to New London, to the newly established submarine base there, and in command of the Simon Lake-designed *G-1*.

The *G-1* was not suited to war service, and Lockwood envied his more fortunate submarine comrades who had better boats and were sent to European waters. After the war, however, he was lucky enough to be sent across the Atlantic to bring back *UC-97*, a surrendered German submarine. He records that after they had learned to understand the German gauges and instructions, he and his prize-crew grew to like the efficient craft assigned to them, and were sorry finally to have to relinquish her to be sunk as a target. Prior to this, of course, all possible information had been extracted from her for the benefit of our own submarine designers and her American skipper. His last submarine command, the brand-new and handsome *V-3*, was commissioned in 1926. (The pace of submarine development and the rapid sequence of design improvements is shown by the speed with which we raced through the alphabet during those early years, skipping only the building of a '*U*'-class.) The *V-3*, later called *Bonita*, was six times the length of the old *A-2*, and more than twenty times her displacement. At some 350 feet in length overall and some 2,000 tons, she was a full-fledged ship, a major war vessel, and was so recognized; but the submarine fraternity had got into the habit of calling their craft 'boats', and a boat she remained.

This anachronistic habit of thought and nomenclature persists even now among old submariners, even though the crew of the nuclear-powered *Nautilus* – with the full support of by-then-retired Vice Admiral Lockwood – referred to their own marvellous boat as a ship, and the follow-on *Triton* of round-the-world renown made it official with a ship's order to that effect. Now that the huge Trident-class submarines, as big as World War One battleships and packing ten thousand times the destructive power, are a fact of life, 'ships' they are and 'ships' they are commonly called. In official US Navy parlance, they are designated as 'major commands', and their skippers are full-fledged captains, four-stripers. The term 'boat', no longer appropriate, has been relegated at last to affectionate memory of old times.

But it would not be correct to argue that the term 'boat' is merely an outgrown routine appellation, or that Lockwood or any of his contemporaries during those early submarine days saw it as such. 'Boat' is expressive of fond familiarity growing from the days when submarines were indeed simple little boats, albeit capable of something no other war vessels could do. The tradition then was that one 'knew one's boat', in ways no surface-ship sailor could, or might even aspire to. Life or death in even the simplest manoeuvres almost always hung directly on how well everyone in a submarine knew everything about what all other crew-members had to do. Everyone's job, in this largest sense, was everyone else's business. A bonded brotherliness thus existed in the submarine crew that occurred nowhere else in the navy.

This sense of togetherness was a driving force in Lockwood's entire life, a compound, naturally enough, of his own propensities for fellowship with men whom he commanded. It was a facet of his personal leadership style that never left him. All submariners of that period felt the bonding of the boat culture, though their individual personalities applied it in different ways, but in Charlie

Lockwood, from ensign to vice admiral, the aphorism reached its highest development. He served in, and was of, the boats all his life, and all the members of that small subculture of the larger navy society loved him for it. He became, in time, the submarine father-figure.

The between-wars years were the halcyon days. The *V-3*, or *Bonita*, must have seemed – to an outsider – the answer to submariners' dreams. Streamlined and slinky, as a submarine should be, dramatically beautiful to look at (on the surface at least), she seemed every inch the sea-going, submersible, fighting ship. Nevertheless, in spite of their apparent promise, these first three 'V-boats' of the US Navy were not successful, the strenuous efforts of a succession of dedicated commanding officers notwithstanding. The three big sister ships were simply not able to fulfil designed operational specifications. They looked the part, but that was all. What they did do, and well, although one might argue it was the expensive way, was to provide a platform from which Lockwood and the other commanding officers could propose improvements – and this the skippers did, with gusto. Charles Lockwood's days in the old *A-2*, *B-1*, *G-1* and the German prize-of-war, the *UC-97*, in which he had had personal experience with the most basic practical aspects of how to operate an underwater ship, now stood him in excellent stead, along with his direct first-hand observation of *Bonita*'s deficiencies. Many were the design modifications he by consequence advocated. The submarine organization being the small, closely knit group that it was, every one of his suggestions received a careful hearing, and nearly all of them were adopted. Most were only logical, but the point was that even to the oldest designer submarines were a new field.

In the last month of 1928, Lockwood's time in command of submarines came to an end. He was then thirty-eight years old and had commanded a total of eight submarines, plus several incidental, mostly old and tired, Asiatic Fleet surface ships. He married at the relatively elderly age of forty, having, in his own words, believed until then that a life dedicated to the often recalcitrant ships that went under the sea did not mix well with marriage and family responsibilities. Alternate shore duty and surface-ship sea duty became his lot for the next few years; then the submarines reclaimed him to be a submarine division commander once again, this time of new and modern 'fleet' submarines with *Bonita*'s lamentable faults corrected.

The mid-1930s were splendid years for US Navy submariners. Once the early development had been done, the inevitable growing pains overcome, the trained officers who were its principal product found a ready reception for the new ideas with which they were all filled. New and improved submarine boats were being designed on a nearly continuous basis. Imaginative ideas were flowing for exercises, for improving fire control and torpedo accuracy, for building faster, longer-ranged boats able to dive deeper and carry more torpedoes, for better habitability in a dozen cumulatively important ways. A Submarine Officers' Conference had been established, including submariners across the board from all pertinent parts of the Navy Department, and this active group met often. Lockwood, as division commander of brand-new submarines in San Diego, found himself frequently back in Washington and, willy-nilly, in the forefront of the discussions. His background of information on the more primitive submarines of his early service provided a ready store of enterprising ideas for the new ones, and soon he found himself detached from his division and ordered to Washington as the new chairman of the Submarine Conference. From here, early in 1941, he went to London, where he was at the time of the attack on Pearl Harbor, beginning his campaign to return to sea.

It was not until well into 1942 that the sought-for orders finally arrived. Captain Charles Lockwood, US Naval Attaché in London, was selected for the rank of rear admiral, detached from duties at the Embassy and directed to proceed to Perth, in Western Australia. There he was to report as Commander, US Submarine Forces, South-west Pacific, with operational control of Allied submarines based in Fremantle, Perth's seaport city at the mouth of the Black Swan river. He arrived at his new post just before the Battle of Midway took place. At that distance, the great significance of Midway was somewhat attenuated, but it was clear that the war had entered a new phase. More to the submariner's pressing interest was the war-fighting potential of the boats for which he was responsible. The new fleet submarines were exactly what Lockwood had been advocating during all those Submarine Conference years in San Diego and Washington. The battle between the officers who favoured small submarines (like the Atlantic-oriented German boats that were doing such damage to England) and those who wanted bigger, longer-ranged 'fleet submarines', better suited to the Pacific, had been won by the fleet-boat proponents. Now, in Pearl Harbor and bases in Australia, that decision was vindicated by the distances the submarines had to travel and the time they were nevertheless able to spend on station. Officers and crews of the weatherbeaten boats coming back after two months at sea on patrol were high in praise for the performance and habitability of their ships.

Disquieting, on the other hand, were numerous indignant reports of torpedo deficiencies that were also coming Lockwood's way. Perhaps there will someday be a careful study of the problem and how it came to be, but it was long ago, and there are more pressing matters. However, to any wartime submariner of the US Navy, now benefiting from 100 per cent hindsight, the torpedo situation during the first half of the war was a national disgrace, and the negligent perpetrators responsible should have been severely punished.

More to the point, today, is the care being taken with the much more potent weapons of the nuclear age, in which total testing is the mandatory requirement. One hopes (and believes) the lesson of our World War Two torpedo fiasco, which rendered nearly useless the primary weapon of one of the most important branches of the US naval service, has been well learned. In 1942 our Bureau of Ordnance could not, or would not, believe the evidence coming in from the submarines on patrol: that there was something wrong. That the conditions described were not identical led to dismissal of all such reports as excuses for poor performance.

Since his days in antique submarines, Lockwood, the consummate submariner, had been steeped in the 'make-do' technique. In addition he had faith in the young skippers and torpedo officers whom he had to lead. The multiplicity of failures, extending even to torpedoes that were seen to explode (apparently) against the side of an enemy ship, convinced him that more than ineffective performance on the part of his submariners must be involved. He decided that in the absence of Bureau interest the operating forces themselves must resolve the contradictions.

It took him more than a year of unremitting effort, beginning with the simplest experiments for what looked like the simplest problem – namely, that the depth-control mechanism seemed to be faulty. The obvious solution for this was to shoot some torpedoes through fishnets and then measure the locations of the holes they made. This he did, just outside Perth's Fremantle Harbor, only to receive back from the Bureau of Ordnance the fatuous statement that his experiments (none of which had the Bureau tried anywhere) were insufficiently rigorous for a true scientific study!

On top of Lockwood's primary job, running an independent submarine command in war, the Bureau was requiring him to redo his firing tests to comport with its ideas on data collection before that misbegotten outfit would even look into his allegations. One would have thought that the mere complaint by a responsible wartime commander, with or without tests, would have sent the Bureau's torpedo department into a frenzy of action. Not so; Lockwood had to do it himself, out in the war zone, under the shadow of an implacably unbelieving Bureau. Then, in January 1943, with the torpedo job still far from finished, came the unexpected call to Pearl Harbor to assume overall command of our Pacific Fleet submarines. Fate, through an aeroplane crash that killed his predecessor, had laid its hand on his shoulder. The assignment as wartime ComSubPac, for which he had trained all his life, had arrived.

For two things US submariners of World War Two will always remember – indeed, virtually worship – their overall commander, Charles Lockwood. First, it was he who finally tore the curtain of obfuscation from the disgraceful torpedo performance with which they had been afflicted, and second, his every move testified to the regard in which he held them, the lengths to which he would go to support them. Their job was to fight the enemy, not the Washington bureaucracy, and they received continual evidence of the effectiveness of his intervention on their behalf. The torpedoes were of course the biggest order of business, and it turned out that there were multiple faults in them and their design, not merely one easily repaired deficiency.

In brief, and in the order discovered (getting ahead of the story), the torpedoes ran deeper than set, and on a sort of sine wave, up and down, so that a perfect shot frequently, but not always, ran beneath the target. Second, the secret magnetic exploder had been designed for the earth's magnetic lines of force in the Rhode Island area where it had been developed, so that the stronger lines of force inherent in ships near Japan often caused the warhead to explode just before it reached the target, thus looking like a perfect hit to the anxiously-watching submarine skipper. By this time all skippers were setting their torpedoes as shallow as they thought they could be made to run, despite categorical orders to set them ten feet deeper than the target's draft, and some, also contrary to instructions, had deactivated the magnetic exploders. But then came the cruncher: the 'back-up' exploder, intended to go off on striking the target's hull, was so delicate that a perfect broadside hit deformed its mechanism before it could function. Small wonder that US submariners were frustrated! To the operational force, led by Lockwood, goes the credit for discovery of the many causes of the many different troubles, and their repair. To the US Navy Bureau of Ordnance goes the discredit, which no wartime submariner will ever forgive.

There was, in fact, a fourth deficiency in the torpedoes, not discovered during the war (though there were some complaints), for only two submarines had survivors to tell the tale, and all of these spent the duration in Japanese prison camps: under some circumstances the torpedoes ran in circles, thus endangering the firing ship. Two US submarines, in documented cases proved after the war, were sunk by their own torpedoes. By statistical analysis there may have been as many as eight, but unless the sunken hulls are sought and found, and the cause of loss discovered, this can never be proved.

Historians are fond of calculating the cost of poor US torpedo performance in terms of ships that should have been sunk. It was far more than that. Although consideration of this leads directly into speculation of what might (or might not) have been, it is not hard to imagine the outcome had a force as effective as Dönitz's [*q.v.*] of 1939 (an almost identical number of around forty submarines fit for war service) opposed the Japanese landing in the Philippines in 1942. The US was able to sink only one transport; the U-boats would have sunk dozens. The invasion might even have been frustrated, certainly delayed. By some estimates as many as 3,000,000 Filipinos, most of them civilians, not to mention thousands of American soldiers, could have been saved.

Of most direct wartime concern to Charles Lockwood, he was forced to relieve skippers, in whose motivation and effectiveness he strongly believed, for inability to perform. At great personal trauma, many of them, some tearfully, themselves requested reassignment. More subtly, Lockwood's own leadership, and that of all the other force commanders, was also greatly affected. Instead of giving confident encouragement to his officers and crews, he found himself constantly – and sometimes speciously – trying to raise morale which he himself felt was justifiably low. To prosecute the war effectively, he needed aggressive skippers; but aggressive or not, nearly all returned from patrol despondent because of poor results. The effect was natural and inevitable: they experienced failure after failure, and by consequence, no matter how hard they tried, failure was what they expected. With a ship and crew to think of, not to mention themselves, they naturally concentrated on plans and tactics to follow expected failure, instead of how to exploit unexpected success. Their pessimistic predictions proved nearly always accurate; the want of consistent success made them cautious; and the need for continual caution made them timid.

More and more, Lockwood realized his biggest enemy was not Japan but the entrenched bureaucracy that refused to acknowledge or even investigate deficiencies reported to it. In desperation, he turned to his own resources, again shooting torpedoes through a series of nets *en echelon* to discover the depth at which they actually ran, simulating the effect of varying the earth's magnetic field on exploder mechanisms to prove they went off prematurely, even sliding torpedoes down a greased wire to impact at different speeds and various angles with a piece of steel plate representing the hull of a ship. Then the inert exploders were disassembled to discover what had actually happened to them.

With every experiment his indignation grew, to the point where, as he reached the high stages of fury, he began to report what he had found to his submarine skippers and their entire crews, at sea and in port. No more for him the theory that research into malfunctioning weapons should be on some more rarefied plane, away from the ken of those who had to use them in war. Some faith had to be kept with the men risking life with these ridiculously poor torpedoes, and he had had enough of the ineffectiveness in Washington. And so there came to be sent a daily message, in a code selected for its ready availability to all submariners. Described were the details of the experiments, statistical analysis of results to date, planned future tests and the procedure by which anyone could propose new ones. Through this means all US submariners were in effect participating. Nothing could conceivably have been more important to them at this time. The thought that at last they were taking matters into their own hands, with the personal assistance and supervision of their big boss, was of itself a tremendous shot in the arm for morale, something that will never be forgotten by those who experienced it.

Lockwood also, of course, kept the parent Bureau aware of these activities. He even made a special trip to Washington to confront its chief – a respected senior officer and personal friend – with the results, but to no avail. Finally, faced with continued Bureau inaction, Lockwood went over its head and appealed to Admiral Nimitz himself for permission to modify the errant mechanisms in his own submarine base shops. For Lockwood, still a very junior rear admiral, this was a risky manoeuvre. Bureau power, in the desk-bound tradition of the navy of those days, was formidable. But he knew his man and had kept him informed, as he did the men who worked for him in his boats and in his repair crews.

Nimitz, old submariner that he was, had in effect orchestrated the trail by which the necessary modifications would, if required, have the full power of his position as Pacific Fleet Commander behind them. His approval of Lockwood's proposal was immediate; and finally, in October 1943, the problem was at last laid to rest. USS *Barb* (SS-220), recently transferred from deployment in the Atlantic, went on patrol loaded exclusively with the modified torpedoes. The *Barb* had an aggressive, innovative skipper, and now he had the dependable weapons all of them should have had from the beginning. From this moment she began to hang up a series of outstandingly successful war patrols, and is remembered as one of the United States' best wartime submarines. (Her skipper, Medal of Honor winner E. B. Fluckey, is likewise known as one of the best US skippers.) It had, however, in effect taken almost exactly half the war to get the *Barb* ready.

There were twenty-two more months of desperate conflict, but Charles Lockwood had accomplished the most important of his life's works. From here onward the effectiveness of American submarines grew rapidly, for they found themselves operating as they should have been from the beginning. Self-confidence now asserted itself. US submarines charged into convoys on the surface at night, shooting torpedoes that functioned and did heavy damage; they sneaked into enemy harbours, past the defensive guns, minefields and patrolling escorts, sought out the important targets and fired torpedoes that sank them – or, if they were loaded with ammunition or petrol, blew them up, sometimes with spectacular effects of light and sound. Taking a leaf out of a World War One submarine exploit, one submarine (the *Barb* again) landed a small gang of intrepid (if amateur) saboteurs to blow up a train that had been seen running along the sea coast of Japan.

One of Admiral Lockwood's special projects, near the end of the war, was to despatch a specially fitted group of submarines into the hitherto nearly inviolate Sea of Japan, between Japan and Korea. In a sense, he did this to avenge the famous submarine *Wahoo* that had been lost there, with Morton, her legendary skipper, after one of the most outstanding records of any submarine. No submarine had been sent into the Sea of Japan since her loss, for the only entrances into this sea, north and south, were blocked by rows upon rows of lethal submerged mines. The penetration through Tsushima Straits, in 1945, completed the total isolation of Japan. I participated in this myself, in my first command, and well do I recall Admiral Lockwood's personal involvement in our preparations. He was literally on board my boat every day until satisfied that our mine-detection equipment functioned properly. From then on, US submarines ringed Japan's home islands, and nothing moved at all. Her merchant marine lay on the bottom of the sea, two-thirds of it sent there by US submarines. Her navy lay there too, one-third of it sunk by American submarines. Had we had to carry through with our planned landing on Japan's shores, our submarines would have been beacons at night and signposts during the day.

All this was accomplished by approximately 1 per cent of the US Navy. Under Charles Lockwood's clear-sighted direction, America's Pacific submarines became by far the single most cost-effective arm of her entire fleet.

Twelve US submarines and one submarine tender were present for the surrender in Tokyo Bay. As was only right and proper, they were represented at the surrender ceremony aboard the *Missouri* by their own admiral, Uncle Charlie Lockwood. Nothing could have been more appropriate. It was an important moment for all; but in Charles Lockwood's mind, as he stood there, the war had been won just two years earlier, at last, when the *Barb* went to sea with a full load of torpedoes that he knew beyond any doubt would work as they were designed to work. And nothing could remove from his mind the certainty that, had they worked as well from the beginning, the cost of the war, and the time it had taken, would have been much, much less than it was.

After the war, Charles Lockwood, now a vice admiral, was appointed Navy Inspector-General, in charge of making sure everything worked properly. After thirty-nine years of naval service he had run his course, and he retired from active duty in September 1947. By then, he had seen the beginning of nuclear power, and as a retired officer was invited to go to sea aboard the Nautilus *and experience the new power for himself. About this time he began a second career, writing books about the navy to memorialize the period he knew. One of his visions – which he lived to see come true – had been of a new era of navies, in which high-speed submarines would dominate the oceans with extraordinary weapons. He died on 6 June 1967, aged seventy-seven.*

PART FIVE

Anti-Submariners, Tactical and General

21

Captain

Frederic Walker
CB, DSO***
Royal Navy

1896–1944

by
David Hobbs

*F*REDERIC *John Walker, born 3 June 1896, second son in a family of three sons and four sisters; father was Captain Frederic Murray Walker RN. Entered RNC Osborne, 1909; BRNC Dartmouth, 1911. Sports included boxing, rugby and hockey; King's Medallist at Dartmouth. Joined HMS* Ajax *as midshipman, 1914; joined HMS* Mermaid *as sub-Lieutenant, 1916. Later service in HMS* Sarpedon *as part of the Grand Fleet's screen awakened his interest in anti-submarine warfare. Married young in 1919, although early marriages were officially discouraged.*

Post-war, served in HMS Valiant *as a watchkeeper. Appointed to the ASW school, HMS* Osprey *at Portland for specialist training in anti-submarine warfare, 1921. Despite his preference for destroyers, he became Fleet AS Officer Atlantic, 1926–8, and Mediterranean, 1928–31, serving in the flagships* Revenge, Nelson *and* Queen Elizabeth. *Subsequently commanded HMS* Shikari *and HMS* Fleetwood, *the latter being the yacht of the Commander-in-Chief Far East Fleet. While in command, Walker received adverse criticism for his outspoken comments.*

Joined HMS Valiant *as executive officer, 1936. Adversely commented upon by the Captain, who described him as lacking powers of leadership, having felt that he wanted more from him. Appointed executive officer of the AS school at Portland, during which appointment he was passed over for promotion to captain. Appointed Staff Officer (Operations) on the staff of Vice Admiral Ramsay [q.v.] at Dover, 1939. This was a key job involving the protection of the BEF against seaborne attack while in transit to France, and during its return in the Dunkirk evacuation. Important as the work was, it was not what Walker wanted and it took him until 1941 to obtain the appointment he had always wanted, command of the sloop* Stork.

A reserved, quiet youth, Frederic Walker had a brilliant start to his career at

Dartmouth; but successive appointments to battleships and his indifference to their pompous, old-fashioned routines led to his failure to be selected for promotion to captain in the normal zone. Command of *Stork* made him the senior officer of the 36th Escort Group comprising another sloop (*Deptford*) and the corvettes *Rhododendron, Marigold, Convolvulus, Penstemon, Gardenia, Samphire* and *Vetch*. He wrote excellent, succinct orders for his subordinate commanding officers; all knew what he wanted and expected from them without his having to ask. Even after work-up he drove his ships hard, determined to create a formidable fighting team, confident of its ability to defeat the enemy.

Although he had yet to see action, he produced innovative ideas that were soon adopted by the whole of Western Approaches Command. Typical of them was Operation Buttercup. At that time, night-time submarine attacks were often carried out by U-boats trimmed down on the surface, where sonar could not detect them, and where they were most difficult to see. Walker's plan, simple but effective, was to illuminate a convoy attacked at night, using starshell and flares. This would force attacking U-boats to dive, and thus give the escorts a greater speed advantage as well as the possibility of detecting the enemy with sonar.

On Walker's first convoy to Gibraltar, bad weather meant there was no chance to try out Buttercup, and nothing of note was achieved in the subsequent patrol in the Straits. German U-boats were using wolf-pack tactics successfully on the Gibraltar routes and, having perfected co-operation with the Luftwaffe long-range aircraft based in western France, were confident that they could decimate the next Allied convoy to sail in good weather. Against this background the 36th Escort Group sailed to escort Convoy HG76 to the UK on 14 December 1941. The action proved to be a classic, which illustrated Walker's ideas so well that it is worth covering in some detail.

HG76 consisted of thirty-two merchant ships disposed in five columns. In addition to the 36th Escort Group, it was protected by the escort aircraft carrier *Audacity* (with 802 fighter squadron embarked) together with the destroyers *Blankney, Stanley* and *Exmoor* from Gibraltar. The weather was fine and calm throughout practically the whole voyage, but the nights were dark and moonless. Out of her normal complement of six Martlet fighters, *Audacity* had only four serviceable ones remaining due to a shortage of replacements in Gibraltar, but shore-based air cover was available for the first three days. A Sunderland sighted a U-boat on the night of the 14th, and a tanker in a nearby convoy was torpedoed and sunk, but HG76 was not attacked.

At Walker's request a Martlet patrol was flown off at first light on 17 December. Sighting a U-boat on the surface twenty-two miles on the port beam of the convoy, the patrol attacked it with front guns and forced it to submerge. Walker immediately led a force consisting of *Stork, Exmoor, Blankney, Stanley* and *Penstemon* to attack the U-boat. This was a radical move – the conventional tactic would have been to huddle around the convoy defensively, waiting for the enemy to attack. Walker struck first and brilliantly gained the initiative. A depth-charge attack was made at 1050 by *Penstemon*, after which Walker ordered his escorts into line abreast and swept westwards and then eastwards across the convoy front. This deliberate hunt bore fruit at 1247 when *Stanley* sighted a surfaced U-boat bearing 060° and a general chase ensued. A relief fighter from *Audacity* was ordered to attack but was shot down by the U-boat. Meanwhile a gun action at long range continued between the escorts and the U-boat, which sank at 1330. Prisoners identified her as *U-131*. The attack group rejoined its convoy at 1910.

At 0906 the following day (18 December) HMS *Stanley* reported a surfaced U-boat six miles on the port beam and three escorts were ordered to attack it immediately. After a brilliant action lasting thirty minutes, *U-434* was blown to the surface by more than fifty depth charges and sank as her crew abandoned her. At 1130 two FW-200 shadowers were chased off by fighters. At dusk a U-boat was sighted at nine miles on the port beam but a prolonged hunt failed to destroy it. It was, however, prevented from homing other boats to join it.

Early on the 19th, *Stanley* sighted and reported yet another U-boat but, almost simultaneously, was herself torpedoed and sunk. Walker turned *Stork* towards the wreck of *Stanley*, obtained sonar contact and dropped fifteen charges in two attacks, which blew *U-574* to the surface 200 yards ahead. A chase followed with the boat turning just inside *Stork*'s turning circle, near enough for the British ship's First Lieutenant to do great execution with a stripped Lewis gun from *Stork*'s bridge but too close for the main armament to bear. Eventually the submarine was rammed and sunk, although *Stork*'s bow and sonar were damaged in the process. An hour later, *Audacity*, which (as in each of the previous nights) was inside the convoy for protection, was narrowly missed astern by a torpedo. Simultaneously, SS *Ruckinge*, the leading ship in the port wing column, was hit by another, but did not sink. Unfortunately she was prematurely abandoned and had subsequently to be sunk by *Samphire*, thus becoming the first merchant-ship casualty. Later in the day several more FW-200s were shot down or damaged by *Audacity*'s fighters before they could home any more U-boats in on the convoy.

The afternoon fighter patrol on the 20th sighted two U-boats ahead of the convoy which altered 50° to starboard to avoid them. Successive fighter patrols were flown until dusk to keep them down but it was considered too late in the day to send off a surface attack group. A quiet night followed in which, for the first time, *Audacity* elected to zigzag outside the convoy, a corvette acting as escort.

The first air patrol on the 21st sighted two U-boats twenty-five miles astern of the convoy, alongside one another with a plank rigged between them. A front gun attack by the fighters shot three men off the plank, but the submarines made no attempt to dive. Walker realized they must have been damaged in collision and were both incapable of submerging. Learning that they were making off away from the convoy, he promptly despatched a strong force of four escorts under *Deptford* to attack them. Whether this was wise is questionable, considering that the convoy was probably still under observation, and that the striking force, in having to steam at least twenty-five miles directly away from it, would be unlikely to rejoin before dusk at the earliest; but, for a combative leader like Frederic Walker, the circumstances were irresistibly tempting. Walker's action certainly underlined the new British spirit of aggression – which came as a shock to the German submarine force. At 1125 an aircraft reported that the ships were only twelve miles from the U-boats. Unfortunately that aircraft had to rejoin *Audacity*; its replacement could not find the submarines; and so the striking force also turned to rejoin the convoy.

But if they had lost those two, there were plenty more U-boats approaching Convoy HG76. Two were located on the port beam and *Marigold* and *Convolvulus* were despatched to intercept. At 1300 yet another submarine was sighted at ten miles on the port bow. It was at this moment that Walker recognized that the convoy was unlikely to shake off the concentration of U-boats and decided to take it home by the most direct route. With the striking force catching up from astern, he attempted to lure the U-boats on to it, by having the surface ships stage a mock battle after sunset. However, the ploy failed, because when the 'battle' started, the nervous merchant ships fired 'snowflake' indiscriminately, lighting up the real convoy. This brought tragedy.

At 2033 the rear ship in the centre column SS *Annavore*, was torpedoed and sunk. Operation Buttercup Starboard was ordered, but no U-boat was sighted. Meanwhile the escort carrier *Audacity*, having recovered aircraft, was again making her way to a night zigzag position outside the convoy as she had done on the night before. But this time, no escort could be spared for her. Sighting a U-boat, she engaged it with her P2 gun; seconds later, she was torpedoed; and at 2210 she sank, bows first. At 2244, HMS *Deptford* sighted a U-boat on the port beam between herself and the merchant ships. The sloop carried out depth-charge attacks on sonar contacts for two hours and although at the time the result was uncertain, it was later learnt that *U-567* had been destroyed.

The loss of the carrier and a merchant ship depressed Commander Walker considerably; but in fact the worst was over. From the 22nd onwards, shore-based air cover and UK-based escorts joined him; no more ships were lost; and the individual vessels arrived at their respective ports on Christmas Day.

As the facts became clear it was obvious that HG76 represented a substantial victory. A large number of U-boats had been assembled, with the intention of decimating the convoy. Instead of that result, four of them had been sunk, as a direct result of the aggressive tactics employed by the escort group commander. Indeed, in the war diary of Rear Admiral Karl Dönitz [q.v.] (Flag Officer, U-boats), the entry for 22 December 1941 shows the extent of Walker's victory: 'The chances of losses are greater than the prospects of success. No contact with the convoy. Therefore the decision has been made to break off operations.'

Walker was awarded the DSO for his leadership of the escort force and was recognized as one of the most keen and efficient U-boat hunters in Western Approaches Command. The impact of his leadership is indicated by the signal sent to him from HMS *Blankney* when the Gibraltar-based ships had to break off and return: 'Regret very much having to leave you when the spoils of war are still waiting to be plucked. Good luck, am proud to have sailed under your orders.' Similarly, the Convoy Commodore signalled to him personally: 'Despite the loss of *Audacity* and *Stanley* you have won a great victory. On behalf of the convoy, deepest congratulations and many thanks.'

A major conference on anti-submarine tactics was held in January 1942 which gave Walker a chance to expound his views on escort tactics. He spoke highly of *Audacity* and her fighters; describing them as having put up a matchless performance, he clearly felt their loss deeply. Convinced that aggressive convoy protection was essential, he also stressed the need for surface escorts to be used as striking forces during daylight hours. This proved too much for his more conservative colleagues to swallow at once, and he was advised to use caution. Nothing daunted, he resolved to carry on with his own methods, confident that success would prove them right; and it did. Through the early part of 1942, while *Stork* underwent repairs, he led his group from the sloop *Pelican*. In July 1942, though technically too old, he was promoted to the rank of captain in recognition of his outstanding leadership and skill in action against enemy submarines. The war and command of an escort group had given him the chance to show his true worth as no peacetime commission in a battleship had ever done. In October 1942 he was appointed captain (D), in charge of all the escort groups in the command. He operated from an office in Derby House in Liverpool, headquarters of Western Approaches Command, and took the opportunity to lecture his young commanding officers on leadership and his ideas of how to take the fight to the enemy. 'A well-led ship's company', he said, 'can be recognized in any emergency by their ready and intelligent anticipation of orders and the absence of confusion and shouting.'

The new Commander-in-Chief Western Approaches Command, Admiral Sir Max Horton [q.v.], believed strongly in creating hunting groups operating independently of convoys, able to concentrate overwhelming force where needed; and in February 1943, with just such a mission, Captain Walker was appointed Senior Officer of the new 2nd Escort Group. He was to command the new sloop *Starling* (then being built) with *Wild Goose*, *Wren*, *Kite*, *Cygnet* and *Woodpecker*. Many officers and men from the 36th Group voluntarily transferred in order to stay near him – an eloquent testimony to his powers of leadership.

After work-up, the ships were employed in the mid-Atlantic gap. When things were quiet, Walker threw in practice emergencies or other manoeuvres, and there was great rivalry in the group to see who could perform the best. Team spirit was extremely high; experience, collective and individual, was great; and, on 1 June 1943, this enabled Walker to perfect his new style of 'creeping attack' against submarines. Before the development of 'Squid' and 'Hedgehog' – depth bombs thrown ahead of the hunting vessel – an attack on a U-boat entailed the hunter passing above it in order to drop stern-laid depth charges. As it passed above, the hunter was forced to lose sonar contact with its prey, which could all too often escape. In Walker's system of 'creeping attack', one ship held sonar contact on a deep submarine and gave controlling instructions to another to move slowly over it, attacking with depth charges. The first victim was *U-202* on the northern convoy routes – a victory singled out as a classic by naval intelligence. Intelligence also noted that since April 1943 the strength had been ebbing from the U-boat offensive and that their attacks were no longer being pressed home.

Since the fall of France in 1940, Walker had yearned to operate in the Bay of Biscay, in order to blockade the U-boat bases in western France and force them to transit submerged. He was able to do so from June until October 1943, operating closely with Coastal Command air patrols. This was less successful than he had hoped; he was unimpressed by the often poor quality of air surveillance. Strangely, though, he made little attempt to improve tactical sea–air co-operation in these months.

In October he returned to the Atlantic routes with the escort carrier *Tracker* and the sloop *Magpie* added to his force. Back in December 1941 he had spoken highly of *Audacity*, but now he described escort carriers as 'a drag on offensive action, e.g. at night or in poor flying weather'. Where surface vessels were concerned, his ideas on anti-submarine warfare (ASW) were brilliant; but he did not wholly extend the same understanding to aircraft, and made no contribution to the exciting improvements in airborne ASW that were taking place at this time. It is possible that the loss of *Audacity* still haunted him, but more probable that, because he had never come into close contact with aviation throughout his long career, he still regarded it as something apart. With ships, however, his tactics had become legendary and when he visited Halifax in November 1943, he was invited to carry out a lecture tour for the benefit of Canadian and American naval officers.

Early in 1944, the composition of the 2nd Escort Group changed. Walker now led a force consisting of his own *Starling* together with *Wild Goose*, *Wren*, *Loch Killin*, *Loch Fada* and *Dominica*. After work-up in the Irish Sea, the group were used from May onwards to patrol the western English Channel against U-boat intervention in the D-Day landings. This proved an immense burden on Walker, since he was leading unfamiliar ships, manned mostly by reservist personnel, through the minefields and navigational hazards off Ushant. Whenever he had been at sea since the start of the war, he had seldom left the bridge, and now *Starling*'s officers noticed signs of strain they had not seen before. In fact their captain had very little time left to live.

On 2 July the group returned from the Channel to Liverpool for leave and repairs, and Walker learned that he had been awarded a third bar to his DSO. He spent a few days at home with his wife, but then orders came for the group to sail on the afternoon of 8 July. On 7 July he returned on board to discuss forthcoming operations with his second-in-command. After leaving his ship, Walker complained of giddiness and a humming noise in his head. After violent sickness he was rushed to the Royal Naval Hospital *Seaforth*. His condition continued to deteriorate rapidly, and at 0200 on 9 July 1944 he died of a cerebral thrombosis in his sleep. His group was at sea without him.

The stature of the man can be gathered from his obituaries. The American Admiral Harold R. Stark [*q.v.*] said of him: 'The United States Forces in Europe wish to convey their deepest sympathy in the loss of an outstanding fighting naval officer in the untimely death of Captain Walker. Although this loss will be keenly felt by the Allied forces everywhere, his fighting spirit will endure with us.' At the funeral service in Liverpool Cathedral, Sir Max Horton echoed these words, saying, 'Victory has been won and should be won by such as he. May there never be wanting in this realm a succession of men of like spirit in discipline, imagination and valour, humble and unafraid.'

Frederic Walker was buried at sea from the destroyer HMS *Hesperus*. Even during his lifetime, he had taken a place in history as one of the outstanding figures of the anti-submarine war; his ability to inspire his subordinates to do their best was one of his cardinal features. After a shining start at Dartmouth, his disappointing career before the war can be put down to a failure to fit in with the nineteenth-century philosophy of the battleship fraternity. Once he got away from them and was given the chance to show his true worth, he was supreme. He was certainly dogmatic; he certainly made some mistakes; but, apart from the failing (common enough among surface sailors then) to grasp fully the possibilities of air power, his judgements were always based on a sound appreciation of the facts at sea, and he was never afraid to back those judgements to the full. His aggressive hunting policy, his painstaking deliberate searches and his novel tactics (such as the 'creeping attack') are legend. Yet his greatest achievement was his ability to create a united, working team out of men from vastly differing backgrounds, making them want to get the best from their ships and weapons, and above all making them want to win. Many have tried; but few have reached anything like his success.

Select Bibliography

Naval Staff History, *The Defeat of the Enemy Attack on Shipping*, Admiralty, London, 1957.

The Development of British Naval Aviation, vol. II, Admiralty, London, 1956.

The RAF in Maritime War, vol. II, Air Ministry, London, n.d.

Admiralty Wartime Intelligence Summaries, Admiralty, London, n.d.

Robertson, Terence, *Walker RN*, Evans Bros., 1956.

22

Admiral

Sir Max Horton
GCB, DSO**
Royal Navy

1883–1951

by
Michael Wilson

MAX Kennedy Horton, born 1883, second son in a family of four. Entered the Royal Navy September 1898, and soon became attracted to the potential of submarines – the Royal Navy's first was launched in 1901. Began submarine training in 1904, and in 1905 (at age twenty-two) was given command of submarine A-1. With only one exception thereafter, he commanded his own ship until reaching flag rank, and remained an enthusiastic submariner throughout his life. In the forefront of British submariners by 1914, Horton sank a German cruiser in the Heligoland Bight and successfully attacked a destroyer. Thereafter, supporting the Russians in the Baltic, he was responsible for several enemy losses. By the end of the war he commanded his own flotilla, and with it returned to the Baltic in 1919 for operations against Russian Bolshevik forces. Peacetime commands followed, including cruisers and battleships, until he was promoted rear admiral in October 1932. His sea-going career continued until he was appointed vice admiral commanding the Reserve Fleet in July 1937.

'Poacher turned gamekeeper' – such is the title often given to Max Horton in his role as Commander-in-Chief Western Approaches, from the end of 1942 until the end of the war. During that period the German U-boat threat in the Atlantic was first contained and then mastered. His decisive victory over the U-boats was the result of a long battle that the Allies could not afford to lose, and was in its way the critical factor in the winning of the war. Yet for much of his earlier career in the Royal Navy Max Horton was an enthusiastic and distinguished submariner.

Like many a submariner he was an individualist. Like all great men he was a perfectionist and as such was ruthless and intolerant in dealing with inefficiency, and believed strongly in the need for training. His technical knowledge and grasp of detail came as a result of his early success as a submariner. He was a strict but fair disciplinarian – a fact he would have thought unnecessary to state for someone in high authority in the armed forces. Some thought him rude, but this was merely a direct manner which at times showed great kindness and understanding.

Max Horton's war may be said to have begun in the summer of 1937 when he was given the appointment of flag officer in command of the Reserve Fleet. Within the navy the Reserve Fleet was often regarded as a dump for 'passed overs', the below-average officer or for those seeking a quiet time before retiring. Not so with Horton; he was quite convinced that war was coming and he was determined that his fleet would be ready when the time came. His previous appointment had been in the Mediterranean, as the Vice Admiral commanding the 1st Cruiser Squadron. There, he had found himself caught first in the threat of war with Italy over the Abyssinian crisis, and then in the politics of the Spanish Civil War where his firmness and tact did much to defuse a potentially tense situation. He had also obtained first-hand insight of the German and Italian navies, as they too were deeply involved in these sad events.

His task was not easy. The Reserve Fleet was a heterogeneous collection of elderly ships of all types and many classes, laid up in the Royal Dockyards and other ports around the coast of the British Isles. Though some (like Horton's flagship, the cruiser *Effingham*) were fairly new, many had not been in commission since their crews had been demobilized in 1919. The ships themselves were manned by only nucleus crews and maintenance parties.

Horton felt then that his first priority was to ensure that everyone was given a sense of purpose – that they felt that they were doing a worthwhile job, were aware of the likelihood that war was not far distant and, most important, that they were not serving in a dull backwater. An early mobilization exercise revealed many deficiencies which had to be rectified. With much hard work, this was done before the fleet mobilized for real at the time of the Munich crisis in 1938. In August 1939 when the fleet was again mobilized, over 12,000 reservists were called up and in the course of a week 133 ships were commissioned and stored: battleships, cruisers, destroyers, submarines and smaller ships. It was a great achievement, for the official target for these reserve ships to be ready was thirty days after mobilization had been ordered. Only a senior officer with Horton's dedication and powers of leadership could have ensured that this collection of ships, manned largely by elderly reservists and time-expired men, could have been ready for sea in such a short time. The Reserve Fleet then assembled at Portland and was inspected by HM King George VI himself. As the King departed, well satisfied with what he had seen, his signal to Admiral Horton shows that he was well aware not only of Horton's own part in making the event practical, but also of that played by the many reservists who had suffered hardships to be there:

The efficiency and smartness obtained in such a short time after commissioning can only have been achieved by the enthusiasm and wholehearted co-operation of all hands, and it leaves no doubt in my mind that the Fleet will quickly reach a high standard of fighting efficiency.

I realize what sacrifices are being made by many of the retired officers, pensioners and reservists in leaving their work and their homes to make possible this quick and important addition to our naval strength.

Led by Horton in *Effingham*, the ships then went to sea for a series of intensive training exercises, after which they dispersed to their several war stations. It was the first of Horton's appointments that had a direct bearing on the course of the war, and as such he takes great credit for ensuring that in September 1939 the Reserve Fleet was ready for war and able to take its place alongside the ships of the active fleet.

With the outbreak of war on 3 September 1939, and with the Reserve Fleet ships all incorporated in other commands, Sir Max (he had been knighted in the New Year's Honours) became the Vice Admiral Northern Patrol. The patrol's operational area was the 435-mile-long gap between Iceland, the Faeroes and Scotland; its purpose was to intercept any ships trying to break the blockade of Germany. For this task Horton initially had only eight old light cruisers of the C and D classes, all of World War One vintage and short endurance. They were quite unsuited for long patrols in the gale-swept waters of these northern seas in winter and suffered frequent damage, besides making life a constant nightmare for their crews. As the commanding officer of one of the ships, HMS *Colombo*, reported:

> the conditions under which men are living are extremely bad. Due to their low freeboard, upper decks are permanently awash in the normal weather of the Northern Patrol. Sleeping accommodation is quite inadequate; men, most of whom have been living in their own homes, have to sleep on and under mess tables, every slinging berth is occupied. Mess decks are wet and drying facilities are poor with the result that watchkeepers come down from their watch as lookouts etc. (often in northerly gales and blizzards), to great discomfort and little opportunity of drying their clothes.

At first Horton went to sea with them in his flagship – he had always preferred to be afloat if possible. Soon, though, he was obliged to transfer his flag ashore at Kirkwall, as it was totally impracticable for him to co-ordinate the work of his squadron from a ship; at sea he often found himself out of touch with the Admiralty, the Commander-in-Chief of the Home Fleet and the RAF, and as an admiral in a single ship on patrol he was out of place. Nevertheless these ships did have their successes (as the number of prizes that were brought in bore witness), and Horton himself was always present to welcome the battered vessels and tired crews as they returned to harbour.

By the end of September 1939, a number of armed merchant cruisers (AMC) began to arrive to reinforce or relieve the hard-worked light cruisers. The AMCS were large liners armed with ancient six-inch guns. Being large, with high freeboards and a good turn of speed, they were better able to keep at sea in all weathers. They were manned with a mixture of naval reservists and some of their original merchant navy crews under naval discipline. As such they were fine for their task of intercepting any German merchant ships trying to sneak home to Germany, but if they encountered a German warship they would be at a distinct disadvantage. Horton himself met every one of these ships as they joined his command and did his best to put their crews at ease in their strange surroundings. For the merchant crews, naval discipline was unfamiliar, and their duties were liable to be monotonous and uncomfortable. His staff then tackled the problem of their training for the task ahead – training which at best could only be minimal.

Perhaps the most famous of these AMCS was the ex-P&O *Rawalpindi*, commanded by Captain E. C. Kennedy RN. On her first patrol they intercepted two German ships. On her second, late in the afternoon of 23 November, they ran into the German battle-cruisers *Scharnhorst* and *Gneisenau*. Believing that he had met with the smaller pocket battleships (even so, formidable opponents), Kennedy sent off a sighting report to the Admiralty and then turned towards the enemy to engage. Kennedy can have had few illusions about the result of such an encounter, but believed that he might be able to inflict some damage on the enemy and delay their escape into the Atlantic until help arrived. Under heavy fire, the thin-skinned *Rawalpindi* was soon ablaze from stem to stern, and sank after dark, taking Kennedy with her and all but thirty-eight of her crew. Nevertheless, Kennedy did achieve his aim, because the German ships, although undamaged, decided to abort their attack on the Atlantic convoys. Fearing the navy's reaction, as their presence had been broadcast by the gallant Kennedy and his crew, they returned to Germany.

Despite such tragic losses, the work of the Northern Patrol went on; and for Horton the end of the year brought momentous change. He was pleased to receive a letter from Winston Churchill (then First Lord of the Admiralty) offering him the appointment of Vice-Admiral Submarines. The Admiralty felt that this post should be filled by an ex-submariner who had commanded submarines with distinction during the previous conflict. Who better than Horton? Until then the post had been held by a rear admiral rather than a fairly senior vice admiral, but as the First Sea Lord, Admiral Pound [*q.v.*], explained to Horton: 'We want you. Your great knowledge and experience will be invaluable.' Naturally Horton was delighted and his feelings were expressed in a letter to a friend:

The new job is taking over the Submarine Branch, and they must have someone who commanded a submarine in war to take charge of them in wartime – hence me. Always told you when things got bad I hoped they would send for me, and it looks like they have done it. I am so happy, happy, happy at the prospect of what lies ahead. I am almost falling over myself with excitement. I haven't forgotten all I knew and I hope to bring them luck anyway.

The men of the Northern Patrol were genuinely sorry to see Horton go. Though they had been driven hard, they felt Horton understood their problems, recognized their hardships and had fought for their interests. However, their loss was the submariners' gain.

Even by the outbreak of World War One in 1914, Horton (then a lieutenant-commander) had established himself as one of the best and most forceful of the navy's submarine commanding officers. He had made his mark in the fleet exercises of 1912 when (in *D-6*) he had sailed up the east coast of England and then attacked the 'enemy' fleet in its base above the Forth Bridge. To do this he had to proceed at periscope depth up the Firth of Forth, with only brief use of the periscope to determine his position, and then repeat the feat out again after firing his torpedoes. Early in that war, by then in command of a newer submarine, the *E-9*, he had become the first British submariner to sink an enemy ship when he torpedoed the old German cruiser *Hela* in the Heligoland Bight, later sinking a wildly zigzagging destroyer off the mouth of the Ems. For these two successes Horton had been awarded the DSO and recommended for early promotion to commander.

But it was in the Baltic that Horton had made a public name for himself, a small number of British submarines being sent there in 1914 and 1915 to support the Russian Baltic Fleet. The British submariners, Horton among them, maintained an aggressive patrol policy which forced the Germans to take counter-measures out of proportion to the small number of submarines involved. Although not as successful as one of his colleagues, it is a measure of Horton's nature that the Baltic was dubbed 'Horton's Sea' by many, including the enemy. The German Admiral Hopmann was to admit after the war that his navy feared his activities more than all the Russian fleet.

In 1940, as Vice Admiral Submarines (VA(S)), Horton was responsible for the general administration and training of all submarines and (under the Commander-in-Chief Home Fleet) for the operational control of submarine operations in the North Sea and Atlantic. Expecting that the Home Fleet would be based at Rosyth, arrangements had been made before the war for the headquarters of the submarine command to be at nearby Aberdour, in Fife. However, with the Home Fleet based instead at Scapa in the Orkneys, Horton felt that Aberdour was too remote from the Admiralty and proposed a move to London. From there he would just as easily be able to talk to the Commander-in-Chief by telephone. A block of flats in North London, 'Northways', was taken over and Horton and his staff moved there in March

1940, gaining the added advantage of being close to the headquarters of RAF Coastal Command.

However, despite his reputed luck, Horton's return to the submarine world in early January 1940 was marked by the loss of three submarines from the same flotilla – *Undine*, *Starfish* and *Seahorse*. Again it was Admiral Pound who put feelings into words when writing to Horton: 'Losses will occur from time to time, but three submarines from a flotilla in one week is a heavy blow. I cannot say how glad I am that you are VA(S) because it is at times such as these that your knowledge and reputation will be so valuable to the submarine service.'

Horton remained as VA(S) for almost two years. They were years of great change, both in the ways of submarine warfare and in the shape of the war itself. The so-called 'phoney war' (though it was never 'phoney' for the submariners) came to an end with the invasion of Norway in April 1940, followed in the summer by the fall of France, the entry of Italy into the war and the conflict's extension into the Mediterranean. By the time Horton was relieved in 1942 it had become a true world war with Russia, the USA and Japan all involved.

At the start of this period, British submariners were inhibited by having to comply strictly with the Prize Rules. These stated that before being sunk, (if indeed they could not be brought into a British port) merchant ships had to be stopped and searched, and provision made for their crews. None of this was very practicable for a submarine when in enemy waters. As the tempo of the war altered with the invasion of Norway, so were the Prize Rules made less and less restrictive, until, by 1942, British submarines in the Mediterranean were making the supply of Axis war materials to North Africa very difficult.

Submarine operations in the Mediterranean and Far East were not under the control of the Vice Admiral Submarines. Nevertheless, he was able to ensure that the submarines themselves and their crews were fitted for the task to be given them. Despite the large increase in numbers being commissioned (and, sadly, the losses incurred), standards were not allowed to fall. Officers from both the RNR (merchant sailors with naval training) and the RNVR (civilian volunteers with naval training) joined submarines. By the end of the war, both types of Reserve had produced their quota of commanding officers, while 'Hostilities Only' ratings (many never having been to sea before) soon formed a large percentage of the crews. Australians, Canadians and New Zealanders, with no submarines of their own, also volunteered to serve in British submarines.

Among the submarines under Horton's command were those of the Polish, Norwegian, Dutch and French navies which had managed to escape from their own countries before capitulation. As the war progressed these submarines were reinforced by new British-built boats, which were then handed over to be manned by crews from the various Allied navies. The subsequent award by the Queen of the Netherlands of the Grand Cross of the Order of Orange Nassau to Horton is a measure of the respect and admiration that the Dutch submariners, indeed all the foreign submariners, felt for him.

Two important developments in the submarine world took place during Horton's time as VA(S). In a private venture by an ex-submariner in a shipyard on the River Hamble, the first British midget submarine began to be built in 1940. When Horton heard of the new craft, he went straight down to see what was going on and to discuss the project with its designer. He was soon convinced of the importance of these boats and arranged for development to continue with every assistance from the navy. The two prototypes, which came to be called 'X' craft, did not fulfil all the necessary requirements, but they worked, and soon six more improved operational craft were built by Messrs Vickers-Armstrong at Barrow. Horton was largely involved in ensuring that the craft overcame all their many teething troubles and in the training of the crews, but it was left to his relief to see them off for their first operation – the famous attack on the battleship *Tirpitz* in a Norwegian fjord. It was at this time that the 'Chariots', or 'Human Torpedoes', were developed, with all the necessary backing from Horton, who had recognized their potential after the Italians' first use of them against the Mediterranean Fleet in Alexandria Harbour. The US Navy's Commander-in-Chief, Admiral E. J. King [*q.v.*], met Horton at this time too. They did not get on at all. Most visiting American officers liked Horton's energy and drive, and King had a similar forceful personality: seeing the Chariots in Portsmouth, he dismissed them as crazy. The drive back to London was frigid.

Horton himself had actually been promoted admiral on 9 January 1941. The fact that he then continued as Admiral (Submarines) indicates the strength of the Admiralty's faith in his leadership, and the important part being played by the submarines. In November 1942, however, he was appointed Commander-in-Chief Western Approaches with full responsibility for the conduct of the war against the U-boats in the Atlantic. This was the change from poacher to gamekeeper. Naturally he was loath to leave his beloved submarines, but readily accepted the new challenge. He wrote:

> I simply hate leaving submarines. No admiral could possibly have been better and more loyally served than I have been, and the way morale and the offensive spirit have withstood the bitter casualties is a source of overwhelming pride. Nothing can exceed the pride I feel in having run this show for nearly three years, or the poignancy of the extremes of happiness and grief that have happened so frequently, resulting from our victories and losses.

At the beginning of the war the Commander-in-Chief Plymouth, Admiral Sir Martin Dunbar-Nasmith, another ex-submariner and a contemporary of Horton's, was responsible for the protection of all Atlantic shipping approaching the British Isles, whether by the North-western or South-western Approaches. By August 1940, with the Germans occupying the coast of

France, the South-Western Approaches had become untenable for the Atlantic convoys and all shipping had to be diverted round the coast of Ireland. Plymouth became unsuitable for the control of the battle, and Churchill proposed that a new headquarters be set up on the Clyde. The Admiralty was unconvinced that the Clyde was the right place for the new headquarters, which would have to house both naval and RAF elements if it were to work smoothly. In the event, Liverpool was chosen and work was put in hand to transform the interior of Derby House. The core was the Operations Room, known as the Plot, which with its massive wall chart covering the whole of the Atlantic would show the position of every convoy, ship and submarine. Opposite the main plot were two sets of rooms, one set for the Duty Naval Commander and RAF Controller, and the other set for the Naval Commander-in-Chief and the Air Officer Commanding 15 Group, Coastal Command.

Despite priority being given to the work it was February 1941 before the new Commander-in-Chief, Admiral Sir Percy Noble, took over the new command. He remained until relieved by Admiral Horton on 17 November 1942. By then the staff had grown to over 1,000 officers and ratings, including Wrens, while at sea the number of escorts had grown gradually to over 170. Even so, there never seemed to be enough escorts for each convoy; and another critical shortage was in VLR (very-long-range) aircraft to cover the area in the middle of the Atlantic. Thanks to the policy so vociferously undertaken by both RAF Bomber Command and the American air force, who believed that the war could be won only by strategic bombing of German industrial targets and failed to see that it could be so easily lost in the Atlantic, only one VLR squadron of Liberator aircraft was available to Coastal Command at this time.

Out in the Atlantic, November 1942 was a black month for the Allies: eighty-three ships totalling 508,707 tons were lost. This was not the worst month of the year for global losses, but never again would so many ships be sunk so quickly in the Atlantic alone. However, it was not a good month for the Germans either – they lost thirteen U-boats, of which six were sunk in the Atlantic. Many of the escorts had been diverted from normal tasks to escort the troop convoys sailing for the Allied invasion of North Africa, Operation Torch. Inevitably, once they learned of the invasion the Germans sent the U-boats south too, operating with small success off the focal point west of Gibraltar and along the North African littoral. This effectively removed much of the pressure from the transatlantic merchant convoys and may have averted an even worse monthly figure of shipping losses. The scale of the task that faced Horton and the men of Western Approaches Command can be gauged by the fact that at this time there were 385 U-boats in commission, of which 207 were available for operations with the average daily number of boats at sea in the area being ninety-five. These figures were daunting enough but they had yet to reach a peak.

Like Admiral Noble before him, Horton believed that the best way to defend a threatened convoy was to reinforce its close escorts at sea with highly trained support groups, working in co-operation with VLR aircraft and free to take offensive action against the U-boats. Once the threat was over the support group would be moved elsewhere, using tankers to refuel at sea. This increased the range of the close escorts concerned. However, it was early 1943 before there were sufficient close escorts for sixteen to be withdrawn from that role and retrained in support group work. Together with a flotilla of destroyers from the Home Fleet and some American escorts, these sixteen ships were formed into five independent support groups. At the same time another seven squadrons of VLR aircraft were at last made available for duty in the Atlantic, but even with that much enhanced air support, Horton was not to be rushed in committing the ships to action; all were given an intense period of training to adjust and learn to work together.

It was about then that Horton set up an Anti-Submarine School in Larne (Northern Ireland), where escorts could exercise their tactics in detecting and hunting submarines, with some elderly RN submarines playing the part of the U-boats and a millionaire's ex-yacht acting as the convoy. The school served to brush up forgotten skills before the real thing was undertaken against the enemy. This seagoing 'classroom' supplemented the Tactical Unit which Admiral Noble had set up in a building in Liverpool, where tactics could be tried out, problems investigated and officers trained in the comparative peace of wartime Liverpool rather than on the battlefield itself. It was all part of Horton's continual interest in training, in which his ships' crews were pushed to the limit and kept up to the mark. Before long, other schools were set up at other ports around the command.

The part played by the Submarine Tracking Room in the Admiralty must not be forgotten. Here a team under Commander (later Captain) Rodger Wynn RNVR assembled all the available information about U-boat positions and movements, passing the result to Horton and his staff. The information came from many sources, such as actual sighting reports and D/F fixes or bearings from when a U-boat last used its radio – which was often. Most important were the Special Intelligence Signals – or Ultra, as they are known today. These signals contained the decrypts of actual German signals either to or from the boats at sea, and depending upon various factors at different times during the war they were either plentiful and up to date, or sparse and late. At the best of times Winn and his team could provide the Admiralty and Horton with an almost complete order of battle of all the U-boats in the Atlantic. Horton himself was known for his luck, and, since his staff generally was unaware of the extent to which the German Enigma codes could be broken, the use he was able to make of much of this secret information must have added to his reputation.

The story is told that on one occasion Horton was greatly dissatisfied with the appreciation given him by the Tracking Room during a hectic convoy battle. In his usual forthright manner he told Winn of his feelings. In turn, Winn suggested to the Admiral that if he cared to wait half an hour, he would prepare all the information that was available to the Tracking Room at the time in question. Horton could come in, make his own appreciation and see if he came to any different conclusions. When Horton arrived he was confronted with a mass of reports which he immediately began to study. After a while he turned to Winn and confessed that Winn was right. His final comment was, 'I leave it to you'; and he did thereafter.

Whenever the situation allowed, Horton's day routine started with the morning briefing, at which he was brought up to date with events, before dealing with paperwork and a round of visits and calls. Whenever possible he would play a round of golf in the afternoon to help him relax and keep him fit. Once he took along with him a photographer from the American magazine *Life* who had come to interview him, and then for the first and only time in his career did a hole in one. The story and accompanying photographs caught the American public's imagination – a British admiral who directed the Battle of the Atlantic and yet took time off for an afternoon's golf, seemed thoroughly in the spirit of Drake playing bowls before defeating the Armada.

The reality of World War Two convoys meant, all too often, battles fought at night. After dinner, therefore, Horton would appear in the Plotting Room to watch the battle develop, and make his decisions and plans before retiring for the night. If necessary he would return during the night attired in pyjamas and dressing gown, alert as ever and quick to grasp the situation.

Despite his undoubted genius in directing the battle from Derby House in Liverpool, and his ability to make the most of resources that were never more than adequate, Horton was fortunate in the calibre of men who actually had to fight the battle out in the Atlantic. There were men like Captain F. J. Walker [*q.v.*], who became a legend even during the war and whose death in July 1944 (not by enemy action but by a stroke brought on by hard work and strain) shocked the nation. Other experienced escort and support group commanders like Commander A. A. Tait (killed when his ship HMS *Harvester* was sunk in March 1944 in the battles around convoy HX288), Commander (later Captain) D. Macintyre and Commander (later Vice Admiral) P. W. Gretton, to name but a few, were no doubt inspired by Horton's own leadership as they in turn inspired their own ships' companies. Horton was also fortunate in having available Captain Gilbert Roberts, who was in charge of the Tactical Unit in Liverpool and as such was responsible not only for much of the shore-side training but also for the development and original testing of many of the new tactics that were so necessary to win the battle against the U-boats.

May 1943 was the decisive month in the battle. During that month, 163,507 tons of shipping, representing thirty-four ships, were sunk in the North Atlantic – the lowest total since December 1941. At the same time, forty-one U-boats were destroyed during the month, thirty-seven of them in the North Atlantic – a loss which, for the first time since April 1940, exceeded the number of new U-boats commissioning. After the war Fregattenkapitan Günther Hessler, an officer on the staff of Admiral Dönitz [*q.v.*], wrote:

failure in a whole series of convoy battles had shown beyond doubt that the offensive power of the U-boat was incapable of dealing with the defence. The situation was due firstly to outstanding developments in enemy radar and second to effective co-operation between surface escorts, support groups and carrier-borne aircraft.

Dönitz himself ordered the withdrawal of the U-boats from the mid-Atlantic convoy routes at the end of the month. For him the battle was not lost; he believed the disasters of the month were but a temporary setback. After all, there were 428 U-boats in commission of which 214 were operational – still a formidable total. For Horton and his team the worst was in fact over, although there were many tough battles still ahead. Having driven the enemy from the mid-Atlantic they then had to counter all his attempts to resume the offensive.

Mention has already been made of the efforts made by Admiral Noble and then Horton to obtain sufficient escorts to form support groups, and for the formation of more VLR aircraft squadrons to patrol the mid-Atlantic area. To these should be added the use of carrier aircraft. Elderly Swordfish torpedo aircaft, converted to carry a radar set and depth charges, were the main British aircraft in use for this purpose, flown either from specially built escort carriers or from the converted MAC-ships (merchant aircraft carriers). The former were small carriers complete with flight deck and hangar built rapidly using a standard merchant-ship hull, while the latter were essentially merchant ships with a flight deck. The escort carriers could accompany the support groups wherever they were sent, but the MAC-ships were constrained to stay with a convoy. Either way, however, they brought a new and valuable asset to the aid of the convoy defences. Radar was slowly becoming more widely fitted in both ships and aircraft, so that U-boats lost the advantage of darkness; improved design of the equipment gave longer detection ranges, keeping the U-boat further from the convoy on the surface. Ahead-throwing weapons began to replace the depth charge, giving a better chance of a successful attack, though even by the end of the war only a small number of the escorts were fitted with them. All these developments helped Horton and his sea-going commanders to keep ahead of the U-boats' challenge.

The Germans too had their share of the development of new equipment and weapons. Pattern-running and homing torpedoes had their successes until counter-measures could be developed. In the summer of 1944, many U-boats were fitted with the *schnorkel*, a device which enabled them to stay submerged when using their diesel engines either for propulsion or for charging their batteries. No longer having to surface, the U-boats achieved a temporary advantage over the Allied ships and aircraft fitted with radar, until improvements in the latter enabled them to detect even the U-boat's *schnorkel* mast, though at shorter range than a surfaced U-boat. New designs of U-boat, the Type XXI and XXIII, began to appear at the beginning of 1945. These boats designed for ocean and coastal work respectively had a high submerged speed, higher in fact than the full speed of many of the older escorts. But by then it was too late; only one of the ocean-going boats ever went on operational patrol, and that coincided with the end of the war. The effect that they might have had on the battle can only be conjectured.

Such developments are typical of the closing stages of any battle and the Battle of the Atlantic was no exception. There is no space here to deal with the many individual convoy battles that were to take place in the period between June 1943 and the end of the war. It was a continual fight to ensure that the convoys got through, the more essential in the build-up to the invasion of France in June 1944. For the invasion period, many of Horton's escorts and Coastal Command aircraft were diverted to assist escort the invasion force across the Channel, yet it was a time when more and more men, material and supplies were needed from across the Atlantic. Despite the depletion of escorts, they were convoyed across with only minimal loss.

With the end of the war in Europe, the reason for Western Approaches Command disappeared. Horton hauled down his flag on 15 August 1945 and the navy returned to Plymouth. Horton himself retired at that time, as he himself explained 'to make way for younger men'. He was sixty-one years of age. In assessing his part in the winning of the Battle of the Atlantic, it must not be forgotten that a large number of the men involved were those of the merchant navy. For the whole period of the war they were in the forefront of the battle, while the men of the Royal Navy, Royal Canadian Navy, the US Navy and navies of the European allies together with the airmen struggled to beat the menace of the U-boat and allow their merchant colleagues free passage. To the end, the Germans strongly believed that the U-boat was the best hope they had of averting defeat by a nation which was dependent upon seaborne supply. A. V. Alexander, then First Lord of the Admiralty, said as much in the House of Commons in February 1945 and added: 'This is a highly important fact which will, I trust, never be forgotten by future First Lords, future Boards of Admiralty or future governments, or by the people of this country.'

But Horton's personal part in the battle is perhaps best summed up in the citation composed shortly after the war, when he was awarded the American Legion of Merit in its highest degree, that of Chief Commander: 'Assuming his important command at the peak of the German submarine menace, Admiral Sir Max Horton brilliantly directed the control and protection of all convoys in the approaches to the United Kingdom, devising and effecting superb measures to safeguard Allied shipping.'

When Admiral Horton hauled down his flag as Commander-in-Chief Western Approaches on 15 August 1945 he had already decided to retire, and would not accept any further appointment that would be offered him. In fact the strains of war were having an effect on his health and he was to undergo five serious operations in the next six years. Nevertheless whenever his health allowed him he remained active in various different spheres, not the least of which was his appointment as Bath King of Arms, involving him in tiring ceremonial. He continued to remain deeply interested in anything concerning submarines.

Admiral Horton died on 30 July 1951. He was given the exceptional honour of a state funeral which took place on 9 August in Liverpool Cathedral, in the city where for three desperate years he had directed, and won, the Battle of the Atlantic.

23

Admiral

Harold R. Stark

United States Navy

1880–1972

by

B. Mitchell Simpson III

*H*AROLD *Raynsford Stark, born 12 November 1880, Wilkes-Barre, Pennsylvania. US Naval Academy, class of 1903. Served in several ships 1903–17. Commanded a division of five destroyers for voyage from Manila to Gibraltar, 1917. Flag Secretary to Admiral William S. Sims, Commander Naval Forces, European Waters, 1917–19. Executive Officer, USS North Dakota, 1919–21. Naval War College, class of 1923. Executive Officer, USS West Virginia, 1923–4. Shore and afloat staff duty, 1925–30. Naval Aide to Secretary of the Navy. Commanding Officer, USS West Virginia, 1933–4. Promoted to rear admiral, assigned Chief, Bureau of Ordinance, 1934–7. Commander, Cruisers, Battle Force, 1938. Appointed Chief of Naval Operations, 1939.*

When Hitler attacked Poland in September 1939, Admiral Harold R. Stark (just short of his fifty-ninth birthday) had been Chief of Naval Operations for less than one month, and the United States was woefully unprepared for war. As senior serving officer in the US Navy, Stark was not worried about an immediate threat to the security of the United States. The Royal Navy was a potent force in the Atlantic, and when combined with the French navy it could keep German forces confined to the continent of Europe. Moreover, the French army was large, and most informed observers were convinced that it could check any westward thrust of the German army. Events were soon to show the error of these assumptions.

The twenty-seven months that elapsed between the outbreak of war in Europe and the Japanese attack on Pearl Harbor on 7 December 1941 gave the United States time to prepare for war. Stark urged Congress to adopt two naval shipbuilding bills, which produced the 'two-ocean navy' that fought in World

War Two. As CNO, Stark first articulated and then commenced carrying out the implementation of the basic Allied wartime strategy to defeat Germany first. Later, as Commander, US Naval Forces Europe from 1942 to 1945, he gave life to the Anglo-American 'special relationship' and nurtured it with skill and dedication. Stark had the support of President Franklin D. Roosevelt in these endeavours.

The two men enjoyed a happy relationship. They had first met in 1914 when Roosevelt was an Assistant Secretary of the Navy, and Stark was a young lieutenant-commander. From then on, they kept in touch, and it was Roosevelt who appointed Stark Chief of Naval Operations, over the heads of numerous more senior admirals. Roosevelt made this important appointment not so much on the basis of friendship as on the basis of Stark's excellent reputation in the navy as a no-nonsense naval officer and a superb shiphandler and commanding officer, and his known ability to work in Washington with the Navy Department and with Congress. This he had demonstrated in the early days of the Roosevelt administration when he was Chief of the Bureau of Ordnance.

Following the outbreak of war in Europe, Roosevelt's first act was to establish a 'neutrality patrol' in the Western Atlantic. It was a precautionary measure. Stark, as Roosevelt's principal naval adviser, implemented this patrol.

At the outbreak of war in Europe, it was clear to Stark that the United States should embark upon an extensive shipbuilding programme. Ever since the Washington naval arms limitation treaties of 1922, the United States had conscientiously observed their qualitative and quantitative limitations. In 1939 it was also clear (as it had been for many years) that the US Navy's most likely opponent would be Japan. In January 1940, therefore, after consulting with Representative Carl Vinson (chairman of the House Naval Affairs Committee), Stark proposed a shipbuilding programme which would increase the fleet's total tonnage by 25 per cent. During the spring and early summer, Congress held numerous hearings on this programme, and by June 1940 had approved most of it.

The collapse of France in the same month was a stunning victory for Nazi Germany. Great Britain now remained alone to face the fury of Adolf Hitler. Not only had the French army been effectively removed from the war, but the French navy was no longer a certain ally; conceivably, its ships could be used against Britain and, if Britain fell, even against America. This rapid and disastrous turn of events led Stark to propose and Congress to enact a second shipbuilding bill which, upon completion, provided the long-sought two-ocean navy. This bill was rushed through Congress in record time. By July 1940, the United States had embarked on an enormous shipbuilding programme which continued throughout World War Two.

In Washington DC, there were serious worries that Great Britain might have to give up the fight. From London, Ambassador Joseph P. Kennedy sent pessimistic telegrams in which he openly predicted that Churchill's government would fall and that a new government would seek peace with Hitler. Stark shared these anxieties and concerns. However, as the summer wore on, and as the much feared German invasion of the British Isles failed to materialize, it became clear to him that Great Britain, although alone, would continue in the struggle.

With the collapse of France and the entry of Italy into the war on the side of Hitler, only Great Britain stood between the Axis and the Western hemisphere. Clearly, all possible aid must be given to the British, who were surrogate defenders of the Americas. Stark gave all assistance he could on his own authority, but very soon faced an almost insurmountable problem. In August 1940, Roosevelt agreed to transfer fifty over-age destroyers to the Royal Navy in exchange for leases on British territory in the New World where the United States could build naval bases. Under US law at that time, the transfer of the fifty destroyers could be made only upon Stark's certification as Chief of Naval Operations that these ships were not necessary for the defence of the United States. He, however, had asked Congress for supplemental funds to refit them and make them suitable for duty with the US Navy. Clearly this meant the destroyers *were* necessary for the defence of the United States, and Stark could not certify otherwise without irrevocably damaging his credibility with Congress. He told Secretary of the Navy Frank Knox that he was prepared to resign rather than make the certification.

Fortunately, a way was found to permit Stark to make the certification required by law. After considerable discussion in the Navy Department, the Attorney-General, Robert Jackson, suggested that if Stark found that the worth of what would be received (bases in Trinidad, St Lucia, Jamaica, the Bahamas, Bermuda and Newfoundland) in exchange for the fifty destroyers actually showed a net gain for the security of the United States, then he could make the necessary certification in good faith. Stark eagerly accepted this formula, because he wanted to render all possible aid to the British, and he did not wish to oppose the President. Within days the transfers were made, and the Royal Navy had fifty more destroyers for vital convoy duty.

In July 1940, Franklin Roosevelt was nominated for an unprecedented third term as President. The ensuing presidential election delayed high-level strategic decisions. Finally, in early November, the American people returned Roosevelt to office – much to the relief of Stark, who sent a congratulatory note to the President.

Throughout the late summer and early autumn of 1940, Stark and his staff had been busy reviewing and rethinking strategic plans and the assumptions upon which they were based. It became increasingly apparent to Stark that although Japan posed a serious potential threat to American interests in the Pacific – notably to the Philippines and to the sea lanes of communication from Hawaii westward – the more imminent and more dangerous threat was in the Atlantic. Roosevelt's re-election meant that the President would now be in a position to make some necessary strategic and political decisions, or at least acquiesce in them. Stark saw that the time was ripe for a major policy decision, and he took the initiative. Working alone, he produced a rough draft of a document which later became known as the Plan Dog Memorandum. He consulted with members of his own staff until he was satisfied with the first draft, which he then sent to General George C. Marshall, Chief of Staff of the US Army, and to the Secretary of the Navy, Frank Knox. A few days later when he had polished the document to his satisfaction, he formally submitted it to Knox, who in turn sent it on to the President that same day, 12 November 1940.

Stark knew Roosevelt well enough not to expect a formal and explicit presidential decision. Rather, he expected that the President would read it. If the President had no firm objections, Stark would hear no more about it. That would be sufficient for Stark to take action in accordance with the memorandum.

This document was remarkable in several respects. Unlike many defence documents, it was written in clear, concise and standard English, which contributed to the precision of Stark's thought. It was also written without the assistance of civilian political scientists and analysts. In only twenty-six pages, Stark analysed the relationship of the war in progress in Europe, the dangers in Asia and what would be the possible effects upon the United States. From that, he proposed four possible courses of action which he labelled A, B, C and D. He recommended course of action D, which in the phonetic alphabet then in effect in the US Navy was Dog. Hence the document has been known as the Plan Dog Memorandum.

In summary, Stark's memorandum stated that the security of the United States was directly related to that of other parts of the Western hemisphere. The most imminent and the most dangerous threat to the United States was the collapse of Great Britain and the possibility that the Royal Navy would no longer oppose the Germans. For this reason, the continued presence of Great Britain in the war was absolutely essential to the security of the United States. Therefore, because Germany presented the greatest threat to Great Britain, Germany likewise presented the greatest threat to the United States. In a telling and oft-quoted sentence, Stark outlined the possible future: 'If Britain wins decisively against Germany, we could win everywhere; but ... if she loses, the problem confronting us would be very great; and while we might not lose everywhere, we might, possibly, not win anywhere.'

Stark eagerly sought to commence staff talks with the British. Technically, the United States was still at peace, and Roosevelt's re-election had been based, among other things, on the American people's desperate hope that they would not become involved in the war. He could not be seen so soon after the election to authorize staff talks with the British. Nevertheless, Stark plunged ahead. Without specific presidential authorization, he invited the British Chiefs of Staff to come to Washington in January 1941 for a staff conference, codenamed ABC-1. He was convinced that eventually the United States would enter the war in the Atlantic, and thus it was necessary to begin as soon as possible the necessary staff co-ordination with the British. Moreover, the war plans then in effect for the United States provided for its major naval effort to be made in the Pacific in a war against Japan.

The British delegation arrived in the United States aboard the British battleship HMS *King George V*. The President went to meet the ship at Annapolis, ostensibly to greet the new British Ambassador, Lord Halifax. Even though Roosevelt never indicated on his copy of the Plan Dog Memorandum that he had even read that document, he worked closely with Stark in advance of the opening of staff talks with the British, and approved Stark's opening remarks to the ABC-1 conference.

After greeting the delegates, Stark left the meeting and turned over the actual conduct of the conference to his immediate subordinates. The end result of this unique conference was the ABC-1 staff agreement, which was nearly sixty pages long, including five annexes on various specific topics. The importance of this conference and the agreement it produced cannot be overemphasized. Stark succeeded in establishing the defeat of Germany as the principal objective of any Anglo-American military and naval effort, which would be coupled with a strategic defence in the Pacific 'in the event the United States is compelled to resort to war'. Thus the groundwork was laid – first, for the defence of the Western hemisphere, and second, for providing every possible assistance to the British. This became the basic strategy of the Grand Alliance in World War Two.

In June 1941, Hitler, having been frustrated in the west, turned upon the Soviet Union in the east. Unleashing the terrible fury of the Wehrmacht against his unsuspecting Russian allies, he threatened the very survival of the Soviet Union. The immediate effect of this stunning development was to divert the forces of Nazi Germany from the west to the Soviet Union.

President Roosevelt and Prime Minister Winston Churchill agreed to meet at Argentia Bay, Newfoundland, in August 1941. Stark accompanied Roosevelt to this meeting, along with other high-ranking army and navy officers. Stark was particularly anxious to meet his British counterpart, Admiral Sir Dudley Pound [*q.v.*]. The Americans were not prepared to make any particular agreements or to arrive at specific conclusions. Rather, they were more interested in taking the measure of their counterparts and in establishing good personal relations. In this respect, they succeeded admirably.

The summer of 1941 was a time of increasing peril in the North Atlantic. Hitler had not been able to invade England, and in the Battle of Britain the RAF had thwarted his attempts to achieve air superiority. However, the German Navy had a powerful and dangerous submarine force, which was unleashed against shipping in the North Atlantic. In September, a German submarine fired two torpedoes at the USS *Greer*, a destroyer en route to Iceland. In October, another United States destroyer, USS *Reuben James*, was sunk by a German submarine. Stark was convinced that the only way to meet the submarine threat and to keep open the sea lanes to Great Britain was to enter the war against Hitler. He openly favoured a declaration of war. However, Roosevelt was more cautious, and let himself be guided by events. Finally, in the early autumn of 1941, Stark authorized the US Atlantic Fleet to destroy any Axis ships which threatened vessels sailing under the American or Icelandic flags. He was convinced that Britain must be supported even at the risk of war with Germany. He was equally convinced that Hitler would not declare war upon the United States until he was good and ready, and that it would be a cold-blooded decision; yet by the autumn of 1941 the US Atlantic Fleet was already at war in everything but name.

Meanwhile, matters continued to deteriorate in the Pacific. Relations between the United States and Japan became increasingly strained. The United States sought an end to the policy of expansionism of the Japanese military government, while the Japanese in turn sought to eliminate Western influence in the Far East. Tensions continued to mount through October and November 1941. By the end of November, Washington was convinced that Japan would soon attack British, Dutch and possibly American possessions in the Far East. However, there was no information as to where the Japanese attack would come or when it would be made. Meanwhile, a large Japanese naval force had left Japanese waters and, taking a northern route towards Hawaii, was poised on Sunday morning, 7 December 1941, for its historic attack upon the US naval base at Pearl Harbor.

The next day, President Roosevelt asked Congress for a declaration of war which he received almost immediately. Four days later – 12 December – Hitler declared war upon the United States. Although war had come to America suddenly and with surprise, the basic strategic decisions which were to guide the war effort had already been made: Germany was the principal enemy; Great Britain was the principal ally. Japan would achieve sudden and stunning success in the next few months, but its line of advance would eventually be checked and penetrated.

Very soon after America's war officially began, there was a major command change in the US Navy. First, on the advice of Secretary of the Navy Frank Knox, Roosevelt appointed Admiral Ernest J. King [*q.v.*], then Commander of the US Atlantic Fleet, as Cominch (Commander-in-Chief, United States Fleet). This meant that King would have operational command of all US naval forces. Stark would remain as Chief of Naval Operations and be responsible for strategic planning, administration and the creation and organization of naval forces. Stark and King were determined that this partnership would succeed, and it is to the credit of both that it did succeed, despite some minor problems at lower staff levels. King was an energetic, dynamic, firebreathing naval leader. In fact, when Stark was first appointed Chief of Naval Operations in 1939, he told King that he should have had the position instead.

Churchill's almost immediate reaction to the formal American entry into the war was to propose that he go to Washington for a conference with the President. He arrived by the end of December 1941, bringing with him his principal naval and military officers. This first wartime summit, known as Arcadia, produced the Combined Chiefs of Staff and established the principle of unity of command. Under the President and the Prime Minister, this body conducted the Anglo-American war effort. The principle of unity of command meant that in any one area there would be one commander of all Anglo-American forces. Finally, the conference established a personal and (on the whole) a harmonious relationship among the British and American Chiefs of Staff. As CNO, and partnered by Army Chief of Staff General George C. Marshall for the military view, Stark represented the American naval forces in these deliberations.

In March 1942, Stark tendered his resignation as Chief of Naval Operations. He told Roosevelt that King should assume the duties as CNO in addition to those of Cominch. Stark felt that the man in command of the naval forces should also be in command of the naval shore establishment and the planning machinery. He also felt that King's personality admirably suited him for this position. Roosevelt reluctantly agreed and accepted Stark's resignation.

But Roosevelt did not permit Stark to retire. He wanted the Admiral on active duty in a capacity which would utilize his considerable administrative and diplomatic skills. Roosevelt therefore resurrected the command held by Admiral William S. Sims in 1917 and appointed Stark as Commander-in-Chief, US Naval Forces Europe (Comnaveu) with headquarters in London. Within a month, Stark took up his new duties.

Roosevelt sent Stark to London for two reasons. First, the President wanted to have someone whom he knew and trusted on the scene in London, in order to keep him informed of developments through the Secretary of the Navy Frank Knox. Stark was an ideal choice, since he and Roosevelt enjoyed a degree of intimacy, and Roosevelt trusted him implicitly. Second, by posting to London an officer of Stark's seniority, Roosevelt demonstrated to the British that despite Japan's dramatic conquests in the Pacific he had not wavered from the fundamental strategic decision to defeat Hitler first. The British knew that Stark had articulated that fundamental strategy, and his assignment to London emphasized American commitment to its continuation.

On the day of Stark's arrival in London, Winston Churchill invited him to spend the night at Chequers, the official country residence of British Prime Ministers. During a long conversation which extended into the small hours of the following morning, Stark repeated to Churchill the substance of the conversation that he had had with Roosevelt in the White House the day before he left Washington. Churchill was at his exuberant best: indeed, the British in general were delighted to have Stark in London. To mark his arrival, the Lords of the Admiralty gave a luncheon in his honour at Admiralty House, the first such luncheon since the outbreak of war. Churchill was among the guests. The First Sea Lord, Admiral Sir Dudley Pound, assigned Vice Admiral Sir Geoffrey Blake as Stark's liaison officer with the Admiralty. Pound gave explicit directions that all information sent to him should also be sent to Stark. In this way, Stark was swiftly admitted to the inner circle of the wartime British military circles. It was an extraordinary act of trust and confidence, which further enhanced the extraordinary co-operation between the Admiralty and Stark's office, and later on between their fleets.

Stark made every effort to become acquainted with senior British officers. He not only made the courtesy calls required by protocol, but he also travelled about the country. He called upon Admiral Sir Percy Noble (Commander-in-Chief, Western Approaches) at his headquarters in Liverpool. There Stark received first-hand information about the Battle of the Atlantic and the state of Anglo-American naval co-operation. He kept King in Washington fully informed and made many useful suggestions to further co-operation between the two navies. King George VI called him to Buckingham Palace for a private meeting. The two men got on well. At that meeting, the King asked Stark to accompany him on an inspection tour of a United States task force which would soon arrive in Scapa Flow. Stark seized the opportunity, and a short time later took a great deal of pleasure in escorting the King on board various United States ships. (King George, who had served in the Royal Navy and was familiar with warships, was particularly impressed with the cleanliness of the American ships.)

In June 1940, General Charles de Gaulle refused to surrender to the Germans when France fell. Instead, he escaped to England and there he rallied French forces to continue the fight against Hitler and for the eventual liberation of France. After France signed an armistice with Hitler, the French government was removed from Paris to the resort city of Vichy, with the eighty-four-year-old Marshal Pétain, hero of the World War One Battle of Verdun, as its nominal head. As Ambassador to the Vichy French government, the United States sent Admiral William H. Leahy, who had been Stark's predecessor as Chief of Naval Operations.

In 1942, the United States found it necessary to deal with General de Gaulle, because forces loyal to him controlled various portions of the overseas French Empire in Africa and in the Pacific which had become important to the United States in the course of the war. The United States was in a particularly difficult position, because it recognized the French government at Vichy and had to deal with the insurgent General de Gaulle, who stoutly maintained that the Vichy government was illegitimate. The Vichy government in its turn had condemned de Gaulle.

Although the United States could not officially 'negotiate' with de Gaulle, Secretary of State Cordell Hull designated Stark to conduct 'consultations' with him in London. Stark was thus *de facto* Ambassador to de Gaulle, and it became one of his most difficult diplomatic assignments.

When Stark first called on General de Gaulle, he was surprised at the cordiality and the warmth of their meeting. He had been told previously that de Gaulle's ego 'stuck out all over him'. Stark never minced words with de Gaulle.

This candour – along with the fact that Stark, too, was a professional military officer – may account for the success of the relationship. As a direct result of the two men's discussions, the United States was able to gain access to portions of the French Empire which were loyal to de Gaulle, notably New Caledonia and the Wallis Islands in the Pacific.

When American and British forces under the command of General Eisenhower invaded North Africa in November 1942, de Gaulle fully expected to take command of the numerous French forces there. The generals commanding the French armies in North Africa had been appointed by Marshal Pétain and were of dubious loyalty to the Allies. The situation was complicated by the unexpected presence of Admiral Jean Darlan, a high-ranking official of the Vichy government. Bowing to necessity, the United States came to an agreement with Admiral Darlan. This agreement guaranteed that the French forces in North Africa would not oppose the Allied forces in Morocco and Algeria. It also demonstrated that de Gaulle had little, if any, influence in North Africa. De Gaulle was furious. Only Stark's calm and skilful handling of the irate French General prevented him from denouncing the Allies and creating difficulties.

De Gaulle demanded an interview with President Roosevelt. Stark acted as intermediary in making arrangements to send de Gaulle to Washington. However, Washington was not anxious to receive him. The Secretary of State as well as the President were generally unsympathetic to the French General and considered him essentially a malcontent and a troublemaker; and when arrangements were finally made for de Gaulle to visit Washington, Admiral Darlan was assassinated. De Gaulle's trip was abruptly cancelled. At last, when Roosevelt and de Gaulle met briefly at Casablanca in January 1943, the American President publicly shook hands with General Henri Giraud, whom the Allies had placed in command of the French forces in North Africa. Not surprisingly, de Gaulle was incensed.

The result was two rival groups of Frenchmen, both of which created numerous problems for the Allies – problems which were felt on many levels and in many respects. Merchant shipping was one. For the Allied war effort to continue, it was essential that merchant ships kept sailing and that interference with their schedules be kept to an absolute minimum. The crews of some French ships were openly loyal to General de Gaulle, while others were not. De Gaulle's agitators at times would board ships where crews were not loyal to de Gaulle and attempt to enlist them into the Gaullist ranks. In many cases there was controversy and conflict on board the ships which produced unacceptable delays in their sailing schedules. One such merchant vessel was the SS *Jamaïque*. While in the Firth of Clyde, *Jamaïque* was boarded by one of de Gaulle's sympathizers, contrary to the stated policy agreed upon by the British and American authorities. He attempted to enlist the crew in the Gaullist forces. Since it was imperative that this ship sail as scheduled, Stark took the matter up directly with de Gaulle. Stark's forcefulness and insistence carried the day, and the ship did sail on time; but behind her she left acrimony and lingering suspicions. Nevertheless – despite this and other instances – Stark's relationship with General de Gaulle was on the whole amicable and successful.

The invasion of North Africa in 1942 was followed by the invasions of Sicily and of the Italian mainland in 1943. Meanwhile, the Combined Chiefs of Staff in Washington were working on plans for the ultimate invasion of the European continent. During this time, the Battle of the Atlantic took on added importance. German submarines based on the French coast presented a serious threat to the sea lanes of communication between the North American continent and the British Isles and North Africa. By May 1942, the British had driven German submarines away from their home waters and into the Western Atlantic. On 4 November 1942, Churchill personally convened the Cabinet Anti-U-Boat Warfare Committee. Its members included the Ministers of Production, Labour, Aircraft Production and War Transport and Air and the air force and navy officers concerned. Churchill invited Stark to participate in the deliberations of this committee along with another American, Averell Harriman, who was responsible for carrying out America's Lend-Lease programme in Great Britain.

This committee met frequently and because of the high status of its members, any actions decided could be implemented quickly. Stark's participation assured its other members that any response from the US Navy would be authoritative. He was well aware of King's thinking in Washington, and he was able to guide the committee in its deliberations accordingly.

British and American officials agreed that the first priority for anti-submarine forces was the continuing protection of North Atlantic convoys. Heavy bombing of German submarine bases in France had produced disappointing results. Stark was convinced that the best defence against the submarines was to launch an offensive against them as they transitted the broad belt from their bases in Bay of Biscay ports to the North Atlantic. He therefore proposed vigorous and intensive patrols by anti-submarine aircraft, whose presence would require submarines to transit submerged on battery power rather than on diesel power on the surface. If a submarine were to surface in that belt, it would be subject to an immediate attack. This proposal required an additional 160 aircraft. Unfortunately, additional aircraft were simply not available at that time, and the anti-submarine forces had to make do with those aircraft that were available.

By July 1943, the effectiveness of American and British air anti-submarine operations was increasing. The US Army then had two Liberator squadrons totalling twenty-four aeroplanes at its disposal, to which the US Navy added a patrol squadron. All were operated from the United Kingdom under the British Coastal Command. In August 1943, the Admiralty concluded that the air offensive in the Bay of Biscay had (at least for the time being) been successful enough to prevent the continued safe use by German submarines of the French ports of Brest, Lorient, La Pallice and Bordeaux.

Nevertheless, Anglo-American planners were worried that when the time came for cross-Channel invasion operations the Germans would be able to mount subsurface or even surface attacks on the vast Allied armada engaged in that operation. Fortunately, the worst of their fears did not materialize, and by August 1943, the French Atlantic and Bay of Biscay ports were no longer tenable to the Germans. That portion of the submarine threat consequently ceased to exist.

The battle against German submarines was conducted not only at sea, but also in the conference rooms in London. The RAF insisted that so-called strategic bombing of factories was the best way to deal with the submarine threat. Stark and others pointed out the fallacy of this contention, and they also pointed out that even bombing submarine bases had not produced the desired effect. The Coastal Command urged that aircraft be devoted to patrol duties to keep submarines submerged and to attack them when they appeared on the surface. The RAF was consistently immune to these arguments.

Operation Overlord, the cross-Channel operation of 6 June 1944, was the greatest and the most complex military operation in the recorded history of warfare. Stark, in his capacity as Comnaveu, headed the administrative command of all naval forces used in this operation. In 1943, he had been responsible for amphibious training. The logistics and administrative problems he faced were enormous. First, it was necessary to insert large numbers of sailors, soldiers and other military personnel into thickly settled areas of England, along with their large quantities of necessary machinery and other equipment. The Royal Navy turned over the Royal Naval College at Dartmouth to the Americans for use in the build-up for D-Day. Aside from the very real problems of billeting men and transporting them and their equipment, there were also smaller but nevertheless significant problems. For example, Washington either did not know or had forgotten that British electrical power was 220 volts, so that none of the American equipment requiring 120 volts would work on British power. Thus, it was necessary either to convert the machinery or to install generators to produce the right kind of power.

Stark returned to Washington in December 1943 for a series of conferences in the Navy Department. At that time, the US Navy's attention was riveted on the Pacific; little thought could be given to any problems which might exist in the Atlantic, and even less to problems in the British Isles. Stark and his staff were told that many of the decisions that, under other circumstances, could have been made in Washington, would in fact have to be made by them in London. Returning to England, Stark set about opening additional naval bases and naval facilities throughout the British Isles in preparation for the influx of men and material necessary for the invasion of Europe.

The beaches of Normandy chosen as the site for the invasion were open to the whims of the sea and weather. Moreover, though the gradients of the beaches were gentle, the normal rise and fall of the tide was about twenty-five feet. To make matters worse, in many places the currents ran parallel to the beach. In order to make these beaches suitable to receive men, vehicles, other equipment and supplies, it would be necessary to create breakwaters and artificial harbours. Stark's command was thus faced with major engineering and logistic problems.

The organization required to construct these harbours was complex and far flung. Their various pieces were built in the British Isles, and then had to be towed to the French coast. This necessitated assembling an enormous force of tugs. The breakwaters were concrete caissons which, on arriving at the French coast, were sunk in place. Floating them from their English ports proved to be extremely difficult.

There were occasional moments of relief from pressing wartime duties. One such moment occurred in February 1944 when Churchill invited Stark to a small and convivial dinner party at No. 10 Downing Street. The guest of honour was King George VI. It was a pleasant evening which ended at 2.00 the next morning with the King's departure.

On Tuesday, 6 June 1944, Stark was at his headquarters in London when the first Allied troops stormed on to the beaches of Normandy. Three days later, he joined King, Marshall and General Henry H. Arnold, head of the US Army Air Force, in an inspection tour of the front lines. All appeared to be going well; then on 18 June, a north-east gale hit the Normandy coast with full effect. There had been no such weather there in June for twenty years, and it devastated the artificial harbours. Fortunately, the pier heads survived, although they sustained severe damage. The most intensive and prodigious efforts were required to repair the damage to the breakwaters, piers and runways. Without them, the vast flow of material and supplies to the Allied armies ashore would have been interrupted.

As the Allied forces pushed back the Germans, first French ports and then later the Belgian port of Antwerp were liberated. Stark's command was responsible for everything afloat in these ports, including pilotage, harbour movements, harbour nets and ship repairs. The army commander assumed responsibility for matters ashore. In the next few months, many bases in the British Isles became redundant, and they were closed while new bases and facilities were opened on the European continent. Yet in October 1944 port facilities on the continent were still not sufficient to meet the needs of the Allied armies. Stark made an inspection tour to see for himself the condition of these ports. Le Havre was badly damaged, but Rouen was in much better condition. Stark continued on to Paris for a meeting with General Eisenhower. At this time, General de Gaulle was head of the provisional French government. Stark sent word that he would like to make a personal call. After some jockeying back and forth, a meeting was arranged. Officials at the American Embassy were extremely interested in Stark's conversation with de Gaulle, because they themselves had been unable to see the French General.

The last major amphibious operation in World War Two in Europe was the crossing of the Rhine. It was also a naval operation. Much naval equipment was transported by truck over sometimes heavily damaged roads to the banks of the Rhine. Nevertheless, these endeavours were successful, and Allied troops crossed the Rhine and proceeded into Germany.

The war in Europe ended in May 1945. Stark knew that he would soon receive orders to proceed home. Finally, Admiral H. Kent Hewitt [*q.v.*] was named as his successor. Hewitt was due to arrive in London in August 1945. At the specific request of the Admiralty, Stark was retained in London until mid- August so that the British could give him a proper farewell.

Stark's last day in Britain included a private meeting with King George VI, Queen Elizabeth and the Princesses Elizabeth and Margaret at Buckingham Palace. In February, the King had publicly thanked him by creating him an honorary Knight Grand Cross of the British Empire. That evening in the Royal Navy's best tradition, the Lords of the Admiralty fêted him at a dinner in the magnificent Painted Hall at the Royal Naval College at Greenwich. There the British government and the Royal Navy saluted Stark and thanked him for all that he had done for the common cause. The First Sea Lord, then Admiral Sir Andrew Cunningham [*q.v.*], accompanied Stark to Southampton and saw him on board the SS *Queen Mary*, which would take him to New York.

In contrast, Stark's arrival in New York and in Washington the following day went unnoticed, and he went on leave, taking a much needed rest at his family home at Lake Carey, outside Wilkes-Barre in Pennsylvania. But now that peace seemed assured, his least expected and most trying test still lay ahead.

At the end of August 1945, the *New York Times* carried front-page accounts of the various investigations conducted into the Japanese attack on Pearl Harbor. Much to his amazement, Stark found that in his official endorsement to one investigation his friend Admiral Ernest J. King faulted Stark for exercising bad judgement in not predicting the Japanese attack on Pearl Harbor. King's official action was the direct opposite of what he had told Stark in a personal letter at the time he took this action. Moreover, the US Congress was preparing an extensive investigation into the attack on Pearl Harbor. Obviously, Stark's testimony would be required.

The long-standing and well-established policy of the US government was that the US Army was responsible for the defence of the Hawaiian Islands, including the US naval base at Pearl Harbor. The US Army failed to detect the incoming Japanese aeroplanes which attacked and severely damaged the American fleet on 7 December 1941. Nevertheless, throughout his testimony and throughout the course of the investigation, Stark refused to blame the US Army for its failure to defend the naval base at Pearl Harbor. Instead, he simply told the Committee what he knew.

Stark's efforts were crowned with success. The committee reported that Stark, along with General George C. Marshall, US Army Chief of Staff, had acted properly, had exercised good judgement and had performed their duties in an exemplary manner.

Participation in the Congressional investigation was Stark's last act on active duty. In April 1946, he retired, having served for forty-three years as a naval officer.

Awarded honorary doctorate of Civil Laws, Oxford University, 1946. Attended presentation of Williamsburg Award to Winston Churchill, 1955. Chairman, Board of Trustees, Wilkes College, 1959–64. Died, Washington DC, 20 August 1972, aged ninety-one.

24

Admiral of the Fleet

Sir James Somerville
GCB, KBE, DSO, DCL, LLD
Royal Navy

1882–1949

by
David Brown

JAMES Fownes Somerville, born in Somerset, 17 July 1882; joined training hulk HMS Britannia, off Dartmouth, in January 1897 at age fourteen. Third-class pass in seamanship; first-class passes in gunnery and torpedo courses. In 1907, as lieutenant, opted for specialization as a torpedo officer. Branch responsibilites included naval electrics and (from 1901) wireless telegraphy (W/T). Somerville sub-specialized in this last area, and, after sea experience in the dreadnought Vanguard, returned as an instructor at the Torpedo School in Portsmouth. Met and married Mary ('Molly') Kerr Main, 1913. As lieutenant-commander, went back to sea as W/T officer in dreadnought Marlborough, 1914. From February to December 1915, Allied Fleet W/T Officer in Dardanelles. Promoted commander and awarded DSO, 31 December 1915. Second Battle Squadron W/T Officer in King George V January–December 1917, when appointed to new Signal School (separated in 1916 from Torpedo Branch) as Experimental Commander, tasked with improving standard W/T and investigating Radio Telephony (R/T). Executive Officer of Mediterranean Fleet battleship Ajax, 3 March 1920, and of flagship Emperor of India, October 1921. Promoted captain, 31 December 1921; Deputy Director, Admiralty Signals Department. Commanding Officer, battleship Benbow, flagship Mediterranean Battle Squadron, August 1922–December 1924, although badly ill, followed by two years as Director of Signals Department. Flag captain battleship Warspite, 1927–9; on staff of Imperial Defence College, 1929–August 1931. Investigated Invergordon Mutiny. Commodore of Naval Barracks, Portsmouth, October 1932. Introduced Naval Welfare Scheme. Promoted rear admiral October 1933 and appointed Director of Personal Services May 1934. Created CB in 1935 New Year's Honours. Became Rear Admiral (Destroyers), Mediterranean Fleet, (flagship cruiser Galatea), 1936, during Spanish Civil War. Promoted vice admiral September 1937; left Mediterra-

nean April 1938, again badly ill. Commander-in-Chief, East Indies, July 1938, with promise of being made Second Sea Lord subsequently. By beginning of 1939, return of illness, diagnosed as TB by naval doctors, although civilian doctors disagreed. Knighted (KCB) in 1939 Birthday Honours List, and placed on Retired List, 31 July 1939.

Although he was fifty-seven years old and had already had a full naval career, James Somerville had not wished to be retired – indeed, he bitterly resented the doctors' decision – but he had little time for contemplation, for inside five weeks the country was at war with Germany. Without waiting to be summoned he arrived at the Admiralty and, though he had no more than the tacit approval of the First Sea Lord (Admiral Sir Dudley Pound, [q.v.]), occupied a desk in the Signals Division. Besides wireless communications, this was responsible for the development of naval radar. His pre-war successors as directors of the division had seen the potential as early as had their air force opposite numbers; the first radar set had been tested at sea in 1937, and a successful prototype long-range radar was demonstrated on a cruiser in 1938. Other applications (notably for gunnery ranging) were recognized, and it was for these that Somerville's old technical and administrative skills were revived.

Under his supervision, the Admiralty Signal and Radio Experimental Establishment (ASRE) was set up and, with the help of university physicists 'recruited' by Somerville, began to develop radars which worked on far higher frequencies than those invented for the Royal Air Force. Somerville himself showed perfect health, though he worked long hours in Whitehall between trips to ships and research sections as far apart as Scapa Flow and Devonport.

An official but improbable post was found for him in early 1940: Inspector of the Department of Miscellaneous Weapons and Devices (DMWD) – later better known simply as 'Wheezes and Dodges'. For several weeks he devoted his energy to producing workable weapons from sometimes seemingly madcap notions, such as steam jets to propel hand-grenades in front of attacking aircraft. These activities were suspended on 24 May 1940, when the new Prime Minister, Winston Churchill, ordered DMWD to fit 12pdr (three-inch) naval AA guns to lorries as improvised self-propelled anti-tank weapons, for use by the army in France. The equipment itself was quickly put together but, though Somerville himself went to Dover to arrange for the first batch to be taken across, it was already too late; Calais was surrounded by German armoured units.

Warned of this by his old friend Vice Admiral Bertram Ramsay [q.v.], who was then Flag Officer Dover, Somerville nevertheless insisted on going to see for himself. What he saw persuaded him Ramsay was correct. He returned to England in HMS *Wolfhound*, the last warship to leave Calais, and, in the afternoon of 25 May, reported his first-hand experiences to the First Lord and the Admiralty Board. The evacuation of the British Expeditionary Force (Operation Dynamo) from Dunkirk was soon decided and Somerville was despatched back to Dover to understudy the now-exhausted Ramsay. During the week which followed, working watch-and-watch, the two vice admirals and their staff officers organized and supervised the retrieval of over 335,000 Allied troops.

The operation was an outstanding success; Churchill called it a 'miracle of deliverance', but it owed much to the selfless dedication of the amateur and professional Allied seamen who repeatedly risked their lives. Much was owed, too, to the brilliant planning and improvisation displayed by the staff in Dover.

After another risky cross-Channel trip and several hours ashore in Dunkirk, it fell to Somerville to take charge of the organization of what was to be the final night's work in Dover. The last ships sailed from France shortly before dawn, after embarking late arrivals and the 25,000 French and Belgian last-ditch defenders of the port area. At 1030 on 4 June, Dynamo was run down. Somerville went back to London on the same day to report on behalf of Ramsay and himself. On the 5th, he was back at his desk, after his first full night's sleep since 23 May.

Mers-el-Kebir

Somerville remained in the Admiralty, working on radar developments and AA weapons, for just three weeks. During this period, Italy declared war on the Allies, French army resistance cracked irreparably and on 17 June, a new French government sued for an armistice. For ten days, British politicians, diplomats and admirals bargained and pleaded with the French to sail their intact fleet to British ports to continue the war, or at least put the ships beyond the reach of the Axis powers; but to no avail. German armistice terms stipulated that the ships must be demobilized. The only concession the French negotiators were able to obtain was that the ships would remain French, under the French flag and manned by reduced French crews. The British Admiralty trusted the French, but had no faith that the Germans would not break the terms; the fear that the ships would be turned against the Royal Navy could not be allayed.

On 27 June 1940, Somerville was summoned by the First Sea Lord and was informed that he was to command a new mobile squadron, to be known as Force 'H'. Based at Gibraltar, it would keep the Italian fleet in the Mediterranean and carry out offensive operations against Italian coastal targets. Pound and the First Lord of the Admiralty, A. V. Alexander, warned Somerville that his command's first task was likely to be the neutralization of the French fleet assembled in the harbour of Mers-el-Kebir, at Oran, Algeria, and that force might be required. Twenty-four hours later, at 1430 on 28 June, Somerville left Portsmouth in the cruiser *Arethusa*. On the same day, the armistice agreed between France and Italy came into effect.

From the Admiralty, Somerville had three alternatives to offer to the French Commander-in-Chief in Oran. He could steam his ships to a British port; if that was unacceptable, he could scuttle them where they lay; or the ships would be sunk by gunfire. Flag Officer Force H was to take the necessary steps to prepare for the operation.

Somerville's first actions after transferring his flag to the battle-cruiser *Hood* cannot have been regarded with favour in the Admiralty. On the evening of 30 June, he called a meeting of flag officers and captains on board *Hood*, to sound out opinions and to discuss the proposed operation. All were firmly (and some were vehemently) against the use of force, the unanimous opinion being that such action would transform defeated France from a neutral into an active and powerful enemy.

Next morning, Somerville interviewed Captain C. S. Holland, formerly the Naval Attaché in Paris, and two officers who had recently served as liaison officers at Oran and Casablanca. They too were strongly opposed to the use of force.

With such a weight of experience and opinion behind him, reinforcing his own reluctance, Somerville appealed to Pound for a compromise short of firing on the French fleet. His advisers at Gibraltar believed that the Royal Navy's prestige would actually be enhanced if, after inviting the French fleet to sail or scuttle, Force H withdrew without firing a shot. Six hours later, Pound replied: 'It is the firm intention of His Majesty's Government that if French will not accept any of the alternatives which are being sent to you, their ships must be destroyed. The proposals in your [signal] are therefore not acceptable.' Somerville had used up the one protest allowed to him by naval custom and had been 'slapped down' in such terms that there can be no reasonable doubt that the author of the signal was not Pound but the Prime Minister himself. His duty – as his subordinates understood – was now to obey loyally whatever orders came from the Admiralty.

The orders arrived early on 2 July, followed by the texts of a written statement to be handed to Vice Admiral Gensoul (the French commander at Mers-el-Kebir) and a personal appeal to be delivered on Somerville's behalf. The latter gave four options – to sail to British ports and continue to fight; to sail to British ports with reduced crews who would be repatriated, or to French West Indies ports for demilitarization under British or US supervision; or to scuttle the ships. If all four options were declined, then, Gensoul was to be informed, Somerville had been ordered to use any force necessary to prevent the ships from falling into Axis hands.

The sad tale of 3 July 1940 really concerns the negotiations on board the ships in Mers-el-Kebir. Somerville himself took no part in these, but cruised offshore, keeping the Admiralty informed of developments. Flatly rejecting the British demands, the French promised that force would be met with force. Hoping for a peaceful solution, Somerville postponed opening fire, from 1330 to 1500 and then to 1730. Even that deadline was set only after a sharp Admiralty signal ordering him to 'settle matters quickly or you will have reinforcements to deal with'. The one offensive action he ordered during negotiations was the laying of five magnetic mines by Swordfish aircraft across the entrance. If the French ships tried to escape, Force 'H' would have to engage them – even if negotiations were continuing.

The final deadline passed but not until 1754 did Somerville order the capital ships to open fire, at a range of 15,000 yards. The solitary mercy of the next few minutes was the accuracy of the British fifteen-inch gunfire, landing only on the intended targets and not on civilians. When fire was checked, the French guns had fallen silent. The old battleship *Bretagne* had blown up, with the loss of 977 men; her sister ship *Provence* and a flotilla-leader were severely damaged; so was the modern battle-cruiser *Dunkerque*. But one ship – the battle-cruiser *Strasbourg* – escaped with three destroyers to sea and headed eastwards. Somerville, well to the north-west, was completely wrong-footed. He had no plans for this eventuality but took the whole Force 'H' in pursuit, though of his large ships only *Hood* could match *Strasbourg*'s speed. His only hope of overhauling the latter was to slow her by air torpedo attack and when this failed, with the loss of two of the Swordfish involved, Somerville was obliged to abandon the vain stern chase at nightfall, when he began his retirement to Gibraltar.

He appreciated he had made a major tactical error, which added to his thorough disgust at the whole affair. On 4 July he wrote to his wife:

> . . . I shouldn't be surprised if I was relieved forthwith. I don't mind because it was an absolutely bloody business to shoot up these Frenchmen . . . The truth is my heart wasn't in it and you're not allowed a heart in wartime.
>
> We all feel thoroughly dirty and ashamed that the first time we should have been in action was an affair like this.

It was not yet over. In Gibraltar, he was ordered to return to Mers-el-Kebir and finish off *Dunkerque*. On 6 July, his Swordfish carried out a series of attacks on the battle-cruiser, inflicting severe underwater damage which put her out of action for months.

Somerville took no pleasure in the congratulatory telegram from the Admiralty that followed the operation. He no longer had faith in the political leadership, or, to an extent, in his service masters, who could not reason the politicians out of decisions he believed to be unwise.

A major source of concern to Somerville was that the Admiralty, as his direct 'handler', had little understanding of the realities of modern war in a distant theatre. As a commander-in-chief, he would have enjoyed a measure of autonomy to plan operations in support of broad directives from Whitehall; but, as a mere flag officer, he was subject to interference even in routine matters, and his initiative was restricted to giving reasons why one unnecessary risk or another should not be taken. Alive to the personal risk of being regarded as unenterprising or worse, he still had the moral courage to persist: 'My responsibility is very heavy and I'm not prepared to be a "yes-man" so as to provide Winston [Churchill] with some squib to let off in the House [of Commons].'

On 8 July 1940, two days after the follow-up attack on Oran, he took Force 'H' to sea again, this time to fight the real enemy – the Italians. His sortie was intended to divert enemy attention from a simultaneous convoy operation in the Eastern Mediterranean and should have included an air attack on Cagliari airfield, in southern Sardinia. On the afternoon of 9 July, however, the persistent attentions of waves of Italian bombers (which neatly bracketed but did not hit his heavy ships) persuaded him that the diversion had worked, so he turned back to Gibraltar.

Force 'H' raided Cagliari on 1 August, while escorting the old carrier *Argus* as she ferried a dozen Royal Air Force Hurricane fighters to within range of Malta. The Italian air force's tardy intervention was held off by *Ark Royal*'s Skua fighters.

This was HMS *Hood*'s last operation in the Mediterranean. On 10 August, Somerville returned her to Scapa Flow in exchange for the smaller but more fully modernized battle-cruiser *Renown*. During the ten-day round trip, he visited the Admiralty for a conference on policy and operations in his area, and at the end of August Force 'H' went back into the Mediterranean in full strength, to accompany reinforcements eastbound for Alexandria. These included the new armoured fleet carrier *Illustrious*, bearing the first squadron of the new Fulmar fighters and equipped with air warning radar. Somerville's own carrier, *Ark Royal*, was never fitted with this. It was ironic that he who had done so much to promote and procure radar for the Royal Navy, was ill provided with radar-equipped ships throughout his period of command of Force 'H'.

The sortie was completely successful in its main aim of passing the reinforcements through undetected. *Ark Royal*'s Swordfish again bombed a Sardinian airfield and Force 'H' was not attacked.

Shortly after the ships returned to Gibraltar, all except *Renown* and a handful of destroyers were detached to the South Atlantic Station, to join the watch on the French battleship *Richelieu* at Dakar. Separated from his force, Somerville could neither participate against *Richelieu* nor fulfil his primary task of keeping the Italians in the Mediterranean. Of several explanations, the most probable is that he was deliberately excluded from further operations against the French navy, either because he had declined such service during the August conference in London or because those at home lacked confidence in his dedication to such distasteful tasks.

However, during September, Somerville displayed more initiative than the Admiralty against the French. Before dawn on the 11th, three French cruisers, accompanied by three destroyers, were seen passing through the Straits of Gibraltar, heading west from Toulon to Casablanca. Somerville brought *Renown* and the only destroyer present to an hour's notice for steam and awaited orders. A series of Admiralty errors meant that by the time he sailed, with orders to intercept the French squadron and inform the senior officer that he could proceed to Casablanca but not to France or Dakar, the six ships had already arrived at Casablanca. Somerville's force was too small and too short of fuel to establish an effective patrol line. He suggested to the Admiralty that C-in-C South Atlantic should establish a patrol off Dakar; again the order was slow in coming; and by the time British ships reached the area, the six French ships had been in Dakar for several hours.

An abortive attack on the port followed. Somerville was not privy to the plan and went to sea (24–28 September) firstly to avoid French air-raids on Gibraltar which the operation had provoked, and secondly on Admiralty orders, to loiter ready to intercept *Richelieu*, which was believed to be about to leave Dakar for the west coast of France. The mission was the clearest indication that the Admiralty had lost touch with reality – *Richelieu* had been hit by an aircraft torpedo as long ago as 8 July and she was not made seaworthy until mid-1941 – and it was followed by an equally baseless scare that the Germans were about to occupy the Azores, so off went Force 'H' on yet another wild-goose chase.

Somerville half-expected to be blamed for the Dakar débâcle. To his surprise he found that Sir Dudley North (Admiral Commanding North Atlantic Station, at Gibraltar) had been cast as scapegoat for failing to order *Renown* to sea when the French squadron had been reported. But North could not have done – Somerville was not under his orders, but directly accountable to the Admiralty. On 7 October Somerville wrote to the latter to take the full responsibility, plainly stating that Their Lordships had had ample warning. Curtly acknowledged, the letter had no effect. Churchill had nursed a dislike of North since the latter had dared to criticize the Mers-el-Kebir decision and he now had the flimsy excuse he needed to sack the Admiral, who was informed that he 'had lost Their Lordships' confidence'. North remained until the end of the year, his demands for a court-martial rejected then and thereafter; not until some years after his death was he vindicated, the long shadow of Churchill's unchallengeable wartime reputation denying him basic justice.

As for Somerville, the diminution of confidence was mutual. Enforced idleness, while awaiting the return of his carrier and destroyers, did not improve his relations with the Admiralty – he was certainly no longer 'Pound's man'. His staff, too, found him extremely difficult during this period, but Somerville had already inspired such loyalty that they put up with his intolerance, believing (rightly) that it would pass when he was able to resume operations against the Italians.

During this period, he and his staff began to consider how best they might carry the war to the enemy, going over to the offensive instead of being limited to defensively covering convoys and reinforcements in the Western Mediterranean. To this end, models of industrial cities and ports on Italy's west coast were made and studied, and plans were drawn up for attacks by carrier aircraft and Force 'H'. No opportunity presented itself for some months, but the time proved to be far from wasted.

The tempo of Force 'H''s operations soon stepped up smartly. Between 7 November 1940 and early January 1941, five separate convoy and reinforcement missions were carried out. *Ark Royal*, just back from refit in the UK, had one of her fighter squadrons rearmed with Fulmars, but *Resolution* had been damaged off Dakar, leaving *Renown* as the only capital ship; and there were only two cruisers (one twenty years old) and nine destroyers to screen her and the carrier. Nevertheless, this first operation was completely successful. So were the fourth and fifth, respectively in December 1940 and January 1941, meeting only inaccurate air opposition. The second was a comparative failure; on 17 November, due to technical causes, only four of a flight of Hurricanes from *Argus* reached Malta, and the remainder were lost, with their pilots. But it was the third of these five operations which generated the most activity, and acrimony.

On 25 November 1940, Force 'H' left Gibraltar to cover a convoy bearing 1,400 army and RAF personnel bound for Egypt, and to collect a battleship and two cruisers returning from the Eastern Mediterranean. Somerville planned the rendezvous with the westbound warships to occur at midday on 27 November, to the south of Sardinia, where the danger of interception was greatest. He was right and at 1220 the Battle of Cape Spartivento began.

Suffice it to say that it could have been a tragedy for the British, for when *Ark Royal*'s aircraft first gave warning, their message was not received in the flagship, due to a receiver-tuning fault, for nearly an hour and Somerville's ships were still separated, by as much as ninety miles.

This was the most serious situation Somerville had faced in forty-three years as a naval officer. His first preoccupation was for the safety of the convoy, which he turned to the south-east, away from the enemy. Thereafter it was by plain good management of his ships that he managed, after an hour's fighting, to drive off a superior Italian fleet, which included two battleships.

The only vessels to be damaged during the battle were HMS *Berwick*, which was twice hit by eight-inch shells, and the Italian *Fiume*, hit by a 'blind' six-inch shell, during the opening exchange of fire between the cruisers. Although no enemy warships had been sunk, the most important result was that the convoy passed safely through the Sicilian Narrows and arrived at Alexandria without loss. Somerville, who had responded absolutely correctly to a most difficult tactical situation and had outfaced the full strength of the Italian fleet, returned to Gibraltar to a warm naval reception and signals of congratulation from Malta and the Mediterranean Fleet; but there was nothing from Whitehall.

On 30 November, the day after his return, Somerville was astounded to learn that the members of a Board of Inquiry, chaired by Admiral of the Fleet the Earl of Cork and Orrery, were already en route for Gibraltar, to inquire into his conduct of the action on 27 November. There was no precedent for such an inquiry, based solely on the brief initial signalled report made by Somerville himself, and he and his Force were utterly outraged by the insult. But as Lord Cork was to point out, Pound had taken this step to provide a swift professional answer to protect his subordinate from Churchill's wrath. Somerville was completely cleared by the Board, but the Admiralty (or, rather, Churchill) had the last word – FO Force 'H' had been 'over-influenced by his anxiety for the safety of his convoy'.

The trust and respect of his fellow flag officers and of his staff and Force never wavered throughout this distasteful episode. Lord Cork, writing to the aggrieved Somerville, explained the background from the viewpoint of an unwilling participant:

> There are always critics ready to raise their voices and suggest what might have been done although they are quite ignorant of what really happened or of the prevailing conditions.
>
> These people, impatient for results, exist both in and out of the Admiralty (I speak from personal experience) and no doubt have raised their voices on this occasion and the most expeditious way of silencing them has in this case been adopted.

Up to this time, the Force had not had an opportunity for offensive action against Italy except as diversionary activities. Somerville now gained Admiralty approval for a plan which his staff had worked out for a bombardment raid on Genoa, where the battleship *Littorio*, damaged in the Mediterranean Fleet's carrier attack on Taranto (November 1940) was rumoured to be under repair.

The first attempt (1–2 February 1941) had to be abandoned because of severe weather conditions. The second attempt (9 February) was a great success. At 0714 *Renown*, *Malaya*, *Sheffield* and destroyers opened fire on Genoa, hitting the Ansaldo works, the city power station, dry docks, oil storage tanks and a railway marshalling yard in the port area. The bombardment lasted half an hour, during which 272 fifteen-inch shells were fired by the two capital ships and *Sheffield* and *Malaya* fired 782 six-inch shells; the destroyers added another 400 rounds. Air spotting made this a very accurate 'shoot' and severe damage was inflicted on most targets. While this gunnery officers' benefit was in progress, fourteen Swordfish from *Ark Royal*, detached to operate aircraft well clear of the land, dive-bombed the oil refinery at Livorno while four others laid magnetic mines in the entrances to La Spezia.

Well planned and executed as it was, the operation had a fair element of luck as well. Force 'H' had been seen in transit, and before the bombardment the Italian Admiral Iachino (whom Somerville had known before the war) sortied with three battleships, rendezvoused with three heavy cruisers, and during the night passed within fifty miles of Somerville, without either fleet sighting the other. Similarly, after the bombardment, Iachino was drawn away from where he estimated Force 'H' would be (and where they were) by a seemingly reliable sighting report. This turned out to be a French convoy: Iachino missed Somerville by twenty miles and one hour.

Somerville returned to Gibraltar on 11 February to another warm welcome. This time, Churchill sent a personal message of praise – 'I congratulate you on the success of the enterprise against Genoa, which I was very glad to see you proposed yourself' – but for the Admiral it was spoiled by what he interpreted as an implication of previous lack of enterprise.

Somerville remained in command of Force 'H' for the whole of the rest of 1941, a year marked by both loss and triumph. In public eyes, the Force's most notable achievement was the crucial part it, and particularly HMS *Ark Royal*, played 2,000 miles from the Mediterranean, in the hunting and sinking of the 45,000-ton battleship *Bismarck*. On 26 May, the carrier's Swordfish crews were largely responsible for relocating and shadowing the ship, and wholly responsible for the crippling torpedo hit on her rudders, which enabled the Home Fleet battleships to catch her and batter her into pathetic wreckage.

Though less spectacular, the backbone of Force 'H''s work, continuing throughout the year, was the convoying of supplies and aircraft to Malta and of reinforcements to the Mediterranean Fleet in Egypt. This was not without loss; in various operations, one of the Force's destroyers had to be scuttled, another was damaged and a cruiser was severely damaged. But it seemed they could not bring the Italian fleet to battle; either the enemy would not emerge or, if he did, could not find them. Judging by his comments, Somerville grew contemptuous of them – the Italians were 'completely Botched, Beggared and Bewildered'; 'Wops without their Jerries are inclined to go just anywhere'; 'the Italian morale must be very low'. To a large extent he was right, but he began to take uncharacteristic risks. On 27 September, trying once again to lure Iachino into a trap (in which he very nearly succeeded), a freighter in the convoy under his protection was sunk and his new flagship, the battleship *Nelson*, was hit sufficiently to reduce her speed to fourteen knots. Back in Gibraltar, he was congratulated again on another successful convoy, but he realized he had had a close call too, and signalled ruefully to the Admiralty; 'Guardian Angel has been reprimanded and admonished to be more careful in the future.'

Force 'H''s convoy successes and its crucial contribution towards sinking the *Bismarck* had altered Churchill's attitude towards Somerville. Now, in conference during late August, he began to welcome the Admiral's views, and in October – though at first 'very angry at objections and difficulties' – even acceded to Somerville's contrary view on a proposed invasion of Sicily. It was at that time too that Somerville's vital contribution in Mediterranean convoys was recognized by his investiture (24 October) by King George VI as a Knight Commander of the British Empire, to add to his existing knighthood. 'Fancy!', signalled Admiral Sir Andrew Cunningham [*q.v.*], 'Twice a Knight at your age!'

But two other less happy events of note took place around then as well, each a further indicator of Somerville's style of leadership. One was that his Chief of Staff, Captain E. G. Jeffrey, committed suicide; the other was that *Ark Royal* was sunk.

Jeffrey's death may be attributed to the difference in character between the two men. Somerville, mercurial and intuitive, had found Jeffrey's methodical, conventional style so irritating that he would often bypass his right-hand man in favour of advice from more junior members of his staff; Jeffrey, in his resentful unhappiness, could see no form of redress against a superior whose reputation was by now so high. Similarly, the loss of *Ark Royal* on 13 November 1941 (to the U-boat *U-81*) might not have occurred had the carrier been a more efficient ship. But in the previous eighteen months, her Swordfish had only once hit a moving target. The fact that that target was *Bismarck* seems to have obscured the fact that similar opportunities for a similar blow against the Italian fleet, which would have had a great strategic impact, were lost; yet this was Somerville's key weapon, and he should have recognized her short-comings, as no doubt he would have done if one of his capital ships had been found wanting in a primary role.

The Eastern Fleet, 1942–1944

Following the Japanese invasions of the Philippines and Malaya, and the loss in the South China Sea of the British capital ships *Prince of Wales* and *Renown*, together with the death of Admiral Sir Tom Phillips (Commander-in-Chief, Eastern Fleet), Somerville was recalled from Gibraltar at the end of December 1941, to take Phillips' place. He held the command for twenty months – months characterized not so much by a lack of action as by a lack of consequence in the war overall.

This is only in part a criticism of his leadership. To a large extent it was inevitable, the effect of geography – the Indian Ocean was not and could never be a central theatre of operations.

On 29 March 1942 in Ceylon, he broke out his full admiral's flag in the battleship *Warspite*. With five battleships and three aircraft carriers, his fleet was quite strong on paper, and certainly stronger than Force 'H' had ever been. However, four of the battleships were unmodernized 'R'-class vessels, well armed but capable of only twenty knots; his two large carriers were not fully worked up, and the third was too small to carry more than a single squadron of aircraft; and the fleet as a whole was divided between Trincomalee, Colombo and a secret base at Addu atoll in the Maldives. A signal of greeting to Admiral Chester Nimitz [*q.v.*] his US Pacific Fleet counterpart, was frank: 'My fleet consists for the greater part of ships that have been employed almost exclusively on independent duties or are newly commissioned. I am engaged in giving them intensive fleet training and hope before long to report them as fit for offensive operations.'

On the same day he learned that a Japanese carrier strike against Ceylon was expected on or about 1 April. At once he ordered all his ships to concentrate eighty miles south of Ceylon. The rendezvous was successful, but after three days and nights of patrol nothing had been seen and some of the fleet were running short of fuel and water. Suspecting that the intelligence had been mistaken, or that the Japanese had heard of his concentration and were not coming, Somerville took most of the fleet to Addu atoll, and sent his small carrier, two heavy cruisers and a destroyer to Ceylon. It was the worst judgement he ever made, and the luckiest. The fleet he was intending to trap – the Mobile Force, under Vice Admiral Chuichi Nagumo [q.v.] – was far stronger than his own. He had ninety-five aircraft; they had 340, in five fast carriers, and ten long-range reconnaissance seaplanes in two heavy cruisers. Not only numerically but individually the Japanese pilots were superior, and, had Somerville's trap succeeded, the British Eastern Fleet would have been severely defeated. As it was, in two attacks against Ceylon, the Japanese sank all his detached ships – the two heavy cruisers on 5 April, and the carrier and destroyer on 9 April.

One month later, Somerville's old command, Force 'H', mounted a successful amphibious operation to capture the Vichy French port of Diego Suarez, at the north end of Madagascar. Operating from Mombasa, his new fleet took no active part beyond mounting an eastward guard against the possibility of a Japanese intervention. This was actually most improbable, because at the time the Japanese were in the Coral Sea, receiving their first strategic defeat from the US Navy. Three months after that (August 1942), US forces began the Solomon Islands offensive. From then on, the Japanese navy had no chance of adventure in any other theatre; but this was not fully appreciated in the Indian Ocean. Since 8 April, recognizing that he could not challenge the Japanese offensively, Somerville had determined to maintain a fleet in being, exerting influence by its existence rather than by its actions. In practice, the absent Japanese exercised more influence on him than he on them. Though its ships were desperately needed elsewhere, the Eastern Fleet could not be entirely removed.

However, it was run steadily down, to replace losses in the Mediterranean. By January 1943 it had no carriers left and, impotent as an ocean fleet, became a convoy escort force.

Throughout his time as C-in-C Eastern Fleet, Somerville had problems with awkward colleagues who wrongly assumed he was subordinate to them. First was General (Field Marshal, January 1943) Wavell, C-in-C India; second was Acting Admiral Lord Louis Mountbatten, appointed Allied Supreme Commander, South-East Asia Command (SEAC), in August 1943. With Wavell, disagreements over command and strategy reached the point that in March 1943 Somerville offered himself to the Admiralty – his actual operational commanders – for reappointment elsewhere. This was not possible; along with the fleet, albeit depleted, his continued personal presence in the Indian Ocean was regarded as politically essential, a promise to the US that one day the RN intended to return to that ocean in force.

During May 1943, many important Americans got to know Somerville personally, when he attended the Trident conference in Washington. There he contributed considerably to successful British arguments that a major offensive in Burma was impossible before 1944; and, almost as a reward, heard Churchill assure the Americans that the Eastern Fleet would be reinforced with modern ships from the end of 1943. Another personal success (in some ways more difficult) was that Somerville became friends with the notoriously anglophobe American Chief of Naval Operations, Admiral (Fleet Admiral, December 1944) Ernest J. King [*q.v.*]. A further accomplishment of his in Washington was to ensure that if SEAC was established, the C-in-C Eastern Fleet would still be operationally responsible to the Admiralty, and subordinate to SEAC only in support of land campaigns and amphibious operations in the SEAC area. In October 1943 it seemed that Mountbatten had grasped this clearly enough, telling Somerville that he 'would not make the mistake of setting up a separate and independent Naval Staff who would very likely end up by running counter to your wishes and annoying you'. By the end of the year, however, Mountbatten had insisted on almost exactly that, and had a still-growing 'War Staff' (as he called it) of 1,900 personnel, while Somerville's increasing fleet was staffed by forty-nine officers and seventy-five ratings. In addition to the fact that (in what Somerville recognized was a comparatively backwater area of the war) the 'War Staff' churned out impossibly grandiose plans, requiring much comment from the individual service staffs, he also saw SEAC assuming a role which could only be properly filled by the Chiefs of Staff in London. 'Dickie [Mountbatten]', he observed, 'tries to keep the party going when it's obvious there is nothing doing. It's up to the people at home to decide the policy and for us to implement it, regardless of our personal disappointments.'

But, in spite of these command tensions, when a chance came in January 1944 for Somerville to leave the theatre, he was most reluctant to do so. The job he was offered – head of the British Admiralty Delegation in Washington, also known as the Chief of British Naval Staff (Washington) – would bring powers and privileges second only to the Sea Lords themselves. But it would also entail very large personal financial expenditure over the mean allowances permitted, even for an admiral; and, as it happened, the Eastern Fleet was at last receiving its long-promised reinforcements. For that, to a great extent, Somerville had Mountbatten to thank, because the forceful SEAC had pressured the British government to honour its Trident promise concerning the Eastern Fleet. Naturally enough, Somerville was not at all inclined to pay out a lot of his own money for a new job when his existing one was just beginning to show signs of becoming more exciting. But the new First Sea Lord (Sir Andrew Cunningham) prevailed upon him, pointing out that he was the only officer suitable for the task; and before he went to

Washington, there was still time for one last – indeed, almost a first – hurrah for the Eastern Fleet.

It did not come at once. During the fleet's build-up, at the end of February 1944, it was learned that major units of the Japanese navy had arrived in the Singapore area. Their actual purpose was to seek refuge after the US Navy carrier strike on Truk, and the Japanese carriers were even less ready for operations than Somerville's ships, but he was concerned lest the enemy was planning an anniversary attack on Ceylon. He therefore proposed to withdraw his fleet to the westward of the Maldive Islands, leaving Ceylon's defence to local land-based aircraft. While assuring him of full support should he take this step, the Admiralty advised him that there was no evidence of the Japanese concentration being directed against the Indian Ocean, and cautioned him against any withdrawal which might adversely affect morale in the theatre. As they anticipated, the threat did not materialize, and on 6 March, eleven days after the 'crisis' had arisen, Somerville cancelled the movement.

This episode represents the last, but possibly the most important, of Sir James Somerville's questionable decisions or appreciations. For so long the follower of an unavoidable defensive strategy, Somerville had not sensed the 'turn of the tide'. Perhaps he had been in the Indian Ocean too long; certainly he was thinking in a single-service vacuum. By proposing to remove the only mobile counter-strike force out of the enemy's reach, he was effectively proposing the abandonment of Ceylon.

By the end of March 1944, however, his fleet included the battle-cruiser *Renown*, the battleships *Queen Elizabeth* and *Valiant*, the carrier *Illustrious*, the fleet-maintenance carrier *Unicorn*, a dozen modern cruisers, three flotillas of destroyers and no fewer than seventy anti-submarine ships – and, with her own destroyer screen, the American carrier *Saratoga*, loaned to Somerville to enable him to undertake diversionary operations to distract Japanese attention from American activity in the New Guinea area. This was only the third time the US Navy had entrusted one of its fast carriers to a British admiral, and the only time it did so in the Far East (*Wasp* and *Ranger* had been loaned to the Home Fleet in 1942 and 1943 respectively). Having learned a lesson from the loss of *Ark Royal*, Somerville had taken particular care to improve *Illustrious'* operating standards, and, besides tactical and weapons training, the entire fleet had practised refuelling at sea. They now had a two-week work-up with *Saratoga* off Ceylon and in the middle of April 1944 sailed from Trincomalee for Sabang, at the northern end of Sumatra in the Japanese-held Dutch East Indies.

Somerville led the Allied fleet – apart from the British and American units, it also contained Australian, New Zealand, Dutch and French ships – and on 19 April the strike, his first offensive mission since August 1941, was a considerable success. Indeed, Churchill called it 'brilliant' and typically, without reflection, queried the advisability of sending Somerville to Washington. 'Admiral James Somerville has added new claims to our confidence,' he wrote to the First Lord and First Sea Lord. ' . . . Why do we want to make a change here at all? It seems to me he knows the theatre, has the right ideas about it, and is capable of daring action. Does he want to go to Washington and give up his fighting command?'

Shelving the question for the moment, Somerville refuelled his fleet in Australia, then in the middle of May led an attack against the oil refineries, engineering works, naval base and dockyard at Surabaya in Java. The results appeared somewhat disappointing at the time, but post-war inquiry showed the attack to have been so effective that it was probably Somerville's most destructive single operation.

On the fleet's return to Ceylon (less *Saratoga* and her escorts, which had had to go back to the Pacific), Somerville found two crises awaiting him – one operational, the other administrative. The operational difficulty was not well resolved. Of his twenty-four modern destroyers, routine or unscheduled maintenance meant six were out of service at any one time. From June to October, ten of the rest had to be allocated for the escort of troopships bound for India, and the remaining eight – quite apart from being insufficient for major operations – were likely to be reduced by the need to provide escorts for major warship movements. It seemed no major fleet operations could be carried out in the coming months.

He declined a suggestion from Cunningham, the First Sea Lord, that he should use frigates and sloops to escort the troopships, because that would have delayed the formation of escort carrier groups. A few enemy submarines were operating in the area, and (in spite of all the Atlantic evidence against this) Somerville wanted to hunt them with small carriers, rather than waiting for them to come to well-protected convoys. The net result of introducing this policy was that from June to 22 August 1944 (when he left the Indian Ocean), seventeen Allied ships were lost, against a single U-boat sunk in return, and only one more major fleet offensive was undertaken.

The administrative crisis was, characteristically, dealt with more effectively. What had happened was that Mountbatten's Chief of Staff, General Pownall, had been agitating in the UK for the Eastern Fleet to come under SEAC's aegis. On hearing of this, Somerville promptly wrote direct to Cunningham saying that it should not happen as long as Mountbatten continued to regard his own staff, rather than the Cs-in-C, as his main advisers. This provoked a letter in which Mountbatten made it clear that he regarded himself as 'Supremo': Somerville, he said, should not communicate directly with the Admiralty, nor even with the other Cs-in-C of the theatre, except through himself, and was acting improperly in making criticisms of himself and his staff.

Against this were several crucial points: Somerville, being a full admiral in his own right, was senior to Mountbatten, whose substantive rank then was captain RN; Somerville had long years of successful wartime command at sea, whereas Mountbatten had had a series of disasters during his twenty-month command of a destroyer flotilla; and last, but far from least, the Admiralty wanted the C-in-C Eastern Fleet to remain operationally responsible to them, not to SEAC. Mountbatten was obliged to give in; and, after nearly two years' struggle, this – the permanent acceptance of the virtual independence of C-in-C Eastern Fleet – was Somerville's principal legacy to his successor.

There was one more thing to do before he left. On 25 July 1944, James Somerville brought his front-line career at sea to an end with a return visit to Sabang. His fleet included four battleships representing the major events in his career. *Queen Elizabeth* had participated in the bombardment of Turkish batteries in 1915, when he had been present; *Valiant* had been with him off Mers-el-Kebir; *Renown* had been his flagship during the bombardment of La Spezia, one of the many occasions of trying to draw out the Italian fleet; and *Richelieu* was the French battleship which had taken refuge in Dakar. Now all four joined under his command and the protection of carrier-borne fighters to shell the port, defences and barracks. It was a singularly appropriate conclusion to a long sea career.

Washington 1944–1945

After four years and two months of almost unbroken 'front-line' service – a period unequalled by any other sea-going commander – Somerville was relieved by Admiral Sir Bruce Fraser [*q.v.*], who had come from the Home Fleet to lead what was to become Britain's most powerful fleet.

The two months which Somerville spent in England before taking up his next appointment were in no way a restful period of recuperation. His presence was required in Whitehall for briefings and up-dates on planning for Royal Navy operations in the Far East, and on the political and military state of the Anglo-American alliance, and to take part in numerous conferences relating to his future duties as the Admiralty's representative in Washington. His off-duty life was tragically interrupted by his wife's illness: she had suffered a stroke while he was returning from Ceylon and although she was released from hospital a month after his arrival her convalescence was far from complete when he left for New York in the SS *Queen Mary* in the last week of October.

His own health was remarkably good. Indeed it had been so since the notorious decision to retire him, five years before, on grounds of ill-health. He remained physically very active, taking exercise by walking and, whenever opportunity offered, rowing a boat early each morning on the Potomac, and showed no signs of suffering from the effects of over two years spent in the enervating climate of India and the Indian Ocean.

His new job was like no other that he had had. He was a buffer between the Admiralty in London and the US Navy, attempting to further the interests of his own country by interpreting policy and requirements to his hosts, whose points of view, often diametrically opposed to those of the British, had to be explained to his masters. Such a task would have required extraordinary diplomatic gifts even if the US Chief of Naval Operations had not been Ernest J. King.

To say that King was an anglophobe is to do this most competent servant of his country and of the alliance an injustice. Rather, he was such a dedicated 'Americanophile' that he regarded as anathema any distraction from his task of welding and wielding the US Navy as the supreme instrument of victory. His idea of distraction was catholic, for it embraced not only outside ideas and diversion of material but also solemn undertakings made by his own President.

Thus King viewed with complete disapproval the agreement that the Royal Navy should take part in joint operations in the Pacific and, aided by like-minded subordinates in that theatre (notably Halsey [*q.v.*]), he contrived to delay and obstruct such operations.

During Somerville's time in Washington, the arrangements for the employment of the British Pacific Fleet were finally thrashed out. During its initial deployment, off Okinawa between late March and mid-May 1945, the BPF operated apart from the US Fast Carrier Task Force; fortunately, it met all the US Navy's demands for self-sufficiency, which ranked as high as proficiency, and, despite Admiral King's continued objections, it was invited to operate with the US fast carriers during the July to August strikes on the Japanese home islands. Without the solid performance of the BPF, Somerville's advocacy would undoubtedly have failed.

Somerville required all the charm and tact with which he was credited in his own service to deal with King. But although he managed to establish a working rapport (in itself a major achievement for a Briton), he was by no means successful in moderating, let alone modifying, the CNO's xenophobia. The latter fortunately was not emulated by the US Navy staff, with whom Somerville's British Admiralty Delegation staff had to deal, and who worked tirelessly to provide the generous material aid which continued to arrive up to the last day of the war.

On VE-Day, 8 May 1945, Sir James Somerville was promoted to the rank of admiral of the fleet. Besides the professional standing which this demonstrated, it also represented a political accolade, for Prime Ministerial approval was required. Somerville's relations with Winston Churchill had fluctuated but this was a permanent mark of good favour.

He was not in the United States on VJ-Day, 15 August 1945. A week previously, he learned that his wife had suffered a further cerebral haemorrhage and was dangerously ill. He returned to his Somerset home on 11 August to find her in a coma and, although she rallied briefly, Molly Somerville died on 18 August. The couple had been together very seldom during the six years of the war; it was tragic that James was left to mourn just as the rest of the world could begin to rejoice.

Summary and Appreciation

Admiral of the Fleet Sir James Somerville had been a twentieth-century seaman – he was not in the mould of the great naval heroes of the past. A technocrat and staff officer by specialization and inclination, he attained command quite late in his career; once he arrived, however, he appeared to be unstoppable, making a deep impression on seniors and subordinates alike, able to talk easily and colloquially with admirals and able seamen. Indeed, his particular gift was for 'man management' and, had it not been for ill-health, he was destined to become Second Sea Lord and Chief of Naval Personnel, an office which would undoubtedly have suited his personal qualities. Retirement and then war resulted in a quite different career.

There is little evidence to show that Somerville was a notable seaman and it is questionable whether he was entirely suited to wartime command at sea, apart from the steadying influence which he provided in two under-strength commands – Force 'H' in 1940 and the Eastern Fleet in 1942. Few British admirals had so many opportunities for action with opposing capital ships; none 'near-missed' so often. His own admitted tactical blunder allowed the *Strasbourg* to escape from Mers-el-Kebir, but hurried staff work did not help, for his orders made no provision for a French sortie. Off Spartivento, the timely and accurate report from a search aircraft (which would have given Somerville more time to set up a rendezvous and approach, and possibly draw the Italian fleet on to his battleships) was delayed by a wireless-tuning error in his own ship – the flagship of a *wireless specialist*! Months later, in the Atlantic, the *Scharnhorst* and *Gneisenau* were found by his carrier's aircraft, only to escape temporarily under cover of darkness and bad weather. Justifiable caution on his opponent's part, aided by inadequate air reconnaissance, prevented an encounter during the September 1941 'Halberd' convoy.

Finally, in early April 1942, a completely erroneous appreciation of Japanese intentions saved him from an intended engagement with a much stronger enemy. If Somerville did not possess the touch of luck which assists the great commanders to get to grips, he was twice favoured in avoiding contact, off Ceylon and, earlier, to the north of Corsica, when returning from the bombardment of Genoa.

Somerville had little opportunity for offensive action for its own sake. Between July 1940 and August 1944, he planned and led only five major operations of this nature – Mers-el-Kebir, Genoa, the carrier strikes against Sabang and Soerabaya and the final bombardment of Sabang. His reputation at sea was built upon a steady defensive record, of delivering every convoy, troop, warship and aircraft reinforcement entrusted to his care from Gibraltar to the Sicilian Narrows, and of maintaining a fleet in being in the Indian Ocean through 1942 and 1943.

But if Somerville afloat was less than a great commander, ashore he was formidable. His steadying influence at Gibraltar, where sometimes he alone was not affected by periodical 'Spanish scares', his handling of Wavell and Mountbatten in the Indian Ocean theatre in 1943–4 and finally his appointment in Washington marked him out as a great communicator who served his service and his country well.

In Washington DC again shortly after the end of the war, Somerville negotiated the return or disposal of all equipment, aircraft and supplies under Lend-Lease; supervised the run-down of the large RN presence in the USA; and helped work out the opening stages of the two navies' post-war relationship. Left Washington 16 December 1945, having been created Commander of the Legion of Merit by President Truman, and was paid a personal tribute of thanks by Fleet Admiral King. Represented HM King George VI in Rio de Janeiro, early 1946, at inauguration of new Brazilian president. Appointed Lord Lieutenant of Somerset, August 1946. Died 19 March 1949, aged sixty-six.

25

Admiral of the Fleet

Lord Fraser of North Cape

GCB, KBE
Royal Navy

1888–1981
by
John Winton

*B*ORN *in London, 5 February 1888. Joined the navy under the 'Goschen Scheme' in September 1902, aged fourteen. After early service, mostly in battleships, he specialized in gunnery, passing out top of his course at HMS* Excellent *in 1912 and going on to do the advanced gunnery course at Greenwich.*

Gunnery Officer of the old cruiser Minerva, *1914; served in her at Gallipoli. Appointed 'Guns' of the new fifteen-inch gun battleship* Resolution *1916.*

Took fifty sailors from Resolution *by train to Baku, the oil port on the Caspian Sea, 1920, to support anti-Bolshevik forces against the Russian Revolution. Captured. All survived eight miserable months of imprisonment.* OBE *awarded to Fraser for leadership.*

Between the wars he was Commander 'G' at Excellent; *Fleet Gunnery Officer in the Mediterranean; head of the Naval Staff Tactical Section; Flag Captain to the C-in-C East Indies in the cruiser* Effingham; *Director of Naval Ordnance; and Captain of the aircraft carrier* Glorious. *Promoted rear admiral in January 1938, he was Chief of Staff in the Mediterranean during the Spanish Civil War.*

When war broke out in September 1939, Bruce Austin Fraser was at the Admiralty as Third Sea Lord and Controller of the Navy, responsible for the navy's *matériel*, for the design and construction of ships, and for all their machinery, armament and equipment. It was a time of strenuous rearmament and a huge expansion of warship building, including five new 44,000-ton, fourteen-inch gun *King George V*-class battleships, five new 23,000-ton, armoured-decked *Illustrious*-class aircraft carriers, eight new cruisers, and destroyers and *Hunt*-class escorts by the score.

Fraser was involved in the planning and design of the 'cheap and cheerful'

Flower-Class corvettes, which were to bear the brunt of the war around the Atlantic convoys. There were also passenger liners to be requisitioned, armed, manned and commissioned as armed merchant cruisers.

As well as overseeing this colossal building programme, Fraser had to contend with myriad other problems, all complex and time-consuming. He had to decide on the balance of priorities between warships and merchant ships when allocating scarce shipyard building and repairing resources. There were thousands of contracts to be placed, designs to be initiated, joint productions to be co-ordinated, with innumerable manufacturers and firms all over the country. Soon Fraser was dealing with the Americans over the repair in the States of war-damaged ships, and the exchange of bases for fifty aged destroyers.

As a gunnery man, Fraser might have been expected to argue the cause of the big gun. In his opinion, the battleship certainly had its proper place, but everything had to give way to the overriding need to defend the Atlantic convoys. When, in 1940, it was decided to cancel the four *Lion*-class battleships, two of which were already building, Churchill and the Vice Chief of Naval Staff, Rear Admiral Tom Phillips, pressed for a new super-battleship to take their place.

Fraser argued that it would be impossible to build such a ship when so many destroyers were already building. In his view, the destroyers should come first. When Churchill insisted that the battleship could be built in a year, Fraser said flatly that it would take four. (A super-battleship, *Vanguard*, laid down in 1941, took five years to complete and was commissioned in 1946.)

Many of the devices and techniques which eventually were to win the Battle of the Atlantic were first put in hand while Fraser was Controller. Improved Asdic sets, more precise and accurate ship-borne radar, and high-frequency direction-finding equipment were developed. Some merchantmen were fitted with catapults for fighter aircraft, others were themselves converted into small escort aircraft carriers.

Many scientific projects came under Fraser's aegis. When the enemy's magnetic-mine offensive began in the autumn of 1939, it became an urgent strategic necessity to devise a counter-measure; one was found, in the 'degaussing coil', and hundreds of warships and merchantmen had been fitted by the spring of 1940. Similarly, scores of minesweepers had to be equipped with the 'double LL' sweep, effective against magnetic mines.

Fraser was a man of great organizing ability, who could delegate responsibility. He was patient with others' arguments, and broad-minded enough to see other points of view. He handled all his many cares with an easy, imperturbable manner and a sense of humour. In fact, his main problem was not his job but his superior, the First Lord of the Admiralty, Winston Churchill.

On the first day of the war, the Admiralty had sent two general signals to the fleet. One was 'Immediate. Special telegram TOTAL Germany'. The other was 'Winston Is Back'. Churchill wasted no time in taking charge. As he later remarked, the opening hours of war could be vital with navies. Churchill longed to wage offensive war and soon lost patience with those who advised caution. Against his more extravagant ideas, the navy's foil was the First Sea Lord, Admiral Sir Dudley Pound [*q.v.*]. Pound himself could be a difficult man to serve, but despite his faults, he did the navy a great service in the early dark years of the war at sea by his handling of Churchill.

Fraser knew Pound well, having been his Chief of Staff when Pound was Commander-in-Chief in the Mediterranean just before the war. The two men got on admirably, and Fraser was Pound's devoted ally in September 1939 in defeating one of Churchill's earliest schemes, Operation Catherine. This was a plan (similar to one in the previous war) to penetrate the Baltic with specially modified warships, in this case two or three of the old *Royal Sovereign*-class battleships, with extra deck armour and side-blisters against air and submarine attack.

Fraser gave Pound the necessary technical information to prove that the plan could not be carried out without jeopardizing other more important construction and should be shelved. Churchill was convinced, albeit reluctantly, and returned more than once to the subject.

Fraser soon grew used to Churchill's ways and did not resent the innumerable papers which, daily and nightly, flooded on to his desk, especially after Churchill became Prime Minister and Minister of Defence. There were suggestions, criticisms and complaints, some marked in red 'Action This Day', and Churchill's 'Prayers' ('Pray let me know, on one side of a sheet of paper . . . ', but Fraser recognized it was Churchill's duty to prod, to initiate. It was up to his service advisers to show if and where his ideas were impracticable.

Some of Fraser's clashes with Churchill went beyond mere disagreements and became furious arguments. After one of them, all the ministers who had been present, waiting with bated breath to see what would happen, came up and thanked Fraser, saying 'My goodness . . . not many people speak up to him like that.'

Churchill did not hold such incidents against Fraser. They increased his respect for him. He could see Fraser was not concerned, as so many in the Admiralty were, only to fight his own bureaucratic corner. If something could be done Fraser would do it, and willingly. Most importantly, Churchill knew that Fraser had a strong sense of duty and put the navy's welfare above everything else.

Fraser was relieved by Vice Admiral Frederick Wake-Walker on 22 May 1942. Having been promoted vice admiral on 8 May 1940, and being made a Knight Commander of the Order of the British Empire (KBE) in the 1941 Birthday Honours, he had been Controller of the Navy for three years and nearly three months. But what he lacked (as he himself knew) was sea-time, and – with the war in its third year – operational experience. His new appointment – Vice Admiral, Second-in-Command, Home Fleet – would make good that lack.

Fraser hoisted his flag as VA2, Home Fleet, in the battleship *Anson* at Scapa Flow on 28 June 1942. At once he asked his C-in-C, Admiral Sir John Tovey, for permission to go to sea to 'gain experience'. On 1 July he hoisted his flag in the aircraft carrier *Victorious*, which sailed that day from Scapa Flow, with the battleship *Duke of York*, flying Tovey's flag, and the battleship USS *Washington*, flying the flag of Rear Admiral Giffen, USN, as distant cover for Convoy PQ17 to north Russia.

The melancholy story is well known. Pound ordered PQ17 to scatter, against the advice of his intelligence staff, when he concluded from Enigma intercepts that the battleship *Tirpitz* was at sea and about to attack the convoy. In fact, *Tirpitz* was already back in harbour. With no escorting warships, and lacking even the basic protection of convoy formation, twenty-three of PQ17's thirty-one merchantmen were sunk by aircraft or by U-boats (three were sunk before the convoy scattered).

Fraser could hardly bear to discuss PQ17, even to the end of a long life. The whole tragic episode reflected upon the honour of his beloved Royal Navy, and upon his old chief, Dudley Pound, to whom he was always intensely loyal.

In the light of information about Ultra recently made available, Pound's decision was less reprehensible than his critics have always insisted, but it was still a grievous mistake. The lesson Fraser drew – that it was not essential for a commander at sea to maintain radio silence at all times and in all circumstances – was to affect his own future decisions at an equally critical time.

In August 1942, still in search of active sea-time, Fraser asked Tovey for permission to go as an unofficial passenger in a convoy to Malta. He took passage in the battleship *Rodney*, incognito and without flying his flag. However, in deference to his rank he was given the flag bridge from where, with his 'staff' – a Marine orderly and a signalman – he could see everything that happened. A great deal did happen.

Fourteen merchant ships, including the tanker *Ohio*, passed eastward through the Straits of Gibraltar on 10 August 1942, escorted by the battleships *Nelson* and *Rodney*, the aircraft carriers *Victorious*, *Indomitable* and *Eagle*, with *Furious* carrying replacement Spitfires for Malta, six cruisers, the anti-aircraft cruiser *Cairo* and thirty-two destroyers. Over the next five days, before reaching Malta on 15 August, the convoy was constantly attacked by high- and low-level bombers, U-boats and torpedo boats. By the time the tanker *Ohio* reached the island, only four other merchant ships had survived. The other nine had been lost: so had the carrier *Eagle*, the cruisers *Manchester* and *Cairo*, and the destroyer *Foresight*. *Indomitable*, the cruisers *Nigeria* and *Kenya*, and the destroyers *Ithuriel*, *Wolverine* and *Penn* were badly damaged.

In that terrible voyage, watching from his bridge eyrie, Fraser saw the first shots he had seen fired in anger since 1915. On the evening of 12 August, dive bombers attacked the convoy, and hit *Indomitable* with three heavy bombs, putting her flight deck out of action. Fraser's young signalman fired a Bren gun at approaching Stukas and may have scored a hit. Rumour in the fleet was that Fraser himself actually shot down a Stuka, but he always disclaimed the story.

In the following month (September 1942) the distant covering force for convoy PQI8 was formed by the *Anson*, flying Fraser's flag, the *Duke of York*, the cruiser *Jamaica* and five destroyers. On 2 September, forty ships sailed from Loch Ewe, escorted by sixteen destroyers, the escort carrier *Avenger* and the anti-aircraft cruiser *Scylla*, wearing the flag of Rear Admiral Burnett.

PQI8 endured the most intense air attacks so far encountered by any Arctic convoy and lost thirteen ships. Fraser's force, sighted by German reconnaissance aircraft on 8 September, probably prevented the appearance of German heavy ships.

German heavy ships did intervene on 31 December 1942 when – escorted by a deep covering force of *Anson*, wearing Fraser's flag, the cruiser *Cumberland* and five destroyers – the convoy JW51B was menaced by the German heavy cruiser *Hipper*, the pocket battleship *Lützow* and six destroyers.

The German ships were well placed to attack in overwhelming strength and should have annihilated the convoy. But the German commanders hesitated (the Captain of *Lützow* was particularly feeble) and lost their golden moment. The convoy was very gallantly defended by the close escort, led by Captain Sherbrooke in the destroyer *Onslow*, and ably supported by Burnett with the cruisers *Sheffield* and *Jamaica*. The destroyer *Achates* was sunk after a self-sacrificing run across the face of the convoy, but the convoy itself was unscathed and reached Murmansk on 3 January 1943. Sherbrooke lost an eye but won a Victoria Cross.

Overall this convoy's experience was an encouraging opening to 1943, and the regular cycle of convoys was continued. *Anson* gave distant cover for JW52 and RA52 and in March sailed for Hvalfjord in Iceland to give support, if needed, to RA53.

Early in March there had been the usual tell-tale indications – from ULTRA Special Intelligence, air reconnaissance, the transfer of Luftwaffe fighters from airfields in Germany to Norway, movements of destroyers and escorts, increased minesweeping activity in the Baltic and the Great Belt – that a German heavy unit, very probably the battle-cruiser *Scharnhorst*, was about to sail for Norway.

Soon it was confirmed that *Scharnhorst* had vanished from her base at Gdynia. She actually arrived in Altenfjord in northern Norway on 24 March. Ultra confirmed that the battleship *Tirpitz*, *Scharnhorst* and *Lützow* were all in Altenfjord on 5 April.

The presence of heavy ships so close to the convoy routes, the lengthening hours of daylight and the need to divert every available escort to the ongoing crisis in the Atlantic meant that there could be no more Arctic convoys for the time being.

By May 1943, Tovey's term as C-in-C was coming to an end. Fraser had spent ten months as VA2 and was the obvious choice to succeed. On 8 May, Fraser hoisted his flag in *Duke of York* as Commander-in-Chief, Home Fleet. He was then fifty-five years old and at the peak of his sea-going career. Command of a premier fleet in time of war was the summit of a professional naval officer's ambitions.

Fraser was of short stature and stocky build, with a ruddy healthy complexion, fair hair, blue eyes and a perennially cheerful expression. He was a most easy-going and approachable man, with a simple philosophy towards life and the navy: that the Royal Navy was the finest service in the world and that he and everybody else, from admirals to ordinary seamen, were very lucky to be in it.

He knew the fleet well already, of course, and now set about imposing his own brand of leadership. He hardly ever raised his voice. The quiet, cold statement 'That's bad' was severe enough reproof for most people. He would administer a 'JGSU' – 'Jolly Good Shake-Up' – to any ship he thought needed it. But he was still polite and considerate to non-offenders, reserving his 'shaking up' for those who deserved it.

He would not tolerate any ill-feeling between 'Ship' and 'Staff', knowing from past experience how unprofitable and time-wasting such feuds could be. Nobody, under any circumstances, was to 'make a scene'. If anyone felt aggrieved, he was to go to the C-in-C if he was on the staff, to the Flag Captain if he was a ship's officer, and state his case. Otherwise, the penalty was dismissal. One member of Fraser's staff was given half an hour to pack his gear and leave the ship.

Fraser normally got up at 8.45, late for the navy, and at about 9.10 would breakfast alone while he read the overnight signals. Having been forced, as a midshipman, to breakfast with his captain, he vowed never to inflict a similar ordeal on anybody else. After a staff meeting in the Admiral's main cabin at 9.30 and as brief as possible a paper-signing session with his secretary, Fraser set off in his barge to visit his ships – not less than two in a forenoon and sometimes four. The ships concerned would have been warned the night before by signal: 'If convenient, should like to visit you informally and walk round at 10.30: normal routine to continue.' (Needless to say, it always was convenient.)

The visits may have been informal but they were thorough. Fraser attached the greatest importance to them. They were his way of getting to know his ships and of getting himself known to their ships' companies. Often he would concentrate upon one department in the ship, cross-questioning its members on every aspect of their jobs. Fraser's staff would investigate defects or omissions.

Occasionally Fraser would spend a day in the boom-defence vessels which worked the harbour booms of Scapa. Usually nobody visited them or took any notice of them; their crews were delighted and flattered to share their tea with the C-in-C and tell him about their lives.

Fraser was normally back in the flagship for lunch by 12.30, after which he liked to be left alone and undisturbed, sitting in his cabin, puffing at his pipe, just thinking. He would rehearse in his mind his response to every conceivable move an opponent might make, examining possible courses of action and alternative tactics, mentally fighting fleet engagements.

Sometimes Fraser would take some of *Duke of York*'s midshipmen for a *banyan*, a swimming and picnic party ashore. One midshipman, Peter Cree, recorded in his journal some vignettes of Fraser in these unbuckled hours. One day they took steak, sausages, potatoes, tinned peaches and 'the best cheese I have tasted for years' over to the village of Swanbister. 'It was worth a fortune just to see the Commander-in-Chief splashing his flag lieutenant, who was chary of entering the chilly water, bouncing a ball on his secretary sleeping in the sun, and stalking a cow for milk, a bunch of tempting grass in one hand and a glass in the other. . . . '

On board, when tea was brought in at about 4.30, Fraser would emerge from his reverie and be ready to see his staff again. By 5.00 pm he was usually pacing the quarterdeck, which he did for about an hour, while staff or ship's officers joined him for short spells, falling into step with their chief as he walked up and down.

Fraser would then settle down for the day's main session of paperwork which, helped by a glass of gin, would last until dinner. Fraser kept a very good table and was very hospitable, especially to officers of small ships. Battleship, cruiser and other big-ship guests got wine. Destroyer, frigate or submarine officers: champagne.

The day ended with a familiar ritual. The Flag Lieutenant would take in the last bunch of signals just after 11.00 pm Fraser would have a whisky and invite his Flag Lieutenant to join him. When Fraser had read the signals, he would say, 'Right, Flags, what are we going to do tomorrow?'

The summer of 1943 was a lull for the Home Fleet, although Scapa Flow was packed with ships working up to full operational efficiency before departing for the Mediterranean. In July, Fraser took the Home Fleet on a 'coat-trailing' sweep along the Norwegian coast to simulate a large combined operation against southern Norway, hoping thus to activate Hitler's well-known phobia about an Allied landing in Norway. In fact the enemy took little notice. In September, the fleet put to sea as soon as the news arrived that *Tirpitz* and *Scharnhorst* had bombarded Spitzbergen, but was too late to intercept. (This was the only occasion on which *Tirpitz* fired her main armament in anger.)

The Arctic convoys remained suspended for the summer of 1943. Fraser thought that the convoys were no longer vital to Russia's survival and should not be resumed unless they were essential to the war on the Eastern Front – or if they would 'enable the German surface forces to be brought successfully to action'. Thus the Germans were holding their heavy ships in readiness in northern waters to attack the convoys, whereas Fraser thought the convoys would be useful only if they brought the German heavy ships to action. What was prey to one side was bait to the other.

On 22 September 1943 British X-craft 'midget' submarines made a brilliantly daring penetration of Kaa Fjord and placed explosive charges under *Tirpitz* which immobilized her for some months. A day later, *Lützow* sailed south. Her departure was forecast by Ultra. A strike by Fleet Air Arm aircraft was launched, but it was unsuccessful, and *Lützow* reached the Baltic on 28 September.

That a major German warship could pass down the Norwegian Leads in this way and reach the safety of the Baltic, without a finger being laid on her, caused much heart-searching at Scapa and in London. For Fraser, it had ominous implications. If *Lützow* could do it, so too might *Scharnhorst* – now the only operational major German warship left in the north.

As the summer of 1943 passed, *Scharnhorst* came to occupy a special place in Fraser's afternoon reveries. The prospect of engaging and sinking her led him to a most important decision. In September 1943 Dudley Pound had resigned as First Sea Lord (he actually died on 21 October). As Churchill later explained, not entirely convincingly, he did not want to take Andrew Cunningham away from the Mediterranean at that juncture. He summoned Fraser to Chequers and offered him the post of First Sea Lord.

Fraser was naturally delighted, and confident he could do the job. But he refused. He said, 'I think I have the confidence of my fleet, but Cunningham has the confidence of the whole navy. I haven't even fought a battle yet. If one day I should sink the *Scharnhorst* I might feel differently.'

Churchill, as Fraser described it, 'more or less sat back at that and said "Thank you very much."' Cunningham's appointment as First Sea Lord was announced on 4 October. Next day, Churchill wrote to Fraser to say, 'I should like to tell you how becoming your attitude was, and how much I am obliged to you for it.'

But Cunningham got to know of Fraser's decision and of the fact that he himself had been only the second choice. The knowledge inflicted a psychological wound on Cunningham. Relations between him and Fraser, never close, became even more distant.

Meanwhile, it was decided to start the convoys again in mid-November and run them regularly until February. JW54A, of eighteen ships, left Loch Ewe on 15 November and JW54B, of eight ships, seven days later. Both convoys arrived safely. The return convoy (RA54A) arrived at Loch Ewe without loss on 28 November.

JW55A, of nineteen ships, sailed on 12 December with a close escort of destroyers and a distant covering force of *Duke of York*, wearing Fraser's flag, the cruiser *Jamaica* and four destroyers. Fraser reasoned that the risk of *Scharnhorst*'s appearance grew with every convoy, while the danger of air attack was decreasing, so he took *Duke of York* all the way through to Kola Inlet, the first time a capital ship of the Home Fleet had ever done so.

Fraser met the Russian Admiral, Arseni Golovko, whose dark suspicions of his motives for coming to Russia were countered by Fraser's characteristic mixture of leg-pulling and charm. Fraser mentioned that he had been in Russia before, as a prisoner of the Bolsheviks. Golovko replied triumphantly that indeed he knew all about it. Yes, said the Chief of Staff (coached by Fraser), but did Admiral Golovko know that Fraser was *grateful* to the Bolsheviks for this?

Golovko had to admit himself astonished. He was even more taken aback when it was explained to him that 'because Admiral Fraser was badly fed in prison it enabled him to recover from the ulcer that had been plaguing him'. The visit concluded with a somewhat surrealist exchange of gifts: Golovko received a vast quantity of buns which he had tasted and approved of in his tour of *Duke of York* – 'the acme of hospitality' Golovko called them. He responded by giving Fraser a marble desktop because Fraser had admired it. 'But what would happen', Fraser asked, 'if you had come on board *Duke of York* and said you liked her?' 'Oh,' said Golovko, 'I'd treat her as your wife!'

Duke of York, *Jamaica* and the four destroyers, designated Force 2, sailed on 19 December for Akureyri in Iceland, to refuel and prepare for the next convoy, the fast (ten-knot) JW55B, of nineteen ships. This, the 'bait' which was to lure *Scharnhorst* out, sailed from Loch Ewe on 20 December 1943. It had a fighting destroyer escort of five British and three Canadian destroyers.

The return convoy RA55A sailed with its escort from Kola on 22 December. Force 1, composed of the cruisers *Belfast* (wearing Rear Admiral Burnett's flag), *Sheffield* and *Norfolk*, which had covered JW55A, sailed from Kola a day later.

Ultra provided Fraser with a stream of speedy and accurate intelligence on the enemy's movements and intentions: on 18 December, for instance, came the information that the enemy anticipated a convoy at sea, had allocated U-boats patrol areas, ordered air reconnaissance and, most ominously, shortened the notice for sea of *Scharnhorst*'s Battle Group in Altenfjord.

A German aircraft sighted and reported JW55B at 10.15 a.m. on 22 December. Fraser was informed by Ultra signal early the next morning. Force 2 sailed from Akureyri at 10 p.m. the following day, carrying out a 'night encounter with *Scharnhorst*' exercise on passage.

Fraser decided that JW55B was now dangerously exposed, being within 400 miles of Altenfjord and once more being shadowed by the Luftwaffe. The flow of Ultra information helped him to handle his forces in a most imaginative and confident manner. Boldly, he broke silence on 24 December to transfer four of RA55A's destroyers to JW55B and to order JW55B to reverse course for some hours.

Finally, at 0217 on 26 December, the Admiralty sent the dramatic 'Emergency' Ultra signal, '*Scharnhorst* probably sailed 1800/A December.' For those who were not Ultra recipients, the Admiralty broadcast a general signal at 0339: 'Admiralty appreciates *Scharnhorst* at sea.'

Fraser signalled to JW55B to turn north and to Force 2 to raise steam for full speed. He asked Burnett to signal his position, course and speed and, in the same signal, gave his own position, course and speed. Once again, Fraser weighed the risks and decided that it was worth breaking radio silence to keep his widespread forces in touch with him and with each other.

Scharnhorst had indeed sailed, with an escort of five destroyers, on the evening of 25 December, wearing the flag of Rear Admiral Erich Bey, the Northern Task Force commander. From the outset Bey's handling of affairs was uninspired. The Luftwaffe and the German B-Dienst decrypting service provided a mass of valuable information, but the German staff work and their use of intelligence were both poor.

Through bad weather and bad seamanship, the destroyers soon lost touch with *Scharnhorst*, which was therefore alone, as well as surprised, when, at 0926 on 26 December, starshell from *Belfast* burst directly above her. After a brief gun action, *Scharnhorst* hauled off to the north-east at thirty knots. Burnett did not follow, but closed the convoy now approaching from the west, reasoning that *Scharnhorst* would probably try again.

So it proved. Shortly after midday, *Scharnhorst* was surprised by Burnett's cruisers for the second time as she headed for the convoy. After another short gun action, *Scharnhorst* turned and fled to the south-east, steering for home. Burnett in *Belfast* was content to follow in *Scharnhorst*'s wake, transmitting periodic reports of her position, course and speed, knowing that his quarry's course would lead her directly towards *Duke of York*.

Fraser could see the situation developing, just as he had hoped, on *Duke of York*'s plot. Force 2 and *Scharnhorst* were on converging courses. Wearing a polo-necked sweater, an old pair of baggy trousers and a battered admiral's cap, Fraser strode up and down his flag-bridge, puffing furiously at his pipe. He exuded confidence. There were two very young midshipmen on the bridge. Fraser could see they were apprehensive, even frightened. With a wink to the others, he gave the young men small tasks, to keep their minds occupied. In the run to the east leading to the Battle of North Cape, Fraser was a man sure of himself and of the men who served him. 'Shall we have the battle before tea or after?', he asked his staff. 'I think after tea.'

Fraser's staff calculated that the first radar contact of the enemy would be a minute either side of 4.15 p.m. The first contact, range 45,500 yards, or nearly twenty-three miles, was actually at 4.17 p.m. Fraser had decided to steer towards his target and open fire at the comparatively short range of about 12,000 yards. This was taking a risk. Several times during the war the initial German ranging and shooting had been excellent. There was always the chance of an unlucky early hit.

Force 2 steadily closed their target until, at 4.47 p.m. for the third and last time, *Scharnhorst* was caught totally unawares, with her turrets still trained fore and aft, by starshell from *Duke of York*, followed by broadsides from her fourteen-inch guns.

Once again, *Scharnhorst* turned, to the east, but reacted quickly. Within five minutes she was replying with her own main eleven-inch armament and steering a weaving course so as to open her gun arcs.

Fraser's destroyers had been in a good position to attack with torpedoes. However, in a move he later regretted, he had already signalled to them to take up positions for attack but not to fire until ordered. Afterwards Fraser said somewhat ruefully that he rather wished one of his destroyer captains had shown the Nelson spirit and disobeyed him.

Scharnhorst fled to the eastward faster than *Duke of York* or the destroyers could pursue her. Soon it was clear she was gaining and was going to escape. *Duke of York* had hit with almost every one of her first salvo and continued to score hits, but they seemed to have no serious effect, while *Scharnhorst* herself straddled *Duke of York* unpleasantly close.

At 6.40 p.m. a bitterly disappointed Fraser signalled to Burnett: 'I see little hope of catching *Scharnhorst* and am proceeding to support convoy.' It was another signal Fraser regretted but, as he said later, 'I *did* give up hope then, for the moment. Of course I can see now that I shouldn't have sent that signal – Burnett was furious – but what else could I think? We'd tried everything and it wasn't enough.'

But, almost as the signal was being sent, the range steadied, and then began to come down. It is probable that a shell from *Duke of York* hit one of *Scharnhorst*'s boiler rooms and reduced her speed that critical amount. The pursuing destroyers were able to close and fire their torpedoes. *Scharnhorst* turned like an animal at bay to the south-west and then to the north, with her speed down to a few knots. Her hull could be seen as a blazing wreck which eventually vanished in a pall of thick smoke, so that an anxious Fraser had to ask several times for confirmation that she had actually sunk.

Scharnhorst finally sank at about 7.45 p.m. after sustaining at least thirteen fourteen-inch shell hits, possibly a dozen lesser-calibre hits from the cruisers and destroyers, and eleven torpedo hits. There were only thirty-six survivors from a ship's company of about 2,000.

Duke of York's gunnery, the destroyers' torpedoes, Fraser's judicious breaking of radio silence and the all-pervasive influence of Ultra, which haunted *Scharnhorst* until her final hours, had all combined to give the Allies a great victory. It was the last major naval action to be fought between capital ships with no direct intervention from the air. It was, in this sense, a slogging match between dinosaurs.

Fraser was made a Knight Grand Cross of the Order of the Bath (GCB). The Presidium of the Supreme Council of the USSR also conferred on him the Order of Suvorov, First Degree. Fraser would have much preferred a DSO. He knew he was too senior, but he would have liked some sort of special dispensation to make him eligible. 'I would probably have got the GCB anyway,' he said. 'But I've got no other medals, nothing to show I've ever been in action. A DSO would at least prove I'd been fired at.'

Tirpitz was now the only remaining German heavy ship in the Arctic. The

Germans worked through the winter of 1943–4 to repair her damage. Progress was closely monitored by a Secret Service observer in Altenfjord, by photo-reconnaissance flights and by Ultra. By March 1944, these showed that *Tirpitz* was about to go to sea for trials. On 21 March, a few days before a large convoy, JW58, was due to sail, Fraser received an Ultra signal: 'It should be assumed that *Tirpitz* may be operationally effective and battleship cover for convoy JW58 should be given.' Fraser decided to combine the covering operation for JW58 with an attack by carrier aircraft on *Tirpitz* (Operation Tungsten).

JW58, which sailed on 27 March 1944, was the largest Arctic convoy of the war with forty-nine ships, and a huge escort of over thirty warships, including five sloops of Captain F. J. ('Johnny') Walker's [*q.v.*] famous 2nd Escort Group, and two escort carriers.

Fraser, in *Duke of York*, with his VA2 Vice Admiral Sir Henry Moore in *Anson*, accompanied by *Belfast*, the aircraft carrier *Victorious* and five destroyers and designated Force 1, sailed from Scapa Flow on 30 March. They were joined at sea by Force 2: the cruiser *Royalist*, with the aircraft carrier *Furious*, the escort carriers *Searcher*, *Emperor*, *Pursuer* and *Fencer*, with *Sheffield* and *Jamaica*, five destroyers and two oilers.

Hearing that JW58's powerful escort had sunk four U-boats and shot down six German aircraft, Fraser decided he need no longer cover the convoy and could concentrate upon Tungsten. When Ultra revealed that *Tirpitz* would very probably sail for sea trials on 3 April, Fraser brought forward the strikes by twenty-four hours.

Two strikes, one hour apart, were flown from *Victorious* and *Furious*, of forty Fairey Barracudas escorted by eighty fighters. *Tirpitz* was caught by surprise, as she was preparing to go to sea. She was hit by several bombs, a large fire started on her upper deck amidships and some hundreds of her ship's company were killed. A second attack on the following day was cancelled.

Fraser had decided against another strike; but Cunningham insisted. Fraser gave his reasons: *Tirpitz* would not be caught by surprise again, the nights were shortening, JW58 was the last northbound convoy that spring, so there would be no convoy at sea to distract the enemy's attention. The strikes were unlikely to have surprise and good weather again, and would only sacrifice valuable crews and aircraft needlessly.

Cunningham still insisted and recorded in his diary for 13 April 1944 that he found Fraser in a 'most truculent and obstinate mood'. Fraser had made the decision not to repeat Tungsten after consulting with his admirals and captains, and he would not alter it. According to Cunningham, Fraser implied that if he were ordered to repeat Tungsten, he would haul down his flag (this was later denied by Fraser). Cunningham told Fraser to sleep on it and call him up in the morning.

Next morning Cunningham thought he had obtained Fraser's agreement but later the Vice Chief of Naval Staff, Admiral Syfret, told Cunningham that Fraser was still talking of hauling down his flag. This Cunningham could not allow. He delayed sending the signal ordering the strike to be carried out and drafted another asking Fraser to come down to London and see him. Later, what Cunningham called 'wiser counsels' prevailed. 'Some manoeuvrings on a lower level' made Fraser 'more tractable'.

So the ships sailed for another strike (Planet), planned for 23 April but cancelled because of bad weather. The aircraft attacked shipping in Bodo Harbour instead. Another strike flew off on 15 May (Brawn) but was frustrated by thick cloud over the target area. Yet another strike on 28 May (Tiger Claw) was abandoned because of bad weather. More strikes followed later in the year, but on 16 June 1944 Fraser was relieved as C-in-C Home Fleet by Vice Admiral Sir Henry Moore.

Fraser was no intriguer and abhorred 'office politics', but through no fault of his own his next appointment was clouded by controversy. He was appointed C-in-C Eastern Fleet, relieving Admiral Sir James Somerville, who was to go to Washington.

The Eastern Fleet had been reinforced with battleships, carriers, cruisers and many destroyers since the beginning of 1944. It seemed hard to send Somerville, who had been C-in-C through the lean years, to a shore desk just as his fleet was gathering strength and could start to hit back at the enemy. But a 'heavyweight' personality was needed in Washington to stand up to the obsessively Anglophobic US Naval Commander-in-Chief, Admiral 'Ernie' King [*q.v.*]. Furthermore, there was personal friction between Somerville and Mountbatten, Supreme Allied Commander, South-East Asia.

It was not just that Somerville was eighteen years older than Mountbatten and a substantive admiral whereas Mountbatten was a captain who had been advanced to acting admiral. Somerville was responsible for the SEAC area but also for the Persian Gulf and much of the east coast of Africa – outside SEAC. Therefore he could be responsible to the Admiralty or to Mountbatten for any of his ships depending upon where they were and what they were doing. This anomalous situation was not improved by Somerville's independent attitude towards Mountbatten.

Churchill approved Fraser's appointment but then said he wanted to leave Somerville where he was. He finally yielded to the arguments of Cunningha ` and A. V. Alexander, the First Lord, who knew that if Somerville were not relieved Mountbatten would ask for his removal.

Fraser hoisted his flag as C-in-C Eastern Fleet on 23 August 1944. Typically, he took a much more co-operative and conciliatory line. As he said, 'One can't fall out with one's Supreme Commander.' Mountbatten later wrote that matters 'improved beyond recognition in August 1944'.

Fraser was C-in-C Eastern Fleet only for a short time. At the Octagon Conference in Quebec in September 1944, Churchill offered President Roosevelt a British fleet in the Far East, an offer which was accepted, although King quibbled and cavilled, both then and later. Fraser was to be the fleet's C-in-C. In October he flew to London to discuss its formation. On his way back he stopped in Cairo to see Vice-Admiral Sir Bernard Rawlings, Flag Officer Middle East, who was to be his second-in-command.

Rawlings had already had a hard war. He was wounded when his flagship was bombed off Crete in 1941. But Fraser found him 'fit and well and I was delighted to have him. Afterwards Rawlings told me he knew he was being vetted!'

As C-in-C BPF designate, Fraser found that every proposal he made about his fleet was turned down by the Admiralty. At last he wrote to Cunningham early in November to point out that these constant rebuffs were causing him to lose credibility in his fleet and he thought it time someone else was chosen as C-in-C. Cunningham called it an 'unpleasant letter' and took no action.

Thus, on 22 November 1944, Fraser hoisted his flag in the battleship *Howe* as C-in-C British Pacific Fleet. His second-in-command, Admiral Sir Arthur John Power, became C-in-C East Indies Fleet.

As C-in-C BPF, Fraser faced immense and unprecedented difficulties. He commanded the Royal Navy's largest fleet of the war with – at 12,000 sea miles from home – the longest line of communication of any British fleet in history. For the conduct of the fleet, he was answerable to the Admiralty. For fleet operations he was responsible to Admiral Chester Nimitz [*q.v.*] at Pearl Harbor. For the supply and shore support of the fleet he negotiated directly with the Australian and New Zealand governments.

Fraser was determined his fleet should take part in the main carrier war against Japan, in the Central Pacific, and not (as was mooted more than once) be shunted into seeming sideshows in the South-west Pacific. Fraser recognized that it was essential for him to have good relations with the Americans and it is greatly to his credit that he succeeded so well. He strongly advocated changing to US communications procedures (against opposition from the Admiralty) and was always punctilious in such matters as wearing khakis to conform to American dress.

In December 1944 Fraser flew with a small personal staff to Pearl Harbor to meet Admiral Chester Nimitz, C-in-C Pacific. The two men liked and respected each other from the start. 'I congratulated Nimitz on what the American fleet had done,' said Fraser. 'He said, "Yes, I think we have done well. There's only one thing we envy you – your British tradition. It's the one thing you've got which can neither be bought nor sold. Guard it with your lives." Wonderful thing for an American admiral to say.'

Nimitz and Fraser signed the Pearl Harbor Agreement: Fraser was to report his fleet for duty to King, who would assign it either to Nimitz or to General Douglas MacArthur; Rawlings would have the same status at sea as an American task force commander, but could be placed under American orders if the tactical situation demanded it; the British would adopt American signal methods and procedures; the fleet was to have an intermediate base at Manus in the Admiralty Islands.

From Pearl Harbor, Fraser went to Leyte to meet MacArthur. Significantly, no agreement was signed although in theory the BPF was as likely at that time to serve under MacArthur as under Nimitz. At MacArthur's invitation Fraser took passage in Vice-Admiral Jesse B. Oldendorf's flagship, the battleship *New Mexico*, to witness the Lingayen Gulf landings in the Philippines.

Fraser was on *New Mexico*'s flag-bridge when it was struck by a Japanese kamikaze on 6 January 1945. General Lumsden (Churchill's representative on MacArthur's staff) and Fraser's secretary were killed. Fraser was badly shocked but unhurt.

The BPF, when it arrived in Australia in February 1945, was a balanced fleet of battleships, carriers, cruisers and destroyers which, had it been available to Somerville two years earlier, could have altered the course of the war. Its main strike force was the four fleet carriers, with 238 aircraft, commanded by Rear Admiral Sir Philip Vian [*q.v.*], the navy's stormy petrel of World War Two.

On passage to Australia, the BPF's aircraft carried out strikes – requested by Nimitz, discouraged at home, but insisted upon by Fraser – against two large oil refineries at Palembang in Sumatra. Despite some losses of aircraft, the strikes reduced the refineries' capacity by more than half.

The BPF sailed from Sydney on the 28th, Rawlings flying his flag in the battleship *King George V*, and arrived at Manus on 7 March. There followed a most uncomfortable, hot and tedious wait, while the fleet's fate was debated at a high political level. At last, on 15 March, the BPF was allocated to Nimitz for operations connected with the invasion of Okinawa (codenamed Iceberg) on 1 April.

For Iceberg the BPF, designated Task Force 57, was stationed semi-independently on the left of the US Fifth Fleet's battle-line, off the islands of the Sakishima Gunto, south-west of Okinawa. Its task was to prevent the Japanese staging aircraft reinforcements from Formosa up to Okinawa, by neutralizing the airfields on the islands of Miyako and Ishigaki. It was a necessary but unglamorous assignment, with no chance of glory and every chance of being attacked.

In grinding down the airfields of the Sakishima Gunto, TF 57 spent sixty-two days at sea, broken by eight days at Leyte, flew some 2,500 sorties, and destroyed fifty-seven enemy aircraft for the loss (mostly not for combat reasons) of 203 of their own. All five carriers taking part in Iceberg were hit at least once by kamikaze suicide bombers.

After Iceberg the US Navy accepted the BPF. Although King remained eternally suspicious, Nimitz and his two fleet commanders, Raymond Spruance [*q.v.*] and 'Bull' Halsey [*q.v.*], welcomed the British, provided they were self-supporting. In practice, the BPF benefited enormously from the splendid 'can do' spirit of the US Navy.

The fleet returned to Australia where Fraser, who had his headquarters in Sydney, had been fighting battles on the diplomatic, political and logistical fronts. The Australian Labour government thought Australia had 'done enough' in the war, while the unions, especially the dockers and the shipwrights, were positively hostile to a British fleet. Much depended upon Fraser's personality and the 'Fraser touch'. Once he had to make the official speech of thanks for a cheque subscribed by munitions workers for the British Centre, established for the entertainment of British sailors in Sydney. 'I noticed', he began, with an innocent expression, 'the cheque is for fourteen hundred pounds, eleven shillings and threepence. If the girl who subscribed the threepence would be good enough to come up on to the platform I should like to give her a kiss!'

Fraser's most intractable problem was finding enough ships for the Fleet Train – the tankers, store ships and ammunition ships which supplied the fleet at sea. The Royal Navy was simply not used to operating for such long periods and over such vast distances as in the Pacific. Although the Fleet Train performed magnificently, in spite of their many disadvantages, they remained a motley collection of vessels, with polyglot crews, assembled from scratch in a matter of months.

The BPF sailed again on 28 June and this time, designated Task Force 37, took its place on the right of the line. In the final operations against the mainland of Japan in July and August 1945, TF 37 played its full part in air strikes and bombardments and overcame its many handicaps to strike relatively blow for blow with the US fleet almost until the surrender of Japan. At the end, to their bitter disappointment, most of TF 37 had to withdraw for lack of fuel.

Flying his flag in the battleship *Duke of York*, Fraser joined his fleet at sea off Japan on 16 August. There was no love lost between *Duke of York* and *King George V*, which had been Rawlings' flagship since Iceberg. *King George V*'s sailors conceded that *Duke of York* had sunk the *Scharnhorst*, but she had done precious little in the Pacific, arriving only after the atomic bomb had been dropped and the shooting had stopped.

Feelings ran so high that Fraser visited *King George V*, had her lower deck cleared and in a straight speech left them in no doubt of his own views. The medicine worked, as it did when *Duke of York* was booed by the cruiser *Euryalus* as she entered Hong Kong after the war. Fraser visited *Euryalus*, too; as somebody who was present said, 'You could have heard a pin drop, but the point was taken.' Fraser had the impression that even Bernard Rawlings, the most generous of men, felt that he had rather usurped what should have been his, Rawlings', rightful role at the surrender of Japan.

Attended by Rawlings and Rear Admiral Brind, Fraser signed Japan's surrender document on behalf of Great Britain at the ceremony on board the US battleship *Missouri* in Tokyo Bay on 2 September 1945. It was a solemn proceeding. 'The silence was complete,' Fraser said, 'except for the whirring and clicking of cameras, and one could feel that all present at that gathering were struggling to adjust themselves mentally to the fact that they were witnessing the act which put an end to a long and bitter war.'

*

Fraser was made a baron in the New Year's Honours List of 1946, taking the name North Cape in his title. He came home and struck his flag at Portsmouth in July 1946. Became C-in-C Portsmouth in May 1947; First Sea Lord and Chief of the Naval Staff in September 1948, and during his First Lordship presided over the beginnings of NATO. Promoted Admiral of the Fleet in October 1948. He went on half-pay in April 1952. He had a long and happy retirement (although technically an Admiral of the Fleet never retires) and died on 12 February 1981. He never married.

26

Admiral of the Fleet

Sir Philip Vian

GCB, KBE, DSO**
Royal Navy

1894–1968

by
Stephen Howarth

PHILIP Louis Vian, born 15 June 1894, London. Joined RN College, Osborne, Isle of Wight, 1907; passed out of Dartmouth as cadet 1911, and later promoted midshipman; served in training cruiser Cornwall *and battleship* Lord Nelson. *Transferred to cruiser* Argonaut, *1914, then to destroyer* Morning Star; *witnessed Battle of Jutland, 1916. Promoted lieutenant 1917; served as first lieutenant in destroyers* Ossory *and* Sorceress. *As lieutenant, trained as gunnery officer and served as such in* Australia, *cadet training battleship* Thunderer *and* Empress of India. *As lieutenant-commander (1929) served in* Kent, *flagship of China Station. Married Marjorie (née Haig), 2 December 1929. Two years working on statistics in Admiralty. Divisional leader of 3rd Destroyer Flotilla (Mediterranean), HMS* Active, *1932; promoted captain, 1934; commanded 19th Destroyer Flotilla, then 1st Destroyer Flotilla (both Mediterranean), 1935–6. Royal Naval College, Greenwich, 1936; flag captain to Rear Admiral Lionel Wells in* Arethusa, *flagship of 3rd Cruiser Squadron (Mediterranean); relieved and appointed to command boys' training establishment at Shotley, Suffolk, August 1939.*

When it was all over, Philip Vian had a very distinct recollection of the mood of August 1939. 'Whereas in 1914', he remembered, 'most of us stood in dread that we should *not* honour our bond, in 1939 we had hoped to the last for peace.' In 1914, he had been a young man, only twenty years old; in 1916, as a sub-lieutenant in HMS *Morning Star* ('the latest and fastest destroyer in the Grand Fleet'), he had witnessed the Battle of Jutland, and though his ship had not taken direct part in the action he had been mightily 'impressed by the thunder of the broadsides of the battle fleet'. By 1939 that time of comparative freedom was long gone, and he was a captain of five years' seniority, with experience of commanding destroyer flotillas in both the Italian–Abyssinian war zone and that of the Spanish Civil War.

Before Germany invaded Poland on 3 September 1939, Vian's mood was not coloured by cowardice, or fear of the likelihood that he would have to take responsibility in war for several ships and many lives; it was simply that, like almost everyone else in Britain who had lived through the Great War, he had hoped the nations would never have to fight again. But if they did, they did, and it was the job he was trained to do. There was, perhaps, one thing in its favour; he had never been happy with shore billets, and no sooner was he ordered to run the boys' training establishment at Shotley in Suffolk than the order was cancelled. Instead, he was directed to take immediate charge of a reserve destroyer flotilla, based at Plymouth in Devon. This was the first posting of what proved to be a brilliant wartime career, distinguished particularly by his outstanding successes as a tactical commander; and by September 1945 Captain Vian would be Vice Admiral Sir Philip Vian, KCB, KBE, the holder of three DSOs and the French Croix de Guerre, and a member of both the Légion d'Honneur and the Legion of Merit.

'His terse war memoir, *Action This Day*, is characterized', according to one authority, 'by generosity to those who served with him.' This is true. The autobiography is also characterized by a modesty which, looking at his war record, seems excessive; playing down his successes, which were many, he details his failures, which were comparatively few. Together, these character-istics of the book naturally suggest to the reader that modesty and generosity were two of the aspects of Vian's make-up; yet even one of the grateful beneficiaries of his generous writing, Rear Admiral Royer Dick, later dismissed the idea of modesty – 'He wasn't like that at all.' Speaking shortly before his own death in April 1991, Dick agreed that Vian was (at least in later life) vain and snobbish, socially awkward and rude; but Dick was at pains to emphasize the clarity, economy and precision of his writing.

Blessed with a good memory and a ready pen, Reginald ('Bob') Whinney – one of those who served with Vian – was able, many years later, to write his own vivid autobiography, *The U-Boat Peril*, in which he explains well the difference between Vian the commander and Vian the writer. Assuming accuracy, the best naval reports are the simplest and shortest. Vian, a thoroughly profes-sional officer, 'had no surfeit of false modesty, yet his written reports were brief to the point of being self-effacing'. Once gained, this was a habit he never lost; yet it means that a reader relying solely on Vian's autobiography, *Action This Day*, would not even learn about his DSOs – even though there were very few others who gained so many, and only one man who gained four.

Similarly, there are two factors concerning Vian about which everyone who served with him agrees, yet neither emerges from his autobiography at all. The first is that he was a superb sea-warrior. 'When it came to contact with the enemy,' says Whinney, 'Vian was gifted as few before.' The second – and Vian can be forgiven for not saying this about himself – is that both inside and outside the navy he was stupendously rude.

Some of the great naval leaders of World War Two have been written about very often, and now, half a century after that war, are almost as famous now as they were then. Others whose work was equally vital – particularly those in the field of intelligence – were not widely known at the time, for obvious reasons, but have come to prominence with the passing of the years. However, Philip Vian falls into neither category. At the time in Great Britain he was publicly celebrated, his name common knowledge; today, outside the diminishing circle of those who knew him personally, he is largely forgotten. Still more oddly, among those who did not know him but do know his name, one of the few things 'remembered' about him is that he won the Victoria Cross; indeed, in at least one book of great weight and authority this is plainly stated as a fact, and that he won it as a reward for the legendary *Altmark* episode. Yet though he earned five Mentions in Despatches, two knighthoods (first of the Order of the British Empire, later of the more senior Order of the Bath), a DSO and two bars, and a clutch of foreign awards, he never actually won a VC.

Perhaps he should have; certainly, in the days of his fame, many believed he deserved one, and they may have been right. But today, when myth is attached to legend, when those who knew him grow fewer each year, and when there is still only one book – his own – about him, it is appropriate to try and clear up some of the muddle, and find out not only the simple facts of his career, but also something of what he was like.

His command of the reserve destroyer flotilla at Plymouth was brief: it began in September 1939, and finished before the end of December. Yet even in that short period, he came to close action with the enemy, when his ancient destroyer *Mackay* surprised a surfaced U-boat, as it sat shelling a tanker which it had already blown in two. *Mackay* – a veteran of World War One – charged into the attack, only to find, as she made ready to depth-charge the swiftly diving submarine, that the speed of her advance had shaken her Asdic (the equipment for detecting submerged submarines) to pieces. So the U-boat escaped, and there was nothing left for *Mackay* to do but finish sinking the tanker, which otherwise would have been a hazard to shipping, and pick up the survivors.

It was not a very auspicious start, but lessons were learned about antiquated Asdic and the need for base repair staff; and from the beginning of 1940, when Vian moved on from Plymouth, he seemed always to be at sea wherever the fighting was hardest. 'You only know Philip Vian', said one of his colleagues, 'when you've seen him in a fight.' So what was he like? How do those who saw him in a fight remember him? The *Altmark* episode is a good place to begin, because it was both the first time he came to public prominence, and the occasion which spawned the myth of his VC.

The background was this. *Altmark* was the tender to the 11,900-ton *Admiral Graf Spee*, one of three *Panzerschiffe*, or armoured ships, as the Germans called them. With a cruiser's displacement, they were built like battleships, and the British called them pocket battleships. At the outbreak of war, *Graf Spee*'s task was to be a surface raider, attacking individual enemy merchant ships whenever she happened to find them. This *guerre de course* was a traditional strategy for any comparatively weak navy; both the French and, in their time, the Americans had employed it against Britain's Royal Navy, and *Graf Spee*'s short career was efficient and humane. In three months she sank nine British ships, reputedly without the loss of a single British life. Prisoners were put ashore when possible, and kept in *Altmark* when not; and, after the Battle of the River Plate (13 December 1939), when *Graf Spee*'s Captain Erich Langsdorff scuttled his ship rather than surrender, *Altmark* returned to European waters (a nine-week voyage, undetected the whole way) with 299 British prisoners on board.

At noon on 15 February 1940, with her guns removed so that she looked like an ordinary tanker, she passed the Norwegian port of Bergen. The same evening, the Captain of the *Tribal*-class 4th Destroyer Flotilla, based at Rosyth in Scotland, received a signal from the Commander-in-Chief, Home Fleet; '*Altmark* your objective. Act accordingly.' Vian did so, sweeping his flotilla of one cruiser and five destroyers through the night, and feeling, at first, full of uncertainty. Poor visibility was made worse by the black background of Norway's rocky coast; no one was sure what their quarry looked like – the only picture they had of *Altmark* was from the *Illustrated London News* – and to make matters trickier there was a question of legality. Norway then was still neutral, so if *Altmark* had prisoners on board and if she went inside neutral territorial waters they would be entitled to release. Whether they would be released or not was another matter, and, if they were not, Vian's warships might also have to enter neutral waters.

That was precisely what happened. *Altmark* was located on the evening of the 16th, escorted by two Norwegian torpedo boats, whose senior officer said she had been examined three times without any sign of prisoners being on board, and who – when Vian demanded to have a look for himself – trained his torpedo tubes on the British ships. *Altmark* took shelter in Jössing Fjord, near Stavanger. As night wore on, timing became critical; German aircraft could be expected at daylight. Requesting instructions from Whitehall, Vian was ordered to board the German, while using minimum force against the Norwegians. The latter withdrew, sensibly deciding that honour was satisfied by the threat of superior force. Inside the confines of the narrow fjord, there was brisk manoeuvring as *Altmark* moved smartly astern, attempting to dazzle and ram Vian's flagship, the destroyer *Cossack*. 'Normally', said Lieutenant-Commander Peter Gretton (later Vice Admiral Sir Peter), 'Vian was not an above-average ship-handler but, as always in an emergency, his performance was immaculate.' It had to be; the fjord was little more than an inlet, about a third of a mile wide and a mile and a half long, and a Norwegian pilot book says it 'can only be taken by small vessels with local knowledge'. But at last *Cossack* was close enough for the First Lieutenant, Bradwell Turner, and Petty Officer Norman Atkins to leap from one vessel to the other. The boarding party followed; there was a short, sharp, hand-to-hand fight before *Altmark*'s crew was overcome; then the locked hatches of the holds were broken open and Turner bellowed: 'Any British down there?' A clamour of voices came back: 'Yes – we're all British!' 'Come on up then,' Turner called, and someone on deck shouted: 'The navy's here!'

During their visits, the Norwegians (who had not actually searched the ship) had missed the 299 prisoners because the German crew had made the maximum possible noise with winches and hoses, to cover any sound from the holds. To the British public, the whole exploit was so dashing – especially given the otherwise inert state of the 'phoney war' – that it and the memorable phrase, 'The navy's here', naturally became very famous very fast. 'I received many letters from the public after this affair,' said Vian in his autobiography. 'A number wrote to say that, as I had failed to shoot, or hang, the Captain of *Altmark*, I ought to be shot myself.'

Instead of that fate, both he and Lieutenant-Commander (later Commander) Turner were awarded the DSO. Although it was a small episode in the course of the naval war as a whole, the *Altmark* affair is important for a number of reasons. It illustrates how astonishingly quickly true stories can become distorted, with misapprehensions becoming accepted as fact. Despite the statements in Vian's autobiography and any number of newspaper reports, Turner was not the man who shouted 'The navy's here!' He says so himself – 'right words, wrongly attributed'. The phrase was used, but by whom? No one, not even those who were present, actually knows for sure. Similarly, the well-known painting of the incident shows *Cossack*'s forecastle, crowded with men, close to *Altmark*'s waist, with the German vessel aground by the stern. Spectators assume this shows the moments before boarding; in fact, when Turner made his jump, it was on to *Altmark*'s starboard quarter, when she was trying to ram *Cossack* with her stern. The ships parted soon after, when it became apparent that *Altmark*'s speed was going to take her aground, and when *Cossack* returned to take off the boarding party and the rescued prisoners, the ships lay bow to bow. In short, dramatic as it is, the moment depicted in the painting never actually took place, any more than the award of a Victoria Cross to Vian.

Close knowledge of the episode also emphasizes the element of luck present, as in any conflict. *Cossack* happened to be in the right place at the right time, trawling, so to speak, for any stray German merchant ships on their way home; she was not at first looking specifically for *Altmark*. Further, *Cossack* happened to have an officer on board (Pay Sub-Lieutenant Geoffrey Craven RNVR) who spoke both German and Norwegian fluently; the ship also happened to be carrying a good number of extra hands, whose own ships were refitting, and so could make up a boarding party without depleting her crew; and her freeboard happened to be almost identical to *Altmark*'s, making their decks nearly the same level, and Turner's jump a practical method of boarding, when ice floes in the fjord prevented the use of boats.

Finally, and most pertinently for this chapter, the episode emphasized Philip Vian's personal qualities of leadership, particularly his ship-handling in emergency – 'deft', 'magnificent', 'immaculate', say those who were there. It was also interesting for Turner to see how, after the action, Vian 'completely unbent'. At 2 a.m., while the flotilla sped homeward, he summoned Turner to the charthouse to help compile their official report. 'Now,' he said, 'we've got to make up the story.' It was perhaps an unfortunate phrase, given the later mythology, but as they worked together, sharing mugs of hot cocoa, it showed Vian relaxing in a way he never normally did.

Vian's six years of war divided into four broad but distinct periods and geographical areas. These were firstly (September 1939 to October 1941) the North Sea and its fringes, from the Eastern Atlantic to northern Norway and right into Russia; secondly (October 1941 to September 1943 including a break when he was ill) the Mediterranean; thirdly (October 1943 to October 1944) the English Channel; and lastly (November 1944 to the end of the war) South-East Asia and the Western Pacific.

His conduct during that first period may be judged simply from the list of his awards while captaining HMS *Cossack*. He was Mentioned in Despatches for his part in the withdrawal from Namsos (May 1940); he won a bar to his DSO for Operation DM, the destruction of a German convoy off the Norwegian coast (October 1940); and he won a second bar for his part in the pursuit and sinking of the 45,000-ton battleship *Bismarck* (24–26 May 1941). In other words, within two years of the outbreak of war, *Cossack* had become one of the Royal Navy's best-known destroyers, and Philip Vian one of its most highly decorated captains. Small wonder, then, that – describing him as a 'top-class wartime captain' – Bradwell Turner still said (just a few weeks before his own death in the spring of 1990): 'I would have followed him anywhere.'

'P.L.V. was a man who lived on his nerves – and very resilient they must have been,' said Lieutenant (later Captain) Bob Whinney. Joining the ship when she was already famous, Whinney could see clearly both the cause and the effect of the *Altmark* episode and other successes. 'As compared with other ships I had known in those early days of the war,' he wrote later, '*Cossack*, leader of the 4th Destroyer Flotilla, was a very efficient ship, had good officers, and the Captain was trusted by his officers and men alike as one who would pursue the enemy effectively and hard but would never take a risk rashly or by accident.'

Yet in those two years, the risks had been many and great, and Vian and his flotilla had not come through them entirely unscathed. Less than two months after the *Altmark* affair, strained Anglo-Norwegian relations deteriorated further when (on 8 April 1940) British warships began mining the approaches to Norway's territorial waters, with the object of preventing the transport of war materials, particularly iron ore, from Sweden to Germany. Norway's whole population numbered only three million, and its army only 13,000 – small opposition for the Reich if, as Norwegians feared, the British action dragged them into the war. In fact, with or without British mines, the war was about to be brought to Norway; the following day (9 April), seaborne German troops invaded at six points, from Oslo in the south to Narvik in the north. Eleven hundred miles of coast separated them, yet the operation was so efficient that all landings took place simultaneously. Spirited Norwegian opposition was confused by treacherous radio broadcasts from Vidkun Quisling, and within a few hours all main ports were in German hands.

The last time German warships had advanced up the North Sea in strength was April 1918. Then, the Royal Navy was able to bring thirty-five capital ships, twenty-six cruisers and eighty-five destroyers against them; now, as the brief and bitter Norwegian campaign began, Britain had only three capital ships, six cruisers and twenty-one destroyers in the same area. The widespread, co-ordinated German initiative perplexed the British: for example, just before noon Vian (temporarily in the destroyer *Afridi*) was ordered to prepare to take seven destroyers from the 4th and 6th Flotillas up the long fjord to Bergen; then just after 2 p.m. the order was cancelled. Instead, with little or no information about shore batteries, booms, port defences or berthing arrangements for ships actually in the harbour, British cruisers screened by destroyers approached the port directly. Soon they came under heavy air attack from the Luftwaffe. With waves breaking over their foreturrets and spray blinding their gun-directors above the bridge, the destroyers found themselves much handicapped. To improve her attack position, HMS *Gurkha* (Commander Sir Anthony Buzzard) turned out of the screen. Later, with mournful hindsight, Vian said: 'I should have recalled him at once.' But there was at that time no firm doctrine for surface forces countering air attack. He let *Gurkha* go; the separated ship rapidly became an easy target; and, under concentrated assault, she was sunk shortly after nightfall.

The episode was tragically typical of British efforts over the next three weeks: the bravest of intentions undone by lack of experience of or preparations for what was still essentially a new form of warfare. British troops were successfully landed at various points, while at sea there were some notable victories – especially the First and Second Battles of Narvik (10 and 13 April), when ten German destroyers were sunk at the cost of two British destroyers. But by the beginning of May it was evident that, for the time being at least, the troops would have to be evacuated and the campaign abandoned; and on 3 May Vian's own ship *Afridi* met the same fate as *Gurkha*.

The occasion was the evacuation of troops from the central Norwegian port of Namsos. Located at the head of another long, narrow fjord, the harbour was already untenable to Allied warships during daylight because of the close proximity (and even closer attention) of land-based enemy bombers. The operation was therefore planned to be carried out over two nights, but bad weather meant only a single night was available. *Afridi* was first of the evacuating vessels in, and last out, her final action within the harbour being to destroy by gunfire the abandoned vehicles on the quayside. Outside the fjord, the ships (commanded by Admiral John Cunningham – later Admiral of the Fleet Sir John, unrelated to Admiral of the Fleet Sir Andrew Cunningham) were attacked by Junkers-88 bombers and Stuka dive bombers, and soon two destroyers (the French *Bison* and British *Grenade*) were sinking. Fuel oil from *Bison*'s tanks spread over the water and ignited, so that the sea itself was on fire. Nevertheless, *Afridi* managed to take on sixty-nine survivors – but then she too came under Stuka attack. By that time, experience had shown that the best defensive manoeuvre was a violent turn towards the attacking aircraft, whose angle of descent – if it was to succeed – would become impossibly steep. As the turn was being done, another Stuka came in from the opposite side. Vian overruled a suggestion that the turn should be instantly reversed. 'This', he later wrote frankly, 'was fatal. The first bomb hit us just behind the bridge, exploded in the foremost boiler-room, and started a devastating fire. The second hit us just ahead of the bridge. . . .'

Despite every effort, *Afridi* sank that afternoon. 'We lost 49 officers and men, 13 soldiers, and more than 30 of the twice unlucky *Bison*'s.'

It is a terrible thing to survive such an event knowing that one's own decision led to the deaths of so many of one's own men. Even so, when Bob Whinney compared Vian and the glamorous Lord Louis Mountbatten (then also a destroyer captain), the difference overall was clear: while Mountbatten supervised 'a series of glorious disasters', 'it was he, Vian, who remained successful in action'.

Certainly the loss of *Afridi* did not do irreversible damage to Vian's standing in the navy. The first time Whinney saw action under his command was Operation DM, a successful night-time ambush of a small German convoy. Once again, there was no firm guidance on how such a thing should be done, and with minimal information Vian had to pose and answer his own questions: whether to attack the escorts or the convoy first; whether to use inflexible close order, or flexible but potentially uncontrollable independent order; and, given that the flotilla was much faster than the convoy, how to remain in action – whether by often reversing course or by circling in restricted sea-room. 'The plan as evolved was imperfect, as hastily conceived plans will be,' said Vian. The self-deprecating tone of the remark is typical of his writing, but not so of the man. Whinney is more forthright: 'At such close range there was no fancy fire-control. . . . There was not much missing the target, and with our own ships in line ahead, it was safe to assume that anything seen on either side was enemy. . . . P.L.V. was at his best; no cursing, no swearing.'

Inside a quarter of an hour after they had been found (off the Norwegian coast, close by the Egero Light), two of the four convoyed ships had been sunk and a third was on fire, while the fourth and the escorts – which had also been heavily attacked – had vanished, presumably sunk or sinking elsewhere. 'Unnerving?', said Whinney. 'No. It was exhilarating to us all.' And Vian got the first bar to his DSO.

Whinney was also present during the battle against *Bismarck* (24–27 May 1941), when Vian – still in *Cossack* as Captain (D) of the 4th Destroyer Flotilla – earned his second bar. In Whinney's striking phrase, the 45,000-ton German battleship was 'new, fast, large, very heavily armed and armoured, magnificent'. Speaking about another officer, Vian had recently remarked to him: 'Any bloody fool can make things complicated. It takes a little more to make them simple.' Thus, in his own mind, Vian was able to reduce the situation posed by *Bismarck* to 'a classic one; enemy battleship with speed reduced, but probably still faster than our own battleships, which were closing in. Our destroyers attack, reduce enemy's speed still further and bring in the heavy ships to deliver the *coup de grâce*'. In fact, as he soon realized, *Bismarck* was already considerably slowed. The main task therefore became the shadowing of the enemy through the night, attacking, when possible, with torpedoes. Severe weather and *Bismarck*'s fifteen-inch shells did not make this any easier or more pleasant, but the destroyers managed to stay in contact, and in the morning, after withstanding what Vian thought was 'a really incredible amount of punishment' from the British battleships *Rodney* and *King George V*, *Bismarck* was sunk.

The action demonstrated again Vian's great ability to handle groups of destroyers in more or less any circumstances. But it also showed one area of weakness in him: an impatient disinclination to make full use of new naval technology. Certainly no sensible commanding officer will clutter his mind with superfluous detail, but as an anti-submarine specialist Whinney (and it should be remembered that he admired his captain very much) had already found Vian – a gunnery specialist – to be just not interested in AS techniques. Similarly, during the *Bismarck* action, Vian simply shut off the bridge voicepipe to the radar room, when the primitive machine could not provide the kind of information he wanted. To Vian, says Whinney, 'simplicity and clarity meant everything, tolerance very little and . . . good manners depended on how he was feeling'.

Nevertheless, the First Sea Lord, Admiral Sir Dudley Pound [*q.v.*], liked the way he worked, and very soon after the *Bismarck* action Vian was given early promotion to the rank of rear admiral (July 1941). He was just forty-seven years old.

At once he was flown to Russia on a quasi-diplomatic mission. Hitler's treacherous attack (22 June) on the Russians, his former allies, had radically altered the maps of war, and Vian's task was to arrange naval co-operation with the Soviet Union against Nazi Germany. But the Russians, shocked, bewildered and deeply distrustful, proved obstructive in the Kremlin and unready in the ports; the mission was a failure; and back in Britain Vian learned

499

at first hand how political considerations could override military advice. Pound arranged for him to present his analysis to the War Cabinet. Round-the-clock summer daylight, the lack of Russian defences and warning systems and the proximity of German submarines and airfields all pointed to the rashness of sending surface ships. In Vian's assessment, one submarine, or at the most two, should be sent until the Russians were better organized, and the situation then reviewed. The Chiefs of Staff agreed, but 'the Foreign Secretary, Mr Eden, regarded my recommendations as calamitous'.

The outcome was the creation of Force K, designed to prepare the way for regular convoys to Russia. Working out of Scapa and led by Vian in the cruiser *Nigeria*, this short-lived group was much more successful than anyone could reasonably have expected. Within a few weeks they had blown up the weather-reporting station at Bear Island and destroyed the coal-mining facilities at Spitsbergen, denying these important strategic aids to the Germans; they had evacuated the Norwegian and the Russian inhabitants of Spitsbergen; and early in September they had fought one of the closest actions of the war. Searching for a reported German convoy, Vian took his cruisers at full speed, in the dark, into Hammer Fjord in the far north of Norway. The convoy was found, battle was joined at such close quarters that one enemy ship actually passed too close to be fired on, and – reverting unintentionally to an older form of warfare – *Nigeria* rammed the convoy's escort leader (the training cruiser *Bremse*) and cut her in two.

Vian really had been lucky that time: no one had seen *Bremse*, and the shock of the impact was so great that at first he was sure *Nigeria* had been torpedoed. *Bremse* was left to sink; the battered British flagship was nursed back across the North Sea at eight knots; and a few weeks later (28 September 1941) the first of the Allied Russian convoys sailed from Iceland. Since it was no longer needed, Force K was dissolved. *Bremse*'s spectacular end was also the end of Vian's time in the North Sea. Pound had a new job in mind for him.

'Prime Minister to Commander-in-Chief Mediterranean, 25 Mar 42: I shall be glad if you will convey to Admiral Vian and all who sailed with him the admiration which I feel at this resolute and brilliant action.' Six months after the dissolution of Force K, Winston Churchill was thrilled to learn of Vian's latest achievement: the successful defence, against strong Italian attack, of a convoy from Alexandria in Egypt to the beleaguered island of Malta. 'That one of the most powerful battleships afloat,' the PM's telegraph continued, 'attended by two heavy and one light cruiser and a flotilla, should have been routed and put to flight with severe torpedo and gunfire injuries in broad daylight by the fire of British light cruisers and destroyers constitutes a naval episode of the highest distinction. . . . '

Malta, in the middle of the comparatively narrow channel between northern Africa and southern Europe, had been the British Mediterranean Fleet's base for nearly 150 years, until 1939, when the base was switched to Alexandria. But as the crossing point of Mediterranean communications, both north–south and east–west, Malta continued to be vital; its defeat or successful defence would probably decide the war in Africa. In February 1942, an Allied three-ship convoy was destroyed by air attack; early in March, Vian's own flagship, the cruiser *Naiad*, was sunk by a U-boat; and it was forecast that, unless further supplies were transmitted, by May the island's stocks of food, aviation spirit and fuel oil would be so low that famine would begin, and defeat must ensue.

It was imperative for a convoy to get through. Four ships, carrying 26,000 tons of supplies, were placed under Vian's protection. In their voyage, the battle which came to be known as the Second Battle of Sirte took place (22 March). On Vian's part, it was a fantastic demonstration of bravery and tactical skill. Naval mathematics said he should have been defeated: his force was made up of four light cruisers and eleven destroyers, while the Italian Admiral Angelo Iachino's force included ten destroyers, one light cruiser, two heavy cruisers and the battleship *Littorio*. But the same two admirals had already met and fought in the First Battle of Sirte (17 December 1941). On that occasion, Vian had fought his light cruisers and destroyers so boldly that Iachino, believing there must be British battleships close at hand, withdrew his own battleships and heavy cruisers. In Alexandria, Admiral Sir Andrew Cunningham, Commander-in-Chief Mediterranean [*q.v.*], followed the Second Battle's progress intently. Among his staff, Colonel R. B. Moseley – an army liaison officer – marvelled at the speed of naval communications and watched Cunningham with fascination. The Commander-in-Chief never interfered with Vian's conduct of the far-distant battle, but as it unfolded on the charts he was 'continually making comments such as "Good boy!", "That's correct," then "Now's the time for a daylight destroyer attack,", "One hit on *Littorio* and they'll all group round in protection." A few minutes later came the signal from Vian for his destroyers to attack. "There you are! He's right again!"'

Diverting the merchant ships, Vian's ships interposed themselves between them and the enemy while making a very heavy smoke screen. 'The tactics pursued by the several divisions', Vian later explained, 'were to emerge from the smoke screen, engage the enemy until the fire from his heavy guns became dangerous, and then re-enter the pall.' It was simple in theory, audacious and extremely difficult in practice; and as ever there was a matter of luck in it which Vian never mentioned. His flagship, *Cleopatra*, was hit once, early on, by a six-inch shell. The ship's Captain, Guy Grantham, saw it 'coming apparently straight at me . . . it sheered off at the last moment and hit the starboard fore corner of the bridge'. That was where Vian normally stood or sat; but at that moment 'he was luckily having a quick look at our position in the chart house'. One officer and fourteen men were killed and the radio aerials knocked out by that single hit; it was the purest chance that Vian survived to continue the fight.

After the battle, because he would not be able to refuel on the island, he was obliged (as had been expected) to leave the four merchant ships before they were finally in harbour, and in the end – after they had endured more air attacks – only 5,000 tons of supplies were landed. It was not possible for any more to be sent for three months; nevertheless, through Vian's victory the island was able to hold out.

In addition to the Admiral's tactical expertise, the battle's strategic value is evident. In Churchill's view, it 'entitles all ranks and ratings concerned, and above all their Commander, to the compliments of the British nation', and King George agreed: on 31 March it was announced that Vian was to be knighted.

In the middle of June 1942, Sir Philip's last attempt at convoying supplies to Malta was (in his own words) a 'distressing failure'. Despite having a stronger force under his command, he still had far too little air cover, and opposition from the Italians was so great that the convoy was recalled to Alexandria. Later, Vian wondered if he should have ignored those orders: 'A more resolute commander than I was, on this occasion might have held on regardless. Something might have got through.'

Though written eighteen years after the event, the words reflect his despondency at the time. By September 1942, he had been in command at sea for three unbroken years, under the most testing wartime conditions, and the strain was telling on his health. Sent back to England for a period of recuperation, he had the bad luck to contract malaria on the way, when the aircraft carrying him broke down in West Africa. He was seriously ill for six months, and in April 1943 was judged fit for shore service only. He would have loathed it; but (rather as happened at the start of the war) when he was on the brink of taking up his appointment, it was changed. The commander of an amphibious force destined to take part in the invasion of Sicily had been killed in an air crash, and Vian was to replace him; so instead of joining the staff planners for the invasion of Europe, he was sent back to the Mediterranean – 'but', he said, 'a Mediterranean transformed'. The war in the desert was turning decisively in the Allies' favour, with direct and beneficial effect on the war at sea. For example, in October 1942, Vian's successor was able to sail a convoy to Malta almost undetected. Vian said honestly that he was very envious of this, adding that such a voyage was one which 'after so much effort and so many failures, I deeply craved'.

It was indeed a pity that that satisfaction was denied him: for, with the coming of his new role, not only the Mediterranean but Vian's part in the whole of the rest of the sea war was transformed as well. During Operation Husky, the invasion of Sicily (9–10 July 1943), he commanded an amphibious assault force; during the subsequent invasion of Italy at Salerno (9 September), he commanded five escort carriers, three cruisers and ten destroyers, providing fighter cover and tactical support; during the invasion of Normandy (6 June

1944), he commanded half the naval side of things, in the shape of the Eastern Task Force (the Western being commanded by an American); and finally, between November 1944 and the end of the war, as a vice-admiral he commanded the carrier task force which spearheaded the British Pacific Fleet – the so-called 'Forgotten Fleet', Britain's inevitably limited contribution to America's massive efforts in that ocean.

In short, after his return to the Mediterranean, Vian was never again able to be in direct command of the weapon he knew best, small groups of small ships; and that may have been a mistake. Not that he ever lapsed into gross incompetence, or anything like it: even though his exploits had made him something of a favourite with Churchill, any serious lack of ability, any indication that he had been promoted beyond his level of competence, would have seen him quickly on the sidelines. Nevertheless, his later actions lacked the dash and flair that had so distinguished his tactical command of small ships. Of course the command of a large fleet is fundamentally different, but the chances of distinction it offers are not necessarily less; and it is notable that although his knighthood was enhanced to KCB for his services in the Normandy landings, and though he received four more Mentions in Despatches, he won no more British action awards. There were still episodes of considerable drama, such as four carrier attacks on Japanese oil installations at Palembang in Sumatra (December 1944 and January 1945), yet Sir Philip Vian was no longer an exceptional sea-warrior, but only a good, competent manager of sea warfare.

In this connection, it is worth recording that during his command of aircraft carriers in the Pacific his pilots believed (and told him) that he was not using them in anything like the best way. His system was to set a series of targets for the day. Targets A, B and C would be attacked by the first sortie, B, C and D by the second, C, D and E by the third and so on. Inevitably this meant the first attacks would be blind; but all aircraft were equipped with vertical and forward cameras, and because the carriers contained very good photographic units with skilled photographic interpreters, it was possible for the pilots of the first sortie to brief those of the second, indicating true targets and decoys on the photographs. Such, at least, was the way the pilots worked, as Lieutenant-Commander (later Captain) Alfie Sutton remembers. He and his colleagues adapted the system from RAF techniques, and it resulted in an extremely high score of enemy aircraft killed. But it was not the way Philip Vian wanted his pilots to work. 'Livid with rage', Sutton recalls, he told them 'on no account to divert from the primary target; there should be no sweeping elsewhere and no photography; and if we had any other relevant intelligence, it should be submitted to the flagship'. But Vian's veto on photography meant that the pilots were effectively forbidden to gather intelligence; and in any case the speed of operations was too fast for intelligence to be centrally submitted. The pilots found this 'dangerous and ineffective', and said so – indeed, shouted so. 'Once we'd settled down to obeying orders,' Vian told them at a briefing, 'the ship had done all right, and was more or less up to the standard of the others.' But when he refused to accept that his orders sent them into unnecessary danger and rendered them less effective than they could be, the pilots booed and jeered, shouting catcalls at him.

It is not surprising that Vian was furious, 'white with anger'; it took a considerable effort on the part of the Commander (Air) to placate him. What is more surprising are the obscenities he shouted back, the kicking of people who found themselves in his way. But this leads us to the least attractive aspect of Philip Vian's wartime leadership. As his responsibilities increased, so his temper (at least in professional dealings) shortened. Years earlier, as a lieutenant-commander, he had come over to Bob Whinney as 'quiet, efficient and . . . kindly, if serious', someone quite happy to teach a younger colleague the rudiments of polo. Correctly suggesting that this is an unexpected tribute, quite unlike the senior officer, Whinney continues: 'As a captain, he was unbelievably rude, hot tempered and frequently needlessly offensive; one had to stand up to him and be right – or make him think so.' Bradwell Turner agrees: 'When he was blowing you up, six times out of ten he'd be right. Three times you might not be sure. But if you stood up and fought back, once at least, he'd respect you.' 'In action,' Whinney continues, 'he was quiet, calm and very, very quick; and anyone who raised his voice unnecessarily did not do it twice. Otherwise, some distance beneath his ferocious exterior, he could be a man of surprising kindness.' 'A complex character', said Peter Gretton. In his assessment, Vian 'needed knowing well by his junior officers if they were to retain his confidence, and his inherent shyness seemed to produce an offensive approach'.

That may be merely charitable; no one else accuses Vian of being inherently shy. While readily acknowledging that he was 'a terribly brave fighting admiral', Sutton also states firmly that he was 'a very unpleasant man', and Turner asserts that his sometimes overwhelming rudeness was a matter of calculation, not merely of losing his temper. Gretton concedes that 'he had his faults; an apparent intolerance of officers who did not measure up to his high standards of efficiency and initiative, and resentment of any differences of opinion in public. He was then abrasive and sometimes abusive. But in private there was no more charming man, and no one with whom matters could more easily be discussed or even argued.'

He had other drawbacks too: blind spots – or at the very least, initial weaknesses of comprehension – regarding anti-submarine warfare and the use of air power. But these were common faults in men accustomed by long training to regard sea war as essentially surface warfare, fought out by the skilful use of ships and guns; and it remains to Vian's credit that he learned as much as he did about forms of warfare which he seems to have found fundamentally alien. Content to describe him simply as 'the great P.L.V.', Bob Whinney concludes: 'In some ways, he was a genius.' When he was in his natural setting, the tactical command of a small group of small ships at close quarters, this was true. No one can demand that their leaders be likeable, and in war it is better to be led by an unpleasant winner than a likeable loser. If his officers had a misfortune, it was that he chose outrageous verbal abuse as a command tool; but Philip Vian was one of the best tactical commanders in the Royal Navy's history, and if he had a misfortune, it was in a system which took him away from that setting.

Fifth Sea Lord, in charge of naval aviation, 1946–8. DSM (United States), 1946. Medal of the Order of St Olav (Norway), Order of the Dannebrog (Denmark). Admiral, 1948. Commander-in-Chief, Home Fleet, 1950–2 (flagship, Vanguard). Retired, 1952: created Knight Grand Cross of the Bath and specially promoted to Admiral of the Fleet (normally reserved for First Sea Lords) in recognition of unique record of unbroken combatant service in World War Two. After retirement from the service, became a director of the Midland Bank and of the North British and Mercantile Insurance Company. Died at Ashford Hill near Newbury, Berkshire, 22 May 1968.

27

Admiral

Arleigh A. Burke
United States Navy

1901–

by
David Alan Rosenberg

*A*RLEIGH *Albert Burke, born 19 October 1901 on a farm near Boulder, Colorado. Appointed to US Naval Academy despite having no high-school diploma. Graduated seventieth in his class, 7 June 1923: married Roberta ('Bobbie') Gorsuch that afternoon. Five years in battleship* Arizona; *postgraduate education in ordnance. Gained* MSE *in chemical engineering from University of Michigan, 1931. Served as main battery officer in heavy cruiser* Chester; *with Fleet Base Force Camera Party recording gunnery exercises; and in ammunition and explosives section of Bureau of Ordnance. Executive officer of new destroyer* Craven, *1937–9; commanding officer of sister ship* Mugford, *1939–40. Assigned to Gun Factory, summer 1940.*[1]

On the evening of Saturday, 6 December 1941, Lieutenant-Commander Arleigh Albert Burke USN sat in Quarters 'M' of the Washington Navy Yard, having an after-dinner brandy with a visiting former shipmate, Marine Major H. D. 'Bucky' Harris. Burke was an inspector of broadside and anti-aircraft gun mounts at the Naval Gun Factory. Harris was an infantry officer who had attended the French Ecole Supérieure de Guerre and served with the French army. He regaled Burke with stories about how the French had been caught unprepared by the Germans in 1940, and expressed the opinion that the United States had similar blind spots. In particular, the American navy at Pearl Harbor appeared terribly vulnerable to a Japanese attack. Maybe, he suggested, they should send a telegram warning of the possibility. Who would listen to a pair of crazy drunk poops?, said Burke. Somebody out there must be

[1]David Alan Rosenberg, 'Officer Development in the Interwar Navy; Arleigh Burke – The Making of a Naval Professional, 1919–1940', *Pacific Historical Review*, XLIV (November 1975), pp. 503–26.

thinking about the problem already. After another brandy the two officers went off to bed.[2]

On Sunday morning Burke went into work, walking across the Navy Yard to his office. Harris went with him to observe gun production that was now going on round the clock. Early that afternoon, word was flashed of the Japanese attack on Pearl Harbor. Harris immediately reported to Headquarters, Marine Corps, while Burke briefly pondered the conversation of the night before. He knew war was coming, but he had not thought it would come that quickly. As off-duty personnel reported into the Gun Factory, a staff meeting was held in the Chief Inspector's office. Production was to be increased immediately, with quality improvements frozen to speed delivery of guns and mounts to the fleet. Contractors were called that afternoon, and on oral instructions orders were increased and weapons manufacture accelerated. On Monday, Burke submitted an urgent request for orders to sea duty in the Pacific Fleet 'as soon as practicable', as captain or executive officer of a combatant ship or, failing that, command or department head of any ship. It took nearly two weeks for a reply, but the commandant of the Gun Factory declared that 'the services of this officer cannot be spared'. The Chief Inspector agreed to have an appointment with Burke every Friday afternoon to review Burke's standing request.[3] Nearly a year would pass before Arleigh Burke would finally receive orders to return to sea.

The bind that Lieutenant-Commander Burke found himself in was of his own making. There were only 220 ordnance specialists available in the entire officer corps to handle duties at sea and ashore. Burke was one of forty-six designated ordnance 'design and production specialists', and one of only nine specializing in explosives. To be released immediately for sea duty, as he hoped in December 1941, was therefore out of the question.

As of 1941, BuOrd was utilizing forty-three active (including Burke) and twenty-two retired line-officer ordnance specialists to run its factories, train its officers and inspect the growing flood of guns, torpedoes and ammunition pouring from America's mobilizing industry. Forty additional officers were ordered detached from the fleet prior to Pearl Harbor to billets in Washington and BuOrd's growing field activities, but even these were hard pressed to meet the demands of the American industrial juggernaut.[4]

[2]Author's interview with Arleigh Burke, 19 June 1981.

[3]Memorandum, Lieutenant-Commander A. A. Burke to Chief of the Bureau of Navigation, Subject: Request for Change of Duty, 17 December 1941, and 1st Endorsement by Rear Admiral George Pettingill, same date, in Personal File (PF), Papers of Admiral Arleigh Burke (BP), Operational Archives, Naval Historical Center, Washington DC (NHA); author's interview with Burke, 19 June 1981.

[4]These data on the Bureau of Ordnance are taken from Buford Rowland and William P. Boyd, *U.S. Navy Bureau of Ordnance in World War II* (Washington DC, n.d.) pp. 461–9; Rear Admiral Julius A. Furer, *The Administration of the Navy Department in World War II* (Washington DC, 1959), pp. 312–51; and US Navy Department, *Register of Commissioned and Warrant Officers of the United States Navy and Marine Corps, July 1, 1940* (Washington DC, Government Printing Office, 1940).

Much of Burke's time was spent travelling the east coast and mid-west, inspecting, encouraging, suggesting and cajoling, putting the 'Prod' in the increased production of guns and mounts, while reserve officers were carefully trained to take up inspectors' posts. On 19 December 1942, after repeated requests for sea duty, he convinced his bosses that his relief was at last available. Burke received orders to detach in January 1943 and proceed to the South Pacific to take command of Destroyer Division 43.[5]

While Burke had remained tied to his inspector's duties ashore, the United States Navy had been sorely tried in mortal combat with a skilful and intelligent enemy. In the Pacific, friends and classmates had put to the test the tactics and techniques of naval warfare developed and practised in the inter-war period. During the Guadalcanal campaign, many of these had been found wanting. In leaving for the theatre of war so long after hostilities had begun, Burke had a year's worth of combat to catch up on. The changes in naval warfare had been tremendous and it would take all his talents to master them.

Burke worked at the Gun Factory right up to his detachment date, hurriedly vacating his quarters on 10 January and catching a train for the west coast amid an evening snowstorm. Finding his division divided between two ships working up on the east coast, and two just deployed to the Solomons, he 'naturally' chose to join the two already overseas. Unable to find air transportation to the South Pacific, he volunteered to serve as the naval troop commander of the 10th Marine Replacement Battalion on the transport *President Monroe* en route to New Caledonia and spent the three-week trip reading long-neglected books and keeping his charges clean, fit and fed.[6]

Burke boarded his flagship, the destroyer *Waller*, at Havannah Harbour, Efate Island, in the New Hebrides in the early afternoon of 14 February 1943. The Guadalcanal campaign had ended, with the last Japanese evacuation operation and the American occupation of the Russell Islands both completed earlier that month. US forces now had a breathing spell, as planning for future operations in the central Solomons awaited the build-up of the amphibious forces necessary to accomplish them. The build-up went on for more than four months, giving Commander Burke (who had discovered that 'things have changed a lot' since he was last at sea and felt 'pretty stupid') the opportunity to become acquainted with the ways of naval warfare in the South Pacific.[7]

This occurred in a number of ways. The first was through conversations with more experienced commanders during trips ashore or in port at Nouméa, Efate or Espiritu Santo. The men leading the navy in the South Pacific were

[5]Transcript 'Interview with Captain Albert O. Momm' by Stan Smith, n.d., PF, BP; Orders from Chief of Naval Personnel to Commander Arleigh A. Burke, No. 65481, 19 December 1942, Official File (OF) BP.

[6]Narrative by Commodore Arleigh A. Burke, USN, Destroyers South Pacific, New Georgia Campaign, DesDiv43 and 44, Task Group 31.2, Film No. 411, recorded 31 July 1945, BP, p. 1; letters, Arleigh Burke to Roberta Burke, 21 January–4 February 1943, PF, BP.

[7]War Diary, Commander, Destroyer Division 43, 14 February–1 April 1943, BP; letter, Arleigh Burke to Roberta Burke, 7 February 1943, PF, BP.

predominantly surface officers who had first commanded at sea in the inter-war period, and who knew each other personally or by reputation. Burke had served with many of them before, and their discussions over drinks at the makeshift officers' clubs or at wardroom dinners were filled with professional lessons learned. The second was through day-to-day operations. DesDiv 43's ships were scattered, but *Waller* was at sea almost constantly conducting patrols, training, or escorting surface units ranging from oilers to the carrier *Saratoga* and battleship *Colorado*. Burke gained much experience in these operations in air defence and anti-submarine screens of task groups.

Finally, Burke read action reports of previous actions, and, beginning in April, benefited from the new secret *Battle Experience* publication put out by Commander-in-Chief, US Fleet, in Washington. This series examined the combined action reports of earlier battles, particularly the many surface night engagements off Guadalcanal, and pointed out areas where pre-war doctrine and wartime practice had failed, and how such wartime innovations as radar could improve American combat performance.[8]

On the night of 6–7 March 1943, Burke saw his first combat as *Waller* led Rear Admiral A. S. 'Tip' Merrill's three light cruisers and two destroyers into Kula Gulf to bombard the airfield at Vila. The force met two Japanese destroyers and sank them with gunfire and a torpedo spread from *Waller*. *Waller*'s captain, Lawrence Frost, initially ordered all ten of the destroyer's 'fish' ready for firing, but Burke told Frost to shoot only five at the two ships. A brief but heated argument ensued as Frost countered that he was 'not here to save torpedoes', but Burke prevailed. At least one torpedo hit. The experience taught Burke that he had to know his subordinate captains' plans and they had to know his thinking about combat beforehand, not when battle was imminent.[9]

By April, the other three ships of DesDiv 43 had arrived in the South Pacific, and Burke was able occasionally to operate them as a unit, as 'dog boss' (destroyer commander) of Merrill's cruiser task force. No actions with the enemy ensued, but the periods at sea gave Burke the chance to develop a concept for night surface actions. He presented it to Merrill on 7 May. The concept, he averred, was not original. 'The ideas are other people's and the conclusions have been reached by Captains' [*sic*] of this Division.' He then proceeded to lay out, cogently and convincingly, the rationale for a new approach to the use of destroyers in the cruiser task force. 'I've written a long letter about how to fight these destroyers,' he wrote to Bobbie on 9 May 1943. 'It's a question which people have very fixed opinions on and which they like to

[8]See in particular Commander-in-Chief, US Fleet Secret Information Bulletins 2, 3 and 4 on 'Battle Experience, Solomons Islands Actions, August and September 1942', 'October 1942' and 'November 1942', issued 1–25 March 1943, US Naval War College Library.

[9]Commanding Officer, USS *Waller*, Action Report, Engagement of 5 March 1943, 7 March 1943; transcript 'Interview with Admiral Burke re Admiral Frost' by Stan Smith, n.d.; and transcript 'Interview with Rear Admiral Frost re Admiral Arleigh A. Burke' by Stan Smith, n.d., all in PF, BP.

air so I've stirred up a hornet's nest. Since my opinions favor bold radical action every body is like to take a crack at it. It may get me into hot water in many ways – if it's the fighting way so that I have to try out my own ideas I have enough confidence in them to prove them. If I have to fight for them over the conference table I may very likely lose the battle and be labelled a sap in addition.'[10]

Burke's idea, in essence, was that destroyers should lead surprise attacks on enemy formations, not be held in reserve. The practice of stationing destroyers as a submarine screen was of limited value at night, he argued, since (if German and American practice was any guide) Japanese submarines were unlikely to travel submerged after dark. Furthermore, when the enemy was sighted, screen assignments forced destroyers to scramble into battle formation ahead and astern of the cruisers. Even in daylight it was difficult to do this neatly. At night, in the confusion of battle, with communications limited or impossible, destroyers would invariably lose track of each other, get in the cruisers' way, and end up out of formation, making it hard to tell friend from foe on the radar screen. The fact that destroyer commanders were not supposed to fire their torpedoes without explicit instructions from the task force commander made matters worse. They could easily be left on the sidelines, unable to use the resources at their command to contribute to the battle.

The solution, Burke argued, was routinely to station all destroyers *ahead* of the cruisers, in battle formation, from thirty minutes after sunset until thirty minutes before sunrise, with permission to attack as soon as an enemy was sighted. 'Destroyers', he wrote, 'are offensive weapons of opportunity. They have for their protection strong hitting power, high speed, and surprise. . . . The only position for destroyers to utilize fully their maximum opportunity is in the van.' If the DDS were prepared to attack without waiting for orders, in formation and at full strength as soon as enemy ships were sighted, they could readily disrupt or disable a small force to the point where the cruisers would have little trouble demolishing it. If the enemy force was too powerful, they could at least distract it with torpedo salvoes, giving the cruisers time to withdraw.

The crucial problem, Burke thought, was whether task force commanders would be willing to delegate the initiative in opening fire. If the destroyer captains had to wait for orders, with the enemy possibly listening in on communications, the critical element of surprise would be lost. The DDS had to be free to attack immediately, without prior communication with the flagship. Delegating authority is always difficult, he wrote, and doubly so when it 'may result in disastrous consequences if a subordinate commander makes an error', but in this case the risks were worth it: 'There is no panacea which will insure success in battle. There are no rules or doctrines made before a

[10]Letter, Arleigh Burke to Roberta Burke, 9 May 1943, ibid.

battle which if rigidly followed, will prevent loss of ships or even a battle. The best that can be done is to train individual units for battle, place them in the positions where they will most probably be effective and then aggressively fight the action under competent bold leadership.' The outcome might well be a matter of luck, but, Burke added, perhaps summing up his philosophy of warfare, 'if history has been written correctly, luck usually rides with the bold'.[11]

Admiral Merrill was an old destroyer hand, and understood Burke's arguments well. He regarded them cautiously, for the same reasons Burke had noted in his memorandum, but allowed Burke to test them as the cruiser–destroyer task force worked to train as a combat team. Unfortunately, there was no chance to test the task force in battle. To Merrill's regret, Burke was transferred at the end of May to command DesDiv 44.[12] He languished aboard the battleship *Maryland* at Efate until 8 June before breaking his burgee in *Conway*. The next six weeks proved to be exceedingly frustrating ones. Where Burke had been able briefly to concentrate the four DDS of DesDiv 43 to train together and operate with Merrill's cruisers, DesDiv 44's ships were constantly being sent on various escort duties around the South Pacific. Ostensibly assigned to escort Rear Admiral Harry Hill's battleship task force, Burke instead found himself bored and frustrated, taking *Conway* and another DD on repeated escort missions for escort carriers or tankers, back and forth to the Solomons. These missions provided little excitement save occasional alerts against air or submarine contacts.[13]

The South Pacific campaign was accelerating. New Georgia was invaded by US forces on 21 June, followed by Rendova on the 30th. Cruiser–destroyer task forces led by Merrill and Walden Ainsworth conducted repeated night bombardment missions in support of the New Georgia operation, and Ainsworth's ships twice engaged the enemy in night surface actions in Kula Gulf and off Kolombangara in early July. On the 19th, Burke was assigned as ComDesSlot in charge of all DDS in the vicinity of Guadalcanal and the 'slot' of water between the Central Solomons. On the 23rd, he took four destroyers from various units up to Enogai on New Georgia, as escort for four fast transports conducting a night resupply of the Marine raiders attacking Bairoko. Shelled by Japanese shore batteries on Kolombangara, Burke received a flesh wound in his back from a piece of shrapnel and dislocated two ribs when *Conway*'s mast was struck by a shell and, as the ship lurched from the impact, a signalman fell on him from above.[14] Unfazed, he took six DDS up to

[11]Letter, Commander, Destroyer Division 43, to Commander, Task Force 19, Subject: Employment of Destroyers, Secret Serial 37, 7 May 1943, ibid.

[12]Letter, Rear Admiral A. S. Merrill to Commander, Destroyer Squadron 22, Subject: Performance of Duty by Commander A. A. Burke, 29 May 1943, ibid.

[13]War Diary, Commander, Destroyer Division 44, 31 May–30 June 1943; and letters, Arleigh Burke to Roberta Burke, 2 June–17 July 1943, ibid.

[14]Commander, Destroyer Division 44, Action Report, Action Report for Night of 23–24 July 1943 – The Bombardment of Enogai and Kolombangara, Serial 002, n.d., ca. September 1943, BP; Arleigh Burke, Comments on Stan Smith's Book Second Draft, n.d., ca. 1966–7, PF, BP.

Munda on the morning of the 25th, to carry out an extensive bombardment prior to the land assault. DesDiv 44 was then ordered back to Espiritu Santo, but Burke received permission to shift his flag to a ship outside his division and continue as ComDesSlot. On the night of 1–2 August he took six DDs up to search waters north of Kula Gulf for Japanese destroyers making resupply runs to Kolombangara, but no contact with the 'Tokyo Express' was made. When Burke returned to Guadalcanal, he was ordered to return to his division; then on the 6th he received orders to take command of Destroyer Squadron 12, on board the flagship *Farenholt* at Nouméa.

By this time Burke had further refined his ideas on night surface combat, building on US radar superiority and surprise. The plan of attack used two divisions of destroyers steaming in parallel columns. The first division would attack with torpedoes immediately after the enemy was detected, while the second would cover with guns ready to fire in case the first division's attack was discovered. As soon as the first division had fired its torpedoes, it was to change course 90 degrees, get out to gun range and cover the second division's torpedo attack. 'We felt that this way the enemy would be continually surprised,' Burke noted later, ' . . . because if they sighted one attacking force coming in and started to fire at them and another force unbeknownst to them up to that time, opened fire on them, we thought that they would be confused and in the resultant confusion one or both divisions would be able to get in the fatal lick before the Japanese recovered from their surprise.'[15] He had hoped to try the plan out on the night of 1–2 August, and was itching for another opportunity when he was transferred.

DesRon 12 was a bigger job but, once again, Burke rarely had more than one or two of his seven ships available to command and train. To make his frustrations worse, on the night of 6–7 August 1943, Commander Frederick Moosbrugger, an Annapolis classmate who had relieved Burke as Com-DesSlot, took six DDs (four of which Burke had commanded on the 1st) into Vella Gulf, and following Burke's battle plan (which had been pressed on him by the second division commander, Rodger Simpson) sank three of four Japanese DDs without suffering a loss.[16] Burke wrote to Bobbie: 'I'm disappointed in a way for altho' everybody tells me I did a good job – and my plans were good – they were mostly used by my successor in my last job – and they worked for him. So long as they worked I suppose I should be happy for that's what counts – and of course that is a lot of satisfaction. Still I'd liked to have done it myself.'[17]

Opportunities to try his plans in combat did come more frequently as ComDesRon 12 than they had in his previous jobs. Burke served as

[15]Narrative by Commodore Burke, Film 411, 31 July 1945, p. 18. The plan is contained in Commander, Destroyer Division 44, Memorandum for Destroyers of Task Force 31, 22 July 1943, and Battle Plan, 1 August 1943, PF, BP.

[16]Letter, Simpson to Burke, 28 August 1943, PF, BP; Samuel E. Morison, *History of US Naval Operations in World War II*, vol. VI: *Breaking the Bismarcks Barrier* (Boston, 1950), pp. 212–22.

[17]Letter, Arleigh Burke to Roberta Burke, 8 August 1943, PF BP.

ComDesSlot between 8 and 23 September, and took four DesRon 12 ships and other destroyers up the 'slot' four times. No contacts developed. On 28 September, Burke received word that he had been 'spot' promoted to captain, but *Farenholt* then spent most of October on training and escort duties between Espiritu Santo and Guadalcanal. Burke's promotion had been no accident; he had come to the attention of Admiral William F. Halsey [*q.v.*], Commander South Pacific Force, and Rear Admiral Robert 'Mick' Carney, Halsey's Chief of Staff, and they had plans for him. So too did 'Tip' Merrill, who had long desired to bring his innovative former screen commander back to Task Force 39.[18] On 19 October, on the first day of a long-planned liberty in Sydney, Australia, Burke received orders to report immediately to Commander, Destroyer Squadron 23, as his relief. DesRon 23's next assignment was to serve as the screen for Merrill's cruisers in the imminent invasion of Bougainville.

ComDesRon 23 was a plum assignment. The squadron's eight new *Fletcher*-class destroyers had come to the South Pacific in the spring and summer of 1943. The previous squadron commander had been less aggressive than the assignment had required and had been relieved, but the individual ships and their skippers were well trained and anxious to prove themselves in combat. The ships had been in the combat zone long enough for their officers to become familiar with the evolving tactical doctrine for night surface actions designed by Burke and proved by Moosbrugger.[19] Burke wasted no time. By six o'clock the next morning he was on a plane from Australia, and assumed command of the squadron on board *Charles Ausburne* in Espiritu Santo at 0845 on 23 October. Later that morning he met with Merrill's staff and confirmed that the doctrine he had proposed the previous May would govern Task Force 39's night surface actions. That afternoon, Burke met with five of his captains and the commander of DesRon 23's second division, DesDiv 46, Commander B. L. 'Count' Austin. At the meeting, Burke handed out his famous statement of DesRon 23 doctrine which began 'If it will help kill Japs – it's important; if it does not help kill Japs – it's not important.' The doctrine was a concise distillation of his previous thinking and continuing experience in anti-air warfare and anti-submarine screening as well as night surface combat. Its aggressive combat tenets were greeted with enthusiasm, as was Burke's terse explication of non-battle doctrine: 'None! . . . Corrections to this section will not be permitted.'[20]

Burke sailed the next morning for Purvis Bay across the 'slot' from Guadalcanal. On 26–27 October, two cruisers and Burke with five DesRon 23 DDS covered the landings on the Treasury Islands south of Bougainville.

[18]Letter, Carney to Burke, 7 October 1943, and Naval Messages, Merrill to Burke, 180617 October 1943, and Burke to Merrill, 180625 October 1943, all PF, BP.

[19]Author's interview with Rear Admiral L. K. Reynolds, USN (Ret.), Former CO of USS *Charles Ausburne*, 2 August 1986.

[20]Destroyer Squadron 23 Doctrine, n.d., PF, BP; interview with Reynolds, 2 August 1986.

Merrill's four light cruisers and all eight of Burke's destroyers then sailed in the early morning of the 31st to bombard Buka and Bonis airfields on Buka Island off the north-west tip of Bougainville that midnight, and to shell Shortland and Ballale Islands off the south-east coast of Bougainville at dawn on the 1st. The first of November was D-Day on Bougainville as the 3rd Marine Division landed at Cape Torokina on Empress Augusta Bay. Task Force 39 was assigned to protect the landing force. Merrill's cruisers and the 4 DDs of Count Austin's DesDiv 46 stood by off Vella LaVella that afternoon while Burke took DesDiv 45 to refuel from a barge in Hathorn Sound at the head of Kula Gulf. Reconnaissance aircraft reported tracking a Japanese force steaming south-east from Rabaul, and Burke rapidly completed his fuelling and headed north at thirty-two knots. Halsey ordered Merrill to a position west of Empress Augusta Bay to intercept the enemy while the amphibs retired for the night to the south-east.[21]

Burke rejoined Merrill late on the 1st and the task force formed for combat with Burke's four DesDiv 45 DDs in line ahead and to starboard of the cruisers and Austin's in line behind and to port as a rear striking force. DesRon 23 was freed of the cruiser's apron-strings to operate flexibly and offensively with torpedoes before the cruiser guns were in effective range. The enemy force of two heavy and two light cruisers and six destroyers was contacted on radar at 0227 on the 2nd and Burke's van DDs charged the contacts, firing twenty-five torpedoes nineteen minutes later. Merrill's cruisers turned 180 degrees and opened fire. Burke's division broke away to the north-east, intending to regroup and rejoin the cruisers. At the time he believed he had done considerable damage but later reports indicated that because the Japanese had turned away to avoid the cruisers' fire, none of Burke's 'fish' found their targets. Task Force 39 ultimately claimed one cruiser and four DDs sunk and two cruisers and two DDs damaged, but actual enemy losses were one cruiser and one DD sunk and two cruisers and two destroyers damaged.

After the first attacks, the battle became a mêlée. Voice radio instructions intended for the cruisers were mistakenly followed by two of DesDiv 46's destroyers, whose captains did not yet recognize the sound of Burke's voice over the TBS (bridge-to-bridge voice circuit). Unwilling to permit his division to fight dispersed, Burke spent precious minutes getting DesDiv 45 reassembled before resuming the attack. By then he was effectively cut off from the cruisers, and fought the rest of the battle as an independent unit, pursuing enemy ships and finishing off those damaged by the cruisers' fire. Meanwhile, DesDiv 46's problems continued. The destroyer *Foote* was hit by an enemy torpedo and lay dead in the water directly in the path of Merrill's

---

[21] War Diary, Commander, Destroyer Squadron 23, 23 October–30 November 1943, BP, pp. 1–14; Narrative by Commodore Arleigh A. Burke, Destroyers South Pacific, Battle of Empress Augusta Bay, Film 411-1, recorded 31 July 1945, ibid., pp. 2–7; Commander, Task Force 39, Action Reports – Task Force 39 covering operations for Empress Augusta Bay and Treasury Island Echelons, period 31 October to 3 November 1943, Serial 0062, 3 November 1943, ibid.

cruisers. Two other DDS collided at thirty knots while manoeuvring to avoid the damaged *Foote*, although both continued to operate. Differentiating friend from foe on the flickering early model radar scopes in the absence of a reliable IFF (Identification Friend or Foe) transponder also proved to be a problem. When Burke's two divisions finally re-established contact with each other, Burke mistook Austin's flagship for an enemy, and fired several salvoes, none of which, luckily, found its target. It was better, Burke noted, to fire than not to fire on a suspected enemy, but it would be better still to know where all your own ships were at any given time so that the confusion would not arise. At night, he concluded, that could be achieved only by staying concentrated and maintaining formation as much as possible.

Burke's destroyers spent the rest of the night pursuing the retreating enemy, rejoining the cruisers shortly after dawn. Task Force 39 then retired to the south-east with the torpedoed *Foote* under tow. An intense 100-plane Japanese air attack followed but fortunately the only hits were on a catapult on one of the cruisers. Despite its mishaps, the action was a clear American success. Two enemy ships were sunk and four damaged against one US ship damaged and three Americans dead. The Japanese, who had mistakenly estimated Task Force 39 as constituting, at minimum, seven heavy cruisers and twelve destroyers, had been prevented from attacking either the transports or the troops ashore. The lessons of the engagement, Burke observed, were once again the importance of surprise, the necessity of having a clear battle plan in advance and the value of permitting destroyers to operate with a degree of independence, so that no time was wasted and no opportunities lost while seeking permission to open fire. In particular, 'it is necessary that [commanders] realize the value of time. It's the only commodity which you can never regain.'[22] Although they had encountered problems in keeping concentrated, his captains, Burke thought, had acquitted themselves very well. 'Their action was not the passive acceptance of finding themselves in a fight and then conducting a good battle,' he wrote at the time. 'They went out looking for trouble, they found it, they sank it, and then they looked for more.'[23]

The remainder of November proved equally busy. Task Force 39 stood by off Bougainville covering the transports in Empress Augusta Bay through the 3rd and then returned to Purvis Bay to rearm and refuel. The next day, the force escorted the second echelon of transports to Bougainville and remained there on alert against the Japanese fleet coming out from Rabaul until the 7th, all the while subject to periodic enemy air attacks. A one-day stint in Purvis Bay

[22]Narrative by Commodore Burke, Film 411-1, 31 July 1945, p. 13. The Japanese side of the story is contained in Document No. 15685, 'Historical Reports, Naval Operations' prepared by Allied Translation and Interpretation Section, Supreme Commander, Allied Powers, Japan, 15 March 1946, and an Office of Naval Intelligence Report 'Narrative of Japanese Operations – Empress Augusta Bay – 31 October–November 1943', Op-23F14, 1 February 1946, both NHA.

[23]Commander, Destroyer Squadron 23, Action Report of Night Engagement off Cape Moltke on the Night of 1–2 November 1943, Serial 012, 4 November 1943, Enclosure (A), BP.

was followed by five days covering additional forces headed for Bougainville, again under constant threat of air attacks, one of which put a torpedo into cruiser *Denver*. Returning to Purvis Bay on the 14th, DesRon 23 received orders to proceed independently the next day to cover the additional echelons of forces heading up to Empress Augusta Bay.

During the brief respite, Burke and *Ausburne*'s skipper, L. K. 'Brute' Reynolds, took a stroll around the deck of the flagship. They spotted the drawing of a little Indian a torpedoman was painting on the after torpedo mount. Intrigued by it, they asked what it meant. The torpedoman replied that it was an American symbol. Burke asked to use it for the squadron. *Ausburne*'s crew had already taken to calling themselves 'beavers' because of their busy schedule the last month, and someone suggested that the Indian boy be named 'Little Beaver', after Red Ryder's sidekick in the popular cowboy comic strip. The symbol was painted on the DesRon 23 bridge wings and, from 15 November on, Burke's command became known as the 'Little Beavers'.[24]

DesRon 23's orders were to destroy any enemy surface forces encountered. If none were contacted, Burke's ships were to bombard the airfield on Buka. This they did on the nights of 15–16 and 16–17 November and then covered another echelon movement to Bougainville before returning to Purvis Bay. On the 22nd, Admiral Halsey ordered Burke back up to Bougainville to destroy any enemy force headed to Buka from Rabaul. No enemy was contacted that night, so DesRon 23 refuelled in Kula Gulf and the next night covered a minelaying operation in the Shortlands south-east of Bougainville. On the afternoon of the 24th, after repairs to a troublesome boiler on *Spence* that had restricted the speed of the ship (and DesRon 23) to thirty knots, Burke reported his ships proceeding at his preferred non-battle formation speed of thirty-one knots from Kula Gulf to a late-evening rendezvous point south-east of Bougainville.[25]

DesRon 23 had been ordered up the 'slot' because the 21 November Commander-in-Chief, Pacific Fleet, Daily Intelligence Bulletin had reported 'several hundred aviation personnel soon to be evacuated from Buka to Rabaul employing three destroyers'.[26] Based on Japanese coded messages intercepted at listening stations in Australia and on Guadalcanal and analysed at the Combat Intelligence Center at Pearl Harbor, this bulletin provided Ultra radio intelligence to selected operational commanders including Admiral Halsey. Halsey's operations officer, Captain Ray Thurber, an old squadron mate of Burke's, had followed DesRon 23's actions under Burke's command, and put the squadron where it 'could do the damage'.[27] Despite the missed

[24]Narrative by Commodore Burke, Film 411-1, 31 July 1945, pp. 15–16; interview with Reynolds, 2 August 1986.

[25]Commander, Destroyer Squadron 23, Action Report of Night Engagement off Cape St George on the night of 24–25 November 1943, Serial 0018, 26 November 1943, Enclosure (A), BP.

[26]Cincpac RI Secret Message 210243 November 1943 in US Navy Commander-in-Chief, Pacific Intelligence Bulletins (#534–#655), 1 September–31 December 1943, SRMN-013, Part III, NHA.

[27]Letters, 'Mick' Carney to Burke, 22 December 1943, and Burke to Thurber, 30 December 1943,

contact on the 22nd, further Japanese evacuation operations were expected, and on the afternoon of the 24th the Cincpac Bulletin predicted 'transportation operation to Buka by destroyers' that night. Thurber, recalling Burke's previous reports of *Spence*'s boiler problems and impaired formation speed, drafted a classic op order which Halsey immediately signed out: 'Thirty-One-Knot Burke get athwart the Buka–Rabaul evacuation line about 35 miles west of Buka. If no enemy contacts by 0300 Love [Local Time], 25th, come south to refuel same place. If enemy contacted you know what to do.'[28]

Halsey's prior messages and DesRon 23's operations during the previous two nights had led Burke to anticipate this action and he had shared his intentions for the night of the 24th–25th with the squadron over the TBS even before the 'Thirty-One-Knot Burke' despatch was received. Nevertheless, he found the new orders 'ideal. . . . they gave us all the information we needed, and how we did the job was entirely up to us'.[29] Burke planned to arrive at the Buka–Rabaul line at 0145 on the 25th and to intercept any enemy contacts from the north-west (towards Rabaul) where the US ships would be least expected. At 0141, radar picked up surface contacts 22,000 yards to the east. Ninety seconds later, Burke called to the squadron, 'Hang on to your hats, boys, here we go,' and led DesDiv 45's three DDS at the enemy at twenty-five knots while Count Austin's two ships provided support in accord with DesRon 23 doctrine.

After World War Two, Burke discussed his doctrine and its performance in this battle, which became known as the Battle of Cape St George, with some of his former foes. He was chided for his 'unconventional tactics', where DesDiv 46 was held in reserve while DesDiv 45 launched the first attack. If the Japanese had realized they were being attacked by a force weaker than their own, Burke was told, they would have concentrated on DesDiv 45 and manoeuvred to separate the divisions and wipe them out in parts.[30] But Burke's attack came as almost a complete surprise. The two enemy screen destroyers spotted DesDiv 45 (which the Japanese identified as 'three cruisers') but hesitated to take evasive action. They were both hit by DesDiv 45's torpedo salvo and one sank immediately. DesDiv 45 then accelerated to thirty-three knots and began a stern chase after the three-DD transport unit

---

PF, BP. Information on Ultra Radio Intelligence is taken from Captain W. J. Holmes, 'Narrative, Combat Intelligence Center, Joint Intelligence Center, Pacific Ocean Area', SRH-20, NHA.

[28]Commander, South Pacific Force Message 240552 November 1943, quoted in Destroyer Squadron 23 Action Report, Cape St George, 26 November 1943.

[29]Narrative by Commodore Arleigh A. Burke, Battle of Cape St George, Film 411-2, Recorded 1 August 1943, BP, p. 2.

[30]Letter, Rear Admiral Arleigh Burke to Professor E. B. Potter, 1 March 1953. PF, BP. The Japanese side of the battle is contained in ATIS document 15685, 'Historical Reports, Naval Operations' and Chief of Naval Operations Pacific Intelligence Section, 'Allied Claims and Enemy Confirmation of Damage to Japanese Ships (October–December 1943)', SRH 184 (Part II), NHA.

that had just landed 900 troops and evacuated 750 aviation personnel from Buka, while DesDiv 46 finished off the screening DD still afloat. At 0215, on a hunch, Burke ordered DesDiv 45 to make a radical course change, and thereby avoided a Japanese torpedo spread. DesDiv 45 came within gun range of the last three ships seven minutes later. In an hour-long running gun battle, a third enemy destroyer was sunk. By 0405, DesRon 23 was unscathed but low on ammunition and was closing St George's Channel leading to Rabaul. Unable to catch the last two ships, Burke reversed course and under welcome air cover headed for Purvis Bay.

The Thanksgiving day victory made Burke and DesRon 23 famous. Congratulatory messages were passed from Admirals Merrill, Halsey and Nimitz, from Admiral Ernest King's staff in Washington, and General MacArthur, while news reports spread the name of the newly christened 'Thirty-One-Knot Burke' throughout America. A subsequent analysis by the Naval War College described Cape St George as 'an almost perfect action' and one 'that may come to be considered a classic'. In Purvis Bay, the exhausted squadron and its commander held heartfelt Thanksgiving services, 'proud of [their] accomplishments, but . . . also humbly aware that those accomplishments were made possible by a force beyond the control of the squadron'. Burke was awed by his squadron's dedication: 'there was no person who did not know that we were far away from any air or surface support and there was no one who did not believe that some of our ships would be damaged in battle. Yet every ship threw itself into battle with a cheerful willingness that I hope is an American trait.'[31]

Burke spent four more months commanding DesRon 23, but despite repeated forays up to Buka and beyond he never again led his command in night action against major enemy surface forces. This was not for lack of trying. DesRon 23 sortied up the 'slot' four times in December escorting echelons of US reinforcements to Bougainville. The squadron bombarded Buka twice, and patrolled the Buka–Rabaul evacuation line eight times with no contacts. January 1944 brought much needed rest, including liberty for Burke and *Ausburne* in Sydney, Australia. By February, Halsey's headquarters had learned that the Japanese would not be planning any more surface evacuation operations, relying instead on submarines. DesRon 23 hunted 'barges, bogies [enemy aircraft], subs, [but] no chances of surface battle' off Bougainville during the first part of the month, screened the invasion of Green Island along with Merrill's cruisers from the 13th to the 17th, and on the 18th steamed far into enemy waters to search for shipping traffic and bombarded Kavieng Harbour on the northern tip of New Ireland. Burke and his five DDs went back

---

[31]Destroyer Squadron 23 Action Report, Cape St George, 26 November 1943, Enclosure (A), p. 17. The Naval War College analysis is contained in President, Naval War College to Commander-in-Chief, US Fleet, Serial 4181, 13 January 1944, PF, BP. The growth of Burke's fame is recorded in congratulatory messages and letters, November–December 1943, in PF, BP, and Album S-100-I, Arleigh Burke Collection, Photographic Section, Naval Historical Center.

to New Ireland on the 20th to look for enemy ships, sank two merchantmen, three barges and an old minelayer, and circled the island, ending up with a brief bombardment of Rabaul Harbour as they steamed past.[32]

After a year in the combat zone, Burke had clear ideas about who he was and where he wanted to go. More than ever, he wanted to remain at sea. It was not that he was 'ungrateful to BuOrd'; it was just that 'I do feel I am in a fighting service – and not a service of supply – I can fight and a lot of people can't.'[33] DesRon 23 was well broken in as a combat outfit, and he hoped to stay with them until June, or at least April. He stood the rigours of combat command well; in fact he told Bobbie, 'the pace is fast but I seem to get fat on it'.[34] He also had a clear sense of what was important: 'We didn't care about regulations by this time, nor did we care what people thought of us. We felt that if we did the job the best we could, and the way we wanted to do it, that if somebody didn't like it, well, they wouldn't like it.' Further, 'things that used to be very important were completely unimportant now. Good food was important, a glass of beer was important, what your shipmates thought of you was important, but what was written down on a piece of paper, or what somebody who was not fighting thought about how you were fighting, that was completely unimportant.'[35]

Burke's tour as ComDesRon 23, however, was coming to a close. The campaign to isolate Rabaul was winding up, with one more operation, the invasion of Emirau, north-west of New Ireland, set for 20 March. Burke hated 'to give up my Beavers but the [South Pacific] area is well cleaned out now'.[36] Indeed, DesRon 23 was scheduled for transfer to the Fifth Fleet in the Central Pacific, and Burke was told that he was being slated for a new job. Friends back in Pearl Harbor were pushing to get him assigned to command one of the first squadrons of new 2,200-ton destroyers now being formed, and by 12 March Burke had received orders sending him back to the States. Fate then intervened in the form of an order from Commander-in-Chief, US Fleet, that 'aviator flag officers having surface officers under their command [should] have non-aviator line officers as chiefs of staff'.[37]

In recommending this new policy to Admiral King, Vice Admiral John S. McCain, the first Deputy Chief of Naval Operations (Air), meant to ensure

[32]Narrative by Commodore Arleigh A. Burke, Destroyers, Strikes, Kavieng, Rabaul, etc., DesDiv 45 and 46; DesRon 23, Film 411-III, recorded 8 August 1945, BP, pp. 1–14; War Diary, Commander, Destroyer Squadron 23, for the months of December 1943 and January–March 1944, and DesRon 23 Action reports for that period, ibid.; and 'Allied Claims and Enemy Confirmation of Damage to Japanese Ships (January–February 1944)', SRH 184 (Part III), NHA.

[33]Letter, Arleigh Burke to Roberta Burke, 25 January 1944, PF, BP.

[34]Letters, Arleigh Burke to Roberta Burke, 22 December 1943 and 6 January 1944, ibid.

[35]Narrative by Commodore Burke, Film 411-III, 8 August 1945, p. 15.

[36]Letter, Arleigh Burke to Roberta Burke, 24 March 1943, PF, BP.

[37]Naval Message, Commander-in-Chief, US Fleet, to Commander, Carrier Group 3, 111700 March 1944, ibid.; for efforts to send Burke to a new command, see letters, Commander Gelzer Sims to Burke, 16, 25 February and 11 March 1944, ibid.

-aviators commanding forces containing any of the new fast carriers
ator chiefs of staff to provide expert air-minded counsel. But the
a bit both ways, to Arleigh Burke's regret. The message conveying
King's order to Rear Admiral Marc A. Mitscher [*q.v.*], Commander Carrier
Division Three, and Fast Carrier Task Force 58, included Burke's name on a
list of four surface line captains from whom Mitscher could choose his new
Chief of Staff. Mitscher, a pioneer naval aviator who had commanded the
carrier *Hornet* at the Battle of Midway and Fleet Air Solomons in 1943,
resented having his personal staff interfered with, especially since he already
had a good *aviator* chief of staff in Captain Truman Hedding, and refused to
deal with the matter. Hedding picked Burke on the basis of his combat record
and the advice of Mitscher's departing operations officer, Commander C. D.
'Don' Griffin, who had been Burke's shipmate in 1932–3. Burke received his
new orders on 16 March. He was disappointed because it meant leaving his
beloved Little Beavers, without any leave at home, for a staff job he knew
nothing about, rather than a potential combat command. DesRon 23 left the
Solomons after covering the Emirau landings, and rendezvoused with Task
Force 58 on the 27th. Burke transferred to Mitscher's flagship, the carrier
Lexington, that afternoon.[38]

Mitscher, newly promoted to vice admiral, was normally a taciturn man,
and beyond offering Burke use of the in-port flag cabin did little to make his
new Chief of Staff welcome. With Hedding on loan to a task group staff, there
was no one to ease Burke's entry into naval aviation. Task Force 58 had just
sortied to strike Palau and Woleai. The planning for that operation was largely
complete, and the staff was already busy on the next. As Burke wrote to
Bobbie, 'I don't know my job and there are many things I should know I don't
and I feel lost.' There were 'compensations': 'ice cream – air conditioned cabin
– a bed – a tremendous cabin, excellent food – and all the luxuries I haven't
had[,] but I'd swap them all for one good job I knew I could do well'.[39]

The raids on Palau and Woleai were followed by operations in support of
General MacArthur's invasion of Hollandia, New Guinea on 21–24 April and
the second fast carrier strike on Truk on 29–30. Feeling all but useless, Burke
was ready to request a transfer. But when Hedding returned he convinced
Burke to stick it out, insisting that if he learned naval aviation and got on top of
the job, he would come to admire Mitscher. Burke accepted Hedding's advice
and threw himself into 'learning the bird man's lingo'. He flew as much as
possible, and got 'lots of training in handling the fleet'. It was not until the staff
flew to Pearl Harbor for planning meetings in early May, however, that Burke
'really cracked the ice' with the aviator admiral. Mitscher was pleased with

[38]War Diary, Commander, Destroyer Squadron 23, 16–27 March 1944; on King's decision and
Mitscher's choice, see Thomas B. Buell, *Master of Sea Power: A Biography of Admiral Ernest J. King*
(Boston, 1980), pp. 371–2; Theodore Taylor, *The Magnificent Mitscher* (New York, 1954), pp. 189–98;
and author's interview with Admiral C. D. Griffin, 12 December 1978.

[39]Letters, Arleigh Burke to Roberta Burke, 4 and 11 April 1944, ibid.

Burke's short, concise plans, tailored not to the eyes of posterity but to the needs of those doing the fighting. He peppered Burke with questions, and found that his Chief of Staff had acquired a solid knowledge of aviation capabilities and procedures. The admiral even permitted Burke to introduce some innovative air tactics in the plans for coming operations.[40]

Despite this thaw and his own growing confidence, Burke still found the job tedious. He longed to command destroyers again, and responded enthusiastically to a proposal by Commander, Destroyers, Pacific, to form a two-squadron force that he, Burke, could lead on forays in the North Pacific.[41] He seldom saw the sun and soon lost his South Pacific tan. When the task force was at anchor he spent his days battling paperwork in the flag office beneath the flight deck, and during the long periods at sea he practically lived in flag plot or the shady flag-bridge in the carrier's island. The reading load was tremendous: action reports, operations orders, landing plans, technical bulletins on radar, air warfare, anti-air warfare and anti-submarine warfare, captured enemy records and reports, and intelligence reports. Mitscher would personally debrief aviators returning from scouting and combat missions from his seat on the flag-bridge and Burke would attend most of those sessions. Burke was cleared for certain communications intelligence, including regular Ultra reports on the disposition and intentions of Japanese forces, and reports from the mobile radio intelligence unit attached to the Task Force 58 staff that monitored Japanese air communications in the task force's operating area and assisted in intercepting enemy air-raids. Where Mitscher viewed this sensitive intelligence with scepticism, preferring instead to trust in the eyes of his fellow pilots, Burke found it a critical component in planning.[42]

The Chief of Staff spent most of his time co-ordinating the work of his twenty-five officers as they stood watches in flag plot and flag radio, established standing operating procedures for the carrier task groups, developed plans and instructions for at least the next two upcoming operations, and wrote up the reports on the operations just completed. Burke wrote the main section of every operation plan and usually found himself writing the action report narratives as well. Planning involved something new or different in every operation. Between March and June 1944, Task Force 58 added two heavy and two light aircraft carriers, another full task group. Multi-carrier task group

[40]Transcript of interview with Admiral Burke by Stan Smith, 12 July 1965, PF, BP, pp. 23–4; letter, Arleigh Burke to Roberta Burke, 15 April 1944, ibid.; Arleigh Burke, 'An Article for Press Forlag', unpublished draft autobiography completed December 1981, pp. 39–47, BP; Arleigh Burke, 'Admiral Marc Mitscher, A Naval Aviator', *U.S. Naval Institute Proceedings*, vol. 101, pp. 57–8.

[41]Burke to Rear Admiral J. L. Kaufmann, 24 May 1944, in reply to Kaufmann to Burke, 27 April 1944, PF, BP.

[42]Author's interviews with Former Task Force 58 Intelligence Officers E. Calvert Cheston, 26 September 1986, and Byron R. White, 9 July 1984. Burke's Chief of Staff duties may be ascertained from a review of the Commander, First Carrier Task Force War Orders and Records of Pacific Operations, 1944–1945, Federal Records Center Suitland (1 CVTF), particularly the Secret and Top Secret Files. See also letter, Arleigh Burke to Roberta Burke, 12 May 1944, PF, BP.

operations were a new development in naval warfare, and the demands of planning for and operating fifteen carriers together effectively was a heavy load to place on the shoulders of an ex-destroyer squadron commander whose previous planning involved no more than eight DDs. When the Marianas campaign began, Task Force 58 contained nearly 100 ships and 900 aeroplanes and Burke struggled to 'get into the habit of dealing with forces instead of ships – and planes instead of guns'.43 The worst part of his job was serving as Mitscher's 'hatchet man', telling 'those few of his senior commanders who failed that they were relieved of duty' because of poor performance. The part he most enjoyed was manoeuvring the vast formation by voice command over the TBS, but even that was a far cry from leading DesRon 23 in combat. He later noted that during his sixteen-month tour as Mitscher's Chief of Staff, 'I have never worked so hard in my life, either before or since, and I don't believe any other person in that staff did either.'44

Mitscher took little interest in staff work, for the most part listening passively to the reports and recommendations presented to him. As Burke proved himself, the Admiral let him handle nearly all the details of Task Force 58's administration, planning and operations. But by the time the carriers left Majuro on 6 June 1944, bound for the invasion of Saipan, Burke had discovered that there was a great deal hidden behind that quiet façade. Mitscher knew how to make quick, bold decisions when decisions counted, and his mastery of naval aviation was unparalleled. 'The boss is a good hard fighting little shriveled up pleasant man,' Burke wrote to Bobbie in May. 'If you ever get a chance to meet him. You'll like him – and you'll have fun because he's full of fun,' and, he added, 'I admire him very much.'45 Although Burke still felt he was an outsider in the world of naval aviation, he and Mitscher were becoming an effective team, bound together by mutual respect, and an aggressive combat spirit.

It was the Marianas campaign and the Battle of the Philippine Sea that solidified Mitscher's reliance on Burke, and welded the destroyer commander to the carrier admiral for the remainder of Mitscher's life. Based on the staff's 'estimate of the situation', Burke and Mitscher believed that 'the Marianas was to be a crucial operation and its success would determine the outcome of the war. If the Japanese were successful, they could sue for peace with the probability of obtaining reasonable peace terms. If the United States were successful, the Japanese Empire was doomed.'46 Thus the Japanese navy would defend the islands with all its resources, creating the possibility of a decisive battle. The staff focused on the courses of action open to the enemy, in

43Letter, Burke to Roberta Burke, 15 April 1944; Memorandum from Chief of Staff to Staff, Subject: Operation Plans, Preparation of, 20 April 1944, PF, BP; Burke, 'Article for Press Forlag', pp. 42–3; Narrative by Commodore Arleigh A. Burke, Carrier Forces Pacific, Battle of the Philippine Sea, Film 417, recorded 20 August 1945, BP, pp. 1–13.

44Burke, 'An Article for Press Forlag', pp. 42, 52–3.

45Letter to Roberta Burke, 12 May 1944.

46Commodore Arleigh Burke, 'The First Battle of the Philippine Sea, Decision Not to Force an Action on the Night of 18–19 June', special dictated narrative, ca. 20 August 1945, BP, p. 1.

particular whether the Japanese could execute a surprise flanking manoeuvre. They concluded that this 'was not a serious consideration' because a northern 'end run' would cost the enemy too much scarce fuel oil, and a move from the south could involve only a small fast diversionary force. In fact, 'there was nothing the Japanese could do with their fleet to affect seriously the occupation of the Marianas so long as the Fast Carrier Task Forces could engage the major portion of the Japanese fleet'. 'There appeared no reason for not steaming directly for the Japanese fleet' because 'we could attack a diversion-ary force as easily from a position 300 miles west (downwind) of the Marianas as we could from the near vicinity of Saipan'.47

When American submarines located the Japanese fleet on 18 June, and the opportunity arose for initiating a major battle overnight or the next morning, Burke was disappointed that Admiral Raymond Spruance [q.v.], in command of the Fifth Fleet, twice vetoed Mitscher's recommendations to send the carriers west. Spruance made those decisions, Burke believed, because he did not appreciate that the fast carriers were capable of both preventing a flanking attack on the amphibious force at Saipan and striking decisively at the enemy. Burke was also disappointed when Vice Admiral Willis Lee, in command of the battle-line, emphatically recommended against seeking a night surface action with the enemy. Burke thought that Lee, a fellow gunnery expert who had himself pioneered night surface actions, would jump at the opportunity. It seemed, he wrote after the battle, that air and landing forces were 'carrying the entire load', while the surface fleet stood on the sidelines.48 It was a bitter pill for the destroyerman to swallow. There were naturally cautious commanders, and naturally audacious ones, he told himself, and both had their strengths and weaknesses. But those who erred on the side of caution should probably choose aggressive chiefs of staff to spur them on. Spruance had been advised by a staff chosen months before who reinforced his conservatism instead of challenging it.49

American carrier planes decimated the attacking Japanese naval air force in the 'Turkey Shoot' air battle on the 19th, and sank a light carrier and two oilers in a long-range strike on the 20th, but Burke 'felt particularly bitter' at the missed opportunities. His draft action report criticized 'the undue caution with which we seem to be so amply supplied' that had given the enemy a chance to delay 'the eventual outcome of the war' by using their navy in 'small concentrated attacks' designed to make future US operations 'so expensive that we will be willing to accept peace terms fairly advantageous to the Japanese'.50 At Burke's request, Mitscher, who so trusted his staff's reports that he usually

47Commander, Fast Carrier Task Forces, Pacific, Draft Action Report, Operations of Task Force 58, 11 June through 21 June 1944, Serial 00298, 27 June 1944, PF, BP, pp. 7–8.

48Letter, Arleigh Burke to Roberta Burke, 27 July 1944, PF, BP.

49Burke, 'Decision Not to Force an Action on the Night of 18–19 June', pp. 8–12.

50Draft Action Report, 27 June 1944, last page (unnumbered); letter, Rear Admiral Arleigh Burke to Theodore Taylor, 8 December 1953, PF, BP.

signed them without reading them, reviewed Burke's conclusions. The Admiral reminded him that there are always some mistakes in battle: 'This time we were right, because the enemy did what we expected him to do. Admiral Spruance could have been right. It was his job to protect the landing force. Forget the criticism and rewrite the last pages.'[51] It was a lesson in leadership Burke never forgot.

By the time Task Force 58 left the Marianas, Burke knew that he would probably not be going back to destroyers. 'This job looks as if it might be a permanent one for me,' he wrote to Bobbie in late July. 'I don't know whether it's my ideas – my hell raising or cutting down paper work they want – for I know I'm not a very good chief of staff and think they should get somebody here who would really like it.'[52]

Mitscher, however, found Burke's work more than adequate. On 13 August he wrote to the Secretary of the Navy recommending that Burke be immediately promoted to temporary rear admiral in 'the best interests of the service'. Burke promptly fired off a letter objecting to the recommendation. 'Of course, I would like to be a Rear Admiral,' he wrote, 'since that is what I have worked for all my life; but, in fairness to a lot of other people and to the Navy, I feel that I do not deserve this promotion now.' It would just cause jealousy, he explained to Bobbie, 'and I don't think it would be particularly good for the Navy – which is the important reason. I can't think of any way the Navy could get any more out of me if I wore two stars.'[53]

At the end of the Marianas campaign, Admiral Spruance and his staff went ashore to plan new operations. Admiral Halsey came in as relief, Fifth Fleet became Third Fleet, and the fast carriers were designated Task Force 38. Mitscher chose not to relinquish command for three months, until after the next major operation. Halsey and Mitscher were both aviators and aggressive combat commanders, and Halsey's Chief of Staff, 'Mick' Carney, was a strong friend and supporter of Burke's. But the command arrangement left Mitscher with less freedom of action than he had enjoyed under Spruance. When the task force sailed, Halsey often assumed tactical command, and, despite his lack of recent experience with the fast carriers, rarely asked Mitscher for advice. The Task Force 38 staff planned and executed the operations against Palau, the Southern Philippines, the Ryukyus, Formosa and Luzon, but by the time the Leyte invasion began on 20 October Halsey was consistently bypassing Mitscher and was giving orders directly to the four carrier task groups. Tired from months of combat, possibly ill with a heart condition, and discouraged by his lack of

[51]Burke, 'Admiral Marc Mitscher', pp. 59–60.

[52]Letter to Roberta Burke, 27 July 1944.

[53]Letter, Arleigh Burke to Roberta Burke, 18 August 1944; and Burke to Rear Admiral J. L. Kaufmann, 12 August 1944, both PF, BP. Mitscher's nomination is in Commander, Fast Carrier Task Forces, Pacific, to the Secretary of the Navy, Serial 202, 13 August 1944, Folder P14, Box 351725, 1 CVTF.

influence on the battle preparations going on around him, Mitscher spent much of his time in his sea cabin.[54]

During the Battle for Leyte Gulf, Mitscher and Burke were largely spectators. When the battle opened on 24 October, *Lexington* was with Task Group 38.3 attacking Luzon, and was too far north to participate in the strikes Halsey ordered against the Japanese Central Force in the Sibuyan Sea. Burke was concerned that evening when Halsey ordered all three available task groups north to engage the carriers of the Japanese Northern Force. If the enemy carriers were anything but decoys, Burke told Mitscher, they would have mounted a co-ordinated attack against Task Group 38.3 that morning. The real threat remained the Central Force, which had turned back but now appeared to have regrouped and was heading for San Bernardino Strait. Mitscher agreed that Burke was probably right, but did not pass on to Halsey his recommendation that the battle-line be detached to guard the Strait. Halsey had all the same information, and would draw his own conclusions, Mitscher stated, and if he 'wants my advice he will ask for it'.[55] The best Mitscher thought they could do would be to press north as fast as possible, hoping to destroy the weak Northern Force by early morning, and then speed south to take on the Central Force. Even this plan was frustrated, however, when Halsey ordered the carriers to slow down, fearing they might miss the Japanese in the night. When Halsey led the battle-line in a hasty return to Leyte Gulf on the 25th, Mitscher's remaining two task groups mopped up the Northern Force. Four enemy carriers were sunk, effectively ending Japan's naval air power. Despite Burke's own doubts about the wisdom of leaving San Bernardino Strait unguarded, he always afterwards defended Halsey's decision to take the Northern Force seriously. Knowing what forces are necessary to take on a particular threat, he pointed out, is always 'much easier when the battle reports are in than when the contact reports are in'.[56]

At the end of October, Mitscher and Burke went ashore to rest. Burke was promoted to the temporary rank of commodore, effective so long as he was serving in his chief of staff billet. Following a trip to Washington, where he briefed Admiral King's staff on recent operations, had a welcome reunion with Bobbie and participated in some public appearances in support of the war effort, he spent December 1944 and January 1945 at Pearl Harbor planning the campaigns against the Bonins and Ryukyus. On 20 January, the staff released a comprehensive set of instructions on fast carrier operations, the first

---

[54]Interview with E. Calvert Cheston, 26 September 1986; US Naval War College, *The Battle for Leyte Gulf, October 1944: Strategic and Tactical Analysis*, vol. II (Newport, Rhode Island, 1957–8), pp. 31–2; Taylor, *Magnificent Mitscher*, pp. 248–59.

[55]Burke, 'Admiral Marc Mitscher', p. 61; letter, Rear Admiral Arleigh Burke to Captain Samuel E. Morison, 5 April 1951, PF, BP; E. B. Potter, *Bull Halsey* (Annapolis, Maryland, 1985), pp. 296–301.

[56]Letter, Burke to Rear Admiral R. B. Carney, 9 December 1944, Miscellaneous Papers Folder, Box 351729, I CVTF.

of its kind, to guide the task force in the coming campaign.57 As important as the work was, Burke rapidly tired of pushing papers. He continued to feel out of place, and the disdain of 'brown shoe' aviators for 'black shoe' surface officers galled him. But he was by now convinced that carriers were the future of the navy and sometimes angered 'black shoe' friends by saying so. 'The trouble with [one such friend]', he wrote, 'is that he doesn't want to admit a non-aviator is washed up. He knows it – but he struggles still. I know it – and am comfortably resigned to a happy and early retirement.'58 Before retiring, however, he wanted one more crack at the enemy in his own cruiser command. This appeared unlikely, however, for no matter how much he hated staff work, he knew he would not leave Mitscher so long as the Admiral needed him.

In late January, Spruance relieved Halsey, Mitscher relieved John McCain, and Task Force 38 was again designated Task Force 58. On 10 February, the fleet sailed from Ulithi. The return to shipboard, in new flagship *Bunker Hill*, lifted Burke's spirits: 'We are back home again,' he exulted, 'not in the same ship – but at sea.'59 Following strikes on targets in the Tokyo area on 16–17 February, Task Force 58 provided support for the Marines battling on Iwo Jima for three days, then returned to Japan to strike Tokyo again, and on 1 March pounded Okinawa. Despite the bitter cold and high seas, this two-week cruise was a simple matter compared to the two-and-a-half-month ordeal that followed. In preparation for the invasion of Okinawa scheduled for 1 April, the carriers sailed on 14 March to raid airfields on Kyushu and the Inland Sea. This began 'the longest sustained carrier operation of World War II'. From 18 March until late May, elements of Task Force 58 were 'under almost continuous attack'.60 Beginning on 23 March, the fast carriers remained tethered to Okinawa, flying patrol and support missions, except for five days in May when Kyushu was struck again. Damage from air strikes and kamikaze attacks kept the task force at three task groups throughout the majority of the campaign. As a bone-weary Burke described it on 6 April, the day before the super-battleship *Yamato*'s final sortie: 'we are in the middle of the most fantastic battle that was ever waged – gruesome, unbelievable, a nation committing suicide, an all-out effort on its way to death taking as many with it as it can'.61

World War Two combat ended for Burke and Mitscher in a flurry of suicide attacks – 'the complete course in suiciders, including the postgraduate course'

57Commander, First Carrier Task Force, Pacific, Task Force Instructions, *FirstCarTF1A*, Enclosure to Serial 003, 20 January 1945, NHA. Burke co-ordinated production of this several-hundred-page document and wrote the sections on cruising instructions and surface operations himself.

58Letter, Arleigh Burke to Roberta Burke, 9 February 1945, PF, BP.

59Letter, Arleigh Burke to Roberta Burke, 27 January 1945, ibid.

60Taylor, *Magnificent Mitscher*, p. 279.

61Letter, Arleigh Burke to Roberta Burke, 6 April 1945, PF, BP. The Okinawa campaign is best described in Commander, Task Force 58, Action Report, 14 March to 28 May 1945, Serial 00222, 18 June 1945, NHA.

– in May.[62] On the 11th, flagship *Bunker Hill* was hit by two kamikazes; 352 men were killed, including thirteen of Mitscher's staff. A basic surviving staff transferred to *Enterprise* but a kamikaze hit her on the 14th, destroying her forward elevator, forcing Mitscher and Burke to move again, this time to *Randolph*. On 27 May, Halsey again relieved Spruance, and the next day McCain relieved Mitscher. Within a week, Burke was back in Washington, and after a brief leave was assigned to Fleet Admiral King's Cominch staff as head of newly formed Section F49, charged with attempting to solve the kamikaze problem. His wartime service had brought him full circle, and, when Japan surrendered, Arleigh Burke was once again at a desk in Washington.

The job was different, however, and so was the man. Before the war Burke had been a promising technical officer, one of the navy's conservative brain trust in BuOrd. Now, he was not only one of the most successful surface combat commanders of his generation, but he was also one of the very few 'black shoes' accepted within the 'brown shoe' fraternity of naval aviation.

Assigned to BuOrd as Director of Research and Development, October 1945. Returned to sea duty early 1946 as Chief of Staff to Admiral Mitscher, accompanying him (October 1946) when Mitscher became Commander-in-Chief, Atlantic Fleet. 1947–55: Director of division attempting to limit unification of the armed services; Deputy Chief of Staff to Commander, US Naval Forces Far East, during first year of Korean War; member of first United Nations Korean Truce Negotiating Team; head of navy's Strategic Plans Division, Washington DC. Selected (August 1955) over ninety-two senior flag officers to be CNO; remained in post for unparalleled triple term of six years. As one of the navy's most effective peacetime leaders, he maintained the fleet at high readiness through some of the worst Cold War crises; accelerated the introduction of new technology throughout the navy; and initiated and protected the project which became Polaris. Retired 1961. In the 1980s Burke became the first living US Navy officer to be honoured by having a class of ship – the Arleigh Burke *guided missile destroyers – named after him.*[63]

[62]Letter, Arleigh Burke to Roberta Burke, 19 May 1945, ibid.

[63]Forrestal to Rear Admiral James Foskett, 6 February 1947, attached to W. R. Smedberg to Burke, n.d., PF, BP. On Burke's subsequent career, see David Alan Rosenberg, 'Arleigh Albert Burke' in Robert W. Love Jr (ed.), *The Chiefs of Naval Operations* (Annapolis, Maryland, 1980), pp. 262–319.

PART SIX

Unsung Heroes

28

Admiral

John Godfrey

CB
Royal Navy

1888-1971

by
David Brown

JOHN *Herbert Godfrey, born 18 July 1888, into a middle-class Birmingham family without naval connections. Career decided for him by strong-minded mother and elder brother. Joined training ship* Britannia *at Dartmouth, 1903; decided to specialize as a navigating officer. Served first in a river gunboat on the China Station then as the flotilla (N) of the 4th Destroyer Flotilla, Home Fleet, 1911–14.*

Joined cruiser Charybdis, *flagship Rear Admiral Sir Rosslyn Wemyss, commanding the 12th Cruiser Squadron, 1914. Remained with Wemyss for three years, as his staff (N) and subsequently, when the Admiral became C-in-C Egypt and East Indies, as Assistant to the Chief of Staff. Saw action at Gallipoli, off Cape Helles and Suvla; served in the Red Sea, 1916. Organized a coastal survey of the Red Sea; was responsible for the practical aspects of the introduction of an Allied system of trade protection in the Indian Ocean. Continued this last main occupation while within the Mediterranean, as Assistant to the C-in-C's Chief of Staff, 1917–18.*

Returned briefly to navigating duties, November 1918; planned, and drafted orders for, the Mediterranean Fleet's passage through the Dardanelles. With this safely accomplished, continued staff work (now in the Black Sea). Returned to Britain for leave and reappointment, August 1919.

Eighteen months on the staff of C-in-C Home Fleet; promoted to rank of commander, June 1920, just before his thirty-second birthday – one of the youngest commanders in the navy. Next served in the Admiralty Plans Division, then became one of the first members of the Royal Naval Staff College's directing staff. Although eminently suited to the job, and despite his excellent record, it nearly cost him promotion, for which he needed sea-time as the executive officer of a major warship. He did not make matters easier by applying for a cruiser on the New Zealand Station, for while he broadened his experience between 1925 and 1928 in HMS Diomede, *he was too far from those who influenced promotion. Not until his last chance, in June 1928, was he selected; although still just under forty, he had been left behind by some contemporaries and even overtaken by juniors.*

After two months at Sidney Sussex College, Cambridge, where he broadened his acquaintance to include many eminent dons of the day, Captain Godfrey returned to the RN Staff College to serve as a memorable Deputy Director. Commanded a heavy cruiser, HMS Suffolk, *on the China Station, 1931–3. Acquired the reputation of being somewhat aloof, but ashore he continued to make new friends, including the head of the Shanghai Reuters agency office, who introduced him to a wide circle of publishers and journalists.*

Deputy Director of the Plans Division 1934–6; created a naval policy from the wreckage left behind by years of recession and pacifism. Others supervised the subsequent rearmament programme, for in 1936 Godfrey left the Admiralty to take command of the battle-cruiser Repulse *and to return to the Mediterranean Fleet. Impressed his C-in-C at Malta, Sir Dudley Pound.*

These were two eventful years in the Mediterranean, with unrest in Palestine and the Spanish Civil War calling for Royal Navy presence at opposite ends of the Station. Godfrey did stints as Senior Naval Officer in both areas, evacuating British citizens from the one and keeping Arabs and Jews apart in the other, and also served as the naval diplomat who restored friendly relations with the Turkish authorities in the Aegean. Made Companion of the Bath (CB), in the 1939 New Year's Honours, a distinction normally awarded only to officers of rear-admiral rank.

John Herbert Godfrey's was one of the more extraordinary naval careers of World War Two. Between 1939 and 1946, he held only two appointments and although neither was in sea-going command, his influence extended worldwide. Respected by his contemporaries, the true value of his contribution to Britain's 1940–1 survival and Allied victory was not fully appreciated until thirty years after the end of World War Two.

As a young and junior officer (he was still under thirty when World War One ended), he had been given a very heavy load of responsibility, and had acquired a remarkable range of experience, not only in naval staff work but also in dealing with allies and civilian administrations. Commodore Burmester, who had been his immediate superior through the last five years, said of Godfrey: 'Ability considered to be exceptional . . . an extraordinarily zealous, loyal and hard-working staff officer who appears to me to be marked out for employment on the War Staff'. This appraisal did not draw attention to the young lieutenant-commander's wide-ranging interests, which went far beyond his undoubted professional expertise, or to his gift for making genuine friendships with key individuals, government officials, bankers, industrialists and members of the great trading houses. To these may be added a quest for knowledge acquired through personal experience and an intellect capable of pulling together all these strands.

In February 1939, John Godfrey became the Director of the Naval Intelligence Department, in succession to Vice Admiral J. A. G. Troup.

'Quite the most interesting job', said Godfrey, 'for a Director at the Admiralty.' His entire career to date had fitted him for the task of heading the Naval Staff's oldest and most senior division: he had seen much of the world and experienced many of its current problems at first hand; he could talk on equal terms with intellectuals, industrialists, financiers, press barons, even if it was considered by some of his naval contemporaries that he lacked the common touch. Above all, his personal qualities – catholic tastes, sound intellect and energy – meant that the Admiralty had the right man at the right time. On 22 February, Godfrey was promoted rear admiral, in advance of the normal half-yearly list. His personal future looked very promising.

Although British naval intelligence has been glamorized and portrayed as an all-seeing Machiavellian organization, running daring spy networks and making full use of technology to obtain facts which it deployed for its own purposes, only during World War One, under the renowned Captain 'Blinker' Hall, did it ever approximate to this image. By 1939, its own sources and methods were strictly 'legal' and its efficiency was dependent upon meticulously maintained and filed index cards, containing information obtained by British naval attachés (openly) and from foreign naval attachés accredited to London, from reporting officers attached to British consulates, from the British and foreign press and from Royal Navy vessels visiting foreign ports. Such 'illegal' material as was obtained came from the Secret Intelligence Service, which was a Foreign Office fief. Codes and ciphers were not NID's responsibility – that lay with the Government Code and Cipher School, another Foreign Office dependant, with whom NID maintained a close liaison – but the running of the Admiralty's direction-finding and monitoring networks was.

The raw material provided the data from which were updated at intervals the routine handbooks giving details of foreign navies, their ships and building programmes and their harbours and coast defences. There was also a section which handled technical information, but here assessment was largely left to the technical specialist departments, such as the Director of Naval Construction or the Gunnery Division.

Besides the recording and internal dissemination of foreign information, DNI controlled the Admiralty's press department, releasing Royal Navy information to the media – effectively Fleet Street and Broadcasting House. By a supremely logical extension, the man responsible for the release of information was also in charge of the procedures for preventing unauthorized disclosure of documents – better than anyone, he could assess what would be of value to a foreign power. For the same reason, the security of naval communications, a vast field which included wireless traffic patterns and operator technique as well as counter-'code breaking', was DNI's responsibility.

Godfrey inherited from Troup one completely unique section, which had no parallel elsewhere. Unlike his fellow Chiefs of Staff, and even contemporary chiefs of foreign naval staffs, the First Sea Lord was not just the senior professional member of a policy-making board, he was also an operational commander, supplied with communications which enabled him to receive information and give orders to commanders and individual ships worldwide. Tactical decisions would always have to be left to the man on the spot, but the Admiralty, with its broader sources of information, could often get him there in the first place. An essential element in the Admiralty assessment process was a knowledge (or at least an intelligent deduction) of the positions of enemy warships and it is surprising that not until 1936 was an organization formed specifically for this purpose. The Operational Intelligence Centre, under Paymaster Lieutenant-Commander 'Ned' Denning, had won its spurs in the autumn of 1938, during the Czechoslovakian crisis, when it tracked the day-to-day movements and assessed the likely intentions of Italian and German warships and merchant shipping. Godfrey immediately recognized the significance of OIC and one of his earliest decisions was to revive a Submarine Tracking Section, under one of its World War One staff, Paymaster Commander Thring, as part of the OIC organization.

The essentials of NID were already in place when Godfrey arrived; his job was to manage their expansion, to be ready for war. The department was undermanned, with barely fifty serving officers and civil servants for its numerous and disparate tasks, but Treasury sanction for expansion, even in the post-Munich climate, was given only after protracted haggling and even obstructionism. In the meantime, Godfrey went out to his influential acquaintances and got them to identify suitable individuals who could be put into uniform for NID's benefit in the event of war. The best known of these recruits was Ian Fleming, the thirty-one-year-old stockbroker who joined John Godfrey as his personal assistant on the recommendation of the Governor of the Bank of England, but there were dozens of others who served no less ably in less high-profile NID appointments.

One of John Godfrey's most valuable talents was his ability to delegate authority effectively. The operational decision-makers – Pound [*q.v.*] and his Vice, Deputy and Assistant Chiefs of the Naval Staff and the Directors of the Operations and Trade Divisions – were encouraged to communicate direct with NID section heads, to obtain information and assessments straight from the experts. Thus, by leaving to his trusted deputies and assistants the day-to-day running of their sections, he was 'freed for my rightful duty, which was to organize, sustain and supervise a machine that was to grow from a few dozen to over a thousand individuals in three years of war'.

The key to DNI's continued ability to remain in touch with his sections and with the outside was the Co-ordinating Section, which occupied Room 39, in the Old Block of the Admiralty. Here, an unusual array of talented individuals from many disciplines acted as a clearing-house for ideas and facts and provided a pool from which Godfrey drew those who would represent him on inter-departmental committees.

An essential part of his 'rightful duty' was liaison with other intelligence authorities. At an early stage in his tenure, he was involved in discussions with

French naval intelligence, to make arrangements for co-operation in the event of war. There could, of course, be no official contact with German intelligence agencies, but in July 1939 he met the head of the British section of German military intelligence, who had come to London to assess for himself Britain's will to fight and had chosen the DNI as the most suitable source of information. This was, of course, the myth in action, but Godfrey was able to oblige, arranging meetings with a selection of individuals, businessmen, politicians and Foreign Office officials, as well as service representatives.

More important, however, was the need for co-ordination and co-operation between the domestic intelligence agencies, civilian and military. To assess the validity of the reports and rumours which abounded during the pre-September 1939 war of nerves, Godfrey was instrumental in the creation of a Situation Report Centre, in which representatives of the service intelligence divisions and the Foreign Office collated information and issued daily situation reports for the benefit of the decision-makers. This body was soon amalgamated with the existing Joint Intelligence Committee, a long-term assessment organization which had hitherto lacked Foreign Office representation: at Godfrey's insistence, the latter department provided the permanent chairman of the JIC. Thus tied in to the main military and political briefing source, full co-operation from the Foreign Office-controlled SIS and Code and Cipher School was guaranteed.

With this assurance, Godfrey now made one of his most important contributions, insisting that 'raw' intelligence from all sources should be passed unprocessed to the OIC, where it would be collated and assessed in the light of the overall picture and situation. Selective dissemination of the digested results was to be the responsibility of the Admiralty, using its wireless communications network. This eminently sensible arrangement, which, with NID's responsibility for naval security, had the merit of protecting sources, was opposed by many who had seen opportunities for themselves in various influential areas and who now saw themselves cut out of the chain. Whatever may have been Godfrey's stated views on devolution, these did not apply to the close interest that he took in the OIC's output, but there is nothing to suggest that he used the knowledge for personal power.

The arrival of Winston Churchill as First Lord of the Admiralty on the outbreak of war obliged Godfrey to modify his style somewhat. Unlike the majority of First Lords who had been in office since his own departure in 1915, Churchill interfered continually in operational matters and seldom hesitated to use knowledge for personal ends. This brought him into immediate contact and conflict with Godfrey, who was responsible for naval 'public relations'. Churchill insisted upon being the bearer of good news to the public and, after Godfrey's deputy in this area had anticipated him on two or three occasions, not only was the individual appointed away to sea (the First Lord being responsible for officers' careers) but, after a 'lively scene', Godfrey was relieved of his PR responsibilities.

NID's Statistical Section, intended to serve the Admiralty as a whole, went next, to become a tool to be used by Professor Frederick Lindemann, Churchill's scientific adviser, for his master's benefit. Worst of all, the First Lord, in November 1939, brought to an end the circulation of a weekly anti-submarine situation assessment which was providing figures of U-boat losses and building rates which clashed with his own over-optimistic announcements. Godfrey maintained his personal integrity and did not allow the prohibition, which remained in force until the end of 1940, to prevent him from keeping those who needed the details informed.

For all Godfrey's preparations, NID took many months to work up under war conditions, not least because his civilian recruits had to learn their way around a completely new world. Lack of reliable information was another problem – the first German ciphers were not read before April 1940, coincidentally with the first useful strategic air reconnaissance operations. Only the briefest warning of the German intention to invade Norway was given (and went unheeded by the First Lord and First Sea Lord) but subsequent small successes during the campaign which followed established some confidence within the department and among its users.

On 13 May 1940, a new codeword was coined, as a prefix to denote to recipients the reliability of information provided by the Admiralty for *tactical* use. Naval Ultra signals contained details obtained only from decrypts of enemy signals and analysed by the OIC. With the exception of a brief period in May, however, the German navy ciphers were not read until May 1941.

French naval ciphers which fell into NID's hands in late June were of brief use only, for the terms of the Franco-German armistice prohibited their use. These did provide useful information about the concessions which the French had managed to wring concerning the basing of their fleet but Churchill, by then Prime Minister, did not choose to view them as sufficient reason to cancel the attack on the French squadron at Mers-el-Kebir. Godfrey did not describe his own contribution to this affair in his unpublished memoirs, which are otherwise very full, but from peripheral sources it would appear that he did nothing to deter Churchill from ordering the use of force.

With Britain alone, it was clear that the only possible ally had to be courted assiduously, and from the summer of 1940 Godfrey took the US Naval Attaché more and more into his confidence. In May 1941 Godfrey flew to Washington with instructions from the Chiefs of Staff to arrange for a combined co-operative US–UK joint-services intelligence organization. Although the US Navy, Army and State Department were individually interested in co-operation with the joint British system, they could not agree to collaborate with one another and only a meeting between Godfrey and the President himself resolved the impasse by the creation of the Office of Strategic Services, under Colonel William Donovan, who was to head the US intelligence effort.

Such success, although ultimately invaluable to the US agencies and thereby to the Allied war effort, was not welcome to all of his peers. The NID, thanks to the simultaneous break into the U-boats' cipher, had begun a nine-month run of success at a time when the other services were not enjoying similar fortune. Godfrey, after over two years as DNI, had acquired authority as well as experience and his repeated assumption of the lead or initiative in 'joint' projects caused stresses within the Joint Intelligence Committee, where his was undoubtedly the outstanding service intellect. By the beginning of 1942, his fellow Directors of Intelligence had asked their Chiefs of Staff to request Admiral Pound not to renew Godfrey's appointment; and because at CoS meetings, the DNI had occasionally pooh-poohed assessments dear to the military and air force hearts, the Chiefs of the Imperial General Staff and the Air Staff willingly obliged.

Pound did not speak to Godfrey on the matter. Nor did the VCNS, Vice Admiral H. R. Moore, who was tasked to investigate the situation. On 15 September 1942, John Godfrey was promoted to vice admiral, an unusual promotion for one who had not been to sea as a rear admiral. The bad news was that on the same day, Pound sent for him and informed him that Moore considered 'that co-operation among members of the JIC . . . was not possible as long as you were a member', and that Godfrey's relief had been judged necessary.

This unceremonial sacking was a manifestly unfair decision; and the fact that it was taken in the interests of inter-service amity, against the one individual who had done most to promote joint-service efficiency in his field, must stand against the reputations of those involved. Godfrey had already accepted without demur a ruling of Pound's in the spring of 1941 that his chance of sea-going command was ended, but the First Sea Lord, perhaps through his illness, showed no recall of the Royal Navy's dictum that loyalty goes down as well as up the chain of command.

Godfrey was relieved at the end of November 1942 by Captain Edmund Rushbrooke, who inherited an efficient and effective machine. In March 1943, Godfrey himself took up his new appointment as Flag Officer Commanding, Royal Indian Navy (Focrin). If his supersession was genuinely due to inability to co-operate with the other services, then this was indeed an odd appointment for Focrin, although the Admiralty's link with the Government of India, was responsible not to the Viceroy or any naval representative on the viceregal staff but to the C-in-C of the Indian Army, whom he served as naval adviser.

Independent of the C-in-C Eastern Fleet, Admiral Sir James Somerville [*q.v.*], he nevertheless had to liaise closely and co-operate with this senior RN commander, whose area of responsibility extended beyond the Indian theatre. Focrin himself had no operational responsibilities beyond local defence and control of Indian ports, for as soon as RIN warships had commissioned and completed trials they were allocated to the operational control of the Royal

Navy. His main purpose was therefore to recruit, train and adminster the personnel of the service whose much expanded wartime form had been bequeathed to him by his predecessor, Vice Admiral Sir Herbert Fitzherbert.

The rapid expansion of the RIN was at the root of many of Godfrey's problems. Too often the ratings were not the pick of the crop, for military tradition in India was predominantly army and the latter was responsible for all recruiting in inland districts. The main deficiency was, however, the shortage of experienced officers and senior ratings, which the Admiralty could do very little to alleviate: sufficient of good quality could be found for sea service and for the naval headquarters staff, but this left too few to provide a wholly reliable cadre for training and discipline in the many shore establishments.

Matters were not made any easier by the complex system of pay, allowances and entitlements administered by the army-orientated bureaucrats of the Military Finance Department. Godfrey's attempts to improve pay and conditions were continually frustrated by the latter and he was not supported by his superior, Field Marshal Auchinleck, on the one occasion that a cast-iron case was presented to the Viceroy's Council – the equivalent of the Cabinet. Such failures did nothing to enhance, on the part of the RIN, either confidence in naval headquarters or affection for a chief who was deeply respected but, according to his own Flag Lieutenant, not a popular figure. Even when he did succeed in establishing fleet clubs in the main ports, an efficient canteen service (RIN ratings were not allowed to use British NAAFI facilities in India), a Welfare Service and a Benevolent Fund, all of which were superior to any Indian Army equivalent, the dissatisfaction over pay remained.

One undoubted personnel success was the creation of a Naval Wing of the Women's Auxiliary Corps (India), in 1944. Previously dressed in army-style uniform, but now in white, the ladies eked out the scarce competent manpower and, against official opposition, styled themselves 'WRINS'. Unlike the majority of Godfrey's innovations, they did not survive long after the end of the war.

Planning the peacetime shape and size of the Indian navy began as early as 1943. The operational success of the sloops, corvettes and minesweepers secured military support for Godfrey's blueprint, which included cruisers and destroyers, even though civilian (specifically financial) and, surprisingly, Royal Navy enthusiasm was less marked. Godfrey did not see himself as being the man to implement the transition from wartime to post-war conditions, having advised the First Sea Lord late in 1943 that he believed that his appointment should be for no more than two years. Auchinleck, however, considered that this period was too short and Godfrey was still in India in April 1945 when the Admiralty informed him that he would be offered no further employment on the Active List; he would be promoted to the rank of admiral and placed on the Retired List in due course. By the time this occurred, in September 1945, Auchinleck had asked that he should continue as Focrin, whichever List he was on, until March 1946.

The war had meanwhile ended, somewhat earlier than expected, thanks to the use of the atomic bombs. Naval headquarters had already done much work to prepare for demobilization: Bombay was to be the centre and it was planned that 500 men would be discharged each week so that the RIN would be reduced from 27,000 men down to its peacetime level of 11,000 by June 1946. Unfortunately, bureaucracy could not keep pace with plans and the Naval Pay and Accounts Department (of the Military Finance Department) took its time in closing individual pay accounts, insisting that every detail should be settled and agreed before a man could be discharged; further delays were likely to occur if there were appeals – and there were many – against settlements. The Bombay shore establishments filled with men who waited longer and longer for discharge; the overcrowding led to lower standards in food, and recreational facilities were inadequate for so many idle men. To make things far worse, the general political climate was deteriorating rapidly with Hindu and Muslim nationalists alike agitating for British withdrawal from India.

Godfrey recognized the potential for trouble early and in August 1945 created a Morale Section at naval HQ, to monitor the situation and take action if necessary. This section was ill-served by the officers in ships and establishments who were supposed to report on morale and discipline, and several weeks went by before it became clear that general dissatisfaction was increasing, as were, on a lesser scale, acts of organized indiscipline. Godfrey asked an Indian Army colonel to conduct an independent investigation into the state of the naval establishments in Bombay and his report, completed in December 1945, identified the specific problems and grievances.

Godfrey pointed out to his senior staff officers that all the traditional ingredients of serious lower-deck disturbances were present – complaints about pay, accommodation and food, lack of interest on the part of many officers in their men's welfare – complicated by the communal differences peculiar to India. He ordered immediate action to retrieve the situation, promising to seek support from Auchinleck if difficulties could not be resolved locally or within naval HQ. The measures were left to his subordinates.

Focrin then spent January 1946 touring the coastal and island establishments aboard the sloop *Narbada*. With hindsight, it is easy to comment that he had chosen the timing of his absence badly – that he should have remained in Delhi to monitor a serious situation. But Godfrey's style of management leaned heavily upon devolution and delegation and, with only two months left before his scheduled departure, he had to allow Rear Admiral A. R. Rattray RIN, who was in charge at Bombay, to take the necessary steps.

On 18 February 1946, ratings at the Naval Signals School, HMIS *Talwar*, mutinied, their long list of demands including better food and pay but also political concessions which were clearly inspired by current Indian Congress

Party propaganda. During the next three days the mutiny – which the participants had initially called a 'strike' – spread to ships and establishments in Bombay, elsewhere in India and as far as Aden and Hong Kong. In Bombay, shots were exchanged between the Indian Army and the mutineers and several ships trained their guns shorewards (but did not open fire).

The men returned to duty on 23 February, after Godfrey had made a personal statement – not an appeal – on the radio. Only in one ship, the sloop *Hindustan* at Karachi, was force needed to suppress the mutiny and life lost, seven men being killed.

It was a very sad end to Godfrey's worthy career. The official Indian government inquiry, which appeared months after he had left the country, on 9 May 1946, was somewhat biased, particularly against the British element in the Royal Indian Navy and the naval headquarters staff, but blame was not attached personally to Focrin. The general informed impression was that he had been beaten by a combination of circumstances and 'the system' – the inertia and apathy of the Indian establishment.

John Godfrey received no honours or awards for his wartime service, the *only* full Admiral (or equivalent in the other services) to be thus snubbed. Auchinleck had proposed that he be created a KCSI (Knight Commander of the Star of India) but the mutiny forestalled that and the British Labour government, courting the future ruling party of India, took no action. He deserved better of his country, and of India. To the first he gave an excellent naval intelligence organization working within an Allied framework which he had done much to create; in India he left a naval administration which was later proved to work well under an independent government. Neither ever acknowledged the debt formally.

Edited the secret history of the Naval Intelligence Division. Chairman of the Management Committee of the Chelsea Group of Hospitals. Founded the Cheyne Centre for Spastic Children. Wrote memoirs for private circulation. Died of a heart attack, 29 August 1971, aged eighty-three.

29

Captain

Joseph John Rochefort
United States Navy

1898–1976

by
Roger Pineau

JOSEPH John Rochefort, born 12 May 1898, Dayton, Ohio. Graduated Polytechnic High School, Los Angeles, 1918. Enlisted in Naval Reserve, April 1918, and sent to OTC Engineering course. Stevens Institute of Technology, Hoboken, New Jersey, 1918–19: reserve commission as ensign, June 1919. Various sea duties to watch and divisional officer, battleship Arizona, December 1924. Assigned to Office of Naval Communications (ONC), October 1925, under Lieutenant Laurence F. Safford. Jointly developed crypto correspondence course; jointly taught basics of cryptanalysis by Agnes Mayer Driscoll. Became OIC of ONC Crypto Section, 1926; sea duty, September 1927; language studies (with Lieutenant (j.g.) Edwin T. Layton), Tokyo, 1929–32; ONI, October 1932; assistant ops officer and staff intelligence chief, battleship Pennsylvania, 1933–6; intelligence officer 11th Naval District, San Diego, 1936–8; navigation officer, heavy cruiser New Orleans, 1938–9; intelligence officer, flagship Indianapolis, September 1939–May 1941.

On 2 June 1941 Lieutenant-Commander Joseph J. Rochefort reported for duty as head of Station Hypo, the naval communications intelligence office in Pearl Harbor. Under his longstanding colleague and friend Commander Laurence F. Safford, the US Navy's crypto section had grown immensely. Safford had begun OP-20-G – the G (security) section of the 20th (communications) division of US naval headquarters – back in 1923, with only one assistant. By 1941, expanding in accordance with its mission of naval radio intelligence and communications security, it contained 700 officers and men. Its headquarters, known as Negat, were in Washington DC; Hypo – later known as Frupac (Fleet Radio Unit, Pacific) – was an outstation covering the 14th Naval District (ND). Cast, another outstation on Corregidor in the

Philippines, was relocated by submarine early in 1942 to Melbourne, Australia, just before the Battle of the Coral Sea, and thereafter renamed Frumel. In the summer of 1941, however, Safford had decided to concentrate on Hypo and build it up, if necessary at the expense of the home station in Washington. He and Rochefort had already discussed this in personal letters over the years, and one of Rochefort's conditions for taking the job was that he should have his pick of personnel. Safford's response was simple: 'You can have anything you want.'

For Rochefort, that meant that he could immediately take on the services of Thomas H. Dyer, and later also Wesley A. ('Ham') Wright. These three had first met in 1933, as shipmates in the battleship *Pennsylvania*, flagship of Admiral Joseph M. Reeves, commander battle force, US Navy. Rochefort then had been intelligence chief and assistant operations officer on Reeves' staff, earning high praise from the Admiral – he was, said Reeves, a 'general encyclopaedia of information and usefulness', and 'one of the most outstanding officers of his rank', whose 'judgment and ability are truly remarkable'. Noting that Rochefort was not a Naval Academy graduate, which 'makes his ability and performance of duty all the more remarkable', Reeves predicted that sooner or later Rochefort would 'advance to positions of high rank and great responsibility'. In those *Pennsylvania* days, Tommy Dyer had been in charge of *Pennsylvania*'s number-three turret, and Ham Wright had been fresh from cryptanalytic training in Washington. Together, during the months after Pearl Harbor, these three and Safford worked extraordinarily well together.

Able to choose the pick of the crop for Hypo, Rochefort placed Dyer and (later) Wright as cryptanalysts, and took on traffic analysts Thomas A. Huckins and John A. Williams, as well as linguists Major Alva B. ('Red') Lasswell USMC and Lieutenant-Commander Ransom B. Fullinwider. Rochefort himself worked as both a linguist and cryptanalyst. In September 1941, these seven men were augmented by Forrest R. Biard, Allyn Cole, Bankson T. Holcomb and Gilven M. Slonin – four language students whose schooling in Japan had been terminated because of the threatening war conditions – and, after 7 December and the attack on Pearl, the Japanese linguist group was further increased by the addition of Joseph F. Finnegan and Arthur L. Benedict from battleship *Tennessee*, and, in February 1942, John G. Roenigk from destroyer *Edison*.

In a recent account, Captain Roenigk recalled clearly his arrival at Hypo.

Rochefort ordered me to first take a 'few days' to become acquainted with the office, the people, the routine, etc. The third day he handed me a sheaf of papers containing coastwatcher reports from New Guinea and comint [communications intelligence] estimates from Tommy Dyer's office. 'Study these,' he said, 'and let me know what the Japanese may be planning to do down here.' I worked on it all day and into the night. I wrote up my estimate and delivered it to him next morning. Glancing at my work he said, 'No, I'll tell you what they are going to do. They plan to capture Port Moresby. You couldn't know that, Roenigk, because you haven't been following it closely for a week or more, as I have.'

By so doing, he let me off the hook gently and I developed confidence in him, especially after several weeks when it was proven that the Japanese were really out to capture Moresby.

Roenigk's appraisal continued:

He was highly motivated and made immeasurable contribution to winning the war in the Pacific. By his example, subordinates flocked to his assistance, tried to learn from him, and tried to emulate his savvy.

Joe was not a slave driver. His own example of working around the clock was enough to motivate anyone associated with him. He seldom left the office, but napped on a couch. He was a great judge of the capabilities of subordinates in placing them where they could best contribute. He had a photographic mind and never, to my knowledge, forgot a single detail.

He was an uncanny card player and problem solver. To accomplish this he had to research every clue, and every piece of a puzzle had to fit snugly or be thrown out.

Safford, now designated EDO (engineering duty officer) and thus with no further obligation for sea duty, seemed securely in charge of communications intelligence (OP-20-G). He was, however, still operating under ONC. This surfaced an unresolved ONC–ONI conflict, which eventually would seriously disrupt Rochefort's career.

At Hypo, as at Negat and Cast, intercepted Japanese radio messages were received from US naval communications listening posts scattered throughout the Pacific and as far distant as Winter Harbor, Maine. Traffic analysts, by studying the externals of these coded and enciphered messages, learned to identify and locate the originator, the call sign of the addressee and the importance of the transmission. The intercepts were scanned for duplication before being examined to recover additives, code entries and any plain-language text. Cryptanalysts then cut through the ciphers and codes to reveal as much of the original Japanese as possible. Finally, linguists translated identifiable groups and occasionally made educated guesses at filling blanks. These tasks were closely correlated, and cryptanalysts tested the translators' guesses against other occurrences of unidentified groups for verification or rejection. Translated texts were promptly shared among the three stations to assure uniformity of information and to avoid duplication.

Information derived from radio intelligence was correlated with data from all other sources to provide estimates of the situation for the High Command. In Washington this was Admiral E. J. King [*q.v.*], the Commander-in-Chief, US Fleet and Chief of Naval Operations (CNO); at Pearl Harbor it was Admiral Husband E. Kimmel and, from 31 December 1941, Admiral Chester W. Nimitz [q.v.], his successor as Commander-in-Chief, Pacific Fleet

(Cincpac); and in the Philippines it was Admiral Thomas C. Hart as Asiatic Fleet commander. A daily report of information derived from Rochefort in Hypo was delivered to Edwin T. Layton, Cincpac intelligence officer, who briefed Nimitz and his staff every morning.

Strangely, there were still some custom-encrusted officers in the naval establishment who sneered at the very idea of electronic 'spying', but under Safford communications intelligence achieved a position of respect. While he ran OP-20-G the development went smoothly. His subordinates had confidence in him, and he in them.

Safford's informal style of running OP-20-G worked well in peacetime, but was less appropriate for coping with burgeoning demands of wartime. He wanted to assign even more independence to Joe Rochefort at Hypo, but this infuriated certain ambitious naval officers such as Rear Admiral Richmond Kelly Turner [*q.v.*], Director of War Plans, who wanted to retain control of intercept work in Washington. Among Safford's virulent detractors, in addition to Turner, were Captain Joseph R. Redman, Deputy Director of ONC, and his brother, Commander John R. Redman, a Safford deputy.

Although the Redman brothers were later shown to have exercised poor judgement, they were adept politicians. Safford played into their hands with a 23 January 1942 proposal to decentralize and streamline OP-20-G, in which he suggested that 'certain personnel' be transferred to Hypo. In the ensuing skirmish, Safford's role in OP-20-G was reduced to one of administrative support and research.

The close relationship between Negat and Hypo, which depended on the Safford–Rochefort friendship, abruptly ended. The Redman brothers and their supporters moved in to take over OP-20-G. Their reorganization disturbed career relationships that had been so productive in the creative effort of code breaking. At the same time, their determination that Washington dictate and control the intelligence function brought clashes over jurisdiction and personalities. These exacerbated the inevitable differences that emerged with Rochefort in Hypo.

Disagreement over the organizational home for communications intelligence had festered for years. ONC insisted on keeping control because it provided the technical intercept facilities. ONI, as the distributor of intelligence and supplier of Japanese linguists, felt that it should be in charge of comint.

This disagreement still simmered on the fair and fateful morning of 7 December 1941. All three stations had lost track of the Japanese aircraft carriers in early November because they had vanished from the air waves. The Pearl Harbor attack was so surprising because it was known that the Japanese were planning aggressive moves in the South-West Pacific – probably Indo-China, Siam, maybe the Philippines – and it was 'inconceivable' that they could launch two major strikes at the same time. Although the Hawaii attack itself was well planned and executed, the wisdom of Japan's strategy remains questionable. The one certain way to unite the 'neutral' and divided United States was to attack Americans on that 'day of infamy'.

Nevertheless, although the three comint stations could not reasonably have predicted the Pearl Harbor attack, Joe Rochefort felt a personal responsibility. He maintained until his death that it was an intelligence officer's job to inform his commander of enemy intentions, and Rochefort had failed, as he said in a 1969 interview: 'I took it as my job, my task, my assignment that I was to tell the Commander-in-Chief today what the Japanese were going to do tomorrow.'

Rochefort meant for comint to serve as it did for Admiral William F. Halsey's [*q.v.*] fast carrier strikes of early February 1942 on the Gilbert and Marshall Islands. Rochefort had provided Halsey with a mobile RIU (radio intelligence unit) for flagship *Enterprise*. This team consisted of Captain Bankson T. Holcom USMC and two radio operators. At a critical moment during Halsey's approach, Holcomb was able to assure the Admiral that the task force was undetected and unsuspected by the Japanese garrisons. So highly were such mobile RIUS valued thereafter that most admirals insisted on having one for every operation.

Combat intelligence also performed well at the Battle of the Coral Sea in early May 1942. As early as March, Rochefort had predicted that the next Japanese campaign would be in the New Guinea area, and that the Japanese navy would follow that up with an all-out offensive in the Central Pacific some time in the summer. These predictions were followed by careful analysis of the movements of enemy forces, which enabled the Allies to thwart Japan's plan – the capture of Port Moresby – for the first time.

In June 1942, the overriding purpose of Admiral Isoroku Yamamoto [*q.v.*], the Commander-in-Chief of Japan's Combined Fleet, in attacking Midway Island was to draw the United States Pacific Fleet into battle and defeat it decisively. He also planned to occupy Midway as well as Aleutian bases. He was frustrated by one man. Rochefort's understanding of enemy intentions enabled him to give Admiral Nimitz the information that made the difference between fighting blindly and fighting with knowledge of where the enemy would be, and when.

Following the Coral Sea battle, Rochefort's prediction of an all-out offensive in the Central Pacific took on reality as a large volume of Japanese naval messages flowed into Hypo, Negat and Frumel, designating the primary objective as 'AF'. Cominch believed AF to be Hawaii or the Panama Canal, the army thought California, but Rochefort was convinced it was Midway Island.

In mid-May 1942 Rochefort put to Tommy Dyer, Joe Finnegan and Jasper Holmes the problem of proving that AF meant Midway. Holmes observed that fresh water was a constant problem at Midway, and suggested sending a cable message there telling the island to send a plain-text radio message reporting (falsely) an evaporator breakdown and water shortage. With approval of Admiral Nimitz the ploy was tried, and it worked. The next day Japanese radio intelligence at Wake Island (which Japan had captured on 23 December 1941) reported that AF was short of fresh water. Finnegan decrypted this message, and it was in Nimitz's hands within a few hours of its broadcast from Wake.

Rochefort's analysis and proof persuaded Nimitz and his staff. 'It required no exceptional stretch of intelligence to appreciate that AF would have to be Midway,' said Rochefort. His OP-20-G antagonists in Washington finally had to agree.

Admiral King was also persuaded to agree with Nimitz that Midway was Yamamoto's immediate objective, and approved Nimitz's tactical plan. Even if the United States miraculously had three aircraft carriers available for action, they would still be heavily outnumbered by the Japanese. Everything depended on Rochefort's balancing the odds by learning the Japanese battle plan.

Finnegan discovered that the enemy air attack would be launched from north-west of Midway, but the date–time cipher eluded him. He sought Ham Wright's help, and they worked throughout 26 May and into the night on the problem. Everyone pitched in. Finnegan finally hit upon the Japanese method of disguising their date–time groups, and Ham Wright developed the solution table.

This table enabled Rochefort to break out data from intercepts showing that the Japanese carriers would probably attack on the morning of 4 June, from the north-west on a bearing of 325 degrees from Midway. He predicted they would launch planes about 175 miles north-west of Midway at around 0700 local time.

Admiral Nimitz called a staff conference for 27 May at which he set the Midway defence plan, based on estimates by Rochefort and Layton. It was one of the rare occasions when Rochefort was summoned to attend. He was half an hour late, dishevelled and bleary-eyed from lack of sleep. He apologized, and explained that he had been reviewing last-minute intelligence. 'The atmosphere was very impersonal,' Rochefort would later remember.

Admiral Nimitz asked me a question, and I would look over there and see four stars. I would answer that to the best of my ability I was sure of my facts, but stressed that they were only deductions. I could not have blamed him if he had not accepted my estimates. I think, looking back, that it was obvious when Nimitz sent for me that he had already decided on his course of action. My appearance at this final staff meeting was to ensure that everyone was thinking alike.

The Midway battle of 4–6 June 1942 reversed fortunes in the Pacific and started Japan down the road to ultimate defeat. Her eventual loss was far greater than the battle casualties: four aircraft carriers, one cruiser, 2,500 men and 322 aeroplanes. Although Japanese naval forces still outnumbered those of the United States, Yamamoto's grand strategy for quick victory through a decisive naval engagement was wrecked. The Americans lost 347 lives, aircraft carrier *Yorktown*, a destroyer and 147 aeroplanes. But Midway marked the beginning of the end of Japanese naval power in the Pacific.

Nimitz called another staff meeting on Sunday morning, 7 June, to which he again invited Rochefort and declared, 'This officer deserves a major share of the credit for the victory at Midway.' Nimitz also noted with a smile that the Rochefort–Layton estimate of where the Japanese striking force would be found was 'only five minutes, five degrees and five miles out'.

As it turned out, Washington thought differently. Neither Redman brother acknowledged that Hypo had made any contribution to the victory. Thanks to their ready access to senior members of the naval staff in Washington, they circulated the word that Midway was the result of work by their team, and not Rochefort's Hypo. Furthermore, they claimed that their operation had broken out the date that allowed Nimitz to get his carriers on station.

The charges made by the Redmans were contradicted by the facts. As Captain Dyer observed years later, the Redmans' 'slur' against Hypo's achievements was 'more than amply refuted by the record'. The two brothers led a conspiracy, knowing that they could count on a receptive audience in Admiral King's staff for their contention that radio intelligence should continue 'under the control and administration of the Chief of Naval Operations' with the Director of Naval Communications in immediate charge.

Shortly before his death in 1985, Dyer wrote: 'I have given a great deal of thought to the Rochefort affair, and I have been unwillingly forced to the conclusion that Rochefort committed the one unforgivable sin. To certain individuals of small mind and overweening ambition, there is no greater insult than to be proved wrong.'

At Frupac, Joe Rochefort, fatigued from his work on the Midway battle, grew irascible. When the Redman brothers asked what they could do to help, Rochefort replied, 'Send me more people, but leave me alone.' He railed about the Redmans and talked of 'seceding' from ONC, to which his Hypo unit was still subordinate. The Redmans naturally resented these intemperate statements, especially from a non-Academy officer.

Then came a new element of friction. Cominch asked the 14th Naval District commandant to recommend awards to comint people for the Midway battle. The request came to Rochefort who believed that such awards should be avoided in wartime because the recognition might jeopardize security. He passed the task to Jasper Holmes, who with Hypo veterans Jack S. Holtwick and naval reservist Thomas Steele prepared a list of names headed by Rochefort's, for whom they recommended the Distinguished Service Medal. Holmes delivered this list to the commandant, Admiral David W. Bagley, who consulted with Nimitz, and both concurred in the recommendation. Rochefort learned of the recommendation for his DSM only after Nimitz and Bagley had endorsed and forwarded it to Washington.

The recommendation moved through channels, accumulating fourteen forwarding comments, mostly negative. The final one said in effect that Rochefort not only did not deserve any credit but should probably not be kept in the Hypo unit. Joe Rochefort realized that for Cominch to approve any credit to Hypo would have been a tacit admission that the principal breakthrough had been made there. That would have laid the Redman prestige on the line, and denied their claim that Negat was responsible for the cryptanalytic success. Rochefort let it be known that he wanted to be left to the more important matter of working for Cominch and Cincpac, getting on with the war and not being involved (as he later said, quite undiplomatically) 'with you clowns back in Washington'.

The response of the 'clowns' was to reassign Rochefort as officer in charge of Icpoa (Intelligence Center, Pacific Ocean Areas). He saw this as a means of getting him away from communications intelligence, and flatly refused to have any part of that. These exchanges ended with Rochefort's being ordered to Washington in October 1942 on 'temporary duty' for ten days of consultation, to gather up loose ends of relations with OP-20-G.

Rochefort realized that he had lost. He told friends, 'When I leave Pearl, I'm not coming back.' While he was en route, the temporary orders were changed to permanent, relieving him of command. On 15 November, notice of this change reached Nimitz – by surface mail rather than cable – so it was too late for him to intervene.

Rochefort arrived in Washington exhausted. Informally he was accused of 'squabbling' with Cincpac staff, opposing the organization of Icpoa, and not keeping Cominch informed on intelligence matters. All of these charges could easily have been disproved but, instead of being decorated or given a spot promotion for what has been judged the greatest intelligence achievement in the navy's history, he was relieved of duty in radio intelligence. For more than a year his unsurpassed technical qualifications and his analytical ability were lost to radio intelligence at a time when the navy needed them badly.

He justifiably resented this shabby treatment. 'I made several mistakes in a great big hurry, one of which compounded the other,' he later admitted in an interview. 'And the net effect was that I flatly refused the offer of special work in Washington.' He insisted on sea duty, but it was against standing regulations to send anyone with comint experience into the war zone. After some minor postings on the west coast, he was assigned in June 1943 to command a floating drydock under construction at Tiburon, California.

There he remained until April 1944, when he returned to Washington and joined the Pacific Strategic Intelligence Group, to provide information for future planning of fleet operations. When he proposed that comint material be incorporated into long-range planning, he was placed in charge of OP-20-G50 to organize Pacific Strategic Intelligence Studies (PSIS). As his assistant in these studies, I had no awareness, from him or anyone else, of his prior World War Two experience. He got along amicably with officers of his rank. To us reservists all senior officers seemed to be Academy graduates, and it never occurred to me at the time even to wonder about his professional credentials. One thing was certain, however: he knew the Japanese language and people, and knew them very well.

Looking back, today, I recall his not being one for spit and polish; and there was no academic haughtiness in his attitude towards juniors. When he commented on our work – good or bad – it was direct and to the point, but with an avuncular air, usually a friendly hand on our shoulder if he stopped by our desk. Corrections were usually made with a tolerant smile, as though he had been there himself, as indeed he had. I never heard an unpleasant comment about him from my reservist colleagues, and that is quite remarkable for a bunch of civilians in uniform such as we were, who usually were ever ready to pass unhappy judgement on superior officers.

I experienced first hand Rochefort's readiness to stand up for his subordinates when he believed them to be in the right. When I proposed giving Japanese typewriter lessons to enlisted ratings it seemed a far-out idea to some, but Rochefort approved, and we achieved round-the-clock expertise on the complex Japanese machine by yeomen who had never studied a word of Japanese.

Rochefort and I became friends in his retirement years, but I never heard a word of acrimony or complaint from him about his wartime treatment. He did say that he might have been better off if he had gone to the Naval Academy, as it could have taught him to be more reserved and less caustic in his opinions.

He was an inspiring leader and morale-builder, with a genius for organization, as he quickly set an uncharted course for some 300 young people – officers and enlisted – in a project that produced lasting results.

PSIS work was useful as a part of the overall intelligence organization, and had many spin-offs. It helped to resolve mysteries of unexplained ship losses, battle credits and disparate claims. It was a solid demonstration of applied intelligence, generated some information, and, as Rochefort later said, 'possibly some thoughts'. His PSIS assignment ended in September 1946, after which he served on general court-martial boards until being placed on the Retired List on 1 January 1947. Yet thinking of his naval career as a whole, and in particular of his unequalled work prior to Midway, I cannot but agree with an observation by the respected historian Edward L. Beach, who, in his book *The United States Navy: 200 Years*, wrote: 'To Commander Joseph Rochefort must forever go the acclaim for having made more difference, at a more important time, than any other naval officer in history.'

Rochefort's naval career had been most unusual – indeed unique – and, some might say, ultimately a sad one. After the long training, there had been the fantastic achievement of Midway, surely the pinnacle of intelligence; and then the years of embittering anger and frustration, energy dissipated in fighting against a mean-minded, jealous conspiracy, when he wanted only to be able to carry on his unequalled work. But these were not the only unusual aspects of his wartime naval career – for its story did not end with his retirement, nor, indeed, until nearly ten full years after his death.

Recalled to active duty in an evaluation group for the Pacific Fleet, 1950–1. Strategic and tactical studies, Naval War College, Newport, Rhode Island, 1951–3. Returned to Retired List, March 1953. Participated in community affairs in California. Acted as consultant for the motion picture Tora, Tora, Tora. Died at Torrance, California, 20 July 1976.

Second plea for a DSM for Rochefort made by Fleet Admiral Nimitz, instigated by Jasper Holmes, 1958; rejected on the ground that World War Two awards were closed. Captain Holmes published Doubled-Edged Secrets, dedicated to Rochefort, 1979. Third plea for a (now posthumous) DSM for Rochefort made by Rear Admiral Donald M. ('Mac') Showers (Holmes' wartime assistant at Hypo), 1982. Full dossier compiled by Showers, based on personal experience, recently declassified documents and data from Rochefort's private files discovered during research for Rear Admiral Layton's memoir, 'And I Was There': Pearl Harbor and Midway – Breaking the Secrets. Dossier circulated and gained support within the navy, but apparently destined for rejection by Secretary of the Navy, 1985. Powerful lecture by Showers at Annapolis, autumn 1985, prior to publication of Layton's memoir, brought admission from member of Secretary of the Navy's office that Secretary had not yet seen the dossier. Two weeks later, Secretary Lehman authorized the award of the DSM to Rochefort. The Baltimore Sun: 'Rarely has a book righted an old wrong even before it is published, but the memoir of Admiral Layton has accomplished this remarkable feat.' Posthumous Distinguished Service Medal presented to Rochefort's son and daughter by President Reagan at the White House, 30 May 1986 – the week of the forty-fourth anniversary of the Battle of Midway.

30

Vice Admiral

Ben Moreell
CEC
United States Navy

1892–1978

by
Paolo E. Coletta

*B*EN *Moreell born Salt Lake City, Utah, 14 September 1892; raised in St Louis. Graduated in civil engineering from Washington University, St Louis, and for his first job worked in the Engineering Department of that city. Appointed Lieutenant (j.g.) in the US Navy's Civil Engineer Corps (CEC). Spent World World One in the public works office at Ponta Delgada Naval Base, Azores. There he impressed the Assistant Secretary of the Navy, F. D. Roosevelt, who visited the island. Served as plant engineer at the destroyer and submarine base at Squantum, Massachusetts, 1919–20; public works officer in Haiti (where he learned French) and Norfolk, 1924–6; assistant design manager in the Bureau of Yards and Docks (BuY&D), 1926–30, Bremerton and the 13th Naval District, 1930–2; and planned the Ship Model Testing Basin – later the Admiral David W. Taylor Model Basin, 1930–2. After studying in France, 1932–3, he served as project manager of shipbuilding and repair facilities in the storage and sub base section of BuY&D, 1935–7, and as public works officer of the Pearl Harbor Naval Base and 14th Naval District at Pearl Harbor, 1935–7. In December, 1937, President Roosevelt overrode Bureau recommendations and appointed him Chief of Bureau and Chief of the Civil Engineers in the grade of rear admiral, the first non-Academy man to be so honoured and one of the youngest to hold that rank. Inspected docking, repair and base facilities in the Atlantic and Pacific. To prepare for possible war, he had two giant graving docks built at Pearl Harbor. Devised the sectional dry dock, any section of which could be towed to a chosen site and connected to form a dock of desired size. In addition, recalling that a naval construction regiment had been formed at Great Lakes during World War One, he obtained permission to recruit naval construction men who could be sent overseas, and late in December 1941 founded the Naval Construction Battalions – or Seabees, or 'Can-do boys'.*

Rear Admiral Ben Moreell kept his people informed via a Bureau of Yards and Docks Quarterly Bulletin, a weekly News Memorandum and, from 31 December 1943 to 6 July 1945, via *Seabee News Services*. These included policies he adopted; reports on current Bureau work; notes on new tests of designs, construction and materials; administrative matters; legislation affecting the Civil Engineer Corps; abstracts of government reports, books and articles on engineering matters; and notes on the accomplishments of Bureau personnel. With the nation at war, there were added copious descriptions of the geographic sites in which BuY&D people would work.

Until 1941, construction work had been supervised by the CEC, the staff administrative organization of BuY&D. The actual work was done by private contractors using civilian labour. Projects recommended by local Shore Station Development Boards or devised by BuY&D were evaluated with a list of projects prepared by a Shore Station Development Board comprised of officers representing every bureau and the Chief of Operations (CNO). In consequence of the Vinson Bill of 17 May 1938, warship construction would increase by 20 per cent and the number of aircraft built would rise to 3,000. To recommend expansion of required shore facilities was the task of the 1938 Board (chaired by Rear Admiral Arthur J. Hepburn) which had one CEC officer as member.[1] Following the outbreak of war in Europe, however, Moreell advised Secretary of the Navy Charles Edison that a new, permanent board should be established to consider new construction on its merits rather than in competition with other projects, and that its recommendations be used to write the public works authorization and budget bills. Edison approved. For fiscal year (FY) 1940, Moreell's expenditure of $102 million for public works was greater than that for any year since 1918. He was then faced with providing support for a navy increased by 11 per cent in June 1940 and in addition a 'two-ocean navy' expanded by 70 per cent. To fund his projects he asked the Secretary to have a study made of what expansion should occur and of its cost. This matter was tackled by the Rear Admiral John Greenslade Board, created on 11 September 1940. For public works alone, in domestic and overseas bases, in fiscal year 1941 Moreell spent three times as much as in fiscal year 1940.[2]

In mid-February 1941, President Franklin D. Roosevelt asked Congress to fortify Guam and Samoa. Several witnesses opposed doing so, but Moreell upheld the President and was supported by officers representing the CNO, Admiral Harold R. Stark [*q.v.*]. In the end Guam was not built up, but Samoa and the Aleutians were, with the construction task falling to Moreell.[3] Another blow came when he visited President Roosevelt after the latter had signed the Lend-Lease Bill in March 1941 and was told that Lend-Lease materials would have to be provided by the army and navy.[4] A further problem he constantly

[1] Moreell in *Annual Report of the Secretary of the Navy, FY 1939* (Washington DC 1939), p. 1, para. 3.
[2] Moreell in *Annual Report of the Secretary of the Navy, 1940* (Washington DC 1940), paras 5–7.
[3] Moreell in *Annual Report of the Secretary of the Navy, 1941* (Washington DC, 1941), paras 4–10
[4] *New York Times*, 15 February 1940, 4: 6, and 16 February 1941, 25: 1; David O. Woodbury, *Builders for Battle: How the Pacific Naval Air Bases Were Constructed* (New York, 1946), pp. 45–54.

faced was the approval by the CNO of 'command facilities' that contributed to the comfort of officers rather than to wartime needs.[5] In any event, with the Greenslade report approved by the naval Secretary on 14 May 1941, Moreell could now seek approval for its recommendations. Much of his time was spent in preparing appropriation requests and defending them before Congress.[6]

Projects Moreell undertook between 1 July 1940 and the attack on Pearl Harbor included housing for civilian workers in overcrowded areas, section bases that would support local defence forces, and base construction at sites from Newfoundland to British Guiana which the British permitted the United States to use in exchange for fifty destroyers. His expenditures for the year exceeded $1 billion.[7]

Although precedent called for rotating officers in principal positions, on 3 November 1941 President Roosevelt renominated Moreell for a second four-year term and complimented him on the manner in which he had geared his Bureau to the needs of the expanded defence programme. Easily confirmed by the Senate, he took his oath of office on 1 December.[8] Six days later the Japanese attacked Pearl Harbor.

With the nation at war, Under Secretary of the Navy James V. Forrestal relied upon six admirals to speed output. These included the chiefs of the Bureaus of Ships, Ordnance, Aeronautics, Supplies and Accounts, the Chief of the Office of Procurement and Material, and Moreell. While Forrestal took care of contracts, the others saw to their production and payment.

Moreell advised his workers to proceed with 'certainty, speed, and economy'.[9] As for his management style, in the words of Forrestal's biographers, Moreell 'used methods as successful as they were unconventional in meeting the unprecedented demand for new facilities both stateside and in the newly won Pacific region. He considered time a much more vital wartime factor than cost, and without too much regard for red tape, he achieved virtual miracles.'[10]

[5]*New York Times*, 12 March 1941, 3: 3; Robert Greenhalgh Albion and Robert Howe Connery, *Forrestal and the Navy* (New York and London, 1962), p. 121.

[6]*Hearings before the Committee on Naval Affairs United States Senate, Sundry Legislation*, 77th Cong., 1st Sess. (Washington DC 1941).

[7]*New York Times*, 5 June 1941, 6: 2.

[8]Ibid., 4 November 1941, 10: 3, and 2 December 1941, 18: 4.

[9]Albion and Connery, *Forrestal*, pp. 60–1.

[10]In the autumn of 1939, when Roosevelt told Stark that he wanted some seaplane bases built along the South American coast, Stark spoke with Moreell, who said that he had no money and that all construction must be authorized by act of Congress. However, in view of Roosevelt's 'limited national emergency', a dummy account could be set up and then eliminated by a defence appropriation. Would the President sign a paper authorizing such a procedure? When Stark offered the suggestion to Roosevelt, the latter became exceedingly angry and asked who had made the proposal. Stark protected Moreell by saying that it was 'just a general feeling'. Roosevelt replied that the bureau chiefs would get something on a piece of paper that they would not expect. Moreell then told Stark that the bureau chiefs would follow an order from the Secretary of the Navy to proceed contrary to law. With both the

To handle the war load, the 125 men in the CEC on 6 December 1941 swelled to 10,860 by war's end, 97 per cent of them being reservists. Further, Moreell engaged a management-engineering firm to recommend a reorganization of his Bureau. In consequence, on 1 December 1940 the Bureau was reorganized. Prior to this time, officer personnel matters and cost analyses had been taken care of in the Chief's office; the major divisions included Maintenance and Operation and Construction Division Contracts, a Design Manager and Chief Clerk. In addition there were seven project managers. The new organization called for five major departments: Administration and Personnel, Progress Control and Statistics, Finance and Operating, Planning and Design, and Construction. Long after the Seabees were created, on 5 January 1944, a sixth department, the Advance Base Department, was established for them.[11]

Among the emergency war demands Moreell faced were the provision of training and housing facilities for enlisted navy personnel (who mushroomed from 125,000 on 30 June 1941 to about three million); fleet operating facilities; naval air stations for the Marine Corps and for naval lighter-than-air stations; new highways to relieve traffic congestion near industrial establishments engaged in navy shipbuilding; and, in addition, the facilities needed by all the other bureaus. He was perpetually in competition especially for critical materials with the demands of the other services. He therefore directed that materials be conserved and that research be undertaken to find substitutes for scarce ones.[12]

To speed up construction, the Shore Development Board was abandoned in favour of having projects sent directly to Moreell and his own suggestions forwarded for approval via the Vice Chief of Naval Operations to the Assistant Secretary of the Navy (Shore Establishments Division). The VCNO would judge strategic and military needs; BuY&D, technical and engineering requirements. The civilians and naval personnel involved in building bases worked for a single organization known as CPNAB (Contractors, Pacific Naval Air Bases) – a partnership between the navy and eight big-time construction firms.[13] Under cost-plus-percentage contracts, contractors spent as much as they could; under cost-plus-fixed-fee contracts, spending money reduced profit. Moreell preferred the latter, because profit was limited to 10 per cent and permitted work to begin before plans and specifications were complete.

Secretary and Assistant Secretary absent, Stark, acting as Secretary, assumed the responsibility. Ibid., pp. 87–88.

[11] For the organization and duty of each department, seè US Navy Department, Bureau of Yards and Docks, *Building the Navy's Bases in World War II*, 2 vols (Washington DC 1946), vol. 1, pp. 62–70.

[12] Ibid., vol. 1, pp. 41–2. See also, Washington, National Archives, Bureau of Yards and Docks, Records of War Plans Division, RG 71, Entry 98, and Records of Advance Base Division, Entry 99. Hereafter cited as NARG 71 with entry number.

[13] Woodbury, *Builders for Battle*, pp. 60–5.

For the duration, said Moreell, his contractors could not undertake other than naval work without his permission.[14]

Moreell centralized policy-making, overall planning and management controls, but he decentralized operations. Each of his department heads subdivided this work into sections and subsections, but all such heads, with the assistant chief, collectively served him as an advisory board. The supervision of actual construction was undertaken by a CEC field representative who often doubled as the public works officer of a naval district, navy yard or other naval station. Field representatives were overseen in seven geographical areas by senior superintending civil engineers. These men, authorized to act in his name, reported directly to Moreell. For overseas operations there were area directors, originally for the Atlantic, Pacific and Alaskan theatres, who also had additional duty on the staff of fleet commanders operating in their areas. On 30 June 1945, there were 1,211 civilians working in BuY&D in Washington but 24,000 in field activities.

To build and maintain the bases and facilities the navy needed during World War Two, Moreell spent $9.25 billion, with $3.18 billion going to advance base construction. Included were naval air stations, shipbuilding facilities, housing, hospitals, ammunition depots, fuel storage dumps and shipbuilding, graving and floating dry docks. Wisely, he employed local contractors as often as he could.[15] In 1943 he concentrated on the west coast for a vastly enlarged amphibious warfare programme, technical training schools and shipbuilding and aircraft-building projects. For public works in FY 1943 he expended $3.1 billion.[16] However, with the mass movement of army personnel overseas, in 1944 he was able to take over surplus army installations valued at $250 million.[17] Of the grand total of $8.1 billion spent between 1 July 1940 and 30 June 1945, advance base procurement took the largest amount ($1.9 billion), while aeronautical facilities came second at $1.6 billion, with ordnance facilities and shipbuilding and repair facilities ranking third and fourth at $717 million and $686 million, respectively. The greatest percentage increase in growth, of 2,139.1 per cent, went for aviation fuel storage.[18]

On 6 December 1941, about 70,000 men were engaged in construction projects at Argentia, Iceland, Puerto Rico, St Thomas, Trinidad and Jamaica in the Atlantic and Caribbean, and at the Galapagos Islands, Alaska, Aleutians, Hawaii, Midway, Wake, Guam, the Philippines, Samoa and Palmyra and Johnston Islands in the Pacific. They were neither part of a military organization nor subject to military discipline. They not only lacked arms and

[14]Ibid., pp. 131–2, 230–1.

[15]*Annual Report of the Secretary of the Navy, FY 1921* (Washington DC 1921), pp. 44–7; Woodbury, *Builders for Battle*, pp. 84–5.

[16]*Annual Report of the Secretary of the Navy, FY 1942* (Washington DC 1942), pp. 37–8.

[17]*Building the Navy's Bases in World War II*, vol. 1, pp. 1–23.

[18]*Annual Report of the Secretary of the Navy, FY 1945* (Washington DC 1945), p. A–96. Photographs of new construction and of alteration work remain in NARG 71, Entry 78.

military training, but could be considered guerrillas if they tried to defend themselves from attack. Nevertheless, those whom the Japanese captured at Wake, Guam and the Philippines were regarded and treated as prisoners-of-war rather than civilian internees. As Moreell described this unfortunate arrangement, 'Our experience at Pearl Harbor, Midway, Wake and elsewhere demonstrated that it was neither fair to the individuals concerned, nor in the interest of over-all military efficiency, to call upon civilian workers, untrained in combat duties, as a measure of self-protection, to work under enemy fire.'[19] The navy was not legally responsible for their welfare and wages, and cost-plus-fixed-fee contracts made it almost impossible for contractors to do so. Moreell thereupon got contractors to pay the families of the captured men $100 for the months of January and February 1942 before getting President Roosevelt to have the government continue to do so.

Moreell remembered that Captain William A. Moffett (commander of the Great Lakes Naval Station during World War One) had used about twenty-five sailors to help with local construction. Moffett's Public Works Officer expanded these into Public Works Companies of sailors with construction experience. By 1917 there had been 3,000 of them at Great Lakes and 300 overseas. Recalling this, Moreell told the Chief of the Bureau of Navigation (Personnel) on 28 December 1941 that advance base construction could proceed only with military personnel under direct military command, and that he immediately needed three battalions for the purpose. Navigation approved the request on 4 January 1942, and a request for additional battalions on the 21st.[20]

Some men, earlier detailed to work in Iceland, joined a contingent of general service personnel known as 'Bobcats' (after the codename of their base), and left the United States early in January 1942 to build a base at Bora Bora in the Society Islands. Simultaneously, Moreell drafted plans for domestic and overseas military construction organizations. The first step was to recruit the first Construction Battalion, or Seabees, of 3,000 men representing sixty trades. Rather than remaining safely at home and enjoying wages three to four times as high (a boot recruit received only $140.00 a month), volunteers came forth in droves. The first Seabee Battalion was commissioned at Great Lakes on 28 December 1941. Two innovations were authority to grant commissioned civil engineers naval rank up to lieutenant-commander, thus giving them command status, and from petty officer to warrant ratings for enlisted recruits. Because many of the men had either

---

[19]Moreell in William B. Huie, *Can Do: The Story of the Seabees* (New York, 1945), p. 9; Records of the Progress Division, NARG 71, Entry 100; Fleet Admiral Ernest J. King, *Navy at War: Official Reports to the Secretary of the Navy* (Washington DC 1946), p. 29; Woodbury, *Builders for Battle*, pp. 391–2, 398.

[20]Admiral Ben Moreell (CEC) USN, 'The Seabees in World War II', USNIP, 88 (March 1962), p. 86; Records of the Construction Division, NARG 71, Entry 94; *Building the Navy's Bases in World War II*, vol. 1, pp. 133–4.

worked for or owned construction companies, the average age of the enlisted men was about thirty-one years, that of the officers about twenty-eight years. Moreell assuaged organized labour by promising that Seabees would engage only in construction work overseas or in work undertaken within the continental limits for training purposes, with all other work at home to be undertaken by private contractors and civilian labour.

While he was friendly to labour, on 30 September 1942 he told a convention of the Building and Construction Trade Department of the American Federation of Labour that the nation could not live without labour but could live without labour unions, as Germany, Italy, Japan and Russia were doing. Labour was not wholly responsible for failure to produce all the war materials needed, but labour's wartime record, said the *New York Times*, 'in many instances, does not make the best of reading'. If labour struck, the manager's wage kept coming. The one who got hurt was 'the boy on the firing line, who needs the bullets you are making, and, second yourselves'. If labour unions condoned work stoppages, they would lose public support. Labour should renounce peacetime jurisdictional rules that interfered with maximim efficiency. If labour leaders could not maintain discipline, they should be removed. Labour should 'get in there and pitch'.[21] Prompted by the prospect of year-round rather than merely seasonal work, labour agreed to obliterate trade lines and have men perform whatever work they were assigned.

With no camps yet available for them, Seabees were assembled in groups of 300 men and given military training by Marines at the Naval Air Station, Quonset Point, Rhode Island, and at National Youth Administration camps located in Illinois (three), New York (one), New Jersey (two) and Virginia (one). They and other men would later comprise battalions (of thirty-two officers and 1,079 men) that would undergo an eight-week assembly and training period. Special stress was placed upon erecting portable fuel tanks, welding and the operation of mobile and portable construction equipment. A typical battalion consisted of a headquarters company of 173 men and of four companies, each with six platoons. The platoons served, respectively, in Maintenance, Construction (two), Blasting and Excavation, Waterfront (Longshoremen), and Tanks, Steel and Pipe. Except for medical, dental, supply and chaplain officers, the rest were CEC. They had to be prepared to offload equipment and supplies in undeveloped areas, build bases ranging in size from section bases to the equivalent of a large city, and provide them with all needed facilities – housing fit for the climate (quonset huts or tents), messing, roads, hospitals, offices, communications, water (including fire-fighting), refrigeration, laundry, electrical supply and distribution systems, waterfront structures, storehouses, sawmills, rock crushing and asphalt mixing plants and repair shops. Granted priority for transportation, the 1st and 2nd Battalions left the west coast early in February 1942 for the South Pacific. The 3rd went to the Fijis; the 4th to Dutch Harbor; the 5th to Samoa.

[21]*New York Times*, 1 October 1942, 1: 2; Woodbury, *Builders for Battle*, pp. 136–7.

By 17 January 1942, ground for a Naval Construction Training Camp (NCTC) was broken at Camp Allen, which with Camp Bradford, at Little Creek near Norfolk, would suffice for one regiment. Camp Peary (outside Williamsburg, Virginia) had a capacity for 40,000. Camp Endicott (Davisville, Rhode Island) cost $20 million. Commissioned on 11 August and opened on 11 November 1942, it had capacity for 42,000 men. In dedication ceremonies held there on 4 April 1943, with more than 12,000 Seabees and civilians present, Secretary of the Navy Frank Knox lauded Moreell for his work and especially for his being the 'father' of the Seabees. Other encomiums came from Admirals E. J. King [*q.v.*], Harold R. Stark and Chester W. Nimitz [*q.v.*], and General Thomas Holcomb, Commandant of the Marine Corps. The praise Moreell enjoyed most was being called the 'King Bee of the Seabees'.[22]

Starting with eighty-five acres adjacent to NAS Quonset Point, Davisville eventually spread four miles to the west and included 1,900 acres. There, railroad tracks, waterfront piers and more than fifty buildings were erected in a renamed Advanced Base Depot, for (in addition to training more than 100,000 Seabees) Davisville manufactured quonset huts and other materials to be sent to Argentia, Newfoundland, and the United Kingdom. Other camps were established at Quoddy Village, Maine; Gulfport, Mississippi; Camp Parks, Livermore; and Port Hueneme, California. The last, begun in early 1942 as a mere receiving barracks for transient Seabees, by 1945 had messing facilities for 21,000 persons and was shipping out 225,000 long tons a month. In addition it trained units to build what were known as Lions (bases of about the size of pre-Pearl Harbor); Cubs (one-fourth the size of Lion); Oaks (major airbase); Acorns (small airbase); and Arguses, a shore-based unit to provide fighter direction, air warning, surface warning, combat information services and co-ordination of a base's complete radar defences. In August 1944, all Seabee training was placed under the cognizance of the Bureau of Naval Personnel. By early 1945, NCTC Norfolk was disestablished; thereafter, all training was concentrated at Camp Endicott, with emphasis now on training only replacement men.[23]

Learning from experience (for in the beginning carpenters, concrete workers, wharf builders and surveyors were all classified as carpenter's mates), changes were made in the sixty ratings that served in the Seabees. Similarly,

---

[22]Reports of Battalions, Recruiting Division, NARG 71, Entry 74; *New York Times*, 5 April 1943, 2: 2; Commander Edmund L. Castillo USN, *The Seabees of World War II* (New York 1963), p. x.

[23]For details on the construction units and the bases they built, see *Building the Navy's Bases in World War II*, vol. 1, pp. 115–32; Paolo E. Coletta and K. Jack Bauer (eds), *U.S. Navy and Marine Corps Bases*, 2 vols, (Westport, Connecticut, 1985); the appendix in William B. Huie, *From Omaha to Okinawa* (New York, 1946); Hugh B. Cave, *We Build! We Fight!* (New York, 1944); Nathan A. Bowers, 'The Seabees in the Pacific', a series of articles in *Engineering News Record*, 1944; the maps in Simon Skordiles, *The Seabees in War and Peace*, vol. 1 (Monterey Park, California 1972); and histories of naval construction battalions separately issued. An excellent photographic work is Henry Terry (ed.), *Seabees Can Do! A Pictorial History Commemorating the Silver Anniversary of the United States Naval Construction Battalions* (Marcelline, Missouri, 1967), with foreword by Moreell.

special training had to be provided for the operation and maintenance of pontoons, stills and purifiers, and mobile generators. As the battalions grew, they were organized into twelve brigades.

As Moreell later put it: 'The contract for the Pacific Naval Bases is the greatest single construction contract in history in the world in point of money value, diversity of character, and dispersion over vast distances.'[24] Civilian crews sometimes would not work while under fire or before 0800 or after 1600, so, because of the great need to unload freighters, stevedore battalions were organized in the autumn of 1942. At their prime, these consisted of thirty battalions of 3,000 officers and men each. These proved that they could unload ships twice as fast as civilian crews. The first such battalion went to Guadalcanal. In addition there were more than one hundred Construction Battalion Maintenance Units (CBMUS), each comprised of 60–250 officers and men, which maintained bases after these had been built. Even smaller units, of 5–600 men, comprised Construction Detachments. These were used for replacement or strengthening purposes. Among special units were Pontoon Assembly Detachments, Truck Operating Detachments, Spare Parts Units and Underwater Demolition Teams. By 1943, training was extended to three months, including Marine Corps instruction in beach landings, and jungle warfare extending to judo and bayonet tactics. The mission of training camps was 'to train officers and men to fight and build'.[25] The insignia adopted was a bee, fighting mad, with a white hat on his head, a spitting tommy gun in his forward hand, a wrench in his midship hand, and a carpenter's hammer gripped in his after hand – an apt symbol, for the Seabees provided US forces with many valuable 'extra hands'.

On 4 May 1942 (the very day Japanese landed at Guadalcanal), a detachment of the 1st Seabees landed at Efate, New Hebrides. Their mission was to build a hospital to care for Americans wounded on Guadacanal, and an airfield and seaplane base from which the island, 700 miles to the north, could be bombed before the Japanese could complete Henderson Field.

To get closer to Guadalcanal, an airstrip was carved out of jungle at Espiritu Santo, a vital link between the fields at Efate and Nouméa (North Caledonia) and Henderson, on the last of which Marines began landing on 7 August 1942. Meanwhile other Seabees worked at Palmyra, Johnston and Canton Islands, in Samoa, and in the Fiji and Ellice island groups. A vital ingredient for their work was the pontoon, the 'Magic Box', designed in 1939 by Captain John W. Laycock CEC. Constructed of sheet steel into $5 \times 7 \times 5$-foot cubes, these could be used as building blocks for landing barges, piers, causeways, floating cranes, finger piers, even floating dry docks; and, when fitted with an outboard motor, served as a self-propelled barge. In the Normandy landings they were called 'rhino' ferries. Moreell inspected them as well as all other landing

[24]Moreell in Introduction to Woodbury, *Builders for Battle* p. vii.

[25]Nathan S. Raitt, *The Navy Seabees: Their Early Days* (Venice, Florida, 1983), p. 14. Moreell described a Seabee as 'a soldier in a sailor's uniform, with Marine training, and doing civilian work at WPA wages'. In 'The Seabees in World War II', p. 93.

equipment prepared for the invasion of Normandy.[26] They were used at Sicily and Salerno as well as in the Atlantic and Pacific. With the waters south of Sicily too shallow for ships to close the shore, the Germans expected an attack on its northern shore. Pontoons permitted a landing on the southern shore and became a standard part of every invasion. In descending order, Moreell's greatest production items were pontoons – 557,207; tents – 395,629; and quonset huts – 140,734.[27] Another prime ingredient was the bulldozer; still another the demolition teams or 'hard rock' men. Very quickly, although they severely joshed each other, the Seabees were welcomed as a bride at a wedding and became integral parts of Marine combat divisions.[28]

While 25,000 Seabees worked on the road from Seattle to Attu, other thousands built the 'Ring Around Rabaul' in the form of airfields on Rendova Island, Munda, New Georgia, Vella Lavella, Treasury Islands, Bougainville, the Green Island, Emirau Islands, along the north coast of New Guinea in General Douglas MacArthur's sector. When Moreell visited MacArthur in Brisbane, Australia, in February 1944, the General said: 'The only trouble with the Seabees [is] that you do not have enough of them.' They then worked in the Philippines, Marianas, Iwo Jima and Okinawa. The asphalt used on the runways and taxiways on Tinian alone would have built a road twenty feet wide from Boston to Washington. Following an inspection trip to Pacific bases early in 1944, Moreell praised the Seabees highly, especially those engaged in stevedoring tasks, for their valour in 'fighting and then going back to work'.[29]

For the Okinawa campaign, the three Seabee brigades, US Army Engineer troops and a contingent of British engineers would have numbered 110,000 if hostilities had not ceased on 14 August 1945. Moreell's plans to use similar numbers during the invasion of Japan were never, of course, implemented. As of 31 August 1945, most of his Seabees (129,101) were in the Central Pacific, the second largest number (56,747) in the South Pacific. Only 125 remained in the North Atlantic.[30] With the co-operation of construction companies and of

[26]Huie, *Omaha to Okinawa*, photograph on p. lx.

[27]Moreell, 'The Seabees in World War II', p. 87; *Annual Report of the Secretary of the Navy, 1945* (Washington DC, 1945), p. A-102.

[28]Huie, *Can Do*, pp. 179–80. For how John Wayne trained his hardhats for war in the Pacific, see the video *Fighting Seabees* (Evanston, Illinois, 1944), V-WRX007CO, 100 min. The Rogers and Hammerstein play (and film), *South Pacific*, was also largely built about Seabees. Major-General Alexander A. Vandegrift, commanding the Marines on Guadalcanal, told Moreell 'I do not know how we would have gotten along without the Seabees, and I trust that they will be in every future operation in even larger numbers than at Guadalcanal.' Castillo, *The Seabees of World War II*, p. 79.

[29]Moreell, 'The Seabees in World War II', p. 98; *New York Times*, 11 February 1944, 4: 1; Records of the Naval Construction Battalions, Naval Construction Battalion Headquarters, Port Huememe, California. MacArthur cited in Castillo, *The Seabees of World War II*, p. x. Among the many stories about Seabees was the one about the chap who drove his bulldozer off a landing craft in the face of enemy fire. He raised its blade and proceeded directly to the Japanese machine-gun nest, which he promptly buried under a load of earth. The technique was adopted by both the army and navy. S. J. Woolf, 'Admiral of the "Can Do" Boys', *New York Times*, 12 August 1945, 6: 18.

[30]*Annual Report of the Secretary of the Navy, 1945* (Washington DC, 1945), p. A-104.

labour unions, Moreell's CEC had swelled to 360,000 officers and men, 83 per cent of whom had worked overseas. Before the war ended, they had built 300 domestic bases and 600 advance bases in the Atlantic and Pacific, some of them as large as Peoria, Illinois. After VJ-Day, moreover, various construction groups left Guam, Saipan and Iwo Jima to build or rebuild Japanese harbours. Other units went to China to support US Marines engaged in repatriating Japanese troops. Still others prepared for the atomic tests held at Bikini.[31]

On 2 February 1944, President Roosevelt nominated Moreell as one of three bureau chiefs for promotion to vice admiral. Although there was no opposition to the men involved, the question immediately arose whether such promotion would set a precedent for men in such positions, whether there would not be too many vice admirals, and whether admirals commanding operational forces, like Ernest J. King and Chester W. Nimitz, should not be promoted to fleet admiral. With no challenge to the proposal by the Bureau of the Budget or the Controller-General, and the Judge Advocate-General ruling that such promotions were legal, on 10 February the Senate quietly agreed to them. Moreell – still only fifty-one years old – thus became the youngest vice admiral in the navy, and also the first CEC officer to hold that rank.[32]

The post-war demobilization of the Seabees, Ben Moreell's creation, was as rapid as with other forces – by 30 June 1946, their numbers had been reduced to 400 officers and 20,000 men. However, their skills, and Moreell's unique experience, were used in both 1945 and 1946 to overcome military and naval supply problems associated with national oil and coal industry strikes. Moreell served finally as Director of Procurement and Materials, until on 1 October 1946, at the age of fifty-four, he was placed on the Retired List. He then headed the Turner Construction Company, and was Board Chairman and Chief Executive (1947–58) of the Jones and Laughlin Steel Corporation. Board Chairman of Americans for Constitutional Action, 1960s; received twelve honorary degrees, four engineering society awards and numerous American and foreign service medals. Died Pittsburgh, 30 July 1978, aged eighty-five. Buried with full military honours, Arlington National Cemetery, 3 August 1978.

[31]Details can be followed extensively in the Central Files of BuY&D at National Archives and Records Administration, Suitland, Maryland, briefly in *Building the Navy's Bases in World War II*, vol. II, pp. 413–16, and in the excellent chapter on BuY&D in Rear Admiral Julius A. Furer USN (Ret.), *Administration of the Navy Department in World War II* (Washington DC, 1959), pp. 399–428.

[32]In his reports to the Secretary of the Navy, Admiral King spoke very highly of the building and fighting of the Seabees. *Official Reports*, pp. 29, 197–8.

31

Lieutenant-General

Holland M. Smith
DSM***
United States Marine Corps

1882–1967

by
Benis M. Frank

*H*OLLAND *McTyeire Smith, born 20 April 1882 in Seale, Alabama. Graduated from Alabama Polytechnic Institute in 1902 and two years later from the University of Alabama Law School. After practising law for a year, he obtained a commission in the Marine Corps. His early career was a mix of foreign expeditionary duty, sea duty and stateside assignments at various Marine Corps posts and stations. In World War One, he arrived in France in early June 1917 with the 5th Marine Regiment in command of a machine-gun company. Shortly after his arrival, he became adjutant of the 4th Marine Brigade, participating with that unit in the fighting in the Verdun Sector, the Aisne-Marine Defensive, which included the famed Battle of Belleau Wood. In July 1918, he was transferred to the 1st Corps, First US Army and fought in the major offensives which led to the end of the war. During the inter-war period, his assignments included study at the Naval War College and the Marine Corps Schools, sea duty and expeditionary duty in Haiti. In 1937 Colonel Smith was assigned as Director of the Division of Operations and Training at Headquarters, US Marine Corps, and later as assistant to the Commandant of the Marine Corps. In 1939, Brigadier-General Smith took command of the 1st Marine Brigade, later the 1st Marine Division, taking it from Quantico, Virginia, to Guantanamo Bay, Cuba, for an extended period of amphibious training. All during the 1930s, he was deeply involved in the development of amphibious warfare doctrine. In June 1941, General Smith was detached from command of the 1st Marine Division to take command of the organization which eventually became the Amphibious Training Command, Atlantic Fleet. When America went to war, he was the leading exponent of and most experienced practitioner in the art of amphibious warfare in the armed forces of the United States.*

When the United States went to war on 7 December 1941, Holland M. Smith was a major-general, US Marine Corps, with more than thirty-six years of active service. By 1941, General Smith had held a number of important varied commands. At fifty-nine, he was both mature and vigorous, and at the height of his professional life at a time when most other men were contemplating retirement. When war came, Holland Smith was both mentally and professionally ready. He was of medium height, perhaps 5 foot 10 inches or so, with a moustache once black but, like his hair, now grey, somewhat pudgy or frumpy, bespectacled, and an inveterate cigar smoker. Normally quiet-spoken, he was aroused only when someone – generally a senior navy or army officer – spoke disparagingly about his beloved Marines or Marine Corps. Then, his temper would rise and he would become the 'Howling Mad' Smith of reputation. Actually, he was very paternal in his relations with his junior officers and enlisted Marines. His contemporaries knew him by his nickname, 'Hoke'.

During the inter-war period, he had attended top-level schools – the Naval War College at Newport, Rhode Island, and the Marine Corps' Senior School at Quantico, Virginia. General Smith had been the first Marine officer to serve on the Joint Army–Navy Planning Committee. He also played an important role in training both Marines and army units in the conduct of amphibious operations employing the concept and doctrine of amphibious warfare developed by the Marine Corps in the 1930s. Among other things, Smith was also instrumental in pushing forward the development of appropriate landing craft for amphibious landings – the Higgins boat (LCVP, or landing craft, vehicle and personnel), and the amphibian tractor (LVT or more popularly, amtrac), both of which were essential vehicles to carry troops from ship to shore as well as keys to a successful landing.

In the years immediately preceding the Japanese attack on Pearl Harbor, Colonel Smith was the Director of Operations and Training at Headquarters, US Marine Corps in Washington DC. He commanded the 1st Marine Brigade before the war, directing it in a number of fleet landing exercises, and when the brigade was redesignated the 1st Marine Division in February 1941, he was its first commander. In June that year, he left the division to command the new I Corps (Provisional) of the Atlantic Fleet, which later became the Amphibious Force, Atlantic Fleet. The primary mission of this command was to ready the 1st Marine and army 1st and 3rd Infantry Divisions for amphibious landings in combat.

In May 1942, the 1st Marine Division was detached from Smith's command for combat operations in the South Pacific. At that time, the Joint Chiefs of Staff (JCS) decided that amphibious training and operations in the Atlantic should be the province of the army, and that all Marine divisions should be deployed to the Pacific. In August of that year, General Smith turned over his command to the army and went to the west coast where he relieved Marine Major-General Clayton B. Vogel as Commanding General, Amphibious Corps, Pacific Fleet (Phibcorspac). At this time, Vogel took command of

I Marine Amphibious Corps (I MAC) in Nouméa, New Caledonia, a combat command that Smith would dearly loved to have been given. As head of Phibcorpspac, General Smith was a trainer, not a combat commander, and he seriously worried that he would never get a combat command in the Pacific, although promised one by Lieutenant-General Thomas Holcomb, Commandant of the Marine Corps.

In his west-coast headquarters at Camp Elliott, just north of San Diego, California, Smith continued his supervision of the amphibious training of both army and Marine divisions. The 3rd Marine Division had recently been formed with units at both Camp Elliott and Camp Pendleton, just up the coastal highway from Elliott. In late 1943, the JCS decided to take action against the Japanese forces which had occupied several islands in the Aleutians, and designated the army 7th Infantry Division as the assault unit. The Joint Chiefs directed General Smith and his Phibcorpspac to train the soldiers. When the invasion force left San Francisco in late April 1943 and set a course for Attu, Smith and some of the Marines on his staff accompanied it as observers with no responsibilities whatsoever. While they had trained units in amphibious operations for a number of years, this was to be the first actual amphibious landing they would experience under combat conditions.

The 7th Division landed on Attu on 11 May under less than optimum conditions. There was a heavy fog the day of the landing and the troops landed on two beachheads which were widely separated from each other. As Smith was to complain in later operations he directed when he had army troops under his command, the soldiers in the Attu landing were not aggressive enough and moved too slowly. So slowly, in fact, that the army General in command of the landing was relieved. If experiencing an amphibious assault under conditions of combat was a 'lesson learned' for the Marine General, he learned another one eighteen days after the initial landing when the Japanese mounted a massive *banzai* attack against the Americans and overran some units. Smith had never seen anything like this before and it profoundly impressed and alerted him to the potential of other like attacks facing the Marines in future operations in the Pacific.

Shortly after the Attu landings, Admiral Ernest J. King [*q.v.*], US Chief of Naval Operations and Commander-in-Chief, US Fleet (he liked the title Cominch) and Admiral Chester W. Nimitz [*q.v.*], Commander-in-Chief, Pacific Fleet/Commander-in-Chief, Pacific Ocean Areas (Cincpac/Cincpoa), met in San Francisco, as they were to do periodically for the rest of the war. Smith was present to give his views on the operation. He had served under King when the latter commanded the Atlantic Fleet's Amphibious Training Command. King both liked Smith and respected his professionalism and ability to get things done, as well as the fact that Smith wanted to fight, a plus in King's book. Smith and Nimitz had not met before, and the Marine General was anxious to meet and impress Cincpac with what he had to offer as an amphibious commander. He obviously succeeded, for Nimitz invited Smith to return to Honolulu with him, and then to accompany him further on a tour of the South Pacific.

After stopping over at Nouméa and Efate, in the New Hebrides, where Marine units were training for the assault up the chain of the Solomon Islands, they visited Guadalcanal. Here the 1st Marine Division had landed on 7 August 1942 in the first major offensive of the Pacific War and proved the soundness of Marine amphibious doctrine and the worth of the training it had received under Smith. There were three Marine divisions in the South Pacific now – the 1st, and the 2nd and 3rd – both of which had also been trained by Smith; they were now in General Vogel's 1 MAC. For a number of reasons, Admiral William F. Halsey [*q.v.*], Commander, South Pacific and South Pacific Forces (Comsopac), was dissatisifed with Vogel's performance and recommended his relief by Major-General Alexander A. Vandegrift, who had led the assault on Guadalcanal. The change in command was made and, as Smith noted in his controversial post-retirement autobiography, *Coral and Brass*, on the return trip to Pearl Harbor he was depressed by the fact that offensive operations in the Pacific were accelerating and he was returning to a training rather than a combat command. At one point in the flight, Nimitz called Smith over to his seat in the plane and told him of his plans to bring him out to the Pacific in the autumn of 1943 to command all Marines in the Central Pacific. For the elated Smith, this was the turning point in the war for him. He was now going to lead his beloved Marines in combat.

Upon returning to California, he resumed his Phibcorpspac command and began training a joint US–Canadian force for a landing on Kiska. After a period of amphibious training off the coast of California, the invasion force staged to Adak for rehearsals. As in the Attu operation, Smith and his staff went along in observer roles only. Two weeks prior to the scheduled D-Day, pilots flying reconnaissance missions over the target reported no activity on the ground. At that point, Smith suspected that the Japanese had quietly left, and he voiced this opinion to both the navy and army commanders of the planned assault; they were not convinced by Smith's arguments. When the landing was made on 15 August, the Marine General was proven right. Despite a lack of opposition – in fact, no Japanese were found – there were casualties, all caused by friendly units firing on each other.

Not long after the operation was ended, and Smith had returned to Camp Elliott, the orders to the Pacific Nimitz had promised him arrived. He and his staff were ordered to Pearl Harbor and his Phibcorpspac was redesignated V Amphibious Corps (VAC). After he arrived, he was awarded the first of a number of decorations he was to receive in World War Two, a Distinguished Service Medal for 'his capable performance on duty on both coasts of the United States . . . training . . . practically all American units, including, at various times, the First and Third Marine Divisions, the First, Seventh, and Ninth Infantry Divisions of the Army, and numerous other Marine Corps and Army personnel'. Before the war was over, he was to be decorated with the DSM three more times.

By agreement among the Anglo-American Combined Chiefs of Staff, the American Joint Chiefs of Staff (JCS) were responsible for the conduct of the war in the Pacific. This decision was made in March 1942, when the Combined Chiefs of Staff approved a dividing line that separated and assigned spheres of command in the Western Pacific. Burma and all South-east Asia west of a north–south line between Java and Sumatra were added to General Sir Archibald P. Wavell's India Command, and the British Chiefs of Staff were charged with the strategic direction of this theatre. The whole Pacific east of the new line was assigned to the JCS, who then divided the Pacific into two strategic areas. The one in which the navy would have paramount interest was the Pacific Ocean Areas (POA), and the other in which the army would be dominant was the South-west Pacific Area (SWPA). In mid-March, General Douglas MacArthur was designated Cincswpa; Admiral Nimitz was at that time designated Cincpoa. At the Cairo Conference (Sextant) the next year, President Franklin D. Roosevelt and Prime Minister Winston S. Churchill agreed upon a grand plan that dictated the thrust of two concurrent and mutually supporting series of operations across the Pacific towards the heart of the Japanese Empire. These drives along separate approach axes would establish bases from which a massive effort could be launched against the Formosa–Luzon–China coastal areas in the spring of 1945. One drive, to be mounted by Allied forces under MacArthur, was to move along the northern coast of New Guinea; in the second, Admiral Nimitz's forces, which contained both army and Marine units in addition to his naval task forces, would push through the Central Pacific to the core of Japanese island defences guarding the heart of the Empire. During this two-pronged advance, the major components of the Pacific Fleet, under Nimitz as Commander-in-Chief of the Pacific Fleet, would support, as assigned, specific amphibious operations within both strategic command areas, and at the same time contain the Japanese fleet. The Cincpac mission to push through the Central Pacific was to be Smith's main concern for the rest of the war.

In planning for the Central Pacific thrust, King and Nimitz met in San Francisco in June, July and August 1943. They discussed many options for the direction of the war. One option was to capture the Gilberts to acquire an airbase from which air coverage and photo-reconnaissance missions could rise over future targets. A six-phased plan of future operations was agreed upon. The first targets would be the Gilbert Islands and Nauru, to be followed in turn by the Marshall Islands, Ponape, Central Caroline Islands, the Palaus and Yap, and the Mariana Islands. In his autobiography, *Fleet Admiral King: A Naval Record*, King said that he wanted to use Marines in these operations because he felt that by their training, organization and temperament they were the troops best suited for amphibious assaults against island fortresses. Besides, he might have been prescient enough to foresee a post-war unification fight, in which case he wanted to keep the navy-Marine Corps team intact to prevent the army from usurping the Corps' amphibious assault mission and absorbing the Corps itself.

In their July conference, both Nimitz and King agreed to the necessity of appointing a corps commander for expeditionary troops and that Holland Smith should be that man. Smith would come directly under the commander of the Fifth Fleet's 5th Amphibious Force, led by Rear Admiral (later Vice Admiral) Richmond Kelly Turner [*q.v.*]. His ascetic and academic demeanour hid his true personality, which was characterized by his nickname, 'Terrible Turner'. Actually, Holland Smith's command was subordinate to three naval commands – Nimitz's Cincpac; Vice Admiral Raymond A. Spruance's [*q.v.*] Fifth Fleet; and Kelly Turner's 5th Amphibious Force. Smith got along well with Spruance, who is considered to have been one of the great naval tacticians and leaders in World War Two. His relationship with Nimitz was on the outside respectful and calm, but Smith could never be certain either that that respect flowed downwards or of Nimitz's support, especially when it came to the matter of inter-service conflicts with the army. By the end of the war, there was no love lost between Smith and Nimitz, and they came mutually to dislike each other.

Like a number of other admirals in the Pacific involved with amphibious operations, Turner thought himself the equal of Marine commanders in knowledge of and expertise in ground tactics and tended to maintain control of the troops once they had landed. Actually, *Fleet Training Publication 167*, a navy reprint in 1938 of the Marines' 1934 publication, *Tentative Manual for Landing Operations*, was the Holy Writ for the conduct of modern amphibious warfare. Among other related matters, the publication quite clearly laid out respective responsibilities in amphibious landings. It stipulated that once the troop commander was ashore and had notified the amphibious force commander that he had taken command of his troops, the amphibious force commander would relinquish his control of the troops and assume a supporting role in the operation. Despite the fact that this doctrinal matter was reaffirmed after Guadalcanal, Kelly Turner apparently did not get the message. This led to a number of quite heated arguments between him and Smith in about every operation in which the two participated.

Throughout their relationship in the Pacific War, it was as though Turner and Smith agreed to disagree. In almost each case, it fell to the fleet commander at the time, either Admirals Spruance or Halsey, to referee their disputes whenever it had to do with strategy, tactics or the conduct of operations ashore, or anything else under Smith's cognizance in which Turner decided to interfere. As a biographer of Smith noted, 'the two men clashed early, loudly, and often'. Turner continually attempted to browbeat and bully subordinates whose intellect he thought was inferior to his own. Smith wouldn't take this abuse and fought back, thus, in a convoluted way, earning Turner's respect. As Smith remarked in his autobiography, 'our partnership, though stormy, spelled hell in big red letters to the Japanese'.

Different people in authority had different views of Smith. In general, he impressed them with his aggressiveness and willingness to march to the sound of guns as well as his expertise in amphibious operations. He was Spruance's choice for amphibious corps commander. After General Holcomb telephoned Smith to tell him that he was getting the Central Pacific command, the commandant turned to a senior headquarters Marine officer who had overheard the conversation and said, 'The reason I am appointing Smith is that there is going to be a lot of trouble with the navy over rights and prerogatives and such things and Holland is the only one I know who can sit at the table and pound it harder than any naval officer.'

When Smith arrived in Pearl Harbor, his troubles with the navy began at once. He was assigned to quarters not commensurate with his rank and he complained loudly about it until given the flag officer's quarters he rated. The navy's explanation was that the billeting officer had made an error. Smith didn't believe this for one moment and determined that he was not going to take such treatment from the navy. He was not only fighting for what he believed he rated as a general officer of Marines, but in a sense he was fighting as well for the principle of equal treatment for his men. It soon appeared that as the Marine Corps' most senior officer in the Pacific, he was going to have to fight not only the Japanese but the US Army and Navy as well to ensure that Marines were not going to be treated as second-class citizens and received the respect they deserved for their combat record.

Immediately after arriving in the Hawaiian Islands, Smith and his staff became deeply involved in the planning for the Gilberts operation, codenamed Galvanic. Just as immediately, he had his first conflict with Turner over the relative roles of the amphibious force and expeditionary troop commanders in an amphibious assault. Smith made it quite clear that no admiral would ever give an order to his troops on the beach. He told his aide that he once said to Turner, 'I don't try to run your ships and you'd better by a goddamn sight lay off of my troops.' The squabble continued for some time, threatening to disrupt the planning for the Gilberts operation. The argument was settled according to the precedent established in *FTP-167* – the landing force would remain under the control of the naval commander until the troop commander sent a message stating that he was ready to assume command on the shore. While this settled matters for a while, another problem arose.

When Cincpac published the troop list for the Gilberts landing, vac headquarters was not listed. It was extremely galling to Smith that, after training the troops and helping plan the operation, he was to have no part in it. To Smith, it appeared that this was just another example of his less than even-handed treatment by Nimitz and his staff, and there was more of this yet to come. Turner and Spruance were equally surprised, and the Fifth Fleet commander immediately issued orders for Smith and his staff to accompany the invasion force. The omission of his name from the troop list reinforced Smith's belief that some senior naval officers thought that they needed no assistance from Marine commanders in the conduct of combat operations ashore.

Besides planning for future operations, Smith and his staff continued to hone and refine all aspects of amphibious operations with which he had been involved during the pre-war fleet landing exercises on the island of Culebra off Puerto Rico. Throughout this early period, the navy fought the Marine Corps in the matter of command relations, the development of necessarily appropriate landing craft, and, equally important, the development of naval gunfire support doctrine, its employment and techniques. Quite simply, the navy did not want to wear out the tubes of its guns in supporting a landing, but preferred to save them for a ship-to-ship naval battle on the high seas. When he arrived at Pearl, Smith pressed for the establishment of a naval gunfire range where all ships of the Pacific Fleet had to qualify before being sent to the forward area. For this range, the island of Kahoolawe in the Hawaiian group was obtained and a naval gunfire training unit set up in September–October 1943. With a view to improving another combat supporting arm, General Smith had a bombing range established in the Pali Valley of Oahu to train navy and army air forces pilots in the techniques of close air support of ground troops, which Marine Corps aviation had developed and refined in the 1930s.

The initial JCS order for Galvanic called for simultaneous landings on Tarawa atoll in the Gilberts and the island of Nauru, the two targets separated by a distance of 380 miles. Because only the 2nd Marine Division and elements of the army 27th Infantry Division were allocated for the operation, and because Nauru promised to be a much more difficult target for the forces allotted than the planner anticipated, Butaritari in Makin atoll in the Gilberts was substituted instead. Earlier in the war, in August 1942, Makin was the target of a raid from submarines by the Marine 2nd Raider Battalion.

In the revised Galvanic plan, there were now to be three targets in the Gilberts: Makin, to be taken by an infantry regiment of the 27th Division; Tarawa, some 300 miles south of Makin and one which promised to be a much more difficult objective, assigned to the 2nd Marine Division; and Apamama, to be captured by a company of Marines landed from a submarine. Turner was in charge of the whole operation, and also commanded the Northern Attack Force for Makin. Smith was to accompany him aboard his flagship as an adviser on the employment of reserve units. Rear Admiral Harry W. Hill commanded the Southern Attack Force, whose objective was Tarawa. His landing force was the 2nd Marine Division commanded by Major-General Julian C. Smith. Much has been written about the seventy-six-hour assault of Tarawa, its many difficulties and high cost in casualties. The primary target of this triangular atoll was Betio, defended by approximately 5,000 veteran Japanese troops. It bristled with well-dug-in guns of all calibres in solid concrete and sand and coconut log mutually supporting emplacements impervious to all but direct hits from large calibre shells or heavy bombs. All of this was on an island three miles long and approximately 600 yards across.

Holland Smith and his staff argued with the navy about the length of time given to naval gunfire preparation of Betio before the landing and whether to land artillery on a nearby island of the atoll. The navy was concerned about exposing its ships in a restricted area to potential air and submarine attacks. In the end, Smith was forced to agree with the navy's plan. Another major factor in the planning was his decision to hold one regiment of the 2nd Division in reserve for employment at either Makin or Apamama if needed. In the strategy of the operation, this deprived Julian Smith of the benefit of landing troops and artillery on another island of the Tarawa atoll at the same time as the main landing on Betio. He was therefore forced to launch a frontal assault without enfilading artillery support.

While the 2nd Marine Division was committed to landing on Betio by first crossing a fringing reef 600 yards offshore, the army's 27th Infantry Division, under Major-General Ralph C. Smith, had as its objective lightly defended Butaritari Island in Makin atoll. Butaritari was approximately eight miles long and was 500 yards wide on the average. The 27th was a New York National Guard unit which, unlike other National Guard organizations, was not reorganized when mobilized and its personnel redistributed to other army divisions to break up political cliques and, more importantly, to prevent an inordinate number of casualties from one city or town should the original unit remain intact. The 165th Infantry, descendant of the legendary 'Fighting 69th' of World War One and movie fame, was the assault force. Facing it on its objective was a garrison estimated at 500–800 Japanese – less than on Betio – and far fewer fortifications than on the Marine target. According to intelligence estimates, the 165th enjoyed an advantage in numbers of six to one, while the 2nd Marine Division would have a superiority of slightly more than two to one, far less than it would have liked.

D-Day for both objectives was set for 20 November. Turner's Northern Attack Force, with Holland Smith on board the flagship *Pennsylvania*, set a course for Makin, departing from Pearl Harbor on 10 November, the 168th birthday of the Marine Corps. The 2nd Marine Division in the ships of Hill's Southern Attack Force steamed from Wellington, New Zealand – where it had trained – and headed for Tarawa and Apamama with a stopover at Efate for rehearsals. Major-General Julian Smith was on board Hill's flagship *Maryland*.

The landing on Butaritari was unopposed. According to official army figures after the battle, the island was defended by 590 Japanese, of which only 250 were combat troops, the remainder naval air personnel and labourers. Against this military force hardly worthy of the name were 6,400 assault troops. Butaritari should have been a walkover, and yet it wasn't. Sniper fire from a single rifleman was enough to slow the advance of an infantry battalion to a standstill. It soon appeared to Smith and Turner that the army regiment was not up to the job. By the end of the first day ashore, troops of the 165th Infantry had captured less than one third of the island. Holland Smith was deeply disturbed at this desultory performance. He related in his memoirs that even while at Pearl Harbor before the operation he had doubts about the 27th's capabilities, and now these doubts were confirmed. The second day went not much better than the first and Smith charged ashore in an attempt to speed up the advance of the troops. His efforts were not successful, for it took the army three days, rather than one day, to secure the island given the nature of the defences. The 165th suffered 66 dead and 185 wounded. Smith estimated that, because of the excess of 'trigger happiness' of the green troops, more than half of the casualties resulted from accidental shooting. One veteran civilian correspondent on the scene said 90 per cent of the casualties were caused by intramural shooting by the army units.

Holland Smith called the capture of Makin 'infuriatingly slow' and the performance of the 165th less than impressive. Thus began a feeling on his part about the regiment and its parent division, the 27th, which was to participate in a future operation which the Marine General would direct. The 165th's cautious conduct in taking Makin was strongly defended by Lieutenant-General Robert C. 'Nelly' Richardson Jr, commander of US Army forces in the Pacific Ocean Area and, like Smith, subordinate to Nimitz as Cincpoa. Richardson quoted the low casualty figures on Butaritari in defence of army tactics and as an argument against Smith's insistence upon aggressive tactics in the attack. This argument, too, was to carry over to the next operation in which Smith commanded army troops.

Richardson was constantly criticizing Marine tactics, troops and commanders to anyone who would listen and to Nimitz in particular. In fact, not long after completion of Galvanic, Richardson wrote a 'Secret – For Adm Nimitz Eyes Only' memo. In this letter, he discusses and criticizes the role of General Smith and the V Amphibious Corps in the Pacific War. The letter foreshadows what came to be known as the 'Smith vs Smith controversy' on Saipan, where Marine General Smith relieved army General Ralph Smith, commander of the 27th Division. In paragraph eight of his nine-paragraph, four-page letter, Richardson wrote: 'I feel that as a tactical headquarters the fifth [*sic*] Amphibious Corps is an unnecessary echelon of command and that it has no means, combat or service, to further the successful capture, defense, or development of bases in the Central Pacific.' He then made two recommendations: 'a. The responsibilities assigned to the headquarters of the Fifth Amphibious Corps be restricted to administrative duties in connection with USMC troops in the Central Pacific area. b. When the time arrives for the employment of a tactical corps as such in the Central Pacific Area, both the corps headquarters and the corps troops, combat and service, be furnished by the Army.'

Nimitz apparently sent the letter for comment to General Vandegrift, who had become Commandant on 1 January 1944, and who reacted to Richardson's letter ten days later in a five-page reasoned response, rebutting all that the army General had written. With respect to Richardson's attack on Holland Smith, the Commandant wrote:

Sub-paragraph 'e' constitutes a gratuitous insinuation concerning the professional ability of the Commanding General, Fifth Amphibious Corps, and by inference, states that General Richardson considers himself more thoroughly qualified to pass on the tactical plans for difficult amphibious operations. Major General Holland M. Smith has for the last four and one-half years commanded units engaged in training for, and the conduct of amphibious operations. . . . It should be pointed out that at least three Army Divisions, the 1st, 3rd, and 9th, which have actually executed amphibious operations, received a considerable portion of their training under General Smith's command.

There is no indication of any further correspondence or action in response to Richardson's letter. Judging by Nimitz's actions or lack of them with respect to the Smith–Richardson confrontations, one can infer that Nimitz successfully stayed aloof from these inter-service rivalries, or, in Smith's view, leaned over backwards in favour of the army. While it is true that these conflicts had no place in a wartime situation, the fact that they did exist had to have some effect on the conduct of the war in the Pacific. The truth is that Nimitz never appears to have supported and defended Smith fully. That Richardson was a hair-shirt to Nimitz may be seen in the recollection of a Marine general of the time he and General Vandegrift called on Nimitz en route to the States after a visit to the South Pacific. They 'were about to tell him good-bye, and Nimitz said, "Well, I'm glad to see you. I'm in for a hard hour. Richardson's coming and it's always unpleasant when he comes."' As will be seen, not only did Nimitz not put Richardson properly in his place, it would appear also that he gave Holland Smith and his Marines little support or credit for their successes and achievements.

At the time the Makin operation was under way, Smith's heart was really with his Marines on Tarawa. He had no idea of what was going on, for communications in the Tarawa operation were particularly bad, so bad that even Julian Smith on the *Maryland* at too many times had no contact with the command ashore and did not know how the battle was going.

The assault of Tarawa began in the pre-dawn hours of 20 November 1943 with the naval gunfire preparation of the target, and, as would happen again at Iwo Jima, a controversy arose over the amount and length of that pre-invasion bombardment. Not only did the navy turn down Julian Smith's plan for a preliminary landing on a nearby island of the atoll, it also refused his request for three days of naval gunfire on the objective; the operation plan required less than four hours and the naval force actually fired for only two and a half hours. While this was the heaviest naval gunfire delivered on an objective the size of Tarawa to that date in the war, it was less than needed in both quantity and quality. Because of the many lessons learned at Tarawa – the first major operation in the Central Pacific – greater importance was given later to the role of naval gunfire in an assault on a strongly defended island. Tarawa proved that in order to soften up the target sufficiently for an unopposed landing, the preliminary bombardment had to be heavier and sustained for a longer period. To reduce casualties in the assaulting force, enemy emplacements would have to be destroyed rather than just neutralized in a short period of firing, as at Tarawa. Another important lesson learned in this operation was the necessity of reducing the time-lag between the lifting of fires and the touchdown of the leading wave in order to prevent the defenders from recovering from the shock of the bombardment too soon. Essentially, anticipating what was to be the nature of enemy defences on the islands of the Central Pacific scheduled for future attack, the performance of naval gunfire had to improve immeasurably.

The first three assault waves heading for Tarawa's beaches in amphibian tractors were able to negotiate the fringing reef off the island and head right into shore and dump the Marines at the seawall. Because of low tide, subsequent waves in LCVPS could not float over the reef and the Marines aboard had to jump over the sides into waist-high water and negotiate the 800 yards into the beach in the face of heavy machine and anti-boat gunfire. Many Marines were killed as they jumped into the water, others died as they became entangled in offshore barbed-wire defences. When they saw on large movie screens the Oscar-award-winning, Marine-made movie *With the Marines at Tarawa* and newsreel films of the landing, shot by Marine Corps combat photographers, many Americans were shocked by the scenes of the bodies of Marine dead in the waters just offshore, floating slowly in and out with the waves.

About the first indication Holland Smith had of how the Marines were faring was a message from Julian Smith after noon of D-Day, when he requested release of the 6th Marine Regiment from corps reserve. The message ended with the bare statement, 'The issue is in doubt.' With but little discussion with Kelly Turner, he approved the request of the 2nd Division commander. It was not until late afternoon of D plus 1 that the Marine commander ashore at Tarawa, Colonel David M. Shoup, who was awarded the Medal of Honor for his heroic achievements in the battle and later became Commandant, sent Julian Smith a situation report. It ended with the words, 'Combat efficiency – we are winning.' Betio was finally officially secured on D plus 3, 23 November, after seventy-six hours of the most intensive, continuous fighting in the war to date. Casualties were 1,000 Marines dead, including the navy hospital corpsmen attached to Marine units, with 2,000 wounded. The Japanese suffered an estimated 5,000 men defending to the death; very few gave themselves up as prisoners, and those who did were in the main Korean labourers.

Holland Smith arrived on Tarawa on 24 November and was appalled at what he saw and smelled. The battleground had not yet been completely policed. Hundreds of bodies, Americans as well as Japanese, were still found all over the island, bloated and stinking, where they had fallen. Marine graves registration personnel worked long and hard in the gruesome task of preparing the dead for suitable burial. Together with Julian Smith, Holland inspected the island, and was overwhelmed with what he saw. He was profoundly impressed by the nature of the Japanese defences, which had frustrated the efforts of normal naval gunfire. In the end, it fell to the heroism and bravery of individual Marines, who, in the face of unbelievably heavy enemy fire, raced to burn Japanese defences out with flame-throwers or to blow them up by tossing hand grenades or satchel charges in the embrasures of the pillboxes.

Smith's bitterness against the navy grew even deeper after Tarawa, especially when he read Nimitz's statements about the battle in a Honolulu newspaper, not least Cincpac's comment that 'our casualties on Tarawa were relatively light'. In his post-retirement memoirs, *Coral and Brass*, Smith faulted the navy for a sinfully inadequate pre-landing naval gunfire preparation of the target, and for the presumptuous comment by a senior naval officer that the island would be 'obliterated by naval gunfire'. However, as a number of students of the war in the Pacific have pointed out, while the naval gunfire was admittedly inadequate, the gunfire plan had been prepared by Smith's VAC naval gunfire officer working together with Admiral Hill's, and that Smith had approved it. Also the need for a speedy conclusion to both the Tarawa and Makin landings to ensure that the naval forces would not become sitting targets for enemy air and submarine attacks precluded a lengthy naval gunfire preparation. Because the Makin operation was inordinately dragged out by the army forces, the navy lost the carrier *Liscome Bay*, which was torpedoed twenty miles off Makin with the loss of 540 officers and sailors. Richardson neglected to add these casualties to the army's when the total cost of Makin was computed and when he defended the army's 'methodical' conduct of the operation.

Smith's post-war memoirs were controversial for the many directions in which he struck out at real and imagined enemies and for the release of his bitterness pent up during the war. One of his most controversial statements was his allegation that 'Tarawa was a mistake' on the part of the Joint Chiefs because it was strategically worthless; for the JCS to have conceived of it being otherwise was a monumental error. This conclusion was not upheld by his closest naval colleagues in the Pacific – Nimitz, Spruance, Turner and Hill, all of whom insisted that the capture of Tarawa of necessity was the prologue to future operations in the Central Pacific, and the Marshall Islands in particular. Further, Tarawa was close enough to Kwajalein for launching reconnaissance and bombing flights to the next American objective. Perhaps the accusation regarding Tarawa which damaged Smith's credibility the most was his insistence after the war that he had opposed the landing. There was nothing in the record then or now to support this. As a matter of fact, as he was reminded by Julian Smith and others at the time his memoirs were published, nothing he said at the time of the landing or immediately after led anyone to conclude that he believed Tarawa a mistake.

Two months after Tarawa, the Marshalls were assaulted. The lessons learned at Tarawa at the cost of considerable blood, sweat and tears were meaningfully studied by those directed to carry the battle further to the Japanese. Those lessons were the need for a thorough preparation of the objective by naval gunfire, the importance of having a sufficient number of amphibian tractors in the assault waves, the employment of co-ordinated close air support during the assault phases, and the necessity for landing field artillery on islands in close proximity to the objective. General Smith also made recommendations relating to changes in combat loading of supplies aboard combat transports and agreed with Turner in the use of underwater demolition teams for conducting pre-invasion reconnaissance of the target beaches and clearing obstacles from those beaches prior to the landing.

After the capture of Tarawa and Makin, a pattern evolved which was to prove eminently successful in subsequent operations in the Central Pacific. Initially, carrier- and land-based aircraft would strike future objectives, acquire aerial photography and at the same time destroy everything possible on land and sea in the target area. Next would come the naval task forces comprised of battleships, cruisers and destroyers to give the objective a thorough working over. Finally, in the assault phase, troops would land to secure the objective. They would be followed by Seabees and other construction personnel to build or improve airfields from which Allied planes could fly to attack targets closer to the home islands of Japan, and then the cycle would be repeated.

General Smith and his staff, as well as the staffs of Nimitz's Pacific Fleet headquarters, Spruance's Fifth Fleet and Turner's 5th Amphibious Force, were now all focused on the Marshall Islands and their coral atolls. Smith and Turner were at this point working smoothly and well in harness. While a mutual respect marked the Turner–Smith relationship, Smith had to protect his flanks from Richardson and other detractors of the Marines. In his extensive correspondence with General Vandegrift, Smith repeated every slight he received from the army commander, and also related the constant sniping Richardson conducted against the Marines whenever he met with Nimitz, and which Nimitz repeated to the Marine commander. Smith was sensitive to all of this, but promised Vandegrift that he would 'continue to exert every precaution to prevent any unfriendly feeling on the part of the Army'.

For the Marshalls, Smith planned a simultaneous attack on Wotje and Maloelap on the eastern fringe of the island group and then use them as bases from which Kwajalein, a large island in the middle of the Marshalls, could be assaulted. Spruance, Turner and Smith were shocked to learn in December that Nimitz wanted a direct assault on Kwajalein. Despite their good and sound arguments against this decision, Nimitz held firm. Within the Marshalls, Kwajalein atoll consists of a triangularly shaped group of small coral islands with Roi–Namur – twin islands connected by a causeway – and Kwajalein Island, about forty-four miles to the south, the most significant targets of the operation. For Roi and Namur, the 4th Marine Division, recently activated at Camp Pendleton and commanded by Major-General Harry Schmidt, was assigned. Army Major-General Charles H. Corlett's 7th Infantry Division was given Kwajalein as its target. Additionally, Majuro, a lightly defended island in the south-eastern section of the Marshalls, was to be taken by the 106th Infantry of the 27th Infantry Division. Holland Smith would be in direct command of all three operations once the troops landed on D-Day, 31 January 1944.

In comparison to Tarawa, for Roi–Namur and Kwajalein, nearby islands were to be seized on D-Day on which field artillery would be landed to support the main landings. More amphibian tractors would be available in this operation than at Tarawa to continue the momentum of the attack of the troops ashore. Preliminary naval gunfire preparation of the objectives would be longer and heavier – it would begin one day before the initial landing and two full days before the main assaults. Further, destroyers would move in close to the shore and continue firing almost until the assault waves landed to keep the enemy pinned down. Finally, for the Kwajalein landings, new landing craft, the LCI (landing craft, infantry) gunboat, mounting rockets, 40mm guns and machine guns would immediately precede the assault waves, taking up the fire where the destroyers left off.

Most commentators have called the Marshalls operation the 'best planned and executed operation of the Pacific War'. The Marines secured Roi–Namur in twenty-four hours. It took the army troops almost four days to capture Kwajalein against the same opposition found by the now-blooded 4th Marine Division on Roi and Namur. Once again Holland Smith had cause to be displeased with the performance of army units. The difference between army and Marine conduct of the assault was that the army's was a slow, deliberate, carefully planned advance, while the Marines conducted a continuous, aggressive advance in which lightly held positions were bypassed and left to be mopped up by accompanying troops. According to Jeter A. Isely and Philip A. Crowl, authors of the classic *The U.S. Marines and Amphibious War*, the army's method was to advance deliberately to hold casualties to a minimum. The differing philosophies were to result in an inter-service controversy of major proportions which was to reach from the Pacific to Washington before long.

The next operation was Eniwetok, an atoll on the western edge of the Marshalls. Neither Smith nor Turner were to be present for this landing. With a D-Day of 17 February established, the objective consisted of three islands – Engebi, Parry and Eniwetok. Marine Brigadier-General Thomas E. Watson led the mixed landing force comprised of the 22nd Marines and two battalions of the 106th Infantry, another regiment of the 27th Division. The Marines landed and secured their objective in six hours, with mopping up completed the next day. The 106th landed on Eniwetok on the 18th and didn't secure it until the 21st. The next day, the Marines landed on Parry, and secured it by nightfall. Eniwetok held 725 Japanese troops; Parry, over a 1,000. In his correspondence with the Commandant and statements to close associates, Smith again voiced his displeasure with the performance of a unit of the 27th Division. It was almost a foreshadowing of things yet to come. For his part in taking the Marshalls, Smith was decorated with a gold star in lieu of his second Distinguished Service Medal and on 14 March 1944 was given the richly deserved and long overdue third star of a lieutenant-general.

This promotion came only after Turner and Spruance were promoted to vice admiral and admiral respectively, and Vandegrift told King that the Marine Corps deserved a lieutenant-general in the Pacific. He reinforced his argument by saying that the Marines felt that they were being discriminated against and that the esprit and morale of his Marines would suffer if Smith's worth was not recognized. This rationale convinced King, who then supported the promotion. Smith was aware of all the backstairs play going on and it just seemed to embitter him further against the navy in general and Nimitz in particular. Smith felt strongly that Nimitz considered the Marines to be second-class citizens and he just as deeply resented the fact that in his war communiqués Nimitz deliberately downplayed the role and accomplishments of Marines in the Central Pacific operations, while giving full credit, and identification by task force, to ships which were involved. Secondly, as mentioned earlier, Smith believed that Nimitz was unwilling to support him when he and his Marines were attacked by Richardson. Meanwhile, Smith made no effort to get along with Nimitz except on a professional basis, and, as the war proceeded, the personal relationship got no better.

Smith ran a happy ship as far as his V Amphibious Corps headquarters was concerned. He chose competent staff officers, recognized their worth and accomplishments and had them promoted on the basis of merit rather than seniority. His staff thought of him as a kind and considerate leader, almost a father-figure to the men who served him loyally. There are any number of stories told about his thoughtfulness and many kindnesses to his officers and enlisted Marines, and his concern about their welfare. He was best described by one of the staff officers closest to him, who said: 'he was an impressive leader . . . everybody recognized him. They knew him. His troops knew him and he spoke to them. He knew how to talk to a Marine. He loved his Marines and I think they had a high respect for him.'

In his post-retirement oral history interview for the United States Naval Institute Oral History Program, Admiral Hill, who liked and, in his own way, admired Holland Smith, gave the following assessment of him:

He was basically a great show-off. A great talker, he liked to dominate the conversation – and usually did so in a rather loud voice. But his men loved him for it. He was their type of tough fighter, and they knew that in him they had a leader who would stand up for them to the bitter end. He was a 100% Marine, and would fight at the drop of a hat if anyone suggested the Corps could ever make a mistake . . . he was . . . a rough, tough leader itching for a fight with the Japs. Naturally, he was hard to work with. No one ever accused him of brilliance, but everyone learned quickly that he had many positive ideas of his own, and changing any of them was sure to be a long and difficult struggle.

The next operation, Forager, with three targets in the Mariana Islands – Saipan, Tinian and Guam – was scheduled for the summer of 1944. It was to be the largest campaign yet mounted in the Pacific and Smith was to command all ground forces in the three operations. He would head the Northern Attack Force for landings on Saipan and Tinian, and Major-General Roy S. Geiger, commander of III Amphibious Corps (IIIAC), would lead the Southern Attack Force for the retaking of Guam. In VAC, Smith would have five divisions (for Saipan and Tinian the 2nd and 4th Marine Divisions and the army 27th Infantry Division in floating reserve; for Guam, the 3rd Marine Division and the 1st Provisional Marine Brigade), and the 77th Infantry Division in general reserve in Hawaii, a total of 130,000 troops in all. Again Richardson complained that the Marine Corps did not have enough trained officers to man a corps staff, much less a field army, which the aggregate of troops scheduled for the Marianas represented. His proposal to relieve Smith by an army general was turned down by both Spruance and Nimitz.

D-Day for Saipan was 15 June, when two regiments each of the 2nd and 4th Marine Divisions landed on the west coast of the island – 2nd Division on the left and 4th Division on the right. The landings were bitterly opposed, with heavy enemy fire coming not only from positions on the beach, but also from artillery in the hills overlooking the beachhead. American casualty figures mounted rapidly. In face of the heavy fighting and the unrelenting resistance of the Japanese, two regiments of the 27th were landed (the 105th and the 165th; the 106th was kept on ships as floating reserve). The Guam landing scheduled for 18 June was postponed, and the Guam Attack Force designated the reserve for Saipan, so doubtful was the situation ashore. Smith's plan of manoeuvre called for the 2nd Division to pivot to the north once its regiments were in order, while the 4th drove across the island, cutting it in half, and then turned north on the right flank of the 2nd. The 27th Division was to advance on the right flank of the 4th and then head southward to secure that part of the island. Holland Smith moved his command post ashore on D plus 2. By the end of the 18th, the 4th Division had reached the east coast of Saipan, while the next day the two regiments of the 27th ashore reached the east coast in their zones and prepared to turn south to continue their mission. As in previous operations, the forward movement of the 27th's regiments was slow and the leadership of some of its units lacked aggressiveness. Because Japanese resistance in all zones became so dogged, Smith called for the 106th ashore and inserted it into the line with the rest of the 27th Division.

It was clear by 21 June that the enemy's main line of resistance was in the northern part of the island and Smith decided to attack in that direction with a full-scale effort. The 27th was designated corps reserve for the push to the north. Meanwhile, two battalions of the 105th Infantry – with one in reserve – remained in the south cleaning up the enemy remaining on Nafutan Point. Again, army forward movement was sporadic, testing Smith's patience. In a conference at corps headquarters with Ralph Smith on 22 June, Holland Smith stated his concern about the slow advance on Nafutan and urged the division commander to push his subordinate commanders harder. Later that day, Ralph Smith was informed that the 27th Division – less one battalion remaining at Nafutan – would be placed in the middle of the line between the two Marine divisions for the drive to the north to begin the next day.

The attack began badly on the 23rd because the 27th was fifty-five minutes late in jumping off. When it finally moved, the left regiment hit heavy resistance and did not advance at all, while the right assault regiment advanced only 400 yards. Meanwhile, the forward movement of the Marines on the flanks caused the front line to assume the shape of a 'U' and the Marine divisions began to lose contact with the army division in the centre. By the end of the day, Holland Smith was quite concerned with the army's progress and asked army Major-General Sanderford Jarman, who was to be island commander of Saipan when the fighting was over, to speak to Ralph Smith in an effort to get the division moving.

On the 24th, again both of the Marine divisions made slow but steady progress, yet in the centre neither one of the army regiments made any appreciable progress in a rugged area the soldiers called 'Death Valley'. At this point, Holland Smith's patience with Ralph Smith and the 27th Division was exhausted and, after explaining the situation to both Admirals Turner and Spruance, he obtained their approval to relieve Ralph Smith and replace him temporarily with General Jarman. In his memoirs, Holland Smith recalled that he had told his naval superiors that 'Ralph Smith has shown he lacks aggressive spirit and his division is slowing down our advance. He should be relieved,' and they agreed. This relief was to become the centre of a bitter inter-service controversy in which there were no holds barred. Even with a new division commander, it was six days before Death Valley was taken.

After some of the most difficult fighting since Tarawa against a determined enemy well dug in in difficult terrain which favoured the defence, the final phase of the battle began on 1 July as the Japanese were compressed more and more into strongly defended pockets of resistance. At this point, Smith anticipated a massive *banzai* attack. His predictions came true early the next morning when more than 2,500 of the enemy charged into a gap between the 1st and 2nd Battalions of the 105th Infantry. Both battalions were surrounded and suffered heavy casualties; one group of the enemy struck the 3rd Battalion, but was repulsed. The Japanese then attacked the positions of the 3rd Battalion, 10th Marines, an artillery unit of the 2nd Marine Division. The Marine artillerymen were forced to fire their howitzers point-blank into the frenzied mass threatening them, and shut off the attack only after taking up rifles, pistols and automatic rifles to hold their ground as infantrymen. Meanwhile, the 106th Infantry, the 27th Division reserve, was committed to fill the gap and restore the line.

The Saipan operation was declared secured on 9 July, although mopping-up operations continued for several days. The taking of Saipan was costly in terms of American casualties of 16,525 (3,426 killed), of which 12,934 were Marines. From the point of view of the Japanese, the loss of Saipan, one of the strongest points in the outposts of the Empire, was the beginning of the end.

Holland Smith's relief of Ralph Smith became known as the 'Smith vs Smith controversy'. While Ralph Smith was one of five army generals relieved in combat during the Pacific War, he was the only one relieved by a Marine general. As might be anticipated, Richardson rushed into the fray, first by convening an army board of inquiry at Pearl Harbor on 4 July and then by showing up at Saipan eight days later. Without even the courtesy of reporting in first to Spruance, Turner or Smith, he proceeded to the command post of the 27th Division to review its troops and award decorations without the approval of Holland Smith, who still had operational control of the division. He began questioning the 27th's officers about the relief of their commander, and then called upon Holland Smith and began to berate him in front of the 4th Division commander, Harry Schmidt. Anticipating a blow-up of this nature, Turner had earlier had Holland Smith pledge to suffer in silence, and he did. Among other derogatory comments by Richardson, Smith (and Schmidt too), later recalled him saying, 'You and your commanders aren't as well qualified to lead large bodies of troops as general officers in the army. We've had more experience in handling troops than you've had, and yet you dared remove one of my generals! You Marines are nothing but a bunch of beach runners anyway. What do you know about land warfare?'

After this outburst, Richardson went to see Turner, who was not under any pledge of forbearance as was Smith. Turner had already been informed of Richardson's arrival, activities and statements, and was waiting for him to appear. Turner later reported to Nimitz and Spruance that he began by telling Richardson that he, Turner, was the commander of the Joint Expeditionary Force and asked by what authority Richardson was exercising command functions ashore at Saipan. Richardson replied that he had verbal orders from Nimitz, but refused to demonstrate any proof of his authority or to even state the terms of his orders. Turner further reported that he attempted to determine if Nimitz had actually authorized Richardson to conduct an investigation of either army or Marine troops; if such authorization had not been given, then he would protect the interests of Holland Smith against any irregular interference in the performance of his duties. There was no question then or now but that Richardson was totally out of line and completely unprofessional in his actions.

Back in the States, a newspaper chain which was to promote General Douglas MacArthur's candidacy for the presidency published a series of editorials critical of Holland Smith and the naval leadership in the Pacific, and demanded that supreme command in the Pacific be given to the army General. The editorials alleged that under Marine command excessive casualties were suffered on Saipan and claimed that Ralph Smith was relieved because he favoured 'more deliberate, less costly tactics'. Until this time, reports of the events on Saipan were largely favourable to the army. Nobody, least of all Nimitz, chose to defend the attacks on Smith and his Marines. Nimitz simply took no action on Turner's report on Richardson's reprehensible activities, a report which Spruance fully agreed with and endorsed.

Finally, the story of the relief and the events leading up to it were reported by *Time-Life* war correspondent Robert Sherrod, whose articles appeared in an August issue of *Life* and a September issue of *Time*. The publication of these articles not only brought the issue out into the open but exacerbated the situation caused by the relief itself. Richardson and Nimitz objected to their publication, and Nimitz recommended to Admiral King that Sherrod's press credentials be revoked and that he be kicked out of the Pacific theatre. King sent Nimitz's letter to General George C. Marshall, Chief of Staff of the army. In his endorsement, King identified Sherrod as the author of the two articles and said, 'His article in *Life* contains nothing derogatory to the 27th Division; it may possibly give the Marines too much credit, but this does not warrant barring Mr. Sherrod as a correspondent. The article in *Time* was presented for review to War Department Public Relations and Navy Publication Relations. Neither took exception to it. In the circumstances, there is no ground for rescinding the accreditation of Mr. Sherrod.' Responding to King, Marshall concurred and then noted that 'relationships between Marine and Army forces on Saipan deteriorated beyond mere healthy rivalry. Corrective measures are needed if we are to remove the potentiality of similar troubles in our future operations.' He also told Admiral King that Ralph Smith was transferred from the Pacific theatre 'in order to obviate all possible embarrassment to the Joint Command'. And there the matter stood, waiting to be revived in the post-war period when personal memoirs, official studies and popular histories were written, and retired senior officers' axes were ground.

Although this was popularly called the 'Smith vs Smith controversy', the roots of it went deeper than just Holland Smith's unhappiness with the performances of Ralph Smith and his 27th Division. It was an inter-service dispute when each of the services was setting up a doctrinal position and was a harbinger of the post-World War Two unification fight when each of the services fought for a slice of the defence dollar as well as for a mission. Moreover, this event was to cloud army–Marine Corps relations for a long time after. As far as Holland Smith was concerned, he was deeply hurt by the fact that neither Nimitz nor, apparently, Vandegrift came to his defence. Nimitz wanted the story kept quiet and went to great lengths to ensure that it would be. As far as Smith was concerned, he was convinced that he acted correctly, and he told Sherrod at the time, 'I don't care what they do to me. I'll be 63 years old next April [1945] and I'll retire any time after that. . . . My sun is setting. I'm just doing my duty as I see it. My conscience is clear.' He wrote to Vandegrift shortly after, saying, 'my duty was clear. It is my belief substantiated by every Army officer here that he [Ralph Smith] would never fight his division as it should be fought. . . .' Although Richardson recommended that no Marine general ever command another army division, when General Simon Bolivar Buckner Jr, commander of the Tenth Army in the Okinawa operation, was killed, Marine General Geiger took over command and ended the campaign successfully. Incidentally, Buckner headed the army board of inquiry that Richardson convened at Pearl Harbor to investigate the relief of Ralph Smith.

With the Saipan operation secured, the next target was Tinian, just four short miles from the southern tip of Saipan. Before the end of the Saipan campaign, Smith had thirteen battalions of artillery lined up almost hub to hub in the south, firing continuously on Tinian in preparation for the attack. The taking of Tinian turned out to be a classic amphibious operation. The only difference was that instead of a ship-to-shore landing, it was to be a shore-to-shore landing as the invasion troops boarded landing craft at Saipan for the assault of Tinian. Other than participating in the initial planning, Holland Smith had no role in the Tinian operation, for he turned V Amphibious Corps over to Harry Schmidt and became commander of a newly activated senior Marine command in the Pacific – Fleet Marine Force, Pacific (FMFPac).

Now that Saipan was over and Tinian under way, Smith paid attention to the Guam landing on 24 July of Roy Geiger's III Amphibious Corps. In the assault were the 3rd Marine Division and the 1st Provisional Marine Brigade, later to be joined by the army's 77th Infantry Division. While Smith was at times impatient with the progress of the 3rd Division, he was never critical of the direction of the campaign by his old friend, Roy Geiger. The army division performed well and Smith sent Major-General Andrew D. Bruce a letter commending his command. Guam was declared secure on 10 August, and thus the Marianas campaign was ended. For his part in a long and difficult series of operations, General Smith was awarded his third Distinguished Service Medal.

Fleet Marine Force, Pacific, with headquarters at Pearl Harbor, was, like Richardson's Pacific Army command, a type command in that it was responsible for the administration, supply and training of Marines, and he would not command troops in combat. Based on directives from the Joint Chiefs, the next two operations in 1945 that FMFPac Marines prepared for were Iwo Jima first, and then Okinawa; the first in February and the second in April. Command of the Okinawa operation, which should have gone to Smith as the senior amphibious commander in the Pacific, went instead to Lieutenant-General Buckner, at first blush further demonstrating that the army was not about to permit Marines to command army troops. This appointment further discouraged Smith. However, given that the troop list of the Tenth Army for Okinawa contained only three Marine Divisions against five army divisions, the rationale behind Buckner's appointment was valid.

Deprived of one command that he wanted, he was given one that he didn't want – command of Expeditionary Troops for the Iwo Jima landings. Spruance and Turner wanted him to take this command, and insisted upon it, despite the fact that Smith protested that Harry Schmidt, as commander of VAC, was a competent leader and didn't need him, Smith, looking over his shoulder. This appointment was an ambarrassment to both Marine generals.

As in previous operations, there was much Marine concern about the length of the naval gunfire preparation of Iwo Jima before the landing. The Marines wanted ten days, which was refused by Spruance and his subordinate naval commanders on strategic and logistical grounds. Holland Smith took no part in the discussion because this was Schmidt's show. In letters to Vandegrift, Smith woefully predicted that Iwo was going to be worse than Tarawa and with heavier casualties. His predictions sadly were to prove valid.

Smith sailed to Iwo on Turner's flagship, *Eldorado*. His assignment was merely to retain control of the Expeditionary Force reserve. Other than that, he had no part in the twenty-six-day bloody battle. While this was true, he made his presence felt to the Marine commanders on shore with short pithy messages of praise or prodding. One decision he did make brought him considerable criticism, and that was not to land the 3rd Marine Regiment, the only unit of Major-General Graves B. Erskine's 3rd Marine Division not to go ashore at Iwo. Holland Smith felt that the battlefield was too crowded as it was with three divisions, less an infantry regiment, on the beach and in the attack. Despite mounting casualties and requests from Schmidt and Erskine (who had been Smith's Chief of Staff for four years), for a fresh regiment in the line, both Smith and Turner refused. Smith told Schmidt that, unless he could certify that without the 3rd Marines he could not complete the operation, no new regiment would be put ashore. Schmidt couldn't and the 3rd Marines, resentful at not having been part of the operation, sailed back to Guam. For this action, Smith was criticized both then and after the war by some of his closest friends and admirers. At the same time, news reached Iwo Jima of criticism of the conduct of the operation and the heavy cost in lives appearing in stateside newspapers. Again, a certain segment of the press pushed for MacArthur as Supreme Commander in the Pacific.

Before Iwo Jima was secured, Turner returned to Guam to prepare for Okinawa, and Smith moved over to the *Auburn*, the flagship of Harry Hill. According to Hill's oral history, Smith was morose and depressed, so much so that Hill feared he might try to harm himself. Others who saw Smith at this time agreed that, while his mood was down, there was no chance of his trying to take his own life. For his role in the Iwo Jima operation, he was awarded a fourth Distinguished Service Medal. In what must have struck Smith as the supreme irony, Richardson sent him a message reading, 'Please accept our warm congratulations for the magnificent fight which has been made by the gallant Marines in the capture of Iwo Jima. It makes one proud to be an American in thinking what these brave men have done.'

Holland Smith left Iwo Jima to return to Pearl Harbor, with a stopover at Nimitz's forward headquarters at Guam. From Pearl he watched the progress of the Okinawa campaign, noting with no satisfaction that his prediction of heavy casualties in Operation Iceberg was coming all too true. While the Okinawa operation was going on, General Vandegrift paid Smith a visit and recommended that the FMFPac commander should return to the States for a well-deserved rest. The Commandant also recommended that Smith turn over FMFPac to Geiger when the Okinawa campaign was secured and fly to California to take over the Training and Replacement Command at San Diego. Smith agreed and on 3 July he relinquished command of all Marines in the Pacific to his old friend, Roy Geiger, by now a lieutenant-general also.

Smith's farewell to his staff was very emotional. As described by an FMFPac public affairs officer:

> He stood there proudly, tears rolling unchecked and unashamed down his cheeks. 'Au revoir, God bless you . . . and I believe in you.' With that, Howlin' Mad Smith took leave of his Pacific Marines. He stepped down from the little bandstand and his fingers pushed underneath his horn-rimmed glasses to brush away the tears.
>
> He wasn't the only one. Next to me stood a young Raider colonel. He had been crying, just as unashamed, from the moment the Old Man had stepped up to make his last impromptu speech to the command. And there were dozens like him all over the room. The leather-faced old men who'd come up through the ranks with him, and the kid majors and the young lieutenants who loved him. They had gathered in the low-ceilinged officers' club at Camp Catlin . . . in their last little tribute to the man from Alabama who had inspired them across the Pacific. . . . Then he told of the Marines who had 'marched across the Pacific' . . . and he tolled off the bloody stepping stones from Tarawa to Iwo Jima which the men under his personal command had taken. . . . 'Out there are the bodies of 15,000 Marines (and he choked a hurt sob) that lie buried under the burning tropical sun. Remember them. . . .' His staff of the Fleet Marine Force went out there to the airfield in the gathering dusk to see him off from his last mission. He said a few words to each one of them. Nothing trite or hasty nor in bravado because he couldn't. . . . What little he said hit the men around him below the belt. And the cold-blooded beachhead veterans cried again because this was finality. The lovable and brilliant Old Man was going home from his last war.

Smith took up his San Diego command as the war was winding down. His enemies were not done with him yet, however, for Nimitz was going to disappoint him one last time. This concerns the surrender ceremony on the deck of the battleship *Missouri* in Tokyo Bay. In all of the official photographs taken of that grand finale to the Pacific War in which Marine ground and air units played such a major role, the only two Marines noticeable are General Geiger and Brigadier Joseph H. Fellows. Where was Holland Smith? Why wasn't he present at the ceremony? Harry Hill relates in his memoirs that when he noticed the guest list for the surrender proceedings, Holland Smith's name was conspicuous by its absence. Feeling that he had been overlooked in the press to organize the ceremony, and believing that as head of V Amphibious Corps, Smith 'definitely deserved a prominent place alongside of Spruance . . . on that famous day', Hill sent a message to Nimitz recommending that Smith be invited and offered to have the General as his guest. Nimitz sent a one-word reply: 'Negative.' Holland Smith later noted in his memoirs that his failure to receive an invitation to the surrender ceremony greatly disappointed him after having fought all 'those weary miles from Tarawa'.

As Marine historian Colonal Robert D. Heinl Jr recalled in his oral history interview:

I saw that photograph of the people assembled on the quarterdeck of the *Missouri*, and the only Marine in sight was Roy Geiger. This is not in denigration of Geiger, who was one of the greatest officers we ever had and whose staff I served on, but it thunderstruck me, and it thunderstruck everybody else, all the people I talked to . . . that they had not had the grace to fly Holland Smith out from San Diego, where they had him on the beach, to take part in the surrender ceremony, which ended a war that he had done so much single-handedly to win. . . . that photograph still angers me when I see it to this day.

Lieutenant-General Holland M. Smith retired from the Marine Corps on 15 May 1946 at the age of sixty-four after over forty years of active service. For having been decorated in combat, he was promoted to general upon retirement, only the third Marine general officer to that date to wear four stars.

Retired to La Jolla, California, a suburb of San Diego, April 1946. Published highly controversial autobiography, Coral and Brass, *1948. While the book did not harm the Marine Corps, as was expected by some, it certainly fixed Smith's image in the public mind for his criticisms of the army and navy in the Tarawa, Saipan and Iwo Jima operations, rather than for the many contributions in planning for and conducting them. Though containing hundreds of factual errors and a number of faulty conclusions, the book made the bestseller lists, and for the author it was a financial success. After the book was published, he never again made any comment about World War Two except in private conversations and correspondence. Became active in civic affairs and, in 1950, hosted a television series,* Uncommon Valor, *which was th. story of Marine Corps operations in World War Two.*

In 1952, at age seventy, he visited the Marines then fighting in Korea. During his retirement years, he kept current with world affairs. At the beginning of the American build-up in Vietnam in 1965, General Smith predicted with some prescience that all that could possibly come from the fighting there was a stalemate.

He suffered a heart attack in November 1966, remained ill for two months, and died in January 1967, just short of his eighty-fifth birthday.

Index

591